HONOR BOUND

HONOR BOUND

American Prisoners
of War in Southeast Asia,
1961–1973

Stuart I. Rochester

AND

Frederick Kiley

Naval Institute Press
Annapolis, Maryland

Naval Institute Press
291 Wood Road
Annapolis, MD 21402

Originally published in 1998 by the Office of the Secretary of Defense, Historical Office. Naval Institute Press edition 1999.

Library of Congress Cataloging-in-Publication Data

Rochester, Stuart I., 1945–
    Honor bound : American prisoners of war in Southeast Asia, 1961–1973 / Stuart I. Rochester and Frederick Kiley.
    p. cm.
    Originally published: Washington, D.C. : Historical Office, Office of the Secretary of Defense, 1998.
    Includes bibliographical references (p.   ).
    ISBN 1-55750-694-9 (alk. paper)
    1. Vietnamese Conflict, 1961–1975—Prisoners and prisons, North Vietnamese.   2. Prisoners of war—United States. 3. Prisoners of war—Indochina. I. Kiley, Frederick T. II. Title.
    DS559.4.R63   1998b
    959.704'37—dc21
                                                                98-39818

Printed in the United States of America on acid-free paper ∞

06 05   04   03   02   01   00   9 8 7 6 5 4

Contents

Foreword

This book and its companion volume on prisoner of war policy in Southeast Asia were prepared at the request of former Deputy Secretary of Defense William P. Clements, Jr. Many years in the making, this study of what happened to American prisoners of war during captivity in Southeast Asia (Vietnam, Laos, and Cambodia) between 1961 and 1973 is the product of painstaking research in the official records and relevant literature and extensive interviews with many former prisoners. Its thorough and meticulous documentation give it the stamp of scholarly authority. The research even extended to one of the authors, Frederick Kiley, undergoing some of the tortures suffered by the prisoners, including the rope treatment, "just to get the feel." Even so, it must be recognized that this cannot be the last word on the subject. History is always being rewritten as new evidence becomes available, especially of an experience as complicated and opaque as the PW/MIA subject has been.

Vietnam and its aftermath have remained an unhappy memory for much of the American public for the past 25 years and more. Those concerned with the fate of the unaccounted for American prisoners and the missing in action have inspired a sympathetic Congress and sympathetic administrations to direct the large-scale determined effort by the Department of Defense to seek a conclusive accounting for the fate of each and every PW and MIA. This extremely demanding and complex undertaking may never be able to resolve the most difficult cases.

Honor Bound is the result of a fruitful collaboration between Stuart I. Rochester and Frederick Kiley. In examining the lives of the prisoners in captivity, it presents a vivid, sensitive, sometimes excruciating, account of how men sought to cope with the physical and psychological torment of imprisonment under wretched and shameful conditions. It includes insightful analyses of the circumstances and conditions of captivity and its varying effects on the prisoners, the strategies and tactics of captors and captives, the differences between captivity in North and South Vietnam and between

Laos and Vietnam, and analysis of the quality of the source materials for this and other works on the subject.

Frederick Kiley holds a Ph.D. in English from the University of Denver. Commissioned in the Air Force in 1953, he was a professor of English at the Air Force Academy and served in Vietnam in 1968-69 as an adviser to the Vietnamese Air Force. After retirement from the Air Force in 1984, he was Director of the National Defense University Press until 1997. Among his book publications are *Satire from Aesop to Buchwald* and *A Catch-22 Casebook*. He has also published articles on prisoners of war and literary and linguistic subjects. This book would not have been possible without the prodigious and intensive research performed by Kiley during his years in the OSD Historical Office.

Stuart I. Rochester earned a Ph.D. in history from the University of Virginia and taught at Loyola College in Baltimore for a number of years before joining the OSD Historical Office in 1980. He is the author of books and articles, including *Takeoff at Mid-Century: Federal Civil Aviation Policy in the Eisenhower Years, 1953-1961* and *American Liberal Disillusionment in the Wake of World War I*. He became Deputy Historian of the OSD Historical Office in 1987, subsequently writing much of the book and seeing the effort to completion.

This publication has been reviewed and its contents declassified and cleared for release by concerned government agencies. Although the manuscript itself has been declassified, some of the official sources cited in the volume may remain classified. This is an official publication of the Office of the Secretary of Defense, but the views expressed are those of the authors and do not necessarily represent those of the Department of Defense.

ALFRED GOLDBERG
OSD Historian

Preface

Thin and pale, clad in the drab civilian jacket and trousers issued by the North Vietnamese only the day before, the first of the returning American prisoners of war stepped through the door of the Air Force C-141 transport that had flown him and 39 fellow PWs* from Hanoi to Clark Air Base in the Philippine Islands. He paused a moment to square his shoulders, descended the ramp to the flight line, saluted the admiral and general waiting to greet them, shook hands, exchanged a few words, then moved to the microphones prepared for the occasion. Navy Capt. Jeremiah Denton, senior officer among the prisoners on this first aircraft, spoke the brief message he had written during the trip from Hanoi: "We are honored to have had the opportunity to serve our country under difficult circumstances. We are profoundly grateful to our Commander in Chief and to our nation for this day. God bless America."

Thus ended the longest wartime captivity of any group of American prisoners in U.S. history. This alone made them remarkable, the longest held among them spending nearly a decade in confinement. But there were other factors that explained the high drama surrounding their return and indeed the attention they attracted throughout much of their incarceration. Certainly it was not sheer numbers that made them special. One hundred and fifteen men followed Denton out of North Vietnam that raw, overcast day of 12 February 1973, with another 475 American prisoners evacuated by the end of March. Counting those who escaped, died, or were released prior to Operation Homecoming, the Vietnam War claimed fewer than 800 U.S. PWs altogether, including civilians—by far the smallest group of Americans captured during any major war in this century. By comparison, more than 4,000 U.S. servicemen were taken captive in World War I, 130,000 in World War II, and more than 7,000 in Korea (see Appendix 1).

---

* Throughout the book, rather than "POW" we use the abbreviation "PW" commonly used by the military services.

From the beginning, from the very first capture incidents, the PWs of the Southeast Asia conflict had an influence and importance disproportionate to the size of their ranks. Part of the reason was the peculiar nature of the war itself, a contest waged, especially by the North Vietnamese, with powerful propaganda as well as military weapons. In a war that was never declared—in which the United States never mobilized, never called up its Reserves, never mounted a ground invasion of the North Vietnamese homeland, even as it committed millions of service personnel to the combat area—Denton and his comrades found themselves at the center of an unconventional struggle, unprotected by normal wartime constraints and at the mercy of captors long experienced in political and psychological warfare. The North Vietnamese labeled them variously air pirates, mercenaries, and imperialist agents, threatened them periodically with war crimes trials, and dangled them as pawns in an effort to wrest concessions from the U.S. government and sympathy from the American public and international community. They were paraded before Vietnamese civilians to arouse anti-American sentiment, released on occasion to coincide with antiwar activities in the United States, and used as bargaining chips in the protracted peace negotiations. Their resistance or cooperation affected morale on both sides, and revelations of their conduct and treatment through released photographs and tapes (in which they often sabotaged their captors' intentions) influenced perceptions worldwide. From 1966 onward, the "PW issue" abided at the highest levels of the American government, at times seemingly attracting more notice than the war effort itself. Toward the end it became a key link in the final political settlement of the conflict.

Beyond the longevity of their confinement and their central role in an unconventional war, unusual credentials and seniority also contributed to their high visibility. The American prisoners of this war were mostly officers, and glamorous aviators at that,* which added to their media celebrity and to their exploitative value. That many already had prominent reputations and impressive records when captured further enhanced their image. No doubt, too, each attained a higher profile as one of a small group than if he had been submerged in a much larger PW population.

The stature of the aviator-officers, the heroes' welcome accorded the returning PWs by a nation anxious to salvage some measure of pride and honor, and the tendency of participants in their postwar memoirs to accent

---

*All but 80 of the 566 military personnel repatriated at Operation Homecoming were commissioned officers; fewer than two dozen of the officers were not fliers.

the positive and downplay (or remain silent on) the embarrassing—all gave rise to what has recently been referred to as the "official story" of the captivity. By this account, which became standard in books and articles in the decade after the war and is still popular today, the PWs were, almost to a man, stalwart warriors who resisted to the maximum under the most abominable and abusive conditions. Patriotic and inspirational, the standard rendition was shaped by memoirs, interviews, and other firsthand accounts immediately following homecoming and then confirmed in an expansive book, *P.O.W.: A Definitive History of the American Prisoner-of-War Experience in Vietnam, 1964-1973*, written by John G. Hubbell and published by Reader's Digest Press in 1976. Hubbell and a small research team interviewed many of the returned PWs during their first two years of freedom. Without access to official documents or to the large number of studies commissioned by the military services, the Office of the Secretary of Defense, and the Defense Intelligence Agency, Hubbell sketched the broad outlines of the story and, with considerable anecdotal detail, skillfully wove the many strands into a vivid and coherent narrative. However, the limited record on which it was based, the absence of footnotes and bibliography, and a highly personal, journalistic style weakened the claim, suggested in the title and again in Hubbell's preface, that *P.O.W.* would be the last word on the subject. Although Hubbell supplied a useful framework for future chroniclers, *P.O.W.* was more a paean, a salute to valor, than an authoritative history.

Critics of the "official story" argued that there was no single, monolithic PW experience, that in fact there was evidence of weakness, laxity, and recurring internal dissension even among the officers (which Hubbell acknowledged though he cited only the most notorious cases with which he was familiar), and that life in Hanoi's prisons, so often a bed of pain and suffering, could also be as humdrum as it was harrowing. In a review essay of the PW literature in 1983, historian Joe Dunn chided Hubbell for stressing "the sensational, the dramatic, the greatest horrors, and the 'exceptional' POWs." The leading proponent of the newer, more critical interpretation, Craig Howes, coined the term "official story" in his 1993 study *Voices of the Vietnam POWs*. "By carefully selecting, excluding, proportioning, and orchestrating their materials," Howes contended, "the senior officers and their historian [Hubbell] wrote both an official defense of the POWs' performance, and a parable for a nation they believed had lost sight of its own greatness."*

* Dunn, "The POW Chronicles: A Bibliographic Review," *Armed Forces and Society* (Spring 83), 501-02; Howes, *Voices of the Vietnam POWs: Witnesses to Their Fight*, ch 4 (82, quote).

If there is some validity to the argument that the original interpretation embellished and ennobled the typical prisoner's experience, the corrective has sometimes been cynical or trivializing. The truth, inevitably, lies somewhere in between; getting to it—arriving as objectively as possible at an understanding of what the PWs did and did not accomplish—is the guiding purpose of this volume. Even as we sought to refrain from the sentimentality of the popular version and to maintain detachment in dealing with so emotional a story, we were convinced in the end that, on the whole, the PWs of the Vietnam War were indeed an extraordinary company of men who endured an extraordinary captivity, though not without chinks in the armor. Viewing the legend objectively still left an epic, the reality being that both suffering and valor, tragedy and triumph, occurred on a large scale. Revisionists like Howes fail to appreciate the terror and vulnerability that those who fell into enemy hands in so hostile an environment must have felt even in the least threatening circumstances, or to grant that those spared the worst atrocities still faced much misery and torment. Nonetheless, it is equally true that individual prisoners experienced a wide range of conditions and exhibited a wide range of behavior. Not every prisoner in North Vietnam, for example, encountered horrible torture or even excessive duress; for those seized late in the war, the experience, in most cases, was much less arduous than for their predecessors. Even among those in custody for the better part of the decade, there were notable variations in treatment—and performance—from one individual to another depending on where exactly he was held, the shifting character of the camps themselves, the extent of one's injuries, varying tolerances for pain and degradation, and many other factors of time, place, and personal idiosyncrasies. With respect to performance, not every PW was a heroic Ulysses any more than all their wives, as one Defense Department official later allowed, were patient Penelopes. If there are dozens of documented, genuine profiles in courage, there are also cases of regrettable conduct and, in a few instances, outright collaboration.

Further complicating and fragmenting the captivity story is the fact that there were prisoners held outside of the North, and outside of Vietnam altogether, many of them having different backgrounds and facing different tests and challenges than the pilots in Hanoi. The "official story" includes only a handful of the PWs confined in South Vietnam and Laos because the prisoners in North Vietnam did not know much about them and because this group consisted largely of lower-ranking noncoms who were less able and less inclined to articulate and publish their own accounts. The record of these PWs in the South and Laos is more difficult to evaluate because of the dearth of published material and also because these captives generally were held in more isolated locations and kept separate from comrades, so what personal accounts we have in the form of debriefings and such often lack corroborating testimony. Furthermore, their death rate was much higher than in the North. Still, the available evidence indicates that here, too, there were both stalwarts and slackers and a range of situations and responses that defy neat categorization.

The problem of separating fact from fiction is not limited to activity in the South and Laos. Memoirs, which comprise the bulk of the published literature, must be viewed with caution, not only because of their discretionary nature but also owing to the lack of an overall perspective beyond the prisoner's own small cell or circle and inevitable memory lapses in the time between living and recording one's experience. Although we had access to returnee debriefings, which have advantages of candor and immediacy over memoirs, confidentiality requirements and statutory restrictions prevented quotation or citation in most instances;* likewise, we turned up other reports and documents that might have lent greater depth and authority to the published sources, but could not cite them because of classification or security considerations. The key limitation, of course, was the inaccessibility of Vietnamese records, Hanoi having given permission to U.S. representatives to review information relating to MIA cases but not yet opening files on the general operation and administration of their prison camps during the war. We had planned a visit to Hanoi in the spring of 1994 to obtain access to such materials and interview former prison officials, but the trip was canceled at the last minute amid controversy over normalizing relations with Vietnam.

For such reasons, then, this history, or any history at this point that attempts to treat authoritatively the experience of the PWs in Southeast Asia, can not claim to be complete much less definitive. Aside from the problem of limited and restricted sources, the historian's task is made more difficult yet by other complicating factors: the uncertain fate of dozens of missing U.S. servicemen who were briefly spotted in captivity by comrades but then disappeared; inconsistencies in the identification of ranks, shootdown and capture dates, casualty figures, and even the spelling of captives' names, in official compilations as well as in memoir references;

---

* To encourage frankness, the services promised returnees that their official debriefings would always be held in the strictest confidence, assuring the men that scholars and researchers would only be granted restricted access and, just as important, no individual's debriefing would ever be made available to another PW. With rare exceptions, that pledge has been honored to this day.

other discrepancies attributable to inaccurate or incomplete reporting during a volatile guerrilla war in which both sides sometimes distorted numbers and manipulated accounting for political effect; and confusion stemming from different time zones that resulted in the same events having different dates in Washington and Hanoi. Countless hours spent addressing these issues have not clarified all the confusion, resolved all conflicts, or filled in all gaps. Finally, although some of the prisoners kept elaborate mental calendars and diaries, conclusiveness with respect to dates and other details is hard to come by where participants left virtually no contemporaneous written record except for censored letters or forced confessions. As one of the ex-captives remarked after coming home, "prison happenings that occurred in 1965, 66, and 67 were already being debated for their accuracy by POWs in detention in 1971," when the mass of the PW population first came together in a single camp and were able to pool their knowledge and information.

Given these obstacles, we have striven to reconstruct the story as accurately and comprehensively as possible, dealing with more individuals (North and South, military and civilian, the heroic and the unexceptional), more events (sensational and routine), more issues, details, and published and unpublished sources than any account of the subject heretofore—and with attention to both the telling of the story and the analysis of it. The result, we hope, is a balanced, objective history as well as an evocative narrative. Warts and all, the experience of the American PWs in Southeast Asia presents one of the most compelling tales in the annals of men at war and one of the more fascinating and significant subplots of the U.S. engagement in Vietnam. When Denton stepped onto the tarmac at Clark, the whole nation smiled with him, but his countrymen could not have imagined how complex and remarkable was the journey behind the homecoming.

This was not an easy book to write, and not only because of the obstacles cited above. If ever there was a work in progress, this was it, its preliminary researching and initial drafting spanning much of one decade and its completion and preparation for publication occupying much of another. The press of other assignments that required putting the project aside for long stretches and the sheer magnitude of the task at times made us wonder if we were not becoming hostages ourselves to an uncertain outcome. With all the interruptions, producing a seamless composition, always difficult in a collaborative effort, became a special challenge. For helping us stay the course and making the undertaking manageable and we hope worthwhile in the end, there are a great number of people who deserve credit and thanks.

We must begin, of course, with the repatriated prisoners of war themselves. Besides providing the authors with a matchlessly stirring subject, they helped ensure with their generous cooperation and assistance, even as they had to reopen bitterly painful chapters in their experience, that the story of their captivity would be recorded as accurately and fully as possible. The frankness and unfailing graciousness with which they responded to our inquiries, granted interviews, and furnished materials informed and enriched this history to an extent we can not adequately acknowledge.

Rather than thanking those former prisoners in some sort of hierarchic order of contribution, we have decided simply to list them alphabetically. The list thus co-mingles individuals whose assistance was ongoing and extensive with those whose contributions were smaller but nevertheless also significant, often shedding light on a specific incident or circumstance where we needed illumination or corroboration. In this latter group were individuals uniquely qualified to offer insight from a particular perspective, for example, those with especially lengthy or brief captivities, those who occupied unique positions in certain prison camps at certain key junctures or intervals, those whose points of view might reflect a distinctly senior- (or junior-) rank attitude, and those of unusual status such as civilians captured in Laos, medical personnel, or early releasees.

The list that follows reflects neither military ranks nor distinctions among services. Nor does it distinguish between military and civilians, or between those captured in South Vietnam versus North Vietnam. It uses the names—sometimes informal—by which the individuals were best known to one another as prisoners. Our most sincere gratitude, then, goes to these former prisoners of war: Everett Alvarez, Tom Barrett, Bill Baugh, Jim Bedinger, Mike Benge, Chuck Boyd, Ernie Brace, Bud Breckner, Norm Brookens, Dave Burroughs, Phil Butler, Ron Byrne, Pete Camerota, Fred Cherry, Larry Chesley, Jerry Coffee, Tom Collins, Ken Coskey, Render Crayton, Ed Davis, Bud Day, John Deering, Jerry Denton, Jim DiBernardo, John Downey, Walt Eckes, Ed Elias, Dick Fecteau, Jack Fellowes, John Fer, John Flynn, Norm Gaddis, Paul Galanti, Dan Gouin, Larry Guarino, Porter Halyburton, Doug Hegdahl, Don Heiliger, Lee Hildebrand, Duffy Hutton, Sam Johnson, Jim Kasler, Tom Kirk, Charles Klusmann, Hal Kushner, Swede Larson, Bill Lawrence, Jose Luna, Tom Madison, Phil Manhard, John McCain, Norm McDaniel, Red McDaniel, Mike McGrath, Kevin McManus, Ike McMillan, Ed Mechenbier, Joe Milligan, Jim Mulligan, A. J. Myers, Norris Overly, Jasper Page, John Parsels, Glen Perkins, Doug Peterson, Charlie Plumb, Ben Pollard, Ben Purcell, Doug Ramsey, Don Rander, Jon Reynolds, Nick Rowe, Bob Sawhill, Ray Schrump, Joe Shanahan, Bob Shumaker, Phil Smith, Charlie Southwick, Larry Spencer, Jim Stockdale, Hervey Stockman, Tom Storey, Dick Stratton,

Tim Sullivan, Orson Swindle, Jim Thompson, Terry Uyeyama, Jack Van Loan, Ray Vohden, Wayne Waddell, Ron Webb, Robert White, and Dave Winn. We regret if we have inadvertently omitted the names of any contributors, or if for want of space not every treasured anecdote or remembered detail found expression.

We learned much also from the ex-prisoners' written accounts, both their published memoirs and the academic papers done at various military and civilian colleges on a broad range of topics from problems of leadership and communication in captivity to the issues of torture and psychological exploitation. Although we cite these sources in the notes and bibliography, special mention should be made here of the set of prison-camp histories compiled by multi-service teams of former prisoners of war under the direction of A. J. Myers at the Air War College. Indispensable for both its breadth and detail, we have found no other report of such quality and accuracy for this or any other PW experience in either U.S. government or private archives.

All historians of the Vietnam War captivity experience must acknowledge an obligation to John G. Hubbell for his pathbreaking work *P.O.W.* That we disagree in places with Hubbell should be no surprise because of the greater access to records and longer perspective on events we enjoyed. We are grateful to him and his team of researchers for their pioneering effort and for Hubbell's courtesy in sharing his materials and thoughts. Early on we benefited, too, from the substantial analysis of PW conditions and performance done after the war by the Air Force's 7602nd Air Intelligence Group, whose tracking and graphic representation of each prisoner's movements from prison camp to prison camp remains among the most valuable documents available for basic reference purposes. Frederic Wolfer, Charles Redman, Claude Watkins, and Jim Monroe of that organization merit special recognition for their contributions to those early studies and for their continuing assistance throughout this project.

Reserve officers from all services took part in the early phases of research for this volume; we owe thanks to many and in particular to Don Jacobs, Bill Sullivan, Steve Ching, and Jack Sullivan. Among other officers who made important contributions along the way, we wish to single out Jim Massaro, Hays Parks, and Mark Sievers.

A fraternity of veteran analysts in the Office of the Secretary of Defense and the Defense Intelligence Agency who have devoted years of dedicated effort to prisoner-of-war matters and later the missing-in-action issue gave unstintingly of their knowledge and expertise. Four in particular lent invaluable assistance: Charles Trowbridge, Gary Koblitz, Sal Ferro, and Robert Destatte. Former Deputy Assistant Secretary of Defense Roger Shields was a constant source of information and encouragement. John Horn of the

Defense POW/MP Office graciously supplied the master list of prisoners that with some modifications appears as Appendix 3.

To our colleagues in the OSD Historical Office we express our deep appreciation for their abiding interest, enthusiasm, and support. John Glennon read the entire manuscript and improved it measurably with his keen eye and cogent suggestions. Ronald Landa, Alice Cole, Max Rosenberg, and Dalton West also offered useful comment and advice. Ruth Sharma was indispensable in both providing editorial assistance and overseeing the preparation of the several drafts and final version of the manuscript. Carolyn Thorne also typed portions of the manuscript.

Kathleen Brassell, director of the OSD Graphics Division, has lent her creative talents to a number of Historical Office publications, matching pictures to words with both dexterity and imagination. She and an able pair at ArtCom Plus, Robert and Eric Seffinga, guided our use of photographs and illustrations and helped shape the overall design and layout of the book. The final production would have been poorer without the reliable assistance of Kelly Jamison and Kyle McKibbin of Output and Tony Ngo of the Defense Automated Printing Service.

Special thanks to Mike McGrath, president of NAMPOW, for vital help with distribution of the original volume and revisions for the present book.

Dr. Alfred Goldberg, the OSD Historian, saw the project through its many stages with the wisdom of Solomon and the patience of Job. To him we owe an incalculable debt for giving us the opportunity to do the book and, as editor and supervisor, strengthening it at every turn with his usual extraordinary skill, sound judgment, and unsparing commitment to excellence. For any shortcomings or errors that may have survived his scrutiny, we alone accept responsibility.

Finally, Wilbur Hoare, Ernest Giusti, and Vernon Davis—all former historians with the Joint Chiefs of Staff Historical Division—shared this long endeavor with us. To those dear friends and fellow authors who did not live to see their own considerable prisoner-of-war work published, we dedicate this volume.

STUART I. ROCHESTER
FREDERICK KILEY

And a special salute to Col. Andy Dougherty. No man ever knew a truer friend.—F.K.

HONOR BOUND

1

The Historical Setting

I t was the misfortune of the American prisoners of the Vietnam War not merely to be captured, but to be captured at a time and place that rendered them especially vulnerable. Their experience can be fully understood only in the context of the turbulent history of Southeast Asia, in particular the deep-rooted resentment of foreigners among the peoples of the region and the post-World War II nationalist and Communist revolutions that brought that resentment to a boil by the time the Americans arrived.

The history of Southeast Asia, and Vietnam specifically, became inextricably linked to foreign influences beginning with the Chinese invasion of the Red River Delta some two thousand years ago. From 111 B.C. to 939 A.D., the Vietnamese were subjects of Chinese warlords, required to pay tribute to the Chinese Emperor. After securing independence in 939, they entered upon a period of steady expansion in which over the span of nine centuries they developed a loose confederacy on the Indochina peninsula. They gradually conquered Annam and Cochinchina—which became central and southern Vietnam—by pushing the Khmer races west into modern Cambodia and annexing the Hindu-influenced Champa civilization in the lands south of Hue and down the coast. By the 19th century, they had tightened their control of the peninsula by driving Montagnard tribes like the Meo to the uncivilized highlands of western Vietnam and eastern Laos. An influx of French missionaries and traders after 1700, however, led to widening French influence and eventually, by 1885, occupation and colonial rule.

By the 1930s, with the whole of Indochina under French suzerainty and threatened by intervention from the ascendant Japanese as well, the forces of nationalism and communism coalesced in Vietnam to form a nascent but as yet uncoordinated resistance movement. Lacking sufficient strength and

1

organization, and riven by internal ideological and political differences, the anticolonial forces quickly succumbed to French counterattacks. Leadership of the tattered resistance fell to a remarkable North Vietnamese who had been a Marxist votary from the earliest days of the Communist International. Educated in France, where he co-founded the French Communist Party in 1920, Nguyen Tat Thanh lived briefly in Moscow before settling in China; there, in 1930, under the alias Nguyen Ai Quoc (Nguyen the Patriot), he organized the Indochinese Communist Party.[1] From his China base, traveling occasionally into the West but venturing into his homeland only rarely and covertly, Nguyen directed the underground effort against the French and Japanese during the 1930s and early 1940s, leading in May 1941 to the formation of the League for Vietnamese Independence—Viet Nam Doc Lap Dong Minh Hoi, or Viet Minh. In 1943, when he struck a deal to free himself from a Nationalist Chinese jail to direct guerrilla actions against the Japanese in Vietnam, he adopted the name by which the world came to know him, Ho Chi Minh—He Who Enlightens.[2]

During World War II, the Japanese occupied Indochina and forced the enfeebled Vichy French government in Vietnam to grant them special economic and military privileges. In March 1945, fearing a French revival in Asia following the ouster of the Nazis from France, the Japanese seized power from the Vichyites, virtually eliminating French authority in northern Vietnam and thus creating a vacuum that Ho and his Viet Minh filled when Japan eventually surrendered. On 2 September 1945, Ho proclaimed the Democratic Republic of Vietnam, gaining favor among the poor peasantry in the north by a concerted campaign of political indoctrination and economic reform.

Following the war, with the defeat of the Japanese, the French managed to reestablish their position in the south, where Communist influence was weaker, challenged by both nationalist and religious anticommunist groups. The French missed an opportunity to win the support of these anticommunist elements by reverting to heavy-handed colonial practices, driving many nationalists by default into the Communist camp. Ho actively courted them, maintaining a pretense of patriotism even as he was subordinating the goal of national unity and independence to the consolidation of his Communist regime in the north.

France briefly recognized the Democratic Republic of Vietnam as a free state within the French Union, but disagreement over the terms of the arrangement soon erupted into violence. By late 1946, French and Viet Minh forces were at war. The Viet Minh, whose military arm was led by Vo Nguyen Giap, a former history teacher whose wife and sister-in-law had perished in French prisons, mounted a campaign of terror and guerrilla tactics that further entrenched the Communists in the north and enabled them to penetrate much of the countryside in the south also.* The French countered by resurrecting former emperor Bao Dai from exile in Hong Kong to head a nominally independent State of Vietnam, hoping now to attract disaffected nationalists away from Ho's increasingly partisan regime. But the French gambit came too late, as Vietnamese nationalist leaders had either been eliminated or intimidated by Ho, or simply preempted; in any case, they regarded Bao Dai as a weak and transparent figurehead whom they were loath to support. With the help of Communist China, which supplied weapons, military training, and propaganda instruction, the Viet Minh battled the French to a stalemate. Numbering some 60,000 regulars at the start of 1947 (reinforced by an estimated 100,000 militia and part-time guerrillas), as compared with France's 100,000-man army in Vietnam, the Viet Minh occasionally skirmished with French units and attacked convoys but avoided heavy losses by retreating into the mountains north of Hanoi and to sanctuaries in China, in the meantime enlisting new recruits and extending supply trails and the guerrilla campaign deeper into the south.[3]

By late 1953, after several abortive offensives, the loss of key outposts in the north, and the steady erosion of their position in the south as well, the French decided to deploy a large contingent of troops along a primary Viet Minh supply route near the Laotian border at Dien Bien Phu, hoping to lure the Viet Minh into a decisive battle in which they might deal the Communists a crippling defeat. The Viet Minh outwitted the French by hauling long-range artillery into mountain positions ringing Dien Bien Phu, carrying in tons of supplies and ammunition by bicycle, and digging a network of trenches throughout the combat area to provide sheltered attack and communication routes. Moreover, General Giap assembled three divisions instead of the single division the French anticipated. By May 1954 it was the Viet Minh who had dealt the decisive defeat, driving the war-weary French to negotiate a cease-fire and rely on the recently convened Geneva Conference to salvage some influence.[4]

As the French position in Vietnam deteriorated in the postwar years, the United States faced a serious test of its new containment policy. Prior to 1950, U.S. officials looked on the deepening French predicament in Indochina with only mild concern—too busy addressing European priorities and reordering their own defense establishment to offer much more than token assistance, and in any case ambivalent about backing the French in what appeared

*From December 1944, when Ho and Giap united to form the first platoons of a reconstituted Viet Minh, the North Vietnamese chain of command was divided into a military arm and a political/psychological warfare arm, with the political commander, Ho, supreme. These first platoons were formed south of the Chinese border near Cao Bang, the site in 1972 of "Dogpatch," the last of about a dozen prisons the North Vietnamese would open to house American PWs.

initially to be a struggle for Vietnamese national liberation. During World War II, the American government had in fact courted the Viet Minh as a counter to Japanese advances in Vietnam: Giap's guerrillas had received supplies from American OSS agents in return for intelligence information, help in locating downed U.S. pilots, and harassment of the Japanese, and Ho Chi Minh himself tried to visit Washington to woo U.S. support for an independent Vietnam. (Though denied a visa, he did meet with Maj. Gen. Claire L. Chennault in March 1945. Ho's life, threatened by severe malaria in 1945, was probably saved by medications supplied by a young American agent, Lt. E. Howard Hunt.) The crystallization of the Cold War by 1948, however, brought an end to the flirtation with the Viet Minh and a shift in U.S. policy in Indochina from anticolonialism to support of the French presence there as a bulwark against the spread of communism in Southeast Asia. The victory of the Communists in China in 1949 and the North Korean invasion of South Korea in June 1950 heightened American concern about the region and spurred the United States to become more actively committed in France's behalf.

In March 1950 President Harry S. Truman authorized $15 million in military aid for Indochina under the new Mutual Defense Assistance Program. In September that same year, an American military assistance advisory group was sent to Saigon to assess French needs, screen aid requests, and monitor French use of U.S. equipment. By 1954, on the eve of Dien Bien Phu, 200 U.S. Air Force mechanics were in Da Nang servicing American combat planes flown by French pilots, and total U.S. economic and military aid was verging on $1 billion. Military planners in Washington seriously considered committing U.S. combat forces to rescue the French at Dien Bien Phu, debating the merits of a massive air strike against the Viet Minh and even the use of tactical nuclear weapons; but qualms about diverting troops from the defense of Europe, becoming mired in an expensive and protracted conflict far from home, and inviting possible Soviet or Chinese intervention prevailed, for the time, to deter any further U.S. involvement. Still, the fateful first steps toward direct U.S. engagement in the Indochina struggle had already been taken.[5]

At Geneva in May 1954 representatives of France, the Democratic Republic of Vietnam, the State of Vietnam (the non-Communist government under Bao Dai that still ruled in the south), Cambodia, Laos, the People's Republic of China, the Soviet Union, Great Britain, and the United States gathered to discuss the terms of ending the Franco-Viet Minh war and restoring peace in Vietnam. The Geneva agreements, issued in July, called for a cease-fire; provisional partition of Vietnam along the 17th parallel, with regroupment of the Viet Minh and their sympathizers to the North and the French and their non-Communist allies to the South; and "free general elections" to be held in 1956 with the goal of unifying the country. Objecting that free and democratic elections would be impossible in the North under the Communist regime, and unsure that the Communists would not capitalize on their recent successes to predominate even in a legitimate referendum, both the State of Vietnam and the United States refused to endorse the agreements, although the United States pledged not to use force or the threat of force to disturb the arrangements.[6]

Between 1954 and 1959, the two Vietnams became increasingly polarized. In October 1955 a referendum in the South deposed Bao Dai and established Prime Minister Ngo Dinh Diem as president of the Republic of Vietnam (South Vietnam). Confident of American support, Diem rejected North Vietnamese overtures to hold unification elections, instead seeking to unify the various anticommunist religious and political factions in the South and setting about to rebuild a national army that over the years had been decimated by desertions and defections to the Viet Minh. The United States hardened its own anticommunist stance even as the French collapse placed the burden for defending Indochina from a Communist takeover squarely on the American government. President Dwight D. Eisenhower at a news conference in April 1954 likened the unfolding dynamic in Asia to a "falling domino" process: if one country should fall to communism, those bordering it would follow in rapid succession. In October 1954 Eisenhower promised Diem aid if assurances of "needed reforms," the details of which were left vague, were forthcoming. In January 1955 U.S. military advisers took over from the French the training of the South Vietnamese army, with 121 U.S. officers on hand by July and 189 in March 1956 when the last of the French advisory personnel departed.* In May 1957 Diem came to Washington on a state visit (Eisenhower met him at the airport personally, an honor the president accorded only one other national leader, King Saud), addressed a joint session of Congress, and was widely hailed as the "democratic alternative" in Asia. By the late 1950s, South Vietnam was receiving nearly $200 million annually in aid from the United States.[7]

In the meantime, the Communist government of the Democratic Republic of Vietnam (North Vietnam) tightened its own grip on power, instituting

---

* Diem's coolness toward the French, combined with the Americans' air of superiority, made the French military's last days in Vietnam emotionally wrenching. Ronald Spector notes that the French "were bitter and disillusioned over what they considered Diem's treachery and irresponsibility toward them and angry at what they saw as the ill-concealed eagerness of many American technical and military advisers to shoulder them aside. The South Vietnamese Army's abrupt adoption of American-type uniforms and the American salute and a ceremonial burning by South Vietnamese officers of their French-style insignia of rank were galling to French pride and indicative of the mood of the Diem regime." See Spector, *Advice and Support*, 255.

sweeping political and economic controls so oppressive that by early 1955 some 900,000 North Vietnamese had taken refuge in the South. Ho and his cadres installed a propaganda network throughout the North Vietnamese countryside—broadcasting official statements over village loudspeakers, holding indoctrination and "reeducation" classes for dissidents, and wringing "confessions" from those suspected of plotting against the regime—a system of mind manipulation and control that the Viet Minh had used effectively with French PWs (see Chapter 2) and that American PWs, too, would experience firsthand in the years to come. Ho turned to Peking and Moscow for economic and military assistance, obtaining in the summer of 1955 a promise of $200 million in aid from Communist China and $100 million from the Soviet Union. Bitter over what he perceived to be the subverting of the Geneva accords by Diem and the United States and alarmed by the sudden resurgence of South Vietnam under the American aegis, the North Vietnamese leader encouraged resistance among elements in the South opposed to the Saigon regime.

Despite Washington's prodding to end corrupt and repressive practices that threatened to undermine U.S. assistance efforts, Diem responded to criticism of his administration with a campaign of suppression as brutally authoritarian as the police state crackdown in the North. By 1960, disenchantment with "Diemocracy" lured thousands of recruits to join with the remnants of the Viet Minh underground in the South to form a National Liberation Front (NLF) whose aim was to overthrow the Diem government. Receiving guidance and material assistance from Hanoi, the NLF moved from political agitation to outright guerrilla war, applying the same tactics of terror and attrition that had been successful against the French. These insurgents (the Diem government called them Viet Cong, or Vietnamese Communists, lumping all the rebels under a Marxist rubric and thus hoping to discredit them) gathered strength as Diem alienated additional segments of the population and as Hanoi stepped up supplies and reinforcements.[8]

Conditions in South Vietnam deteriorated rapidly after 1960. The Viet Cong began to attack in larger units and on targets closer to Saigon as their influence spread over a larger area. Compounding the crisis, a civil war in neighboring Laos between pro- and anticommunist factions (see Chapter 3) permitted North Vietnam to use the jungles of eastern Laos to send a stream of ammunition and equipment into the South as well as to infiltrate cadres of trained guerrillas to bolster the Viet Cong effort; by 1965, Hanoi would be sending entire regiments of regular army troops into the South over these trails. Instead of following American advice to reach an accommodation with his domestic critics, Diem resorted to even harsher measures, in one dramatic instance that provoked worldwide outrage, crushing Buddhist dissent

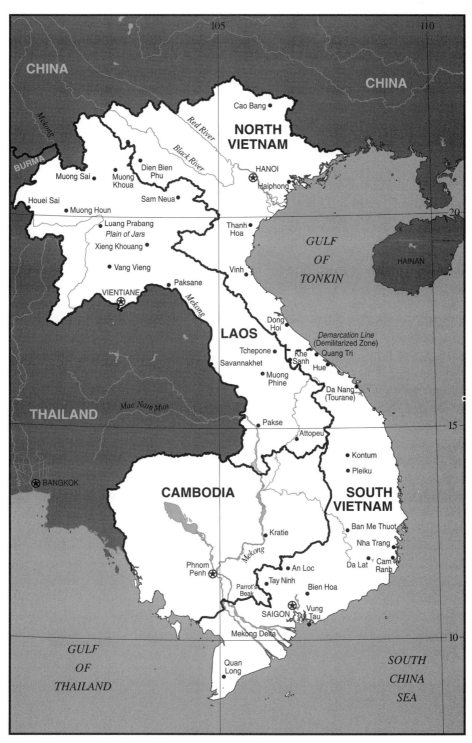

Southeast Asia (1961)

in a violent showdown at Hue in May 1963. By the time Diem was eliminated in a coup in November 1963, the South Vietnamese army was in disarray, the Communists controlled by some estimates more than half of the country, and U.S. policymakers were groping for a solution to a conflict they only faintly understood and only recently had given serious attention. Even as they were finally beginning to recognize the magnitude of Diem's failure and the urgent need for a reexamination of American policy in Indochina, U.S. officials continued to perceive the threat to South Vietnam as a military rather than a political problem—a case of aggression from the North rather than internal upheaval in the South. And so as the administration of President John F. Kennedy reassessed U.S. Indochina policy between 1961 and 1963, it determined that the survival of South Vietnam required additional U.S. military assistance, President Kennedy deciding, over the muted objections of some and apparently despite considerable personal misgivings, to commit more American troops and treasure to the struggle.[9]

By late 1963, then, the United States was knee-deep in what journalists already were characterizing as a quagmire. The number of U.S. soldiers in Vietnam had increased from 342 officers and enlisted men at the time of the Geneva agreements in July 1954 to fewer than 1,000 when Kennedy was inaugurated in January 1961 to more than 16,000 at the time he was assassinated in November 1963. The major new commitment Kennedy authorized in November 1961 following a fact-finding mission to Vietnam by national security aides Walt W. Rostow and General Maxwell D. Taylor (see note 9), although short of committing U.S. combat troops, substantially transformed the nature of the American involvement in terms of the volume of assistance and the numbers of military advisers, significantly Americanizing the war. The casualty rate would increase proportionately. Between July 1959, when Maj. Dale R. Buis and Sgt. Chester M. Ovnand were killed in a Viet Cong raid on an American mess hall at Bien Hoa—the first American advisers to die by enemy action in Vietnam*—and the end of 1963, over 100 U.S. servicemen were killed in action in Vietnam. By December 1963, two dozen American soldiers and civilians had been prisoners of war in Vietnam and Laos, some of them already having died in captivity or been released.[10]

The escalation initiated incrementally by Kennedy accelerated exponentially under President Lyndon B. Johnson. The events that followed Johnson's

* For *official* purposes, Spec. 4 James T. Davis, who was killed on 22 December 1961 (after the Kennedy buildup of November 1961, when official recordkeeping began), is considered the first U.S. fatality in the Vietnam War, although there were others killed earlier in terrorist incidents such as the one that claimed Buis and Ovnand, and 10 U.S. servicemen died in hostile action in Laos in 1961. The names of these earlier casualties were later included in the Vietnam Memorial, although Ovnand's name was initially misspelled "Ovnard" (Stanley Karnow discovered the error while researching *Vietnam: A History*).

succession now read like a litany: the bombing of North Vietnamese PT boat bases and congressional passage of the Tonkin Gulf resolution in August 1964 in response to attacks on U.S. destroyers in the Gulf of Tonkin; the bombing of North Vietnamese and Viet Cong targets in February 1965 in retaliation for a Viet Cong attack on the U.S. base at Pleiku; the introduction of U.S. ground combat forces at Da Nang in March 1965; the key decisions of April and July 1965 that massively increased the U.S. troop commitment, intensified the bombing campaign, and effectively changed American military strategy in Vietnam from defensive to offensive; mounting antiwar protests and draft resistance in the United States as the South Vietnamese government staggered through a series of coups and countercoups and U.S. force strength in Vietnam climbed from 184,000 at the end of 1965 to 486,000 by the end of 1967 (with 16,000 American troops killed in action in Southeast Asia since 1961); the Tet offensive of January-February 1968 which, although a tactical defeat for the Communists, delivered a devastating political and psychological blow to American policy and, especially as portrayed by a cynical press, seemed to confirm the futility of the U.S. effort. By the time Johnson announced his decision in March 1968 not to run for reelection, the U.S. military presence in Vietnam had swelled to 535,000 men, reaching a peak strength the following spring of 543,000 before the deescalation of the war proceeded under President Richard M. Nixon.[11]

Johnson's abdication reflected the growing conviction in Washington that a military victory in Vietnam was impossible—at least on terms that were politically acceptable. Concurrent with his reelection decision, Johnson rejected the request of his commander in Vietnam, General William C. Westmoreland, for 206,000 additional troops, declared a partial bombing halt (which became comprehensive in November), and approved holding discussions with Hanoi over a mutual troop withdrawal. The progress of deescalation, however, was as convoluted as the process of involvement. Even as preliminary negotiations with the North Vietnamese began in Paris in May 1968 and as U.S. forces curtailed operations in the North, the Johnson administration kept up heavy pressure against the enemy in the South, in the meantime moving ahead with a Vietnamization program to upgrade the South Vietnamese armed forces and transfer to them increasing responsibility for the war effort. The continued high level of military activity added 389 Americans to the ranks of captured or missing in 1968 and 189 in 1969.[12]

Under Nixon, U.S. troops were gradually withdrawn, but intensive bombing of North Vietnam was resumed at intervals to maintain pressure on Hanoi for a settlement and buy time for Vietnamization. Moreover, in 1970 and 1971, the Nixon administration expanded the war to Cambodia and Laos. Intended to disrupt Communist supply lines and staging areas and to underscore

U.S. determination to prevent a Communist takeover of Indochina, the Cambodian and Laotian campaigns wreaked enormous destruction and dislocation without appreciably advancing American goals.[13] In an all-out effort to return North Vietnam to the conference table and salvage "peace with honor," Nixon ordered large-scale bombing of North Vietnamese ports and factories in December 1972. Finally, in January 1973, the Christmas bombing having taken its toll on both parties, the United States and North Vietnam, together with representatives of South Vietnam and the Viet Cong, signed accords formally concluding the Vietnam War. Although the bombing of Cambodia would not end until August and there remained the threat of renewed hostilities as the Communists violated the Paris agreement and seized the military initiative in Cambodia and Vietnam following the American withdrawal (Saigon fell to the Communists in April 1975), the United States did not intervene further. The last American troops left Vietnam on 29 March 1973. The last American PW acknowledged by Hanoi, the NLF, and the Pathet Lao was released on 1 April. Thus ended another chapter in Vietnam's long history of foreign intervention, with the United States having exited the way of France, and the Soviet Union and the People's Republic of China (both of which continued to supply North Vietnam after 1973) vying to become the next master of Indochina's destiny.

Neither history nor geography treated the American prisoners of war kindly. Harsh jungle terrain, a monsoonal climate marked by extremes of damp chill and oppressive heat and humidity, primitive sanitation, meager nourishment, exposure to tropical diseases—all would take their toll. But for all of the cruel conditions imposed by geography, life in captivity for the PWs was made more onerous yet by the weight of Vietnamese history and the pressures of Cold War politics.

It was the Americans' misfortune to fall into Vietnamese (and Laotian) hands in the wake of a long and bitter period of Western colonialism and, simultaneously, at the time of a violent internal struggle among the Vietnamese themselves. The Viet Cong and North Vietnamese associated their American attackers with both the hated French and a regime in South Vietnam they regarded as corrupt and decadent. The animus toward their captives was both nationalistic and ideological: the Americans were perceived both as the latest in a long line of foreign invaders bent on conquest and as the agents of a capitalist counteroffensive aimed at subverting the "people's revolution." The Communists not only believed these notions viscerally but used the twin concepts as a double-edged propaganda sword in the battle for public opinion as well.

It was, of course, a tragic happenstance of American history that the PWs were there at all. Had the French made a more graceful exit from Vietnam in the 1940s and not exacerbated the divisions in the country by their prolonged presence, had the Communist takeover of China and the Korean War not coincided with the French collapse and thus not imbued the Indochina struggle with Cold War implications, had skeptical American planners and officials followed their own better judgment and the wisdom of senior hands at the State Department and not acquiesced in successive expansions of aid and advisory personnel until U.S. involvement became irreversible—the United States would never have committed troops to Southeast Asia in the first place. It is an abiding irony of the American experience in Vietnam that the French would later criticize the Americans for attempting to rescue Western interests there when the French were largely responsible for the predicament by their reluctance to relinquish empire. The French had themselves beckoned for U.S. participation earlier to rescue them from their own foundering effort. At that time, a young congressman from Massachusetts realized that such intervention would be a mistake. "In Indochina," John F. Kennedy reported on his return to Washington from a trip to Southeast Asia in 1951,

> we have allied ourselves to the desperate effort of a French regime to hang onto the remnants of empire . . . . To check the southern drive of communism makes sense but not only through reliance on the force of arms. The task is rather to build strong native non-Communist sentiment within these areas and rely on that as a spearhead of defense rather than upon the legions of General [Jean] de Lattre [de Tassigny]. To do this apart from and in defiance of innately nationalistic aims spells foredoomed failure.[14]

There is no better evidence of the gravitational, unthinking nature of the U.S. involvement in Vietnam than the young Kennedy's own shifting position on the issue over the next decade.

Once they were captured, Cold War politics and posturing made the American PWs pawns as well as victims. President Johnson eschewed a formal declaration of war because of domestic opposition at home and concern that such a declaration would put pressure on the Soviet Union and China to intervene formally also. The absence of an official war declaration left the American prisoners in a legal limbo wherein the North Vietnamese could characterize them as "pirates" or "mercenaries" and deny them the protection of wartime conventions. The undefined nature of the war also blurred the distinction between military and civilian personnel, complicating the situation of both. As an Army study noted in 1969, "The Vietnam war was characterized at all times by the lack of . . . precise distinctions between military and civilian personnel, between classical and guerrilla warfare, and between friendly and hostile territory. Accordingly, terror and counterterror in the 'civilian' sector of the conflict rapidly escalated into reprisals and counterreprisals [sic] against 'military' prisoners of war." Thus in 1965, following the execution of Viet Cong terrorists by the South Vietnamese, the Viet Cong executed, avowedly in retaliation, U.S. Army Sgts. Harold Bennett and Kenneth Roraback and Capt. Humbert Versace.*[15] Obviously, U.S. civilians in South Vietnam also suffered by their inevitable association with the war effort and their vulnerability to terrorist ambush. All told, some 60 American civilians were taken prisoner between 1961 and 1973, their fate determined generally by the same twists of fortune and enemy caprice that affected military PWs.[16]

Cold War constraints—the apprehension over Soviet and Chinese intentions, mounting public and congressional criticism of the U.S. military buildup, and the continued reluctance of the Joint Chiefs to divert troops from Europe—also limited U.S. strategic options and encouraged a policy of "graduated response" that held American prisoners hostage to the spasmodic and sometimes fickle shifts in Washington's prosecution of the war. The fitful pattern of bombing pauses and resumptions, intended to moderate North Vietnamese aggression and placate domestic and international public opinion, more often than not emboldened and angered Communist prison camp officials, who alternated torture and leniency according to the fluctuations of U.S. policy. The desire to downplay the scale of the U.S. military commitment no doubt contributed to the 1965 decision in Washington to pursue quiet diplomacy in securing release or better treatment for American PWs. The low-key approach, while accommodating political sensitivities, yielded few tangible results. Only after 1969, when U.S. officials decided to "go public" with the PW issue and revelations of widespread prisoner abuse embarrassed Hanoi, did the conditions of the PWs begin to improve.

No war has been hospitable to its prisoners. The Americans held captive by the Japanese and the North Koreans had to endure their own peculiar horrors, in some respects more brutal than the abuses in Vietnam.[17] But no prisoners were more at the mercy of historical and geopolitical forces beyond the theater of war itself than the Americans in Southeast Asia. (The Korean case was somewhat analogous in its Cold War ramifications, but the U.S. action in Korea did not come on the heels of a century of Western occupation—the North Koreans were perhaps just as xenophobic as the North Vietnamese, but there was not the deep reservoir of anti-Western enmity that

* See Chapters 12 and 13.

existed in Vietnam. And, of course, the period of captivity in Korea was much shorter.) For all the physical discomfort stemming from a lengthy captivity in a harsh environment, it was the intrusion of these larger, murkier forces that made the PW experience in Southeast Asia so precarious. The continual uncertainty over their status and ultimate fate, the emasculating and guilt-inducing manipulation of them for the consumption of the American and international press, and the alternation of hope and despair as the U.S. war effort waxed and waned were more persistent torments than the chronic afflictions of disease and inclement weather. That they could triumph over such adversity was testimony not only to the Americans' physical courage but also to their own strong traditions and sense of purpose and their conviction that history was on their side even as it seemed, for the moment, to be conspiring against them.

2

PWs of the Viet Minh, 1946-1954

By the time Americans were taken captive in Vietnam, Vietnamese Communists had already had considerable experience dealing with prisoners of war, dating at least as far back as 1946, when the Viet Minh took French and French Union* prisoners in the early stages of the Franco-Viet Minh War. By 1950, the Viet Minh had herded several hundred French PWs, many of them civilians, to camps in mountain strongholds north and northwest of Hanoi. Then in October 1950, in battle near the Chinese border, they captured several thousand more French and French Union soldiers. Altogether, including those captured at Dien Bien Phu in May 1954, some 40,000 Frenchmen and their allies are believed to have fallen into Vietnamese hands.[1] So that more than a decade before Americans began filling up Viet Cong and North Vietnamese prison camps, the Viet Minh were overseeing and exploiting a sizable PW population. In so many ways Viet Minh treatment of these French PWs now seems like a rehearsal for the American experience that followed. For this reason it is instructive to review in some detail the nature of the French captivity.

Conditions in the Viet Minh prison camps varied according to location and the progress of the war, but they were without exception wretched. Generally prisoners, upon capture, were placed in small camps supervised by local villagers, then, when circumstances and facilities permitted, moved to larger compounds for permanent internment. The village camps contained as many as 100 prisoners at a time, with 8 to 15 men assigned to a hut that would be guarded by 20 or so Viet Minh. Most huts were confiscated peasants' homes; a few were built by the prisoners themselves. In low-lying areas,

---

* French Union prisoners included Algerians, Moroccans, other African and European Foreign Legionnaires, and Indochinese troops and civilians allied with the French.

14

huts often stood on stilts, both to avoid flooding and snakes and to provide overhead shelter for livestock. The prisoners erected crude partitions for privacy and to segregate the ill. They slept on bamboo floors in whatever clothing they had without any covering. To keep warm in the mountain camps, where temperatures were often below freezing, they built makeshift fireplaces, piled straw collected from rice fields, or simply huddled together when allowed to; they received no blankets until months after capture, if at all.

As they would view the Americans, the Vietnamese regarded the French PWs as criminal aggressors rather than prisoners of war and refused to recognize any rights they had under established international PW conventions. Camp guards, under little or no supervision, abused and beat prisoners at will. In one of the most dreaded forms of punishment, known as the "buffalo treatment," captors confined prisoners in the manure and sewage below a hut floor with dangerous buffalos, foraging pigs, and other animals. Many French PWs died of starvation or infection in these pits or grew so weak that they perished later, some of them while walking to repatriation points.[2]

At a large camp near a village called Nuoc Kay in northern North Vietnam guards routinely jammed newly arrived prisoners, already sick, starving, and exhausted, under the floors of the huts to wallow in offal, denying them medicine, soap, and adequate food for weeks. Finally, jailers removed the debilitated captives and allowed them to walk about the compound for short periods. Later, the Vietnamese permitted them to set up a latrine area for waste disposal and rudimentary cleanliness. They threw the prisoners bits of rice, often putrid and contaminated by rodent feces, and ladled out small cups of thin pumpkin broth—a meager and usually temporary relief before resumption of the abuses.

French soldiers captured in the north in 1951, when the war intensified, experienced a particularly abominable captivity. Forced to lug heavy loads through swampy rice paddies and over rugged mountainous terrain, with scant food, little rest, and no medication, they lived worse than common beasts of burden. After delivering their loads, they were often interned near mountain villages in small compounds containing a hut or two and little else, fenced by bamboo, sharpened sticks, and thorn branches. At capture the Viet Minh confiscated all items of value and personal comfort. A few Viet officers made the hollow gesture of issuing a receipt for valuables, later announcing that a prisoner had forfeited his receipt by improper behavior or a bad attitude. Guards commonly harassed and beat the prisoners, locked them in stocks, or subjected them to a version of the buffalo treatment. They doled out small quantities of rice and salt, leaving the PWs to grind the rice on stones, then find a way to cook it. Occasionally, prisoners stole, butchered, and ate a village dog, always in fear of detection. The wrath of villagers, who raised dogs for food as well as security, could be as cruel as that of the guards.[3]

From time to time in these village camps, PWs who were not too ill "volunteered" for work details outside the compound—carrying supplies, cutting wood, building roads, clearing trails—in the hope of a little extra food or an opportunity to escape. There were attempts at escape but success was rare and failure invited barbaric punishment. Soldiers or villagers, the latter fearful of Viet Minh displeasure, dragged recaptured PWs back to their chief guard for disciplining. In an especially brutal case near Cao Bang, one guard executed two recaptured prisoners by shooting each first in the leg, then the shoulder, then the foot, then the side, then the stomach; a third survived only because the ammunition ran out.[4] All told, some 70 French PWs were known to have died trying to escape or helping others try.

Medical attention, no matter the size of the camp, was virtually non-existent. Bernard Fall, who accompanied French units in combat operations in both Vietnam and Laos and would return to write the most authoritative firsthand accounts of the French experience, reported instances where PWs went eight months with unset fractures. In their weakened condition, prisoners died of snake, lizard, and scorpion bites they would have survived if healthy. Camps typically were located near rivers and inmates usually took their drink directly from the river; waterborne intestinal diseases became rampant and in some camps resulted in mortality rates of near plague proportions. Fall reported that one camp counted 201 deaths out of a total of 272 prisoners between March and September 1952; another, 120 out of 250 men lost in July-August 1954. Crude infirmaries, "equipped at best with antimalaria tablets and a lancet or two," Fall noted, were set up in huts in some of the camps, but the Viet Minh, adhering to a strict policy of segregating officers and enlisted men, refused to allow captured French doctors to treat the injured or ill. More often than not they kept for themselves Red Cross packages intended for the sick. In another grim foreshadowing of the American experience, no French PW with serious wounds of the abdomen, chest, or skull, or experiencing severe psychological disorder, survived Viet Minh captivity. Not until early 1954, just before the fall of Dien Bien Phu, did the Viet Minh establish a few field hospitals for prisoners. Even then the surgery was so primitive, often performed without antibiotics or anesthesia, that French officers saved more lives by preventing surgery than securing it.[5]

Some PWs fared better than others. The Moroccans among the French Union captives, themselves "victims of colonialism" in the view of the Vietnamese, received favored treatment, including relative freedom of movement within the camps and assignment as camp cooks, which assured them extra and better food. A group of Italian prisoners from a French Foreign Legion unit managed to weather some difficult moments because they communicated in a language not understood by the guards and thus were able to organize better to meet their hardship. (The Italians' experience paralleled that of Turkish PWs held by North Korea during the Korean War.) A unit of Spaniards also fared relatively well, possibly because of their stated opposition to Franco's fascist regime in Spain; some of them stayed on in North Vietnam after the war, marrying Vietnamese women and raising families. One might expect the Africans and southern Europeans to have done better, too, because of their easier adjustment to the grueling heat and humidity, though they must have had their own share of problems with the winter chill.[6]

The French, drawing the full ire and attention of the Vietnamese and more debilitated by the climate, had more trouble. The Viet Minh would designate prisoners of their own choosing as camp foremen with no regard to seniority or rank, a practice aimed at destroying all trace of authority among the French officers. Additionally, during 1950-51, they isolated officers of colonel rank and denied communication between officers of different units by confining them to their respective huts. Thus two vital ingredients for successful resistance—leadership and communication, devices that helped the Italians survive and that American PWs would manage to maintain in a continual struggle with their captor—were effectively nullified in the case of the French.

Survivors of the village camps, which served as interim holding areas, were moved eventually to permanent labor camps. Before 1950 there were few such facilities. According to a later report prepared for a U.S. congressional committee, in the early years of the Franco-Viet Minh War, "prisoners were deposited in mountain retreats or carried along with the military forces or simply eliminated when expediency dictated." Gradually, however, as the war expanded, and especially after the disastrous French losses of October 1950, new arrangements were necessary to accommodate the increasing numbers of PWs, and a more conventional and permanent, though still primitive, prison organization emerged.[7] These larger camps, located in remote areas, enabled the Viet Minh to maintain tighter security and, just as important, to subject PWs to an elaborate indoctrination program under the supervision of a trained staff. Indoctrination, a process of educating or "reeducating" prisoners as to the error of their ways, was intended by the Communists both to break down PW discipline and morale and to yield propaganda statements that could be used to discredit the French war effort.

Borrowing methods developed by the Chinese and used in the Korean War, the Viet Minh based their indoctrination program on a Pavlovian system of reward and punishment, alternating carrot and stick to gain the desired confession or information. At one turn the PW would undergo a relatively benign round of interrogation sessions and political meetings where he would be exposed to propaganda lectures and literature, then given an opportunity for reflection and self-recrimination. The Vietnamese would pose as lenient and paternalistic, offering to forgive the criminal act if the prisoner sincerely repented. As a sign of contrition, the prisoner would be asked to write a letter variously extolling the Viet Minh for humane treatment, acknowledging the justness of the Vietnamese revolution, urging French withdrawal from Indochina, or advising a negotiated settlement with guerrilla leaders. At appointed intervals interrogators would follow up with what American PWs would later call "attitude checks." In a typical instance the examiner would instruct his charge that he was

> fortunate enough to be in the hands of the people, who will look after you. Time no longer has any importance for you. Learn to be patient. It needs a great while for a man as corrupted as you to become good. But good you will become. And when the people have completely won the war against the colonialists you will be sent back, an entirely new, entirely regenerated being. . . . One day France too, the whole of France, will come over from the side of falsehood to that of truth.

"We are going to give you the chance of improving yourself," the examiner concluded, "[but] if you remain stubbornly devoted to your wrong way of thinking . . . there will be no pity for you."[8]

To induce compliance, the Viet Minh would manipulate the prisoner's mail, his rations, his freedom of movement. Periods of labor were alternated with the interrogation sessions, intensified or relaxed depending on the progress of the prisoner's reeducation. French Legionnaire troops, for whom the Communists prepared propaganda in several languages (including Arabic and African dialects), were promised early repatriation to their original homelands. In one camp French Union troops were given medical care according to a scale of "People's Democratic urgency" that corresponded roughly to the degree of their commitment to the French cause, those with the strongest affiliation being the last to receive attention. On occasion cooperators would be released, always in a showy display to encourage others to comply. Improving attitude brought reward; resistance, punishment.

What could not be induced was coerced. Indoctrination turned vicious in 1951 at the Cao Bang prison camp near the Chinese border when the PWs there, as a group, refused to sign a manifesto praising the Viet Minh and condemning the French; after a 15-month ordeal, in which two-thirds of their number died from starvation or mistreatment, the group finally capitulated. A special camp was established at Lang Trang in the far north for tough resisters. A French Army chaplain, Catholic priest Paul Jeandel, reported how the Viet Minh resorted to brutal beatings and fake executions from which particular PWs (Father Jeandel was one) obtained a reprieve at the last possible moment. Jeandel, who spent three years in the Communist camps, described the worst aspect of the experience in terms that numerous American PWs would later echo in their own accounts:

> Medieval tortures are nothing in comparison to the atomic-age torture of brainwashing . . . . It amputates your soul and grafts another one upon you. Persuasion has taken the place of punishment. The victims must approve and justify in their own eyes the measures which crush them. They must recognize themselves guilty and believe in the crimes which they have not committed . . . . I have seen men leave camp who were dead and did not know it, for they had lost their own personality and had become slogan-reciting robots . . . . I myself nearly lost my reason.

"The worst wasn't to die," Jeandel reflected, "but to see one's soul change."[9]

Lucien Bodard, author of *The Quicksand War: Prelude to Vietnam*, wrote of the terrible dilemma faced by French soldiers at indoctrination: "Should one refuse and die, maintaining the integrity of a French officer? Or is it not one's duty to use cunning, to pretend to be converted in order to live through it and fight again for one's country another day? But is it possible to pretend without being dragged in, without being a traitor in spite of oneself, and without becoming despicable?" Bodard added that it was a predicament "in which even the strongest ended up by no longer knowing what he was doing, what stage he had reached, or even what he really thought. The men who went through this were marked forever." This sentiment, too, would become a familiar refrain in the Americans' own captivity memoirs and debriefings. Yet another was the recollection of a French lieutenant that however bad the living conditions in the camps, "in the long run the most unbearable thing was . . . the pedantic dogmatism, the presumption of ideological superiority, the know-all school-teacher attitude of the yellow-skinned preachers of world revolution . . . . [The indoctrination effort] was far more unpleasant and far more humiliating than being hungry or ill."[10]

In general, the French broke more easily than the Americans would—partly because of the aforementioned leadership and communication problems and partly because their training had not prepared them for hardline resistance. The training of American military personnel, especially the officer-aviators who made up a large percentage of U.S. PWs, stressed steadfast resistance in the event of capture—a rigid code of conduct deemed necessary to preserve discipline and thus, in the opinion of the drafters, enhance survival. (This code evolved out of the Korean War experience, where there had been an apparent breakdown of morale and discipline among American prisoners and widespread allegations of brainwashing and collaboration.* As we shall see, literal adherence to the post-Korea Code of Conduct's admonition that a PW would reveal only his name, rank, service number, and date of birth became increasingly untenable in the face of interrogation and torture methods used by the Vietnamese. Though adhered to in principle, the Code would often be abandoned in practice and replaced by improvisational survival techniques.) French Air Force training before 1954, by contrast, had prescribed relatively flexible resistance guidelines. The French airman's instructions said simply to do nothing that would hurt another PW or bring harm to French units fighting the war. French fliers were advised to tell interrogators false unit designations whenever possible, give names of senior officers who had previously served in the area and therefore might be known to the Vietnamese, offer basic information about aircraft performance and equipment characteristics without going into details, tell the Vietnamese how good their camouflage was, appear ignorant of any vital information such as codes or other secret knowledge not likely to be given mere air crewmen, and speak accurately on the subject of French Air Force organization (about which the enemy likely already knew and would use to test the credibility of the prisoner's answers).[11] The aim of the French training was to cast crewmen as reasonably cooperative in telling the captor what he already knew, but as neither correct nor well informed about more complex or highly classified matters. As for confessions, token admissions and gestures of compliance were permissible if the prisoner had reached the limit of his endurance. There is much in common between this French approach and that developed under duress later by the Americans, although the Americans, beginning with a tougher resistance stance, as a group held out longer and more effectively.

---

* In truth, the American prisoners in Korea were victimized as much by youth and inexperience as by inadequate PW resistance and survival training. Most PWs in Korea were enlisted men— in most instances lower-ranking and less educated than PWs in Vietnam, the majority of whom were officers and thus could be expected to be more highly motivated and better trained. For the two sides to the controversy surrounding the performance of U.S. PWs in Korea, see Eugene Kinkead, *In Every War But One*, and the revisionist Albert D. Biderman, *March to Calumny*; an excellent historiographical article that summarizes the issues and reviews the literature on the subject is H. H. Wubben, "American Prisoners of War in Korea: A Second Look at the 'Something New in History' Theme," *American Quarterly* (Spring 70), 3-19. See also "POW: The Fight Continues After the Battle," Report of the Secretary of Defense's Advisory Committee on Prisoners of War, Aug 55, Washington, D.C., which provides background both on the performance of PWs in Korea and the development of the new Code of Conduct; and Frederic F. Wolfer, Jr., "The Origins of Affinity for the Armed Forces Code of Conduct Among Prisoners of War Returned from Southeast Asia," Ph.D. dissertation, George Washington Univ, Washington, D.C., Jun 79, which examines the usefulness of the Code for PWs in Vietnam.

The Viet Minh's political warfare specialists waged the propaganda campaign as relentlessly as Giap's guerrillas pursued the military advantage. They exploited confessions extorted from their captives to dramatize alleged atrocities of the French and the legitimacy of their own cause. They attempted to sway French public opinion against the war by publishing fabricated or extorted antiwar statements. Photographs of early PW releases or posed sessions where PWs were being treated kindly were issued to demonstrate the beneficence of the "people's revolution." For three months before the Geneva Conference of 1954, the Communists permitted prisoners at a few camps to elect a camp representative, to whom they granted no real authority, and then photographed the charade to create the illusion of democratic procedure.

Most cruelly, the Vietnamese played a numbers game with PW rosters, making political capital out of French anxiety to determine the number of their countrymen in captivity. As the Viet Cong and North Vietnamese would do in the propaganda war against the Americans, the Viet Minh refused to provide official lists of casualties, or accept lists from the French for confirmation, until it suited their purpose. Without verifying their accuracy, they exploited PW lists tendered by the French as French admission of colonial aggression. They distributed by turns incomplete and inaccurate prisoner rosters because they knew the French people expected a thorough accounting from their own officials and such pressure would cause the French government to grant concessions in return for PW information.* [12]

The French had good reason to worry about the fate of their PWs since Communist regimes had a notorious record for dealing severely with captured prisoners. More than one million World War II Soviet-held PWs were never accounted for; thousands of those who were accounted for died from inhumane treatment in captivity. In one tragic episode in the Katyn Forest in 1941, the Russians were believed to have slaughtered between 5,000 and 16,000 Polish PWs, mostly officers—executions they admitted to in 1990. As negotiators gathered in Geneva in 1954, the Communist record in Korea became available: of 75,000 South Korean and United Nations prisoners taken by the North Koreans and Chinese, 60,000 never returned; and the early evidence indicated also that several thousand Americans may have died or been executed in Korean PW camps. Moreover, Vietnamese sale of bones to French representatives, in a grisly scheme to profit from French desire to

---

* The North Vietnamese attempted to turn the PW issue to similar political advantage against the United States, denying for six years U.S. requests for a list of American PWs. Not until late 1970 did Hanoi release one, sending it to noted war critics Senators J. William Fulbright and Edward M. Kennedy and through the auspices of the antiwar group COLIFAM, headed by Mrs. Cora Weiss. Not until the final accounting of captives in 1973 did Hanoi give the American government an official list.

have remains returned for burial service, hardly inspired confidence about the well-being of Viet Minh-held PWs.[13]

With respect to the fate of American prisoners in the Korean camps, it should be noted that the aftermath of the Korean War brought much the same rumors and recriminations concerning MIAs (personnel missing in action) as would occur after the Americans departed Vietnam. The following passage extracted from testimony before a subcommittee of the House Foreign Affairs Committee in May 1957 could as easily have been written in 1974:

> While the possibility exists that there may still be some personnel held, alive and against their will, we do not have any further positive information or intelligence from any source that such is the case. Because of the lack of positive information to support the contention that any of our military are still held, as well as a lack of conclusive information to indicate that they are all deceased, I am sure you will realize the difficulty we face in attempting to comfort the next of kin and to satisfy the understandable and patriotic concern which has been expressed by so many Americans on this subject.
>
> We are in the extremely difficult position of not being able, in all honesty, to hold out much hope, while at the same time we cannot in good conscience completely foreclose the possibility that some may still be alive. In any event, the information we demand can only come, in the final analysis, from the . . . Communist . . . authorities.

"Since the end of the war," wrote a discouraged Defense Department official to the Assistant Secretary of Defense for International Security Affairs in 1967, "we have pressed the Chinese . . . to provide information about these Americans but have consistently been rebuffed." As late as 1970, U.S. representatives would still be lamenting the lack of Chinese cooperation in resolving the cases of some 389 missing Americans whose fate remained uncertain 20 years after the Korean armistice.[14]

French concern about their own PWs and MIAs in Indochina turned out to be justified. According to Bernard Fall, of an estimated 37,000 French and French Union soldiers reported "missing" in Indochina, most of whom were assumed to be PWs, only some 11,000 were known to have survived, "most of those . . . walking skeletons in no way different from those who survived Dachau and Buchenwald." The others either died in captivity or were never accounted for. (An even grimmer fact revealed by Fall: fewer than 10 percent of France's Indochinese allies believed to have been taken prisoner—chiefly South Vietnamese—were ever released or accounted for.) The French chief of staff, General Paul Ely, in his 1964 memoirs, reckoned that of 32,000 to 45,000 French and French Union personnel missing in action, at least 20,000 had probably been PWs. These figures are supported by other sources, though official French figures are hard to come by and have varied over the years. When President Nixon at a news conference in June 1972 cited a figure of 15,000 French PWs who were never accounted for, French authorities, responding defensively, insisted that the total was closer to 6,000 and that most of those were Indochinese and Legionnaires of non-French ethnic origin who likely disappeared into the society, returned anonymously to their homelands, or, in the case of the Vietnamese, were inducted into the North Vietnamese armed forces.[15]

The Viet Minh used their PW chips to the very end. In the spring of 1954 they introduced the prisoner of war issue in negotiations leading up to Geneva, gaining Viet Minh admission to the conference as a full participant in exchange for returning a number of French wounded. They stalled the opening of the conference, scheduled to begin 26 April, until 8 May, the day after the fall of Dien Bien Phu, thereby assuring themselves a negotiating advantage of another large body of prisoners, including many French regulars. The PW additions increased the Communists' leverage and enabled them to gain more at the table in Geneva than they could have achieved with additional divisions on the battlefield.

How badly the Viet Minh wanted a military victory at Dien Bien Phu to support diplomacy at Geneva may be judged by the price they paid to attack when and as they did. General Giap, as part of his siege plan, had ordered new channels cut for the surrounding mountain streams, channels designed to inundate French fortifications through a trench network dug by his troops and coolies. Yet, with Geneva approaching, he did not wait for the imminent seasonal rains, sacrificing thousands of lives by assaulting through the dry trenches. (After the French surrender, the Viets herded prisoners back to the battleground to reenact the fight in a staged scene before movie cameras. They could not film, however, because by that time the rains had arrived and the battlefield was under water.) Had Giap delayed until the rains fell, the French would have been flooded. He instead ordered the costly assault because the Viet Minh needed the victory in order to negotiate from strength at Geneva. As for the PWs taken at Dien Bien Phu, ironically and tragically, many died in a forced march over 500 miles of jungle terrain on the way to prison camps and repatriation holding areas and never did figure in the Geneva calculus.[16]

Even after the signing of the Geneva agreements in July 1954, the North Vietnamese, as they would do after the Paris accords in 1973, obstructed efforts to expedite PW exchanges. Article 21c of the Geneva pact stipulated that all prisoners, foreign and Vietnamese, were to be given "all possible assistance in proceeding to their country of origin, place of habitual residence or zone of their choice." Unlike the more specific repatriation safeguards which

the United States had incorporated into the 1953 Korean agreements to protect captured North Koreans, this broad statement and ambiguous language
in effect granted the North Vietnamese control over the disposition of thousands of PWs. They proceeded to pervert the intent of the article, forcing
captured Indochinese into slave labor or military service in the Democratic
Republic of Vietnam and returning many Eastern Europeans, captured with
French Legionnaire units, to jail or death behind the iron curtain.* Thus
when the PWs had served their purpose as puppets in the propaganda campaign and bargaining chips in the peace negotiations, they continued to be
used by Vietnamese Communists as pawns in the ongoing Cold War.[17]

From capture through indoctrination and final release, in terms of
physical abuse, psychological torment, and political manipulation, French
captivity under the Viet Minh broadly foreshadowed the American PW experience a generation later. This is not to say that there were not conspicuous
differences in the two experiences: most of the French PWs were ground
troops and most of the Americans were airmen; the type of warfare was different; and circumstances of capture were much different. These contrasting
factors in themselves affected the physical condition and treatment of the
respective PW groups. Other differences, some quite significant, have
already been mentioned. Still more distinctions were drawn by Anita Lauve,
an expert on the French situation, in testimony before a House committee
investigating the issue of American MIAs in 1976. Lauve remarked that,
although the French enjoyed the advantage of having cultivated friendlier
native contacts at least among some elements of the populace, they fought
a more conventional ground war deep behind enemy lines and so were more
susceptible to mass captures and the harsher conditions of an itinerant

* The ordeal of these Eastern European Legionnaires, most of them political exiles originally,
has never received wide publicity. The Viet Minh claimed first that they had deserted voluntarily
to the Vietnamese cause, then (after holding them captive for two years after Geneva before
deporting them) that they freely chose repatriation to their original homeland. In one instance
a group of German and Hungarian PWs escaped from Viet Minh prison camps and appealed
to the International Control Commission for asylum, reporting that hundreds of others were
being similarly detained. The ICC responded quickly, but failed to find any prisoners once
they had located the camps in question because the Viet Minh usually knew ahead of time
when the ICC planned such inspections and moved the prisoners into the jungle. When on
one occasion they were surprised by an ICC team asking to examine a certain village, Viet
Minh escorts led the ICC team astray to a village with the same name but in a different locality,
where there were no PWs; by the time the ICC recognized the deceit, they had lost several
days, during which time the Communists had shifted the prisoners to another remote village.
Appeals by the ICC to the Red Cross to investigate claims of forced detention and illegal
deportation proved unavailing.

captivity in remote and makeshift camps.[18] (In this latter respect, the French experience more closely paralleled that of those U.S. PWs caught by the Viet Cong in the guerrilla war in the South.) By the 1960s the North Vietnamese had developed a much more elaborate prison system that resulted in generally better conditions for American prisoners but also more calculated and sophisticated punishments.

Despite these many variances, one remains impressed by the degree to which the two experiences were comparable. If there were significant differences, there were also striking similarities. In the end, both groups of PWs suffered in the extreme. If the Americans who emerged from their homecoming transports were not the "walking skeletons" that Fall referred to in his Dachau analogy or the "living skeletons with burning eyes, lost in their clothes" that Dien Bien Phu chronicler Jules Roy described,[19] it was only because of a relatively benign pre-release period in which to recuperate and a short bus ride to the release itself, whereas many of the French were marched long distances wounded or in poor health to their repatriation points.

The nature of the Vietnamese Communists' treatment of French PWs "needs to be known in the West," Fall warned in December 1958, "since future complications in the area may compel friendly forces to face the same foe once more under similar conditions."[20] Fall's admonition, prophetic as it was, came somewhat belatedly, as even before he wrote these words the United States was already reprising the French experience. A harbinger of what lay ahead for the Americans occurred in June 1954, as the French affair in Indochina was winding down just after Dien Bien Phu and the United States, willy-nilly, found itself filling the vacuum left by the French demise. A brief and rather uneventful episode, it nonetheless provided an early glimpse of the shifting stage and new cast of characters.

On 14 June 1954, U.S. Army Pvts. Doyle Morgan and Leonard Sroveck and Air Force Airmen Ciro Salas, Giacomo Appice, and Jerry Schuller became the first Americans captured in the Vietnam wars. Viet Minh soldiers seized them at a beach near Tourane (Da Nang), in Quang Nam Province, after they had borrowed a French military vehicle to go swimming. The men had been part of a U.S. maintenance crew supporting French supply units. Their capture immediately triggered action at high levels at the Pentagon and State Department. U.S. troops, with French cooperation, instituted a covert search, but their efforts at discretion failed when a Hong-Kong-based UPI reporter quoted a Civil Air Transport pilot who had revealed the capture of the Americans. The story appeared in the *Washington Post and Times Herald* on 18 June.[21]

As the French pressed the search, they learned that Americans in swimming trunks had been sighted among a group of about 20 prisoners in Viet Minh hands south of Da Nang. In Washington, the State Department feared Communist exploitation of the capture at the Geneva Conference then in session. Several American reporters on assignment to Indochina, particularly Marguerite Higgins of the *New York Herald-Tribune*, urged U.S. officials to appeal directly to the Viet Minh, but U.S. Chargé d'Affaires in Saigon Robert McClintock recommended against such action, which he felt "would merely invite contemptuous propaganda." He favored a confidential appeal through the French, leading to a secret exchange of prisoners. After gaining Secretary of State John Foster Dulles's approval, he won the cooperation of the French High Command and its chief, General Raoul Salan. Salan reported that French PWs released by the Viet Minh had confirmed the captivity of the five U.S. servicemen. The French then privately requested that the Viet Minh release the Americans.[22]

On 30 August the Viet Minh informed General Salan that they would release the five the following day at Qui Nhon, a coastal city south of Da Nang. The release occurred without incident, whereupon the State Department allowed the press to speak with the men. Their captivity, it turned out, had been unpleasant though not brutal. They received medical attention, ample food, and regular baths, no doubt benefiting from the relaxed atmosphere in the aftermath of the just-concluded truce between the French and Viet Minh. For several days after their capture in fact, their keepers had assumed them to be French because of the vehicle they drove. Their identity was discovered only after one of the prisoners of Spanish-American extraction was questioned by a collaborating French Foreign Legion PW who spoke Spanish.[23]

U.S. Air Force debriefers determined that during the first week they had been marched through a series of villages, with stops at peasant huts for meals, rest, and interrogation, before arriving at a permanent PW facility on 23 June. At the new facility each was given a "personal history form" to complete that requested information about their military unit and duties and personal items such as names and ages of parents and dependents, civilian occupations and property holdings, and organizational affiliations. (Intelligence experts recognized the forms as virtually identical to those used by the North Koreans and Chinese with United Nations PWs during the Korean War.) The men were told that the purpose of the questionnaire was to obtain information for notifying their service and families of their capture.[24]

There followed, according to the Air Force report of the incident, several interrogation sessions where they were asked about the personnel of the Tourane air base, the numbers of Americans there and their duties, numbers of aircraft, the locations of fuel supplies and ammunition dumps, and the like. The questioning was informed and persistent but without threats or pressure even when the prisoners responded evasively. U.S. debriefers were convinced that the lenient treatment, at times even solicitous—as when the men complained about aching feet—and seemingly innocuous interrogation were intended to soften up the prisoners for indoctrination. A Viet Minh officer regularly visited the men, typically three times a week for an hour or two on each occasion, to engage in "friendly political discussions," explaining the Communists' "clemency" policy, contrasting the treatment they were receiving with alleged mistreatment of Communist PWs by the U.N. forces in Korea, extolling the struggles of the Vietnamese people against imperialist aggressors, and professing an interest in Shakespeare, American novels, and life in the United States. That the Americans were favorably impressed if not converted was attested by their comments following repatriation. Upon their release, the Viet Minh broadcast on the radio a prepared statement, attributed to the five Americans and circulated in the world press, that suggested how successful the Communists had been in conveying their point of view: "Since our capture we slowly came to realize American intervention in the Indochina war was against peoples fighting resolutely for independence. Had we realized the truth beforehand, we would not have agreed to come to this country."[25]

The propaganda statement, even to its phrasing, presaged the content and style of many others broadcast a decade later by Hanoi and the National Liberation Front Radio in South Vietnam and attributed to American PWs. Those statements would come usually after rougher treatment, more often than not after unbearable torture and degradation, but the precedent had been established here as early as 1954. In retrospect, Fall's advice was well worth heeding. For a new enemy of the people's revolution, there would be much to learn from the French experience. Indeed, for those familiar with the details of the French captivity, the American PW experience would create a sense of déjà vu that was at times positively haunting.

3

Laos: Prisoners of the Shadow War

Although the United States steadily increased its presence in Vietnam following the French departure, it was not until the fall of 1961, when threats to the Diem regime from within and without reached critical proportions, that Vietnam became a preoccupying issue for American officials. As the reins of policy shifted from Eisenhower to Kennedy early in 1961, it was not Vietnam but rather Laos that presented the more immediate threat to U.S. interests in Southeast Asia and therefore commanded more urgent attention. The *New York Times* Index for 1961, for example, shows 8 columns of entries for Vietnam, 26 on Laos. When Eisenhower briefed Kennedy the day before the inauguration, he reportedly remarked that "Laos was the key to the entire area of Southeast Asia" and that it was "imperative that Laos be defended" against a Communist takeover. According to Arthur M. Schlesinger, Jr., and Walt W. Rostow, aides to the incoming president, Kennedy could not remember Ike even mentioning Vietnam.[1]

Even as the springtime news out of Saigon sounded alarms, the new administration kept Diem's problems in South Vietnam on the back burner while resolving to confront the Communists in Laos. While pursuing a diplomatic solution and resisting direct military involvement, Kennedy authorized covert actions, including increased reconnaissance flights. On 20 April 1961 he ordered U.S. military advisers in Laos to wear their uniforms,* established officially a military assistance advisory group, and instructed the MAAG to train Laotian rightists in combat operations. Though the administration was

---

* Some 400 U.S. advisers had been sent to Laos by Eisenhower in 1960, but, so as not to violate terms of the 1954 Geneva accords that prohibited military missions in Laos other than by the French, they dressed in civilian clothes. The uniform decree followed by three days the date of the Bay of Pigs invasion. For a discussion of the effect of the Cuban fiasco on U.S. policy in Laos and Southeast Asia generally, see *U.S. Government and the Vietnam War: Part II, 1961-1964*, 23-26.

intent on keeping the American force in Laos clear of combat engagement, contact with the enemy, as in Vietnam, became inevitable as the war expanded and intensified. On 16 December 1960 an American reconnaissance aircraft flying over Communist positions in Laos had become the first U.S. Air Force plane fired at in the Southeast Asia conflict. The shootdown in March 1961 of another reconnaissance plane marked the first American aircraft lost to enemy action in Indochina. Such incidents produced casualties—and prisoners. Thus it happened that the first Americans who could truly be called PWs in Indochina (the group captured by the Viet Minh in the summer of 1954 were taken prisoner but detained for only 10 weeks and released without harm) fell into the hands of *Laotian* Communists.[2]

Although Laos would shortly become a sideshow to Vietnam, it acquired and retained a special notoriety for prisoners of war held there. Because the Laotians were more primitive and impoverished than the Vietnamese and operated with even less regard for international conventions, Americans taken captive by them often fared even worse than in Vietnam. The ordeal of Walter Moon, Grant Wolfkill, Dieter Dengler, and a dozen or so other Americans captured in Laos in the early 1960s introduced another chapter in the evolving PW experience in Southeast Asia and offered early evidence of the particular horror of captivity in "the shadow war."

Bucolic, sparsely inhabited, mostly unremarkable through a sleepy history dating to 1353, when Lao migrating from China founded the kingdom of Lan Xang (Million Elephants), Laos acquired increasing significance after World War II as a buffer state between competing geopolitical and ideological rivals on the Indochinese peninsula. French Vietnam, Thailand, and China all had a stake in the disposition of Laos, as did the various Indochinese nationalist and Communist movements spawned in the war's aftermath. Furthermore, because the United States and the Soviet Union, with like myopia, looked upon Laos as having surpassing strategic importance for the security of their interests in (and beyond) Southeast Asia, they were headed for a showdown there as an early test in the developing Cold War. The languorous Laotians were hardly stirred by all this attention, but there were leaders among them alert to the new dangers and opportunities who maneuvered determinedly for control of the postwar situation. Although in the main their purpose was to preserve Laotian integrity and prevent their country from becoming a bloody battlefield for the competing outside interests, their inability to compromise their own differences plunged Laos into a ruinous cycle of civil war and political chaos that left the Kingdom of a Million Elephants more than ever at the mercy of external forces.

By 1950, a tripartite struggle had evolved among the Laotians, gathering around three native princes and arraying the forces of nationalism and communism in an often confusing alignment. Prince Boun Oum represented the dominant "royalist" faction, which welcomed a retention of French influence,* and support from Thailand and the United States as well, in order to prevent a takeover of Laos by surging Indochinese Communists. Prince Souvanna Phouma headed a neutralist group that hoped to remove the vestiges of Western colonialism while resisting the intrusion of Asian communism. Souvanna Phouma's followers were Laotian nationalists in the purest sense and had to contend with partisan pressures from both the right and the left. Prince Souphanouvong, half brother to Souvanna Phouma, was a dedicated nationalist but also an impatient opportunist who drifted into the Communist camp and an alliance with the Viet Minh as a means to free Laos from France and protect it from Thailand. Charging Boun Oum's royalists with being puppets of the anticommunist Western powers, he became a puppet of Hanoi.

As happened in Vietnam, the Communists capitalized on postwar dislocation and anticolonial sentiment to mount a strong drive in the outlying provinces. Souphanouvong, who married a North Vietnamese woman sympathetic to the Communist cause, formed a Laotian Communist party, the Pathet Lao (Lao Nation), in 1949. With the aid of an expanding corps of Viet Minh advisers, the PL undertook a guerrilla war against the French and their royalist supporters. By 1953, they had established a headquarters at Sam Neua and a network of highways linking Pathet Lao strongholds in northern Laos with Communist outposts in North Vietnam (thus creating the sanctuaries and supply trails that would become so famous during the period of American involvement). After the fashion of their Viet Minh mentors, the Pathet Lao engaged in a systematic campaign of terror and intimidation to cement their position, executing or ousting former village leaders and arranging election of PL agents in their place.

The French, confronted with a deteriorating situation in Laos at the same time that they were losing ground in Vietnam, threw their support to the neutralist Souvanna Phouma, who received substantial aid, too, from the United States. When the neutralists could not stem the Pathet Lao momentum, and appeared in fact to be cozying up to the Communists, the United States (left to go it alone after the French collapse in Indochina) backed a rightist reaction in 1960 led by Prince Boun Oum and General Phoumi Nosavan, the latter

---

* France established a protectorate over Laos late in the 19th century. Except for a period of Japanese occupation during World War II, the French maintained sovereignty until an agreement was signed in 1949 granting Laos limited independence within the French Union. It was contention over that grant of limited autonomy that precipitated the internal political struggle.

a powerful and ambitious politician with connections to the American CIA and the ruling elite in Thailand.

The rightists, assisted by U.S. military advisers and Filipino technicians, succeeded for a time in stymieing the Communist advance and securing their own position, arresting a number of leading Pathet Lao officials. But Souphanouvong and his followers managed to escape to North Vietnam to regroup. And another faction, led by Kong Le, a young paratroop commander who sought to rid Laos of all foreign influences and backed the fallen neutralist Souvanna Phouma, mounted a strong challenge to the new regime. Kong Le had briefly seized the Laotian capital at Vientiane in August 1960 before being turned back by Phoumi and forced to withdraw to the Plain of Jars in north central Laos.

Civil war ensued, with the United States stepping up assistance to Phoumi and the right-wing royalist government and Kong Le gravitating reluctantly into an alliance with the Pathet Lao and accepting aid from the Soviet Union. Through 1961, the U.S. ferried in transports to fly support missions for Phoumi's units and contributed Special Forces soldiers to train personnel. Soviet airlifts kept Kong Le's army supplied, and North Vietnamese advisers trained his men in the use of Russian weapons. Kong Le's campaign took on increasing importance for the Communists when the Viet Cong in South Vietnam escalated attacks against the Diem government. The VC required a supply route through eastern Laos; the Pathet Lao cultivated their newly struck relationship with Kong Le to insure the flow of supplies down what came to be called the Ho Chi Minh Trail.

A lengthy stalemate resulted in a convening of the Geneva Conference on Laos in May 1961 and, eventually, in June 1962, a pact by Princes Boun Oum, Souvanna Phouma, and Souphanouvong to end the civil war. Souvanna Phouma became the prime minister of a coalition government that would continue to be buffeted by coup attempts and insurgencies from the left and right, with the Pathet Lao solidifying its control of eastern Laos and Souvanna Phouma coming to be identified increasingly now with the anticommunist right and relying more and more on U.S. aid to check the Communists. As the "shadow war" polarized and widened through the 1960s, it ensnared a growing number of Americans, who likely did not much understand the vagaries of this complicated intramural conflict but who, as PWs, found themselves confronted with the stark reality of captivity in a strange and forbidding land.

The first American to fall captive in Laos was Charles Duffy, 52, a civilian with the U.S. mission in Vientiane. Duffy was taken prisoner while hunting

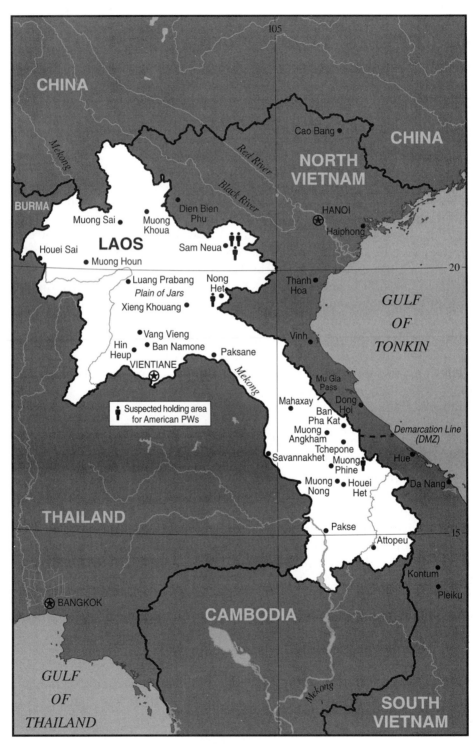

Laos (1963)

with a Laotian companion in a wilderness about 35 miles northeast of Vientiane. What happened after that is unclear. After capturing the two men on 13 January 1961, the Pathet Lao apparently marched them northward toward PL headquarters at Sam Neua. The companion escaped during this trek, later reporting the incident to Royal Lao forces, but Duffy's fate remains clouded. A Pathet Lao official told NBC cameraman Grant Wolfkill (himself a prisoner) in August 1962 that Duffy had starved to death. A report reached American officials in 1964 that Duffy had died in captivity in 1962 after suffering a series of illnesses, dehydration, exposure, and a general deterioration of health following the rigors of his long march. No other American nor any Royal Lao member saw Duffy after capture. No report, either admitting or boasting, of his capture emanated from the Pathet Lao. Americans held in Communist jails in 1962 and in 1965-66 heard from guards that Duffy may have died on a forced move between Pathet Lao camps. In the absence of definitive evidence of his fate, the U.S. government listed Duffy as a prisoner—technically a detainee because he was a civilian—for 15 years, after which a final review presumed that he died while in captivity.[3]

Much more is known about the second American captured in Laos, Army Maj. Lawrence Bailey, who returned to relate a detailed account of his experience.[4] On 23 March 1961, a U.S. C-47 transport, carrying an Air Force crew of six and two Army officers headed for leave in Saigon, made a reconnaissance sweep over a part of southern Laos and the Plain of Jars before continuing on to Vietnam. Such flights had become routine as U.S. forces aided the Royal Lao in their struggle against the Communists, proceeding usually without incident or casualties. Suddenly, however, the C-47 burst into flames from a hit on its right side. The crew chief threw open the escape hatch, but as he distributed parachutes the aircraft went into an uncontrollable spin. Major Bailey, fortunate enough to have his chute already buckled, bailed out, as did a second man, whose identity is unknown. As Bailey drifted to earth, this second man, unable to work his parachute, plunged to his death among the ancient crockery jars for which the plain is named. The other six men never left the stricken plane, perishing together as it spun into the ground, disintegrated, and burned.[5]

Bailey landed roughly, struggling free of his parachute as pain shot from his left arm, shoulder, and knee. Knowing he was close to the area in which royalist troops operated, he felt he had a chance for rescue even though the C-47 crew had clearly not had time to radio a distress message. Unable to put weight on his injured leg and suffering from shock, he collapsed after crawling a short distance. Sometime later—in his dehydrated state he lost track of the time—Bailey spotted soldiers running across a nearby ridge. His shouts attracted the Laotians, who turned out to be Communists. They took his equipment, lifted him to his feet, and moved him to a small camp, where they held him six days until they could fly him to Sam Neua. Lawrence Bailey thus began a captivity that would last 17 months.

At Sam Neua the Pathet Lao maintained a field hospital staffed by Vietnamese. Here Bailey received an injection of saline solution and a cast for his injured arm. His leg was not broken, as he had first feared, but damage to the tissue would keep him flat on his back for a month. Medical personnel fed him a gruel of condensed milk and soup, so unpalatable it caused him to vomit. Having had only milk and water at the previous camp, he had gone without solid food for a week before they provided small amounts of rice and fish. About 3 April, an English-speaking interrogator quizzed him regarding his aircraft's mission and U.S. policy in Laos, the first of a series of interrogations that would repeat the same line of questioning and last until the end of May.

As the days stretched into weeks, Bailey grew increasingly concerned about his status. Was he a prisoner of war or a political prisoner? His assignment to the Army Attaché in Laos, known to his captors, was technically a military assignment but still bore the appearance of a political post because of the mission's close connection with the U.S. Embassy. At one point during his hospital stay, officials brought in a neatly typewritten document for Bailey's signature. It stated in English that he had been injured, had had a corrective operation, would receive further treatment, that the other seven men on the plane were dead, and that their bodies had been given to the Royal Laotian government. Though he had not had an operation, Bailey felt it would be quibbling to deny the signature and could see no value in arguing against what he believed was essentially a statement of the truth.

After a month, Bailey's leg had mended well enough for the Lao to move him to a nearby building for incarceration. The cell, about 12 by 15 feet, was dark except for a small patch of light emanating from a sealed window. Cobwebs covered the dirty plaster walls. The room seemed to have served other purposes in better times, for the floor was a brick tile and held a fireplace. The two blankets given him at the hospital kept him warm enough through most of the year, but when November came, he, like many other prisoners in Southeast Asia, learned how cold a "tropical" climate could be. By then Bailey had cultivated good relationships with two of the guards (see below), who gave him extra clothing for cold weather and even on occasion let him build a small fire in the fireplace.

In the meantime, the interrogation sessions continued. Bailey came to know his chief interrogator well. The man wore what Bailey took to be a Pathet Lao uniform with a pistol belt, holster, and an American .45. He first described himself as a field marshal but later told Bailey that he, too, was a major. He spoke English adequately, and on those occasions when he was accompanied, he would interpret for the visitor. Almost never did he ask a question to which the prisoner could answer a simple "yes" or "no." Bailey fended him off with equivocations and professions of ignorance. Without actually being conscious of doing so, he resorted to one of the most effective techniques of resistance: being dull. Americans in Vietnamese captivity later would learn that, especially with certain higher ranking and fluent inter-rogators, dullness could be a disarming weapon. It bored and frustrated inquisitors, often leading them to abandon a prisoner as a poor source of information. For Bailey it bought precious time.

The interrogations, frequent during April and May, ceased for several months before resuming in November. Bailey's confidence grew with experi-ence. When the interrogator threatened to kill him for not revealing the whereabouts of Phoumi's troops, Bailey countered, seemingly resigned to his fate, "You can do what you want with me or to me, but I have told you I don't know." That statement usually drew the line. Back in his cell, Bailey reviewed what he had told them and what he had denied knowing. Never during the later interrogations did he provide information he had denied knowing in an earlier session. Apparently this tactic made his denial cred-ible. What might have happened under torture, no one can surmise, but under these pressures short of torture, Bailey was satisfied that he protected classified information.

During the summer and autumn of 1961, Bailey made friends with two of the regular guards, who responded with good treatment and occasional favors, especially when their comrades were absent. One, whose name was Sweetavong, learned English words from the prisoner. During their conversa-tions, Bailey gathered news from the outside world. From the second guard, Tong Sing, he received extra food, cigarettes, and a pair of socks. Tong Sing sometimes washed Bailey's clothes for him, a gesture of great kindness under the circumstances. From time to time, Bailey thought of escape. He went so far as to joke with Tong Sing about it, suggesting they escape together to visit a popular night club in Vientiane. Tong Sing enjoyed the jest but motioned to Bailey how difficult escape would be, indicating that numer-ous guards patrolled the routes leading from the camp and that there were "beaucoup Vietnamese" in a certain direction, betraying a fear of the Viet-namese which impressed Bailey. This sober, evidently sincere, warning of the near impossibility of escape shelved Bailey's plans.

On 18 October hospital officials handed Bailey two telegrams trans-mitted through the Red Cross, one from his wife, one from his mother. Although they were brief, a few words saying everyone was well and hoping to hear

from him, they buoyed his spirits greatly. He felt now that he would survive. In November, two other pieces of mail came—a card from his children
and a letter from a cousin.

His own deliverance was still a long way off. He passed a cold, uncomfortable winter with little relief from the darkness and isolation. In January
1962, Sweetavong introduced an English-speaking friend, who told Bailey
that peace negotiations had begun. This news was the last he had until
late July, when a Laotian official in charge of the area briefed Bailey about
release. Freedom came two weeks later, suddenly and almost anticlimac-
tically. On the flight to Vientiane, the first leg of the journey home, Bailey
would be joined by five other prisoners who had been held in camps further
to the south. Then he would discover how benign his treatment had
been compared to that of other Americans captured by the Pathet Lao,
who were denied medical care, cruelly abused, and, in at least one instance,
brutally murdered.

Charles Duffy had been captured in January 1961 in the hills above
Vientiane, in the southern part of central Laos, his fate uncertain. Lawrence
Bailey had been captured in March in the middle of the Plain of Jars, then
imprisoned at Sam Neua in northeastern Laos. In April and May the American PW ranks in Laos suddenly multiplied with the addition of four U.S.
Special Forces advisers, the pilot and flight mechanic of an Air America helicopter, and an American news photographer captured in two separate
incidents. Of this group, all but two, who disappeared shortly after capture,
were brought to a camp at Xieng Khouang east of the Plain of Jars.

In April, the town of Vang Vieng, located halfway between Vientiane,
the administrative capital, and Luang Prabang, traditional seat of the royal
family and center of power of Prince Souvanna Phouma, became the site
of a battle between pro- and anticommunist forces. Capt. Walter Moon,
advising the rightist General Kouprasith, and Sgts. Roger Ballenger, Gerald
Biber, and John Bischoff, training advisers to a battalion of Royal Laotian
infantry, were trapped in a Pathet Lao ambush north of the town. Moon,
wounded in the fighting, was taken prisoner. Radioman Biber and medic
Bischoff escaped the area in an armored car but, according to reports from
surviving Laotian soldiers, ran into a second ambush farther south. Whether
they died in the ambush or later as captives is not known, but they were
never seen again alive.

Ballenger eluded capture with the aid of three friendly soldiers and
made his way to Vang Vieng, only to find it in Pathet Lao control. Undaunted,
he organized a plan with the three Laotians to steal a canoe and paddle

downriver towards Vientiane and safety. For two days, they traveled undetected, but then were trapped by a squad of Pathet Lao, who tied them and rowed them back upstream to a Communist-controlled village, from which the group walked three days to Vang Vieng. Here, Ballenger and the Laotians were separated. A week later Ballenger was moved to Xieng Khouang, a Pathet Lao enclave in a high valley east of the Plain of Jars used by the Communists as a training area and prison.

Captain Moon, suffering from additional head and shoulder wounds incurred while attempting to escape, was already at Xieng Khouang when Ballenger arrived. Both men were placed in solitary confinement for refusing to cooperate with Communist interrogators. The Pathet Lao considered them tough resisters, guarded them closely, and treated them harshly. Communication between the two soldiers was limited until the arrival of news cameraman Grant Wolfkill, Army Capt. Edward Shore, and Navy Seaman John McMorrow, captured 15 May 1961 after their helicopter crashed during a troop transport mission.

Wolfkill, 38, a former Marine twice wounded in combat in the South Pacific in World War II, had been covering the Laotian civil war for NBC television and other news organizations and was gathering material for a story on the upcoming Geneva Conference on Laos, scheduled to open on 16 May. On 14 May, he was present when the several Laotian factions signed a cease-fire agreement before the International Control Commission and two dozen newsmen in an old one-room schoolhouse in Ban Namone, a town south of Vang Vieng on the route to Vientiane. When he learned of Pathet Lao shelling of rightist positions near a village called Pa Dong, in the hills to the northeast of Vientiane, he decided to cover the action, catching a flight back to Vientiane and arranging the next morning to go by helicopter to the shelled area. Shore, 27, a captain in the Army Transportation Corps, was the pilot of the Air America helicopter on which Wolfkill found a seat among a squad of Laotian soldiers. McMorrow, 20, was the mechanic.

A few minutes into the flight, about 12 miles south of Ban Namone, the chopper developed severe vibration, forcing Shore to cut power and make a crash landing. The crippled machine settled into a row of trees and probably would have crashed more seriously had Shore not given the engine power at the moment of impact. The final descent thus partially controlled, no one was injured. The eight Laotian soldiers on the chopper climbed out. Shore tried to radio a distress call to Vientiane, but the crash had snapped off the tail antenna. The motorized radio failed also, and two flares sent up at passing C-46 transports did no good. Wolfkill suggested to the Laotians that they fan out and guard the area in case anyone came to investigate the crash site. He was not alarmed because the area was outside Communist-held territory. As they waited near a small hut, bullets suddenly flew through the branches all around them, sending them diving for cover. The Laotian soldiers drifted away, deserting the Americans, who had only two rifles, a pistol, and a few shells, no match for the automatic weapons now zeroing in on them. Wolfkill reasoned that the attackers could be no worse than neutralist troops of the Kong Le forces; because the cease-fire had been signed, he surmised, surrender to them seemed the best course. The others agreed, hid their weapons, and gave up.

The attacking force turned out to be a dozen Kong Le soldiers, who soon bound the three men with rope and herded them off toward a nearby village. None of the three expected the 15-month captivity which lay before them, but none was aware of the degree to which the Kong Le faction had gravitated into the Communist camp. For the next few days they moved on foot and by dugout through four more village areas in a westerly direction toward the road from Vientiane to Vang Vieng. During the journey, they saw transport planes and helicopters flying search patterns, looking for them. Shore was angered when the helicopters flew past at safe altitudes, taking precaution against ground fire, because he himself had flown search missions looking for Sergeant Ballenger at considerably lower altitudes and well before the cease-fire. They came close to being spotted when a Heli-courier observation plane flew over, but the plane dropped its left wing as it passed with the men to its right, obscuring the pilot's view from his seat in the left side of the cabin.

On the third and fourth days, pneumonia drained Wolfkill's strength. At a rest point, when he appeared unable to go on, Shore and McMorrow, fearing one of the guards might shoot him, supported him and helped carry his bag. They spent the fourth night in a village hut, their arms and necks tied to a wall as they were kicked and choked by one of the local functionaries. As the situation was looking grim, Wolfkill managed to free his hands and, gripping them together in front of him as if shaking hands with himself, he said, "Souvanna Phouma, Kong Le." It worked. The guards removed the neck ropes, and the villagers brought in food and water. A crisis had passed.

Still exhausted but no longer so close to collapse, the three Americans walked the next day through hillside and jungle paths, passing columns of Pathet Lao soldiers taking up new positions, movement specifically prohibited by the cease-fire but that would secure more territory for the Pathet Lao at the final settlement.* Late in the day, they reached a roadway Wolfkill

---

* The Geneva Conference on Laos met intermittently between 16 May 1961 and 23 July 1962. Throughout the talks, which were more eagerly pursued by concerned officials in the United States and the Soviet Union than by the warring factions in Laos, the cease-fire agreement would repeatedly be violated as each side sought to consolidate and strengthen its position.

recognized. A dirt track with the ominous name Highway 13, it was the link from Vientiane to Luang Prabang. Wolfkill knew they were near a village called Hin Heup and that not far north were Ban Namone and Vang Vieng. The men's spirits soared when an old U.S. Army truck splashed to a halt in the mud nearby to pick them up for the journey north. They had to travel directly through the little town where, less than a week earlier, the cease-fire had been signed. Wolfkill felt certain that the ICC officials, perhaps some newsmen, and maybe even some anticommunist representatives would still be there. But his optimism faded when the truck stopped on a hillside and the guards ordered the prisoners out. After a few minutes, another truck pulled off the road to deliver an officer in a Pathet Lao uniform who snapped an order to the senior guard. Wolfkill was certain the officer was not Laotian, but a North Vietnamese in Lao uniform. He remembered debating with other journalists whether General Phoumi's claims about North Vietnamese officers present in Laos were truth or propaganda, and now he had the bitter answer.

The sound of helicopter engines startled the men. Minutes later, three American choppers passed over, heading south toward Vientiane. With their passing went hope for quick release. The men were too discouraged to look each other in the eye. Guards ordered them back into the truck and drove them into Ban Namone. As they reached the town, Wolfkill stood and told the others to do the same, hoping someone would see them and report their presence. The guards did not seem to mind, and the bold move paid off. A man emerging from a hut by the little schoolhouse, seeming to recognize Wolfkill, waved to him. Wolfkill never learned who that man was, but news of the journalist's capture soon reached the outside world.

At Vang Vieng, guards tied the three men and a Chinese prisoner under a tarpaulin for the trip through town. On the other side of Vang Vieng at a Pathet Lao camp, soldiers took all their possessions, offered perfunctory medical attention (by a nurse whom Wolfkill had photographed a few days earlier working in a *rightist* camp treating Phoumi troops), and then ordered guards to tie them flat on their backs on the ground. It rained nearly all night. By morning the four were chilled to the marrow, shaking violently, and in pain, when more trucks arrived. Kong Le officers greeted the prisoners, offered cigarettes, and told them that they were to be driven to Xieng Khouang, one man to a vehicle. As the convoy departed the camp, two newsmen stepped from a hut—one of them a Chinese whom Wolfkill had seen earlier at the cease-fire ceremony in Ban Namone. The Chinese filmed the men with a movie camera, the other man with a still camera. The filming rekindled hope that they might be released. The trucks paused at a building further down the road, where the men were questioned by a Laotian whom Wolfkill recognized as a former valet to Kong Le, now advanced to an important position. This man wrote down their names, Wolfkill making certain the spellings were correct. As the interrogation ended, Wolfkill, interpreting in French for the others, asked how long they would be held. The interrogator promised release when a neutralist government was formed, probably in two months. He ordered the men to write statements about the helicopter crash, which they did, telling the truth about the engine failure because they felt the truth was their best hope for gaining their freedom.

Instead of improving, conditions worsened once they left Vang Vieng. Guards soon forced them into a single truck, trussing them up like the pig who shared the truck's floor with them. The truck moved slowly north and west for seven days along the roundabout road to Xieng Khouang, but halted halfway when the road washed out. The guards then herded the prisoners back to Vang Vieng on foot, a difficult trip, especially for Wolfkill, whose feet were badly infected. As they reentered town the second week of June, they saw the same newsmen who had photographed their departure three weeks earlier. Wolfkill managed to secure an audience with Peng Pon-sovan, neutralist leader in the area, a man he had met briefly once before. Ponsovan promised good treatment at Xieng Khouang if they would write statements condemning the American presence in Laos. The men refused that, but they did make general statements supporting neutrality for Laos. After the audience, they were forced to pose again for the Chinese camera-man while a Laotian officer conducted a mock questioning.

The men remained a fortnight in Vang Vieng. As they waited, they noticed that a small aircraft flew in and out regularly. Although Wolfkill thought their escape chances better if they killed the guards and fled over land, Captain Shore preferred to steal the liaison plane from the nearby airstrip. Shore felt confident that the Beaver would start at once and they could take off quickly. They agreed to try the first time the plane remained overnight. Ironically, the very next afternoon the Pathet Lao had difficulty in starting the little plane, having to work on it for 20 minutes before the engine caught. Shore had nightmares about sitting in the plane's cabin while the engine cranked and cranked but did not start. They never had another chance to escape because the following day, 24 June, they were taken aboard a DC-3 with Russian markings and a Vietnamese crew and flown to Xieng Khouang. Aboard the plane also were Peng Ponsovan and a Kong Le colonel, both of whom assured them that their stay in the new camp would be pleasant and brief. Their reception at the flightline in Xieng Khouang was uneventful. Not until guards rudely thrust them into a dark room and nailed the door shut behind them did they realize they had again been deceived.

The prison at Xieng Khouang was called La Trang. Captain Moon, Sergeant Ballenger, and several Royal Lao soldiers were already there. Conditions were horrible: wretched food, no medicine or vitamins, little sunlight, no opportunity to exercise. Everyone suffered from dysentery, nausea, and skin diseases. The guards were Meo tribesmen; cruel, capricious, and stupid, they abused the prisoners at will. When the new arrivals spotted Moon and Ballenger through a crack in the door, they made enough noise for Ballenger to hear them. Two mornings later, when Wolfkill peeped through the crack, he saw the name BALLENGER printed in charcoal on a scrap of paper. He and the others acknowledged the communication by conversing loudly, pointedly mentioning names and passing what news they could. Ballenger prepared another sign the next day, telling them that Moon was there. Lorenzo Frigillano, a Filipino mechanic captured during Kong Le's coup in Vientiane who would eventually be released with four of the Americans, was also in a nearby cell with Laotian prisoners.

The daily routine began when one of the Meos pounded upon a metal pot. Similar clanging marked all the major activities during the day. The strict regimen and the clanging which punctuated it were North Vietnamese procedures, not Laotian. (PWs held in Hanoi after 1964 would recognize it.) Wolfkill later described the morning routine in a published captivity account:

> CLANG, CLANG, CLANG-A-CLANG, CLANGCLANG, CLANGCLANGING . . . Darkness. What guards on today? Machine Gun Kelly, Gray Cap, Dirty Mouth and Baby Doll—what a crew! Door opens; walk out; along the path, we scavenge for tin cans, paper, sticks, anything of value; pick leaves; toilet; dawn sun rises; wash in stream; dally on walk back; sweep and clean cell; July 4 crossed off calendar, the fifty-first day as prisoners. Independence Day, whistle "Yankee Doodle"; door closes; darkness, waiting for morning meal; darkness till door opens for the morning meal; the guards were not out in full armed force this morning, so we could eat in peace, but the rotten food was the same—rice, rock salt, weeds.[6]

Twice in July, the five Americans, Frigillano, and the Laotian prisoners were driven to the airport, where heated discussions (translated for the Americans by Frigillano) took place between Laotian and North Vietnamese officials. Only the insistence of one of the Laotian neutralists that the North Vietnamese and Pathet Lao had no permit to move the men prevented their departure for Hanoi. This official was the friend of one of the Lao captives, a Maj. Ban Lang. Ban Lang told the others on the way back to prison that they would be transferred in two days to the control of the neutralists and that their treatment would then improve. The return to prison the second time was a severe blow to Captain Moon, who by now was in poor condition, his head and shoulder wounds becoming more serious and causing delirium. Moon fiercely resisted being thrust back into his cell. Wolfkill intervened between Moon and the guards, but Moon nevertheless was beaten with rifle butts, blows which he did not seem to notice. The others feared for his life because he was now clearly out of his senses.

The promised improvement, once again, never came. The guards' treatment of the PWs grew rougher. They began to shoot into the rooms occasionally, just for a laugh. One shot blew a concrete fragment into Wolfkill's ankle; another missed McMorrow's head by inches. McMorrow was in misery from severe dysentery; the others forced him to eat even though they knew he would lose the food quickly. Appeals for medicine fell upon deaf ears. Release finally came for the long-suffering Moon. In addition to his wounds at Vang Vieng and during his attempted escape, he had evidently suffered a brain concussion. When the Pathet Lao wired a speaker into his room to broadcast a constant stream of propaganda, the wounds, the psychological torture, and the despair of isolation took their toll. On 22 July, as he and Ballenger were let out to relieve themselves, Moon demanded to see the camp commander and refused to obey his guards. The other prisoners heard six shots fired, then saw one guard, whom they called "Ichabod," back out of the cell, his rifle pointed at the floor. The guard commander, "Wild Eye," ran in. The men heard two more shots, this time from Wild Eye's pistol. Then Wolfkill, peering through the door crack, saw two guards drag out the body, Moon's blood staining the cement in the cell corridor.

Shore, Wolfkill, and McMorrow resolved to unite with Ballenger, afraid that he, too, would be killed if he remained isolated. The guards became lenient for a spell, allowing the four to use the latrine and wash in the stream together. The contact reinforced morale for all. Ballenger was a tough, resilient, resourceful man, a demolitions expert, and the most likely of the group to survive the rigors of a harsh captivity. He had used junk in his cell to create a variety of games, drawings, and various objects to occupy his mind. His accomplishments inspired the others to organize their time and exercise their minds.

In September 1961, Wolfkill received a package. Two-thirds of the contents had been removed, but what remained was a treasure—dysentery medicine, candy, powdered coffee, soup, milk, and a letter from Wolfkill's Japanese girl friend. Two days later a Laotian doctor arrived to tell the men that Souvanna Phouma would soon form a government and that their release was close. Wolfkill took advantage of the situation to ask that the men be allowed to use the latrine more often and that they be permitted to barber themselves. For a while they enjoyed a respite from the stifling routine. The ever-inventive Ballenger surprised the others by sniffing the powdered coffee rather than drinking it, explaining that it left a good sensation in his head for the whole day.

On 17 September, the four Americans were herded onto trucks and tied for a two-day journey into the mountains, where they were locked up in an old fortress near the Laos-North Vietnam border at Nong Het. Ballenger was more suspicious than the others. He recalled the pattern of their captivity and noted the Chinese method of breaking a prisoner's resistance by building up hope for release, then dashing it, then slowly building it up again, then dashing it. His suspicions proved correct, as a North Vietnamese man in charge of guards supervised the construction of a gruesome single set of leg stocks to hold the Americans through the cold mountain nights.

The stocks were made from one heavy beam, cut lengthwise so the upper half could be lifted. The ankles fit into eight grooves on top of the lower beam; then the other beam was wedged down into place. The grooves were too small to accommodate the ankles thrust into them, so that almost at once the ankles bled and became infected. When the infections caused the ankles to swell, the pain became excruciating. The most agonizing instant was the moment when the guards sledgehammered the wedges into place. The blows vibrated through the ankles, legs, and groin, causing so much pain that the men flinched and held each other trying not to cry out. Aggravating the pain were sensations of panic, claustrophobia, and choking. The men could barely move as they attempted to shift their weight to ease the pressure on their ankles. They constantly touched or overlapped each other's bodies; when one man moved, the others felt it. They had to endure not only the press of the stocks and the painful stiffness from lying in one cramped, cold, damp position through the night, but also the pain of bladders unrelieved for 12 hours or the humiliation and degradation of incontinence.

As the weeks passed, dysentery and diarrhea, heretofore chronic, became unremitting. The pain of the stocks was attended now by the filth and discomfort of the diarrhea. The two men lying on the inside had a small advantage whenever they became ill at night, because a man on either side could help raise the sick man's body and try to hold a cup underneath while he forced out the putrescent feces. This agony often continued unabated through an entire night. The prisoners' pleas for medicine to control the diarrhea went ignored. For weeks at a time they tried to deny themselves even the momentary relief of passing gas for fear that the movement would turn liquid, soil them and their clothing, and lead to infection. During this period, with no opportunity to wash, they developed boils, rashes, and hemorrhoids.

Wolfkill feared the Pathet Lao would never release any prisoners they had so confined and so treated. Ballenger, however, told the group that he knew, from his survival training courses at Fort Bragg, North Carolina, that prisoners locked into stocks during the Korean War had come home. Ballenger explained that because the stocks prevented the men from attempting escape, thus risking death, they protected the men against themselves. It was a white lie, but it sustained morale. Besides the filth and agony of the stocks, the men were also the victims of petty harassment by the Meo guards and Laotian officers. Guards kicked the men, pointed loaded guns at them, fired near them, jabbed at them with bayonets, ridiculed them when they were sick, forced them to cross ditches filled with sharp-pointed punji stakes in order to defecate, withheld mail, stole from Red Cross parcels, and in other brutish ways demeaned and hazed their captives.

After two months of these abominations, in November 1961, the four prisoners were suddenly roused from their cell and taken back to La Trang prison near Xieng Khouang. The trip required six days, a welcome break from the recent routine. Their new cell, the one formerly occupied by Frigillano and the Laotian PWs, had been cleaned and ventilated. There were openings for sunlight. The men hoped treatment would improve, and this time they were not disappointed. They had a good meal, a decent night's sleep under blankets and without leg stocks, and, the next day, a visit from International Red Cross representative Andre Durand. For the occasion, the four Americans were allowed to bathe in a nearby stream (with the great luxury of a bar of soap), then enjoy their first hot meal in months. The experience was darkened by the presence of the Lao prison officer Wild Eye, the same officer who had killed Captain Moon. Wild Eye watched them closely during this period and carefully supervised the actual meetings with Durand.

During the initial session, the Pathet Lao set up certain rules: Durand would be allowed only 10 minutes per man; they would all speak in French; the entire visit would be recorded on tape. Durand argued with Wild Eye about the taping, doubtless because he knew it would make the prisoners uneasy and could be used against them later. During the argument, Wolfkill's eyes brightened as he saw two letters lying on a table to one side; they bore the NBC trademark, sure evidence that people at home knew he was alive. The visit degenerated into a continuing discussion about the tape recorder until Kong Le representatives in attendance declared that they would have to consult with Souvanna Phouma before proceeding. Since Durand's plane was leaving that afternoon, well before an agreement could be reached, the interviews with the prisoners had to be postponed.

Three days passed before Durand's return. During this time, the PWs regained vigor as a result of the improved food and a chance to exercise. Although, like the food, it had to be rationed, they also took turns luxuriating in the sunlight before an open window for a few minutes a day—this after months of sometimes such complete darkness in stocks in their old cell that they could not see each other a few feet away. Their renewed health inspired their statements to Durand, the meetings now conducted without the tape recorder. Wolfkill, celebrating his thirty-ninth birthday that very day (29 November), immediately let Durand know that they lacked shoes, blankets, and medicine, had been confined in stocks in darkness, and had received their first mail just two weeks previously. Having to speak in French was a handicap, as was the 10-minute time allowance—Wolfkill was not sure he conveyed to Durand a clear message about the leg stocks—but at the end of the session he was satisfied he had in the main accomplished his purpose.

The Americans had prepared well for the meetings, composing a master list of questions, then dividing the list into quarters so that they would waste no time with repetition. Durand knew his business also. His first question to Ed Shore, the second interviewee, was, "I assume you need everything that Wolfkill needs?" Shore, allowed to answer in English with his responses translated into French, went on to enumerate the deficiencies in food, exercise, hygiene, sunlight, and fresh air. Roger Ballenger then covered other problems, as did McMorrow in his turn. Durand did what he could for the men, and, of course, he carried word of their condition to the outside, which as much as anything else improved their chances for release.[7]

After the humanitarian show, the Laotians were no longer interested in treating the four men so well. In fact, they sent them back to the dread compound at Nong Het, where the prisoners endured four more months in the same misery they had suffered prior to the Durand visit. Several captured local tribesmen joined them in the darkness of the cell. The guards used the ankle stocks to restrain all eight prisoners, each by one ankle, making living conditions doubly miserable, especially for the Americans after their few days of decent food, cleanliness, and sunlight.

In April 1962, they were moved a few miles to a mountain camp run by a North Vietnamese officer. Here conditions were adequate. They worked in a cornfield, ate regular meals, had regular toilet times, and slept on beds. In August, as news of a genuine cease-fire circulated in the camp, the four Americans and Lorenzo Frigillano were helicoptered back to La Trang to undergo another interrogation by Pathet Lao officers and Chinese journalists. During this questioning, Ballenger refused to give any information beyond that required of a prisoner of war, a stance that enraged the senior Lao interrogator, who threatened the sergeant with further solitary confinement and punishment. Ballenger reiterated his position, his recalcitrance blunted some by Wolfkill's translation of his words into French and subsequent translations, in turn, into Laotian, Vietnamese, and Chinese. Eventually, the furious Pathet Lao colonel stormed from the room. His threats had been empty; he had been bluffing.

On the fourth day back at La Trang, a Russian jeep drove into camp to deliver a gaunt, bent, bearded American clutching a few letters. Wolfkill, assuming it to be Charles Duffy, the missing civilian captured while hunting in 1961, introduced himself. As it turned out, the stranger was not Duffy but Army Maj. Lawrence Bailey, the captured Army Attaché assistant who had been held at Sam Neua.

The six prisoners recounted their experiences and savored the anticipation of release, which was finally, after so many false hopes, at hand. Within a week of Bailey's arrival, they boarded a Russian aircraft for the flight to Vientiane and freedom, passing on the way out of the compound the cement floor still stained with Captain Moon's blood. During the flight, the Pathet Lao in charge told Wolfkill that Duffy had starved to death, but that he knew nothing of Gerald Biber and John Bischoff. Shore, watching the terrain intently to be certain they were heading for Vientiane and not Hanoi, suddenly exclaimed to the others that they were flying right over the area in which their chopper had come down 15 months earlier. Then they spotted the wreckage despite the jungle canopy, and Wolfkill gave Shore the traditional thumbs-up sign of victory, remembering a moment later that he had made the same gesture after Shore had successfully crashlanded.

The formal release was concluded without incident. A plane awaited Bailey, Shore, McMorrow, Ballenger, and Frigillano to fly them to the Philippines. Wolfkill was soon among friends in the press community at Vientiane, who gathered to greet him. From the joyous throng appeared the owner of the hotel in which he had stayed, carrying a tray. On it were two ham-and-cheese sandwiches and two cold beers—the same meal the newsman had eaten before leaving on the day of his capture.[8]

Less fortunate than the Wolfkill group was another aggregation of PWs captured between 1963 and 1966 and interned in a series of crude camps in southeastern Laos. Wolfkill's group suffered a hellish captivity but all (not counting Biber and Bischoff, who disappeared almost immediately and whose fate is unknown) except Walter Moon survived. Of the seven captured in this subsequent group, only two are known to have returned alive and those after daring escapes.

On 5 September 1963, an Air America C-46 flying supplies to a Royal Lao unit battling Pathet Lao northwest of the town of Tchepone was shot down in this Communist-controlled territory that protected the supply and infiltration route between North and South Vietnam. Killed in the crash were the pilot, Joseph Cheney, and co-pilot Charles Herrick. Aboard the C-46 were Eugene DeBruin, an American working as a cargo kicker; radio operator To Tik Chiu, a Hong Kong citizen of British-Chinese extraction; and three Thai crewmen—Pisidhi Indradat, Prasit Thanee, and Prasit Promsuwan.

Left to right: DeBruin, Indradat, Promsuwan, Thanee, Chiu at Ban Thapachon, 1964.

Better prepared for the emergency than the crew on Major Bailey's aircraft that went down in the Plain of Jars two years before, the five parachuted safely to earth near a village called Ban Nassong. Quickly captured, they were moved by truck to Muong Phine, where Pathet Lao interrogated them and told them they were to be incarcerated. They then continued by truck to Ban Thak Nong on the northern side of Tchepone, there to be imprisoned until late November.

The United States immediately sought the men's release, but the Pathet Lao issued no acknowledgment of their capture for more than two months. Then, through a message to the International Committee of the Red Cross, the PL charged them with an illegal overflight and intrusion of Laotian territory, which, they claimed, made the captives criminals subject to imprisonment and prosecution. The Pathet Lao proposed negotiating directly with the United States rather than working further through an appropriate intermediary such as the International Control Commission or the ICRC because they believed such direct contact would give them more leverage as well as international recognition. At the same time, the PL announced the possibility of a "people's trial" of the men on criminal charges—a declaration similar to one made by Hanoi in 1966 regarding U.S. fliers captured in North Vietnam.* In this

* See Chapter 10.

instance, negotiations never developed, and the history of the five prisoners from this point on is inexact.[9]

In late November or early December, they left the Tchepone area to travel northwest to Muong Angkham, where they spent at least three weeks and possibly as long as six months, followed by perhaps another three months back at Muong Phine prison, before being hauled by truck northwest to Ban Long Khong. In May 1964, they escaped from camp and eluded guards for four days before being recaptured at a waterhole, betrayed by a local farmer. According to Indradat, friendly forces, troops of General Phoumi, observed their capture from a nearby hill but made no effort to rescue them. From midsummer 1964 to 22 December 1965, they were held at two other camps, Ban Thapachon and Ban Tam, moving between the two camps at least once about October 1964, blind pawns in the confused political contest.*[10]

On 20 September 1965, an Air Force rescue helicopter crewed by Capt. Thomas Curtis, Lt. Duane Martin, and Sgts. William Robinson and Arthur Black was shot down 30 miles north of Mu Gia Pass near Ban Song Khone. Curtis, Robinson, and Black were captured by North Vietnamese and taken to Hanoi, to spend the rest of the war there as PWs. Martin fell into the hands of Pathet Lao as he tried to cross a trail after evading for more than two weeks. Once captured, he was taken south through Mu Gia Pass to join DeBruin and the others at Ban Tam in December, when the group moved southeast to Ban Pha Kat. In February they were joined by Navy pilot Dieter Dengler, who would later escape and relate their story in a published memoir that remains the most graphic personal account of captivity in Laos.†

On 1 February 1966 Lt. (j.g.) Dengler, flying an A-1H attack aircraft along the Laos-Vietnam border in bad weather not far from Mu Gia Pass, was forced to crashland his crippled plane after taking several hits in the right wing. The landing, in a clearing studded with tree stumps, severed the plane's wings and tail and sent the fuselage cartwheeling. When it stopped, Dengler, his helmet ripped off, head gashed, and left leg badly bruised, scrambled out

---

* Russia ended its airlift to neutralist units in the Plain of Jars in 1963, weakening Kong Le's army as a stabilizing force in Laos. The deaths in 1963 of President Kennedy, President Diem of South Vietnam, and Thai leader Thanarat Sarit—all strong supporters of General Phoumi— further destabilized the fragile coalition government; after a series of political assassinations and coup attempts in 1964, Phoumi retired to Thailand. A patchwork neutrality in Laos continued for the next decade, with the Communists steadily gaining strength.

† Some have found Dengler's account to be so incredible as to be either overdrawn or possibly even concocted in places. Hallucinations suffered during the last days of his escape and large doses of medication taken afterwards to relieve a serious malaria condition may have impaired his memory. Noting inconsistencies in his statements and lacking corroborating evidence from other sources, Defense intelligence officers have had difficulty evaluating Dengler's extraordinary story.

and made for a nearby creek. As he heard shouting, he buried his survival gear, radio, and pistol, and moved off to the north, guessing that his trackers would search to the west, toward Thailand. At noon the next day, he too was captured while trying to cross a trail.

The two Laotians who caught him were mountain tribesmen, dressed in American-style shirts and trousers, carrying American weapons, and wearing sunglasses. They tied his arms, then double-timed him for about six hours through a series of villages. Local people guided his captors from one village to the next. Each was dressed differently. None wore military rank. None spoke English. For the night, the Laotians tied Dengler spreadeagled to four stakes. By morning, he was a mass of insect stings and mosquito and leech bites. A week passed in this fashion before the party stopped at a village Dengler remembered as Yamalot. Here a small, chubby, French-speaking Laotian official, possibly the province chief, took charge. He told Dengler he had been four times to the Geneva Conference. He produced a camera and said he wanted to send a photo to Dengler's family along with a letter stating the captured pilot was safe. He gave Dengler paper to write to his fiancee and his mother. Dengler printed letters to both, using the entire paper. The Laotian then asked Dengler to sign a statement condemning the United States. When he refused, guards tied him upside down from a tree and beat him unconscious; later they tied him behind a buffalo and drove the animal through sharp bush that sliced the prisoner's skin. More beatings followed, but on the tenth day since his capture, Dengler was taken from Yamalot with the statement still unsigned.

He and two guards walked to another village, where they spent the night. About midnight, Dengler took advantage of the guards' heavy sleeping to escape. He found his shoes, hiked to the lowest spot around, a creek bed, then followed the stream for two hours, unfortunately returning almost to the place from which he started out. At first light, he began climbing a karst mountain, reaching its peak about noon. He signaled two passing U.S. F-105s, one of which dipped a wing and circled. But no rescue came, and Dengler, exhausted, sick from a poisonous fruit he had eaten, and cut from the sharp karst ridges, climbed back down the mountain, using vines to control his descent. Near the bottom, drained from fatigue, he collapsed into a waterhole. Moments later he was surrounded by a platoon of Pathet Lao, who dragged him out and bound him tightly, cutting the circulation in both arms. As one Laotian tried to club Dengler with a rifle butt, the rifle fired a bullet through the stomach of a comrade, killing him. A third soldier shot the first through both legs before order was restored. Then they beat Dengler and jammed an ant nest over his head. Though in torment, he was lucky to be alive.

By morning, both of Dengler's arms were useless; they would remain numb for more than a month. That night guards stuffed him upright into a hole, at least five of them keeping close watch. At dawn they traveled on, past a North Vietnamese training camp, new buildings, and a new roadway, reaching Houei Het and Par Kung three days later, on the afternoon of Valentine's Day. Here Dengler joined DeBruin, Martin, and the others in a bamboo stockade. Martin and he exchanged tales of evasion and wanted to try an immediate escape, but the others thought it better to wait for the approaching monsoon.

As they waited, conditions worsened at the prison. Guards gave them a small rice ration that they supplemented by killing and eating snakes and rats. Once a day the guards allowed them out to dump their toilet pails, but most of the time they were locked in wooden foot stocks and tied or hand-cuffed. The trip to empty the pail was dangerous because the guards were both cruel and skittish. Sometimes they shot at a prisoner if he moved too slowly or too fast. The men feared being shot if they stumbled or fell. After 10 days, they were moved to a new location and a jungle camp where food was even scarcer. The anticipated rains never came. By June the men overheard guards talking about killing them so there would be fewer alive to eat the precious rations. The drought meant no more drinking water and no baths. The prisoners were covered with lice and full of infections. Chiu and Martin were the sickest. In the escape plan, Chiu was to go with DeBruin and Martin with Dengler so each would have the best possible chance. Thanee, Prom-suwan, and Indradat arranged to go together.

The plan was a good one. They carefully studied the guards for a week, tracing every move, always noting where the weapons were kept. Knowing it was a three-hour hike to the village at Par Kung and that few Laotians would be in the area after dark, they planned to slip out during the guards' supper, seize the weapons, kill the guards, then set up signal fires for a C-130 that passed over every night. With luck, they hoped to be rescued in the morning. On the night of 29 June Dengler loosened his bindings and, crawling under a fence through a hole he had dug out earlier, managed to reach the weapons hut, but just as he began passing rifles to Martin and Indradat the guards discovered the escape. The prisoners blasted away, killing as many as six of the Laotians, but two got away. Now there was no chance to signal the aircraft.

The men split up as rehearsed. DeBruin and Chiu made for a hilltop to wait until Dengler and Martin or one of the Thais could return with help. Dengler and Martin became ill with jaundice and malaria soon after escape and, knowing they could not survive a jungle trek in their condition, decided to risk travel near a creek. For 10 days they stumbled along the creek, which was fast and narrow, with steep, sharp ridges that caused them frequently to trip and fall, until they reached a deserted village, where they rested in a hut. The next evening they floated downstream on a raft they found, at one point startling a local fisherman, frightening him away. They rested for another day, then decided to head directly for the coast, following another stream to a second empty village where they again stopped.

The next day—their thirteenth since escaping—they suffered a severe setback. After they had walked all day and reached an abandoned village, they were shocked to realize it was the same one they had left three days before. Dengler left the now prostrate Martin under cover in heavy bush and backtracked to find bullets they had hidden a week earlier. It took him two days for the round trip, but he brought back the bullets, and with them the chance to build a fire with which they could signal and cook food. Their plan was to ignite leaves and wave them in arcs the shape of S and O when a plane passed at night. It appeared to work. Although several jets passed without seeing the SOS, a C-130 seemed to spot it, dropping flares, which the men took as acknowledgment. They expected rescue in the morning.

But no rescue came. Starved and desperate, they struggled along to another village, hoping to find food. As they neared a hut, a villager sprang out and slashed Martin's leg and shoulder with a machete. He just missed Dengler with a third swipe as Dengler retreated into bush and up a gully. Dengler never saw his escape companion again and assumed Martin, gravely ill and mortally wounded, died in that remote Laotian village.[11] Terrified and furious, he made his way back to their hideout, which, that night, he burned to the ground as a C-130 flew over. Next morning he climbed a ridge and spread cloth from the parachute flares, again dropped by the C-130, in an SOS. No rescue came that day, nor another plane that night. The next day he left the ridge to follow a stream and almost ran into a Laotian search party tracking prints left by him and Martin earlier. The two had walked backwards whenever they crossed the stream to make it appear they went upriver when they went down. Dengler decided to follow the group because, by knowing where they were, he could avoid them if they turned back.

It was a good decision. He needed food badly, and the searchers, whenever they ate, left bits behind—rice, peppers, fish heads and bones. His luck held for four more days. At a fork in the stream, he struck out away from the search party just before he began fading in and out of consciousness and suffering daily periods of hallucination, often imagining that he and Martin were talking. He could easily have given himself away.

He ate snails and leaves, slept under a log one night, on top of a rock next to a waterfall another. He suffered intense pain in his kidneys and coughed blood. Whenever he rested, he needed two hours just to arise and prepare to move again. On the morning of 20 July 1966, he cracked his head on a rock while crossing a stream and stayed there to recover and dry in the sun. As he lay on the rock, an A-1, the same type of plane he was flying when shot down, flew up the stream toward him, shooting over his head. The plane made another pass. Dengler leaped out and tried to spread an SOS with the parachute cloth, but he had forgotten how to make an S. He waved and jumped, and then there were two A-1s—"Spads" the pilots called them because they were World War II relics refitted for current service. The Spads had seen him. One stayed low, the other climbed higher for radio transmission. Had the first plane not been in a bank at exactly the correct spot, the pilot would never have seen Dengler because the Spad's broad cowling and low wings made downward vision poor. Had he flown 20 yards to the right or left, he would not have seen him either because the jungle would have obscured his view. By such a slim margin Dengler was rescued. As he was pulled into a hovering helicopter, Dengler recalled, "this guy was out there, and I grabbed his leg; I wouldn't let go of that son of a gun until we hit Danang. Once I was in the chopper my body gave out completely. My body said that's enough, there is no more . . . . I couldn't lift a sheet of paper, I couldn't turn my head. That was it."[12]

After Dengler's return, Air America searched the Houei Het region for DeBruin and Chiu, but rescuers never found a signal. Rumors and unverified reports suggested that DeBruin had been recaptured, but he was last officially accounted for in May 1966 (before the 29 June escape attempt), when a Pathet Lao representative mentioned his whereabouts to an American Embassy officer. His fate after June 1966, along with Chiu's, remains a mystery.[13] What became of Thanee and Promsuwan also no one knows. Only Indradat besides Dengler of the original seven is known to have come out of Laos alive. Indradat, who parted with the other Thais following the escape, was recaptured after a 33-day evasion and severely beaten, but he held on to be rescued along with 50 other prisoners (none of them Americans) during a raid upon their camp in January 1967—the most successful prison camp raid of the war.[14]

On 6 June 1964, as the DeBruin group was well into its first year of captivity, Navy Lt. Charles Klusmann, flying an RF-8 reconnaissance aircraft over the Plain of Jars, was forced to evacuate when enemy ground fire hit his plane. He never actually felt the shells impact, but just as his wingman radioed that the plane was smoking, Klusmann lost control and had to eject not far from the area he had been photographing. His parachute landed him on top of the only tree in the clearing beneath him, and the 20-foot fall to the ground badly wrenched his right leg and slashed his right arm.

Numbed by shock, he crept into tall grass to treat his wounds. In about an hour two aircraft appeared. One acknowledged his signal mirror; the

Early Laos captives. *Above:* Dengler (left), Klusmann. *Below:* Left to right, Wolfkill, Bailey, and Ballenger at press conference after their release.

other—a helicopter—made a low pass over his position, but took 80 hits from heavy gunfire from surrounding hills and had to retreat. A half hour later, when more helicopters reached the scene, he crawled up to a ridge line, anticipating rapid rescue. However, there were too many Communist troops in the area. They drove off the choppers, surrounded the ridge, and soon had Klusmann at their mercy.

Klusmann's capture began an 84-day odyssey that would end with his successful escape. He and Dengler would be the last two U.S. fliers to manage escape from prison in Laos. Only nine American prisoners captured later by the Pathet Lao would survive to be released in Hanoi at the end of the war, and most of those were captured after 1970, when North Vietnamese regulars often commanded Lao units and supervised prisoners in a more orderly fashion. Had Klusmann not escaped, then, he would probably have perished in Laotian captivity.

His first two days of movement south with his captors were painful but not brutal. They fed him adequately. At a camp the second day, they questioned him but did not mistreat him. The next morning he left with an armed escort on a walk that one of the Laotians indicated would take them to Vientiane. They rested during the afternoon, then moved by truck that night until the vehicle slipped off a primitive bridge across a small stream, sticking the wheels. They continued on foot to a village, where the prisoner became the object of great curiosity the next day. In an interrogation that fourth day, Klusmann recited his name, rank, and serial number but refused to provide other information. His interrogator, as a fellow soldier, was somewhat sympathetic to Klusmann's plight. As they talked, he told Klusmann that release would depend upon the United States stopping its aid to the right-wing forces in Laos. Fearing deportation to Hanoi or even to China, Klusmann resolved to try escape when well enough. The next day, his captors permitted him to write the first of 10 letters he would compose during his confinement.

On the sixth day since his capture, Klusmann developed dysentery and nausea, making resistance more difficult. He affected several pretenses—that he was rather dull, the product of indigent parents, and a man without money himself. His interrogators' perception of him as an ordinary American may have delayed their use of stronger tactics. When they revealed knowledge about reconnaissance missions on the *Kitty Hawk*, Klusmann's carrier, he continued to play the role of the simple pilot, professing ignorance even of what happened to his reconnaissance photos upon his return to the ship. They told him that his treatment would have been worse had they shot him down while he was bombing or strafing. His chief interrogator proved to be an intelligent and patient man, clever enough to extract information from time to time despite the prisoner's dumb posture.

After a few more days of casual interrogation, Klusmann moved (the date probably 14 June 1964) to another camp still in the Plain of Jars. Perhaps eight miles away, this new camp was his fifth. Here he was placed in solitary confinement for two months. The loneliness was oppressive, but his room was of decent size, about 9 by 15 feet, and held a crude bed, table, chair, kerosene lamp, blankets, and mosquito netting—luxurious trappings for a PW in Southeast Asia. He also received toilet articles and a pair of trousers that looked like U.S. issue. Like so many other PWs later, he improvised an exercise routine to stay fit and help combat the isolation. He estimated that 264 crossings of the open floor of his room equaled one mile, and recorded 183 miles back and forth exercising his bad leg. He suffered harassment but no torture. The guards even brought him a deck of playing cards.

The Pathet Lao surrounded his hut with barbed wire the day after he arrived and closely guarded him, even while he slept. For his various ailments they gave him vitamin C and camphor oil, the latter a popular Oriental panacea. They took a number of photographs, many of poses that suggested the pictures were to be used more for propaganda than identification purposes. The interrogations gradually became indoctrinations as the Lao captain in charge attempted to make Klusmann "not a communist but more progressive." Later, when Klusmann received copies of the English-language *Peking Review*, he found in them versions of his interrogator's lectures and assumed the periodical was the source for the material.

After a month, Klusmann began to experience depression from the isolation and prolonged captivity. One rainy afternoon, the Lao captain told him that the Voice of America had announced his death, triggering for the young Navy pilot a period of obsessive brooding about whether or not anyone at home knew that he was alive. Having little else to ponder, he found it nearly impossible to shake his malaise. He tried cussing his guards, who did not understand English. He tried working math problems on the dirt floor of his hut, but had to slow down his calculations to make the diversion last longer. Eagerly he read a book his captors gave him, Thackeray's novel *A Shabby Genteel Story*, and wondered how such a volume came to be in the little Laotian camp. After several days of rain, he tried to dig an escape hole under the wall of his hut, but he gave up when he discovered that the posts driven to support the barbed wire were too deep for him to go under and too close to slip between.

He had no way of knowing that on 16 June a Pathet Lao official named Phoumi Vongvichit told members of the International Control Commission and representatives of the press at Prince Souphanouvong's headquarters that the PL had captured an American flier 10 days earlier. Nor did he know that U.S. Ambassador Leonard Unger, through his own sources, had learned of Klusmann's capture and had written to Souphanouvong in July requesting his early release.[15]

Beginning his second month in isolation, his mental and physical condition deteriorating, he agreed to write a letter attesting his "good treatment" when the Lao promised in return to mail another letter to his wife. Klusmann had been concerned about her health and his father's, too, as both were recovering from serious illness, and he thought this might be his only chance to let them know he was alive. A few days later he realized he had been victimized and, with his remaining resolve, determined again to escape. In August an opportunity came when guards moved him a short distance to a larger building and placed three dozen Laotian prisoners with him. He soon cultivated an acquaintance with three of the captives who claimed to be imprisoned for political reasons. Klusmann was skeptical but had little choice except to believe them. Friendly forces were not far away, and these natives had knowledge of the territory and regarded Klusmann as insurance for their being accepted by friendly Laotian troops once they made good their escape.

When two more Laotian PWs joined the group, the six men agreed that three would escape while the other three covered. They picked a date when moonlight would be minimal and there would be rains to cover their trail, but had to cancel the plan twice when the prison commander unexpectedly placed guards around the building. On the third night, 28 August, when the guards withdrew before dawn, the men seized their chance. The three who had agreed to cover the escape now decided to escape as well. Klusmann and two of the men crawled through the wire and walked quietly to a predetermined rendezvous area. Klusmann made the hike well enough, having been able to exercise recently because his dysentery had subsided. He also had cut grooves into his Navy boots to give him traction, having learned how slippery they were on wet terrain during his march in the first days of captivity.

When the second trio did not reach them within 90 minutes, Klusmann and his companions set out into the darkness, continuing in the morning when they found decent cover along hillsides. One of the Laotians who knew the area well agreed to guide them toward a village held by friendly troops. When the other Laotian left to get food at a farmhouse they were passing, the Pathet Lao soon captured him, then spread the alarm about the other escapees. Klusmann and his companion immediately got to cover and ran as long as they could, doubling back eventually to where they felt the Pathet Lao would not look for them. This doubling back may have saved them because they heard shots a distance away in the direction of their original escape path. Now they headed directly west, maintaining a straight course and avoiding trails. The route was treacherous, as they were frequently lacerated, bruised, and bitten, and had to stop periodically to pull off the incessant leeches. That night, soaked and exhausted, they rested in a bamboo grove, feeling safe enough to keep a fire burning among the trees.

Near the end of the second day, they spotted a mountain that Klusmann's Laotian companion said represented the front line in the war. They spent that night in an abandoned shack where they were able to cook a squash, eat melon, dry out, and rest. By noon of the third day, Klusmann's injured leg had grown so swollen and painful that he had to lift it by hand to keep moving through the high grasses. He was further weakened from the bleeding caused by the leech bites. But his journey was nearing an end. At noon, they crossed a trail covered with tracks like those made by American combat boots. The trail led to a friendly camp; other trails they soon discovered led to fortified hilltops. Klusmann's companion, certain they were safe, approached one of the camps and found anticommunist troops who welcomed the two men and saw them safely before dusk to an airstrip, where shortly an American plane landed to transport Klusmann to Thailand and sanctuary.[16]

In retrospect, Klusmann realized that he had revealed a weak spot—concern for his family and that they be made aware of his status—to his interrogator, who used that knowledge and Klusmann's illness and depression to manipulate him to write the letter in which he said he had been treated well. On the other hand, he was satisfied that he had carried off his pose as an ill-informed pilot, "just an airplane driver," and that he had steeled himself into strong enough physical and mental condition to manage the escape attempt. Those efforts, and a large measure of luck—he received relatively mild treatment compared with the Wolfkill and DeBruin groups, and he was thrown in with Laotian prisoners who spoke English and shared his urge to escape—saved him.*

Lt. Charles Klusmann's tale soon spread throughout military survival training schools. For a time, the happy outcome reassured pilots ordered to fly missions for the continuing shadow war in Laos in the mid-1960s, and it helped some who were downed in North Vietnam. But, by 1968, stories of Laotian barbarism toward captured Americans would become so widespread that U.S. pilots commonly elected to avoid going down in Pathet Lao territory even if it meant nursing a crippled aircraft into North Vietnam.

---

* Questioned thoroughly by Navy investigators upon his return and confronted with evidence of concessions to the enemy, Klusmann was troubled for months by both remorse and concern about his future. He was eventually exonerated and went on to a successful career, holding command positions and retiring with the rank of captain.

4

South Vietnam: Prisoners of the Viet Cong, 1961-1964

Laos would remain the recipient of U.S. attention and assistance through the 1960s as the government of Souvanna Phouma struggled to maintain its authority in the face of continuing Pathet Lao aggression. After 1961, however, the Kennedy and Johnson administrations would increasingly seek to limit the American involvement in that murky conflict and instead draw the line against Communist insurgency in Vietnam, where the sides seemed more clearly defined and the anticommunists appeared more willing and able to fight.

The thickening U.S. involvement in Vietnam in the post-World War II years, traced in Chapter 1, had been fitful but steady. An American military assistance group had been dispatched to aid the French effort there as early as 1950. By 1955, U.S. advisers were training the South Vietnamese army. Finally, in the fall of 1961, President Kennedy made the fateful decision to authorize a significant buildup of the American presence in the South, a major step toward the commitment for the first time of U.S. combat troops in Southeast Asia. That influx of men and materiel began with the arrival of two helicopter companies in Saigon on 11 December.

In February 1962 the Defense Department established a Military Assistance Command for Vietnam (MACV) to oversee the expanded U.S. role, and the *New York Times* reported billets in Saigon so scarce, with new units checking in almost daily, that "the men sleep three in a room at the hotel Majestic."[1] By the end of 1962, more than 10,000 U.S. military personnel were committed to the Vietnam action; 23,000 by December 1964. By May 1964, U.S. forces would have suffered more than 1,000 casualties. Although the U.S. role in the conflict remained ostensibly advisory and auxiliary at this point, the State Department, as casualties mounted, came under increasing pressure to recognize Vietnam as a combat zone so that American soldiers wounded in support operations would be eligible for the Purple Heart and other combat decorations. In December 1964, a 30-year-old Army captain, Roger H. C. Donlon, became the first U.S. serviceman awarded the Medal of Honor for action in Indochina.*

Inevitably, as the magnitude and nature of the U.S. involvement underwent a fundamental change, and engagement with the enemy became a more regular occurrence, the American prisoner of war experience in Southeast Asia also took on new dimensions. The list of U.S. PWs expanded, still incrementally but ever more steadily, until PW matters acquired front-page prominence. Stray Americans would continue to surface in Pathet Lao camps through the decade, but, with the shifting scene, the preponderance of captives would now come under the control of *Vietnamese* Communists. In South Vietnam in these early formative years of the new commitment, before the United States launched operations in North Vietnam, that meant the Viet Cong, heirs to the Viet Minh in their battle against the French and a captor already well schooled and seasoned in the handling of prisoners of war.

In terms of both their background and their fate, the group of prisoners held by the Viet Cong in the three years between December 1961 and December 1964 would be a microcosm of the much larger group taken captive in the South over the course of the decade. In this original group, numbering 29 altogether, were officers, senior NCOs, young draftees, civilians employed by the United States government or by private corporations, and three missionaries, one of whom was a woman; two were Filipino workers hired by U.S. firms and one was a South Vietnamese interpreter employed by the U.S. Army. Of the 29, 14 would be released by the Viet Cong, one after nine years. Two would escape. Six, possibly eight, would be executed or murdered. Five would die of other causes while captive. All told, nearly half the group would die after becoming prisoners.

The following PW list, arranged chronologically in order of capture, identifies the 29 and indicates their status. There may have been more American PWs than the 26 cited here, but, as would be the case throughout the Vietnam

---

* The Associated Press noted that Donlon's medal citation marked the first time the United States officially referred to the Viet Cong as an "enemy." The White House took pains to emphasize that the medal was "the first to be awarded an individual who distinguished himself while serving with a friendly foreign force engaged in an armed conflict against an opposing armed force in which the United States is not a belligerent party." Congress had granted authority to make the award in such circumstances in July 1963 following the controversy over the denial of the Purple Heart. See *NY Times*, 24 Apr 62, 4 Dec 64; *Washington Post and Times Herald*, 6 Dec 64.

conflict (indeed, in almost any combat situation, especially a guerrilla war), circumstances did not always permit positive determination of prisoner status.*

Name	Rank	Captured	Fate/Year
1. Fryett, George	Spec 4/Army	26 Dec 61	Released/62
2. Mungada, Alfred	CV Filipino	Dec 61	Released/62
3. Groom, George	Sgt/Army	8 Apr 62	Released/62
4. Quinn, Francis	Sgt/Army	8 Apr 62	Released/62
5. Marchand, Wayne	Sgt/Army	8 Apr 62	Killed/62
6. Gabriel, James	Sgt/Army	8 Apr 62	Killed/62
7. Gerber, Daniel	CV	30 May 62	Killed/62
8. Mitchell, Archie	CV	30 May 62	Killed/62
9. Vietti, Eleanor	CV	30 May 62	Killed/62
10. Matagulay, Roque	Sgt/Army	23 Jul 62	Released/62
11. Phan Cham Van	CV SVN	23 Jul 62	Released/62
12. Krause, Arthur	CV	8 Jun 63	Released/63
13. Pitzer, Daniel	Sgt/Army	29 Oct 63	Released/67
14. Rowe, James	Lt/Army	29 Oct 63	Escaped/68
15. Versace, Humbert	Capt/Army	29 Oct 63	Killed/65
16. Camacho, Issac	Sgt/Army	24 Nov 63	Escaped/65
17. McClure, Claude	Sgt/Army	24 Nov 63	Released/65
18. Smith, George	Sgt/Army	24 Nov 63	Released/65
19. Roraback, Kenneth	Sgt/Army	24 Nov 63	Killed/65
20. Thompson, Floyd	Capt/Army	26 Mar 64	Released/73
21. Johnson, Edward	Sgt/Army	21 Jul 64	Released/67
22. Grainger, Joseph	CV	8 Aug 64	Died captive/65
23. Laguico, Elpidio	CV Filipino	8 Aug 64	Released/64
24. Towery, Herman	Capt/Army	22 Oct 64	Died captive/64
25. Tadios, Leonard	Sgt/Army	11 Dec 64	Died captive/66
26. Parks, Joe	Sgt/Army	22 Dec 64	Died captive/67
27. Bennett, Harold	Sgt/Army	29 Dec 64	Killed/65
28. Crafts, Charles	PFC/Army	29 Dec 64	Released/67
29. Cook, Donald	Capt/Marine	31 Dec 64	Died captive/65

The first American captured by the Viet Cong was Army Spec. 4 George Fryett (1), seized the day after Christmas 1961. Fryett, a clerk in the office

* For example, in June 1964, Marine PFCs Fred Schreckengost and Robert Greer left their post south of Da Nang and rented motorbikes for a sightseeing excursion. When they did not return, the Marine Corps conducted a week-long search, which finally located the bikes submerged in a canal, but no bodies. Whether the two Marines were killed in an ambush or, as a Vietnamese reported, taken prisoner for a day before being killed, has never been confirmed. In a second example, where the preponderance of evidence indicated a "capture," Army Capt. Herman Towery (24) was wounded, then cut off from his unit in October 1964. A patrol found his body the day after the action. He appeared to have died of his wounds. The enemy held the territory for a time and probably held Captain Towery, but an inconclusive review determined that he may have died before capture. Army casualty officers decided to list him as a prisoner for the two days until his body was recovered.

of the chief of staff at MACV in Saigon, was captured while riding a bicycle on the outskirts of the city on his way to a swimming pool. Two Vietnamese on bicycles approached him from behind and tossed a grenade at him as they passed, blowing Fryett to the ground with numerous shrapnel wounds. The Vietnamese blindfolded him and dragged him into a nearby woods, where they held him until dark. Then they forced him to walk through the night, finally pausing by a stream at dawn. Fryett, bleeding and in pain from his injuries but seeing a chance to escape, worked his bonds loose and jumped into the water. The Vietnamese, reacting quickly, recaptured him, retied him securely, then marched him to a village, where a nurse dressed his wounds. Alfred Mungada (2), a Filipino employed by a civilian contracting firm as a surveyor, was seized about the same time as Fryett and released several weeks later in February, but Fryett's captivity would last into the summer.

During a six-month imprisonment, Fryett's treatment was harsh but not brutal. The Viet Cong beat him when he was uncooperative, fed him little, and several times forced him to dig his own grave. He was perplexed by the inconsistencies in his handling. Initially he was convinced his captors intended to kill him, especially when they first directed him to dig the grave. Later he felt they wanted to keep him alive, though to what end he was unsure. He never knew when they would beat him, interrogate him, or ignore him. Although he dreaded the rough treatment, he also dreaded the periods of indifference for fear that his captors would kill him because he was no longer useful. He thought constantly of escape, but another chance never came and finally it was not necessary. In late June, with little fanfare, the Vietnamese led him to a road and put him on a bus for Saigon.[2]

Army Sgts. George Groom, Francis Quinn, Wayne Marchand, and James Gabriel (3, 4, 5, 6) were captured in April 1962 when their Special Forces camp southwest of Da Nang was overrun by Viet Cong. Marchand and Gabriel, wounded in the fighting, were carried about a mile after capture by Groom and Quinn, until the VC ordered the latter to leave the injured men behind. The Vietnamese assured the Americans that Marchand and Gabriel would be treated by medics, then left for friendly forces to find. When U.S. soldiers did discover them a few hours later, they were both dead, having been shot in the head at close range. Groom and Quinn spent 22 days in captivity before being released upon making statements acceptable to the VC, including promises to leave Vietnam and not return.[3]

On 30 May 1962, near Ban Me Thuot in the Central Highlands region of South Vietnam, the Viet Cong seized three American missionaries working at a Montagnard leprosarium. Daniel Gerber, Archie Mitchell, and Dr. Eleanor Vietti (7, 8, 9) were serving with the Christian Missionary Alliance for South Vietnam. The VC took over the hospital, separated the three Americans, and lectured the rest of the staff about cooperating with the foreigners

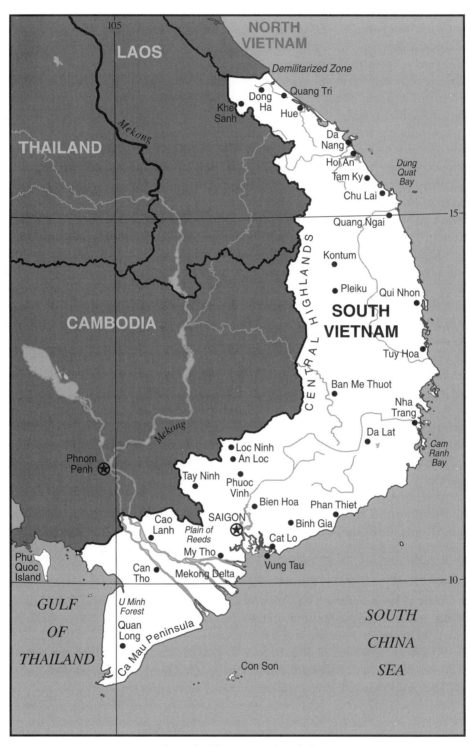

South Vietnam (1964)

who were "oppressors of the people" and "worthy of death." The three were never seen again, although their fate remains uncertain. In November 1962 captured Viet Cong documents indicated they had been killed. In February 1963 Gerber's passport was recovered; it had been used as a VC notebook. Reports circulated among Montagnards that the Viet Cong had tied the missionaries to posts inside a hut and set it ablaze. Other reports claimed that they were captive in the same general area as late as December 1964 and were moved south to Lam Dong Province in 1966. Bernard Fall among others speculated that they were pressed into service treating wounded VC; one report had them treating Communist troops during Tet 1968 at a field hospital back in the Central Highlands.* There has never been any question of their capture, but when or if they died has never been confirmed. As late as 1979 the State Department still listed them as imprisoned or detained.[4]

Army Sgt. Roque Matagulay (10), a Guamanian by birth and an adviser at the U.S. Special Forces Self-Defense Training Center in Phan Thiet, was on a hunting trip in July 1962 near his base with another U.S. NCO, a Vietnamese civilian interpreter, and a South Vietnamese Army private when they were ambushed by several squads of Viet Cong. Two of the group, Army Sgt. Carl Brown and the Vietnamese private, quickly escaped, but Matagulay and the civilian interpreter, Phan Cham Van (11), were captured and held together for the next five months. They were kept in a series of seven camps and another half dozen village and jungle rest areas, always closely guarded, and frequently interrogated and indoctrinated. Two weeks after capture, Matagulay developed an unremitting malaria that left him susceptible to Viet Cong pressure. When his condition worsened in November 1962 the VC elicited from him statements confessing U.S. atrocities against the Vietnamese people, condemning the United States for aiding the Diem government, and petitioning for his release. They did not torture him, but their constant harassment, given his weakened state, wore down his resistance. He later said he did not consider the statements, albeit of propaganda value, serious enough to be worth his life.

The Viet Cong, besides exploiting his illness, held Matagulay at an unusual disadvantage in that his Vietnamese girl friend was pregnant at the time he was captured. He believed they would allow him to write her only if he vilified the United States. In a letter to her he declared his support for the Communist cause, even suggesting that she join him in North Vietnam. At his release ceremony in December, Matagulay made statements praising the Viet Cong, sang their song, and accepted gifts of an engraved spoon and a basket of fruit. Following his and Van's return to U.S. custody,

---

* This may have been a reference to two missionaries captured during the Tet offensive, Henry Blood and Betty Ann Olsen. Olsen was also associated with the leprosarium. See Chapter 21.

Fryett (left), Matagulay: Two early captures released by the Viet Cong.

there was a conflict in testimony between the two, Van accusing Matagulay of substantially weaker resistance than Matagulay recounted. The Army considered charges of collaboration but eventually dropped them, gave Matagulay an honorable discharge, and later permitted him to reenlist with the proviso that he not be eligible for a security clearance.[5]

There was no consistent pattern to these early captivity episodes, but there were already discernible tendencies. The Viet Cong seemed intent on capturing useful enemy, especially American advisers, then moving them to safe areas for interrogation and indoctrination. VC defectors corroborated that such a policy existed and that special briefings before VC attacks had directed units to capture and hold all officers and those enlisted who aggressively resisted, and to release soon after indoctrination those enlisted who surrendered at once and turned over their weapons.

Civilian prisoners in most instances appear to have received the same treatment as captured servicemen. On 8 June 1963, Arthur Krause (12), an engineer employed by Philco, was seized while driving a jeep near a construction site southwest of Tam Ky, 40 miles below Da Nang. He spent five months as a prisoner, underwent indoctrination and propaganda exploitation similar to that experienced by service prisoners, then was released. Less fortunate was Joseph Grainger (22) of the U.S. Agency for International Development, captured while driving a truck on AID business 8 August 1964 in Phu Yen Province, about 230 miles northeast of Saigon; like the three civilian missionaries and Army Sergeants Marchand and Gabriel, Grainger apparently died in captivity. The VC Provisional Revolutionary Government reported in January 1973 that he died 17 March 1965. A Filipino named Elpidio Laguico (23), captured at the same time as Grainger, was released after four months; like Alfred Mungada, captured with George Fryett and released after a short internment, Laguico may have benefited more from his Asian extraction than civilian status.[6]

Prisoners in the South were necessarily moved frequently, as the VC were forced themselves to shift camps often and travel at long stretches with only brief stops at rest areas. Sergeant Matagulay's seven moves in five months would not be atypical. There were no detention stockades at this time, nor would there ever be any large PW camps for Americans in South Vietnam. Because of the nomadic conditions and the relatively small numbers of PWs involved, rare would be the situation in which even a half dozen Americans would be held together in the South. So far as can be verified, prior to 1968 it happened only in one or two instances—in the Tam Ky region and along the Cambodian border near the "Parrot's Beak," the strip of Cambodian territory protruding into South Vietnam west of Saigon. Later, toward the end of the war, there would be more cases as the Communists collected their U.S. PWs and marched groups of them en masse to camps in the North.[7]

VC prisoners received some medicine, including quinine, sulfa, and penicillin, but medical care was no better than the French had experienced under the Viet Minh, and those PWs who died in captivity likely perished as often from neglect as from willful mistreatment or execution. Fryett, Groom, and Quinn reported being given pills and injections for stomach problems and malaria, but as Viet Cong attitudes hardened and medical supplies became scarcer, injuries and illness would increasingly go untreated. The VC would later refuse the repeated pleas of captured Army doctor Floyd Kushner, the only physician among the American prisoners in Southeast Asia, to administer aid to wounded and sick comrades.[8] The lack of medical attention had particularly severe consequences in the South, where swampy conditions and outdoor confinement resulted in a higher incidence of malaria and other jungle diseases than occurred in the relatively cooler and drier North.

Medical neglect was compounded by shortages of food and a diet consisting almost exclusively of rice that was often uncooked and contaminated. Far from supply bases and having no time to cultivate produce, the Viet Cong scavenged as they roamed through the countryside and drew on stores that had been cached in jungle caves and were rotting and vermin-infested. During the wet season even the rice ration was cut by a third. Captain Kushner recalled that in his camp in the rugged northern tier of South Vietnam, where the mortality figure reached 45 percent in 1968-69, "the overwhelming killer was starvation or its complications."[9] Judging from the accounts of prisoners released in the early years, who sometimes ate bits of chicken or dried fish with cooked rice, food may have been more easily procurable then. In any case, there is evidence that throughout the war PWs in the South ate no worse than their captors. Matagulay reported a political officer who ordered Viet Cong soldiers to give their rice rations to new South Vietnamese prisoners. The soldiers went hungry that night so that the prisoners could eat, the officer explaining that the Viet Cong believed so strongly in their cause that such sacrifice was routine. U.S. intelligence officers dismissed such incidents as VC ploys, calculated to ingratiate and thus disarm prisoners upon arrival, but there were numerous PWs released by the Viet Cong in the years to come who would report regularly eating the same rations as their guards, in the case of the Americans sometimes even more when the VC recognized their need for larger quantities.

If there was much that was makeshift and haphazard in the Viet Cong's treatment of prisoners, there was also one abiding consistency—the importance the VC attached to the indoctrination process and to the PWs as propaganda tools. The French had discovered this single-mindedness with the Viet Minh during the first Indochina war, and now the Americans were learning about it as well. Captured VC reported, and released PWs verified, that the Viet Cong were interested in prisoners less as sources of tactical intelligence information (for which they used their own agents) than as grist for the propaganda mill. Groom, Quinn, and Matagulay found that interrogators routinely asked for military information but quickly lost interest when the prisoner resisted giving it. The preoccupation was always with obtaining statements for propaganda purposes.

The methods were similar to those employed by the Viet Minh. VC indoctrinators were themselves thoroughly indoctrinated. They tended to be zealots, many of them veterans of combat against the French. (American PWs would notice after 1963 a dropoff in the skill and dedication of their interrogators as the Viet Cong began to run short of these experienced cadre and as the Northern-trained veterans of the French campaign were replaced by younger, less proficient locals.) The VC tried to convince American (and South Vietnamese) PWs that the Diem government was a puppet regime in the service of U.S. imperialism, likened the so-called "strategic hamlet" program (instituted by Diem in the spring of 1962) to a network of concentration camps, and praised the National Liberation Front as the legitimate instrument of Vietnamese nationalism. It was a familiar litany, passed down from the French days; only the names of the nemeses had changed.

At intervals in the indoctrination process the VC asked the Americans for confessions of criminal behavior, petitions for amnesty, or appeals to their countrymen to withdraw from Vietnam. A tape recorder was generally at hand, ready for an unwitting or broken prisoner to speak propaganda into it. The Communists used every gambit of manipulation, occasionally exploiting a prisoner's illness by having the individual sign a request for medicine and inserting in the request a veiled antiwar statement that could be extracted from context. Usually the statements would be broadcast or published to reflect credit on the Viet Cong and incriminate Diem and the United States. Sometimes they would be used for internal purposes: statements signed by Matagulay and Fryett were incorporated into Viet Cong textbooks as part of a training program for indoctrinators and interrogators.* As with the Viet Minh, the political warfare effort was as well organized as the military campaign.

All in all, as we shall see, PWs in South Vietnam had a more precarious experience and usually suffered a worse fate than PWs in North Vietnam, who, although tortured more systematically and more rigidly incarcerated, had food and medical aid more readily available and had important advantages of leadership and organization accruing from a more homogeneous PW population and larger, more concentrated numbers. By the end of 1964, with the guerrilla war intensifying and PW conditions steadily deteriorating in the South, one out of three Americans taken prisoner by the Viet Cong could expect to die in captivity, a percentage that, with fluctuations, would persist through the decade.[†10]

Among those captured in 1963 and 1964 two groups of Special Forces advisers stand out. On 29 October 1963, Army Lt. James Rowe, Capt. Humbert Versace, and Sgt. Daniel Pitzer (13, 14, 15) were seized in the Ca Mau Peninsula near the tip of South Vietnam's Mekong Delta. Further north, a month later, on 24 November, Army Sgts. Issac Camacho, Claude McClure, George Smith, and Kenneth Roraback (16, 17, 18, 19) fell captive in rubber plantation country not far from Saigon. The Rowe group, joined in 1964 by Sgts. Edward Johnson and Leonard Tadios (21, 25), were confined in a series of camps in the Delta's canals and forests over the next five years.

---

* Prisoners in the Mekong Delta during 1964-67 saw these training manuals and U.S. forces captured some.

† For the entire length of the Vietnam conflict, including short-term confinements early and late in the war, the mortality figure for prisoners held in the South would be closer to 20 percent, as compared with 5 percent in the North. See DIA Intelligence Appraisal, 8 May 73, figures 8, 12.

Left to right: Rowe, Versace, Pitzer.

The Camacho group, augmented by two American servicemen captured at the end of 1964, Army PFC Charles Crafts (28) and Marine Capt. Donald Cook (29),* were held at 10 locations, chiefly northeast of Tay Ninh near the Cambodian border. So remarkable were the experiences of the two groups, each running the gamut from triumph to tragedy and each strikingly documented in published accounts, that these men would achieve a special prominence in PW annals.

Rowe, Versace, and Pitzer were captured when the South Vietnamese unit they were advising fell to vastly superior Communist forces after vicious combat. The Government unit was stationed six miles north of Quan Long in the middle of Viet Cong territory. Diem's forces had won a major victory there against a VC battalion three months earlier, driving the rebels into the U Minh Forest, where they treated their wounded, reinforced their ranks, and resupplied. In October, there was no doubt that new attacks were coming—intelligence had been forecasting them for a month—but when they came, the size of the forces and quality of the weapons far exceeded expectations.[11]

The three Special Forces advisers were lucky to survive the strike on their camp and lucky to fall captive with each other. Rowe and Versace were tough and resourceful West Pointers; Pitzer was the team's medical chief and a stalwart soldier himself. All were wounded in the fighting, the two officers suffering leg injuries and Pitzer catching fragments in his shoulder and badly spraining an ankle. The Viet Cong moved them northwest to a small camp in an area of intersecting canals. Here they received food, medication, and mosquito nets and met with a member of the Liberation Front, who told them the VC had won a great victory in the battle and that it was their policy to treat prisoners well. Rowe soon developed dysentery, but he and the others were relieved to find their treatment decent and thought they might

* A third end-of-the-year capture, Army Sgt. Harold Bennett (27), seized in the same incident as Crafts, died en route to the Camacho camp. See Chapter 13.

be released after a few weeks. Rowe and Pitzer were kept separate from Versace, and when the three were united to have pictures taken, their hopes soared. From this session came a photograph of Rowe with his hands clasped atop his head that was widely circulated; it turned up later in the possession of captured and dead Viet Cong.

On 13 November 1963, after two weeks in this first camp, the prisoners began a trip of several days southward by boat through canals lined with vast rice paddies, coconut groves, and clumps of banana palms before arriving at a more permanent camp in a swampy region deep in the Delta. Here the three underwent interrogation and indoctrination supervised by the camp commander and two political officers, Ba and Muoi. There were lectures and more staged photographs, two of which were found later when South Vietnamese troops overran the area. For his diarrhea, Rowe received an injection of vitamin B-1, a curious treatment that left him praying to escape infection from an unsterile needle.

Late in November, Versace, despite a severely lacerated knee, tried to escape. Recaptured, he resisted indoctrination so vehemently that by the end of December the Viet Cong had marked him as a "reactionary," one impossible to convert to their teaching, and a troublemaker. They began to treat him cruelly, putting irons on his injured leg and leaving him to the mercy of a brutal guard. Pressure mounted for the prisoners to write letters attesting good treatment that would be useful to the Viet Cong as propaganda. Cooperation, the captors hinted, might bring release. Rowe and Pitzer decided to write only a vaguely worded letter to the Red Cross stating that they were captive and asking that their families be informed. This proved unsatisfactory.

Ba, the political officer, returned from a two-week absence with a paper he claimed to be a Red Cross data form. It required, before any personal information could be forwarded, that the prisoners answer a series of questions on military matters, then write a long personal history. He was asking that the men supply the ammunition for their own exploitation. The contest was on, with the captor holding all the trump cards. Rowe and Pitzer, ill and filthy, pressed for proper treatment under the Geneva Conventions. They pleaded for toothbrushes and other items of personal care and asked that the Red Cross be notified. Ba dismissed the Red Cross as an agent of Western imperialism and insisted that the prisoners show proper gratitude to the National Liberation Front for sparing their lives. The two could hear Versace raise his voice in argument with Muoi and the camp commander, Major Hai. So steadfastly did Versace hold his ground that interrogators began conducting their sessions in French and English so that the guards would not understand how well the American captain rebutted indoctrination. Versace, who could speak Vietnamese and French, at some points was debating his inquisitors in three languages. To the younger men, he was a marvel of courage and an inspiring example.

With the onset of the new year came the terrible news that President Kennedy and President Diem were dead. Suspicious and unable to understand the Vietnamese phrase *bi am sat*, which means "assassinated," Rowe and Pitzer dismissed the reports as false. In January, the Viet Cong moved Versace and Pitzer west to yet another camp, which the men would name "Mangrove Motel." Rowe joined them two weeks later. At Mangrove, all three were isolated, placed in small cages ("large enough to sit up in" and "long enough to lay in," Pitzer later described their cramped quarters[12]), and locked in leg irons at night, as the VC intensified their efforts to break the PWs. Ba, formerly a journalist until the Diem government closed down his paper, worked on Rowe and Pitzer. His tendency to philosophize soon earned him the nickname "Plato." He produced the same data card that Rowe had earlier refused to sign, and he tantalized the prisoners with news that the Front had recently released an American.* Rowe now accepted the card for study, intending to convince Ba of his willingness to cooperate but inability to provide the requested information.

As the weeks dragged on, indoctrination sessions became more formal. A team of teachers arrived to supervise a program of lectures, discussions, and readings. Slogans, crudely printed in English, went up on the walls of the indoctrination hut, exhorting the prisoners to "Welcome the lenient policy of the Front toward POW's" and "Oppose the dirty, undeclared war." Miserable as Rowe was with intestinal problems, he drew strength from Versace's unrelenting resistance, the latter continuing to defy his indoctrinators despite obvious physical and mental anguish. In April the VC staged a cruel drama in an apparent attempt to induce Pitzer and Rowe, whom they considered more exploitable than the insolent Versace, to comply. On the morning after a noisy disturbance in Versace's cage, Rowe, as he returned from the latrine, was instructed to walk to the kitchen to get his rice ration—the first time he had been permitted to do so in the new camp. On his way to the kitchen, he passed a small heap of rags and crushed aluminum. The rags, bloody and torn to shreds, were Versace's prison pajamas; the crushed metal, the captain's drinking cup and plate. Rowe walked past the cage that had held Versace and found the bars broken loose as if there had been a fierce struggle. Plato seemed unusually grave when he came for the daily lesson. He told Rowe that Versace had become so recalcitrant that action had to be taken. On the other hand, he added, he had turned in to the Front a good report on Pitzer and Rowe, despite their own lack of cooperation.

---

* Possibly civilian Arthur Krause, if Ba was telling the truth. Krause was let go in November 1963.

The incident had a predictable effect. The two remaining prisoners, presuming Versace dead, felt guilty that they had not resisted as unflinchingly as their comrade, yet now feared for their own lives were they not to cooperate. Rowe, determined to resist Plato's pressures without openly confronting him, insisted he was a simple engineer, unversed in politics or military tactics. He listened patiently to Plato's Marxist discourses on Vietnamese history. All the time gauging his opponent's knowledge of his background so as not to be caught in discrepancies, he talked slowly about schools he had attended and technical training he had received in civil engineering. To mollify Plato he once or twice divulged military information he thought innocuous or possibly capable of confusing the enemy. "The dangers of attempting to lie to my captors were something I'd been warned about at Fort Bragg, in a class on resistance to interrogation," Rowe later explained the dilemma common to all U.S. PWs in Vietnam, "but the theory of holding out no matter what was done to you suddenly became the scenes from the training film and not the reality facing me."[13]

From his cage at the front of the compound, Pitzer was able to see the coming and going of camp officials and observe the arrival of outsiders. He and Rowe worked out a communication method in which they would leave notes in the latrine to keep each other informed and sustain their morale. In May, the communication ended when the VC forced Pitzer, now very ill, to use Versace's old latrine, completely isolated from the one he had shared with Rowe. Rowe, figuring that he could not string Plato any further, decided he would write to the Front in a gesture of cooperation. His letter was simply a request for release. It contained none of the confessions or admissions the Front required. Plato returned it as unsatisfactory, insisting that Rowe would have to repent publicly. The lieutenant countered by asking how he could repent when he was guilty of no crime. The exchange initiated another round of fencing, Rowe again having succeeded in buying time and deferring rough treatment.

Rowe's understanding of Vietnamese improved enough by summer 1964 that he was able to converse with his guards. On one occasion as he discussed with them the Front's lenient policy toward PWs, questioning the sincerity of the policy when the Front had murdered Versace, a careless young guard blurted out that no one had been killed. Buoyed by the revelation that the captain might still be alive, Rowe later overheard other guards talking about the Versace incident, using a phrase, *mau luon*, that he had never encountered before. Several days later in conversation with "Ben," the VC medic (the PWs named him after the television character Ben Casey), he discovered the words meant "eel blood." Camp officials, Rowe realized, had staged the incident, smearing Versace's clothing with blood and fabricating his death in order to intimidate Rowe and Pitzer. When the medic left, Rowe leapt joyfully into the air, driving his arm through the thatch roof of his cage. Versace indeed was alive, and the VC did not know he knew.

Rowe spent the summer battling a severe fungus infection, alleviated only slightly by a Clorox-like liquid supplied by Ben. Partly to take some pressure off Versace, he sent word to Plato that he was ready to talk, then dictated four pages of civil engineering theory to the delighted interrogator, who retired to translate the statement into Vietnamese for his intelligence officer. When Plato gave the translation, which took five days to produce and amounted to technical gibberish, to his superior, Rowe heard the screams all the way back to his cage. He had won a little victory.

The satisfaction did not last long. Frustrated by the incessant indoctrination and in misery from unremitting diarrhea, Rowe lost his temper and slugged a guard, fracturing his jaw and incurring the wrath of the man's cohorts, who rushed in to Rowe's cage and bolted leg irons to his ankles. Muoi directed the men to strip Rowe, add another iron to fasten his arms, and remove his mosquito net. That night, left to wallow naked in his own filth, he endured hundreds of mosquito bites, passing into a coma before morning. Not long after, Pitzer, harassed by the same guard whom Rowe had hit, redislocated the man's jaw and for punishment was spreadeagled outside his cage, his wrists and ankles bound tightly with wire. It was a grim month for the two prisoners until camp officials, eager to resume indoctrination, announced that, as an indication of the VC's leniency policy, the Americans could visit together once a week.

At their first meeting after several months of isolation, Pitzer's appearance shocked Rowe; his health, long deteriorating, had rapidly worsened from the recent punishment. Rowe recalled the sergeant's pipestem legs reminding him of pictures he had seen of prisoners at Dachau. Plato had them listen to a Radio Hanoi broadcast by Robert Williams, a disaffected American living in Cuba, and Anna Louise Strong, the veteran fellow traveler, who praised a "solidarity" conference she and Williams had attended in Hanoi. While Rowe passed the time learning Vietnamese and devising a baseball game from wood splinters and his aluminum drinking cup, Pitzer's health continued to decline, the sergeant crestfallen after Plato backed off from a suggestion that he might be released. Soon the meetings between the two PWs were curtailed, further demoralizing Pitzer.

In September 1964, two new men arrived at the camp, both of them welcome additions. The first was a Vietnamese sent in to improve the prisoners' diet, evidence that the Front fully intended to keep them alive. The second was another American PW, Army Sgt. Edward Johnson, captured in July during fighting 15 miles northeast of the camp where Rowe and the others had been seized. Johnson, a powerfully built black, had been hauled slowly southward by his captors, maintaining good health despite the arduous trek. His robust appearance encouraged Rowe and Pitzer, and the secret exchange of messages with him brought them confirmation of Kennedy's death and refreshing news of the latest automobile models and baseball franchises and a popular rock group called the Beatles. A shortage of prisoner pens forced the VC to place Rowe and Pitzer in the same cage, with Johnson occupying Rowe's old compartment.

In October, Rowe received treatment for a beriberi condition that had caused his legs and abdomen to swell and prevented him from urinating. Ben injected him with strychnine sulfate, a drug that was effective but whose action was excruciatingly painful. Rowe later described the sensation as comparable to having one's legs slashed from hip to ankle and then having alcohol poured over the open wounds. He urinated a gallon of fluid the first night; to his astonishment, the loss of water and remission of the swelling left him looking like the emaciated Pitzer.

In mid-December the guards built a third cage to hold Army Sgt. Leonard Tadios, captured 11 December in an area close to where Johnson had been grabbed.* Tadios had been hit by a mortar round and suffered several fragmentation wounds to his leg, one of them deep and serious. When Rowe heard him stubbornly refusing VC treatment, he got permission to visit the new arrival. He convinced him that the camp medic should take out the smaller fragments but leave the large one for Pitzer to look at and possibly treat later.

On the morning of 23 December a helicopter attack on a camp nearby gave Rowe and Pitzer, who were outside their cage, a chance to make for the woods. They plunged into thick foliage, hoping to get as far away from the guard huts as they could and find a clearing from which to signal the choppers. But they were missed at once and quickly recaptured. After continued strikes in the area, they, Johnson, and Tadios were moved to a temporary camp several miles northeast of Mangrove Motel. The PWs spent a month there, much of it under the watch of younger guards, as the aging veterans of the French campaign were increasingly being replaced by fresh recruits.

Pitzer nearly succumbed to malnutrition in January 1965, but he managed to rally by force-feeding himself rice with help from Rowe. When he improved enough to walk around, Rowe helped him bathe in the canal that ran through the camp. One day they heard a familiar voice coming from an area farther down the canal that was screened from their view by dense vegetation. It was the indomitable Versace, still arguing with his captors. Pitzer

---

* Another Army sergeant, Joe Parks (26), was captured in the Delta about this time, on 22 December 1964, and would eventually join the Rowe group in February 1966. See Chapter 12.

and Rowe spoke loudly, hoping that the captain would hear them. Rowe recalled they felt a sense of reunion impossible to describe to an outsider. It was good that Versace's voice lifted their morale because on 20 January 1965, they, Versace, Johnson, and Tadios began a period of captivity far more brutal than what they had previously experienced. By the time their long ordeal was over, Versace and Tadios would be dead, Pitzer and Johnson would be released, and Rowe would be on the road to fame as a writer and lecturer following a miraculous escape.

One month after the capture of Rowe, Versace, and Pitzer in the Mekong Delta, on 24 November 1963, a second group of Special Forces advisers—Army Sgts. Issac Camacho, Claude McClure, George Smith, and Kenneth Roraback—were taken prisoner in a surprise midnight attack on their camp at Hiep Hoa, about 25 miles northeast of Saigon. In the fighting, McClure received fragmentation wounds and phosphorous burns, and Camacho sustained a head injury when one of the captors struck him with a rifle butt. Camacho and Smith were moved to a hamlet a mile from the point of capture, treated, then marched through a series of villages where they were displayed to the local citizenry. After several days they were reunited with the other pair some distance to the south.[14]

The Americans found the villagers along the way surprisingly restrained and their captors considerate and attentive to their safety. In fact, they were told they would be set free very soon close to Saigon. Extending hope for early release, whether the release was intended or not, had by now become a standard VC ploy, the Communists assuming that a prisoner expectantly awaiting his freedom would be easier to manipulate. The four sergeants must have realized the deception as the VC moved the men by boat and trail through ever smaller villages, farther and farther from Saigon, southwest into the Plain of Reeds, a trackless, swampy morass used by the Viet Cong as a refuge.

On the fifth day of their captivity, Thanksgiving, after paddling through miles of canals and dikes, they reached a tiny island, less than a dozen feet across, where the VC constructed a thatch hut for the PWs. Ten days of recuperation followed during which guards supplied ample food and even toothbrushes, and a Vietnamese medic removed a large piece of shrapnel from McClure's foot and injected him with penicillin. The good treatment was accompanied by casual interrogation and indoctrination. The leader of the guard detail asked for the names of other members of the Special Forces team at Hiep Hoa and produced a statement of remorse attributed to Arthur Krause, the American engineer seized in June and released only a week before the new captures. In his halting English the elderly Vietnamese indicated he wanted similar confessions from Camacho and his group. Later testimony conflicted as to what exactly was conceded, if anything, but McClure recalled they were told to write something like, "My presence at Hiep Hoa is endangering the lives of the people." In signing the statement, McClure spelled his first name "Charred" instead of "Claude," hoping to convey the message that he had been burned.

On 8 December the prisoners were advised that they were to be taken to meet the Central Committee of the National Liberation Front, again with the suggestion that release was in the offing and that they might be home for Christmas. As they traveled northward toward the city of Tay Ninh, anticipation once more yielded disappointment. During the first week of the difficult journey they came within range of Nui Ba Den, the tall mountain and familiar landmark some 50 miles from the site of their capture. From the location of the mountain, they knew they were heading further north, away from Saigon to the east. At night they passed through an extensive canal system, now and then riding by oxcart across grasslands. When they neared the mountain, the party was joined by an English-speaking representative of the NLF, who told them that the guards wanted to kill them but that as long as they obeyed orders and were polite, they would go unharmed. They spent another week traveling by boat and on blistered feet until finally arriving, on 18 December, at the first of 10 camps they would occupy in the general area northeast of Tay Ninh.

At "Sing Sing," as the prisoners named the first camp, they were able to rest for a few days while the VC changed guards under the direction of the English-speaking man from the Front. On the fifth day, they hiked to a second camp, "Bivouac," where they were locked in a large cage that was decorated with propaganda signs and slogans similar to those Rowe and Pitzer were finding about the same time on the walls of their indoctrination room many miles to the south. Their stay in the cage was brief, relieved by a Christmas dinner of chicken and precious bread, before they were moved to a specially constructed hut deep in the jungle. Here, beginning in January 1964, they were subjected to regular and intensive indoctrination sessions.

One by one, the prisoners faced a frail, neat, bespectacled man of imposing manner and impressive credentials, a former university professor, they were told, who had chosen to support the NLF rather than join the Diem government. He talked in competent English about Vietnam's fight for independence and encouraged the PWs to discuss why they were in Vietnam. He assured them that he did not want military information, boasting that the Front had agents so well placed that "we can tell you what will happen in your headquarters tomorrow."[15] To relax the men, he served them tea, candy, and cigarettes.

The indoctrinator, whom the PWs referred to as "the man with the crooked glasses," held many advantages over his charges—aside from their being a captive audience. The four NCOs were relatively unsophisticated, with limited schooling and probably less knowledge of American political theory and history than that possessed by the Front's more educated cadre. Their resistance training, emphasizing absolute noncompliance and silence except for identification purposes, had not prepared them for dealing with a gentle, solicitous, and patient yet tenacious interrogator. Moreover, the group lacked both leadership and cohesion. Camacho, the senior among them, was personally courageous and conscientious about adhering to the Code of Conduct, but he broke under pressure short of torture and also failed to keep the others in line. Roraback, the most uncooperative of the four, was disliked as much by one of his comrades as by the VC.[16]

When the persuasive man with the glasses gave the PWs a history lesson on Vietnam, recounting the long record of foreign intervention and aggression and reciting abuses under the Diem regime—persecution of religious groups, suppression of human rights, expropriation of property, unjust taxation, rampant profiteering and corruption—the young and impressionable Americans were overmatched. Their preconceived notion of the Communists as a sinister force in the South, as outlaws and aggressors—a view already undermined in their eyes by the friendliness with which the Viet Cong were greeted in many villages—no longer seemed so convincing. As the indoctrinator compellingly detailed the evidence against Diem, then asked whether or not the United States could be judged guilty as well because it had supported the South Vietnamese president, he sowed doubt and confusion among the prisoners, drawing them out in conversation as he plied them with more cigarettes and tea. He contrasted their "mercenary" participation (at one point brandishing a U.S. Army pay scale) with the Viet Cong's commitment to a set of principles. The VC, he observed, fought for almost nothing because they believed so strongly in their cause. Finally, he appealed to their instinct for survival by noting that the Viet Cong had no desire to keep them, that they were a burden to the guerrillas, but that they could not be simply let go to fight again. They would, he said, have to promise to repudiate the U.S. involvement and to leave the country. Once he had reached this point with each prisoner, the indoctrinator asked the individual if he would write down his thoughts on what they had discussed, then retired for a time before returning for yet another session.

The Americans were caught in a cruel dilemma. Even though more sympathetic to the Communist viewpoint as a result of the indoctrination exercise, they were mindful of their obligations as professional soldiers and their orders under the Code of Conduct. Even the most naive among them knew that providing the incriminating statements sought by the man with the glasses was a calculated risk, that there was no guarantee that the Front's Central Committee would find the statements acceptable or would not continue to exploit the men for further admissions. Yet they were indeed a burden to the Viet Cong. They had to be fed, moved, and housed. Their only value to the VC was insofar as they could be used to enhance the propaganda effort. They knew, too, that President Kennedy was dead (assassinated just two days before their capture), that the U.S. commitment in Vietnam was still tentative and likely to become even more problematic with the change in administrations, and that the vague and undeclared nature of the U.S. participation left them in the meantime in a legal limbo—without prisoner of war protections and vulnerable to criminal charges. Smith later recalled their predicament:

> All of which put me in the position of being a soldier in an army not at war, captured by an organization that did not exist in the eyes of my government, which was *fighting* that organization. It was straight out of *Catch-22*. Since the NLF was a nongovernment, the U.S. couldn't logically expect it to follow international agreements concerning prisoners, but by the same token the U.S. couldn't negotiate our release without recognizing that the NLF was quite real—something it wasn't about to do.
>
> But on the other hand, the NLF obviously did exist and did hold territory—hell, you could argue that they controlled Hiep Hoa, considering how easily they kicked our ass out of there. By our own government's policy I wasn't at war with them—or with anybody else, for that matter—but by mortaring their farmers and training strikers to go marauding and burn down their houses, by this alone I could be considered a criminal.
>
> Now, according to the Superman Code, the Army wanted me to suffer torture and death rather than give up anything more than name-rank-serial number. I had been captured while guarding Madame Nhu's goddamned sugar mill—while her own soldiers in the mill hadn't fired a shot. Dying for that didn't make any more sense in the jungle than it did when I was crouching in that bunker [at Hiep Hoa] with the bullets going . . . all around my head.
>
> In the end, I decided to write a statement. How much weight could anybody give to a statement written by a POW under god-only-knows what conditions in the middle of the damned jungle? And if the statement *were* released, it would at least tell the Army and my folks that I was still alive.[17]

So for various reasons of shifting sympathies, lack of a clear sense of purpose, fear and uncertainty, and simple fatigue after weeks of skillful indoctrination, the prisoners complied and furnished written statements. Camacho thanked the VC for sparing his life and for the good treatment he received, expressed sorrow for any suffering he had caused the Vietnamese people, and promised never to return to Vietnam if released. Smith, after a half dozen visits with the man with the glasses, and McClure, a black whom the VC evidently baited with appeals to race, were coached into making declarations of sympathy for the Front and recording similar expressions of guilt and regret. Only Roraback apparently held out.*

On 28 January 1964 the prisoners were moved to a new camp, their third in the Tay Ninh area. The new location, a day's walk eastward, Smith named "Auschwitz." It had four large cages, about 50 Viet Cong support troops, and as many as 200 guerrillas coming and going at any one time. Many of the VC there they had encountered earlier at Sing Sing and Bivouac. The camp commander, "Suave," who also conducted political classes and rallies for the regular troops in for rest and resupply, was so called for his neat dress and gentlemanly manner. His assistant, who did the translating for the PWs, they called "Prevaricator" because of his habitual lying and exaggeration. The chief guard, a large, strong professional soldier who dominated the other guards, constantly issuing orders, was "Anus."

The men spent nine months in Auschwitz, settling into a lazy routine that found them now and then doing work around the camp, mostly chopping wood and digging holes, alternately bantering and battling with their captors, and passing the time with whatever treats they could bum from friendly guards, from Cambodian cigarettes to a game of Chinese checkers. Belying the place's nickname, conditions here were markedly better than those the Rowe group faced in the Delta. Because the camp was a sizable guerrilla base with a supply depot and rest facilities, the mood was relaxed, discipline minimal, and food relatively plentiful. Anus played "Battle Hymn of the Republic" for the prisoners on his mandolin, insisting it was originally a Chinese song; he let Camacho play the instrument until the latter broke a string. Tet, the lunar new year, was celebrated with meals of pork, dates, and nuts, in which the prisoners were allowed to share. Noted Australian writer and Communist Wilfred Burchett visited in March, occasioning more ceremony and another special meal of sardines and fresh bread. Burchett spoke with the Americans, posed for photos, and left copies of two of his books, *North of the 17th Parallel* and *Mekong Upstream*, which the VC later gave the prisoners to read. Smith asked Burchett to get word to his mother that he was all right, and Burchett transmitted the message on a radio broadcast, which Mrs. Smith heard.[18]

* Court-martial charges were filed against Smith and McClure upon their release and return in December 1965, the Army judging that they had resisted to a lesser extent and furnished more damaging statements than the others. The charges were later dismissed. See Chapter 13.

Australian journalist Wilfred Burchett meets with, *left to right*, Camacho, Roraback, McClure, and Smith in March 1964.

If life at Auschwitz was not oppressive, neither was it a picnic. The men endured the usual hazards endemic to the jungle—foul water, army ants, venomous centipedes and snakes, sweaty days and chilly nights. Smith was barely able to walk for a day after being stung by a scorpion. All suffered periodically from malaria and malnutrition, despite the relative availability of medicine and food. The special-occasion suppers leavened a mostly unpalatable diet that had them struggling to keep rations down. They lived in constant dimness under the jungle canopy, such that when they were taken to a clearing they squinted uncomfortably. McClure in particular had psychological problems; according to Smith, at long stretches he was listless and despondent. Finally, there were the persisting indoctrination pressures. The man with the crooked glasses made a follow-up visit, leaving notebooks for the PWs to fill with further reflections on the war. Flippantly they drew cartoons instead, until the indoctrinator reacted angrily, whereupon they wrote additional statements condemning the U.S. involvement.

When helicopter activity in the area increased in September, the prisoners were moved briefly to another camp they named "Little Stream," where they continued to suffer from the harsh effects of the environment but were treated with an almost benign neglect by their captors. The PWs lived, ate, and slept side by side with the guards. They dug an air raid shelter, but did little other physical labor. Prevaricator set up a class to teach them Vietnamese. The guards split with them helpings of fish and meat as well as extra rice. As security grew lax—they were chained only at night and then loosely to a pole in the hut they shared with the guards—the men could have escaped from the camp without much difficulty, but, as seems to have been a prevailing attitude among American PWs in the South, they regarded the jungle as just as forbidding and perhaps an even less forgiving enemy than the VC. In any case, after three weeks at Little Stream, they were returned to Auschwitz.

The continuing improvement in their treatment rekindled hopes for release, and this time their expectations were well founded. The Front had in fact been attempting to arrange a release, possibly as a goodwill gesture or as part of a prisoner exchange. Its representatives abruptly terminated discussions, however, when the South Vietnamese government executed a teenage member of the NLF who had been caught placing explosives under a bridge that U.S. Secretary of Defense Robert S. McNamara was expected to cross during a visit to Saigon. The young Communist, Nguyen Van Troi, was executed on 15 October 1964, provoking a sharp reaction from the NLF and causing the Front to cancel plans for releasing the Americans.* "I stopped blaming my captors so much at that point," Smith recalled, remembering his frustration at the prisoners' coming so close to obtaining their freedom only to have the door shut again. "I wasn't mad at the Vietnamese for not releasing us. They weren't going to have a man executed and then go ahead and release Americans . . . . As far as I was concerned the United States and the Saigon government became directly responsible for our captivity from that point on."[19]

As the war heated up late in 1964 and the Viet Cong found themselves increasingly on the run, conditions for PWs throughout South Vietnam steadily worsened. The Camacho group, entering its second year of captivity, was now affected as well. Finding Auschwitz abandoned upon their return, the bars removed from the cages and most of the supplies gone, the group pressed northward to a new camp, which the men named "Big Stream," where they stayed for several weeks until heavy rains and vulnerability to air attacks forced them back to the thicker cover of Auschwitz. At Auschwitz a new commander greeted them. "Oil Can Harry"—the prisoners

* Troi had been captured in May and quickly sentenced to death. The NLF had warned both Saigon and Washington that carrying out the execution would jeopardize the lives of PWs held by the Viet Cong. The United States, maintaining that the punishment of Troi was an internal matter for the South Vietnamese government to decide, did not stop the execution, although it did succeed in delaying it until October.

named him after a sinister, black-attired character in the *Mighty Mouse* cartoon—put the PWs to work milling rice for themselves and the guards. Bad luck soon struck when "Gidget," a young guard, accidentally discharged his rifle, wounding Smith in the leg. The other VC apologized and tended the injury, even supplying Smith with warm milk during his recuperation, but the prisoners viewed the incident as a serious setback to their fading chances for release since the Viet Cong were not likely to let go a recently wounded man: "not much propaganda value in that," Smith recalled his reaction.[20]

With the approach of Christmas, the regular bombing and strafing runs of a B-26 in the area—unsettling the PWs as much as the Viet Cong—ceased temporarily.[21] Oil Can Harry brought in a radio so that the Americans could hear broadcasts from Hanoi and Peking. To keep occupied, Camacho began to teach Smith Spanish, and between them they mischievously wrote a version of *Los Tres Moranitos—The Three Little Pigs—* into Smith's notebook, imagining the livid reaction of the man with the glasses. Thus they passed the time in the jungle camp near Cambodia. Meanwhile, three other Americans were seized east of Saigon—two Army advisers, Sgt. Harold Bennett and PFC Charles Crafts, and Marine Capt. Donald Cook. The new captures were marched toward Auschwitz and the Camacho group. In the nightmarish months ahead, as the Christmas respite gave way to a convulsive new year, two of the three, along with Roraback in the original quartet, would perish.

As the Rowe and Camacho groups struggled through their respective ordeals in the Delta and Parrot's Beak regions of South Vietnam, at the northernmost tip of the country Army Capt. Floyd (Jim) Thompson (20) entered upon a solitary captivity that would keep him in virtual isolation, almost a secret prisoner, for some nine years. Thompson, commander of a Special Forces detachment in Quang Tri Province, was captured on 26 March 1964 while flying on a reconnaissance mission near the DMZ. Severely injured, he would recover to endure a nomadic confinement in a series of tiny, remote camps that, remarkably, would not place him in contact with another American military PW (except for one brief encounter) until a month before his release on 16 March 1973. The Vietnamese always considered him to be a Viet Cong captive, although initially he was incarcerated in camps in Laos and eventually he spent most of his imprisonment in North Vietnam. His near-decade as a PW would make him the longest held prisoner of war in U.S. history. He also was one of the most heroic.[22]

"Old Man of the South"
Thompson

On the day of his capture Thompson and his pilot, Air Force Capt. Richard Whitesides, crashed when struck by ground fire during a low pass over a suspicious jungle area. Thompson, seated in the rear of the small observation plane, survived the crash but suffered a broken back, leg burns, a facial wound, and a concussion that left him fading in and out of consciousness for several days.* His guards, mountain tribesmen (Montagnards, perhaps Meo), lugged him by stretcher along trails from the then-little-known village of Khe Sanh southward through the valleys into Laos to a camp on the Tchepone River, the first of a dozen locations at which Thompson would be held.

The Ranger captain remained at this first camp from 9 April to 1 May 1964. The installation consisted of five huts that were constructed on stilts and made of bamboo and thatched roofing. Montagnard families lived in three of the huts, the guards in another, and Thompson in the fifth. Although the guards were friendly and offered him adequate food, Thompson was too ill to eat and periodically lapsed into coma from the pain of the untreated back injury. Somehow he recovered strength, per-haps sustained by thoughts of the impending birth of a new baby,† enough to begin moving about unaided. Left unguarded one day, he even attempted

---

* Whitesides's body was never recovered. He was presumed killed in the shootdown.
† Thompson's fourth child was born the day after his capture.

escape, but was soon discovered, whereupon he explained he had simply stepped into the jungle to urinate. During two more aborted tries, he repeated the charade when apprehended, finally giving up the escape notion until he could gain more mobility.

By May, the wounds to his face and leg had begun to heal, thanks to medicine and cleaning by the guards, and his back had mended to the point where his captors were able to transport him to a second camp, "Bravo" (Thompson named the camps by the phonetic alphabet, Alpha to Lima), where he spent a month. In June he was taken further southward, still along the Laos-South Vietnam border, to Camp Charlie. During these marches, the guards—usually six in number—whisked him quietly through the mountain villages, slipping in and out under the cover of darkness and concealing his face with a floppy hat and mosquito net so that the locals could not see that he was an American. He was not told the reason for any of the moves, but the reason for the latest became apparent when he was introduced to two Viet Cong political specialists who spoke very good English. At Charlie he was now firmly under the control of VC cadre, and they intended to thoroughly interrogate and indoctrinate their important captive, the only officer prisoner in the northern region of South Vietnam. In fact, Charlie seemed solely designed for that purpose.

The sessions lasted all day, sometimes into the evening, with a pause for rest at noon. The interrogators assured Thompson that their only objective was to educate him, to help him understand the basis for the Viet Cong's struggle, and to prepare him for release. They showed him pictures of U.S. personnel who had been let go after cooperating (Army NCOs George Groom and Francis Quinn and civilian Arthur Krause) and promised him the same outcome if he followed suit. Thompson hung tough, listening blankly for days on end to the Communists' rendition of Vietnamese history, the pain from his broken back growing worse again as he was forced to sit upright during these classes. The VC applied more pressure, increasing the length of the sessions, reducing his rations and making him prepare his own food, and between sessions forcing him to work cutting underbrush.

Physically and mentally exhausted after a month of instruction and finding his interrogators losing patience with his "bad attitude," Thompson decided to attempt escape. Knowing he was near the Laotian border, he thought he could reach friendly forces if he traveled east, toward the coast. As Dieter Dengler did in Laos, he planned to head north first, assuming his guards would never expect him to take off in that direction. His chance came on 21 July, when early in the morning he caught his guard asleep, silently put on his boots,* and slipped off in the direction of the latrine, and then, undiscovered, into the jungle. For more than 10 minutes he moved deeper into the bush before he heard the alarm sounded. The head start was enough to allow him to reach a river by afternoon, still undetected, but when he tried to cross at dusk he was intercepted by Montagnards whom the VC had cleverly posted along the bank.

Upon his recapture and return to camp, he was confronted by Charlie's commander, who, angry and embarrassed by the escape, put Thompson on public display and beat him unconscious. When he awoke he was threatened with execution by an assembled firing squad, then told he would be given one last opportunity to "atone." Another round of intensive interrogation followed. When he remained silent, he was denied sleep, made to do senseless tasks, and whipped repeatedly with a bamboo stick. His only food during this time was a daily bowl of thin rice soup. It took weeks and more beatings, but the Vietnamese finally so weakened Thompson that, on 18 August, while semiconscious and "more dead than alive," he signed a prepared statement attesting to the legitimacy of the Viet Cong's cause and the wrongfulness of American intervention, also recording a few words for broadcast.

Thompson later recounted his amazement at the VC's extraordinary effort to obtain what seemed to him so trivial—a mild propaganda statement. They had constructed a camp in a remote jungle area, staffed it with trained interrogators and guards, and spent more than two months—not to learn vital military information, but to force him to say merely that they were treating him well, that the Viet Cong were good people, and that the United States was interfering in their just struggle. It would be years, not until late in his captivity, before he would realize the importance the Communists attached to such statements. Then he would learn about the antiwar movement in the United States, Hanoi's international propaganda campaign, and the lengths to which the Viet Cong and North Vietnamese would go to present their case.

The day after surrendering to his captors' demands, Thompson was moved a short distance to Camp Delta, which consisted of three thatched

* Thompson, perhaps because of his crippled condition at capture, had been permitted to keep his soldier's boots. Generally, the Viet Cong took them away from PWs, either making prisoners walk barefoot or outfitting them with Vietnamese-style sandals. Sgt. Daniel Pitzer, testifying before a House subcommittee in 1971, noted that he and the others in the Rowe group had their shoes removed immediately upon capture and that for the entire duration of their captivity, four years in his case, they went barefoot at all times. "That was one way of detaining a prisoner or keeping the prisoner from escaping," Pitzer told the committee. See *American Prisoners of War in Southeast Asia, 1971*, 51.

huts by a stream. Here he and his guards lived upon what food was available in the immediate vicinity. The prisoner gathered and split wood, cooked, and cleaned up around the huts. The guards watched him more closely now because of the escape attempt at Charlie. Thompson spent 15 months in this desolate spot, foraging for food, fighting off leeches, mosquitos, and ticks, and trying to preserve his sanity through the oppressive isolation and monotony. Meanwhile, to the north, the North Vietnamese were putting to the test Navy Lt. Everett Alvarez, imprisoned about the same time that Thompson arrived at Delta. North Vietnam's first captured U.S. aviator, Alvarez would be famous from the day of his seizure, his name and picture prominently featured in news accounts on both sides. If secluded, forgotten Jim Thompson became the Old Man of the South, the celebrated Alvarez was destined to become the Old Man of the North. His capture opened a new, pivotal chapter in the American PW experience in Southeast Asia.

5

First Arrivals at the Hanoi Hilton

In August 1964, as the fighting in the South intensified, locking the South Vietnamese army and Viet Cong insurgents in an inconclusive but escalating guerrilla war, the U.S. involvement in the struggle took another fateful turn. On 4 August, while operating in the Gulf of Tonkin some 60 miles off the coast of North Vietnam, the United States destroyers *Maddox* and *C. Turner Joy* reported coming under attack from North Vietnamese gunboats. The *Maddox* had reported a similar incident two days earlier.* President Lyndon B. Johnson, angered by Hanoi's defiance in supplying the Viet Cong despite Washington's warnings and alarmed by what appeared to be increasing North Vietnamese military activity in the South, ordered a retaliatory air strike against North Vietnamese torpedo boat bases and oil storage depots. On 7 August Congress, at Johnson's behest, passed the so-called Tonkin Gulf Resolution authorizing the president to take "all necessary measures to repel any armed attack against the forces of the United States and to prevent further aggression."[1] With the wide grant of authority to the president in the deployment of U.S. forces to Vietnam and with the first attacks on the North, another significant threshold, in

---

* The precise nature of the destroyers' mission and the circumstances surrounding the alleged attacks, whether they were provoked or whether they in fact even took place, subsequently became the subject of a major controversy that has never been fully resolved. For a contemporary account of the episode that supplies information known then, see *Time*, 14 Aug 64, 11-16. Secretary of the Navy Paul R. Ignatius presented evidence supporting the attack claim in a letter to Senate Foreign Relations Committee Chairman J. William Fulbright, 18 Dec 67, copy in OSD Hist. For a historian's estimate that raises questions based on later revelations and a closer examination of conditions and motives, see George C. Herring, *America's Longest War: The United States and Vietnam, 1950-1975*, 119-21. See also *The Gulf of Tonkin, The 1964 Incidents*, Hearing before Senate Foreign Relations Committee, 90 Cong, 2 sess (20 Feb 68); Eugene G. Windchy, *Tonkin Gulf*; and, polemical but useful, Joseph C. Goulden, *Truth Is the First Casualty: The Gulf of Tonkin Affair—Illusion and Reality*.

North Vietnam (1965)

terms of both the deepening American commitment in Southeast Asia and the evolving U.S. prisoner of war experience there, had been crossed.

The air strikes on 5 August, flown from the carriers *Ticonderoga* and *Constellation*, destroyed or damaged 25 North Vietnamese patrol boats and 90 percent of the oil storage facilities at the port of Vinh. The raids, although successful in crippling North Vietnam's limited naval capability and dramatically demonstrating American might and resolve, were not without cost. Two U.S. planes were lost, a third was damaged, and, most seriously—an event having ominous political and public relations implications—North Vietnam claimed its first American prisoner of war, naval aviator Lt. (j.g.) Everett Alvarez, Jr.[2]

Alvarez had been downed by antiaircraft fire after completing a second pass over the PT boat base at Hon Gay. Unable to nurse his smoking A-4 Skyhawk out to sea, where rescue might have been possible, he ejected not far from shore and a half hour later, after a futile attempt to swim to safety, was picked up by several armed Vietnamese in a fishing vessel. They bound him in heavy rope and turned him over to a patrol boat, which delivered him— "pale, weary and awe-stricken," Radio Hanoi reported in its announcement of the capture—to the base he had just attacked.[3]

After taking a series of photographs, North Vietnamese officers interrogated him briefly, gave him a small dish of unpalatable meat, then placed him in a cell with two Vietnamese prisoners. When his cellmates were unusually friendly, one of them speaking English well, Alvarez became suspicious and guarded his conversation. For two days the interrogations continued, his inquisitors telling him that he had been victimized by his own government, that there had been no PT boat attacks on American ships, that the Johnson administration had fabricated the episode as a pretext for its use of force. On 7 August he was taken by jeep inland to spend the next four days at a secluded farmhouse. Here he was quizzed further by an officer whom American PWs would later call "Owl," more for his distinctive features than any special intelligence. At first refusing to talk, Alvarez finally relented, supplying mostly misinformation, when he realized that Owl had read English newspaper accounts of the shoot-down and already knew many details about his family and even his mission. To his surprise, his cryptic responses pleased the officer. Alvarez learned, as others would later, that sometimes any answer would satisfy an interrogator who was under pressure to produce information.

On the morning of 11 August Alvarez and his keepers left the farmhouse for Hanoi, reaching the North Vietnamese capital and its notorious Hoa Lo prison by early afternoon. Hoa Lo, meaning in Vietnamese "fiery furnace," had been built by the French at the turn of the century and was still being used as the main municipal prison in North Vietnam. Surrounded

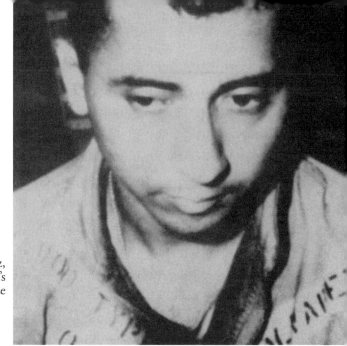

Alvarez,
North Vietnam's
first prize

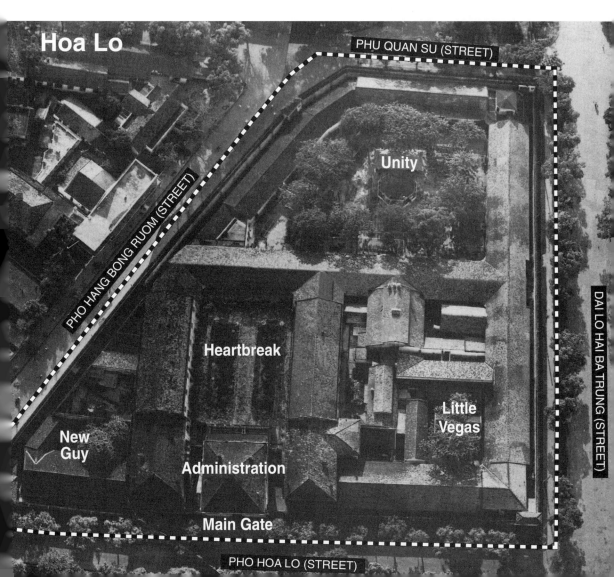

Hoa Lo

PHU QUAN SU (STREET)

PHO HANG BONG RUOM (STREET)

DAI LO HAI BA TRUNG (STREET)

Unity

Heartbreak

Little
Vegas

New
Guy

Administration

Main Gate

PHO HOA LO (STREET)

by thick concrete walls 15 to 20 feet high, it occupied an imposing trapezoidal block in the center of the city. The complex was divided into four general areas that the Americans would name "Heartbreak Hotel," "New Guy Village," "Little Vegas," and "Camp Unity," the latter by far the largest section, opened late in 1970 when the North Vietnamese herded nearly all the PWs into Hanoi. Security at the prison was formidable. Guard towers ringed the exterior walls, which were topped by several strands of barbed wire thought to be electrified and jagged glass shards ("the remnants of French champagne bottles," according to John Hubbell,[4] whose PW history deals at length with the American experience at Hoa Lo). If some-how a lucky inmate made it over the wall, he would wind up on a residential street not far from downtown Hanoi, an unlikely spot for evasion. There was only one entryway to the massive facility, and it was divided by a series of heavy iron gates that sealed shut one after the other. No U.S. serviceman escaped from Hoa Lo, and few considered trying. With grim irony its first group of American occupants soon dubbed the forbidding fortress the "Hanoi Hilton."

Alvarez was placed in room 24 of the Heartbreak section. Heartbreak became the in-processing, screening, and initial interrogation center for most of the new arrivals. It was subdivided into offices, interrogation rooms, torture chambers, a courtyard, and a block of eight cells, each seven feet square with a cement slab bed on either side to which leg irons were attached and a high barred window that was usually boarded. The eighth cell served as a washroom and bathing area. As Heartbreak quickly filled, incoming cap-tives were housed in New Guy Village, which adjoined it. After a period in Heartbreak or New Guy ranging from days to months, the prisoner was usually transferred to another section of Hoa Lo or to a camp outside Hanoi. Alvarez would remain at Heartbreak for 10 months.[5]

Room 24 was outside the cellblock area, twice as large as the regular cells, and not as dreary. Alvarez had a metal frame bed, a mosquito net, table, two chairs, an issue of clothing, and time to spend outdoors in the courtyard. Guards instructed him to say *Bao Cao* (pronounced "Bow cow"), a servile phrase for requesting permission to speak, whenever he wished to address them. To his surprise, his treatment initially was good. But despite the relative advantages he enjoyed while the North Vietnamese had yet to develop rigid confinement procedures, conditions were still horrible. Rats, some over a foot long, invaded his room night and day. The food was sickening—animal hooves, chicken heads, slimy bits of vegetables, cold and rotten fish, unidentifiable chunks of meat covered with hair. In a few weeks, vomiting constantly and suffering from bloody diarrhea, he lost almost 40 pounds. Only when the Vietnamese realized how ill he was did they improve his diet, feeding him rice soup, which alleviated his intestinal problems if not the rat infestation.

Although Alvarez had been careful to dispose of his wedding ring in the water following his ejection—remembering from his survival training that the Communists would exploit the fact he was married—his captors knew of his wife from Western wire reports and tantalized him with two photographs of her clipped from newspapers. (Alvarez kept these photos during his entire captivity and brought them out with him in 1973.) On 20 August, guards took him to a house six miles south of Hoa Lo, where a Japanese camera crew filmed him in his flight suit and helmet. He tried to hide his face from the camera but could not. When Vietnamese radio reporters came to interview him at Hoa Lo a week later, he decided to make a brief tape indicating that he was alive. In a follow-up letter he included a reference to an avocado tree he had planted, so that his wife would know the message was authentic. Alvarez took advantage of the opportunity to write, though he went about it discreetly, mindful not to say or divulge anything that might be of use to his captors. When he mentioned in one communication that the North Vietnamese had told him they planned to try him as a criminal, camp officials, censoring the letter, made him delete the remark. But his letters, at least a dozen of them, reached his wife, and some of hers reached him. Alvarez would treasure this early correspondence. When other prisoners, in larger numbers, began arriving at Hoa Lo in the spring of 1965, none, including Alvarez, would be permitted to write or receive letters regularly.

Beginning on 21 September 1964 a team of officials quizzed Alvarez twice daily for four hours at a time, gently but persistently pumping their prize captive for both biographical and military information. Owl, who had accompanied Alvarez to Hoa Lo from the farmhouse outside Hon Gay, was now joined by a second political officer and a third man to whom both deferred. The Vietnamese mixed interrogation with doses of indoctrination, attempting to manipulate the pilot for propaganda purposes. They prodded Alvarez to compose a letter to Ho Chi Minh requesting release and expressing appreciation for good treatment; he declined. They took him to view wreckage of downed aircraft, using a circuitous route in an effort to disorient him and keep him from realizing that he was still in Hanoi. On one occasion they had him meet with American fugitive Robert Williams, who explained his disillusionment with the United States and urged Alvarez to write to Ho.* Alvarez was unimpressed by the Williams visit but devoured the spread of cookies and fruit that the hosts had arranged to warm the atmosphere.

---

* Williams, a black, had been touring China and North Vietnam with his wife, the two making appearances and broadcasts in behalf of the Communist cause. American PWs in the South James Rowe and Daniel Pitzer were made to listen to one such broadcast by their Viet Cong captors. See Chapter 4.

The two-a-day interrogation sessions lasted for six weeks, until 6 November. Although he found his examiners "amateurish" and easy to divert, the eight hours of questioning each day, combined with the abominable food, the uncertainty about his status (the North Vietnamese, harping on the criminality theme, told him he was not entitled to PW protections because there was no declared war), and an overwhelming sense of isolation took their toll. He coped with the loneliness by carrying on imaginary conversations with a variety of friends, playing out both sides of the dialogue himself. He scratched out an altar with bible passages on a wall outside the room and carved his name and arrival date next to it. (Dozens of American prisoners who would later pass through Heartbreak would notice the signature and be inspired by the scripture.) Prayer and exercise readied him for the next day's encounters. He sidetracked the senior Vietnamese officer, who enjoyed droning on about his country's history and the methods the Viet Minh had used to defeat the French, by pretending to be interested in those topics. He parried questions about carrier operations with prattle on how Americans played football, how the popcorn machine functioned on his ship, how his father worked in a shoe factory called the Foot Machinery Corporation. Alvarez had an advantage here because he was the first American captured by Hanoi and his inexperienced interrogators at this point had only a rudimentary, often mistaken, knowledge of affairs in the United States.

The stall tactics succeeded for days on end, but the relentless grilling eventually wore down Alvarez and caught him in contradictions and obvious lies. In the fourth week the Vietnamese confronted him with evidence that he had not been flying an unarmed reconnaissance plane, as he had insisted, but a fighter-bomber equipped with ordnance. He admitted he had been untruthful and, feigning contrition, threw himself on their mercy, explaining that he feared execution if they learned he had fired on their boats. The senior officer assured him that they had no intention of killing him. The incident, together with the gradual improvement in his diet, convinced Alvarez of his importance to his captors and that they fully intended to keep him alive. What he could not know was that the price of that assurance would be continual torment for some eight and a half years and periods of such suffering that at times death would have been a relief.

Following the Tonkin Gulf confrontation and the retaliatory raids leading to Alvarez's capture, the Johnson administration resisted for a time further escalation of the war. The president chose to ignore a guerrilla attack on the Bien Hoa airbase in November 1964 that killed four American servicemen and destroyed several B-57s. He also rejected reprisals after a Viet Cong attack upon a U.S. billet in Saigon that killed more Americans. But with Diem's successors continuing to flounder and the military situation continuing to deteriorate, the administration faced increasing pressure to intervene more directly if it hoped to avert a Communist takeover of South Vietnam. Finally, in February 1965, when the Viet Cong assaulted the U.S. advisory compound and a nearby helicopter base at Pleiku, killing 8 Americans and wounding more than 100, Johnson ordered the start of bombing operations against North Vietnam.*

The initial strikes, called "Flaming Dart" according to a reprisal plan previously drawn up by the Joint Chiefs of Staff, were conducted by both U.S. and South Vietnamese aircraft and aimed at the Dong Hoi army camp about 50 miles north of the seventeenth parallel dividing North and South Vietnam. When the North Vietnamese responded with further attacks on American installations, including the blowing up of a U.S. enlisted men's billet in Qui Nhon on 10 February that killed 23, Johnson approved a more extensive bombing plan code-named "Rolling Thunder." The new program, which would continue, with incremental expansions and occasional pauses, for three years, began on 2 March. By April U.S. Air Force and Navy planes were flying 1,500 attack sorties per month against the North (a figure that would peak at 4,000 in September before declining with the onset of the monsoon season). The bombing activity had thus progressed from a limited, retaliatory effort to an ongoing, if still carefully controlled, offensive.[6]

Even as the administration stepped up the bombing through the spring of 1965, it pursued a deliberate and restrained policy of "graduated response" calculated to bring North Vietnam to the negotiating table without unduly provoking its Soviet and Chinese allies. Such a policy, entailing strict constraints on the type and location of targets and the conduct of air operations, so throttled the program that Ambassador Maxwell Taylor complained in early March that the North was being struck by "a few isolated thunder claps" rather than "Rolling Thunder." The policy of restraint also straitjacketed American pilots, immensely complicating their job and exposing them to higher than usual risks. Under Washington's close supervision (Johnson allegedly remarked that "they can't even bomb an outhouse without my approval"), pilots had to stay exactly to assigned targets—in most cases,

* The Pleiku attack occurred on the very day, 6 February (Washington time), that Soviet Premier Alexei Kosygin arrived in Hanoi to discuss a North Vietnamese request for additional aid. Some have argued, cogently, that the North Vietnamese timed the attack to coincide with Kosygin's visit; by inviting U.S. retaliation, in this view, they hoped to strengthen their case with the Soviets, who were as concerned as the United States about an expansion of the war that could increase Chinese influence and jeopardize superpower "peaceful coexistence." On this point, see Karnow, *Vietnam: A History*, 411-14.

clearly defined military facilities and transportation and supply lines whose bombing would pose a minimal threat to civilians; fly in and out of designated corridors, the patterns becoming so familiar that the North Vietnamese learned to anticipate them and counter with an effective air defense system; and strike only in weather and at levels that permitted visual identification of the targets (and left attacking aircraft exceedingly vulnerable). Even as the scope and intensity of the air war increased significantly in mid-1965 and restrictions were relaxed to allow some flexibility and initiative in targeting, Air Force and Navy aviators, still prohibited from bombing enemy population centers and confined to raids on peripheral airfields and oil storage sites that had become all too predictable, found themselves flying into heavily defended areas at great peril and with only token results. Such missions produced deep frustration and high casualties. By summer more than 30 American airmen had been killed or were presumed missing in action and a dozen captured. Those captured joined Lieutenant Alvarez in another war.[7]

Alvarez heard of the bombing from North Vietnamese officials, who visited his cell and showed him local press releases detailing the effects of the raids. He reacted to the news with a mix of hope and apprehension. He hoped the attacks would persuade Hanoi to negotiate a quick settlement; yet he also feared for his own life should the destruction spread to Hanoi and rile his jailers. In late February, back in interrogation after a respite of many weeks, Alvarez was confronted once again by Owl, who asked the pilot to explain a set of cards the Vietnamese had obtained. Alvarez immediately recognized the materials as "kneecards"—quick-reference cards carried, usually in knee pockets, by U.S. naval aviators and containing information on weapons loads, release altitudes, rate of fuel consumption, specific tactical angles of attack, and the like. He assumed the cards belonged to Lt. Edward Dickson, a Navy pilot who he learned had been shot down during one of the early strikes following the Pleiku incident. Aware that the war had taken a dangerous new turn and determined not to disclose anything that might harm other American fliers, Alvarez remained silent, telling Owl only that he had never before seen the cards.

From the supply of February news releases, Alvarez learned too that the North Vietnamese had captured Navy Lt. Cdr. Robert Shumaker. Shumaker had been seized on 11 February when his aircraft was hit by ground fire and he was forced to parachute into the countryside near Dong Hoi. Bailing out at low level, deploying his chute less than 100 feet from the ground, Shumaker landed hard in a sitting position and suffered a compression fracture of the lower back. Although not totally crippling, the injury prevented him from escaping, and, left untreated by his captors, would cause him excruciating pain for much of his eight years in prison.[8]

Shumaker was picked up by a ragtag band of non-uniformed militia—peasants armed with bolt-action rifles and rusty bayonets—who were accompanied by a handful of uniformed soldiers with automatic weapons. North Vietnamese officers shortly assumed control of the Navy flier and, on the way to Hanoi and Hoa Lo, displayed him before press groups and assembled crowds at a half dozen stops, where villagers chanted angrily and hurled stones at him. Once at Hoa Lo, he was interrogated 8 to 10 hours a day, listening mutely to questions that seemed to him incredibly naive and often irrelevant. When the endless sitting on a cold chair aggravated his back and he could no longer tolerate the pain, he relented and gave his inquisitors information, and misinformation, about his family. His "breaking," although he had divulged nothing of consequence, produced remorse and guilt feelings that would not diminish for months. The self-reproach was heightened by a series of media events staged by the North Vietnamese through the spring wherein they paraded Shumaker—only the second American in their custody and hence, like Alvarez, the subject of enormous public interest and curiosity—before gatherings of reporters and cameramen, on one occasion trucking him to a hospital in civilian clothes, ostensibly to treat his bad back, and then administering a fake medical examination for the benefit of clicking photographers. An unwitting and helpless party to his own exploitation, Shumaker fretted that somehow he had been derelict and that his lapse had aided the enemy.

Shumaker was placed in New Guy Village. Although Alvarez supposed his Navy comrade was at Hoa Lo, he did not realize for some time that the two were within earshot of each other, even though in different sections of the prison. From his cell in room 24 of Heartbreak, Alvarez could watch the delivery of food trays and estimate from them the numbers of new arrivals as the spring and summer of 1965 wore on. In March he received his second Red Cross package, a cornucopia of cigarettes, dried fruit, cookies, instant coffee, towels, underwear, and toothbrush and toothpaste. With it came "Rabbit," a large-eared, schoolboyish but cocky interrogator-indoctrinator who wriggled his lips as he spoke and who would become a regular nemesis to Alvarez and the other Americans at Hoa Lo. Through much of the spring Rabbit lectured Alvarez on the virtues of communism, exclaiming during one visit: "You Americans, we believe that the mind of Capitalist man is like an old brick from the wall of a water closet. It takes 100 years to get rid of the smell." Rabbit's English was poor at this point—it would improve with practice over the next eight years—and his manner haranguing, making the indoctrination sessions onerous for Alvarez. When the North Vietnamese, beginning in May, halted the visits and left Alvarez in isolation for an extended period, he was lonely but relieved.

There is disagreement among the first group of PWs as to who actually named Hoa Lo the Hanoi Hilton, but the nickname became popular after June 1965, when Shumaker scratched the message "Welcome to the Hanoi Hilton" on the handle of a pail to greet the arrival of Air Force Lt. Robert Peel. By the middle of June, the food trays arriving daily at the Hilton numbered 11. The first Air Force PW was Lt. Hayden Lockhart, downed in an F-100 close to the DMZ. Following him were Navy Lt. Cdr. Raymond Vohden, Air Force Capts. Herschel Scott (Scotty) Morgan and Carlyle Smith (Smitty) Harris, Navy Lt. Phillip Butler, Air Force Capt. Ronald Storz, Peel, Navy Lt. John McKamey, and Air Force Maj. Lawrence Guarino. Storz, flying the dangerous job of forward air controller, crashed his small observation plane in the same vicinity where Lockhart went down. The others were captured throughout North Vietnam as far north as the Hanoi area.[9]

Casualties of the early stages of the Rolling Thunder program, this group, with Alvarez and Shumaker, would form the vanguard of the PW ranks in North Vietnam. As Alvarez and Shumaker had already discovered, these first arrivals at Hoa Lo were entering a different world from the village-style captivity experienced by PWs of the Viet Minh, Laotian, and Viet Cong guerrillas. They, and the several hundred who followed them, would be herded into larger, more permanent prisons (the Hilton was one of some dozen such facilities) that were usually walled, divided into cellblocks, and closely supervised by trained personnel. In this more structured setting, they faced tighter security, more organized routines, and more rigorous indoctrination than did their compatriots in South Vietnam.

North Vietnamese prison procedures evolved over a period of time, but they were already becoming institutionalized with the processing and handling of this initial group. Although Alvarez had been allowed to write letters to his family and had been outfitted with Red Cross-supplied khaki trousers, blue shirts, shoes, and a belt, by April 1965 the writing privilege had been withdrawn, Red Cross packages were being confiscated, and prisoners were being issued a more austere pajama-style uniform and sandals. At check-in they also received a standard issue of mosquito netting, cotton blanket, underwear, toothbrush, water jug and cup, soap, three pieces of toilet paper (to last 10 days), a straw mat for their bed, and a small waste bucket that doubled as a stool.[10] Over the years, whether the result of short supply or willful mistreatment, these basic amenities became sharply curtailed.

For several months during the first half of 1965, the North Vietnamese had prisoner meals prepared outside the compound and brought in. Although poor by Western standards, this food, consisting of sliced bread, meat, and vegetables, was savory compared with what would follow. The food served after July 1965, prepared on the premises, grew steadily worse— from watery soup and a nondescript but edible side dish of greens to the

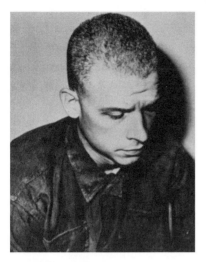

Above: Butler (left), Shumaker in custody after shootdown.

Left: Lockhart, first U.S. Air Force pilot captured.

Below, from left: Morgan, Harris, Peel.

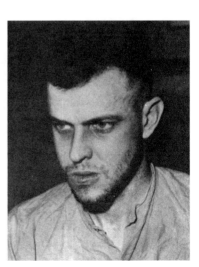

repulsive fare of fish heads and wormy bread that had made Alvarez so ill during his first several weeks at Hoa Lo. Moreover, rations would gradually be reduced from three meals a day to two. Food at the Hilton and elsewhere in North Vietnam would never be as scarce or as vile as in the South, but the diet was horrid nonetheless. And unsanitary living conditions, although again not as primitive as in the South, no doubt contributed to the prevalence of dysentery and parasitical diseases. Initially allowed to bathe and shave daily, by the end of 1965 the PWs were fortunate if they visited the washroom once every two weeks, and during periods of extortion or punishment might not be permitted to bathe for a month or longer.[11]

In other ways, too, the North Vietnam captivity experience was settling into routines and patterns here in 1965 that, with fluctuations according to the progress of the war and the growth of the prison population, would become characteristic for the next several years. Interrogation and indoctrination procedures and propaganda tactics will be discussed in later chapters, but they were well established almost from the beginning, from the time Alvarez entered the system, based on techniques borrowed from the Chinese and Korean Communists and used by the Viet Minh against the French. As Alvarez and Shumaker learned early, what the Vietnamese lacked in sophistication they made up for in persistence. Almost from the moment they were apprehended, even on the trip to prison, the Americans were pressed for information, peppered with propaganda, and exploited at every turn for the consumption of foreign reporters and local crowds. Shumaker recalled how "from the instant of capture" he was surrounded by photographers, cameramen, and combat artists and soon after subjected to news conferences and interviews with journalists. From this record of images and words, much of it staged or extracted from context, the North Vietnamese wasted no time documenting their case before their own people and the world. A photo of Shumaker alongside the wreckage of his plane appeared in *Vietnam Courier* the same month of his capture. A staged capture shot of Lieutenant Lockhart appeared in the April issue of the same newspaper. A film produced by the North Vietnamese in April showed Alvarez walking on a road and later being interviewed, Commander Vohden being carried into a medical building supposedly for treatment, and the Lockhart capture scene.[12]

Hopes that North Vietnam's more legitimate standing and more formalized arrangements (compared with those of the National Liberation Front in the South) would incline its leadership to be more respectful of international conventions were quickly dashed. Threatening Alvarez with criminal proceedings and exhibiting Shumaker before hostile crowds en route to Hanoi—clear violations of the Geneva Conventions—were early indications that the North Vietnamese no more intended to observe prisoner of war canons than had their guerrilla comrades to the south. Already they were labeling the American pilots "criminal aggressors" and "air pirates," staking out a position they would maintain even at the final repatriation negotiations in 1973.

The U.S. Defense Department, acknowledging the increasing number of airmen listed as missing over North Vietnam (more than 50 as of November 1965), many of whom were thought to be held by Hanoi, unintentionally complicated the PWs' plight with a change in the official terminology it used to account for military casualties. In 1962 the Secretary of Defense had instructed the services to submit weekly casualty reports for Southeast Asia; those servicemen believed to have been taken into custody in Vietnam or Laos, in accordance with established policy set by a 1953 definitional directive, were to be designated "captured or interned." To the Johnson administration, anxious to avoid the impression that the military was involved in combat activity in Southeast Asia, these terms perhaps appeared too suggestive of a wartime situation. In any case, following the Tonkin Gulf retaliatory raids, with the list of American advisers being held in South Vietnam lengthening and the prospect that more U.S. servicemen would now fall captive in the North, the Defense Department decided to modify its casualty nomenclature. In a new instruction of 30 September 1964 it substituted for "captured or interned" a blander, more ambiguous category, "detained."* "This terminology," read the memorandum that went to the services from the DoD Comptroller's office, "is more appropriate to present conditions than 'captured or interned' which customarily is associated with a condition of declared war." Having the effect of downplaying the significance of the Communist captures and underscoring the absence of a formal declaration of war, the Defense Department's action unfortunately buttressed the North Vietnamese argument that their American captives were not entitled to prisoner of war protections. Only in July 1966 when Hanoi threatened to carry out war crimes trials did the Pentagon reverse its decision and restore the original terminology of the 1953 directive.[13] In this instance, too, in the early battle of wits and semantics between Washington and Hanoi over the status of the American prisoners, a pattern was developing that would become recurrent: the fate of the American prisoners would be held hostage to the pendular swings of the political and public relations contest.

---

* It is perhaps too easy to impute devious motives to the administration's action. In truth, the PW problem had not yet become a pressing issue and there is nothing in the available record that suggests an outright deception. It may be argued, with plausibility, that the Pentagon's decision simply reflected a desire to conform to the language contained in a recent amendment to the Missing Persons Act. The political ramifications of the decision, however, must have been apparent even if not a paramount consideration.

Indeed, ultimately the fate of the American PWs would hinge as much on shifting public opinion toward the war in the United States as on the policies of the U.S. or North Vietnamese governments. Even as the early arrivals checked into the Hilton in the spring of 1965, the first organized U.S. antiwar march gathered at the United Nations building in New York City and the opening episode in a series of campus demonstrations protesting the growing U.S. involvement in Vietnam took place at Rutgers University in New Jersey. In an ironic counterpoint that dramatized the sharpening division in American attitudes toward the conflict in Southeast Asia, Commander Vohden, a Rutgers graduate, was shot down and captured within a few hours of the rally at his alma mater. The protests would intensify with each escalation of the bombing and with each new commitment of troops, complicating the administration's decisionmaking and exacerbating the predicament of the PWs, who, it often seemed, would be exploited in proportion to their countrymen's uneasiness about the war. Fortunately for Alvarez and the small company of fliers at Hoa Lo, they would gain strength from their swelling numbers and from the special bonds that would be forged among them as they resolved to win their own peculiar war in the bowels of the Hanoi Hilton.

6

Establishing Communication:
The Tap Code and Other Channels

Shumaker spotted Lockhart in the courtyard of New Guy Village sometime in mid-March 1965, not long after Lockhart had arrived at Hoa Lo following a week-long evasion that ended in his capture. Observing that they emptied their waste buckets in the same latrine and that the guards rarely entered the feculent area, Shumaker found a place to secrete a note and scrawled a message on one of the walls alerting Lockhart to the hidden piece of paper. As he waited futilely for days for Lockhart to signal his discovery of the note, Shumaker began to doubt the courage of his fellow aviator. He did not know that Lockhart had waged a one-man war against the local North Vietnamese unit that attempted to capture him after his shootdown; nor did he know that the airman had lost his glasses during ejection or evasion and simply could not see Shumaker's message. Finally Shumaker risked placing a second note in Lockhart's prison uniform as it hung drying in the bath area. When a guard detected it instead, Shumaker was reprimanded and threatened with punishment if he tried to communicate again.[1]

Undeterred, Shumaker waited for another opportunity and, three months after the Lockhart incident, attempted to reach Air Force Capt. Ronald Storz by leaving another note in the latrine. This time contact was made. Storz responded by scratching his name onto a piece of toilet paper with the burnt end of a matchstick. Thus was accomplished the first exchange of messages among American PWs in North Vietnam. Soon the names Vohden, Morgan, Harris, and Butler appeared on handles of food pails and the undersides of plates, as the crude, makeshift beginnings of a communications network took shape in Heartbreak Hotel and New Guy Village. The primary channels initially were voice contact and the note device, but the former was easy to detect and the latter difficult and time-consuming

to execute; discovery of either by guards brought warnings and then reprisals. The most clever technique, and the one which eventually became the
most commonly used by American prisoners in the North, was the tap code,
introduced in the summer of 1965 by Air Force Capt. Carlyle Harris.[2]

In late June 1965, as the PW population continued to expand and prison officials made room for additional captures, Harris, Lt. Phillip Butler,
and Lt. Robert Peel were rounded up and placed in Shumaker's cell in New
Guy. The four fliers, after a spirited reunion and exchange of tales about their
experiences, determined that Shumaker was the senior-ranking officer and
decided on a concerted plan of resistance should they be split up again.
Shumaker rightly assessed that no plan could be effective without communication, and the group searched for a method that would be both
simple and safe. Harris remembered that when he was in survival training
at Stead Air Force Base, Nevada, an instructor during a coffee break had
shown him a code based upon a five-by-five matrix of the alphabet that
could serve as a covert basis for PW contacts.* By dropping K from the alphabet, one arranged the 25 remaining letters as follows:

	1	2	3	4	5
1	A	B	C	D	E
2	F	G	H	I	J
3	L	M	N	O	P
4	Q	R	S	T	U
5	V	W	X	Y	Z

The communicator transmitted a letter by using two numbers, the first
referring to the letter's location in the horizontal rows of the matrix and the
second placing it in the vertical columns. For example, 2-2 signified G; 1-2,
B; 4-5, U. The sequence GBU, an abbreviation for "God bless you," became
one of the most frequently passed messages at Hoa Lo and eventually the
universal sign-off signal. A famous if inelegant early transmission that used
C to denote both C and K was "Joan Baez Succs," sent after the Vietnamese

* The so-called tap code had been used in Korean prisoner-of-war camps, where Americans learned
it from the British. The system dates at least to World War I, and a version of it was used in the
Civil War. Lt. Edward Davis later claimed to have introduced inmates to a version of the code
he learned while watching the film "The Birdman of Alcatraz."

played a recording over the Hilton public address system by the well-known American antiwar activist.[3]

Within days of its conception in Shumaker's cell, the tap code began to circulate throughout Hoa Lo. On 5 July, when guards found a note the Shumaker group had left for Maj. Lawrence Guarino, they returned the four roommates to solitary in various sections of New Guy and Heartbreak. Hoping to thwart further communication, the North Vietnamese unwittingly permitted it to spread, as the transferred men taught the code to other prisoners. Captain Storz, placed in a cell that enabled him to watch guard movements in and out of Heartbreak, assumed lookout duties there, while fellow PWs practiced the system until they became proficient. By August, most of the camp was sending and receiving signals.

Simplicity made the tap code effective; ingenuity made it at times awesome. PW leader Cdr. James Stockdale, captured in September, later remarked that a man could send out a veritable newspaper. With experience the code became a medium for conversation as well as information. Stockdale wrote in his memoir of his communication in the summer of 1966 with Air Force Maj. Samuel Johnson in an adjoining cell:

> Our tapping ceased to be just an exchange of letters and words; it became conversation. Elation, sadness, humor, sarcasm, excitement, depression—all came through. Sam and I would sign off before dark with abbreviations like GN (goodnight) and GBU (God bless you). Passing on abbreviations like conundrums got to be a kind of game. What would ST mean right after GN? Sleep tight, of course. And DLTBBB? I laughed to think what our friends back home would think of us two old fighter pilots standing at a wall, checking for shadows under the door, pecking out a final message for the day with our fingernails: "Don't let the bedbugs bite."

Abbreviation became a necessity because of the physical demands on both tapper and receiver in transmitting long messages. Stockdale learned through one of his first contacts to shorten the sentence "WHEN DO YOU THINK WE WILL GO HOME?" to "WN DO U TK WE GO HOME?" A complicated message passed early in 1966, after the Vietnamese had instituted a torture program, read: "GM LGU Z 12 IN PS ALRDY HIT F BIO X 5 NOW GETG THRTS F BIO X PB LTR FM HOME X LL FOX IS NEW XO X NEW NAME LCDR RENDER CRAYTON NO OTH INFO X PB N BP Q W SPOT SOS." Translated, it meant:

> Good morning. Larry Guarino says 12 men in the Pigsty have already been tortured for biographies. Five men are now being threatened

with torture if they do not write biographies. Phil Butler got letter from home. Looks like Fox is the new executive officer of the camp. A new validated prisoner name is Lieutenant Commander Render Crayton. We have no other information on him. Phil Butler and Bob Peel had quizzes with Spot—same old shit.

The letter X, when tapped alone, signified a sentence break, much as "STOP" does in a telegram.[4]

New prisoners were introduced to the system as soon as possible, although it often took patience and resourcefulness to convey the code to those wholly uninitiated and considerable courage for the newcomers to respond to their comrades' efforts. The new men usually came to the cellblock from a grueling orientation session, where they were put on notice not to talk or communicate in any way. The veterans had somehow stealthily to ease their apprehension and teach them the matrix. Sometimes Morse code served to explain the matrix; other times, the "teacher" had to painstakingly tap 26 times on the wall to convey the notion of an alphabet and then tap out numbers corresponding to letters. If the novice was slow to grasp the concept, the teacher might tap an 8 and then a 9 repeatedly until the sequence "H-I, 8-9, H-I—Hi!" registered. In some cellblocks the men were able to pass the matrix directly by talking through the wall as the listener listened on his side, or through notes slipped into rice bowls or latrine buckets. One new prisoner, hurled to the floor in the Hilton's torture room, discovered the matrix carved on the underside of a table with the exhortation, "All prisoners learn this code."[5]

Navy Cdr. James Mulligan, captured in the spring of 1966, learned the code from Marine WO John Frederick. At first baffled by the strange rapping on his cell wall and frustrated by the refusal of other inmates to return his verbal entreaties, Mulligan, once indoctrinated, became one of the more skillful tappers in the PW community. He later recounted his excitement at discovering the system and his determination to master it:

> I drilled myself without let up. It was like learning the multiplication tables from the good nuns at St. Patrick's School in Lawrence, Mass., my hometown when I was a kid. I stayed awake most of the night engaged in arduous practice as I firmly implanted the new code in my mind. I wanted to be able to communicate with [Frederick] the first thing in the morning. God, was I lonesome for human companionship. The eerie silence of complete solitude was an oppressive load that bore down on me mentally like a ton of bricks. I hated each second of it, but now I had a way out. I only needed to master the POW code, and I would have the ability to join the social structure again.

That first day it took several tries before he understood that Frederick's "RUOC" meant "Are you OK?" Exultantly Mulligan tapped back, "YES, HOW R U?"[6]

Just as in the days of telegraphy experienced operators could recognize different hands upon the transmitting key, in the North Vietnamese prisons experienced tappers developed the ability to recognize the special characteristics—the signatures—of others. The necessity to abbreviate encouraged individualistic dialects as well as personalized patterns of touch, speed, and emphasis. "As we worked the wall together," Stockdale recalled, "we learned to be sensitive to a whole new range of acoustic perception." Alvarez later noted that with little to see or touch, especially for those who spent considerable time in solitary confinement, "hearing . . . [became] our primary sensor," and they became acutely tuned in to the characteristic sounds—coughs, sneezes, even the shuffling of feet—of guards and prisoners alike. From the style of tapping and the information conveyed about home and family, they formed visual impressions of partners in adjoining cells whom they had never met—often to be surprised years later, when finally united face to face, that the companion "did not look at all like . . . [he] sounded."[7]

The capacity of the mind to store and organize under such adverse conditions as existed at Hoa Lo and elsewhere in the prison system proved astonishing. Mulligan became a walking "memory bank" of PW names, compiling a mental list through tap and note communication and able to transmit his bank alphabetically complete with ranks and shootdown dates; upon his release in 1973, he could recite the names of over 450 American prisoners. A prodigious but not atypical display of tap virtuosity occurred one day at "Alcatraz," the small prison near Hoa Lo to which the Vietnamese sent 11 tough resisters in 1967. Stockdale, the senior officer in the group, decided to transmit a series of instructions concerning how the prisoners should combat the "Fink Release Program" (so called because, while Hanoi billed it as a humanitarian early-release plan, hardline resisters like Stockdale viewed it as an extortion scheme to induce prisoners to cooperate). Stockdale composed six 50-word messages that he flashed by finger to Navy pilot Nels Tanner across the courtyard. Tanner, peering under his door, memorized each message, then tapped it on both the right and left walls of his cell, passing it along the cellblock in both directions. Within two hours, the six messages reached all the prisoners, and the policies were committed to memory. Just before guards locked the men into leg stocks for the night, Tanner flashed his usual GN—Good Night—to Stockdale, adding that he had processed 5,000 words that day![8]

As the PWs were transferred among different camps, they brought to their new location fresh tap techniques and variations from their previous

Rabbit   Spot

camps and in turn learned new methods themselves, so that the system was constantly being refined. To prevent the North Vietnamese from solving the code or as an extra precaution in the transmission of sensitive or classified information, the prisoners occasionally rearranged the matrix altogether, altering the code with scrambling techniques that became so sophisticated that sometimes communication failed. When he returned home in 1973, Stockdale challenged experts at the Defense Intelligence Agency to decode a sample that he presented them; so complex was the encryption that the DIA specialists could not decipher it.[9]

As both a tonic for morale and a source of vital news and information, communication proved essential to the well-being, indeed the survival, of the American prisoners of war. Not the least of its benefits was, through shared observations and experiences, to provide the captives with a fund of knowledge about their captors, ranging from the personalities and behavior of particular guards to the policies and procedures of particular camps. Nowhere was the network more active than at Hoa Lo, where the tap code originated and which remained the primary confinement site for most of the Americans.

Through the summer and into the fall of 1965, as communication pulsed from cell to cell along the Hilton's cement corridors, the prisoners determined that a rough hierarchical structure existed in the camp, extending from a PW superintendent and camp commander down through an interrogation and indoctrination staff of political officers to the rank and file of turnkeys, guards, and workers. Since the North Vietnamese rarely revealed their names, the Americans relied on nicknames to identify personnel. "We named every single person we saw," recalled one PW. From personal dealings with them

> we had individually derived names for most guards. When we correlated such things, we found that some of the names for certain guards were quite similar. It was usual to name a guard for some trait; but some were named for a movie actor that he resembled in some way or manner. That is to say a sleepy-eyed guard might be "Robert Mitchum." A large nosed individual might be "Jimmy Durante" . . . . As for medical workers, there were a few "Kildares," "Ben Caseys" and of course, just plain "Doc" . . . . Because of the similarity of names assigned different persons by POWs living separately, we were later to have quite a problem in identifying them and speaking about them to one another.[10]

Gradually a consensus did develop as to the identities of key personnel. "Cat," a highly educated, vain martinet named Bai or Bui, held a major's rank and was evidently the senior officer for the prison system; deferential subordinates let the PWs know he was a member of the North Vietnamese general staff and had handled French prisoners during the Franco-Viet Minh War. "Dog," handsome, intelligent, and fluent in French and English, commanded the Hilton. By turns avuncular and stern, Dog was a model of professionalism when things went smoothly but became flustered in the presence of superiors when PWs did not cooperate; one of the senior prisoners later remembered him as an excellent administrator and, belying his nickname, "the closest thing to a gentleman I ever met in North Vietnam."[11] In a few months Dog was replaced by "Fox," a less sophisticated but tougher officer, hardened by combat. The chief interrogator-indoctrinators were "Eagle," "Owl," "Rabbit," "Mole," "Chihuahua," "Mickey Mouse," and, somewhat later, "Spot." Eagle, graying and older than the others, appeared to be in charge of the group; although he often wore a black coat and hat and on occasion resorted to strong-arm tactics, he usually played good guy to Mole's bad guy during interrogation. Owl—either Alvarez or Scotty Morgan gave him the name and it stuck when the other PWs were similarly impressed by his deep-set dark eyes—claimed to be a college professor serving his nation in time of crisis. The jug-eared Rabbit, young, bright, and coolly efficient, became the best-known and most ubiquitous of the interrogators, both despised and admired by his American subjects; a favorite of Cat, he was only a lieutenant in 1965, but would steadily acquire more responsibility and authority. Mole briefly played the villain during interrogation routines, but, a minor functionary who made little impression on the Americans, he would disappear from the prison system in 1966. Chihuahua, so called because of his frail build and facial resemblance to the excitable canine, was an intermittent presence who quizzed Alvarez and Stockdale among others. Mickey Mouse was a capable junior officer who would advance rapidly, becoming camp commander in 1966. Spot, named for a whitish patch of skin on his chin and neck, possibly from napalm burns, appeared late in 1965 and, like Rabbit, was still around at the final repatriation ceremonies.[12]

"Stoneface" was the chief turnkey during most of the early period, with "Pigeye" and "Dipshit" sharing the duties, the latter also serving as medic. Stockdale later referred to Dipshit as "a sort of Mother Superior" at Hoa Lo, "a part time medic and full time disciplinarian and guard." Generally bumbling and incompetent, Dipshit treated several of the prisoners decently at first, but eventually alienated most of them by his arrogance and careless bandaging of their wounds. "Pigeye," also known as "Straps and Bars" for his favorite torture devices, would become Cat's principal henchman and a master at forcibly extracting information and confessions; a small, muscular man, he was an expert at inflicting pain, as impassive as he was ruthless—"a very impersonal technician," Stockdale described him.[13]

Comparing notes, the prisoners were able to discern a pattern to their treatment. Upon arrival at the Hilton they typically underwent two to four weeks of interrogation followed by an intensive period of indoctrination, during which the cadre of political officers would deliver canned lectures about Vietnamese history, the evils of capitalism, and the like. They could expect physical and verbal abuse, psychological pressure, threats of execution, and, when caught communicating, consignment to isolation. In these first months, although they were occasionally roughed up, some placed in leg irons, they were, as a rule, not tortured. Interrogators used the good guy-bad guy method familiar to PWs from survival training. For example, Mole would rant at a new captive about his "criminal" actions and threaten to turn him over to a mob. He would talk about relatives being killed by the American bombing, seem to lose control, and start slapping and kicking the prisoner, vowing vengeance as he stormed out of the room. After a period for the message to sink in, Eagle would enter, comfort the prisoner, and warn him that Mole had become irrational. It might be wise, he would suggest, to cooperate just a little and show some remorse to mollify Mole. These admonitions might be accompanied by a cigarette, perhaps tea, always conversation about the PW's family or health. Then the scene would revert with

Mole's reentry. After a while, the prisoners saw through this game and scorned the transparent manner in which the Vietnamese played it.[14]

It became clear, too, as prisoners swapped information, that senior PWs were handled more harshly than the younger men. Major Guarino, for instance, seized in June 1965, was for a time the oldest American in captivity in the North. The Vietnamese put him on rations even paltrier than the meager diet they served his younger comrades. They segregated him and subjected him to rougher interrogations, longer indoctrinations, and generally more severe treatment. He was locked in leg irons before any of the junior officers. Although his rank and experience would give him strength over the long haul, his seniority and age, apparently targeting him for abuse, placed him at a disadvantage initially.

Guarino was up to the test. He had weathered a brutal trip to Hanoi, during which his captors exposed him to jeering villagers and tied him so tightly that his arms became infected from rope cuts. Once at Hoa Lo, he refused to be cowed by Owl's interrogation. Because he suffered from ulcers, hunger caused him flaring pain; yet he would not and could not eat the crude meals delivered to his cell. Contact with Lieutenant Peel, who signaled him, lifted his spirits, and he reciprocated by passing on the welcome news that Peel's family knew their son was alive. A message left in Guarino's cell by Captain Storz, the previous occupant, outlining the agenda he would face, further sustained him, dispelling fear of the unknown, one of the PW's worst enemies.

During his second week of interrogation, Guarino met Dog, who stood in the wings during one session, then returned the next day to conduct his own quiz. Dog's intelligence and cultivated manner would have been engaging under other circumstances. He spoke with directness and conviction, and in easy English. Without malice but with a bluntness that was arresting, he told Guarino that the Geneva Conventions did not apply to the Americans because the war they were fighting was undeclared. Furthermore, he submitted, the United States would have to sacrifice the prisoners to avoid political embarrassment. "You must understand," he advised the American pilot, "that your position here is and will always be that of a criminal . . . . You must cooperate and show repentance for your crimes to earn good treatment. Sooner or later, you are going to show repentance. You are going to admit you are a criminal. You are going to denounce your government. You are going to beg our people for forgiveness."[15]

The smell of food wafting from the nearby cell of Navy Lt. John McKamey—fare that Guarino imagined had to be better than the swill he was being served—added to his anguish. Still he continued a virtual fast as Eagle and Dog pursued their inquiry. He stymied their questions with

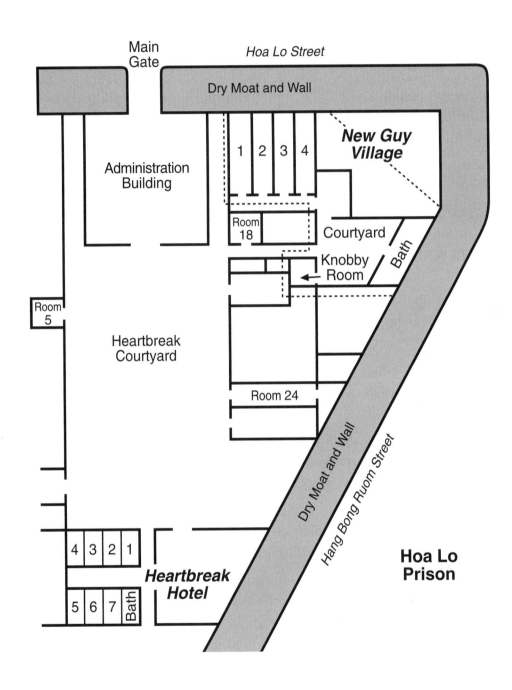

Heartbreak Hotel and New Guy Village

idiomatic responses, confusing the interrogators and stalling the proceedings. Dog, under pressure to produce information, was left to fidget nervously as Guarino successfully denied him intelligible answers. On 1 July the flier's frustrated captors put him in ankle stocks, keeping him there, for all but 10 minutes a day, for weeks.

The communications network, now operating as both gossip grapevine and information clearinghouse, expanded steadily. Access varied considerably depending on an individual's location and condition. McKamey, Lockhart, and several of the others shuffled between Heartbreak and New Guy, relaying news from one section to the other with each transfer. Guarino talked to McKamey while the two were jailed within earshot in New Guy for a few days. Shumaker, Peel, Harris, and Butler were back together in New Guy after two weeks in solitary for attempting to contact Guarino; the latter, not realizing they had risked punishment in the effort to reach him, suspected that the four must have cooperated to gain favorable treatment since they were together in one large cell and in seemingly high spirits. Morgan was in touch with Storz and Lockhart in Heartbreak, with Storz continuing to serve as lookout from a perch that allowed him to follow comings and goings into and out of the cellblock. Storz's whistled "Yankee Doodle" heralded new arrivals, and was often the first signal the newcomers received. Alvarez remained isolated, as did Commander Vohden, who was in agony from a compound leg fracture suffered during a difficult ejection and landing and aggravated by a Vietnamese doctor's bungled attempts at surgery; Vohden's cries for painkillers could be heard by McKamey and others. As an example of the chance, often improbable nature of PW contacts, Vohden and Morgan, who were shot down on the same day, 3 April 1965, would not meet until 1973 just before homecoming.*[16]

The system received an added boost with the arrival of Navy Cdr. Jeremiah Denton, Jr., in mid-July. Denton would eventually devise another form of the tap code, a variation which would be particularly difficult for the Vietnamese to detect. As an assertive senior officer, Denton used the code to coordinate resistance, keep informed of prisoner health and morale, and circulate possible escape routes and methods. Denton's energy and enterprise were remarkable in view of his crippled condition. He and his bombardier-navigator, Lt. (j.g.) William Tschudy, had been downed in an A-6 Intruder, the Navy's newest attack aircraft, during a bombing run over North Vietnam's Thanh Hoa bridge complex south of the 20th parallel. Denton was

* Vohden managed to survive a series of botched operations and savage torture to become, with Morgan, the fifth longest held PW in American history—after Thompson, Alvarez, Shumaker, and Lockhart. After repatriation and medical repair, he would be appointed Principal Advisor to the Secretary of Defense on PW-MIA matters, and then Superintendent of the U.S. Naval Observatory.

injured trying to control the plane after it was hit. A tendon in his left thigh snapped, part of it curling up into his abdomen and rendering his leg useless. He was wounded further when, attempting to evade the enemy by floating down the Ma River, he was attacked by two young men in a canoe and slashed twice in the neck with a machete.[17]

Denton spent the first night of his captivity in a village, where he talked briefly with Tschudy, who had parachuted into a nearby hamlet and was seized without incident. The two never realized they would not see each other again for seven years—"six Super Bowls, and a moon landing before I would meet him again," Denton would later say. They were trucked separately to Hanoi and Hoa Lo, Denton entering New Guy Village on 19 July. After several days of routine questioning by Owl and Eagle, the latter confronted Denton with a list of names of squadron mates from the carrier *Independence*, accurate identification of the aircraft he had flown, and charges that U.S. Secretary of Defense Robert McNamara had ordered him to bomb civilian targets. Denton had reason to be concerned. From press reports the Vietnamese knew that McNamara, on a tour of American bases in Southeast Asia, had indeed witnessed the launch of the Thanh Hoa raid from the flight deck of the *Independence*; that the A-6 was an advanced aircraft with many technical innovations whose elucidation could provide them with invaluable information for their Soviet and Chinese mentors; and that Denton was now the senior American officer in their possession. Faced with these established facts, Denton squirmed but refused to cooperate, and the interrogators finally relented.[18]

Denton and Guarino made voice contact about 21 July. Believing that news of his ankle stocks would deflate Denton's morale, Guarino said nothing about his condition for a couple of weeks. During this time, the two determined that Denton was senior and that a single chain of command would be more effective than separate command structures by service. They also decided to answer notes left by the Shumaker group, and were happy to find that the four had in fact been active resisters and that Guarino's suspicions had been wrong. As days passed, Denton received a flow of information about the layout of the prison, the content of indoctrination sessions, the character of the interrogators, and, from new arrivals, developments on the outside. In turn he disseminated orders and instructions. Everyone would observe the Code of Conduct. Everyone would stick together when he ordered a resistance tactic, such as a hunger strike. Everyone would report key events in their experience, beginning with shootdown, so that Denton would have a complete picture of the PW population and the camp. Everyone would try to wash whenever possible and do all they could to stem the rounds of dysentery. The orders went out and were followed.

Toward the end of July Denton joined Guarino on the punishment rolls. He had pried and twisted loose the metal bar on top of the leg stocks on his bed, intending to use the bar as a tool to remove the frame of his small window and tear an escape hole in his cell wall. He had nearly succeeded when guards discovered him. They moved him to an adjacent cell and clamped him in irons. His communication with Guarino now became more important for both men. Together they battled hunger and the discomfort of the stocks. "The latrine," Denton recalled,

> . . . posed another problem. It was nothing more than five holes in concrete next to the shower. Roaches and huge spiders that I first thought were tarantulas crawled around the openings, and I was reluctant to use them. I did anyway, because using the honey bucket* in my cell was even more onerous. It was too small for the American anatomy, and the cell already smelled bad enough. The problem became an academic one soon enough. With exercise impossible, I became constipated.

Guarino's refusal to eat had nearly killed him. He gained sustenance from the contact with Denton until the Vietnamese finally improved his diet. Rabbit, alarmed by Guarino's condition and professing not to realize he suffered from ulcers, had him fed a chicken soup with celery and a half-loaf of bread.[19]

Even with Denton removed from the network for a time, the prisoners continued to refine communications by adding to the tap code operational signals and backup channels. It soon became evident that only four basic operational signals were necessary, all easily deliverable through the tap matrix. The first and most critical one was a danger (stop, no, negative) signal—one that could warn of the approach of a guard, for instance. The second was the opposite of the first—yes, good, agree, go. The third was "repeat"; the fourth, "wait." Additionally, the unmistakably American "Shave and a haircut . . . two bits" became a popular tapping refrain to "call up" or "roger" a partner in an adjoining cell. Backup systems were crucial should the PWs be discovered tapping and the main system compromised or certain individuals caught and separated from the others. Anything available was used to secrete notes, the notes themselves conforming to the tap matrix. In Heartbreak the singing or whistling of "Pop Goes the Weasel" became a common danger signal, followed by "Mary

---

* The PWs had several euphemisms for their wastecans, the most common one being "honey bucket." Another term widely used was "bo," the Americans' rendering of the Vietnamese name for the receptacle. (The prisoners thought their keepers were trying to say "bowl," but *bo* actually means "bucket" or "bowl" in Vietnamese.)

Had a Little Lamb" as the all-clear. Hand signals, derived from deaf-mute sign language, were used in some instances. Occasionally the tap code was supplemented by Morse code, an efficient and proven system but one that had to be employed with care because it required a consistent hand to avoid misunderstanding and, being internationally known, could be deciphered by a trained enemy ear. In fact, the Vietnamese sometimes stationed a translator proficient in Morse in an empty cell between PW cells to intercept communication; in one instance, in August, when Denton transmitted a joke in Morse to Guarino, the hidden translator laughed at the punch line, betraying his presence and the vulnerability of the code.[20]

July and August 1965 saw an influx of new prisoners, arriving now in increasing numbers and posing new tests—and opportunities—for the Hilton's communications system. Besides Denton and Tschudy, there were Air Force Capts. Paul Kari (shot down on 20 June), Richard Keirn, Kile Berg, Robert Purcell, Norlan Daughtrey, and Wesley Schierman; Navy aviators Cdr. Fred Franke, Lt. Cdr. Robert Doremus, and Lt. (j.g.) Richard Brunhaver; and Air Force Maj. Ronald Byrne. Stockdale, Air Force Capt. Quincy Collins, Navy Cdr. Wendell Rivers, and Navy Lt. (j.g.) Edward Davis followed in early September. Kari was the first F-4 Phantom pilot to be captured; Keirn was the second. Several of the others were downed flying the older F-105 Thunderchiefs.

Kari, on his 64th combat mission in 70 days, went down in the mountains west of Hanoi and was seized immediately. By the time he reached Hoa Lo he had already endured a hellish initiation. Like many others ejecting at high speed and out of control, he suffered a painful back injury bailing out of his plane.* Then his captors furiously stripped him of his flight suit, wrenching his ankles while ripping off his boots. When he reached down to undo the zipper on one of the boots, he was clubbed on the head and lost an eardrum. When the Vietnamese heard attack aircraft buzzing the area, they became frightened and thrust Kari into a hole that turned out to be a giant anthill; for an excruciating half hour he remained lodged there until

* Spinal injuries, prevalent among ditching pilots early in the war, would be reduced markedly after 1967 with the introduction of a refined "rocket" ejection seat that substantially diminished the effect of G forces. See Martin G. Every and James F. Parker, Jr., "A Review of Problems Encountered in the Recovery of Navy Aircrewmen Under Combat Conditions," report to Office of Naval Research, Jun 73, in *Americans Missing in Southeast Asia*, Hearings before House Select Committee on Missing Persons in Southeast Asia, 94 Cong, 1 sess (1975), pt 2, 177-79. On the problems experienced by Air Force PWs during ejection/bailout, see Joseph W. Kittinger and John H. Yuill, "Southeast Asia Escape, Evasion and Recovery Experience of Returned Prisoners of War," in Armand J. Myers et al, *Vietnam POW Camp Histories and Studies*, vol 2, Air War College, Maxwell AFB, Ala, Jun 75, 44-75.

"BAO CAO"

The captors tried to humiliate and control the PWs by forcing them to bow and utter the servile phrase "Bao cao" whenever they wished to speak. PWs who resisted risked punishment.

Standard issue: sandals and the "bo," or waste bucket.

The drawings here and following p. 146 are from John M. McGrath, *Prisoner of War: Six Years in Hanoi* (Annapolis, Md.: Naval Institute Press, 1975). McGrath was a Navy lieutenant when he became a prisoner of war in North Vietnam on 30 June 1967. He sketched these drawings upon his return home in 1973.

Covert communication was the lifeblood of PW resistance. Here, a PW taps a message to another cell while listening through a cup for a reply.

COMMUNICATING WITH
MUTE CODE

A high-speed, single-hand mute code developed by Air Force Lts. Thomas McNish and Michael Brazelton improved communication, especially between distant cells and cellblocks.

the Vietnamese pulled him out. The captor band then dragged him through villages, made him face what turned out to be mock firing squads, and, when Kari destroyed his beacon transmitter that the enemy had hoped to use to lure U.S. rescue helicopters into their gun sights, beat him until they ruptured his other eardrum.

Throughout the ordeal, Kari established an unwavering resistance stance that he would maintain. Before guards trussed him onto the back of a truck for the trip to Hanoi, they shoved him in front of a camera for a staged capture film, which he undermined by gesturing defiantly with his finger. (More than four years later a friend saw the sequence in a survival movie and showed it to Kari's wife, who confirmed the prisoner was her husband.) Once at the Hilton, he was greeted with Storz's "Yankee Doodle." Within a week he was in contact with Storz, Lockhart, and Morgan. They prepared him for the good guy-bad guy ruse, which he promptly encountered in interrogation. They warned him, too, to have a story rehearsed in case the enemy pushed him past the point of resistance. Kari had already decided he would tell them that he had been flying along the Thai border, defending against attacking MIGs, when the call came in to locate a downed pilot, so that his violation of North Vietnamese airspace had been for humane rather than "criminal" reasons. The innocuous, plausible account would buy Kari time but not ultimately spare him punishment. In subsequent years he would undergo severe torture while continuing to lace his statements with lies.[21]

Richard Keirn, at age 41 one of the oldest PWs when seized, was the first of the American pilots to be brought down by a missile. As his F-4 formation approached a target zone west of Hanoi, three surface-to-air missiles, or SAMs, shot up like "telephone poles," one of them damaging two of the planes, including Keirn's. As flames and smoke curled through his cockpit, he managed to work the secondary ejection system, which catapulted him to earth with a bruised shoulder, burns, and a piece of shrapnel in his leg. He hid safely in an area of karst the first night, but early the next morning he was discovered by local militia. His captors displayed him to villagers, then drove him to Hanoi, where he spent a week in isolation at Heartbreak, followed by another month in solitary but also in precious communication with Storz, Morgan, and others. Over the next five to six years, "Pop" Keirn would undergo more than 700 interrogations, live in solitary several times for months at a stretch, be forced to sit on a stool or to kneel for days on end, and be clubbed and kicked into unconsciousness. Previously captured near the end of World War II by the Germans, he had spent seven months as a Nazi prisoner. In 1973 he would say that the German captivity had been "rough," but the experience in Southeast Asia was "completely unbelievable—something not of this world."[22]

Summer 1965 check-ins to the Hilton. *Top:* Kari (left), Keirn; *middle, from left,* Purcell, Schierman, Franke; *bottom,* Berg, Doremus, Brunhaver.

Kile Berg was a spirited addition to the PW ranks. Like Guarino and several of the others, he had had a premonition of disaster before taking off on the mission that resulted in his capture. On 27 July, while making a bombing run against a SAM site, his plane was hit by antiaircraft fire and he was forced to eject. Shortly he found himself at the Hilton, in Heartbreak not far from the badly injured Vohden. Over the next two months he played dumb during interrogations—stammering, stuttering, and generally stalling until Owl or Eagle in exasperation would supply the answer themselves. Berg had a keen imagination and sense of humor that sustained him and lightened the tension for others as well. He combated his initial isolation by negotiating with himself for the design and purchase of an airport. He talked aloud, playing all the roles, keeping the game alive for months. A busy communicator once he had access, he later brought comrades into the game, and years afterwards some would ask him where he had located a certain operation or how much he had paid for certain equipment. Mischievously, he taught a guard, who wanted to learn a standard American expression, to say upon making the rounds of the cellblock, "I'm queer"; the guard proudly greeted inmates thusly for several weeks, nonplused by the prisoners' hilarious reaction.[23]

Twenty minutes after Berg fell captive, another F-105 pilot, Capt. Robert Purcell, went down 30 miles west of Hanoi. Although suffering a serious back compression injury during ejection, Purcell managed to evade capture for 18 hours. Brought to the Hilton, he forced himself to exercise until he achieved mobility; still badly hurting, he performed a number of risky actions to aid fellow prisoners. In the spring of 1966, despite having been roughed up by the Vietnamese for stubborn resistance, the courageous Purcell would remove the access panel in the ceiling of his cell and scramble through the overhead attic joists with food for injured and tortured men and with communication to the isolated and bedridden.[24]

Norlan Daughtrey and Quincy Collins, Air Force captains flying F-105s, were both seriously injured when shot down, Daughtrey on 2 August and Collins exactly a month later. Daughtrey's broken arms were placed in casts in a primitive clinic near the bridge he had attacked. Moved to Heartbreak, after three days of isolation he entered the communication net when jailers allowed Paul Kari to visit his cell to empty his waste bucket for him. Three weeks later Ray Vohden hobbled over to join him in a courtyard cell. Collins remembers nothing of his own shootdown. He went unconscious with the impact of whatever hit him, and he awoke on the ground already captured. His leg had snapped at a right angle, cleanly broken, and soldiers took him to a hospital where it was set. Ten days later he was delivered to the Hilton and placed in the same cell with Vohden, Daughtrey, and Bob Peel, the latter moved there when the Shumaker group was again dispersed; Peel, relatively healthy, gamely nursed his crippled companions. Collins was to have a miserable captivity because of his mangled leg and a series of illnesses. To his benefit, however, his weakened condition reduced his usefulness to interrogators, and as a result he was subjected to fewer quizzes than most prisoners.[25]

Ronald Byrne, felled in an F-105 while on a mission testing new equipment, arrived at the Hilton toward the end of August and was locked in the same cellblock with McKamey, Tschudy, Keirn, Berg, and Purcell. He found early interrogations, which centered on his criminality, degrading and mentally wearing but not physically threatening. When he learned of Guarino's and Denton's harsh treatment, he reasoned, probably correctly, that the examiners spared him further abuse on this point because they were concentrating on the senior prisoners. He was surprised that the Vietnamese placed him in an area occupied by several of his squadron mates. The careless arrangement enabled the fliers to agree on their cover story and exchange information about their quizzes, both valuable advantages when the questioning became more rigorous.

Four Navy airmen—Fred (Bill) Franke, Robert Doremus, Richard Brunhaver, and Edward Davis—were downed in late August around the same time as Byrne and Schierman. Franke and Doremus took a direct hit from a missile near Thanh Hoa, both of them catapulted from their F-4 either by the engagement of its ejection system or from the force of the explosion itself. Others in their squadron, witnessing the uncontrollable spin of the aircraft and then the explosion, would doubt the two survived. Injured but intact, they were captured at once and delivered to Hanoi the next day. Franke's first communication came from Navy pilot McKamey, a veteran of three months at the Hilton; McKamey briefed him on the camp routine and the names of other captures. Franke and Doremus were joined in Heartbreak after a few days by Brunhaver, who had gone down minutes after them on the same mission. The three experienced similar interrogations, except that Brunhaver's first was conducted in the presence of the turnkey Stoneface by a new officer nicknamed "Al Capone." When Brunhaver was uncooperative, Eagle entered the picture and, with a copy of the Americans' Code of Conduct, sought to disarm Brunhaver's defenses. Brunhaver hung tough, aided by McKamey, who explained interrogation procedures and the tap code.[26]

Davis reached Hanoi after the others because he had been captured a couple of days later and farther to the south. While en route he had tried to escape, nearly succeeding before guards caught him climbing out the back window of a confinement building. During the three-week journey to the North Vietnamese capital, Davis was joined by Navy Cdr. Wendell (Wendy) Rivers, shot down on 10 September, and the two arrived at the Hilton together. Davis entered the Heartbreak section and soon gained contact with Franke and Brunhaver. Moved to New Guy on 16 September, he became friends with Commander Denton, who was in a nearby cell. Despite the difference in their ages, the two would develop a deep and mutual respect, forming a special bond that would help them through the dark days ahead.[27]

By his account Davis had communication "within 45 seconds" after guards deposited him in his cell at Heartbreak. Although the Vietnamese would become obsessed with detecting and suppressing communication, supervision at the Hilton in September 1965 was still relatively lax. During the afternoon siesta period, with surveillance slackened, prisoners both tapped and talked openly. Those assigned to wash dishes relayed information by scratching letters and numbers on utensils.

Alvarez was one of the beneficiaries of the loose arrangements. In May, Rabbit, finding him intractable, had left the one-time prize capture sequestered and incommunicado in a remote corner of the prison while the political cadre turned their attention to later shootdowns. Living in solitary for months, depressed and weak from loss of weight after the Vietnamese abruptly cut his rations in half, and moved from the spacious room 24 of Heartbreak to a series of smaller cells, he remembered the summer of 1965 as the "worst" period of his entire stay at Hoa Lo. Even when moved into closer proximity to other PWs and hearing tapping on the walls, the meaning of the sounds eluded him, as he had not yet learned the code. Only in August, when he discovered messages carved on the bottoms and handles of the kitchen utensils and bowls, did his depression subside. He began to exercise and he scratched his own name on one of the dishes. Two days later came back a reply from "Storz," informing him of the prisoner tally: "Hi EA, the score is Navy-7, Air Force-7." (Storz's count was short by a half dozen, as he may have been unaware of a number of the late August additions.) When on the next day, 1 September, while allowed outside to wash, he managed a quick conversation with Larry Guarino, his rejuvenation was complete.[28]

The first American prisoner to arrive at Hoa Lo, Alvarez was the last of the original group to enter the communications network. By the end of September he would know the tap code and become an instructor himself. He and the other veterans passed on encouragement and coping tips to the steady flow of new arrivals, and they in turn coached later newcomers. Occasionally the Vietnamese would shut down one channel or catch and punish an individual, but the system would not stay disrupted for long. As Doremus observed in his memoir:

We had been caught talking, tapping on the walls, handsignal-
ling, making noises with most anything and variations of each
method. Someone even disconnected one of their propaganda
speakers and made static with the open leads which we could read
and understand. The guards caught him and he suffered the consequences for it. Notes were intercepted; signals were understood
by the camp authorities. But as we lost one round, we would shift
to a new method. Sometimes the new method was better. Sometimes we had to lay low and proceed with caution. But sooner or
later we would be in touch again.[29]

Even as the Vietnamese over the years would enforce the prohibition on
communication more strictly, resorting to purges of senior officers, torture,
and other drastic measures to deter contacts and punish violators, the system
could not be silenced. Communication was, quite simply, a primal necessity, as vital and nourishing to the PW's spirit as food was to his body—"the
heart of our existence," Denton called it. To communicate with a comrade—
even when there was no special message or information to convey—became
an elemental drive and a death-risking priority. Alvarez later referred to
sound as "a POW's weapon" and communication, even "idle chatter," as a key
to withstanding the sometimes overwhelming sensory deprivation of the
prison camps.[30] Communication kept the prisoners in touch with reality.
It kept them sane. It gave those in desperate shape, men like Alvarez and
Guarino, hope. It permitted many of the Americans to thrive here at Heartbreak and New Guy in the summer and fall of 1965, and, as conditions and
treatment worsened, it would help many of them to survive.

7

Adjustments, Relocation, and
an Emerging Leadership

In July 1965, President Johnson, increasingly concerned about the security of U.S. bases and installations in Vietnam as well as the progress of the war, approved a major expansion of American ground forces in the South and, moreover, the use of those forces in combat where necessary. Undeterred by Johnson's decision, which committed an additional 100,000 U.S. troops to Southeast Asia over the next six months, the Viet Cong took advantage of Saigon's tottering government and its own gathering support from North Vietnam, Russia, and China to step up attacks in the Central Highlands and the region north of Saigon. The Johnson administration badly misjudged Viet Cong resolve, just as it wrongly assumed that the graduated bombing campaign in the North would bring Ho Chi Minh to the negotiating table. By autumn, North Vietnam was matching the U.S. buildup man for man, steadily infiltrating its own combat units into the South. Meanwhile, the American prisoners of war, in both the North and the South,* found themselves trapped in a lengthening purgatory growing more vicious and miserable by the day.[1]

"I do not know that I shall ever be able to convey the trauma I experienced that day I was shot down," Rob Doremus reminisced about his capture and initial confinement. Doremus described the profound, literally overnight adjustments American prisoners in the North had to make as they entered Hoa Lo. "The quick change from a field grade officer to pajama clad captive; from clean sheeted, foam rubber pillowed bed . . . to cement bed complete with foot stocks" came with an awful suddenness. The squalid conditions at the Hilton—cracked plaster walls, rusty waste buckets, feculent latrines and

---

* The story of American PWs in the South will be resumed in Chapter 12.

open sewers—contrasted sharply with the spit-and-polish gleam of air-conditioned quarters they had occupied days or hours before on U.S. carriers or airbases. Although the first arrivals had been allowed to bathe regularly and were issued a parcel of toiletries, each successive group faced dwindling supplies and more spartan circumstances. Jim Mulligan recalled his thrill at receiving a toothbrush and toothpaste after months of dental miseries; he spent an entire day "brushing each tooth over and over again." Shaving was permitted once every week or two after the fall of 1965; using cold water, an old razor, and a worn and ill-fitting blade to hack a bushy mustache and heavy beard, one inmate remembered his first shave at Hoa Lo leaving his skin looking like "fresh hamburger." Infrequent shaving and washing caused a rash of sores about the neck and face and boils over the entire body, aggravated by mosquitos and maggots that fed upon festering wounds and infections from untreated injuries. Baths came to be relished despite the strong yellow laundry soap and chilling cold water that were the only available cleansers.[2]

There were all manner of acclimations, big and small. Sleep was made more difficult by the cement bunks which, even when a straw mat would be provided as a cushion, caused pressure and then callouses on hips, shoulders, and knees. Filthy blankets offered some protection from Hanoi's surprisingly cold winter, but there was no escaping the stench of sweaty summers. "With the rooms boarded up and no air, and with the temperature going over 100," recalled Navy Lt. Cdr. Richard Stratton, a later captive who arrived at Hoa Lo in January 1967, "we just stunk." At one point Stratton would go 200 days without shaving or having his hair cut, washing only occasionally with a cupful of water. Prisoners learned to hoard water for drinking as well as bathing, and to squirrel away string, matches, nails, toilet paper—anything they could get their hands on that might be used for escape, communication, or simple hygiene. From string and nails were fashioned mosquito nets; matches lit up dark cells and etched notes with their burnt tips; toilet paper, although having by one estimate "the texture of a brown paper bag," was a precious commodity where diarrhea was a constant affliction, and guards would confiscate it to punish disobedience.[3]

"For someone who lived by the clock, who kept his watch as close to the second in accuracy as possible," wrote Doremus, a naval aviator, "the denial of the use of any timepiece was important." Doremus adapted by relying on the position of the sun (whose location could be discerned even through boarded windows), the schedule of the camp radio, and stealing glances at a turnkey's watch. Others learned to tell the time from the sound of the prison gong or chime of city bells in Hanoi and the regularity with which meals were served—a schedule so fixed and anticipated that Stockdale found it "transformed me into a human clock." Keeping a record of the seamless, endlessly repetitive days and weeks was more difficult. Makeshift calendars were scrawled on walls and floors. Navy Lt. (j.g.) Ralph Gaither, captured in October 1965, devised a system using string from his blanket to tie knots to represent days, inserting extra string for special dates (anniversaries, holidays, etc.) and leaving extra space to indicate the beginning of new months. Gaither later said "the string was to grow long and accumulate knots beyond my wildest nightmares."[4]

As much a challenge as tracking the time was finding ways to pass it. Even with communication permeating the silence and filling cherished moments, there was still the matter of how to occupy the long periods of inactivity. "Except during those precious minutes of communication," Stockdale soliloquized, "the prison routine continues to deaden my sensibilities." With wakeup at dawn, long stretches between meals, and opportunities to leave one's cell restricted to emptying a wastecan and small chores like sweeping corridors or washing dishes, boredom was a constant problem. Once the initial interrogation phase was completed, prisoners settled into a stupefying rut where exercise consisted mainly of pacing and recreation of daydreaming. "Even the occasional quiz," Denton recalled, "was a welcome break in routine." Whole afternoons were consumed in passive observation of the insects and rodents that wandered in and out of their cells. During his summer 1965 malaise, Alvarez would stare hypnotically at the steady procession of spiders and scorpions that crawled through his door. Many of the PWs developed a peculiar fascination with the gecko, a multicolored lizard whose mischievous play and efficient devouring of mosquitos and cockroaches made it an agreeable companion. The geckos provided Gaither with "hours of entertainment" and so impressed Denton that he devoted three pages to the subject in his memoir. Others befriended spiders, mice, even the huge rats that were as big as opossums, anthropomorphizing the creatures and following their activities intently as if viewing a pageant.[5]

When the pageant waned or became too familiar, they resorted to mind games for diversion, inventing their own puzzles or projects a la Kile Berg, whose imaginary airport negotiations (see Chapter 6) offered day-long escapes. Doremus restored cars. "I could have told you about the color-coding I would have had for every nut, pulley, accessory underneath the hood," Doremus mused in an interview a couple of months after homecoming. "The more meticulous you got, the more time it would consume." Others built houses, roads, or tunnels, brick by brick and stone by stone, or reconstructed their lives year by year. One drilled oil wells, "although I knew absolutely nothing about oil," and fancied himself a millionaire.

Stockdale computed logarithms "with a stick in the dust" and spent a month contemplating the physics of the musical scales. Mulligan planned an investment fund for his family while Denton rummaged through a mental file of names and faces of long-forgotten grade school acquaintances. Some searched their distant past; others fantasized about the near future. In a resourceful bit of improvised play, next-door neighbors Gaither and Ron Byrne scratched a checkerboard onto the planks of their beds and, using pieces of rock and straw for men, tapped out moves in Morse code.[6]

With activity so constrained and monotonous, even a minor treat or punctuation in the routine became an occasion for celebration. In a world in which receipt of a toothbrush was a notable event, the PWs had to find solace in small pleasures. Except during periods of punishment or where the intrusion of the war caused shortages, the North Vietnamese normally gave the prisoners three cigarettes daily, and for the smokers among them, such as Mulligan, who "savored each drag as if it were nectar," these drafts were often the highlight of the day. For others, meals, bad as they were, served the same purpose. "Eating even the meager rations," Doremus explained, "was something to do." Food, in fact, became an obsession. Little crumbs of bread were lingered over and then devoured as if they were confections of candy. (By 1966 they were just as rare, as a poor-grade rice would supplant moldy bread as the main starch.) With the two daily meals served five hours apart, at 10:30 a.m. and 3:30 p.m., that left 19 hours between dinner and breakfast, ample reason to prolong the evening repast. "They'd bring you a meal which you could finish in about 15 minutes," Doremus recounted.

> But, instead of eating it all, you'd take half of it and decide how you were going to eat the rest. You could even make a sandwich out of rice, roll it in a ball, and divide it. You'd take about half an hour playing around with it before you'd even eat it. Then, you'd chew it very slowly watching for the rocks in it. The Vietnamese, they couldn't believe the way we played around with our food. You could string that whole thing out to about an hour-and-a-half. And that's an hour-and-a-half of your time that's gone.

When they were not eating or stowing food, they were dreaming about it. "The whole process of obtaining sustenance from seed to feed," Doremus wrote,

> was thought about for untold hours, days, and weeks. I have day-dreamed (and night-dreamed) of menus and methods of preparation, until I thought I had eaten the very food I conjectured . . . . For a period of about a year my roommate and I would pass our recommended breakfast menu . . . complete with the wine or

> booze of the day . . . in a coded message to a solo in the next
> cell . . . . We could conjure visions of anything from grits and red-
> eyed gravy to six different styles of cheesecake. I could spend a
> happy, busy, and interesting hour "on the wall" learning someone's
> grandmother's recipe for mince meat pie.

Denton remembered that "every evening, Mulligan would construct a dinner
for Stockdale, patiently working through the soup and salad, the roast beef,
parfait, and even the brandy Alexander and proper cigar. Shumaker was especially good on breakfasts, and each morning we would eagerly await his offering
while the guards were ladling out our miserable fare."[7]

Holidays often brought a welcome change of pace and an improvement, however ephemeral, in both diet and overall treatment. Although
Christmas in Hanoi wore heavily on the soul, it did wonders for the appetite, as the North Vietnamese, more out of calculation than respect or
sympathy, furnished the inmates a small banquet—turkey, duck, fresh
salad and bread, cookies, sometimes a bottle of beer—the proverbial carrot,
invariably followed by the stick. The Vietnamese Lunar New Year, Tet, as
well as other of their festival days, was generally marked by the same pro-
liferation of food and liberalization of policy, accompanied by grating
ceremonies and propaganda displays that some PWs found not worth the
extra victuals. In some years, depending on their disposition, usually when
it was to their advantage for propaganda reasons, the Vietnamese would
also recognize the Americans' Thanksgiving, Easter, or Fourth of July, serving a special mess and even permitting token celebrations or observances,
which they would photograph to demonstrate to the foreign press their
magnanimity. With prison officials practicing a sort of "gastro-politics," the
Americans would eventually be able to ascertain the mood of their captors
and the progress of the war from the holiday bill of fare and telling altera-
tions in the menu at other times of the year.[8]

Manipulation such as occurred with the upgrading of meals at Christmas conferred certain benefits during benign periods, but its malignant side
carried denial and retribution and reminded prisoners how vulnerable they
were to their captors' whims and the vicissitudes of the war. Food, toothbrushes, and toilet paper could be curtailed as easily as dispensed. Privileges—
sunlit cells, outdoor exercise, opportunities for bathing—were alternately
bestowed and rescinded in a usually fruitless but nonetheless unsettling
effort to regulate prisoner behavior. The Americans were at the mercy of
low-level and mean-spirited guards for small favors or concessions; some
of their keepers were decent and considerate men, but even these turned
nasty when the war would be going badly. Mail was another instrument of

manipulation—closely censored, regularly confiscated, and released in a controlled fashion that rewarded or penalized behavior and was intended to sow dissension among the PWs. Medical care, too, was often administered or withheld according to a prisoner's conduct, although, given the crude state of Vietnamese medicine and the limited training of prison doctors and nurses, its denial in some instances was a blessing. Even in such mundane matters as dress, the Vietnamese may have employed subtle methods to demean or demoralize the Americans: sometime late in 1966 a uniform with broad red or plum and gray vertical stripes became the standard prison issue, an outfit so clumsy and degrading that Mulligan referred to it as "the clown suit."[9]

Even as the PWs adjusted to captivity in North Vietnam, some adapting remarkably well, new trials and tribulations continually tested their ingenuity and fortitude. A major stress was having to relocate every six months or so, with cell changes within Hoa Lo and then to outside camps ordered with increasing frequency as the expanding PW population crowded existing facilities. For all the dreariness and monotony of Hoa Lo, at least it offered a reassuring familiarity, enhanced by a well-established communications network and the stores of personal "belongings" that prisoners had collected over time and stashed behind loose bricks and in cracks in cell walls. With the move to a new camp they had to start all over again, with new physical surroundings, uncertain communications, somewhat altered procedures and schedules, and a strange set of guards (though typically several would be transferred along with the prisoners, and much of the guard force would see duty throughout the system, so that it would be rare not to have encountered at least a couple previously). By comparison, many of the later camps—built or converted hurriedly, some intended to be only temporary—lacked even the simple conveniences of Hoa Lo. Relocation generally resulted in inferior conditions.[10]

A case in point was the appearance of two new camps opened by the North Vietnamese in the late summer of 1965 to accommodate the overflow from Hoa Lo. The Hilton, with only a dozen usable cells in its Heartbreak and New Guy sections (other wings of the old prison would be opened and renovated later), had become filled to capacity as a result of the intensified American air activity over the North that accompanied escalation of the ground war in the South. By the end of August Hanoi had bagged more than a score of U.S. fliers, with 11 more seized in September and 14 in October. "Briarpatch," opened the last week in August and named by the Americans for its harsh features, was located 35 miles west of Hanoi in a mountainous region near the town of Xom Ap Lo. Although Alvarez found the food there at first better than at the Hilton, it had no running

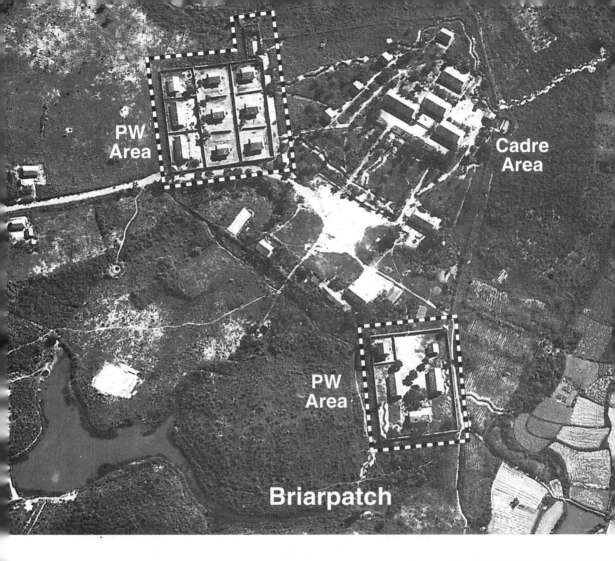

PW
Area

Cadre
Area

PW
Area

Briarpatch

Zoo

water or electricity and, partly owing to its remote location, was the only camp in North Vietnam that would become a match for the primitive captivity circumstances prevailing in the South, with the diet so poor that PWs confined there for any length of time would suffer from serious malnutrition. Briarpatch held 10 PWs initially, all of them among the earliest shootdowns—Alvarez,* Guarino, Butler, Lockhart, Storz, Shumaker, Harris, Morgan, Purcell, and Tschudy; McKamey, Keirn, Peel, Berg, Brunhaver, and Kari joined them shortly (Peel only briefly before being returned to Hoa Lo). After three weeks of operation, the camp was temporarily closed on 20 September when U.S. bombers pounded the area and forced prison officials to herd the PWs back to Hanoi. It was reopened in December and remained in use for more than a year, despite continuing supply difficulties, until February 1967.[11]

Not as primitive or remote as Briarpatch, but in its own way just as desolate, was the "Zoo," the second PW facility opened in August-September 1965. In fact, the Zoo was situated only a couple of miles southwest of Hoa Lo, on the outskirts of Hanoi, but the differences between it and the Hilton were so pronounced it might as well have been located in a separate province. Near Bac Mai Airfield and the village of Cu Loc, it had once been a French film studio and recreation center, possibly a movie or art colony; lying about its grounds were yellowing posters, old film cans, damaged reels, and other remnants from those earlier days. The PWs at first called the place "Camp America" and, with cows, chickens, and other farm animals roaming about, gave the several buildings names like "Barn," "Chicken Coop," "Stable," and "Pigsty." There was a large swimming pool in the center of the main compound, but its fetid water lay thick with garbage and junk. The Americans were dismayed to find guards eating fish raised in the pool. The concrete buildings had adequate tile roofs but otherwise were in varying states of disrepair, their rooms, hastily converted into cells, ranging from musty to putrid. The PWs were scattered among the dozen or so one-story structures, making communication difficult. There were no beds to sleep on, only cement floors. The windows, already barred, were also being bricked up when the group transferred from Briarpatch arrived there the last week in September, shortly after it opened. The louvered French doors, later to be replaced by thicker, more secure ones, were padlocked but had a slight give that allowed prisoners to peek out and observe activities within the compound; they also contained eyeholes that enabled guards, or wandering livestock, to peer in at the prisoners, a feature that contributed to the nickname Zoo, which was adopted in 1966.

* Until placed in a cell with Guarino at Briarpatch on 13 September, Alvarez had not had face-to-face contact with another American in over a year.

As one of the men put it, "It's the first kind of place where the animals come to look at the people." The Zoo would become a primary detention center during the early years, holding more than 50 prisoners by February 1966 and about 120 at the start of 1967. As a rule, after September 1965, American captives would be brought to Hoa Lo for registration and initial interrogation and then moved to the Zoo (or Briarpatch after it reopened in December 1965) for long-term incarceration, periodically to be returned to the Hilton for special punishment or an intensive extortion or indoctrination session.[12]

As isolated and disconnected as their situation was, the majority of PWs never considered themselves divorced from the war effort. For them the prison camps became just another theater, albeit a unique one, with its own peculiar logistical and tactical demands. Their mission had changed, from one of active fighting to one of resistance and survival, but they still had a soldierly function to perform—to disrupt, to stymie, to exhaust the enemy, finally to defeat him, in this case on the battlefield of propaganda and psychological warfare. Indeed, although they were on the periphery of the fighting, they saw themselves at the center of the political struggle and viewed their mission as ever more crucial as they recognized the PW issue taking on increasing political significance. "The conditions under which American POW's existed," one of their leaders later recalled,

> have changed radically since World War II. It is no longer a matter of simply being shot [ejected] into your parachute, going to a reasonably pleasant "Hogan's Heroes" prison camp, and sweating out the end of the war. At least it was not that way in Vietnam. In Vietnam the American POW did not suddenly find himself on the war's sidelines. Rather, he found himself on one of the major battlefronts—the propaganda battlefront.
> . . . For Americans who became POW's in Vietnam, capture meant not that we had been neutralized, but that a different kind of war had begun . . . .[13]

As for the seniors among them, their role, as it had always been, was to provide leadership; to conceive, plan, and coordinate tactics; to create and operate an effective organization; to sustain morale. The tasks of leadership remained constant, but became more complicated and challenging in this unconventional setting. In North Vietnam at least, the leaders had the advantage of handling a fairly homogeneous, well-trained, and experienced group of men. The Navy and Air Force aviators who comprised the bulk of prisoners in the Northern camps were career servicemen for whom discipline and motivation were natural. But this solid corps of professionals would become greatly emasculated and debilitated from imprisonment. Their "fighting" capability had somehow to be restored. The job of leadership was to institute and maintain a semblance of organization, even as the leaders were continually being segregated, and to nourish hope and a will to resist even as the leaders themselves bore the brunt of punishment and were being tested to the limits of their endurance. Fortunately, there were senior officers up to the assignment, a coterie of exceptional individuals who managed to devise a resistance organization with cleverness and skill and who, when singled out for abuse by the Vietnamese for their efforts, and sometimes removed from direct contact or communication with their troops for extended spells, continued to lead by courage and example.

On 9 September 1965, Navy Cdr. James Stockdale, a veteran of air attacks over North Vietnam since the Tonkin Gulf raids 13 months earlier and now the commander of a carrier air wing, was shot down during a reconnaissance run halfway between the coastal cities of Vinh and Thanh Hoa. Fellow senior Jeremiah Denton characterized Stockdale as having "limitless physical courage . . . despite his relatively small size," remembering him "serving as cannon fodder against the huge Navy football team while he was a junior varsity player." Stockdale also was highly intelligent, having earned a graduate degree in international relations from Stanford, where he studied Marxism and Communist affairs and explored the Korean War PW experience. His academic interests and a growing philosophical bent would ripen while in prison and dominate his activities upon release. With a tough but reassuring presence, weathered face, and a shock of gray hair which another senior noted "gave him a remarkable likeness to the writer Carl Sandburg," Stockdale was an impressive figure who elicited respect from both peers and subordinates. Hanoi's biggest prize since Alvarez, in time he would become the sharpest thorn in its side.[14]

Stockdale suffered a broken bone in his back during ejection and further injuries when he parachuted onto the main street of a small village and was beaten by a gang of angry locals. By the time North Vietnamese Army personnel arrived to transport him to Hanoi, his left leg had been severely broken and was dangling grotesquely at the knee at nearly a 90-degree angle. On the way to the capital his handlers stopped at a building, possibly a medical facility, to have the leg checked. When a doctor dressed in surgical garb drew a large saw and scalpels from a satchel, Stockdale implored the man not to amputate. Although the Vietnamese did not appear to understand English, he realized Stockdale's concern and gave the crippled flier an injection that put him to sleep. The doctor was unable to repair the shattered limb, failing to get the knee back in its socket, but he heeded the prisoner's plea. Although Stockdale would never regain full use of the leg, he was fortunate nonetheless. Had he lost it, he likely would not have survived. Whether owing to happenstance or their fear of the resulting bad publicity, the Communists released no maimed American PWs during or after the war, following a pattern established with French PWs during the Franco-Viet Minh War.

Stockdale entered Hoa Lo on 12 September, stretcher-ridden and wrapped in bulky casts to protect his leg and his shoulder where his back had been broken. Placed in room 24, the relatively comfortable space in Heartbreak that Alvarez had once occupied, he was accompanied by Eagle, Owl, and Dog. The last wasted no time introducing himself, evincing respect for the aviator's rank and concern about his condition but proceeding to deliver a tirade of indoctrination about Vietnamese sovereignty and United States interference in the people's revolution. When Stockdale complimented Dog on his English and inquired about his education, the prison commander replied that the *revolution* had been his university, a remark that impressed the cerebral American.

Despite his familiarity with foreign cultures and Communist ideology from graduate school studies, a careless mistake almost did Stockdale in at the outset. When Dipshit, the general prison fetchit, rigged a stool on his stretcher so that he could drink from his soup bowl, Stockdale gratefully responded with "Attaboy." Dipshit recoiled, insisting he was not to be called "Boy" but "Mister." This would be but the first incident among many in which Vietnamese resentment of Western racism and imperialism, the enduring legacy of French colonialism, became clear to Stockdale. ("I was to be paying a lot of French debts," he wrote in his memoir.)[15] It was also one of several instances in which Dipshit's petulance threatened a prisoner's well-being.

As he slowly sipped his soup, Stockdale pondered his predicament, fixing on four main concerns. First, he had to guard against the enemy's brainwashing or manipulating him into making the sort of "treasonous" statements he had read in Korean PW files during his Stanford research. Second, he was convinced the war would stretch on at least five years, requiring planning for a long resistance. Third, he had to conceal from the Vietnamese the extent of his involvement in the Tonkin Gulf raids, some of the details of which they had already obtained from news clippings; if they learned that he was the leader of three of the principal strikes, they could "sink their teeth into a massive piece of propaganda."[16] Fourth, he had somehow to buy time and plot a resistance course while exceedingly weak and vulnerable from his injuries; to gain strength and mobility became an immediate priority.

For two weeks, despite constant pain and worry about his deteriorating leg, his luck held during interrogation. Eagle and Owl did not confront him with evidence that he had led the Tonkin Gulf attacks. In seeking military information, Eagle settled for Stockdale's admission that his carrier, the *Oriskany*, flew F-8, A-4, and A-1 aircraft, and accepted his refusal to divulge additional details. Eagle also settled for Stockdale's explanation that, despite his rank, he was only a functionary with simple maintenance and administrative responsibilities and no knowledge of plans. When he experienced circulation problems in the bad leg, Dog, no doubt concerned about losing his special prisoner, sent a doctor to examine him. The physician removed part of the cast, drew blood from the cartilage in an attempt to reduce the swelling, and departed, to reappear two days later and load the patient onto a truck for an uneventful trip around the city, during which Stockdale never left the vehicle. (Dog possibly had intended to deliver him to a hospital for treatment but failed to make the necessary arrangements in advance.) Back in his cell, the suffering Stockdale stared at the mangled leg, which bent askew and looked almost detached at the knee. Hearing water running and someone whistling "I've Been Working on the Railroad"—which he construed as a fellow airman's allusion to railroad bombing—he responded with "Anchors Aweigh," relieved to hear the Air Force song whistled in return.*

On the night of 24 or 25 September Stockdale was taken to a hospital some six or seven blocks from the Hilton. Although his room and bed were dirty and invaded by rats, the medical staff acted professionally and told him they hoped to rebuild his knee and leg in a series of three operations. The first, in October, left his knee loose. Ten days later, the second operation, an attempt to manipulate the kneebone back into its socket, failed. The doctors promised him a third operation at a later date when he was stronger. One allowed him to write his wife Sybil to tell her that he was alive, but the letter was never mailed. On 25 October Dipshit and Mickey Mouse, the latter apparently delegated responsibility for Stockdale's medical treatment, moved the prisoner back to the Hilton.

Stockdale was too invalided and too isolated at this point to exercise any influence over the band of PWs at Hoa Lo, but the leadership role there was being filled by another senior recently deposited in Heartbreak. Air Force Lt. Col. Robinson Risner—a Korean War ace, a test pilot, and his country's choice to fly the Lindbergh Anniversary Flight in 1957, during which he set a transatlantic speed record—was seized exactly one week after Stockdale. He had already been shot down once over North Vietnam, the previous

---

* The whistler, Stockdale later learned, was Lieutenant Peel, who had been doing a wash for injured cellmates Vohden, Daughtrey, and Collins.

spring, when he was rescued at sea. Ordered home, he received the Air Force Cross, was trotted out at press conferences to explain U.S. goals in Indochina, and became the subject of a *Time* cover story that extolled his achievements and portrayed him as an exemplar of the dedicated and skilled American fighting man in Vietnam. He was downed the second time only a month after returning to his unit in Thailand. Banged up but not hurt seriously when captured, he reached the Hilton on 18 September 1965.[17]

Risner's exploits had been so widely publicized that the Vietnamese had heard of him even before he fell into their hands. They knew of the *Time* article and that he had led several raids which destroyed key bridges and killed many soldiers. For 10 days a steady procession of interrogators, including some obviously of high rank, pressed him to answer questions, but he held his ground, refusing to talk even when Rabbit threatened to try him as a criminal or turn him over to a mob. One even threatened to have him burned at the stake if he did not cooperate, a grisly form of execution that Communist thugs had carried out against mandarins, landholders, and village elders who opposed them in the 1950s and that the Viet Cong had occasionally used to intimidate adversaries in the South.

Risner soon made contact with Air Force buddies Byrne and Schierman, pilots from his own squadron who had entered Hoa Lo a couple of weeks earlier, and Major Raymond Merritt, his wingman, who had gone down the same day as he. To the tune of "McNamara's Band," he sang in a hushed tone when the guards were out of earshot:

> *My name is Robbie Risner.*
> *I'm the leader of the group.*
> *Listen to my story and*
> *I'll give you all the poop.*[18]

His first day in Heartbreak he exchanged news with Byrne and met Navy pilots Franke and Doremus, who advised him to take the opportunity to wash whenever he emptied his waste bucket in the latrine and offered tips on how to protect his food from the rats. In the same cellblock, too, was Navy Cdr. Wendy Rivers, brought to Hoa Lo with Ed Davis on 14 September and destined to become Risner's close friend. Rivers, who narrowly missed rescue by a hovering A-1 when his survival radio did not work, would become an active link in the communication network and a key senior in his own right.

Before going to sleep that first night, Risner learned the tap code. As the senior officer among those known to be incarcerated at Hoa Lo— Stockdale was still incommunicado, and, in any case, it turned out that Risner outranked him by a matter of days—Risner had already begun planning an organization, regretting that he had not paid more attention to the experience of colleagues captured in Korea. Of one, he recalled: "I had never asked him if he had been tortured or had gotten enough to eat . . . . I had been so caught up in my daily activities that I had not bothered to find out more . . . . All my information had come through the survival schools and from what I had read in fiction."[19] About 20 September, assuming command, he directed that all prisoners memorize the tap code and use it wherever they were sent. This instruction, marking the formal adoption of the code as a standard means of secret communication, would be one of the most important orders issued by any of the seniors during the entire period of captivity.

After two weeks in Heartbreak, in early October 1965 Risner, along with Rivers, was shifted to the Zoo. Paul Kari and John McKamey, in an adjacent cell, briefed the senior officers. Risner was elated to find Bob Purcell rooming nearby, the Air Force captain having been reported killed in action. At Purcell's suggestion, Risner requested a talk with the camp commander about improving conditions at the squalid camp. "Spot," a new interrogator, summoned Risner to state his grievances. Risner complained about the unswept quarters, the absence of beds and lights (the prisoners could not even see what they were eating), and the need for exercise and more frequent bathing. When Spot upbraided him for insolence and returned the leader to his cell, Risner issued his first order at the Zoo: the men were to pray for brooms, beds, lights, and outdoor exercise. Risner intended the prayers to unify the group and to instill faith. Even he was astonished when within days their supplications were answered. For beds guards brought in wooden pallets and set them on sawhorses. Mosquito nets were provided, and the men were allowed outside to exercise for 15 minutes at a time. A week later, as if descended from the heavens themselves, light bulbs appeared, dropped through holes in the ceiling.

Another senior arrived at the Zoo in early October—Commander Denton. Denton had been a forceful presence at the Hilton during the summer of 1965 until locked in irons when he attempted to fashion an escape hatch. His injured leg had become infected from a rusty stock and remained swollen even after Dipshit had cleaned the foot and applied sulfa and a nurse inoculated him. Eagle finally released him after he tossed off a glib retort to a question about how long it took the United States to train a reserve Army division. Denton gibed, "Oh, . . . a week, or a month, or a couple of years." Eagle was so pleased to get the hardliner to say something beyond his name and serial number that he promptly freed him. Once at the Zoo Denton resumed his militancy as second in command to Risner. Mulligan rated him "the unquestioned POW leader" during the early years, who, "more than any other senior, gave purpose and direction to the resistance movement."[20]

With Denton, Risner, Rivers, Guarino, Byrne, and Franke all at the Zoo by the middle of October, and with Stockdale hospitalized and then returned to an isolated room at the Hilton, all the seniors were removed for a time from influence over the new men arriving at Heartbreak. The Vietnamese had clearly intended it that way: by removing the veterans, they could put later captives through initial interrogations and indoctrination without them having had the benefit of experience or leadership, thereby rendering them more exploitable. Resistance at the Hilton suffered, but the Zoo became a beehive of countervailing strategy and activity.

The acronym SRO for Senior Ranking Officer quickly became known to all Zoo PWs, and each of the seniors knew where he stood in the chain of command. Should both Risner and Denton be put out of commission or moved, the next man stood ready to take over. Code names were employed to protect identities: Risner, for example, was "Cochise" (later "Abe"); Denton, "Wildcat"; Guarino, "Yankee Boss" or "YKB." Captain Storz, located next door to Risner after the colonel was transferred from the Barn to another building known as the "Garage," functioned as a kind of executive assistant, circulating messages and keeping track of policy and personnel matters for the leadership.

With Risner supervising, the prisoners collected every sort of potentially useful object—bits of wire, soap, cloth, matches, rope, paper, nails. To conceal their activities, they maintained a close watch over their jailers, clocking guard movements and recording their sleeping and recreation habits. Risner urged the men not to needlessly antagonize the detention staff, rejecting flippant behavior as provocative and unproductive. To surmount the communications obstacles at the new camp, which had a more sprawling layout than the Hilton, he had the inmates, using the crude instruments at their disposal, bore whispering holes through the walls between cells; not only could the prisoners thus talk to one another, but they sometimes were able to use the holes as observation ports to see and "visit" their neighbor, a great boost to the spirit. Between buildings a "wastecan express" carried instructions and a map of the camp. From his corner cell in a building called the "Office," Denton whistled names and information to Risner while he was in the Barn. On Sundays Denton led all those within range of his voice in the Lord's Prayer. A whistled "God Bless America" was the sign to commence, with the Pledge of Allegiance usually following the service.[21]

On 24 October, when camp officials conducted their first serious shakedown inspection, they had plenty to find. They discovered a list of Risner's policies in a surprise raid on Storz's cell. As the guards broke in, Storz tried to destroy the sheet of directives along with a master list of PWs. While holding the guards off with one hand, he grabbed one of the papers and swallowed it. Unfortunately, he had snatched the personnel list, less important than the policy list. Moreover, the latter contained Risner's name, and it was his real one rather than the cover identity. Storz was shoved into an empty cell and left there stripped to his shorts for three days without food, water, or blanket. Failing to break Storz when they demanded that he confirm Risner's role as a resistance organizer, the Vietnamese, with a vengeance, turned their attention to the leader.[22]

When Risner likewise refused to admit anything, he was taken before "Fox," a seasoned officer who would shortly succeed Dog as prison commander.* Fox had him gagged, cuffed, blindfolded, and trucked back to Hoa Lo, whose maximum punishment facilities, once used for French offenders, were being readied for the Americans. It was now 1 November 1965. A long siege of torture was to begin for the SRO, as the Vietnamese were in the midst of a brutal crackdown that would soon ensnare the other seniors and eventually most of the junior men as well.

It was something of a coincidence that the triumvirate of senior officers who would lead the American PW resistance in North Vietnam throughout much of the decade of captivity were captured early in the war and at virtually the same time. Air Force Lt. Col. Hervey Stockman, seized in June 1967 and himself a later SRO, commented on the odd parallelism of the trio's experience in a postwar treatise, adding to the threesome of Stockdale, Risner, and Denton a fourth figure, Air Force Maj. Lawrence Guarino:

> It is interesting to note that four prisoners, three senior 05s and one a senior 04 [Guarino], all to assume major roles of leadership in the Hanoi prison system, entered that system within a span of four months of each other in the summer-fall of 1965. All were to experience a portion of The Beginning period in solitary confinement but in communication with other American prisoners, then to be among the first to resist, then suffer but continue to lead in the brutal environment of The Middle Years. Their paths were to cross and recross throughout the entire history of American aircrew detention in North Vietnam. Two were USAF and well known to each other prior to shootdown, two were Naval Academy classmates. All four had different backgrounds, temperaments and personalities, but all four shared a wealth of military experience and moral fiber.[23]

* Apparently, Dog doubled as commander at both the Hilton and the Zoo the remainder of the year and was then replaced by Fox in 1966 when Hanoi installed a firmer cadre of officers to oversee tougher PW treatment.

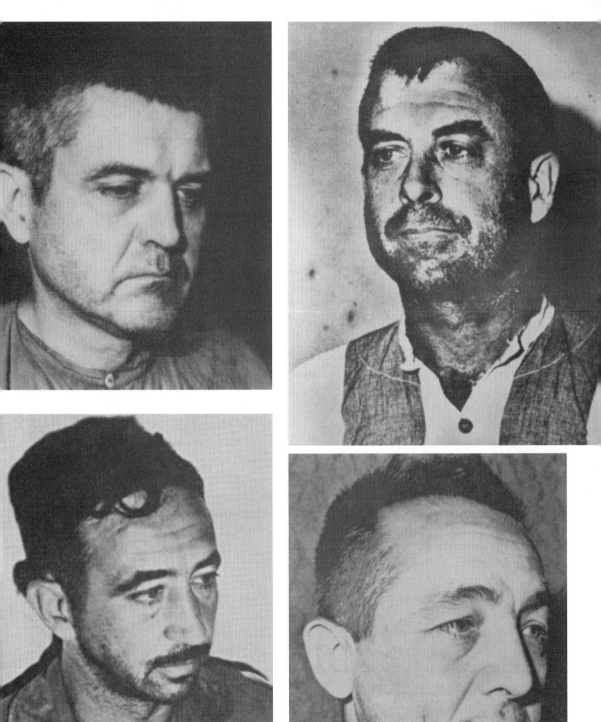

Clockwise from top left: Senior leaders Stockdale, Denton, Risner, Guarino.

To the extent that their situation could be called fortunate, the PWs in the North were lucky to have had such high-caliber leadership from the very beginning. These men knew not only how to command but also how to cooperate, combining personal strength with mutual respect and teamwork. Nowhere was this collaboration more evident than in the determination of seniority, an issue that was potentially divisive owing to traditional service rivalries and that was enormously complicated in captivity by the absence of the normal modus operandi. "Establishing who was the senior ranking officer was no small task," Risner later remarked. There was the matter, first of all, of gathering and communicating information on what seniors were being held and what their relative ranks and tenures were. This knowledge had to be integrated and disseminated even as new prisoners were arriving daily, some of them possible SROs and some with news of battlefield promotions that had been awarded the others while incarcerated. Because verification of the effective date of such promotions was almost impossible, the leaders decided to base seniority on rank at the time of shootdown. Even this proved unsatisfactory with the passage of years, as Stockdale indicated at homecoming: "New guys were coming in shot down as Commanders who had been Lieutenants in squadrons with old guys who had been shot down as Lieutenant Commanders, thus the old guys were now working for their previous wingmen." The system would eventually be changed when it became altogether untenable after 1970, but it would never be without shortcomings.* Finally, there was the matter of where civilian PWs stood in the pecking order. As it happened, the issue rarely surfaced, as there were so few American civilians imprisoned in the North (many more were captured and detained in the South), but General Westmoreland himself raised the intriguing question of "who is the senior— a Foreign Service Officer Grade 3 of the Department of State, a GS-12 employee of the CIA, or an Army Lieutenant Colonel? The three ranks are roughly equivalent."[24]

Despite the many impediments, generally the leaders resolved their differences and any competing SRO claims quickly and smoothly. The subject of seniority arose as early as July 1965, when Denton made contact with Guarino in the New Guy section of the Hilton. "One thing Larry and I had to settle," Denton recalled,

---

* Stockdale's report contains a section titled "Who's On First" where he cites the vital importance of establishing seniority and the maddening complexities that plagued the process. On the confusion resulting from vaguely delineated authority, see Stockman, "Authority, Leadership, Organization," 26, 27-28.

was the chain of command. The Code of Conduct demands that in a
POW situation, command must be established on a rank and seniority
basis; that is, when officers of equal rank are involved, seniority takes
precedence.

Larry thought that was fine, but since he was in the Air Force
and I was in the Navy, what we had was two one-man armies. Eventually, I convinced him that he was wrong. The senior ranking officer
is in command over men of all services. So far as Larry and I were
concerned, that was me. Larry gave in gracefully and agreed to accept
my orders.

Denton in turn unhesitatingly became Risner's deputy at the Zoo, and
Stockdale, though junior to Risner by only a matter of days, would defer to him
in those few instances where the two were in proximity in the same camp or
cellblock. In 1970, all three would recognize a later shootdown, Air Force
Lt. Col. Vernon Ligon, as outranking them. Still later, they would acknowledge Air Force Cols. John Flynn, David Winn, and Norman Gaddis as
seniormost. In almost all cases, a spirit of cooperation and solidarity, spurred
by an understood commonality of interests, prevailed over personal ego and
service parochialism.[25]

"Perhaps it seemed like a Mickey Mouse exercise," Denton wrote of
his discussion with Guarino, "but the question of command soon became
of immense importance." From the standpoint of the PWs waging an effective resistance, it became so important that the Vietnamese would continually try to subvert the command structure, at first by moving the seniors
around or segregating them and later by designating junior officers as
"room responsible" in a transparent attempt to undermine the seniors'
authority. Such measures, although sometimes briefly successful, almost
always failed in the end. The unity and discipline displayed by the seniors
extended throughout the ranks. Guarino later observed: "From our earliest
days of captivity, we had sought out the ranking man in the camp and conducted ourselves in accordance with his orders . . . . The organization was
a joint effort from the first to the last." When the Vietnamese required
the junior officers to be the only point of contact with prison officials, the
PWs thwarted the program by surreptitiously maintaining established organizational arrangements and channels: the junior liaisons ostensibly served
the enemy but actually took their cue from the PW leadership.[26]

In truth, over the years there would be breakdowns of authority, lapses
in the chain of command, intramural squabbling, even instances of resentment
and outright disobedience of the leadership.[27] Especially as the stresses of

captivity mounted and as the prisoner population continued to grow, there would be some erosion of cohesiveness and harmony. The fraternal bonds and close-knit camaraderie that distinguished the PW community in the early years inevitably diminished somewhat as their numbers multiplied and new camps proliferated. But what is more arresting is the extent to which unity and discipline and a working, indeed widening organization persisted. That they perdured in the face of so many obstacles may be attributed both to the constancy and long and skillful tenure of the original seniors and to the character of the brave and highly trained men who, with few exceptions, unflinchingly followed their lead.

8

Tightening the Screws: The Beginnings of the Torture Era in the North

The fall of 1965 happened to be the coldest autumn in Hanoi in many years. At the start of October three dozen Americans shivered in the concrete chill of North Vietnam's prisons; by Christmas, another 30 would join them. One man in four was seriously ill or badly injured or both. The first enlisted men to become prisoners in the North, Air Force helicopter crewmen Arthur Black and William Robinson, captured on 20 September, made the long trek from the DMZ to Hanoi along with their pilot, Capt. Thomas Curtis.* Black and Robinson were destined to become the longest held enlisted PWs in American history, followed closely by Air Force Sgt. Arthur Cormier, downed six weeks later. Among others taken captive in the fall of l965 were Air Force Capt. Philip Smith, downed and imprisoned in China;† Air Force Maj. Fred Cherry, the first black pilot seized by the North Vietnamese; several junior officers seeing their first duty—Air Force Lts. Thomas Barrett, Edward Brudno, and Jerry Singleton, and Navy Lts. (j.g.) David Wheat, Porter Halyburton, Ralph Gaither, and Rodney Knutson; and two senior officers, Navy Cdrs. Harry Jenkins and Howard Rutledge. Capt. Harlan Chapman became the first Marine PW in the North when shot down on 5 November; he was joined a month later by two other Marine Corps fliers, Maj. Howard Dunn and WO John Frederick.

These latest additions to the PW ranks could not have arrived at a bleaker time. The North Vietnamese, increasingly agitated by both mounting PW resistance and unrelenting U.S. bombing raids, rather suddenly stiffened their treatment of the American prisoners. Until November, there had been

---

* Curtis's co-pilot, Lt. Duane Martin, fell into Pathet Lao hands during an evasion attempt and was killed the following year while trying to escape from a Laotian stockade with Navy Lt. (j.g.) Dieter Dengler. See Chapter 3.
† The experience of Americans captured in China is discussed in Chapter 26.

Top: Marine aviators, left to right, Chapman, Dunn, Frederick. *Bottom:* Smith (left) went down in China; Air Force Sergeants Black (middle) and Robinson (right) would become the longest held enlisted PWs in American history.

warnings and threats, an occasional reprisal or strong-arm tactic, mostly aimed at the seniors, but no concerted effort to discipline the Americans— "disorganized harassment and isolated incidents of slaps and cuffs," Hervey Stockman described the climate. The lackadaisicalness of guards and generally loose supervision by prison officials had permitted relatively easy communication among prisoners. This atmosphere of benign neglect changed abruptly following the 24 October incident that turned up the Risner policy list and made prison authorities aware of the degree of clandestine activity among the Americans. It is likely the Vietnamese had been formulating a more rigorous and definitive PW plan for some time, recognizing as surely as their captives that the war might well drag on inconclusively and that they had better prepare for the long haul. A tighter regime at some point was inevitable. The 24 October episode may have prodded the Vietnamese to act immediately. No doubt, together with the spreading bombing damage in the Hanoi-Haiphong area, it shortened tempers. In any case, it gave the Vietnamese a pretext for clamping down. The new era that ensued, so distinct that the PWs in retrospect referred to it variously as the "Middle Years" or "Extortion Era" of the captivity experience, would extend from late October 1965 to the fall of 1969.[1]

Denton had noticed the telltale signs of a changing attitude upon his arrival at the Zoo in early October. "I didn't like the feel of the situation," he recalled. "Both sides, the prisoners and the North Vietnamese, appeared to be feeling their way toward new positions . . . . The guards were becoming meaner, and the officers more wary and oppressive. I couldn't quite put my finger on it, but the atmosphere was changing for the worse." By November, for starters, food rations at the Zoo were cut drastically and kitchen staff were no longer washing off the human fertilizer the Vietnamese used on their crops. The camp took on a decided look of permanence as construction workers busily converted once airy rooms into secured cells with bricked windows and thick wooden doors and raised a low-lying perimeter wall to 10 feet and strung barbed wire along the top. At both the Zoo and Hoa Lo officials posted a set of regulations in every cell addressing the prisoners as "criminals" and ordering them to give full and truthful answers to all questions, obey all guard instructions, bow to all Vietnamese personnel entering their cells, demonstrate a "polite attitude" at all times, and attempt no communication either through signals or tapping. Twenty such regulations directed every routine activity and carried strict penalties for any violation. Additional guards and turnkeys were brought in to enforce the restrictions.[2]

Vindictive as it seemed, the crackdown was as much tactical as temperamental. With the expanding American war effort, prison authorities were under increasing pressure to obtain information and statements that could be used for propaganda purposes. To produce these they had to break down the PWs' resistance. The regulations were intended to do just that—by tightening control, discouraging communication, dampening morale, and nullifying the influence of organization and leadership. At the Zoo, with communication stifled for a time and different buildings reacting without a coordinated strategy to the bowing edict, the Vietnamese succeeded temporarily in dividing the prisoners with a "no bow, no chow" policy, depriving resisting cellblocks of food while feeding complying ones on schedule; by December 1965, absent a common stand, all PWs at the Zoo were bowing. Neither fiat nor intimidation, however, stemmed the resistance for long. An early version of Denton's tap system, virtually impossible for jailers to detect or prosecute, soon restored and in fact improved the communications network. When the rules crackdown failed to achieve the desired result, the

Vietnamese decided to turn the screws tighter, literally, resorting to harsher forms of punishment and finally a systematic program of torture.[3]

Prior to late October 1965, although there were the sporadic instances of "slaps and cuffs," there were no documented cases of outright torture of American PWs in North Vietnamese prisons. Even as the Vietnamese steadily turned to more brutal methods as a matter of course in November and December 1965, they went to elaborate lengths to justify their actions, maintaining all along that they were not abandoning their much advertised "humane and lenient" policy toward prisoners of war. It was the prisoners, Hanoi insisted, who "chose" to be punished by willfully violating established regulations. (The Koreans and Chinese had used the same sophistry to legitimatize mistreatment of their PWs.) The Vietnamese were careful to include among the regulations a promise that any prisoner who followed the rules and demonstrated a "good attitude" would earn humane treatment.

For the Americans, whose Code of Conduct precluded cooperation with the enemy and specifically prohibited responses to questions beyond the so-called "big four" (name, rank, serial number, and date of birth), the end to the era of restraint placed them in a vexing position. There was no way they could comply with both the captor's requirements and their own Code of Conduct. It was one thing to contend with verbal threats and inconveniencing penalties, such as late delivery of food and the withholding of toothbrushes and cigarette privileges, quite another to withstand a gloves-off campaign of physical extortion and retribution. The Vietnamese, who had obtained copies of the Code and studied it for clues on how best to exert pressure on the Americans, assumed that, where persuasion and harassment had failed, brute coercion would succeed; interrogators, though still not averse to using the carrot in certain situations, looked forward to the extra latitude they were now allowed. What they did not realize was how much abuse the prisoners would take before surrendering. Before long, torture, as both an instrument of punishment and a means for extracting information—cloaked in a rationale of legitimacy—became a standard procedure. And the Americans faced a cruel choice between submitting, which under the Code of Conduct could be construed as treason, and suffering.[4]

Navy Lt. (j.g.) Rodney Knutson, a radar intercept operator captured with pilot Ralph Gaither when their F-4 went down on 17 October, became the first victim of the evolving reign of terror. Knutson had been forced to shoot it out with Vietnamese militia who surrounded him after he parachuted to the ground; he killed two riflemen before being grazed himself by a stray bullet.* He and Gaither were taken to Hanoi in separate trucks and would not meet again for several years. At Hoa Lo he immediately underwent interrogation, refusing repeatedly to provide information beyond his name and serial number and finally thrusting the pen with which he was expected to sign a confession through the piece of paper. That evening he was brought a bowl of filthy gruel, which he dumped into his wastecan, falling off to sleep after doing battle with rats, some of which seemed to him as big as jackrabbits.[5]

Over the next week Knutson would pay dearly for his insolence. The lieutenant had violated the recently posted regulations pertaining to inmate cooperation. At the direction of superiors, guards locked him in ankle straps, bound his arms so tightly behind his back they lost circulation, denied him food and water, and, when he still refused to apologize for his behavior, punched him with clenched fists until they shattered his nose, broke several teeth, and caused his eyelids to swell shut. When after three days guards removed him from the stocks, he was unable to straighten up because his bloodied back and buttocks, beaten to a pulp with bamboo clubs, had formed a giant scab. When they released his bonds, he could not believe the intensity of the pain caused by the recirculation of blood into his blackened hands and forearms. When, semiconscious and writhing in agony, he remained silent, the Vietnamese applied a new torture that finally broke him.

In the so-called "rope torture," administered to Knutson on 25 October and soon to become a source of dread throughout the Northern camps, guards forced him face down on his bunk, set his ankles into stocks, and bound him tightly with rope at the elbows. The long end of the rope was then pulled up through a hook attached to the ceiling. As a guard hoisted the prisoner, he lifted him off the bunk enough so that he could not relieve any of his weight, producing incredible pain—with shoulders seemingly being torn from their sockets—and horribly constricting breathing. (An alternate technique was simply to set the prisoner on his bunk or the floor, arch his back with a rope stretching from the feet to the throat, and place pressure on the back until his mouth was practically touching his toes.) Screaming and in tears from this first use of the rope treatment, Knutson at last agreed to talk.[6]

* Like most of the American fliers, Knutson carried a .38 pistol, which was used mostly as a signaling device since it was capable of holding tracer ammunition that could be seen by air rescue units when fired. The use of tracer ammunition against humans was considered to be a violation of international law because of its powerful explosive effect. Knutson, who fired tracer rounds, apparently had no choice, shooting back in self-defense. Others did the same. On the .38, see Blakey, *Prisoner at War*, 377. Risner noted that most aviators carried a .38 as well as a "blood chit," a package with pieces of gold bullion for barter and lengths of silk cloth that had printed on them, in several languages, "I AM AN AMERICAN FIGHTING MAN" and the promise of a reward for returning the bearer to friendly hands (*Passing of the Night*, 7-8). As Knutson's rude greeting attested, the PWs rarely had an opportunity to employ the "blood chit."

What he confessed they already knew, that he had been flying an F-4. They wanted further details, such as who was in the aircraft with him, information which they also already had but which they wanted him to divulge as a show of sincerity. Knutson stalled. He managed to string along his interrogator with a tale about a swimming pool on his carrier and his job as a recreation officer whose responsibility was pool maintenance. When he reported that the Navy used phonograph records rather than tapes, the interrogator was pleased to learn that his small country had a technological advantage over the Americans. Knutson further gulled the examiner with lies about his family, claiming that his father was a chicken farmer who lived in Farm District No. 1 and that he himself had driven a peanut truck selling peanuts to basketball players. Having granted the interrogator at least some conversation, however implausible, Knutson earned the privilege of bathing for the first time since his capture. The crude bath facility had only a cold water faucet, and a prison worker had to bring in a pan of warm water in order for him to get his flight suit off. The outfit had been worn all during his punishment so that it had adhered to his ulcerated haunches. It took two hours of soaking to free him. Guards handed him prison pajamas, a blanket, and rigging for a mosquito net. That night he was able to sleep for the first time in more than a week.

Toward the end of October, on a trip to the latrine, Knutson found a message that had been left for him by Lieutenant Peel. To his amazement, the message noted that their treatment had been fairly good and not to be overly concerned. Knutson shuddered in admiration of the iron men who thought this treatment mild, then slipped into guilt and depression for having succumbed, he felt, too easily. In fact, nothing had been farther from the truth. Later accounts established that he had absorbed more punishment than any of his comrades in the Northern prisons up to that time and had held out magnificently.[7]

As the torture campaign spread through the fall and into the winter of 1965, Knutson's ordeal became a rite of passage experienced eventually by almost every American PW in the North. Returning prisoners later estimated that 95 percent of the men underwent torture of one kind or another.[8] The techniques varied from use of the ropes to cuffs of a ratchet type that could be tightened until they penetrated the flesh, sometimes down to the bone; aggravation of injuries received at ejection or upon landing, such as twisting a broken leg; forcing a man to sit or kneel for long periods of time without food or sleep; beatings with fanbelt-like whips and rifle butts; the application of an assortment of straps, bars, and chains to body pressure points; and

The "rope trick" in extremis. The pain and physical damage are described on pp. 147–48.

Refusal to write propaganda at a "quiz" often led to enforced kneeling. A pencil or pebble under the knee vastly magnified the pain.

To silence screaming, torturers sometimes stuffed filthy rags into the mouth with an iron pipe. Resistance would break teeth and rip the roof of the mouth.

PWs with "bad attitudes" could spend weeks in cuffs or leg irons, unable to lie flat or turn onto their sides. The only relief came at mealtime when their hands were cuffed in front, often numb and too swollen to use.

prolonged solitary confinement, often while in darkened quarters and/or in leg irons and manacles.[9] Just as Denton had discovered that the prison waste buckets, designed for Orientals, were too small for the American anatomy, so, too, were ankle stocks and wrist cuffs undersized—making even simple shackling painful and torture that much more excruciating.[10]

The Vietnamese developed a set routine, using room 18, in a corner of the Heartbreak section just outside New Guy Village, as the primary correction chamber. It was a large area, according to Stockdale about 25 feet by 30 feet, with soundproofed walls (painted at first blue, then ironically a sort of wardroom green, the color the Navy frequently chose for shipboard interiors presumably for its relaxing properties) and an array of menacing contraptions, the most imposing being a giant hook suspended from the ceiling. Cattycorner to room 18, in New Guy, was a second torture room known as the "Knobby Room" for its fist-sized knobs of plaster that had the effect of blunting if not completely muffling prisoner screams. This had been Bob Shumaker's old cell and in fact had become known to the PWs as "Shu's Room." By the spring of 1966 it had acquired a different notoriety.[11] The expert technician who presided over the torture program was a small but powerfully built man whom Stockdale remembered as utterly expressionless and consummately skilled. "Pigeye," or "Straps and Bars," as he would later be known, had put Knutson through the ropes and would shortly become a familiar figure to many others. Stockdale would "go into the ring" with him "8 or 9 times," until "he knew my tolerance for pain, and I knew his skill," the PW leader recalled. Pigeye appeared to take his orders directly from Major Bai, or "Cat," as the Americans called him, the imperious superintendent of the prison system. Whether Cat was the architect of the torture program or was following the instructions of some higher authority in the government, he took a keen personal interest in the program and closely supervised it. Denton described him as "a slender man in his middle forties," intelligent and well-read but a devoted follower of the party line, with "a sinister but somewhat handsome face" that was "accentuated by a merciless nature." "He loved his work," Denton remembered, "in contrast to many other North Vietnamese who loathed the torture or simply closed their eyes to it. He and Pigeye were a great team."[12]

It is difficult to overstate the pain that the American prisoners endured under this regime. Air Force Capt. Konrad Trautman, a 1967 shootdown who would be subjected to the rope treatment on a dozen separate occasions, related the experience in an interview soon after homecoming:

> Let me try to tell you what it really feels like when they tightly bind your wrists and elbows behind your back with nylon

straps*—then take the strap and pull the arms up, up your back, to the back of your head. If you can remember when you were a little boy, the fooling around you did, and someone grabs your hand and just twists your arm up to your back, and says: "Say Uncle." He does it with just one hand. And this, as you remember, is a very severe pain. Well, imagine this with both arms tied tight together—elbow to elbow, wrist to wrist—and then, using the leverage of his feet planted between your shoulder blades, with both hands, he pulls with all his might, 'til your arms are up and back over your head, forcing your head down between your feet, where your legs are between iron bars. The pain is literally beyond description . . . .

Besides the pain itself, you are tied up so tight that your windpipe becomes pinched and you breathe in gasps. You're trying to gulp in air, because your wind passage is being shrunken. Your throat, in a matter of 30 seconds, becomes completely dry . . . .

After about 10 or 15 minutes in this position, tied up so tightly, your nerves in your arms are pinched off, and then your whole upper torso becomes numb. It's a relief. You feel no more pain . . . . The breathing is still difficult, but the pain is gone. You've been anesthetized. However, when they release the ropes, the procedure works *completely* in reverse. It's almost like double jeopardy. You go through the same pain coming out of the ropes as you did going in.

Sometimes the ordeal would be compounded by the ineptness of torturers less proficient than Pigeye, or by the handlers' limited understanding of English which prevented them from realizing that a prisoner was surrendering. In the early months of the program, as in Knutson's case, the Vietnamese seemed satisfied simply to break the prisoner and pry loose any response at all. Later they would demand written apologies and signed confessions. Prior to a round of punishment the prisoner was given an opportunity to offer information as atonement for his transgression; if he refused, he was screwed or cinched a notch tighter; if he complied, the concession would be used to induce yet further cooperation at a later point. Stockdale described the process as "like a ratchet on an auto jack." Col. John Flynn, a 1967 capture who became the highest-ranking senior in the Northern camps, told a news conference upon his return home that after repeated torture sessions the Vietnamese "knew each one of us better than we knew ourselves . . . . They brought me to the point where if they asked me to shoot my own mother, I would have." Many a one prayed for death, but personnel were under strict orders not to lose any prisoners, hence inspiring the title of one of the first published accounts of captivity in Vietnam, Stephen A. Rowan's *They Wouldn't Let Us Die.*[13]

* By 1967, the Vietnamese had in most cases replaced rope with nylon straps, which they obtained from the parachutes of downed airmen.

Navy Cdr. Harry Jenkins, captured on 13 November 1965, was the first senior officer to experience at once the tougher treatment (even Risner, an early victim, had had several relatively easy weeks to settle in prior to the crackdown). Shot down near Dong Hoi, North Vietnam's southernmost major city, on his 133rd mission, Jenkins was brought to the Army head-quarters at Vinh, where an English-speaking officer recognized his name from American news dispatches and an article in *Stars and Stripes* that had identified him as a squadron commander and strike leader. When he reached Hanoi and Hoa Lo after a 10-day journey, including the stopover in Vinh, he was immediately taken to room 18, briefly questioned by the chain-smoking Eagle, then delivered to the Knobby Room, where manacles were clamped to his ankles and a heavy steel bar and several pieces of timber wcrc laid atop his legs. His wrists were tied behind him and his upper arms swathed in rope from the elbows to the shoulders. He lasted perhaps three hours until the wrenching pain and dehydration from soaking perspiration (as with Knutson, jailers had not bothered to remove his flight suit) forced him to cry out for help. Pigeye let him suffer for another 20 minutes before an interrogator entered to ask him if he was ready to talk. He gave the man some basic information, unclassified facts about his carrier and aircraft he was sure the Vietnamese already knew, whereupon guards relieved him from the torture rig. Another week of interrogation followed in which he was pressed for further details. When he again failed to hold the line at the "big four," he became, like Knutson, racked by a sense of dereliction and accompanying guilt—until contact with inmates in Heartbreak sometime later, among them his good friend Jim Stockdale, made him realize that he had been the first senior to be thrust into torture immediately and that others were being forced to bend as well.[14]

Indeed, the same day that the Vietnamese ended Jenkins's interroga-tion, on 29 November, they dragged in Navy Cdr. Howard Rutledge for a session with Pigeye. For three days, Rutledge, who had had to kill a machete-wielding villager at the time of his capture and was subsequently beaten savagely by a vengeful mob, was clubbed and rope-tortured until he, too, yielded. Deposited in Heartbreak, anguished by his capitulation, he was quickly consoled by Jenkins and Stockdale, the latter tapping to him, "Don't feel like the Lone Ranger." Stockdale and the others in the cellblock who had not yet been put on the rack—Chapman, Singleton, Air Force Capt. George McKnight, and Navy Lt. Cdr. James Hutton—wondered whether their number would come up next and whether they would do as well. Rutledge, who would go on to become a key operator in the communications network and a bellwether in the PW organization, would become a regular visitor to the correction chambers. "He was among the top four or

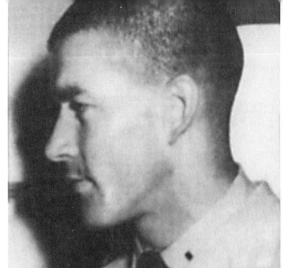

Early torture victims, *clockwise from top left,* Knutson, Gaither, Shankel, Reynolds, and Davis.

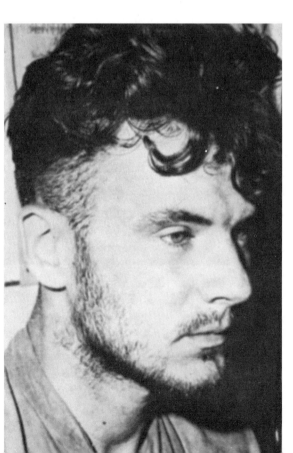

five prisoners in the amount and intensity of torture and mistreatment he received," Denton later noted, calling him a "marked man" because of his defiant attitude and involved activity.[15]

Going through room 18's revolving door about the same time as Jenkins and Rutledge was Air Force Capt. Jon Reynolds, who arrived at the Hilton just after Thanksgiving 1965. During a rough ejection, Reynolds had broken both arms just below the shoulder, fractured his jaw, and damaged his right leg. Because of the arm injuries, the rope torture was especially excruciating, causing him to submit early, though he managed to offer up more fiction than fact. Others terrorized at the Hilton during this period included Navy Lts. (j.g.) Wendell Alcorn, strung from No. 18's meathook after standing up to Eagle's black-coat-and-hat inquisition for a week, and William Shankel, whose dislocated knee was sadistically turned and twisted.[16]

Although the most intensive and sophisticated torture took place in Hoa Lo's specially equipped chambers, the extortion program was implemented elsewhere as well. At the Zoo, prisoners had not only rations but also bathing and latrine privileges abruptly curtailed and were abused at the slightest provocation. When Bob Shumaker was noticed leaning against a cell door, the guard accused him of attempting to escape and hauled him into a pitch-dark corner of the Zoo's "Auditorium," a building that had once housed a movie theater but now was filled with spider webs and crawling vermin and reeked with the stench of urine and excrement. The Vietnamese had constructed a punishment cell in the building with no bunk or mat and only a waste bucket that workers emptied once a day but did not clean. In this black-as-night, fetid stall, Shumaker suffered vertigo, terrible nausea, and an unremitting dysentery that further befouled the room and went unrelieved for two weeks until a guard brought him some pills.[17]

Ed Davis was placed on rations of bread and water and clamped in heavy leg irons and ratchet handcuffs for secretly communicating and refusing to sign a statement agreeing to abide by the new regulations. He managed to persevere when he found a nail in his cell with which he was able to manipulate the lock on the cuffs so that he could get some occasional relief and sleep. However, a new interrogator whom the PWs called "Frenchy" for his French accent (he was also known as "Harelip") made Davis "hold up the wall"—stand facing the wall for long periods with his hands held high—and continued the starvation diet, so that by the end of November the prisoner was down from a pre-capture weight of 165 pounds to a skeletal 110. When guards beat him and put him through the rope treatment, he finally conceded and gave Frenchy sketchy and evasive biographical information. Satisfied with this evidence of compliance, the interrogator dropped the demand for the signed statement.[18]

Ralph Gaither, separated from his radar operator Knutson at capture, was, at 23, the youngest officer at the Zoo when he arrived there in late October, about the time of the Risner incident that had precipitated the crackdown. When the Vietnamese discovered a peephole Gaither had carved into the door of his cell, they reacted viciously. Supervised by Rabbit, who was doing double duty at the Hilton and the Zoo, guards forced Gaither to kneel on the concrete floor for hours while they slapped him around with blows over the ears designed to break his eardrums. They threatened him with execution, then jabbed a bayonet into a wound on his neck. For five weeks he remained handcuffed, until transferred to Briarpatch in early December. Under the pressure of further interrogation and threatened with another round of punishment, he dissembled much like Knutson, telling examiners that his father was a Big Foot Indian, that his family worked for the B.S. Railroad, and that his wingman and briefing officer were named Dave Brubeck and Walter Winchell. When he was questioned again the next day, he announced that the biographical statements were lies and promised that if quizzed again he would concoct another story. Nonplused, the inquisitors withdrew for a time, leaving Gaither, for the moment, to savor a small victory.[19]

Actually, the PWs scored a number of moral victories in spite of the increased surveillance and suppression. At the Zoo, Denton, who replaced Risner as senior when the latter was carted back to Hoa Lo, pursued Risner's policies as best he could under the changed circumstances. Communications were throttled but not silenced, as the prisoners took advantage of guard mealtimes and siestas to transmit news of torture sessions to the uninitiated and words of support and encouragement to victims. Denton, now in Risner's old cell in the Barn, kept in touch with Davis, who was jailed next door, throughout his ordeal, concluding messages with the diverting signoff, ". . . brought to you by the makers of Denton's Odorless Honeybuckets, the Honeybucket with a lid." The SRO, Wes Schierman, and others in the cellblock created a commotion in an effort to get guards to let up on Davis, succeeding at least in summoning Frenchy for a resolution of Davis's fate. In a separate incident in the Zoo's Pigsty, when prison officials, in the company of a civilian inspector, harassed Larry Guarino, one of Guarino's mates several cells down attracted their attention with loud shouts for his wastecan; when the party rushed over to check the disturbance and flung open the door, they were greeted by a large puddle of excrement that sent them dashing off, ridding Guarino of his tormentors and affording the cellblock some much needed comic relief. On still another occasion, when a member of a North Vietnamese political delegation visited Denton and, referring to the fertilizer floating in his soup bowl, remarked contemptuously in English to the American, "Do you know that you are eating shit?," Denton retorted that he hoped there was "some protein in it." Risner and Stockdale, even as they awaited their fate on torture row at the Hilton, oriented new arrivals as they passed through Heartbreak and established a twice-a-day food "bulletin" that circulated the breakfast and dinner menus as the first meals were being delivered to the cellblock holding area. When guards left to take their own meals, the men were able to communicate freely for an hour or so until the keepers returned.[20]

Morale was boosted, too, by the continuing influx of new prisoners that soon crowded even the expanded facilities and forced the Vietnamese to limit solitary confinement to only a handful. Men who had been confined in lonely isolation for weeks, in some cases months, suddenly obtained roommates. Guarino was joined at the Zoo by Ron Byrne on 17 November. The next day Alvarez, who, except for an abbreviated stay with Guarino at Briarpatch in September, had been consigned to solitary from the time of his shootdown in August 1964, was placed with recent capture Air Force Lt. Thomas Barrett. Elated by the turn in his fortunes, Alvarez peppered Barrett with questions about life on the outside while the anxious newcomer pumped the veteran for a lowdown on prison conditions. On 23 December, Dog, perhaps as a Christmas gift, gave Alvarez a letter from his wife Tangee, the first he was allowed to receive since February. When he was given the opportunity to reply, but warned not to make any mention of Barrett, he included in the letter a reference to "Marcia," who, he told Dog, was his wife's niece but which in fact was the name of Barrett's fiancee. Naval Intelligence analysts in Washington, forwarded the letter by Tangee, soon deduced that Barrett, who had been reported missing, was alive and rooming with Alvarez in Hanoi.[21]

The onset of the Christmas holiday, at the same time that President Johnson ordered a bombing pause, ostensibly for the purpose of fostering peace negotiations, brought a respite from the terror in late December. In general, the prisoners' food improved, interrogation sessions were less intense, and punishment abated some. "Full portions of bread and rice returned," Denton noted the turnabout at the Zoo, "and they were now washing the feces off the cabbage, and serving the soup hot!" The Vietnamese distributed blankets, sweatshirts, and sandals*—perhaps in a

---

* Up to this point, although Alvarez and some of the earliest shootdowns had been issued sandals, most of the prisoners had not worn shoes since the removal of their flight boots at capture. They would not be issued socks until well into 1966. See Myers, *Vietnam POW Camp Histories*, vol 1, 129-30. In the South, under the Viet Cong, there were prisoners who went barefoot during their entire captivity (see p. 84n).

Holiday letup: *left to right*, Byrne, Cormier, and Guarino with priest, Christmas 1965.

First 1966 shootdowns Grubb (left) and Coffee.

concession to the Christmas spirit, no doubt partly to insure that their hostages would survive the cold winter ahead while lying on cement bunks and floors. Prison officials called off their goons and engaged in casual conversation with the PWs. On Christmas Day, Risner, only recently out of torture, was ushered into Cat's office at the Hilton for candy and a congenial talk; afterwards, Cat called in Stockdale for tea and a discussion of their mutual responsibility to help "bring this imperialist war to an end"; over at the Zoo, Frenchy chatted pleasantly with Rivers. All the prisoners received a Christmas dinner of turkey, fresh vegetables and salad, cookies or fruit, and, depending on the location, a half-bottle of beer, cup of rice wine, or coffee. As an added bonus, inmates at the Zoo were treated to baths, shaves, and haircuts; for Commander Rutledge, who had been transferred from Hoa Lo on Christmas Eve, these were his first since his capture a month earlier.[22]

From the quiet over Hanoi, contact with recent shootdowns who knew of the plan, or simply observing the sudden absence of new faces entering the system, most of the Americans were aware of the bombing halt. Although they of course welcomed the breathing spell, few were under any illusions that it signaled a change of heart or a genuine reversal of policy on the part of their captors. There were ample reminders of the enemy's treachery. Risner momentarily let his guard down during the visit with Cat, then realized the meeting was being staged and photographed for propaganda consumption. Frenchy had Rivers escorted to the camp library after their chat, hoping his cordiality and the holiday favors would make his quarry more receptive to the stacks of Communist reading materials there. On Christmas Eve, Catholics Guarino, Byrne, and Art Cormier were permitted to leave the Zoo and travel to the Hilton to see a priest for confession and Holy Communion—but accompanied by the officious Rabbit, who, upon delivering them, insisted that they confess their "crimes" against the Vietnamese people; only the priest's intervention separated Rabbit from the ceremony, as the clergyman absolved the three fliers and dispensed communion wafers to them. Although authorities promised mail privileges for good behavior, except in rare instances—the Alvarez case, a letter Guarino received from his wife, an exchange of messages between Stockdale and his wife (granted by Cat in his effort to soft-sell the senior before resorting to torture), and letters dictated by interrogators—they continued to confiscate incoming and prohibit outgoing correspondence.* Perhaps with more mischief than malevolence, Dog broke in the Zoo's new loudspeaker system

* Rob Doremus, captured in August 1965, was not allowed to write home until November 1966 and did not receive a letter until Christmas Day, 1967. Rivers did not receive his first letter until April 1967. Their experience, judging from an examination of debriefings, was typical.

with a violin rendition of "Smoke Gets in Your Eyes," broadcast over and over, to remind the PWs of their flaming ejections; Denton found Dog's twitting uncharacteristically "droll" for the Vietnamese, but others doubtlessly did not appreciate the black humor.[23]

When the Johnson administration extended the bombing moratorium through January, the Vietnamese may have concluded that the American government was weakening in its resolve and was on the verge of abandoning the fight. Possibly looking to the winding down of the war and the impending release of the prisoners, perhaps marking their own Tet holiday with continued indulgences, officials at the Zoo ordered complete physical exams for the men there. When doctors showed concern over the PWs' loss of weight, the officials doubled the men's rations and upgraded the food. Further, they ventilated cells to admit some light and air, gave more attention to hygiene and sanitation, and for the most part maintained the lenient treatment. The reprieve, however, lasted barely a month. Before long it became clear that the bombing pause was more an exercise in public relations than a serious peace initiative. Hanoi and Washington remained hopelessly deadlocked, Johnson and Ho Chi Minh making impossible demands of each other, so that the military stalemate was matched by a diplomatic impasse. Finally, on 31 January, after a suspension of 37 days, the U.S. air attacks resumed, and with their renewal, the persecution of the American prisoners of war recommenced as well.[24]

During 1966 almost 100 U.S. airmen would be added to the PW rolls in the North—compared with 63 captured in 1965. The magnitude and nature of the additions reflected both the ongoing escalation of the war and the changing complexion of U.S. strategy that would find the Air Force flying a steadily increasing number of missions into North Vietnam. Although Navy aviators would bear the brunt of the shootdowns during the first four months of 1966, starting in May Air Force casualties began to catch up as the service's role in the air war expanded. By year's end, the roster of 1966 captures would include twice as many Air Force as Navy personnel. Also of significance, as the year progressed, an increasing proportion of those falling into captivity would be junior officers, in the main Air Force lieutenants and captains, a factor that contributed to the growing prominence of the original seniors, who acquired more influence and responsibility as they struggled to fill the leadership vacuum. The seniormost naval officer claimed in 1966, Cdr. John Abbott, died shortly after being taken prisoner. The highest-ranking Air Force officers were Lt. Col. James Lamar and Maj. Norman Schmidt; Schmidt would be killed by the Vietnamese or die in prison—the circumstances are not clear—a year after his capture. All told, including juniors and seniors, eight of the 1966 group would die in captivity,* evidence of the return to hard times following the Christmas-Tet lull.[25]

The first American airman to be seized in North Vietnam in the new year, Air Force Capt. Wilmer Grubb, apprehended on 26 January, succumbed nine days later, reportedly from a ruptured spleen and other injuries sustained while parachuting.[26] The second American taken prisoner in the North in 1966 was Navy Lt. Gerald Coffee, downed on a photo reconnaissance flight near Vinh on 3 February and fished out of a small bay by Vietnamese militiamen the same day.† It was Coffee's unfortunate lot to fall into Vietnamese hands just as the enemy was resuming the torture program in earnest. En route to Hanoi, the pilot's captors subjected him to a mock execution and a savage version of the rope treatment wherein he was gagged and dangled from a tree. His right arm having been broken and elbow dislocated during ejection, he endured an hour of paralyzing pain in the ropes before satisfying interrogators with trivializing answers to questions about his aircraft and carrier. At that, he fared better than his navigator, Lt. (j.g.) Robert Hanson, who had bailed out and landed in the water with him; a guard informed Coffee that Hanson had been killed.[27] Once at Hoa Lo, Coffee was pestered with more interrogation and indoctrination and wrote an apology for the American air attacks in order to get treatment for his badly swollen arm. In Heartbreak he and two fellow Navy aviators also seized in February, Lt. Cdr. Render Crayton and Lt. (j.g.) Larry Spencer, came under the guidance of SRO Risner, who taught them the tap code, filled them in on prison procedures, and braced them for the trials they would likely face next.[28]

Following Coffee, Crayton, and Spencer into the Hilton was Navy Cdr. James Mulligan. Mulligan, who suffered a broken shoulder and cracked ribs when ejecting from his smoking A-4 Skyhawk, had spent a nightmarish week traveling to Hanoi in the custody of local militia and then a rough band of Army regulars. During the journey, he was lugged blindfolded and without shoes over gravelly roads, pelted by crowds at stopovers, and exhibited before spectators at a circus-like arena. When he was switched to a truck and the vehicle pulled up to refuel outside the capital, one of the soldiers, to entertain passersby, poured gasoline over deep gashes in his

---

* Besides Abbott and Schmidt, Marine Corps WO John Frederick, Navy Lts. James Connell and Terry Dennison, and Air Force Capt. Wilmer Grubb and Majs. Gene Pemberton and Benjamin Newsom.
† Navy Lt. (j.g.) Dieter Dengler had gone down in Laos two days earlier and been captured by Pathet Lao on 2 February. See Chapter 3.

wrists that had been left by the leash used to haul him earlier. Entering Heart-break in a delirious state the last week in March, he was moved to New Guy upon regaining consciousness.

There, denied food and medical attention, made to sit in a crouch-ing position between quizzes, his damaged wrists tied so tightly his hands became black and numb and pus oozed from the broken flesh, Mulligan was harangued by Rabbit and Mickey Mouse and tortured by Pigeye until, force-fed coffee to stay lucid, he taped a "confession" of his crimes. At a nearby hospital facility a physician finally treated his shoulder and wrists and ordered fresh clothing and food for him, but Mulligan balked when the Vietnamese wanted to operate on the shoulder. He had made contact with Stockdale, who warned him against surgery based on his own experi-ence when Vietnamese doctors had attempted unsuccessfully to mend his bad leg. Mickey Mouse accepted Mulligan's refusal to return to the hospital and instead had him transferred to the Zoo.[29]

The latest move was hardly calculated to provide relief. By the time Mulligan arrived at the Zoo in April, conditions at the suburban camp had reverted fully to the murderous atmosphere existing prior to the holi-day recess. Indeed, before the close of January, two Zoo inmates, Wendell Alcorn and "Skip" Brunhaver, had already experienced the new wave of terror there. Alcorn, who had been sent to the camp at the end of Decem-ber, after having spent a difficult week at Hoa Lo following his capture, was strapped to a torture machine that applied pressure by degrees and would have snapped his arm at the elbow had he not complied with Rab-bit's demand for biographical data. Brunhaver, a resident of the Zoo since its opening in September, had become a key man in the camp's communi-cation system as a result of his central location next to a shower room and his contact with a Thai prisoner who enjoyed considerable freedom of movement about the camp and supplied the Americans with valuable in-telligence. Whether Brunhaver was targeted by the Vietnamese for his suspected activities, or, as seems the case, he simply became the victim of a widening, indiscriminate purge whereby the enemy was now torturing even without pretext and for the most routine information, the aviator was dragged to the Auditorium starting on 31 January for a series of grueling extortion sessions. Severely beaten, placed in "hellcuffs" that were clamped high on the forearm and designed to cut off circulation, trussed in ropes for 16 consecutive hours, then having the atrocities repeated day after day for a week, Brunhaver finally broke when, denied all but minimal food and water during the entire period, he was down to little more than 100 pounds and losing his mental faculties. Even then he gave only a smatter-ing of biographical information, much of it false or misleading.[30]

The spring thaw in Hanoi did nothing to mellow the Viets' mood or moderate treatment. Prisoners throughout the system were now being tortured and starved to elicit biography. In a section of the Zoo known as the "Pool Hall," Jon Reynolds (moved there from the Hilton in late December) and Air Force mates Capt. James Hivner and Lt. Robert Jeffrey were able to hold on for a spell when Bob Purcell risked climbing through the access panel in the ceiling of his cell and carried scraps of food and water to them through an attic crawl space. Purcell, who himself had been starved and done time in cuffs and irons for refusing to bow, ran his "catering service" during siesta, narrowly returning to his bunk before the guards made their rounds. Bill Shankel, in the Zoo's Pigsty since late January, went a full week in March without food or water until producing a sham autobiography—"a combination of the lives of Errol Flynn and Cary Grant," his debriefer later observed. In April, Rod Knutson, who the previous October at Hoa Lo had been the first of the PWs to experience the rope torture, underwent several days of abuse in the Zoo's Auditorium and another building behind the Pigsty that the PWs called the "Outhouse" for its overwhelming stench. A new officer whom the Americans named "Dum Dum" (also known as "J.C." for his strutting demeanor) along with two new guards named "Slim" and "Magoo" (the latter resembling the cartoon character) subjected Knutson to a battery of horrors—ratchet cuffs, hours locked in the Outhouse fending off hoards of mosquitos, vicious beatings, gaggings, and finally the ropes—until, his wrists cut to the bone and his fortitude once more drained, he scratched out a personal history, repeating to the best of his recollection the nonsense tale he had supplied earlier about his upbringing on a chicken farm and shipboard duties as a recreation officer. Forced to write an apology as well for insulting Fox, now commander at the Zoo, Knutson scrawled an ambiguous response: "I have been told that I have violated camp regulations . . . and I promise to do a better job in the future . . . ."[31]

In terms of prolonged misery, no prisoners suffered more than the men confined at Briarpatch, the primitive camp situated in the mountains west of Hanoi that had been reopened in December. PWs here were housed in tiny seven feet by ten feet pens in brick huts that had no electricity or plumbing. Even after renovations were made and a bathing area constructed in February, with water drawn from a well, the captives were restricted to one bath every 10 days (usually without soap), a shave every four to six weeks (with five men on a blade), and a haircut every two to three months. During both Christmas and Tet the men had received generous holiday meals but otherwise the fare was limited to a small plate of rice and a small bowl of greens or cabbage soup twice a day with an occasional banana. Unlit cells and shuttered windows accentuated the gloom. A dozen Americans* huddled through the raw winter in perpetual darkness with only thin cotton blankets for warmth. When Ed Davis refused to write a biography, he was pummeled about the face, manacled in torture cuffs, put through the ropes, and made to sit on a concrete stool for a week until he conceded. Navy Lt. Cdr. James Bell was chained to his bed for 35 days. Springtime brought more light and milder weather but even harsher treatment. Ralph Gaither was beaten for getting a drop of water on a jailer's pants while washing dishes. Gaither later recalled the nervous wait for one's turn in the torture chamber as Briarpatch officials systematically terrorized the prisoners to obtain information: "I knew my turn was coming . . . as the men in cells down the hill from me were taken in order . . . to the torture rooms. I could hear my turn coming, and feel it, as cell by cell the ominous pain moved up the hill toward me." By June, additional transfers from the Zoo more than doubled the camp's population,† and the remote compound was becoming a busy interrogation and indoctrination mill.[32]

Both juniors and seniors were victimized following the holiday hiatus, but when the velvet glove was discarded, the fist fell hardest on the senior officers. Jerry Denton, who had been starved and placed in irons but not tortured through the fall of 1965, finally had his "first taste of real brutality" in February. After several unsatisfactory quizzes with Owl and Eagle, he was marched to the Zoo's Auditorium, where, under the supervision of a husky guard he named "Smiley" (also known as "Pigeon"), he was assaulted repeatedly, isolated in darkness, and ratcheted in cuffs so violently that it would take four men three hours to remove them from his shattered wrists. Hallucinating and incontinent, he haltingly scribbled a biography, endeavoring to "concoct a mixture of truth and fiction that would deliver me from that dark room." Deliverance came but it was short-lived. In April, the Vietnamese, angered by his continued resistance and his "inciting" of others, brought Denton to the Hilton for an extended session with Pigeye in which he was mauled, starved, and tortured into unconsciousness. When

* Navy captives James Bell, Ed Davis, Ralph Gaither, John McKamey, Dennis Moore, and Bill Tschudy; Air Force captives Willis Forby, Paul Kari, Scotty Morgan, Wes Schierman, Thomas Sima, and Ron Storz. McKamey, Tschudy, Kari, Morgan, and Storz had been among the original group sent to Briarpatch at its opening in the summer of 1965. They spent autumn at the Zoo, then were returned to Briarpatch in December.
† Nine PWs arrived in April: Phil Butler and David Wheat (Navy); Thomas Barrett, Thomas Collins, Thomas Curtis, George Hall, James Hivner, Hayden Lockhart, and George McKnight (Air Force). In May came Navy aviators Alcorn, Alvarez, and Brunhaver and Air Force fliers Brudno, Jeffrey, Robinson, and Singleton. Another dozen would be sent to Briarpatch in June: Frederick Baldock, Glenn Daigle, John Heilig, Rod Knutson, and Bradley Smith (Navy); Arthur Black, Larry Chesley, Daniel Doughty, Warren Lilly, James Ray, and Bruce Seeber (Air Force); and Marine PW Harlan Chapman.

he awoke, his dislocated fingers were propped around a pen and he was made to write a confession of crimes and then tape a similar statement.[33]

Jim Stockdale had been left alone for the most part in the Heartbreak section of the Hilton following his incarceration in September 1965, allowed time to recover from the injuries sustained during ejection and capture. Cat, however, decided immediately after Christmas to concentrate on breaking him and Colonel Risner, both to derive maximum propaganda advantage from the seniors' capitulation and to set an example for the younger men entering Hoa Lo. To underscore the importance he attached to the effort, the prison superintendent assigned four guards and two inter-rogators, Rabbit and Mickey Mouse, full-time to the task. In January, still on crutches, Stockdale was locked in leg irons and then tortured in ropes until acquiescing to Rabbit's demand for a letter, addressed to the "U.S. For-eign Secretary of State," denouncing the American involvement as illegal and immoral.* Rabbit kept up the pressure through the remainder of the winter and into the spring, applying the ropes to force the crippled flier to complete biographical forms and confessions of misdeeds. Now stashed in an isolated cell in New Guy Village between visits to the Knobby Room, Stockdale waged a war of nerves with his tormentors, stymieing the extor-tion effort with both intransigence and cleverness. When compelled to read a prepared propaganda statement before a camera, he gestured with his first and fourth fingers extended to signal the intent of his remarks. (He would later say that "indispensable attributes in this deadly game of extortion and pain are not only tough-mindedness and physical courage, but skill in the dramatic arts as well.") By the end of May, Cat apparently felt he had gotten as much as he could out of the hard-nosed senior. Stock-dale was permitted his first shower since being shot down nine months before. Early in June 1966, together with recent captures Air Force senior Jim Lamar and Maj. Samuel Johnson, he was jeeped to the Garage section of the Zoo,[†] where he would remain until January 1967.[34]

Robinson Risner—known affectionately as "Robbie" to his Air Force buddies and gradually, as word spread of his heroism, to scores of admiring

---

* Stockdale persuaded Rabbit to have the letter addressed instead to the Navy Department, where he knew superiors familiar with his style would easily be able to detect a spoof. He then proceeded to write a flowery piece replete with double meanings, obscure phrasing, and veiled ridicule. The Vietnamese never used the letter, nullifying Stockdale's effective ruse.

† Stockdale arrived at the Zoo only two days behind Denton, who had been escorted back there on 2 June after winding up his detention at the Hilton. Although senior to Denton, Stockdale was unable to assume command at the Zoo because of the presence of two Thais in an adjacent cell who could not or would not speak English and thus removed him for a time from the com-munication chain. Denton, therefore, resumed command, until Risner, too, was returned later in June. See Denton, *When Hell Was In Session*, 104-05; Stockdale, *In Love and War*, 185-86.

comrades throughout the North Vietnamese camps—absorbed as much or more punishment between November 1965 and the summer of 1966 as many of the men would face during their entire PW term. He had been one of the first victims of the torture program and, owing to both his reputation and his uncompromising stance, remained a prime target throughout the extortion era. Following the October raid on Ron Storz's cell that had identified him as the Zoo's resistance ringleader, he had been hauled off to Hoa Lo for disciplining. Over the next six weeks, almost without letup until the eve of the holiday season, he was exposed to every correctional device and tactic in the enemy's repertoire. He spent the whole month of November and into December, all told 32 consecutive days, in leg stocks with only a daily piece of bread and sip of water for subsistence, forced to lie in his own filth when he lost control of his bowels. Released from the stocks, he was blindfolded with heavy pads so tightly they "seemed as if they were driving my eyeballs right back into my head," dragged through an obstacle course studded with large trees and open drainage ditches, then herded indoors again to be cinched in ropes. Failing to knock himself out by purposely slamming his head against the cement floor, he endured horrendous pain for what seemed an eternity before screaming for relief and agreeing to write an apology. During the respite that followed he made contact with Stockdale in the next-door cell in Heartbreak and gave the Navy commander lessons in the tap code and precious information on Americans at the Zoo. Jon Reynolds, a recent shootdown, brought news of Risner's promotion to full colonel. Apparently, the Vietnamese were aware of the fact also, as around this time, in mid-December, they assigned Risner to washing dishes in an obvious attempt to degrade him. The famished prisoner relished the job, however, as it offered a chance for leftover scraps as well as an opportunity to leave his cell and communicate more freely.[35]

Risner enjoyed a relatively lenient interlude from Christmas through March while Cat was busy with Stockdale. It was during this period that he coached Coffee, Crayton, and Spencer as well as others in the steady stream of new faces passing through the Hilton, dispensing advice and encouragement to the newcomers and then employing them as messengers to convey tidings and instructions to Jerry Denton at the Zoo when, some days or weeks later, they were transferred there. With the approach of spring he felt the pressure increasing again and grew uneasy—for good reason. When Cat finished with Stockdale, he turned Rabbit and Mickey Mouse loose on Risner, and another round of torture began for the tough airman.

Cat had asked Risner to read a prepared newscast on the camp radio. When Risner refused and then compounded the "error" by attempting to communicate with a Vietnamese prisoner, Cat had his henchmen put the American on his knees for two days without food or water. When he was offered another chance and refused again to read, Mickey Mouse ordered a guard to tie him in the ropes. Knowing the ordeal that lay ahead, Risner decided to try to outsmart the Vietnamese while he still had his wits, agreeing to cooperate and using a three-day breather to plan ways to defeat the propaganda effort. He considered killing himself or severing the tendons in his hands so that they could not force him to write a confession, but realizing "it was my voice they wanted most," he determined to damage his vocal cords. When pounding his larynx proved unavailing, he dissolved a portion of his soap bar in a cup of water and gargled, hoping the lye in the soap would inflame his throat and destroy his voice. The acid left his mouth "a raw mess" and his throat "sore as a boil," but he could still talk when Mickey Mouse showed up with a recorder and script. Threatened once more with the rope treatment, he began to read the furnished material. However, he mispronounced words, ignored punctuation, and muttered in a German accent that rendered the tape almost useless. Mickey Mouse recognized the fakery and warned the prisoner he was not through with him, promising another session, but in the meantime the haggard Risner had survived a second round. In June the senior was moved back to the Zoo, where the duel with the enemy would shortly be resumed.[36]

Despite courageous, often ingenious resistance, Denton, Stockdale, and Risner in the end all capitulated to some extent, as had dozens of their junior comrades by the summer of 1966. Jim Mulligan later testified that the North Vietnamese managed to obtain statements from 80 percent of the American prisoners over the duration of the war.[37] For the Risners and Stockdales and others in the early group of captures—those seized during the first two years of the fighting in the North—the odds on holding out were particularly long. Their rapidly growing but still relatively small numbers enabled the Vietnamese to interrogate them more intensively and torture them more methodically, and repeat the process many more times, than would generally be the case with prisoners arriving in later years. Thus, although some in the early group would be among the staunchest resisters, they also were exceedingly vulnerable; for an inescapable fact of confinement in North Vietnam after the inauguration of the torture era was that if the captor exerted enough pressure and turned the screws tight enough, no one, not even the most defiant and strong-willed, could resist indefinitely. Each of the men had a different threshold of pain, but all had an eventual breaking point.

When they broke, the PWs—seniors and rank and file alike—no sooner recovered from their physical trauma than they had to confront another torment that often proved as agonizing as the torture itself. In acquiescing to the enemy's demand for information or a confession, they had violated what they understood to be the cardinal principle of the U.S. military Code of Conduct, which stipulated that, no matter the circumstance, prisoners were to furnish only their identity and nothing more. The acute shame and guilt experienced by the earliest extortion victims—Shumaker, Knutson, Jenkins, Rutledge, Davis—was common more or less to all those who would succumb. The American aviators had assumed that their stalwart sense of duty and superior conditioning, including survival school training, would prepare them to meet whatever test the enemy offered. Only when they realized that that training, and the Code of Conduct, had presumed at least minimal observance by the enemy of the protections guaranteed prisoners of war under the Geneva Convention were the sense of having betrayed their country and subsequent despondency relieved some. As more inmates were victimized and the extent of the extortion, and the "breaking," became more widely known, the conscience-stricken were reassured that they had not been singularly weak or derelict, and the self-recriminating soul-searching was replaced by a growing questioning of the worth and validity of the Code itself. As each of the men had his appointment with Pigeye, the Code increasingly seemed to be a noble but meaningless abstraction that paled into irrelevance before the harrowing reality of the ropes and stocks.

Gradually, then, as the prisoners were subjected to increasingly brutal persecution in 1965 and 1966, a more relaxed attitude toward the Code began to emerge and a more flexible standard of conduct became generally accepted. As Stockdale, who was instrumental in developing the guidelines, later observed: "As POW's who were treated not as POW's but as common criminals, we sailed uncharted waters . . . . The Code did not provide for our day to day existence; we wrote the laws we had to live by . . . . We set a line of resistance we thought was within the capability of each POW to hold, and we [the leaders] ruled that no man would cross that line without significant torture."

A practical problem for the leadership became the determination of what exactly constituted acceptable behavior and then transmitting the modified resistance policy through the camps. There evolved a fundamental set of rules, widely disseminated and understood, that directed the prisoners to resist to the point of permanent injury or loss of mental faculty, and then fall back on deceit and distortion, keeping all coerced answers and activity to a minimum. Denton, who held to a particularly strict standard, instructed his men to "die before writing anything classified," but for personal biographies and such, "take torture and before you lose your sanity, write something harmless and ludicrous." If broken, Denton advised, "don't despair. Bounce back as soon as you can to the hard line."[38]

Even Denton made concessions to common sense and individual discretion in certain situations. Both he and Stockdale gave perfunctory nods to
satisfy the Vietnamese bowing requirement so that they could save energy
for resistance on more substantive issues. Evasions and stalls were permitted
for the purpose of disrupting interrogation or avoiding further punishment, and improvisational techniques—mispronunciations, finger gestures,
reading in monotone, blinking signals with the eyes, and other devices—were
encouraged to nullify the effect of a taping or filming under duress. (The
Vietnamese were so preoccupied with the content of a response, or the very
act of prisoner submission, that they frequently overlooked hidden signals
and telling mannerisms.) However, Denton cautioned his men not to get too
cute, reminding them that any information volunteered—however seemingly
innocuous or utterly false—could be taken out of context and exploited by
the enemy. From his own experience, when he inadvertently supplied Dog
with information on his family that subsequently went out over the Hanoi
airwaves, he knew the risks of going beyond "the big four."[39]

In sum, then, resistance would continue to be based in principle on
adherence to the rigorous requirements of the Code of Conduct, but it was
understood that sticking to the "big four" was the heroic ideal and not an
absolute imperative. In Stockdale's words, the Code of Conduct remained
"the star that guided us."[40] The realistic objective became one of holding
out as long as possible, then giving as little as possible, and using the breathing spell that normally followed a period of torture to recover strength for
the next bout. If everyone abided by this policy, the leaders believed, the
Vietnamese would consume more and more time completing their interrogations and wresting confessions, thus frustrating the enemy's propaganda
agenda, compelling him to divert valuable personnel and other resources
from the larger war effort, and gaining for the Americans precious days
and weeks while the expanding PW population further taxed the enemy's
logistics and stretched out the extortion program. The latter especially would
be no small accomplishment as the captors' alleged "humane and lenient treatment" degenerated ever more savagely into cruel and unusual punishment.

9

Indoctrination: Torturing the Mind

The torture program had the twin goals of disrupting PW resistance and obtaining statements that could be exploited for propaganda purposes. A more subtle tactic directed at the same ends was indoctrination—an ongoing process of "education" or "reeducation" that predated the torture era and that continued (somewhat paradoxically, since one of the indoctrinators' principal ploys was the "humane and lenient" line) through the worst abuses. If torture was intended to intimidate and beat the Americans into submission, indoctrination was designed to confuse them, to sow doubts and misgivings among them as to the legitimacy of the U.S. involvement and the superiority of American values and institutions. The one worked on their bodies; the other, more insidiously, on their minds.

Indoctrination, of course, did not originate with the North Vietnamese. The concept of converting prisoners to one's cause through political education and psychological manipulation has a long history dating in this century at least as far back as World War I, when the Germans attempted to segregate and recruit Irish inmates in their British PW camps and the Turks likewise sought to sway the Muslims among their Indian Army captives.[1] It was the Chinese Communists, as they consolidated their intensely ideological regime in the late 1940s and early 1950s, who instituted indoctrination as a routine and systematic practice, aimed at converting the unsusceptible as well as the susceptible among their prisoners and political enemies, and who refined techniques to include so-called "brainwashing" and a Pavlovian calculus of rewards and punishments.

Writing in 1956 about the Chinese handling of American PWs during the Korean War, Edgar Schein might have been describing a scenario for the American PW experience in Vietnam in the 1960s, so striking were the similarities. The Chinese, Schein noted, told their American captives in Korea that they were misguided innocents "tricked into fighting for an evil capitalist society" in a faraway "civil war"; promised leniency if the prisoners would only avail themselves of the opportunity through education for enlightenment and repentance; used interrogation "in a didactic way" to encourage discussion and explore the PWs' values and beliefs; had prisoners write autobiographies as a means both to obtain exploitable information and to spur self-examination; designated PWs as "reactionaries" or "progressives" depending on their willingness to listen and study, and geared their treatment accordingly; carefully controlled news and information access by stacking camp libraries with Marxist materials and limiting PW contacts with the outside world to interviews with Communist correspondents; and used the device of repetition to both reinforce instruction and exhaust the prisoners mentally.[2] Although Vietnamese Communists never adopted the most extreme Chinese methods and were sensitive to accusations of "brainwashing" in view of the notoriety the Chinese excesses received in the international press, indoctrination became a vital element of their PW operations and they borrowed freely from their ideological mentors.[3] We have already seen how the Viet Minh took their cue from the Chinese in their efforts to indoctrinate French PWs. The North Vietnamese, and the Viet Cong in the South, would follow much the same example with their American captives, and, for that matter, often with political opponents among their own people.

Like Mao Tse-tung, Ho Chi Minh attached such importance to the indoctrination effort and to the political warfare (what the American military would call "psywar") function generally that he placed the latter on the same organizational level as Operations, Logistics, and Personnel—coequal with the major military functions and commanded by men of rank equal with that of other commanders—and assigned it a principal role in the prosecution of strategy. Most of the PW camps in North Vietnam in fact had two "commanders," one the nominal camp commander, who was a Regular Army officer responsible for routine administrative matters such as maintenance and supply, and the other the camp's chief "political officer," who represented the political department in Hanoi and was in charge of interrogation and indoctrination. In an intricate bureaucratic arrangement, the indoctrination responsibility was divided between the Enemy Proselytizing Section of the Political Warfare Office in the Ministry of National Defense and a correlative agency in the Ministry of Public Security.[4]

In the North (owing to obvious logistical disadvantages, the Viet Cong in the South was not nearly so well organized), a prisoner almost immediately upon capture would be interviewed by a provincial or regional political officer to determine his exploitation potential. The examiner prepared a "Preliminary Personal Record" that described the behavior of the PW upon capture and his attitude toward his captors. The Vietnamese used this initial evaluation to classify prisoners according to temperament and posture and to plan a suitable course of treatment. Age, rank, and physical condition at capture were also important determinants of treatment, but the "Preliminary Personal Record," an interrogator-indoctrinator's first impressions of an American arrival, could serve for years as a basis for camp assignments and handling of the individual. The prisoners had no knowledge of these reports—only after homecoming did they learn of their existence through captured enemy intelligence accounts—and so they were often at a loss to explain what seemed to be at times mere caprice on the part of their handlers. Ralph Gaither, trying to comprehend why some of the men in his group were placed together and others placed in solitary, was totally baffled. "We soon quit trying to figure out why the Vietnamese did what they did. Their logic was completely unfathomable," he concluded, not realizing how deliberate actually were the Vietnamese tactics.[5]

The debriefings of returning PWs offer no clear-cut consensus as to the quality of Vietnamese interrogation and indoctrination personnel. Hanoi apparently assigned its most capable people to the task, both because of the priority the government accorded the function and because officials knew that only well-trained specialists would be a match for the better educated Americans; moreover, as an informant submitted, the Vietnamese were sensitive to being considered a backward nation and were as eager to impress as to convert the Americans. Often senior officials handled senior PWs: the ongoing contest between Cat and Stockdale became a classic duel between two consummate professionals. Even the most qualified Vietnamese indoctrinators, however, were hampered by limited language skills and lack of familiarity with American customs and institutions. Lt. Cdr. John McCain III, a prominent 1967 shootdown, remembered trying to explain the concept of Easter to a new interrogator:

> I thought maybe I could do some good here, so I said, "We believe there was a guy who walked the earth, did great things, was killed, and three days later, he rose from the dead and went up into heaven." The guy gave me a very puzzled look, and asked me to explain that again—and again. Then he left the room. A few minutes later, he came back and said, "The other officers tell me you tell nothing but lies, so go back to your room before I have you beat."[6]

Over the years their command of English and grasp of American practices would improve considerably, but a certain naivete would always persist.

"Their awe of paper and writing mystified me," Gaither later wrote, betraying his own cultural prejudices. "They could not understand that when you force a statement out of a man by physical abuse that it is not binding. But their Army life was built around repentance and confession . . . ." Gaither "couldn't help but laugh" at some of the enemy's observations, "like the comment, 'Zohnson must really be hurting for pilots to have an ensign flying a F-4.' They really believed they were shooting down every plane that flew over North Vietnam and that we were running out of pilots." Wendy Rivers later ridiculed attempts to indoctrinate him as "gross and completely unbeliev- able," remarking that "it seemed the indoctrinators would discuss anything with the PWs just to have an opportunity to practice and learn better English." Larry Guarino said "they mixed reality with fiction as though it were all true. It was very difficult for us to separate the real bullshit from the imaginary bullshit." In fact there were many Vietnamese political officers who earned the respect of the Americans and who, despite their relatively primitive ways, managed to win more than a few rounds in the psychological war.[7]

The distinction between "interrogation" and "indoctrination," where one left off and the other began, was blurred by the Vietnamese to the point of insignificance. By definition the former refers to the *extracting* or *eliciting* of information, the latter to the *imparting* of information. But in practice in the Vietnamese camps they became flip sides of the same seamless process, closely intertwined and conducted usually by the same personnel. Interrogator- indoctrinators might commence by asking specifically for military information— for example, pressing a downed pilot to describe the instrumentation in the airplane he was flying—but inevitably the inquiry would at some interval come around to an articulation of the Communist cause and denunciation of the Americans. The PWs referred to all their encounter sessions with the enemy as "quizzes," a popular catch-all term that could be easily abbreviated to "qz" for transmission by tap code, but in general, especially after the initial post-capture grilling, the Vietnamese were interested less in obtaining speci- fic answers than in checking attitudes and encouraging dialogues that might yield propaganda plums or relax the prisoner's hardline posture. The process was so subtle and subliminal that an examinee was often unaware that a meeting had drifted from an orderly interrogation into exhortation and rambling discourse.[8]

Zealous as their proctors were, the prisoners were convinced that the Vietnamese were trying not so much to "convert" them per se as to jade their senses and instill certain precepts that would become, through constant dril- ling, a part of their own intellectual mindset. (Ron Byrne later remarked that most of the Americans "knew more distorted V history than they did

American history.") So that, whether they accepted the cant or not, the PWs could recite it chapter and verse, parroting Communist slogans and doctrines either when physically compelled or, unwittingly, by simple force of habit in the course of conversation with the enemy. Coming from *their* mouths, such pronouncements, as enhanced by Hanoi's media specialists, could produce stunning propaganda. "It is doubtful," Byrne observed,

> that anyone was actually persuaded to the North Vietnamese
> national viewpoint. There was some success, however, in getting
> PWs to retain the information presented. Many PWs could repeat
> the V line almost verbatim, although it was normally referred to
> in a humorous or sarcastic vein. Although some PWs did remain
> affected for a time, in most cases, the program was a failure except
> as a mechanism to provide the material necessary for inclusion
> in forced propaganda statements.

U.S. Air Force analysts concluded similarly in a 1976 report that the PWs were "frequently 'broken' . . ., but for specific objectives other than political remolding. All evidence points to the NVN understanding that they could not ideologically convert PWs—but they could, and did, induce cooperation in sufficient measure to have claimed limited success in the exploitation of their captives."[9]

Beyond generating fodder for propaganda, indoctrination served other uses short of outright conversion of the prisoner. If the incessant drilling did not *re*orient the PW, it might at least *dis*orient him—shake his composure, sap his conviction about the cause for which he was fighting, leave him vulnerable to guilt feelings, convince him of the captor's omnipotence, and generally weaken his resistance. Stockdale believed the Vietnamese goal was to plant doubts among the prisoners as to the wisdom, if not the morality, of the American involvement and to edge them toward some degree of sympathy for the enemy's position, hoping that if indoctrinators could not transform the Americans into full-fledged Communists, they might at least "make 'Dave Dellingers'* out of them."[10]

Most of the PWs received a taste of indoctrination with their very first interrogation at the Hanoi Hilton. No matter who presided—Rabbit, Spot, Dog, Mickey Mouse, Owl, Eagle, or Cat himself—the arraignment was a set piece. The new prisoner was informed that he was a criminal—perhaps the unthinking agent of his government, but a transgressor nonetheless, the latest in a long line of invaders who historically had meddled in the affairs and violated the sovereignty of the Vietnamese people. The Vietnamese, the interrogator would explain, had liberated their country from

---

* A reference to one of the leading U.S. antiwar activists.

Chinese control a thousand years earlier and had more recently repulsed the Japanese and French. The thrust of the lecture was partly nationalistic, partly ideological. The PW was told that the United States had resumed the colonialist role of France in Indochina and that the Saigon government was a stooge for American interests as it had been for the French. The interrogator went on to indict American society itself as decadent and corrupt and dominated by a small ruling class of powerful and wealthy individuals.[11]

These themes were repeated again and again at subsequent sessions, with certain key phrases, like "four thousand years of glorious Vietnamese history," uttered by indoctrinators hundreds of times over the course of a prisoner's instruction. Even those PWs who were familiar with the technique from their survival-training classes on Chinese methods used in Korea, marveled at the monotony and ubiquitousness of Vietnamese indoctrination, as they found themselves marched back and forth endlessly to dimly lit quiz rooms or, if disabled, visited in their cells—learning the catechism so well they could have switched roles and conducted the liturgy themselves. Although the tone and tempo of the meetings might vary—from conversational chats, to screeching tirades, to more programmatic classroom-type exercises—the gist was always the same.

The setting and procedure eventually became as predictable as the subject matter. As new camps were constructed and the Hilton underwent renovation, they were equipped with examination rooms that had virtually identical layouts. The standard quiz room contained a table with a cloth draped to the floor, under which a tape recorder could be hidden; a straight-back chair for the interrogator and a low, perhaps two-foot-high stool for the prisoner (except at the Zoo, where designated rooms had a concrete cube built for this purpose); and an overhead hanging bulb, with a conical shade that could either direct the light at the table or shine it in the face of the PW. The bare surroundings, focused lighting, and superior positioning of the interrogator heightened the captive's sense of isolation and vulnerability. As the prisoner entered the room, he was required to bow to the officer and stand at attention until told to sit down. After a perfunctory and usually reassuring introduction by the interrogator, altogether incongruous given the sinister ambiance, the discussion or instruction would begin, lasting on average anywhere from one to three hours depending on how satisfactorily the interview proceeded and how crowded was the camp's indoctrination schedule.[12]

Contrary to Vietnamese intentions and expectations, the rigorous indoctrination regimen generally did not chasten or soften the men but rather incurred deepening resentment. Familiarity bred contempt rather than passive acceptance. The PWs termed the scripted ideological drills "bullshit

quizzes," loathing especially those administered by rookie interrogators
("kiddie quizzes") who were assigned the duty for no other reason it seemed
than to improve their English.[13] Those prisoners who posed as simple, dull
airplane drivers in order to dodge queries for tactical or technical information invited a patronizing handling that made their sessions particularly
wearing. Although the Americans occasionally found humor in the inflated
assertions and schoolmasterly manner of their indoctrinators, the numbing
routine over a period of time became in its own way as onerous and enervat-
ing as more physical forms of punishment.

It was almost as impossible to maintain silence in the face of indoctrination as it was when confronting torture. To simply respond with the "big
four" would mean more return visits, or, during the extortion era, more
torture. Moreover, prisoners were instinctively tempted, out of their own
sense of intellectual and ideological superiority, to rebut the indoctrination
attempts. The motivation to debate was a natural inclination, particularly
among the more aggressive and intelligent PWs, who saw opportunities
themselves to persuade and convert. Thoughts of indoctrinating the indoctrinators, however, proved illusory. "In the face of open ridicule and known
disbelief," Byrne wrote, "the V would repeat their line." Challengers proceeded at their own risk. "Innocent light conversation could cause an hour
of heartbreaking explanation to keep from being accused of a bad attitude
or worse," Doremus recalled. "A poorly chosen idiom could mean punishment from a quiz-master who must save face if he felt insulted." Once
engaged in discussion, once having become a "player," in Stockdale's term,
the participant found it difficult to withdraw from the contest. At a study
conference in 1975, Stockdale noted that "among the POWs who had
the greatest problems were those with backgrounds in American history or
political science, who thought they could successfully argue with the captors." More than a few times, clever instructors provoked rebuttals that were
exploited out of context, tricking men into making statements harmful to
the U.S. cause when they believed they were engaged in a dialogue defending American principles.[14]

Through experience prisoners learned that "polite silence" remained the
best policy until physical coercion forced a reply.[15] Thus reduced literally
to a captive audience, they had to withstand an assortment of carrots and
sticks calculated to break their will or at least draw them out. Just as the
Chinese would take recalcitrant Indian PWs to the bank of a freezing river
and then warm them with tea and cigarettes,[16] so the Vietnamese would alternately menace and massage their American subjects with "bad guy-good guy"

charades (the political officer usually playing the good guy role, rescuing the prisoner from the bullying camp commander or his henchman)* or the manipulation of diet and privileges. Jim Mulligan recalled being courted with cigarettes, salt, and bananas before being asked to sign a document. Rivers received a sweater and blanket prior to one session. On the other hand, Bob Shumaker told debriefers of threats of physical abuse "if you didn't 'see the light' and 'cross over to the people's side,'" his captors resorting also to "psychologically disturbing" methods such as withholding mail and conveying news depicting only the depressing aspects of American life.[17]

Rivers found the friendly "hour of charm" approach the most difficult to resist, "because Americans are decent human beings, and when someone is polite to them they are friendly and polite in return," but he was exposed, too, to "the despair approach, the exhaustion method, . . . disgrace approach, dire consequence approach," and solitary confinement. Byrne, writing a chapter for a PW study some years later, noted that "pressure used to force a PW to repeat indoctrination material for propaganda was the same as that applied to gain intelligence, ranging from a simple request and veiled threat to full torture." "The lengths to which an interrogator could go to extract material," Byrne added, "seemed to vary with the political climate, orders from above, etc."[18]

Race was another factor that figured in the indoctrination contest. The Vietnamese targeted black prisoners as prime candidates for indoctrination because of past injustices suffered by African Americans and their presumably lukewarm attitude toward fighting a war on behalf of the "ruling class." Appeals to PWs on the basis of race or ethnicity, as we have seen, were not without precedent: there were the aforementioned efforts during World War I by the Germans to set Irish prisoners against their British comrades and Turkish overtures to Muslims among their Indian captives; and when the Chinese captured Indian prisoners during border clashes in the early 1960s, they placed Gurkha and Sikh soldiers in separate companies and attempted to subvert loyalties with preferential treatment and inflammatory assertions. Although ordinarily not segregated in the Vietnamese camps, black PWs received special attention. In both the North and the South they were told they were fighting on the side of racial and economic inequality and thus helping to perpetuate a system that had enslaved them. Indoctrinators urged them to reflect on the plight of their people back home, refuse to fight, and counsel others not to serve. The release of black Army Sgts. Edward Johnson and James Jackson by the Viet Cong in October 1967 was accompanied by a statement expressing "solidarity and support for the just struggle of the U.S. Negroes . . . for basic national rights" and linking the

* See Chapter 6.

Cherry

Halyburton

American civil rights cause with the U.S. antiwar movement. American servicemen in the South in November 1967 heard a broadcast telling them:

> It is a fact that 1 out of every 10 young men in America is a Negro, but two out of every five men killed in the war in Vietnam are Negroes. Second, the Vietnamese people have done no harm to the Negro people. "No Viet Cong ever called me a nigger," said a Negro. Third, colored people in America and in Vietnam are victims of the same policy of the Johnson administration. Negroes are fighting for the same goal—freedom.
>
> It is time for the Negro GI to find a way out of Vietnam. He should not go along being used to fight for an administration that never fought for him . . . .
>
> When it comes to a choice between life and death at the most critical moment on the battlefield, the best way for the Negro GI is to let himself be taken prisoner rather than be killed. Negro GI's in South Vietnam, for your survival rise up and oppose this Johnson war and press for your repatriation. All Negro people and progressive Americans are behind you.[19]

Statements such as the above were intended for domestic and international consumption as well as for weary American troops regardless of race, but they had a particularly sharp edge for those blacks in captivity when combined with other indoctrination. Air Force Maj. Fred Cherry, the highest-ranking black captured in the North, was informed of Dr. Martin Luther King's murder and told that in the riotous aftermath blacks were being slaughtered in the streets. "They tried to make me different," Cherry recalled. "They tried to exploit me . . . . They knew we had a race problem back home. And they used it to try and turn me against the white POWs in camp." At one point he was convinced his captors meant to release him and frame him as if he had cooperated with them. In another instance they had him listen to a recording by "black power" advocate Stokely Carmichael and tried to persuade him to prepare a similar tape. They thought "if they could get the first and most senior black POW to denounce the war, they could play that tape to young black soldiers in the field and get them to drop their weapons," Cherry told a University of Maryland class in 1989.

Suffering extensive injuries when shot down in October 1965, Cherry, perhaps by chance but likely by design, was placed in a cell with young Navy Lt. Porter Halyburton, a white Southerner with a pronounced accent. Although the two were initially suspicious of one another—Halyburton did not know that the Air Force had black pilots, and Cherry suspected his cellmate of being a French spy for the Vietnamese—the relationship became a close one and Cherry later credited Halyburton with saving his life when his injuries became infected from medical neglect and he had to be hand-fed and helped with his bodily needs. Stout resistance to the Viets' racial propositioning ticketed the black flier for some of the severest torture of the extortion era (93 straight days at one stretch) and almost two years of solitary confinement, including 53 consecutive weeks.[20]

Denton noted admiringly in his postwar memoir that the Vietnamese "gave up on" Cherry.[21] In fact, among the two dozen or so blacks known to have been taken prisoner,* there is scant evidence that any were swayed at all—though Johnson and Jackson were among those, black and white, who made statements under pressure that reflected Vietnamese tutelage. As Jackson remarked several months after his release, the race-baiting may have prompted him and some of the other black prisoners to "think" about the matter of racial inequality in their own society, but the issue neither confused nor demoralized them. Army Sgt. Donald Rander, seized early in 1968 in the South and jailed in the North, "threw the propaganda back" at his agitators. "Don't you realize that I'm just a black soldier and the white

---

* The official compilation at the time of homecoming in February 1973 showed 72 black servicemen as captured or missing, with 16 (9 enlisted and 7 officers) returning (not including several, such as Sergeants Johnson and Jackson, who had been released earlier) and 2 having died in captivity. Although the numbers were subsequently updated, most of the 54 designated as missing on the 1973 list remain unaccounted for and are presumed to have died in action rather than captivity.

man don't tell me nothing?" he complained to a persistent interrogator. "The white guys go out and do all that important stuff. They wouldn't let me do anything like that."[22]

In the end, the Vietnamese had no more success with their black prisoners than with other targeted groups, such as Hispanic prisoners or younger PWs, who they supposed would be more impressionable and less knowledgeable and therefore more pliable. As indicated earlier,* the American prisoners in Vietnam, whatever their color or age, because of the high proportion of officers among them, on the whole (and even allowing for the higher percentage of enlistees captured in the South) tended to be more experienced, better trained, more committed, and generally more mature—and unyielding—than American PWs of previous wars.

Disappointing results only made the Vietnamese try harder. The standard examination room quizzes were supplemented by visits to reading rooms and museums, lectures by political commissars, audiences with touring antiwar celebrities, and broadcasts over a blaring loudspeaker system—all intended to reinforce the one-on-one encounter sessions.

Prisoners at the Hanoi Hilton would occasionally be taken around the city to visit the War Museum, a cavernous warehouse of military artifacts that traced the centuries-old Vietnamese struggle for independence; contemporary art exhibits that exuded Communist and nationalist themes; or photographic displays depicting both U.S. damage to Vietnamese civilian institutions (churches, leprosaria, schools, and hospitals) and damage inflicted by the Vietnamese on U.S. military installations and personnel. Tours of devastated areas were coordinated with local authorities to turn out the victimized masses to intimidate the escorted PWs. Although dreary and unpleasant, such excursions were welcomed by the prisoners as a change of pace and scenery, especially when not accompanied by camera coverage of the event that turned the outing into a filmed propaganda exercise. The seniors did what they could to discourage such trips, recognizing their propaganda value to the enemy even when the activity did not serve its didactic purpose.[23]

Perhaps twice a year in the North the prisoners gathered in groups to view movies. Most of the camps had a large room or center courtyard that functioned as a screening facility. The Zoo's "Auditorium" was strung with blankets to separate aisles and prevent PW recognition and communication; elsewhere, too, darkness, seating arrangements, and strict controls limited PW contact. Presentations ranged from footage of Viet Cong "victories" in the South and bombing raids and casualties in the North to diverting short

* See Chapter 2, p. 20n, and Chapter 4, note 10.

subjects such as song and dance skits and scenes from the Moscow air show and circus, the lighter fare inserted possibly to make the propaganda segments more palatable. Dick Brunhaver and Phil Butler among others viewed a propaganda film at the Zoo in the spring of 1966 entitled "Sons and Daughters" that featured U.S. antiwar leaders Jerry Rubin and David Dellinger and a protest march by University of California students carrying Viet Cong flags. Bob Shumaker's group at Briarpatch witnessed a color film with lovely Vietnamese girls in a bright setting that shifted dramatically to black and white clips of U.S. air attacks. Jerry Coffee, who reported seeing "two or three movies per year" between 1965 and 1969, noted how during the course of a film "the same clip of an aircraft being shot down might be used half-a-dozen times, to signify great U.S. air losses." In at least some instances, prisoners could elect not to attend the movie sessions and would not be forced to, but, again, for the sake of a break in the monotonous routine as well as to avoid a "bad attitude" label, most chose to go. In later years, after 1969, moviegoing would be more frequent, relaxed, and entertaining, although not without continuing propaganda messages.[24]

Late in 1965 and through the spring of 1966, the North Vietnamese opened reading rooms, first at the Zoo, later the Hilton, and after that at Briarpatch, in which they placed stacks of Communist and pacifist literature. In these cell-size "libraries," as they called them, they laid out glossy magazines with such titles as *Vietnam Pictorial* and *Soviet Union*, English-language newspapers like the *Vietnam Courier*, a series of paperbacks on cultural and political topics called *Vietnam Studies*, and the writings of well-known Marxists like Wilfred Burchett and Felix Greene. From time to time, carefully edited American magazines appeared that carried antiwar stories or news calculated to deflate PW morale. Within a week of his capture Coffee was reading reports of U.S. and South Vietnamese military casualties in the *Vietnamese Courier* and shown grisly photos of North Vietnamese bombing victims in *Vietnam Pictorial*. The prisoners were required to spend a specified amount of time in the reading rooms—20 minutes to an hour twice weekly at the Zoo in 1966, for instance—but that varied over the years and from camp to camp. Sometimes materials would be brought to an individual's cell. Later in some camps the PWs were encouraged to reproduce their own articles and art work, heavily censored by officials and limited to approved subjects but collected in magazine format and circulated like a campus newspaper. These publications, with names like *New Outlook* and *New Runway*, became a source of contention among the prisoners. Some felt they were harmless and offered an opportunity to sneak satirical pieces and cartoons

Clockwise from top left: Alvarez, captured August 1964, "on the town" with a smiling attendant; captured pilots meeting with a West German delegation; Lt. Cdr. William Hardman, captured August 1967, made to view bomb damage; propaganda reading room.

past unsuspecting Vietnamese editors, while others frowned on them as improper and detrimental collaborations with the enemy.[25]

Also late in 1965 and into 1966 the North Vietnamese installed loudspeaker systems at the Hilton, Zoo, and other camps as they became operational. The PWs were well familiar with the apparatus, as it was widely used in the countryside to disseminate propaganda among the Vietnamese populace and when new captives were marched through villages on their way to Hanoi they heard news and propaganda broadcasts almost everywhere they traveled, later saying the operation reminded them of Orwell's *1984*. "Hamlets, no matter how remote," remembered Navy pilot Charles Plumb, a 1967 shootdown, "could not escape the rebounding echoes of a Ho Chi Minh speech or a military march. When I was moved from camp to camp, I saw villages which were absolutely destitute—no water or sewage system, no secure shelter, no electricity. No electricity, that is, except for a single strand of wire strung around bushes and branches and bamboo poles leading to a shining multi-kilowatt speaker often as large as eight feet in diameter . . . . Even the forbidding jungles granted no deliverance from the propaganda."[26]

Once incarcerated the PWs found the prison speaker systems just as ubiquitous. Day after day, with up to five hours of programming daily, the green boxes poured out a stream of Voice of Vietnam radio broadcasts, propaganda pronouncements delivered by impassioned Vietnamese or disaffected Americans, and distortions of the news or personal apologies read by the prisoners themselves under pressure. The English-language short-wave Voice of Vietnam broadcasts, beamed to U.S. troops in the South, ran for 30 minutes in the morning and again at night, at 6:00 a.m. and 9:00 p.m., and featured three female announcers who mimicked the style of World War II's "Tokyo Rose" and were dubbed "Hanoi Hannah" by the Americans. In May 1966 the North Vietnamese introduced a program on the history of Vietnam that reran a segment on the battle of Dien Bien Phu over and over again while guards forced the PWs to sit at the foot of their beds listening silently and attentively as they monitored their reaction through open doors. Special broadcasts might include a tribute to Ho Chi Minh on his birthday or, on Sunday evenings, a program called "Radio Stateside" (or "Stateside Special") that cultivated black servicemen by interspersing racial-oriented news with recordings of currently popular black music. Taped appeals from prominent American peace advocates, many of them visitors to North Vietnam— personalities such as Jane Fonda, Joan Baez, Stokely Carmichael, and Ramsay Clark—at once incensed and demoralized the prisoners.* Fred Cherry heard

---

* The House Committee on Internal Security compiled a list of U.S. nationals involved in such broadcasts between 1965 and 1972, with dates and circumstances. See *Restraints on Travel to Hostile Areas H.R. 1594* . . ., Hearings before House Committee on Internal Security, 93 Cong, 1 sess (9, 10 May 73), 7682-87.

Jane Fonda's voice over a camp public address system in October 1967 as he was in the midst of an extended torture siege; he became so enraged by her allegations of cowardice on the part of American pilots because they bombed at night and killed women and children that he "tried to tear [his] irons from the walls."[27]

News reports on the radio, as on film and in available published accounts, dwelled on negative events such as antiwar demonstrations and political assassinations. "They told us the day that Martin Luther King was shot, they told us the day that Bobby Kennedy was shot," John McCain later remarked, "but they never bothered to tell us about the moon shot." Listening to the same Hanoi Radio broadcasts in the South, Nick Rowe felt that "the most devastating" blows to the prisoners' morale were "quotations by [antiwar] Senators Mansfield, Fulbright, and McGovern. We got every one of those just as soon as they came out," he told a debriefer. "The anti-war movement in the U.S., the racial problems, the campus disorders, the draft card burners, the deserters, and the self-immolations; all of this was given to us immediately. Their stuff . . . we could disregard. But when they started quoting *Newsweek*, *Time*, *Life*, *Look*, the *Washington Post*, columnist Walter Lippmann . . . ."[28]

Repetitive and incessant, the loudspeaker barrage was made all the harsher by poor fidelity, ear-splitting amplification ("two decibels above the threshold of pain," Doremus estimated), and no way to control the volume or program selection. Nevertheless, the system did have its occasional redeeming moments, as when a camp radioman mistakenly tuned in a Manila broadcast that told the prisoners there had been a coup in Indonesia that threw out the Communist government there. Sometimes on Sunday afternoon, whether on purpose or by accident, the radio at the Zoo would pick up a BBC Far Eastern broadcast of classical music. (New Zoo arrival Larry Chesley remembered his delight at hearing a Chopin piano piece and assuming it was a regular occurrence.) The North Vietnamese quite likely intentionally gave the PWs a periodic dose of Western music as part of the carrot-and-stick strategy, just as they alternated Hanoi Hannah with Christmas carols to mellow their captives during the holiday season. With regard to the latter, 1966 shootdown Air Force Capt. Norman McDaniel recalled hearing "Ave Maria" over the Zoo's PA system his first Christmas in the camps and experiencing "the greatest sadness and deepest longings in my heart that I have ever known." Howard Rutledge granted that the carols were a ploy to manipulate the homesick Americans but welcomed the holiday music nonetheless. Catching portions of an awful recording of "Silent Night," he found the hymn, "scratches and all . . . beautiful beyond describing." Several of the PWs later termed some of the programming decisions "bizarre," Shumaker citing a series of Eddie Fisher records played during Christmas 1969.[29]

As the enemy worked harder at indoctrination, the prisoners resisted harder in an escalating contest that became at times as much a battle of wits as a test of wills. When McDaniel, who the Vietnamese somehow learned could sing, was himself made to perform over the PA system, singing carols to his comrades, he attempted to frustrate the plan by stumbling through the lyrics. Risner, as we have seen, administered judo chops to his throat and then gargled with the residue from a bar of lye soap in a desperate effort to avoid reading a doctored newscast over the Hilton's radio; when finally forced to comply, he gave an incoherent rendition.* At Briarpatch, cellmates Air Force Capts. Warren (Bob) Lilly and Richard Bolstad (captured the same day, 6 November 1965), required to read the news, mangled the names of North Vietnam President "Horseshit Minh" and Australian Communist "Wellfed Bullshit" and devised exaggerated Southern, Italian, German, and British accents that had long-suffering colleagues howling with laughter. Many prisoners followed Stockdale's example of undermining coerced propaganda statements by slipping in obscene gestures before the camera. When Doremus and several of his mates were forced to "audition" for a camp radio production, he and the others "flunked with flying colors," treating their fellow PWs to a babble of stutterings and mispronunciations.[30]

A favorite tactic of the Vietnamese that served both their PW indoctrination and external propaganda purposes was to schedule press conferences or interviews in which select prisoners (usually those thought to be vulnerable because of youth, race, or previous cooperation) would be mustered for meetings with foreign press delegations, representatives of pacifist organizations, or visiting dignitaries or antiwar celebrities. By showcasing their captives in a "humane and lenient" atmosphere—press rooms were typically furnished with flowers, cookie trays, and the like—the Vietnamese sought to buttress their case with their own constituencies and world opinion as well as to lull the prisoners into letting down their guard in the presence of less threatening "outsiders." Between 1965 and 1967, Shumaker, whose emotional response to a question about his family at one such session may have marked him as a leading candidate for subsequent appearances, met with a New Zealander, a Chinese delegation, expatriate American Communist Anna Louise Strong (joined by a group of British and Japanese reporters), and, with Bob Peel, members of the World Peace Council. At first disarmed by the seemingly innocent nature of the exchanges, Shumaker became steadily more aware of their perils and by the time he and Peel were trotted out for an

* See Chapter 8. Risner recounts the incident in a chapter in his memoir entitled "Tryouts for Radio Hanoi" (*Passing of the Night*, ch 14).

interview with East German newsmen in the summer of 1967 they were successfully thwarting the staged conferences with "bad performances."* [31]

Perhaps because of his youth, Phil Butler was another prisoner the Vietnamese thought could be exploited at these media events. They trucked him to meetings with Soviet and Oriental reporters and before a group called the "World Federation of Trade Unions," which included Strong and another exiled American Communist, Sidney Rittenberg. Although the propaganda ministry managed to obtain from these "photo opportunities" a batch of exploitable snapshots and film footage, Butler, at the risk of severe punishment, stymied other efforts by sticking out his tongue at the camera and refusing to talk beyond giving his name, rank, and service number. [32]

Because of their propaganda value as star attractions, the seniors, too, were sometimes dragged out before the media, especially in the early period before the Vietnamese realized how counterproductive such sessions could be with a wily and determined resister. For three consecutive days and nights in May 1966, forced to go without sleep, Denton was drilled intensively by Mickey Mouse on the "truth" about the war and then was taken for separate interviews with a Japanese reporter and Wilfred Burchett. In both instances he ignored the script and defended United States policy in Vietnam. Before the Japanese newsman, with cameras rolling, he blinked against the glare of floodlights, at first reflexively and then, nimbly seizing the opportunity despite his extreme fatigue, in calculated movements that spelled "TORTURE" in Morse code. Naval Intelligence would later review the videotape, which was bought by a U.S. television network and widely circulated, and pick up the message, the first indication the U.S. government had that the American PWs were being tortured. [33] When Risner met with author Mary McCarthy in 1967, so wary had the Vietnamese become of the seniors' craftiness that they were convinced Risner's raised eyebrows (his reaction to a McCarthy comment) and McCarthy's knocking on wood (to underscore her hopes for an early end to the war) were secret signals.†

---

* Shumaker became a pillar of the PW community. He earned high praise from Denton, who considered him "brave, but not foolhardy" and "in a class by himself" as an ingenious communicator (*When Hell Was In Session*, 37, 149-50). When Stockdale bumped into Shumaker at Hoa Lo in 1967, he noticed "the cuffs of his prison pajamas bore the unmistakable rust rings of continuous stays in irons" (*In Love and War*, 261).

† Risner's and McCarthy's versions of their meeting differ sharply, beginning with the question of whether McCarthy, as Risner maintains, requested to see him in particular and including descriptions of each other's physical appearance and details of their visit. The encounter apparently left such a bad taste for both that they carried on something of a feud even after Risner was released —Risner drawing an unflattering portrait of McCarthy in his memoir and McCarthy challenging the credibility of Risner's captivity account generally. See Risner, *Passing of the Night*, 173-75; McCarthy's review of Risner's volume in the *New York Review of Books*, 7 Mar 74; and Doris Grumbach, "Fine Print: The Art of Reviewing by Innuendo," *New Republic*, 16 Mar 74, 32-33, a review essay that excoriates McCarthy.

Stockdale went relatively unscathed through the remainder of 1966 after his rough bout with Rabbit early in the year,* but not before he was brought before Nguyen Vien, a well-traveled Communist intellectual and propagandist who had been a key agitator in the Viet Minh campaign against the French in 1953-54. Still at New Guy Village in the Hilton, about a month before his transfer to the Zoo in June, Stockdale listened while Vien compared LBJ to Hitler and asked where the American military professional drew the line in obeying authority when orders conflicted with conscience. The "hour-long verbal Ping-Pong game" (the normally circumspect senior apparently disregarded his own advice here in engaging the enemy in debate) ended with Vien coolly remarking: "Our country has no capability to defeat you on the battlefield. But war is not decided by weapons so much as by national will. Once the American people understand this war, they will have no interest in pursuing it. They will be made to understand this. We will win this war on the streets of New York."[34]

Many of the prisoners welcomed the media attention for the chance it offered "to get your name out" and inform their families of their survival and condition. But the high-profile sessions, rarely yielding the results the Vietnamese hoped for, were usually followed by reprimands and reprisals. Risner, for example, noted that the visit with McCarthy, and other appointments around the same time with East German and North Korean delegations, worsened his situation. "I know I suffered," he later said, "and to my knowledge she did absolutely nothing to help our cause. This was true of all the appearances."[35]

A defiant gesture such as an undisguised finger obscenity or outright refusal to talk would bring down the full wrath of prison officials. To avoid torture, PWs who were asked to read statements before cameras or at press conferences came to rely increasingly on more subtle body language and a simple lack of spontaneity or enthusiasm—a deadpan expression, a listless monotone, a glazed or robotic look of the type Navy pilot Richard Stratton would later affect in perhaps the most publicized media episode[†]—that would convey to observers a lack of sincerity and effectively defeat the Vietnamese plan. Of course, the degree of conviction was in the eye of the beholder and an overly subtle performance might not get across the desired point. Hence globetrotting American antiwar liberals Staughton Lynd and Thomas Hayden, predisposed to looking favorably on the Communists' treatment of

---

* See Chapter 8. Stockdale surmised that Cat, Rabbit's superior, decided not to expend so much time and energy on one man and to "stash" him until they were ready for him again. "I had failed Cat in the clutch and he temporarily dropped me out of his personal surveillance stable and put me on ice," Stockdale jotted in his memoir (*In Love and War*, 184).
† See Chapter 18.

PWs, dismissed Ron Byrne's "mechanical" response and "blinking gaze" during a 1966 interview as merely the behavior of a prisoner under stress, exceedingly cautious, and "grappling for self-control," when in fact Byrne may have been attempting to signal his callers that he was being persecuted.[36]

Prisoners at Briarpatch took to using the opposite hand when forced into writing propaganda, both in coerced confessions and on those few occasions when they were allowed to pen even censored letters to relatives. The tactic not only served to cast doubt on the validity of such scribblings but also enabled the men to prolong the writing process and the breathing spell it offered away from more unpleasant activity. After 1970, when the PWs were permitted to write more regularly and under more relaxed circumstances, several of the Briarpatch group, Ralph Gaither for example, continued the practice, causing their families and officials in Washington to continue questioning the authenticity of the letters right up to homecoming. Stockdale referred to an alternative, "slant" technique used by captives in other camps.[37]

Communication was an important PW weapon not only in delivering the desired message to the outside world but in briefing one another inside the camps on indoctrination and propaganda developments. Just as comparing notes helped the men to weather interrogation and torture, so it prepared them for what to expect in the way of indoctrination. Sharing insights on misinformation and distortions enabled the prisoners, under certain conditions or with particular personnel, to employ a method of news interpretation they referred to as "180 degree decoding," meaning they believed exactly the opposite of what indoctrinators told them. They learned to read between the lines, to discount casualty reports, and to recognize that indoctrination became more strident and preposterous as the war was going badly for the enemy. The North Vietnamese, Coffee later reflected, "made up for significant set-backs by describing greater imaginary victories." Coffee recalled that a favorite saying among PWs after a new round of indoctrination was, "The Vietnamese people have suffered another great victory."[38]

To survive the loudspeaker "onslaught," Coffee said they learned how to "tune in" and "tune out" the camp radio and "turn off" the speakers "mentally."[39] As long as the contest was played on the level playing field of the mind, the Americans could devise means to resist and deflect the captor's best indoctrination efforts. Indeed, the PWs proved time and time again they could prevail in a battle of wits, but in a test of wills, at least one that came down to brute force, the outcome would be different.

The torture and indoctrination programs became almost indistinguishable during that period late in 1965 and through 1966 when the "political climate" that Byrne cited as a key determinant of Vietnamese treatment of the PWs soured and the captor turned vicious. The interrogator whom the

PWs called "Frenchy" left the Zoo in January to assume command at Briar-patch and proceeded to make a bad situation at the isolated camp even worse. Guards wore tennis shoes so they could sneak from cell to cell without being heard, catching Butler among others in forbidden communication and subjecting violators to savage punishments. Gaither remembered a loud-speaker being installed in his cell in the spring of 1966 (as Briarpatch had no electricity, the system was powered by a gasoline generator) and Hanoi Hannah beginning every program with a quote from Alaska Senator Ernest Gruening telling the American soldiers their dead comrades "have not died for their country . . . but have been mistakenly sacrificed in part of an inherited folly." With Frenchy "after 'results' at any cost," Ed Davis recalled the Vietnamese mixing indoctrination and pressure for propaganda state-ments indiscriminately, "the sessions rapidly [progressing] to harangue and harassment and finally to threats and actual torture."[40]

Elsewhere, too, indoctrination took on harsher dimensions as instructors came under increasing pressure themselves to supply propaganda materials for the psywar. Sam Johnson and Jim Lamar were beaten soon after arriving at Hoa Lo in May 1966, both having suffered broken and dislocated limbs during shootdown that were damaged further when interrogators yanked and twisted them until the prisoners almost passed out from the pain. Lamar, forced to meet an Asian press delegation his second day in Hanoi, grimaced at photographers and told reporters he had been physically compelled to face them. At the Zoo in June Denton detected "a strange and ominous mood . . ., a feeling that a purge was coming." Within the next month at all the camps the prisoners would be required to "make a choice" between two courses. As Gaither remembered the options offered by their captors: "On the one hand, you can side with the Vietnamese people and live, some-day maybe to return to your families and loved ones; on the other hand, you can side with your government and its policies of war and criminal aggression against the Democratic Republic of Vietnam. That is the side of death."[41]

Cat (Major Bui) told Dave Dellinger in 1967 that the North Vietnamese did not attempt to "brainwash" the prisoners but rather simply to "talk" with them and "explore as fellow human beings" the state of the world and the social and political ramifications of the war.

> Of course we give them books like Felix Greene to read and the text of the Geneva Accords and I myself often talk with them for an hour or two. But you can be sure that there are no pressures brought and that we simply explore as fellow human beings the kind of world it is and the kind of world we would like it to be.

> I don't know. Perhaps some Americans would consider that brainwashing but we don't, and I don't think the prisoners do either. And they are free not to talk with us and not have such conversations if at any time they find them offensive.[42]

As indicated earlier, it is accurate to say that the Vietnamese did not engage in the more elaborate conditioning exercises and blatant "mind control" techniques favored by their Chinese mentors. Byrne allowed that the effort to reshape their thinking was more "an annoyance rather than a serious threat,"[43] and it may even be conceded that there were relatively benign intervals when the indoctrination process contained civilized and "conversational" exchanges. Nonetheless, Cat was being grossly disingenuous. Hanoi's Enemy Proselytizing Section may have subordinated pure indoctrination—the actual ideological conversion of their prisoners—to exploitation for propaganda purposes—getting the Americans to utter damaging statements whether they believed them or not—but its officers could be just as tireless and ruthless as the Chinese in pursuing their objective. Cat's reference to "no pressures" being exerted was, of course, a colossal deceit, as the Briarpatch gang and victims elsewhere in the system in the spring of 1966 could testify. The North Vietnamese may have been averse to brainwashing, but not to physical coercion, and when they exhausted their supply of carrots and when their appeals to reason and good sense proved unavailing, they did not hesitate to resort to torture.

Of course, in resorting in the end to physical brutality, prison officials effectively discredited their own indoctrination program, which was based on the alleged justness and humanity of their cause. Although indoctrination eventually produced and enhanced propaganda statements, it failed to accomplish its larger purposes. Prisoners accept and adapt to captivity insofar as they are able to sustain their convictions. The Vietnamese had hoped, by challenging those convictions, to block the adaptation process and render their captives more tractable—and, by unsettling enough individuals, to disrupt the broader PW organization. A heavy-handed indoctrination program only hardened the Americans' convictions and strengthened their faith in the integrity of their government and rightness of their cause. If the resistance continued to buckle under the unbearable pressures, the Americans' contempt for their captors intensified and with it the determination to somehow triumph over an increasingly loathsome enemy.

10

The Hanoi March and the
Issue of War Crimes Trials

All the time that the North Vietnamese were waging their war of nerves with the American PWs they were, of course, engaged in a larger political and propaganda war with the U.S. government for the hearts and minds of the international public. A leading element in this overriding "psywar," becoming ever more prominent by the summer of 1966, was the threat to prosecute American PWs as war criminals. From the beginning of the U.S. involvement, Vietnamese Communists in both the North and South had referred to the Americans variously as pirates, mercenaries, and criminals. But officials in Hanoi now talked increasingly of actually bringing the prisoners to trial. Without access to DRV records, one can not determine with any certainty, in this matter as in so many others, what motives and calculations underlay Hanoi's actions. What is clear is that however spontaneous and emotional the talk of war crimes trials may have been initially, the North Vietnamese eventually saw in such an exercise a way to discomfit the American government on a sensitive issue and to provide fuel for the mounting anti-American propaganda campaign in Vietnam and growing antiwar sentiment in the United States and Western Europe. The result was that the American PWs found themselves pawns in an escalating political contest spanning several continents as they fought their ongoing personal battles in the Indochina prisons and jungles.

As early as September 1965 North Vietnam indicated it intended to try captured U.S. airmen as criminals. In response to appeals from the International Committee of the Red Cross for the warring parties to observe the 1949 Geneva Convention on prisoners of war, Hanoi replied in a letter dated 31 August: "In order to compensate for its defeats in the undeclared war of aggression in South Vietnam, the United States Government has, without any justification, given orders to its air and naval forces to make surprise attacks on the Democratic Republic of Vietnam . . . . The people and the Government of the Democratic Republic of Vietnam consider the actions of the United States Government . . . as acts of piracy and regard the pilots who have carried out pirate raids . . . as major criminals . . . ." Following American bombing in the area of Vinh Linh, the DRV Foreign Ministry announced that U.S. pilots "who have destroyed property and massacred the people" would be prosecuted as criminals under Vietnamese law. Later in 1965, Radio Hanoi repeated the threat, this time citing public meetings that "unanimously" demanded "punishment" for attacks on "market places, hospitals and schools." In February 1966 the Cairo newspaper *Al-Ahram* reported that the North Vietnamese ambassador had informed the Egyptian foreign minister of North Vietnam's decision to try the Americans.[1]

In an orgy of what Henry Kissinger would later refer to as "ferocious self-righteousness,"[2] North Vietnamese officials went to great lengths to justify legally as well as morally the arraignment of captured Americans and to defend against similar indictments of their own regular and guerrilla forces. They argued that theirs was a war of national liberation—internal (though with warrantable "international" assistance from other Communist states), defensive, and just—as opposed to the American intervention, which was an external aggression, unjust, and in any case undeclared and thus having no claim to entitlements under international protocols. Confronted with the fact that North Vietnam was a signatory to the 1949 PW Convention, the Communists reminded critics that their representatives had signed the Geneva agreement in 1957 with the specific reservation (to Article 85) that "prisoners of war prosecuted for and convicted of war crimes or crimes against humanity, in accordance with the principles established by the Nuremberg Tribunal, [shall not benefit from] the present Convention."[3] By pointing up the absence of a state of declared war and also invoking the Nuremberg reservation, the DRV was covering all bases, strengthening its contention that it had no obligation whatsoever to treat the American captives as legitimate PWs. North Vietnam's interpretation of the struggle not only had legal and propaganda utility, but offered considerable practical advantages as well. By regarding its captives as criminals rather than PWs, it could release individual prisoners when it wished, at politically timely intervals and without protracted negotiations or regard for formal repatriation. Further, because it recognized no obligation to follow Geneva Convention procedures, it could hand over whomever it wanted rather than releasing first the ill, injured, longest held, and those with family emergencies.

U.S. officials scrambled to develop their own legal brief, insisting that the military activity in Southeast Asia, although not a declared war, still constituted an armed conflict within the meaning of Article 2 of the Geneva prisoner-of-war convention* and hence qualified American PWs for its protections. Endeavoring to seize the high ground, U.S. Secretary of State Dean Rusk wrote ICRC President Samuel Gonard on 10 August 1965 that "the United States Government has always abided by the humanitarian principles enunciated in the Geneva conventions and will continue to do so." Rusk added that the U.S. government was reviewing conditions under which Communist prisoners were being held in the South to see that they met the Geneva requirements and expected North Vietnam to do the same for American prisoners. With respect to the "war crimes" charges themselves, the Department of Defense's Office of General Counsel noted that the U.S. bombing raids, targeting military production or support facilities, were legitimate combat operations consistent with conventional military practice, thus captured fliers were entitled to full and fair hearings in any "war crimes" proceedings. In March 1966 State Department Legal Adviser Leonard C. Meeker drafted a memorandum for the Senate Foreign Relations Committee on "The Legality of United States Participation in the Defense of VietNam." Meanwhile, Pentagon planners took the Vietnamese threats seriously enough to map contingency plans, including possible reprisals, in the event of trials and/or executions.[4]

This account primarily of the captivity experience is not the proper place for discussion of the complicated legal questions that the Indochina conflict posed regarding the nature of the hostilities and the status of the combatants, but let it suffice here to say that both Hanoi and Washington devoted considerable energy to denying or establishing the rights of the American PWs and that semantic fencing and sophistical posturing enabled each side to build a persuasive case. As A. J. Barker observed in a 1974 study that placed the legal problem in historical context, by 1960 the prominence of cold war and guerrilla war since World War II had blurred the traditional definitions of "war" and "peace" and the role and status of combatants, obsoleting much of the language and provisions of the 1949 PW accord. "When the revised Geneva Convention was framed in 1949," Barker wrote,

> its prescriptions for the treatment of prisoners of war were written against the background of two World Wars. War was seen in traditional terms as an open conflict between two or more sovereign nations. There was simply 'war' and 'peace' and the problems that are now associated with 'cold war' and ['freedom fighters'] were not apparent. Thus there was no provision for Gary Powers to claim

---

* Article 2 provides that "the present Convention shall apply to all cases of declared war *or of any other armed conflict* which may arise between two or more of the High Contracting Parties, even if the state of war is not recognized by one of them." (Emphasis added.)

POW status when his U-2 was shot down over Russia, although he was on a military mission.[5]

The American prisoners in Vietnam found themselves caught in the same legal limbo if not the same circumstances. The ICRC supported the U.S. interpretation of the applicability of the 1949 accord to the Indochina situation but international law was equivocal or murky on many aspects of the war crimes issue.* If the U.S. position tended to prevail in the court of international law, the Vietnamese often seemed to trounce the Americans in the all-important court of public opinion.

In the end, the North Vietnamese elected to rely chiefly on the Nuremberg argument, the war crimes issue, which they evidently judged to be more compelling legally and more appealing morally than the increasingly moot matter of whether an undeclared war came under the jurisdiction of the Geneva code. Whatever the precise thrust and timing of their thinking—and again, lacking access to DRV sources, one can only surmise—we know that through the first half of 1966 the Hanoi news media stepped up the drumbeat of accusations. What seemed to have originated as a natural, impulsive

---

* Princeton University international law professor Richard A. Falk maintained in 1971 that a case could be made for the criminality of U.S. pilots' actions if one accepted North Vietnam's allegations that the United States bombed both military and civilian targets indiscriminately:

> On the merits, . . . North Vietnam had a reasonable basis for regarding the captured pilots as potential war criminals. International law experts and moralists have been divided on the legality of indiscriminate aerial bombardment of populated areas. The use of air power in the 1930s by Mussolini's Italy against Ethiopia and by Nazi Germany on behalf of Franco's forces in the Spanish Civil War were occasions of universal public outrage. These instances of high-technology societies waging war against relatively helpless low-technology societies (with no capability for self-defense or retaliation) were apt precursors of the air war against North Vietnam . . . .
>
> In the view of North Vietnam and many independent specialists in international law, the air war constituted a war crime both in aggressive intent and in its daily execution. The air war, by bringing the war to North Vietnam, by its indiscriminate patterns of bombardment, and by the widespread use of such prohibited weapons as anti-personnel cluster bombs and delayed action bombs, clearly raised issues of criminality.

See Richard A. Falk, "The American POWs: Pawns in Power Politics," *The Progressive* (Mar 71), 13-21. It should be noted that Falk was an outspoken critic of the U.S. intervention whose judgment may have been colored, too, by the Kent State tragedy and My Lai massacre revelations, both coming about the time he was writing. For a treatment of the issue more sympathetic to the American side, see Lewy, *America in Vietnam*, 396-406. Lewy stresses the unintentionalness, and often unavoidableness, of the harm to civilian personnel and property, and calls attention to the restraint and care exercised by the American pilots (that ironically placed them in greater peril themselves). For a deeper examination of the subject, see the massive collection of essays by Falk, ed, *The Vietnam War and International Law*, 4 vols; for balance, Telford Taylor, *Nuremberg and Vietnam: An American Tragedy* and Peter D. Trooboff, ed, *Law and Responsibility in Warfare: The Vietnam Experience*.

ventilating of anger steadily acquired the complexion of an orchestrated public relations campaign, as the North Vietnamese began systematically compiling evidence attesting to the criminal nature of the American activities.

In February Hanoi's Ministry of Foreign Affairs published a 77-page pamphlet documenting the war crimes case with a text of charges accompanied by photographs of bomb damage. Entitled *US War Crimes in North Vietnam*, the pamphlet alleged that U.S. planes attacked densely populated areas, killing and maiming civilians; shelled kindergartens, hospitals, pagodas, and nursing homes; and employed inhumane and outlawed weapons such as napalm, phosphorous bombs, and fragmentation rockets. The report cataloged the purported atrocities in grim detail: 18,000 U.S. bombing sorties between February and November 1965; 63 raids on the city of Vinh alone; 30 hospitals destroyed or damaged; 10 days of shelling that gutted 160 buildings at the Quynh Lap Leprosy Center; 120 schools demolished; the names of priests and monks killed at their churches or pagodas; lists of other civilian buildings destroyed. Thirty pages of photos showed the ruins of homes, schools, and dams and the corpses of old people and young children.[6]

The February pamphlet gave the North Vietnamese not only an imposing courtroom exhibit but also a powerful and effective propaganda vehicle. Printed in English and other languages, it became grist for the gathering antiwar movement both in Europe and America. It provided bountiful testimony for a War Crimes Tribunal being organized by the British philosopher and pacifist Bertrand Russell, a largely symbolic but widely publicized effort to try American leaders in absentia. And it strengthened the convictions and facilitated the efforts of antiwar activists in the United States, three of whom—Herbert Aptheker, historian and theoretician of the American Communist Party, Staughton Lynd, an assistant professor of history at Yale, and Thomas Hayden, a founder of Students for a Democratic Society—had just returned from a visit to Hanoi. During their tour they posed for photographs next to several of the bombed-out buildings pictured in the Ministry of Foreign Affairs publication and interviewed an American PW, Ron Byrne.* Upon their arrival home, they recorded their impressions in two accounts published later in 1966 that buttressed the war crimes case.[7]

Other PWs were visited in the spring of 1966 by Wilfred Burchett and by agents of Lord Russell, Burchett and Russell assembling evidence for their own respective investigations. Using a false name, Burchett interviewed Larry Guarino, Ray Vohden, and Jerry Denton. Ralph Schoenman, an American who was Secretary General of Russell's Tribunal, passed through the camps while collecting information for the legal defense of David Mitchell, the first American to refuse service in Vietnam on the grounds of it being a

---

* See Chapter 9.

criminal war under the Nuremberg charter. Schoenman met briefly with Jerry Coffee, who wrote a letter with concessions to the propaganda line in order to be sure that the missive would get out to his pregnant wife. Through their own grapevine as well as from the occasional news selectively filtered in by the Vietnamese, the prisoners were aware of the Russell inquest and of incidents such as the death of Norman Morrison, the Quaker who immolated himself near the steps of the Pentagon in November 1965.* Few, however, realized at this early point how organized the opposition to the American presence in Vietnam was becoming and how significant a seemingly innocuous letter might be in the hands of a polemicist like Schoenman.[8]

The charges propagated by Hanoi and recited by the Aptheker and Russell groups found a receptive audience among pacifists and anti-colonialists on both sides of the Atlantic, with veteran crusader types joined now by impressionable youths caught up in a groundswell of protest. In the United States, the crowded spring of 1966 saw scores of teach-ins, marches, vigils, picketings, and other demonstrations on college campuses and street corners of every major city. By midsummer the antiwar movement in the country had become alarming enough to conservatives in Congress to cause the House Un-American Activities Committee to subpoena prominent activists, and Nguyen Vien's taunt to Commander Stockdale that "we will win this war on the streets of New York" seemed less and less an empty rhetorical threat and more a purposeful plan of action.

Fortified by the warming antiwar climate, the North Vietnamese turned the heat up another notch in June, making direct comparisons between the U.S. bombing raids and Nazi World War II assaults and drawing the obvious parallel to the Nuremberg offenses. On 16 June Hanoi Radio reported widespread meetings and petitions urging punishment of the American pilots and a campaign to bring them to trial. While there was nothing new in all this, the U.S. embassy in Saigon noted "unusual intensity and shrillness" in the latest round of denunciations and reiteration of the word "immediately," which indicated the trials might be imminent. Following air strikes on oil depots near Hanoi and Haiphong on 29 June, ordered by President Johnson after repeated warnings to North Vietnam to stop its infiltration into the South, Hanoi Radio broadcast that huge crowds were milling about and shouting "death to the U.S. imperialists!"[9]

---

* Almost overnight Morrison became a martyr to the antiwar cause and a cult figure within North Vietnam itself, the Communists adorning factories and schools with his photograph, naming streets after him, and celebrating his memory in song and poetry. See Aptheker, *Mission to Hanoi*, 54. Morrison was eulogized by Communists in the South, too, the Viet Cong hanging his picture beside that of Nguyen Van Troi, the teenager executed by the South Vietnamese government in October 1964.

On 7 July the official Czech news agency claimed in a dispatch from Hanoi that North Vietnam might soon begin trials of captured U.S. airmen, and that death sentences could result for some. The Czechs believed the trials would commence either on 20 July, the anniversary of the signing of the 1954 Geneva Agreements on Vietnam, or on 4 August, the second anniversary of the Gulf of Tonkin incident. Although the U.S. government was still uncertain as to whether Hanoi was planning full and serious legal proceedings or mock show trials, State Department and Pentagon strategists circulated a "draft scenario" outlining a "menu of actions" that was designed to register U.S. disapproval swiftly and aggressively in either event. Finally, on 6 July—as it turned out, a day before the Czech dispatch—the several months of ferment came to an abrupt and dramatic climax in an episode that had far-reaching repercussions for both the American PWs and the psywar.[10]

At Briarpatch prisoners knew something was amiss when they were awakened early in the morning, ordered to shave, and without explanation told to hand over a set of their pajamas. Hurried through their afternoon meal, they were issued new uniforms that had three-digit numbers stenciled across the back of the shirts. Alvarez recalled being given a shirt stamped "206" and wondering why, since there were only a quarter of that number of PWs in the camp. Some of the men, having heard Hanoi Hannah's broadcast report of the renewed air raids, construed the high numerals to signify that the North Vietnamese were indeed shooting down large numbers of American pilots. Others surmised that the Viets were up to their old tricks, intending the three-digit figures, which ran into the 500s, to suggest they were holding many more prisoners than they actually had—though it was not yet clear for what purpose exactly.

That same afternoon PWs at the Zoo, issued similarly stamped shirts, also stirred nervously over changes in the normal routine. Rob Doremus noticed how speedily guards responded to his and his cellmate's request for medication for their diarrhea. Denton thought jailers making their rounds at the Pool Hall were more tense than usual. Jim Mulligan was taken into a quiz room next to the Auditorium for a photo session and on the way back to his cell spotted a heavily camouflaged truck in the courtyard.[11]

The accounts of repatriated prisoners differ significantly in their recollection of details surrounding the 6 July events (e.g., the numbers of men who received stenciled shirts and whether the shirts were distributed that morning or the day before), but there is general if not unanimous agreement that 52 of the PWs from the two camps, 16 from Briarpatch and 36 from the Zoo,[12] were assembled in the late afternoon, blindfolded, handcuffed in pairs, and taken in trucks to downtown Hanoi. Risner remembered one odd detail being that the Zoo PWs were outfitted with sandals secured with gauze strips as if to prepare them for some treacherous going. Those left behind at the camps were either seriously injured (Mulligan, Stockdale, and Fred Cherry, for example) or had not yet had their names released as prisoners of war.[13] In the latter case, the Vietnamese doubtlessly wished to keep the identities of these captures a secret, which they would not long have remained under the circumstances that were about to unfold.

Once in Hanoi, the Briarpatch convoy, which had come a considerably longer distance, made a rest stop at a sports stadium, where the men were fed rice and bananas and allowed to relieve themselves. Toward evening, with darkness descending, the two groups rendezvoused at a park area not far from the stadium and near the Hoa Lo prison complex. Still blindfolded and in cuffs, the prisoners were aligned in rows of two along a narrow road that emptied into the main street of the city. Rabbit, who functioned as a kind of coordinator for the operation, advised them that they were about to "meet the Vietnamese people."[14]

Although anxious as to what lay in store, the Americans were ecstatic over the reunion with so many comrades, nudging elbows or knees to communicate by code or talking openly until ordered to stop. "What [the enemy] had not learned," Risner later observed, "was that having a handcuff between us was just like a telephone. All either of us had to do was move the handcuff or put pressure on it, and we could communicate."* Some of those shackled together were already cellmates, but at least a dozen of the prisoners had been in solitary and, for them, being joined with a fellow countryman, even in chains, was cause for jubilation. When their blindfolds were removed, the men searched excitedly for familiar faces. Risner discovered he was now paired with Alvarez, with whom he had once communicated through a cell door but had never met face to face.[15]

The high spirits were soon deflated by Rabbit's snarling command to move out and by the spectacle ahead of floodlights, whirling cameras, and grandstands of menacing crowds lining the route to the main thoroughfare. As the men were prodded forward with bayonets, Bob Purcell shouted mockingly, "Oh boy, I love a parade!" Rabbit admonished them to show humility and bow their heads, but Denton and several others passed the word to look proud and stand tall.

---

* While boarding a truck at the Zoo for the ride into Hanoi, Risner had been cuffed to Air Force Lt. Jerry Driscoll. Driscoll had been jailed near him in Heartbreak a couple months before but was then unable to respond to communication because of a head injury suffered when he bailed out of his plane. With Driscoll having regained consciousness and Risner beside him during the trip into the capital, the two made up for lost time.

Hanoi March before guards lost control. *First row* (left to right): Keirn and Berg; *second row,* Shumaker and Harris; *third row,* Byrne and Guarino.

Bill Tschudy and Al Brudno, wearing numbers 381 and 399, were at the front of the column, followed by Phil Butler and Hayden Lockhart and then Risner and Alvarez, about 10 to 15 feet separating each pair. A cordon of red-scarved political cadre escorted the procession. According to North Vietnamese personnel captured in 1970, the political officers, hoping to win increased support from Hanoi's patrons, deliberately marched the group past the Soviet and Chinese embassies to impress officials there with the numbers of PWs the DRV held. As the column turned onto the main avenue, the prisoners were met by larger and noisier crowds, in some places massed 10 deep (John McKamey estimated as many as a hundred thousand altogether). Cued by a chanting Rabbit and incited by blaring loudspeakers and marshals with bullhorns, the throng erupted into a frenzy as the PWs filed past.

The hostile galleries cursed the prisoners, hurled bricks and bottles, and pressed close enough to pummel them with outstretched arms while guards grabbed the men by the hair or used rifle butts to force them to lower their heads. Scores of spectators broke through the makeshift barriers, darting in between the Americans—kicking, screaming, spitting, striking the defenseless men with clenched fists as they stumbled along dazed and now frightened. Alvarez heard someone profane his name and looked up to find a Cuban cameraman calling him a "traitor" and then smashing him behind the ear with a piece of equipment. He and Risner helped steady each other as they staggered under savage blows that dropped them to the ground. Tschudy, Brudno,

Butler, and Lockhart were brutally assaulted. A famous photo shows Lockhart holding up a dazed Butler after he had been hit by a bottle. Moments later, Lockhart was stunned by a punch; the two kept each other upright the rest of the way. Denton was felled by a rock, dragging Bob Peel down with him. As Peel helped him to his feet, the senior was slammed in the groin and took several more punches from the same assailant until he and Peel synchronized a maneuver to jab back with their free hands and also deliver a hook with their manacles.

The ordeal continued for perhaps two miles and for what seemed to Alvarez and Shumaker to be about an hour. Ed Davis and Jim Hivner took a vicious pounding, as did the other twosomes—Shumaker and Harris, Brunhaver and Singleton, Guarino and Byrne, Storz and Schierman, Coffee and Cormier, and on down the line. Others running the gauntlet included veterans Dick Keirn, Kile Berg, Wendy Rivers, Bill Shankel, Duffy Hutton, Porter Halyburton, Tom Barrett, and Bruce Seeber and 1966 captures Dick Ratzlaff, Cole Black, Charles Boyd, Alan Brunstrom, Darrel Pyle, David Hatcher, and Alan Lurie. Over the last third of the route, with the tattered column headed back toward the stadium where the Briarpatch group had stopped on their arrival in Hanoi,* the parade fully degenerated into a riot, the surging hordes completely out of control, until the political officers feared for the Americans' safety and the guards themselves began to panic. The latter tightened the ranks and now shepherded the bloodied and battered PWs toward the stadium gates. For the last 50 yards guards and prisoners alike forced their way through to sanctuary.

The final tandem of Ralph Gaither and Jim Bell just barely made it. Bell's left shoulder was still dislocated from his shootdown nine months earlier, and his right arm was handcuffed to Gaither's left, requiring Gaither to battle like a demon against the mob, which threatened to seal the two shipmates off from the others already inside the stadium. As they clawed their way along, they recited the 23rd Psalm. Gaither described the final 100 yards:

> There was no path through the tightly packed crowd. When the team of prisoners made it to the gate, it was opened for them and closed immediately once they were inside.
>
> We had a hundred yards to go. The crowd was hysterical. Every person there tried to get at us with their fists and rocks and shoes and spit.
>
> It took us fifteen minutes to make that hundred yards, and everything we had been through during the previous hour was

---

* Butler was later told by a camp officer that the march was to have culminated in a war crimes trial at the stadium but that the plan had to be abandoned as a result of the confusion and pandemonium. Alvarez and several others could not resist pointing up the obvious analogy between their situation and the Christians being led to the Coliseum to be thrown to the lions.

compounded in that raging crowd, a crowd that could only be described as raving mad.

Finally, the gates opened for us . . . .[16]

The inside of the stadium looked like a combat evacuation zone, with the men sprawled on the grass by the cinder track, tending to wounds while the guards took a head count. Nearly everyone had suffered injuries of one sort or another, some serious. One of the blows to Denton's groin had caused a partial hernia. Others nursed loosened teeth, broken noses, blackened eyes, and various bumps, bruises, and lacerations. As if to rub salt in the wounds, a voice over the loudspeaker system, still manipulating the crowds outside, proclaimed that for their crimes the prisoners had experienced the just wrath of the Vietnamese people.

Navy Lt. Cdr. Cole Black, captured only 15 days earlier and bleeding from cuts over both eyes, asked innocently, "Do they do this often?"[17] During the march Black had been chained to another recent shootdown, Air Force Capt. Charles Boyd, who, unfairly, chewed him out for bowing when Boyd mistook him for the taller Jerry Singleton, to whom Boyd had been cuffed originally on the trip into Hanoi. While blindfolded and amid the chaos of ducking bottles and dodging punches, Boyd did not realize that the Vietnamese had given him a new partner and that Black had in fact acquitted himself as well as anyone. As the two sat recuperating and chatting, Boyd recognized his error and dissolved in laughter despite his pain, perplexing Black again with his seeming bluster. Explanations for Boyd's puzzling behavior would have to await their next encounter, which would be many years later, for guards silenced them and they would not meet again until they were on their way home in 1973.

After a half hour or so to allow the crowds to disperse, the prisoners were loaded again onto the trucks and returned to Briarpatch and the Zoo. In the tumult surrounding their departure, the camp officers had failed to take the usual precautions, so that Risner and Denton were inadvertently seated together. When guards drifted to the back of their truck to get fresh air, the two seniors thus had a rare opportunity to compare notes. As Denton updated Risner on the condition of his squadron mate Ray Merritt and on the status of other downed fliers, he missed a signal that guards were approaching and was whacked senseless by one of them, but not before the two leaders had exchanged valuable information.[18]

The Briarpatch convoy reached camp about midnight, when the exhausted PWs were mercifully returned to their cells. At the Zoo, Dum Dum, furious at the conduct of several of the prisoners, ordered guards to gag Denton, Coffee, Hutton, Keirn, and Purcell, strap them to trees, and administer another beating. Others, still blindfolded, were led into walls and posts. Shumaker hit his head on a stone archway and was thrown into his cell unconscious. Guarino and Byrne were kicked in the testicles. Risner was run into the back of a truck and down a flight of concrete steps and so badly mauled from the day's abuses that his roommate Jim Lamar counted himself lucky for the severe arm injury that had kept him from making the trip.

By dawn, most of the Zoo participants were back in their cells. So ended what Gaither called "one of the blackest days of my captivity." It remained for Denton to have the last word with their tormentors. "Prepared for the worst" when taken at bayonet point before Fox, the Zoo commander, he was asked by Dum Dum (interpreting for Fox, who knew little English) what he thought of the march. Exploding with pent-up rage, he proceeded to denounce the parading of prisoners in the streets as "a return to barbaric times" and said he had nothing but contempt for the Vietnamese officers' "utter cowardice," predicting that the spectacle would "bring a wave of criticism from the world." Fox, with Dum Dum again translating, responded with unexpected solemnity: "I have something to say to you and I request that you remember it for a long time. These words are important. Do you understand? . . . The march was not the idea of the Army of Vietnam. The march was the idea of the people." Denton understood perfectly. Fox was telling him that the North Vietnamese Communist Party had ordered the march and that the Army did not necessarily agree with the decision. Upon later reflection, Denton would realize that Fox, as a professional soldier, was concerned that should the United States defeat North Vietnam, the Vietnamese military would be tried for war crimes if implicated in such transgressions. The brief exchange was an ironic epilogue to the hellish affair, as the war crimes issue had come full circle.[19]

As Denton predicted, the march proved a serious mistake for North Vietnam. One of the government's principal objectives in staging the event had been to produce film that could be used in the psywar. The organizers' intent was to show cowed Americans slinking cravenly through the streets of Hanoi before the jeers of a victimized but orderly populace. What they got instead was footage of manacled prisoners comporting themselves with admirable dignity and courage against an unruly mob. Rather than dramatizing the war crimes issue and arousing international sympathy for their cause, the march provoked an embarrassing backlash.

U.S. officials were quick to condemn both the march and the unrelenting threat of trials. Washington's response, heretofore measured on the war crimes subject out of concern for both domestic and North Vietnamese reaction, was now forthright and unequivocal. "We feel very strongly . . .," who are military men, who are carrying out military assignments in line of duty against military targets, are not war criminals and should not be treated as such." The notion "that these American boys have committed war crimes," Johnson told the nation, "is deplorable and repulsive. Your Government has taken every step that it considers appropriate to see that proper representations on this subject have been made." Secretary of State Rusk instructed all U.S. embassies and missions to be prepared to launch a diplomatic offensive should Hanoi proceed with trials and in the meantime to request host governments to advise North Vietnam that any move to try the American PWs would be a grave error. On the matter of the march, Rusk lodged a strongly worded protest with the ICRC, pointing out that such acts of public incitement and humiliation directed against prisoners of war were clear violations of Article 13 of the Geneva Convention.[20]

In a bipartisan burst of indignation the administration was backed by "hawks" and "doves" alike. Nineteen senators who opposed the widening U.S. involvement in Vietnam issued a "plea for sanity" to Hanoi, noting that any further violence against the captives would spark a public demand for retaliation "swift and sure." Democratic Senator Richard Russell, chairman of the Senate Armed Services Committee, warned that the United States would make "a desert" of North Vietnam should trials occur, while Russell's Republican colleague, Senator George Aiken, predicted the "complete destruction of North Vietnam" in the event that harm came to the American prisoners. Gauging such pronouncements as more than mere saber rattling, *New York Times* columnist James Reston thought putting the PWs on trial would be a gross miscalculation by the Communists. "There has been much stupidity but very little jingoism in America's conduct of this war," Reston wrote on 12 July. "The American people have been troubled but calm. With one or two exceptions, the President and his aides have avoided appeals to emotion and no effort has been made to arouse a spirit of hatred toward the political leaders or the soldiers of North Vietnam . . . But all this could easily be changed by howling mobs, drum-fire courts and firing squads in Hanoi." The *Times*, *Philadelphia Inquirer*, *Newsweek*, and *U.S. News & World Report* were among those publications that carried stories and pictures of the march, *Newsweek* titling its article "Trial and Error?" and the *Inquirer* decrying in an editorial "the cowardly abuse of defenseless prisoners" that "can only produce worldwide shock and revulsion."[21]

The march indeed produced shock waves both at home and abroad. It also compelled the Johnson administration to come to grips with the PW issue as a day-to-day problem that would require ongoing attention and carefully coordinated policy. For months, even before the springtime unease over Hanoi's escalating war crimes rhetoric, there had been mounting concern within the government over reports of Viet Cong and North Vietnamese execution and mistreatment of American prisoners.[22] Yet even as staffers in the State and Defense departments hurriedly developed information and plans, the handling of PW affairs continued to suffer from neglect and confusion. The political sensitivity of the issue, the still relatively small numbers of captured, the conviction that the plight of the men would only be complicated by official statements and public disclosures, and loose organizational arrangements that fragmented responsibility—all help to explain the government's halting, somewhat fitful approach to PW matters prior to July 1966. As a congressional report later noted:

> Even the term "prisoner of war" went largely unused until 1966. At this time, the U.S. Government believed that to publicize any details about the missing or the treatment they received would jeopardize those still held by the enemy, both in the jungles of the South and in the prisons of the North. Occasional public releases of POW/MIA information in 1965 merely identified the numbers involved. The brutal treatment of known prisoners was rarely presented by [Defense] Department spokesmen for public information. DOD had not yet created a special office to oversee policy for all POW's; each Service continued to minister to its own. The Joint Chiefs of Staff were preoccupied with fighting the war; other problems of Vietnam overrode the POW issue.[23]

By late April the threats out of Hanoi and the internal bureaucratic disarray had become serious enough to spur the White House to establish a special interdepartmental Committee on Prisoner Matters headquartered in the State Department, and, shortly afterwards, to consolidate the PW responsibility under State's veteran diplomat, W. Averell Harriman. The Pentagon itself recognized the need to give more attention to the prisoner problem, the Deputy Under Secretary of the Air Force writing to the Assistant Vice Chief of Staff at one point in May to complain about the lack of up-to-date files on known PWs and absence of "a central monitoring office to keep in close touch with OSD, State and the other Services."[24] The spring storm clouds raised eyebrows and consciousness levels all around but it was the July march that focused public interest and high-echelon official attention on the PW question as never before.

Harriman wasted little time assuming his coordinating role. He pursued a wide range of contacts with foreign governments and international leaders, including solicitations of support for the U.S. position from Moscow and the Vatican, consultations with Red Cross and United Nations representatives, and a bold if ultimately abortive attempt to initiate a dialogue with the North

Vietnamese chargé in Laos to discuss the PWs and other matters.[25] As a goodwill gesture he offered to arrange the repatriation to North Vietnam of Communist PT boat crewmen captured in the South by U.S. forces, and through intermediaries engaged in secret talks with the National Liberation Front to obtain the release of Americans held by the Viet Cong.*

Seeking the Pentagon's cooperation, Harriman telephoned Assistant Secretary of Defense John McNaughton on 19 July and asked for a complete list of "US personnel missing and known to be or possibly detained in North Vietnam together with appropriate data on the mission on which they were lost." In order to respond to Hanoi's charges about U.S. attacks on civilian facilities, Harriman also wanted "the fullest and most detailed information that can be developed concerning accidental bombing/strafing of non-military targets in North Vietnam." Additionally, Harriman conveyed to Secretary of Defense McNamara his view that the military services should not be excessively harsh in judging the Code of Conduct performance of returned prisoners lest the North Vietnamese and Viet Cong exploit the "heartless" treatment of returnees for propaganda advantage. Mindful of the "extreme sensitivity" of the subject within the services, the ambassador stressed that he was

> not talking here about prisoners who may have betrayed their comrades, or who have actively and obviously lent themselves to furthering the enemy's propaganda purposes. But where the alleged misconduct consists of isolated and possibly ambiguous statements, and where much of the evidence comes from post-release debriefings of the prisoner himself, I would propose for your consideration that a decision to proceed with formal investigation or indictment, or a public announcement thereof, might be held in abeyance pending high level review, perhaps by yourself personally.[26]

---

* Shortly before the Hanoi March, Harriman undertook a clandestine effort to secure the release or exchange of American prisoners in the South. Although he managed to open a channel of communication with the NLF and though there were some men released on both sides eventually as a result of the initiative, in general the code-named "Operation Buttercup" had only limited success owing to mutual distrust, unacceptable demands by the Communists, including U.S. recognition of the NLF, and breaches of secrecy that hindered negotiations. In the case of the PT boat captives, the U.S. overture was stymied by North Vietnam's characterization of its captured personnel as kidnapping victims rather than prisoners of war, Hanoi preferring for propaganda reasons to perpetuate the fiction that it had ordered no troops outside the North's borders, that it was waging a purely defensive war. (The sailors were after a time released anyway. See memo ASD(ISA) for DepSecDef, 6 Mar 68, sub: Responsive Release of North Vietnamese PWs Held by US.) The subject of prisoner exchange and release efforts, an intriguing and significant but little known aspect of the Vietnam PW story, is treated at length in Davis, *The U.S. Government and American PWs in Southeast Asia*, ch 5 (ms).

So that Hanoi could not point to South Vietnamese abuse of captured Viet Cong and North Vietnamese troops as a pretext for mistreating American PWs, Harriman followed up Rusk's 1965 review of conditions in the South Vietnamese camps with several actions to insure that the camps were being operated in accordance with the Geneva requirements. These steps included the construction of improved facilities, the training of South Vietnamese personnel in proper screening and processing techniques, and elaboration on previously implemented JCS directives regarding such matters as the clothing, feeding, and physical examination of enemy PWs. At a conference of Asian leaders in Manila in October, Harriman secured passage of a resolution reaffirming the Geneva principles and calling on full compliance by all parties. By November work was completed on a new prisoner camp at Da Nang and the Red Cross was reporting favorably on the progress in the treatment of Communist PWs in the South.[27]

While Harriman coordinated the diplomatic counterattack, on the juridical side government attorneys prepared legal defenses for the U.S. PWs, formulating a rebuttal to a brief that East Germany had furnished Hanoi citing grounds for war crimes trials based on the Nuremberg cases. Lights burned late in State and Defense legal offices through the summer of 1966 as researchers sifted mounds of files to assemble support for the government position. Reinforcement came from the legislative reference service of the Library of Congress, which, responding to urgent requests from members of Congress, found no precedent in international law for treating pilots as war criminals and determined that the Nuremberg Judgment not only did not give Hanoi authority to try captured fliers but that it specifically prohibited such trials as themselves violations of international law. In the event that Hanoi proceeded with the trials, the administration readied plans to obtain counsels for the prisoners.[28]

To aid the government's case, the Joint Chiefs of Staff declassified parts of the operating rules of engagement to establish the American pilots' innocence with regard to unavoidable civilian casualties. Further, the services, led by the Navy, proposed scrapping the policy of categorizing the prisoners as "detainees" (the customary way the State Department identified U.S. citizens held against their will in another country) and reinstituting the more specific and straightforward "captured or interned," which the military had used prior to October 1964.* "As our level of involvement has increased and as the problem of missing and captured personnel has taken on major significance," Assistant Secretary of Defense for Manpower Thomas D. Morris advised Deputy Secretary Cyrus Vance on 19 July,

* See Chapter 5.

the use of the "detained" language, particularly in the press release format . . ., has become increasingly troublesome. At the present time, Hanoi refers to captured U.S. fliers as "pirates" and "war criminals" and publicly threatens to try them as criminals. Any usage of terms by us which tends to derrogate [sic] from our prisoners' entitlement to the rights of "prisoners of war" is potentially embarrassing to the major effort now in progress to force Hanoi, as a signatory to the Geneva Conventions, to accord our personnel the rights of prisoners of war . . . .

Vance implemented the nomenclature switch in an order dated the same day as Morris's memo, directing also that captured personnel were now to be referred to in official correspondence and public statements as "prisoners." Moreover, the services redesignated several men carried previously as "missing," Alvarez for example, as prisoners. The changes, entirely semantic, were intended to remove the PWs from any legal limbo should trials occur. By August the military services had newly prepared instructions and freshly designed forms in use in their casualty offices.[29]

To monitor more accurately numbers and treatment of prisoners, as well as North Vietnamese intentions with respect to trials, U.S. intelligence agencies, throughout 1966 but with ever increasing urgency after July, upgraded their PW data collection and analysis efforts. Assuming a steadily broadening role, the Defense Intelligence Agency provided PW-MIA intelligence to the Office of the Secretary of Defense, the Joint Chiefs, and the State Department, and by the end of the year would be coordinating regularly scheduled interagency meetings among intelligence personnel from DIA, the individual services, and the Central Intelligence Agency. The CIA and the National Security Agency lent their support by passing all PW information to DIA and by assigning its collection a high priority. Codenamed "Brightlight," the overall program soon took on special importance. Throughout the intelligence community there was a ready willingness to share resources and expertise in the interest of determining the status and prospects of American servicemen captured or missing in Southeast Asia.[30]

Film of the July marchers permitted analysts to identify several of the individuals whose fate had been unknown, but ascertaining names and numbers of captured among those reported missing, especially in the case of airmen downed over the North, remained a vexing problem. Estimates varied widely and fluctuated regularly, as the Communists' propensity for secrecy and disinformation in the handling of PWs made confirmation of capture reports and prisoner sightings a formidable, frequently frustrating task. The services' own strict categorization criteria, requiring concrete and corroborating evidence, disposed casualty administration officers, in the absence of over-whelming proof of capture, to opt for the safer, more inclusive "missing" designation. To determine who among the MIAs might be in Vietnamese cus-tody, investigators had to rely on random and often shaky sources—intel-ligence from captured enemy personnel; reports from journalists and other visitors returning from North Vietnam, often Communist sympathizers inclined to distort the facts; and information trickling out of the camps themselves, either supplied intentionally by the Vietnamese in propaganda statements* or by the prisoners themselves in ways Coffee and others noted in their memoirs.† Because the prisoners were kept segregated and sometimes received their information second- or third-hand from fellow PWs passing through the system, even their figures were deemed undependable, although there were exceptions, notably the highly accurate information relayed by Jim Mulligan. Officially the U.S. government counted only 45 airmen as prisoners in the North as of August 1966; later evidence would place the total at closer to 150. The PW accounting would become as much a political and public relations affair as a numbers exercise, as Harriman, service casualty administrators, and government spokesmen, prodded by the press and fami-lies of the missing, were already discovering.[31]

If the war itself remained the preoccupation of U.S. civilian and military authorities dealing with Vietnam matters in the summer of 1966, there was in this flurry of diplomatic and bureaucratic activity indication that the PW issue had evolved from a peripheral concern to a subject warranting ser-ious debate and deliberation and that the Johnson administration was finally confronting squarely its many troubling aspects. To be sure, the adminis-tration remained ambivalent about publicly spotlighting the issue for fear of further harm to the prisoners and adverse domestic political repercussions—the so-called "Go Public" campaign of the Nixon administration was still several years away—and there were those both in and outside of the government who continued to feel that PW matters were not receiving sufficient priority. Owing in no small measure to the ill-conceived Hanoi March, however, the

---

* North Vietnam's eagerness to exploit such statements occasionally backfired. In late July, Hanoi's daily newspapers printed a photograph of Air Force Capt. David Hrdlicka, downed over Laos in May 1965, with a statement that he was "horribly lonely" thinking about his wife and three children and "all the more furious because while I am a prisoner here, the authors of the war policy are happy in the bosom of their families" (FBIS, 22 Jul 66). When Hrdlicka later dis-appeared in the prison system, either in Laos or North Vietnam, Hanoi was caught in a trans-parent lie as it attempted to deny he was ever in custody.
† See Coffee, *Beyond Survival*, 172-73; Mulligan, *Hanoi Commitment*, 116-21 (also Hubbell, *P.O.W.*, 228-30); Rick Maze, "Revelations in POW's Book Concern Pentagon Officials," *Air Force Times*, 8 Oct 84.

prisoners' fate and the policy decisions relating thereto were at last getting high-level scrutiny in Washington.*

With regard to the immediate concern, the danger of trials, Rusk's appeals to foreign governments and Harriman's patient backstage diplomacy were rewarded with a chorus of international protests denouncing the march and beseeching Hanoi to drop the prosecution idea. Prime Ministers Gandhi of India and Wilson of Great Britain, visiting Moscow, lobbied the Soviets to restrain the North Vietnamese. United Nations Secretary General U Thant issued a statement expressing disapproval, as did Pope Paul VI and the World Council of Churches. The International Committee of the Red Cross sent a cable reminding Hanoi of its Geneva obligations. And much of the world press chimed in.[32]

Recognizing that the propaganda war was being lost on the issue of the trials and wary of the possibility of U.S. retaliation, the North Vietnamese decided, apparently as early as the third week in July 1966, to abandon any plan to prosecute the American fliers. A message from Ho Chi Minh to U.S. socialist leader Norman Thomas and other American antiwar activists on 20 July referred to the DRV's "humanitarian" policy regarding captured enemy troops and conspicuously omitted mention of "war criminals." On 23 July Hanoi announced the formation of an 11-man committee to investigate "war crimes of U.S. Imperialists in Vietnam," but the move was probably a face-saving gesture calculated to buy time, as the same day Ho told a Columbia Broadcasting System representative that there was "no trial in view." The retreat seemed complete when a few days later Ho was quoted as remarking to a group of visiting journalists that the "main criminals" were not captured pilots "but the persons who send them there—Johnson, Rusk, McNamara— these are the ones who should be brought to trial."[33]

Newsweek reported on 1 August that "almost literally overnight, Hanoi [had] softened its tone significantly—and the sighs of relief were as audible

---

* Through 1966 and 1967, Defense would defer to State in most PW matters, such as efforts to gain prisoner release, attempts to persuade the Vietnamese to comply with the Geneva Convention, and determinations on what information to furnish next of kin. Pentagon representatives, however, voiced increasing unhappiness with their secondary role, with what they perceived to be State's oversensitivity to the political ramifications of prisoner-of-war policy decisions, and with State's general lack of assertiveness in holding North Vietnam to account (disapproving, for example, of State's reliance on ICRC inspections of prison camps). By July 1967, growing dissatisfaction among the services and in the Joint Chiefs of Staff led to creation of a top-level PW Policy Committee within Defense. Placed in the Office of the Secretary of Defense—clear testimony to the importance the Pentagon attached to the issue— the committee would exert steadily increasing influence. Davis, *The U.S. Government and American PWs in Southeast Asia*, a comprehensive study of the evolution of PW policy and organization within the Defense Department during the Vietnam War, treats the State-Defense frictions and the formation of the new Pentagon committee in ch 2 (ms).

in Washington as they were anywhere." In fact, the retreat was only a "tactical withdrawal," as the State Department saw it, North Vietnam denying only its intention, not its right, to try the prisoners. The trial threat would resurface periodically, if never again as dramatically, with Lord Russell's Tribunal serving Hanoi's purpose as a surrogate hearing in the meantime. Despite the muted language of Ho's 20 July communication, the war crimes rhetoric continued unabated. Having judged the trials themselves as counterproductive, Hanoi sought to turn the setback to advantage by attributing its decision not to proceed with prosecution to its "humane and lenient" disposition rather than any change of heart regarding the gravity or culpability of the pilots' actions.[34]

Although the North Vietnamese had lost a key round in the psywar, they remained convinced they would prevail over the long haul. Indeed, in a series of dispatches from North Vietnam in late December 1966 and early January 1967, *New York Times* assistant managing editor Harrison Salisbury did much to undermine the U.S. position and restore Hanoi's credibility with new disclosures of U.S. bombing damage to Vietnamese cities and civilians. Salisbury's reports, which were printed almost daily in the *Times* and published in book form in April 1967 and quoted in newspapers around the world, turned out to be suspect, based in large part on unverified information supplied by Communist sources, including a North Vietnamese propaganda pamphlet distributed shortly before his visit. The *Times* issued a belated and partial retraction but stood by the main thrust of Salisbury's account. The sensational impact of the respected newsman's articles from "behind the lines" demonstrated how mercurially the momentum could shift in the psywar.[35]

With the legal ambiguities relating to the nature of the conflict and the status of the American captives going unresolved and the military situation seemingly locked in a stalemate, the psywar promised to gain in both intensity and significance. By the end of 1966, in the wake of the Hanoi March, it had already become a major battleground, engaging high-level elements of both governments, entailing elaborate tactics and strategy, and ensnaring not only Salisbury but the likes of CBS News correspondents Charles Collingwood and David Schoenbrun and award-winning journalist Harry Ashmore.[36] If the North Vietnamese continued to view the prisoners as an asset to be exploited to advantage in the propaganda contest, the goal of American officials was now to persuade the enemy that the PWs were more a liability than a prize in this respect.[37] In effect, the prisoners were working from the inside to achieve the same result, although they hoped, of course, to remain valuable enough to their captors to be kept alive and well. If there was any satisfaction derived from the march by the PWs, it was that the event had given their plight critical public exposure, even as the sour outcome spelled more trouble for them.

11

"Make Your Choice": Another Round of Terror

Fox's disavowal of responsibility for the Hanoi March unfortunately did nothing to alleviate the mental or physical anguish the exercise inflicted, or to soften the treatment that would follow. The frustration and embarrassment that resulted from the misadventure left the North Vietnamese in a foul mood and more determined than ever to establish U.S. criminality. Pressed to back up earlier assertions and regain lost ground in the propaganda war, the Communists undertook an all-out campaign to wring corroborating confessions from their captives as to the illicitness of the U.S. involvement and the American pilots' own actions. Thus, even as the threat of actual trials gradually receded, the PWs faced no letup of persecution or exploitation.

In the days and weeks following the march, the Vietnamese hammered away at the war crimes theme at every opportunity. They released individual photographs of Jim Mulligan and Dave Hatcher (the first their families and authorities learned they were alive) with alleged statements by the two men condemning the war; identified Ed Davis, Bruce Seeber, Cole Black, and Air Force Lt. James Ray, the latter captured in May, as prisoners, with pointed references to the airmen as "criminals"; and disseminated pictures of new shootdowns in humbled or sinister poses. In two films made about the time of the march, Air Force Capt. Murphy Jones, seized on 29 June, was shown first bandaged and dirty, clad in underwear, then, more provocatively, aboard a truck in his flight suit.[1]

The Mulligan and Hatcher depositions were aired over official radio on 7 July, only hours after the marchers had been returned to their respective camps. Mulligan was quoted as acknowledging that he was shot down on a mission "attacking your country" and that he had "killed many innocent people and destroyed civilian property." "This war in Vietnam," the apology continued,

Jones paraded in truck.

had no appeal for me for it was an unjust war against a people who never did anything to the detriment of the U.S. interests. My military obligation forces me to participate in this war; many other military men share this same attitude, as do numerous other groups forming against this unjust and unlawful war in the United States and contributing to a groundswell of war opposition on the U.S. homefront. . . .

For my own crime I beg your forgiveness and request that you treat me humanely and allow me to have some part in ending this dirty war waged by our government.

The statement attributed to Hatcher was virtually identical in both style and substance. Hanoi's official newspaper supplemented the broadcast confessions with an article appearing on 11 July under the headline, "Confessions By The U.S. Aggressor Pilots [Bare] The Johnson Clique," in which Seeber, Jones, and Ray were quoted as conceding the illegality of their government's actions and expressing gratitude for their "humane" treatment. Seeber was said to have realized that "the war waged by my government in South Vietnam and the bombing of North Vietnam do not conform to the U.N. Charter and are contrary to the 1965 Geneva agreements."[2]

Such confessions, when authentically signed or spoken, could have been extracted only under extreme pressure. To obtain them, the Vietnamese, beginning immediately after the march and continuing for the remainder of the year, required the Americans to "choose" between cooperation and resistance, the one path, the captives were told, boding good treatment and perhaps early release, the other torture and possibly death. Although the Communists introduced the so-called "Make Your Choice" (or "Choose the Way") proposition as if it were a new initiative, the program was little more than a formalization of longstanding practice whereby the enemy sought to legitimatize punishment by shifting the burden of responsibility to the prisoners themselves. What was new about the program had more to do with thrust than substance: whereas previously such an extortion tactic was used primarily to cripple resistance, the singular objective now was to obtain the coveted confessions of criminal wrongdoing that could be exploited in the propaganda war. The PWs had an inkling of what was transpiring, but they attributed the stepped-up quiz activity to the need for evidence specifically for the Russell Tribunal, not realizing the much wider audience to which Hanoi's political warfare office was playing.

Given the constraints of even a modified Code of Conduct, "Make Your Choice" was, of course, a proposition offering no choice at all. Later there would be a few instances where American PWs would elect to cooperate—as we shall see, several of them would be charged with treason by fellow PWs upon their return to the United States—but at this point in the summer of 1966 there is no recorded case of a prisoner in the North who did not follow the seniors' instructions to hold out as long as possible.* The only question was how much torture a man would or could take before submitting. As always, thresholds differed from one individual to another, but from the testimony of prisoners observing prostrate comrades being delivered, one by one, to their cells after interrogation sessions, it is safe to say that no one went unscathed during this period and that many endured extraordinary suffering. Denton went so far as to state in a homecoming report that "the month of July 1966 was perhaps the most torture filled month of the PW history."[3] Depending on when they and those in proximity to them went to quiz, others would say the same of August through November.

As usual, Colonel Risner was at the center of the latest confrontation. A few days after the march, elaborating on the seniors' earlier general order to resist to the utmost, give as little as possible, then recover to resist again, Risner issued guidance advising PWs who were being forced to read indoctrination materials at the Zoo library to hold out indefinitely but not past the point where they risked "permanent loss of a limb or of sanity." He intended

---

* One marginal case, though his identity remains a secret and the details sketchy, is discussed in Myers, *Vietnam POW Camp Histories*, vol 1, 95.

especially to reach the junior officers at the Zoo and later arrivals who might not have received the earlier instruction. When one of the prisoners tried to circulate the message by scrawling the word "RESIST" in six-inch-high letters on the ground in the exercise area, it was Risner who was called to account.

Guards placed the aviator in the tiny, unventilated punishment pen in the Zoo's Auditorium, where he remained for three days in the brutal heat of Hanoi's midsummer, suffering from diarrhea, sores, and boils, his hands cuffed behind his back, and his body clothed in heavy, long prison pajamas. On the third day, and daily for the next week, they ran him back and forth between the Auditorium and his cell, requiring him to listen to radio propaganda broadcasts while in his room and tightening the cuffs another notch on each visit to the "hot box." When he attempted to communicate with Jim Lamar and was accused of concealing a nail that had been planted by a turnkey—the Vietnamese would frequently plant an object such as a nail or razor blade, then conduct an inspection to "discover" the item and have yet another pretext for interrogating and threatening the offender—he spent another night in the Auditorium, during which he was beaten and his cuffs were ratcheted to the last possible notch. In excruciating pain, he confessed to communicating, ordering the resistance, and secreting the nail, but refused to write that he had committed crimes against the Vietnamese people. Only when yet another stretch of torture threatened the loss of use of his arms and wrists did he finally accede to the fourth charge. His continuing ordeal—the price of leadership and of his own hardline defiance—bad as it had been, would somehow grow ever worse. Dragged aboard a truck with recently captured Navy Lt. Paul Galanti, he was returned to Hoa Lo in late July, to begin what he would later term "the longest six weeks of my entire life."[4]

Meanwhile, at Briarpatch the arrival of another 15 prisoners on 11 July brought to 54 the number of Americans there.* As camp commander, Frenchy implemented the "Make Your Choice" program with ruthless efficiency, combining it with a campaign of harassment that required the PWs to bow or face harsh penalties. Certain guards, particularly "Magoo" and "Slugger," regularly struck the men without provocation, on occasion forcing them to run barefoot and blindfolded through the compound or dragging them by nooses around their necks. Even "Flower," a pudgy "chow girl," and "Johnny Longrifle," a water hauler of 15 who was shorter than the rifle he later carried as a soldier, took to insisting on bows from the Americans. When new SRO Larry Guarino instituted a do-not-bow policy, a number of prisoners observed it to the letter, taking torture almost to the point of permanent maiming.

---

* The precise figure remained in flux, as prisoners were rotated in and out of the remote camp for various reasons, for example when serious illness or injury necessitated sending an individual back to Hanoi for treatment (as happened with Jim Bell and John Heilig).

Guarino rescinded the order because of the rough and disproportionate punishments it brought, but his communication did not reach everyone, so that several endured further agony for what seemed a relatively minor infraction.[5]

The misery was compounded by reduced rations, heavier doses of radio indoctrination, and a decision by the Vietnamese to keep cell windows shuttered even through the summer months, turning the rooms into steam baths. Guards poked long sticks through cell bars to inflict still more torment. Treatment at Briarpatch always seemed to be more vicious than elsewhere in the system, perhaps because of the camp's atavistic character and isolated location that gave staff somewhat freer rein and that heightened tensions and irascibility all around. An undesirable assignment for prison personnel and PWs alike, there was a tendency for "bad attitude" cases on both sides to wind up there, making an already grim situation even more combustible. Whether in truth or for effect, Frenchy explained to the Americans that guards that summer were in an especially ugly mood because of reports of relatives killed by the U.S. bombing and because President Johnson's resumption of air attacks had destroyed half of North Vietnam's petroleum supply and was severely impeding the effort against the South.[6]

The "Make Your Choice" program began in earnest at Briarpatch in August with the arrival of a political commissar the prisoners nicknamed "Doc" and a new extortion specialist who soon earned the moniker "Louie the Rat." They joined the despised holdover "Bug" (known also as "Mr. Blue," for the color of the camp's torture room), a physically repulsive, emotionally unstable interrogator whose wandering right eye, constantly jabbing index finger, and harping "You have murder my mother" evoked alternately scorn and terror. When Doc's appeals to reason and for voluntary statements proved unsuccessful, the bad guys took over.

Paul Kari was taken to interrogation on 5 August, followed in rapid succession by his roommate John McKamey, Alvarez, Tom Barrett, and Scotty Morgan. All were brutalized, their screams heard by the others over several days and nights, until the captors extracted the requisite confessions and apologies. Alvarez described the ritual in his memoir, remembering vividly the encounter with Bug and his henchmen and how "for the first time in my life I felt sheer hatred":

> August 9 was my day of infamy. They came in early and . . . took me to the quiz room. They eyed the blank piece of paper. I tried to make light of it, nervously remarking, "See, I haven't written anything."
> "You want me to punish you?"
> "Well . . . I guess . . . ."
> "That's the only way you're going to get anything."

> To help him put on the cuffs, [Bug] summoned J.C.* I knew
> what was ahead and prayed I would be able to withstand it. They
> held my hands behind my back and closed the ratchet cuffs around
> my wrists, squeezing the metal to the last notch. But my wrists are
> smallish and they could see that the cuffs were not biting in hard
> enough. They opened them up, bent my arms as close together as
> they could and fastened the cuffs tightly a few inches below my
> elbows. The pain was excruciating. It felt like a hacksaw had stuck
> deep in my flesh. The cuffs seemed to cut through to the bone. My
> head was pushed far forward and all I could do was yell and scream
> to ride with the pain. They left me alone for quarter-hour spells and
> then returned, yanking my arms up and squeezing the cuffs tighter
> yet. The worse it got the louder I shrieked. The more I howled the
> more they slapped and punched. J.C. preferred to strike from behind
> but when he came from in front it was always with the underside of
> his closed fist. My eyes felt like popping. My veins wanted to explode
> in a gush of boiling blood. J.C. was joined by "Ichabod Crane,"†
> a spindly 6′2″ turnkey with a drooping head, blazing dragonian
> eyes and clothes that were too short and tight-fitting. Together they
> worked me over heartlessly, like a couple of kids pulling wings off
> flies. "Write!" they shouted as they struck with their fists and feet,
> knocking me off the stool, hoisting me up again and using me as a
> punching bag.

By mid-day Alvarez was ready to write, though it would be a few hours
before he could hold a pencil, his hands "attached to the ends of . . . [his]
arms . . . like frozen gloves." It would be two years before they would regain
their natural color.[7]

Jon Reynolds was told to write on one of two topics, "Follow the Way of
Ho Chi Minh" or "Follow the Way of LBJ." When he refused the bait and
wrote nothing, guards forced him to sit on a small cement block, tightly
handcuffed, for four days and nights until he wrote that he followed the way
of LBJ. Having made the wrong choice, he was cuffed and confined in darkness for several more days until he finally admitted, craftily, that he was sorry
"for the miserable Vietnamese people." Others, too, dissembled as best they
could. A battered, feverish Al Brudno, agreeing to write after handcuffs were
ratcheted through to both wristbones, said he regretted coming to Vietnam
because the Vietnamese people had been "truly revolting" for 4,000 years.[8]

Ralph Gaither's appointment came on 10 August, Phil Butler's on the
11th. Cellmates Bob Shumaker and Smitty Harris were summoned on the

---

* J.C. was the name some prisoners used for Dum Dum. However, by most accounts the latter
remained at the Zoo after the Hanoi March and was still there at the close of 1966. Alvarez,
then, may well have been referring to a different officer (or guard) altogether.
† Also known as "Beanpole."

15th. Gaither's two days in the "Blue Room," poignantly recounted in his memoir, left him with lasting nerve damage to his hands and an "unspeakable agony of soul" in the aftermath of his surrender. Butler and Shumaker, finding the pain of the "hell cuffs" intolerable, each tried to commit suicide by bashing his head against the stone wall of the torture chamber. Rod Knutson, his forehead split open from a hammering with rifle stocks, was convinced he was going to be beaten to death.[9]

With the air war penetrating deeper into the North, the Vietnamese appeared to grow increasingly concerned about the possibility that Briarpatch might be raided. Sometime in mid-August they instituted a series of precautionary measures, including cuffing the prisoners routinely for much of the day (after several weeks, the cuffs were replaced by a rope tied only to one wrist); dressing the men in long-sleeved pajamas so that they could be evacuated on short notice; and digging trenches and building fortifications throughout the camp. The prisoners would later disagree as to whether Frenchy was acting out of genuine (if unfounded or exaggerated) fear of an attack or if he was merely contriving new ways to pester his charges. Whatever the motive, the result was yet more distress for the Americans, as the bindings and heavy clothing added further discomfort to already sweltering conditions and the trenches were used for evacuation drills that caused the men, who were blindfolded and manacled during these exercises, more bruises and lacerations. Moreover, deep holes dug beneath cell bunks, ostensibly as bomb shelters, became convenient punishment stalls. Reynolds, Brudno, Butler, Lockhart, Bell, and McKnight were among those required to spend a month in the dank, vermin-infested pits for communication violations.[10]

On 17 September the camp underwent a reorganization, a shuffling of bunk assignments that seemed designed to separate those prisoners who had already been tortured from those still awaiting their turn. At the same time, Frenchy conducted a communications purge that snared the Reynolds group mentioned above and others who were managing to transmit messages by tapping along the walls—"like earnest woodpeckers," Alvarez remembered—or rattling wastecans or dishes in code. Until the summer of 1966, much of the communication activity at Briarpatch had occurred in the bath area, where the men had in fact established a "mailbox" drop, but the stiffer regimen installed after the Hanoi March, which limited bathing and interaction in general, made contact more difficult and dangerous. Still, the men managed to improvise, even after the September crackdown. Ed Davis, worked over for a week when he and roommate Jim Hivner were accused of relaying information to comrades, tapped out a message to Alvarez and Barrett that he had discovered how to use a piece of straw to loosen his cuffs. Gaither and Bill Shankel held a communion service by tapping on the bars of their adjoining

"Briarpatch Gang" victims.
Top: Tschudy (left), Brudno;
middle, from left, Barrett, Bell,
McKamey; *bottom,* Chesley,
Ray, Singleton.

cells.* Kile Berg, who replaced Barrett as Alvarez's roommate, showed the veteran PW how to cushion his buttocks against the jagged edges of their shared toilet bucket by squatting on his rubber sandals.[11]

The second batch of prisoners went through much the same paces as the first group, with a few new features added to the program in late September. Shankel, Jerry Singleton, Larry Chesley, and Wendell Alcorn were among those who were run barefoot through the evacuation trenches and then stashed in five-foot-high caves dug into the sides of the ditches. The combination of bloodied toes and ankles, poor diet, and the onset of cooler weather produced a painful beriberi-like condition that came to be called "Briar-patch feet" and that, according to Chesley, afflicted almost all the men who took torture in September and October. Where necessary, the ratchet cuffs followed or accompanied the trench detention. By fall, "LBJ all the way" had become the stock refrain for PWs being asked to make their choice, but for the second wave, too, compliance was only a matter of time, and in the end they capitulated also—like their precursors, doing their best to render confessions useless by contorted grammar or idiom or clumsy penmanship. The resourceful Berg convinced an interrogator that Batman and Robin were real and had the Vietnamese pumping him for information on where the crime-fighters lived and to what political party they belonged.[12]

Toward the end of November, with the entire camp having been tortured for statements (some twice), Briarpatch returned to what sufficed for "normalcy." Improvement in treatment coincided with the departure of the increasingly psychopathic Bug, who was transferred to the Hilton. The prisoners were now allowed outside, one cell at a time, to get fresh air and even start a small garden. Frenchy initiated a camp cleanup that utilized the PWs to hoe weeds, bury rubbish, and lime the refuse pit. The men fertilized the garden plots with feces from the dump area, planted greens, and watered them with urine. Just before the prison closed in February 1967, the PWs would dine on some of this hardy produce.[13]

The relaxation extended through Christmas, when the Americans were permitted to sing holiday carols, play chess and checkers, eat a large meal that included turkey and carrots, and decorate a tree. They were also encouraged to tape greetings to relatives, an invitation that some, whose families had no other way of knowing they were alive, eagerly accepted, but others rejected on the assumption that the enemy would exploit the recorded seasonal messages to lend credibility to its "humane and lenient" claim. For the same reason—that the activity might boost Vietnamese propaganda more than

---

* Shankel, who occupied a cell next door to the Blue Room, overheard every torture session and attempted as best he could to tap news and encouragement to the victims when they were left alone. He estimated that on average the PWs lasted two to three days before breaking. His own turn came in late August, but he received a reprieve on 2 September when a national holiday intervened.

their own morale—the prisoners were divided over whether to participate in the recording of holiday music. Deciding to tape songs while taking care to avoid anything that smacked of an antiwar anthem, Art Black treated his comrades to a drum solo of "Jingle Bells," Jim Ray sang "Puff, the Magic Dragon," and Gaither strummed a medley of Christmas tunes and for good measure played "The Wabash Cannonball" and "Malagueña" on a crude Czech guitar the Vietnamese provided.[14]

All told it had taken a protracted three to four months for the Briarpatch authorities to pry loose the formulaic statements of confession and apology. The "Briarpatch gang" would become famous when tales of their extraordinary ordeal and remarkable valor would circulate among, and become an inspiration to, later captures. Although they surely deserved their exalted stature, it should be remembered, in the interest of perspective, that they had no monopoly on horror or heroism. The fact is that prisoners throughout the system faced much the same hardships during this period and generally performed at the same impressive level.

The experience of PWs at the Zoo, for example, paralleled that of the Briarpatch group almost to a man. The Zoo had its own special cases, and, owing to differences of geography, numbers (it contained twice as many PWs), and other factors, its wave of terror exhibited its own peculiar tendencies, but in the final analysis one would be hard pressed to say which group suffered more or coped better. As at Briarpatch, Zoo officials were preoccupied in the summer of 1966 with obtaining propaganda materials to support the Russell Tribunal and other psywar efforts, "Make Your Choice" becoming the prime vehicle for accomplishing that goal. Risner's treatment at the ramshackle camp during the week after the Hanoi March signaled the start of a new round of torture there that followed the same basic pattern as the persecution at Briarpatch, peaking in the early fall and winding down to a Christmas recess.

Because of the camp's proximity to Hanoi and Hoa Lo, prisoners at the Zoo were often taken into the Hilton for their interrogation and torture sessions. Risner was regularly shuttled between the two.[15] In July, Wendy Rivers, Jerry Coffee, Ray Merritt, and Duffy Hutton were quizzed at the Ministry of Justice building across the street from the downtown prison, then put in ropes until they produced incriminating letters, which they were forced to tape as well. Rivers recalled that when he and Hutton compared notes afterwards, the latter had a sagging right eyelid "and it appeared that every blood vessel in his face had ruptured." Guarino, just before being shipped to Briarpatch, spent a long night in the ropes at Hoa Lo in which he was spreadeagled and gagged before surrendering. Also passing through Hoa Lo at this time were new shootdowns undergoing their initial interrogation, men like Paul Galanti, Darrel Pyle, Alan Lurie, and Leonard Eastman, the newcomers receiving their baptism under particularly nasty circumstances.* [16]

Rabbit, Pigeye, and Mickey Mouse supervised the process at Hoa Lo, with Fox, Dum Dum, Spot, and "Lump," a political officer with a large tumor protruding from the middle of his forehead, presiding at the Zoo. Lump impressed the Americans with his smooth English and overall bearing but was viewed warily as a soft-sell artist who could coolly make the transition from carrot to stick if he did not get results; in this respect, he may have assumed a role similar to Doc's at Briarpatch. [17] As for torture instruments, Pigeye was partial to the rope treatment, but the ratchet cuffs that were used so efficiently at Briarpatch were employed at the Hanoi prisons, too.

As at Briarpatch, guards assaulted and tormented Zoo inmates indiscriminately between formal quizzes. Turnkeys purposely left cell doors unlocked after evening meals so that cohorts could enter, in twos and threes, and administer random beatings. For full-fledged extortion sessions, the men, when they were not brought to Hoa Lo, were sent to the Auditorium, Outhouse, or "Gatehouse," a long, bunkerlike concrete building near the front entrance to the camp that had been converted into a punishment facility. Except for larger dimensions, the Gatehouse's cells resembled Briarpatch's notorious pits: darkened, unventilated, fetid, without mosquito netting, and with oven-like summer temperatures (by one estimate, registering over 100 degrees at midnight). The Auditorium's single cell—cramped, pitch black, strung with cobwebs, and teeming with maggots—the PWs likened to a closed coffin. In one pen or another, sometimes hauled between buildings or tortured in their own cells when Gatehouse's torture row was fully occupied, over 100 Zoo residents paid their dues between July and December 1966. [18]

Victims that summer included Howard Rutledge, John Borling (an Air Force lieutenant captured 1 June), Norlan Daughtrey, Larry Spencer, Al Brunstrom, Jim Mulligan, and Jerry Denton. Rutledge entered the Outhouse on 8 August and did not leave until signing his confession on the 31st, spending the better part of a month in anguish—legs in irons, hands cuffed behind his back, surrounded by "a pile of human excrement crawling with countless moving things," only a small bowl of rice to eat each day with two cups of filthy water, and so ravaged by heat, dysentery, hunger, and pain that he

---

* Navy pilot Galanti and Air Force officers Pyle and Lurie were captured in the same vicinity within days of each other in mid-June. Captain Lurie spared the other two some pain by taking the lion's share of abuse with recalcitrant behavior at holding camps on the way to Hanoi. All, including Eastman, a Navy lieutenant seized on 21 June, experienced a rough reception at the Hilton before being trucked to permanent quarters at the Zoo. The four completed their initiation in time to participate in the Hanoi March.

"could remember I had children but not how many." Borling took several severe beatings and suffered infections over much of his body, counting some 30 boils at one point.[19]

Mulligan, whom the Vietnamese seemed to shift constantly from one building to another—between July and September he occupied the Barn, Garage, Auditorium, and Stable before landing in the Gatehouse—was one of the few who was not shackled during the course of "Make Your Choice," probably because of his grave physical condition that was exacerbated now by starvation and dehydration.* Dave Hatcher reported to Denton in mid-September that "Mulligan looked like a survivor from a Nazi concentration camp and weighed no more than 100 pounds." The Navy commander had verged on collapse after spending five days entombed in the Auditorium until the Vietnamese finally permitted him to wash and brought him tea and a decent meal. The stay at the Gatehouse caused his condition to worsen again, such that as he lay on his floor pallet he was "ready to die," when a medic gave him pills for his dysentery that again revived him.[20]

Denton was one of those who preferred the traumatic but relatively quick torture of the ropes or hellcuffs to the drawn-out endurance sessions in the punishment pens. He was already well familiar with both techniques and now experienced each anew. He spent most of the summer and fall alternating between the Auditorium and his cell at "the Gate" next to Borling's, as the Vietnamese pressured him to rewrite his springtime confession according to the new format. When Lump asked him to supply information on the PW communications network and he refused, he was placed in a gruesome contraption that utilized ankle restraints, a rope, and an iron bar in a pulley-like operation. Lump released him from the apparatus after 10 days and nights of daily tightening had nearly severed the senior's Achilles tendons.[21]

By October, a combination of circumstances—the rush of events with the impending commencement of the Russell proceedings, a brimming camp population, and continued PW resistance that prolonged the extortion process—caused Zoo authorities to resort increasingly to the intensive approach.† With the Auditorium and Outhouse being utilized round-the-clock, the Gatehouse filled to capacity, and the Hilton itself crowded with new shootdowns, Lump and his henchmen, including a strapping youngster the PWs called "Big Ugh,"‡

---

* Curiously, Mulligan was also the only PW to wear a blue-colored pajama suit, which he received early in his captivity. He liked its distinctiveness because it enabled other PWs to spot him easily.
† Denton later remarked that "the resistance was so stiff . . . they were running out of torture equipment." He recalled seeing a guard "taking apart a huge metal sign and cutting it into pieces with an acetylene torch to make more traveling irons" (*When Hell Was In Session*, 123).
‡ Stockdale described him as "a moon-faced big country boy of about seventeen who had just joined the army and was strong as a horse" (*In Love and War*, 187). See, too, Mulligan, *Hanoi Commitment*, 114.

began torturing prisoners in their regular cells at the Barn and other build-ings in the compound. Air Force Lt. Fredric Flom, who had been seized in August and stayed long enough at Hoa Lo to have his shattered arm placed in a cast, was observed by Denton absorbing repeated beatings in his Gar-age cell. Flom's squadron leader, Maj. James Kasler, the subject of a *Time* article that lauded him as a Korean War ace and one of the "hottest" pilots in Southeast Asia,* suffered a hideous leg fracture upon ejection that did not prevent Dum Dum from working him over in the Stable.[22]

At the Office a goon squad visited Air Force Capts. Wilfred Abbott and Robert Waggoner and Lts. Ralph Browning, Edward Hubbard, Martin Neu-ens, and Leroy Stutz (all summer 1966 captures except Stutz, who was seized in the fall). Abbott, on loan to the Navy and downed while flying an F-8 Cru-sader off a carrier, broke a leg on ejection much like Kasler. Browning, whose father had spent 19 months as a German PW at Stalag 17 during World War II, became a father himself around this time, but would remain unaware of his son's birth: his wife Ann wrote him almost daily, but no letter would reach him until April 1970. Stutz went down with badly injured Capt. Robert Gregory, who never made it past Hoa Lo. When Stutz asked about his mate's fate—they reached the prison together but Gregory soon disappeared—a Vietnamese told him cryptically, "Many men die in war."[23]

The Pool Hall, with Denton in command and Mulligan quartered there after 21 September, became something of a "Dirty Dozen" menagerie of hard-liners and hospital cases. Hatcher occupied cell 2 (between Denton and Mul-ligan); Brunstrom and Render Crayton, cell 6; Bob Purcell was in 7; Coffee, 8; Daughtrey and Ray Vohden, 9. In cell 4 or 5 (Denton and Mulligan have different recollections here) were Quincy Collins, the crippled September 1965 shootdown, and Air Force Capt. Armand Myers (captured the same day as Borling, 1 June), both hobbling about on cane and crutches. In cell 10 were recent captures Navy Lt. Cdr. Jack Fellowes and Air Force Lt. Ronald Bliss. Fellowes, whom Denton would praise as "one of the toughest men in prison," had lost the use of his arms when tortured for information on the EA-6 (an electronic version of the A-6) at Hoa Lo soon after his incarceration. Bliss, though disabled himself with a serious head injury, attended to Fellowes and, by several accounts, including Fellowes's own, literally kept his cellmate alive until he was well enough to feed and bathe himself.[24]

Although it is difficult to exaggerate the travail experienced by the Ameri-can PWs during the "Make Your Choice" campaign, it must be noted that even reigns of terror have their subtleties and vicissitudes—that there were exceptions, anomalies, aberrations from the norm that here and there relieved the picture somewhat, at the Zoo as at Briarpatch. Both Mulligan and Coffee

* Kasler was shot down on 8 August—incredibly, the very day the *Time* story appeared. The North Vietnamese wasted no time capitalizing on their prize catch, promptly reporting his capture and showing him off to the foreign press.

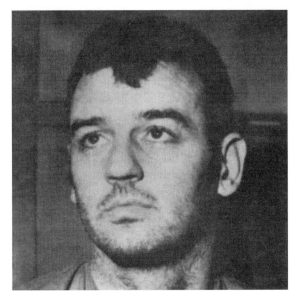
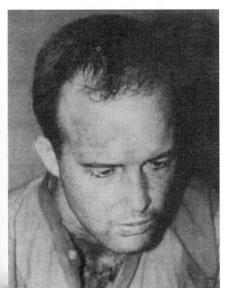

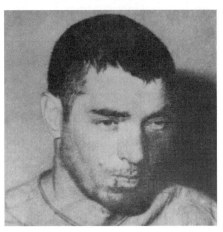

"Pool Hall" residents, *clockwise from top left,* Daughtrey, Vohden, Collins (with crutch), Hatcher, Fellowes, and Bliss.

remembered fondly a Zoo jailer they called "Happy," "a decent sort" whom
Denton, too, found sensitive and considerate. Coffee's and Rivers's recollections among several others are surprisingly restrained in recapitulating this
period, suggesting it was less eventful and trying for some of the men than
it was for others. Rivers mentioned that on five separate occasions, inexplicably, Zoo PWs received a ration of beer. Kasler conceded that Vietnamese
medical personnel set his damaged leg and gave him a shot of penicillin even
as they verbally assaulted him and repeatedly applied and removed a body
cast for the benefit of photographers.[25]

Moreover, as at Briarpatch, even the darkest hours were brightened from
time to time by small victories and moments of levity that, however ephemeral,
sustained pride and morale. Fellowes gulled an interrogator into believing
that movie star John Wayne was a pilot in his squadron but had refused
combat duty and was ordered to remain in the United States. Prisoners viewing a propaganda film late in 1966 managed to clasp hands despite the elaborate precautions taken by officials to separate the men. Denton circulated Ed
Davis's method of loosening and removing cuffs and then devised a technique
of his own, though when guards detected it, Denton recalled in his memoir,
the Vietnamese "procured a heavier type of cuffs made in China from which
no one could escape." By dislodging panels in doors and windows, several
men fashioned peepholes for intelligence-gathering or simple "viewing pleas-
ure." Mulligan got a chuckle out of watching a group of Vietnamese peasants
stealing bricks from a Zoo storage pile.[26]

And finally there was the anodyne of communication, at once balm and
tonic, available, as always, even where there seemed to be insuperable obstacles. "By applying our communication system persistently and creatively,"
Coffee later wrote, "we [breached] barriers of brick and concrete and vast
spaces in between." Barn resident Harry Jenkins used his height to send signals and messages over the top rim of the shower stalls above the heads of
unsuspecting guards. Mulligan managed to transmit to Jim Stockdale, who
remained isolated in the Zoo's Garage during the summer and fall of 1966,
a map of the camp and his memorized, ever-expanding list of PW names,
using toilet paper and the pen that Dum Dum obligingly provided for his
"Make Your Choice" statement. He and Coffee "talked through the wall" in
adjacent cells at the Pool Hall, the latter establishing an "all clear" procedure
and using the noon siesta hour to convey news and words of support to his
long-suffering comrade. Denton's ragtag band at the Pool Hall, in between
torture sessions and licking wounds, clocked guard movements and recorded
the comings and goings of vehicular traffic outside the cellblock. The Zoo's
scattered layout, with prisoners dispersed over several buildings, normally
made camp-wide communication more difficult there than elsewhere, but

Fox's policy after July of shuffling the men between facilities and between the Zoo and Hoa Lo—intended to disrupt communication channels further—actually resulted in an enhanced networking.[27]

Beginning around Thanksgiving, again following the Briarpatch pattern, treatment steadily improved. On 8 December 1966 Denton watched intently as guards retrieved cuffs and irons from cells; shortly afterwards, for the first time since spring, he received a ration of cigarettes, was allowed outside for 15 minutes a day for exercise, got a haircut, and was permitted to bathe and shave at regular intervals. Mulligan reported that all quiz activity came to a halt in the Pool Hall. Veritable "banquets" were served both Thanksgiving and Christmas, replete with turkey, vegetables, and hot tea and coffee. Christmas was observed with lights, festivities—and propaganda. "I'm sure these clowns are putting on their Christmas act tonight," the sequestered Stockdale thought as he heard a busy commotion outside his cell. Indeed, nearby in the "Coop," Fox and Lump were receiving prisoners in a room decorated with a tree, ornaments, and an old nativity set ("probably left behind by the French," Rivers surmised), dispensing oranges and cigarettes as photographers clicked away. Earlier the men had been escorted individually through the Auditorium, again cameras snapping in the background, to view a grisly exhibit of pictures of mangled and mutilated bodies, allegedly victims of American bombing attacks. As the PWs gathered there for a movie the day after Christmas, an air raid siren went off when a U.S. low-level reconnaissance plane flew over the camp, giving the Vietnamese shudders and the Americans yet another lift.[28]

By January 1967 the weather in North Vietnam had turned a bone-chilling cold and the sweatboxes of July and August now became deepfreezes. Mulligan remembered rolling up in his blanket New Year's Eve at the Zoo "chilled to the marrow" and shivering "like a rattling bag of bones covered by a loose shroud." As bad as the heat and humidity were in summer, most of the prisoners would later have more vivid and bitter memories of Vietnam winters, and by many accounts the winter of 1966-67 was among the harshest. Norm McDaniel, who spent January in solitary confinement at the Zoo, wrote that prior to his capture he thought of Vietnam as "a tropical country with year-round warm weather. But after I spent my first winter in North Vietnam [that season], that image was dispelled . . . . Although I have some skin discolorations from heat rash and tropical itch, my most painful climatic experience was with cold weather."[29]

The frigid elements posed as many problems as the enemy and as challenging a test of the Americans' ingenuity. Rivers recalled "experimenting" with his two thin blankets and two long pairs of pajamas in various layers to achieve maximum warmth. Alvarez remembered the grounds at Briarpatch frosting over at dawn and he and his roommate Kile Berg huddling together and dreading the next call to interrogation. He noted in his memoir that one of the best ways to be prepared for the sudden summons to quiz during the winter was to be "overdressed," to wear both sets of pajama shirts and trousers for extra insulation against the numbing cold of sleepless nights and prolonged stays in the quiz and punishment rooms. Stockdale learned from comrades Jim Lamar and Sam Johnson how to protect his feet by putting his pants on upside down, that is, by hitching the open pants legs up to his waist and using the closed drawstring end of the pajamas to create an insulated pocket for his toes.[30]

The start of a new year brought plenty of opportunity to apply the "cold war" tactics. As surely as winter followed fall, the relative benignity of the holidays gave way again to meanness in a cycle that was becoming all too familiar to the PWs. Although "Make Your Choice" had run its course by December, January witnessed another binge of brutality as remorseless as the weather. When caught tapping to Bill Shankel, Ralph Gaither was cuffed and stuffed in a pit filled with waste, then beaten and gagged. Bob Shumaker was asked to tape a confession stating that he had been shot down while attacking a population center, the city of Dong Hoi. When he resisted, guards dragged him to a new torture room on a hill 100 yards above Briarpatch, where they put him in ropes, applied ratchet cuffs, and bashed him with metal rods for 20 minutes, then took his clothing and threw him into a muddy ditch with icy slush up to his bare ankles. After being extricated, he was dragged around the camp on a leash and returned to the torture room for another flogging until finally yielding and taping a statement to Frenchy's satisfaction.[31]

Others, too, had to deal with the inclemency of both the season and the captor. In mid-January occupants of the Zoo's Pool Hall were marched to quiz one by one, some taking torture for the third time in six months. Meanwhile, downtown at the Hilton, Pigeye was busy initiating a new arrival with his nefarious assortment of "straps and bars." Navy Lt. Cdr. Richard Stratton, seized on 5 January 1967, the first American pilot bagged by North Vietnam in the new year, "was a Communist propagandist's dream," author John Hubbell observed. "He was just what the Vietnamese were waiting for, a big, heavy-set, dark-visaged, tough-looking . . . American imperialist."*

As Pigeye administered the rope treatment, Stratton, his wrists already shredded from hellcuffs, felt the pain beginning instantly, "as if someone had

---

* In a 1978 self-characterization, Stratton agreed that he fit the stereotype perfectly: "I've got the big nose, sloping forehead, the crew cut, the pot belly; I'm everything their cartoonists use to portray the typical American aggressor on the land, sea, or air; and I've got the loud mouth; I was the arch-type of what the mad bomber was going to be." See Blakey, *Prisoner at War*, 110.

thrown a switch," the sensation "indescribable," his shoulders seemingly "trying to roll out of their sockets." In repeated efforts to get the aviator to admit that his plane had been felled while bombing Hanoi, Stratton was beaten to a pulp, burned with a cigarette, had his thumbnails bent back, and was twice left cinched in the ropes. After two weeks he capitulated, but not before urinating on the confession papers. Stratton's defiance would soon manifest itself again in an episode that would cause Hanoi considerable grief and deliver another serious blow to its psywar campaign.[32]

Fortunately, just as the Vietnamese appeared to be resuming full-scale extortion operations, another holiday, Tet, intervened and this time ushered in an extended period of remission that finally brought the curtain down on the post-Hanoi March round of terror. With U.S. pressure having effectively silenced talk of war crimes trials by year's end and secret discussions underway between the North Vietnamese government and Johnson administration, the PWs benefited from a general relaxation of tensions beginning in late January and lasting into the spring. During Tet Risner had a genial session with Cat, who, he recalled, "was in a good frame of mind, helped by drinking several glasses of wine. He could turn it on and off like a faucet, but now he was quite jovial and friendly." Rivers recalled that it was about this time that the Vietnamese first issued socks to the prisoners: "They were poorly made and ill-fitting [but] they did help keep his feet warm." Mulligan and Denton would each later reminisce about their mutual elation at discovering they were to become cellmates after long terms in solitary, Mulligan saying it was the best day he would ever have in Hanoi "save one . . . the day I was repatriated."* [33]

Denton's and Mulligan's happy arrangement was short-lived—Mulligan referred to it as a "three day honeymoon"—but not because of any new crackdown. Rather, the two were separated when the Communists decided to close Briarpatch and transferred several dozen PWs from both Briarpatch and the Zoo to expanded facilities at Hoa Lo. Briarpatch was vacated, including every pig, duck, and piece of furniture, on 2 February. The Vietnamese claimed that an acute water shortage necessitated the evacuation but they may have wanted to relocate the prisoners closer to Hanoi in the event of a cease-fire and possible early repatriation. Except for a brief period in February 1971 when it was reactivated to hold a small group of PWs captured outside North Vietnam, the frontier camp would remain shut for the duration of the war.[34]

---

* As bad shape as Mulligan was in, he thought Denton looked "a helluva lot worse," with sunken eyes, a skeletal frame, and a week's growth of beard that made him appear "twenty years older than his actual age." Mulligan used the same concentration-camp analogy to describe Denton's condition that Dave Hatcher had applied to *him* (in a report to Denton no less) the previous September.

The system-wide overhaul, carried out the last week in January and first week in February, marked the conclusion of one phase of the captivity experience and the inauguration of another, as the revamping of the physical setup was accompanied by a fundamental shift in the captor's philosophy and policy. The "Make Your Choice" program that dominated the PWs' lives between July and December 1966 was not exactly mothballed—it would be reinstituted again and again in one form or another over the next several years as an instrument of intimidation and torment—but it was never again employed as systematically or as feverishly. "By no means were mistreatment and torture to end," Hubbell noted; "for the Americans, the worst periods of the long captivity still lay ahead. But henceforth, pressure was to be applied on a somewhat more selective basis and for specific purposes, not merely to make men utterly submissive or to cow the United States." In Denton's words, torture would still be "used for punitive purposes—even, at times, on a camp-wide basis—for such things as escapes and the discovery of sophisticated command and communications systems. Prolonged spot purges against specific groups were also conducted for propaganda exploitation, and new prisoners were tortured individually for military information. But routine subjugation purges against the entire mass of prisoners did not continue."[35]

Denton attributed the policy change to the prisoners' stout resistance: "The North Vietnamese had thought the Americans would be easy touches, and when they were not, the whole program of total subjugation was thrown into chaos. There wouldn't have been much point in torturing us to death. What they wanted was to subdue us and then win us over to the point where we would routinely do their bidding. They failed." The PW leader could not bring himself to acknowledge what the majority of his comrades painfully conceded, that they had in fact been subdued, if only after barbaric brutalization. Denton misread the Communists' primary objective as subjugation rather than obtaining propaganda statements and overlooked the importance of external events and Hanoi's own miscalculations in explaining the ultimate failure of "Make Your Choice." Most of the men had melancholy rather than proud recollections of the affair. Typical was Gaither's solemn epilogue to the Briarpatch segment of his captivity account: "So ended my stay in Briar Patch. As unpleasant as some of the incidents were that I revealed in these chapters, they were not the worst. Many terrible things happened at that camp, things that I cannot bring myself to write down in this book. That men can perform the inhuman acts to other human beings that I saw in Briar Patch is a hard fact that is unfathomable in its reason and incredible in its cruelty."[36]

Even if Denton misstated somewhat the significance and outcome of the post-Hanoi March terror, the American PWs clearly had given the Vietnamese all they could handle. The ordeal that was, in Gaither's phrase, an "agony of soul" had also become a testament of faith. "You build up experience," Shumaker later said, referring to his own stay at Briarpatch. "You go through that thing, and you learn that they didn't really kill you, and they probably have an interest in keeping you alive. And this makes you a little stronger to hack it the next time." Risner wrote in his memoir how around Thanksgiving 1966 he would shout encouragement out the window of his cell in New Guy Village to anxious arrivals entering the Hilton, his hollers bouncing off the walls of the cellblock as if the sound were coming from the ceiling.

> Before we were released, I had guys come up to me who knew I was in New Guy Village for a long time. They would ask, "Did you ever sing out the window?" I said, "Yeah." They would say, "You know what? I was standing in the room in there after my capture, and heard a voice come out of the ceiling singing, 'Have faith. Don't give up. Keep your chin up.' I would look all around and it was just like a voice right out of the sky!"[37]

12

The Middle Years in the South: Nick Rowe's Group in the Delta

I n 1965 U.S. troop strength in South Vietnam grew from about 25,000 at the start of the year to over 50,000 in June, and, following the installation of Prime Minister Nguyen Cao Ky and Chief of State Nguyen Van Thieu, to approximately 180,000 in December. By the end of 1967, the total would soar to almost a half million. Along with the soldiers came also thousands of civilians—engineers, technicians, mechanics, teachers, contractors, program administrators—to work in support capacities. The steady Americanization of the war exposed both U.S. military and civilian personnel to increased dangers, including risk of death or capture. The number of U.S. combat fatalities in the South climbed from 245 at the end of 1964 to almost 16,000 through December 1967. The number of captured did not match the total in the North but was significant nonetheless, reaching nearly 50 by the time of the Hanoi March in July 1966 and upwards of 100 by the end of 1967, as many as a score of them civilians.[1]

Because they were fewer in number, more isolated, usually of lower rank, and engaged in less glamorous and publicized actions than the aviators who went down over the North, the Americans held by the Viet Cong in the South, with some exceptions, have generally not received the attention given to the Briarpatch gang and other PW groups in the Northern camps. This is unfortunate. Imprisoned in the deepest recesses of Indochina's jungles, they underwent their own physical and spiritual agonies, in many cases even more excruciating because of the dearth or complete absence of comrades with whom to compare notes and share food or feelings. A nomadic captivity in the custody of guerrillas meant less regimented discipline and fewer episodes of planned, organized torture but also a more chaotic, brutish daily existence. They were placed in bamboo cages and huts rather than concrete cells, were required to move long distances in deteriorating condition, and were more at the mercy

Cage used for American PWs in the South.

of the elements than their compatriots in the North, who suffered terribly from extremes of hot and cold weather but whose cement walls at least afforded some protection from blistering sun and monsoonal rains. Describing "the torment of the rain-forest prison camps" that lay ahead of captured civilian Douglas Ramsey, seized by the Viet Cong in January 1966, Neil Sheehan, author of *A Bright Shining Lie*, cited the virulent forms of malaria and beriberi common in the South, "the leeches, the cobras that were to curl for the night under the bunk of his cage, the forced marches whenever the exigencies of the conflict required a shifting of the camp, the terror of the B-52 strikes by his own Air Force, the guards who stole food the prisoners needed to survive because they were hungry themselves, the hideously cruel interrogators who were embittered toward all white men by too many years of war and fugitive jungle existence."[2]

Despite marked differences in the captivity environment as well as in the sociological makeup of the respective PW populations,* there were also inevitable similarities between the Northern and Southern captivity experiences. In an interview with *U.S. News & World Report* following his release in 1973, Ramsey voiced many of the same sentiments expressed by Northern returnees at their own homecoming debriefings, alluding, for example, to the chronic

* See Chapter 4, note 10.

problem of boredom (to occupy his mind, he devised and solved mathematical puzzles) and the wide variation in the temperaments of his guards (some being "fairly decent" and others "something out of the Marquis de Sade"). Clothing (Ho Chi Minh-style pajamas) and shaving and bathing privileges were roughly comparable, if the former was in shorter supply and the latter more problematic in the South. (Prisoners in both regions complained about the lye soap—in the words of a Southern PW, "the only thing I've ever seen that will go through two layers of skin without touching the dirt.") Robert Browne's study of the treatment of U.S. military personnel captured in the South examines a range of subjects from interrogation and indoctrination procedures to daily routines in terms that are sometimes indistinguishable from characterizations of prison life in the North. Our own previous discussion of VC indoctrination (see Chapter 4) indicates that it had much the same priority and was conducted in much the same fashion as under the North Vietnamese (see Chapter 9), though perhaps with more local discretion and improvisation owing to the guerrillas' greater autonomy.[3]

Granted certain common themes, it is still accurate to say that, on the whole, conditions in the South were harsher and less forgiving. Captured Viet Cong documents may have stipulated that American hostages were not to be mistreated and were to be carefully handled and cultivated for purposes of political exploitation. In practice, however, with the VC's roving bands often unaccountable to superiors, one was more likely to find in the South rogue individuals and maverick units who ignored prescribed procedure and, as evidenced in several cases mentioned in Chapter 4, abused or murdered their charges without apparent authorization.[4] As noted previously, approximately 20 percent of the prisoners captured in the South eventually perished, as compared with 5 percent in the North. Even where American PWs were not willfully mistreated in the South they fell victim to the more spartan circumstances, the greater severity of the environment, and in general the more punishing day-to-day physical hardships. Soap and towels may have been issued in the jungle, but they were replenished less frequently; pajamas and mosquito nets were more threadbare; and the mosquitos were more vicious and ubiquitous. A captive in the Mekong Delta called the mosquitos there "unbelievable," saying "you look down at your bare feet [in the morning] and it looks like you're wearing black socks." As Lt. Col. Michael Murray observed in a study for the Naval War College, "many men died in captivity [in the South] simply because it was too hard to live."

> Pleas to men, who had just laid down to await death, went unheeded. Even slapping them to get them angry in hopes of inspiring some motivation to live did not succeed. Captured in November 1967 with a bullet wound in his left shoulder, a broken wrist and two

fractured teeth, Dr. Kushner* was given two asprin [sic] for treatment, and the bullet was removed without anesthesia. This treatment was typical rather than exceptional. The death rate in the South was extremely high, and was due principally to conditions of filth, deprivations in diet and treatment, and sickness.[5]

Deficiencies in training and mental toughness among the high percentage of enlistees and civilians confined in the South may have contributed to a greater degree of malaise and fatalism among Southern PWs, but certainly one could make the case that environmental factors alone can explain their lower morale and lesser fortitude. Kushner spent time incarcerated in both the North and South and although his stay in the North came toward the end of the war when conditions had radically improved there, even taking that into account, he found "no comparison" between his three-and-a-half years in the jungle and his two years in Hanoi's concrete jails. "In our camps in SVN," he stated upon his return in 1973, "every day saw a grim struggle for survival. In NVN we simply waited—we waited in cold (or hot depending on the season) dark cells, subsisting on meager diets; but there was not a daily active battle for survival." Northern PW Richard Stratton later conceded: "It was better for us than for [those in the South]. . . . We were less isolated in urban areas than in the jungle, so for every [piece of] bad news we heard on the radio from Hanoi Hanna, we heard good news from a downed flier or another new prisoner. They tried to keep us isolated, but they couldn't keep us from communicating. We knew we had each other."[6]

Prisoners in the South did have one option that for the most part was not available to PWs in the North: they could, and did, escape on occasion. The same lack of sheltering walls that left them exceedingly vulnerable to the inclemencies of climate removed a principal barrier to breaking out and slipping away—and, once having accomplished that, they had a chance to make their way to friendly in-country forces or natives. Not that it was easy or that it happened with any regularity. In transit the Americans were usually bound with rope, then at night shackled or chained to trees or poles. Temporary camps were surrounded by a punji-staked or fenced perimeter, with watch-dogs, roaming guards, or booby traps also placed in the vicinity and the prisoners sometimes blindfolded as well. If these security precautions somehow failed, the would-be escapee still had to navigate dense jungle without a compass or provisions, typically minus shoes, and in a debilitated state. "You can walk out of the camp," 1968 escapee James Rowe later contended. "But they don't really worry about you getting away. They found that everybody that tried . . . either blundered into more troops, ran into another camp, or become [sic] disoriented." Proceeding overland through thick brush

---

* Army physician and PW Capt. Floyd Kushner (promoted to major while in captivity in June 1969). See Chapter 4.

during the rainy season, Rowe said, "you leave a path that looks like Fifth Avenue . . . ."[7]

Despite the overwhelming odds, some succeeded. Rowe's stunning escape after five years in Viet Cong custody is treated on p. 241. Marines James Dodson and Walter Eckes, captured and held together in May 1966, took advantage of guards' carelessness to make their getaway on 18 June, reaching friendly lines four days later after trekking through miles of rough terrain. Most of those who were successful managed to escape within days or weeks of their capture, when they still had the strength to pull it off. Army PFC Bruce Graening was seized 9 March 1967 and during the night of 17 March overpowered a single guard and made it to U.S. control the next morning. Army Spec. 4 Donald Braswell and civilian Dewey Holt freed themselves within 24 hours of their capture, untieing their bonds as their two guards slept, shooting the VC with their own weapons, and fleeing to safety the same day. An unusual case was Spec. 4 Thomas Vanputten, who in 1969 escaped after more than a year in captivity and survived 18 days wandering in the jungle before a U.S. helicopter spotted and evacuated him. Issac Camacho, like Rowe, escaped after a long confinement, but had the advantages of help from a couple of comrades and knowledge of the approximate location of Government troops.[8]

Including several individuals who were in custody less than 48 hours, about two dozen American PWs escaped from Viet Cong captivity.[9] Though not a large number, that was still two dozen more than successfully escaped from North Vietnam prisons,* and over 10 percent of the total number seized in the South. Though a high-risk undertaking, with failure bringing almost certain reprisal, it must not have seemed like much of a gamble when compared to the alternative—enduring the known and unknown perils of a jungle captivity at the mercy of treacherous natural forces and an equally cruel and capricious enemy. The one course held out the prospect of freedom; the other, even more so than in the North, slow starvation, deterioration of body and soul, and eventual demise.

"It is probably the most hostile natural environment that an American could face." Thus did one commentator at a 1975 PW conference describe the region south of the Mekong River, a watery maze of snaking canals, infested swamps, and thick mangrove forests. If PW survival was chancy everywhere

* There were a few notable if ultimately abortive escape attempts in the North, including instances where prisoners made it out of permanent detention facilities and temporarily eluded recapture. These, along with the controversy over the matter of escape policy and the application of the military Code of Conduct's escape doctrine in such problematic situations, are discussed in later chapters.

in the South, nowhere were the odds worse than in the Mekong Delta. Here prisoners were confined in cages that hovered on stilts just above the water, contracted unremitting and often fatal diseases, and had to subsist, as did the VC themselves, on a scavenger diet and what scarce supplies the VC were able to float into the area on sampans and other small boats. Of the 14 Americans known to have been captured in this region, one was rescued soon after being caught, three were released early and one at homecoming, two escaped, five died in captivity (including one who was executed), and two remain unaccounted for. Significantly, only one of the four seized after 1968, when conditions and treatment steadily improved elsewhere, survived in the Delta.[10]

Lt. James (Nick) Rowe, Capt. Humbert (Rocky) Versace, and Sgt. Daniel Pitzer had been in Viet Cong hands since October 1963. Late in 1964 they were joined by Sgts. Edward Johnson and Leonard Tadios. For months the group had been hauled from camp to camp through the Delta's rice paddies, their rambling captivity punctuated by failed escape attempts, extended bouts of dysentery, and dashed hopes for release.* January 1965 found them on the move again. They reached a stand of crude huts on 25 January and put up there until 7 February while guards fenced in a new compound the men called "No-K Corral." Here the prisoners savored the opportunity to walk about without sinking to their knees in mud. For Rowe and Pitzer it was the first time in 16 months they felt solid ground.[11]

By late March, all except Versace† were back at a detested site Rowe labeled "Mosquito Junction" for another round of indoctrination, this time led by a political officer named Mr. Hai. Hai, nicknamed "Goldie" for his gold-capped teeth (he was also known as "Mafia"), had a better command of English than the previous indoctrinator, Mr. Ba, and was considered by Rowe to be shrewder and more effective. But the techniques were basically the same that had been employed earlier: droning discourses on Vietnamese history and the virtues of communism, the alternation of threats and punishment with overtures and blandishments, the manipulation of expectations, the resort to a Red Cross data card to elicit information, and attempts to play on rank and race to divide the Americans. With regard to the latter, Rowe remarked during a 1969 debriefing that "Pitzer was prejudiced, and Johnson was a racially conscious Negro" and the VC tried to exploit the friction between them.[12]

---

* See Chapter 4.
† The recalcitrant Versace was kept separate from the others, and so his whereabouts are difficult to reconstruct. He was last seen shortly before the group arrived at No-K, when Rowe spotted him, looking white and gaunt, near a canal bank. Pretending to address a guard, Rowe exchanged a message with the hardline resister: "Nick here, Rock. All of us still hanging in and pulling for you." Rowe remembered Versace responding faintly: "Thank God you're here, Nick. God bless you." It was the last communication any of the group had with their courageous comrade, who would be executed several months later. See Rowe, *Five Years to Freedom*, 150-51.

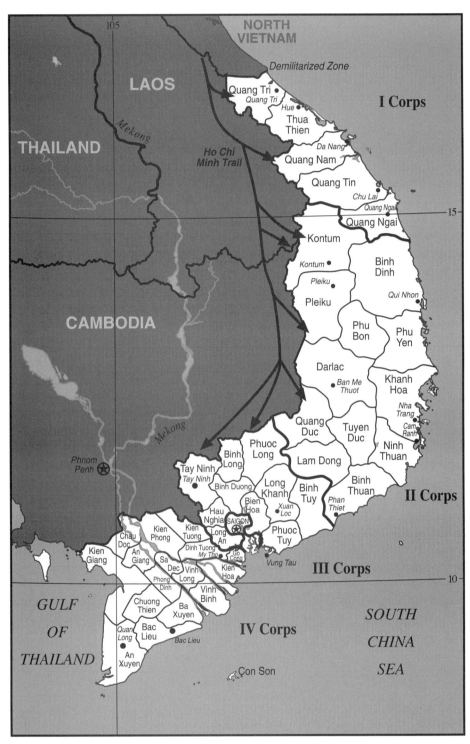

South Vietnam Provinces and Military Regions (1965)

The prisoners were aware of the enemy's gamesmanship and equivocated and dissembled as best they could when finally forced to write, but in the end they had no choice but to cooperate.

Rowe stuck with his fabricated cover story so long he was sent to a "punishment" camp, where additional indoctrination was interspersed with wood-gathering details and phony air raid drills in which he was made to walk barefoot over sharp weeds that shredded his soles. In May he was joined at "Salt Mines" by Len Tadios, who had attempted escape, avoided capture for two days, but wound up at the punishment camp in heavy leg irons. There followed "two and a half months of utter desolation and hopelessness,"[13] according to Rowe, with infrequent meals, long stretches without water, and a persisting fungus affliction that now threatened Rowe's eyesight. Only the drenching downpours of the rainy season saved them from dehydration.

In late August, their strength ebbing, they planned yet another escape, Rowe fashioning a flotation device from a pair of old pajamas and the two whistling show tunes ("Tonight" from *West Side Story* and "Old Man River") to coordinate a midnight getaway. Woozy from malnutrition, plagued by swarms of mosquitos, confused by a heavy cloud cover that prevented them from using stars for a compass, and having to tramp through chest-high grass that left an obvious trail in their wake, they barely made it to daybreak before a search party discovered them. Returned to Salt Mines, they were clamped in straitjacketing arm irons along with leg irons and spent a week writhing in their own diarrhea until Rowe promised they would not try to escape again.

On the evening of 7 September 1965 Rowe and Tadios rejoined Pitzer and Johnson at No-K Corral. The reassignment, ostensibly a reward for cooperation, provided little relief. On 26 September the quartet listened to an English-language broadcast out of Hanoi on a radio supplied by guards, riveted by the words that "the execution was carried out at ten o'clock" and then learning that "Captain Humbert Roque Versace" and, amid the static, a prisoner named "Coraback"* had been killed "in retaliation for the murder of three patriots in Danang." The startling announcement plunged them further into despair.[14]

Rowe was convinced that he had become a marked man himself, having "failed" his indoctrination lesson and been targeted as a troublemaker much the same as Versace. (He told a debriefer in 1969 that Mr. Hai later confirmed that he had in fact been on a short list for execution.)[15] With Pitzer, he passed his second year in captivity on 29 October, reckoning that, whether by slow death in the jungle or quick death by killing squad, he was destined to pay with his life. The more protracted the captivity, he realized, the less chance they had. George Fryette, Roque Matagulay, Arthur Krause, and others released by the VC in the early years, Rowe later explained, were held for not

---

* Sgt. Kenneth Roraback, a member of the Camacho group. See Chapters 4 and 13.

more than six months. "During this period of time they're capable of providing for a man . . . . But after six months, this sort of falls away. They have neither the desire nor the ability to keep a man over an extended period . . . ."[16]

Trapped in what the Special Forces lieutenant referred to as "a tightening vise,"[17] Rowe drew on all his training and mettle to survive. He later credited his rudimentary understanding of medicine with helping him through his malaria and dysentery. During punishment periods he diverted himself by reciting the names of state capitals and recalling from memory verses of Chaucer's *Canterbury Tales*. He maintained muscle tone by hoarding any greens he could find and walking or running in place the equivalent of a kilometer each day. By sheer will he managed to keep down protein-laden snakes, dogs, and fish, however rotten or nauseating, closely observing his guards' habits for tips on edibility and flavoring. And, like American prisoners in the North, he gradually adapted the Code of Conduct to circumstances that did not permit the traditional "heroic" posture, resisting behind an occasional "facade of courtesy and cooperation" and relying on guile rather than insolence or unacceptable silence while hatching escape plans. Of Versace, Rowe later said the senior set an example that was "unbelievable" but unrealistic: "He followed the Code of Conduct to the letter, and he was executed because of it. Now, it's true they got nothing from him, but we lost a fine officer." Although he felt guilty at having perhaps compromised the Code and feared punitive action should he make it home, Rowe remembered that "his thoughts of the indoor toilets at Levenworth [sic] made that appear to be a very attractive alternative to his captivity experience."[18]

Few PWs, in the North or the South, combined survival skills and steely temperament as proficiently as Rowe. And, unsurprisingly, few—in the South, only a handful—fared as well. Among Rowe's noncom cohorts, Pitzer had nerve and guts but suffered crippling injuries during his capture that hampered his adaptation. Tadios was brave but unseasoned and also impaired by serious wounds. In even worse shape was Army Capt. O. J. Walker, who had been held captive and in isolation for almost a year when he linked up with the Rowe group in a bivouac area on 7 January 1966, in Rowe's description, "a hulk of human wreckage." It had been a dreadful period for Walker in which he had lost 100 pounds, developed a pronounced stoop from long intervals of enforced squatting, and been ravaged by a series of infections and ulcerations. He had attempted one escape and resisted staunchly until starvation and infection drove him close to death. Why the Viet Cong transferred him to the Rowe camp is hard to fathom, though Rowe speculated they may have thought the company of other Americans would revive him. Walker was overjoyed to be united with his countrymen and was deeply moved at the attention given him by medic Pitzer and Rowe, but the rehabilitation was too little and too late. So severe was his ringworm-type infection that one hand had swollen to four or five times its normal size and when Pitzer lanced it, Rowe later recalled, "it looked like somebody had shot [Walker] with a 45." His mates kept him alive for 28 days, but he had deteriorated to the point where Rowe doubted he would have survived even at the best stateside hospital. On 4 February, under orders from guards, Pitzer, Rowe, and Tadios carried the comatose Walker on a litter to a boat in a nearby canal, which one of the Vietnamese said was to transport him to a VC field hospital. The last the other Americans saw of Walker was his still figure stretched out in the bottom of the vessel as two guards poled it quickly down the canal and out of sight.[19]

A month after Walker's departure, Tadios's condition suddenly took a grave turn. Like Walker, Tadios had had trouble eating without vomiting. Additionally, he had a terrible case of hemorrhoids, the result of an impacted bowel, that caused profuse bleeding. For all the sergeant's physical problems, Rowe felt that Tadios in the end succumbed to psychological pressures. He "saw Walker go and it looked like an easy way out," Rowe remembered. "Immediately after Captain Walker died, Tadios turned the whole thing off."[20] After badgering by Rowe, the Vietnamese did provide some medicines, but to no avail. Cruelly, Rowe and Pitzer were made to repeat the Walker rite, placing their comrade aboard a boat for the hospital, never to see him again. This time they were left with the memory of a tattoo on Tadios's left shoulder—a black panther with claws extended and the motto "Death before Dishonor." It had been the gritty sergeant's personal coat of arms and now it became his epitaph.

Between the Walker and Tadios demises, Army Sgt. Joe Parks, captured during a firefight with the Viet Cong on 22 December 1964 (only 11 days after his arrival in Vietnam), appeared in camp. For more than a year Parks had lived with captors who treated him decently and fed him adequately, so that when he joined the Rowe group in February 1966 in a new location the men dubbed "Neverglades," he was in good physical condition. Parks was well liked and respected by the others. Intelligence reports later noted how stubbornly he resisted after capture, in one instance refusing to be photographed with an unloaded pistol handed him by VC for propaganda effect. But Parks, too, wilted under the strain of continuing confinement in the rain forest, especially after the group in late June was moved west and then south to a more overgrown and inaccessible area and placed in cages again. (At Neverglades they had enjoyed the freedom of open huts.) Although the prisoners were allowed out of the cages to gather and cook their own food* and even

---

* After the deaths of Walker and Tadios and fearing they might lose the others also, the VC permitted the men to fish for themselves and collect and prepare their own food, initially under close supervision but later with surprising latitude. Pitzer discounted the significance of the loose arrangements, noting they were always "more a prisoner of the terrain than . . . of the Vietcong guards themselves" (Pitzer testimony in *American Prisoners of War in Southeast Asia, 1971*, 51). See, too, Rowe interv in *Southeast Asia Survival Journal*, 132-35.

play a waterlogged version of volleyball, the summer days hung heavy with oppressive humidity and renewed indoctrination and Parks in particular slumped into depression.

August 1966 brought yet another addition to the fold, Special Forces Sgt. James Jackson now joining Rowe, Pitzer, Johnson, and the failing Parks. Jackson had been captured about the time of the Hanoi March near the southern tip of the Delta. A medic, he and Pitzer had once trained together. His first night in camp he almost strangled on a piece of paper wedged inside his rice— a note from the other PWs informing him of the camp organization. Jackson and Pitzer helped stabilize Parks, who, like Walker and Tadios, had stopped eating. In November, however, Parks developed beriberi and the intermittent medication provided by the enemy could not stem the disease, which soon overwhelmed him. On the first day of the new year, 1967, Parks died. The Americans cleaned their friend and tried, futilely, to obtain a good pair of pajamas for his burial. Once more they carried a fallen comrade to a waiting boat and a river of no return.

1967 brought some improvement but it was still a time of elemental endurance—"struggling to keep our heads above water," as Rowe phrased it with more literalness than he probably intended.[21] In March, Rowe, Pitzer, Johnson, and Jackson were taken to No-K Corral, the third stay in that camp for all but Jackson. The quartet was stuffed into a single low cage, requiring them to hunch and crouch anytime they made a move. The new camp commander, Mr. Sau, was a dedicated and soulless fanatic, a southerner trained in the North and reinfiltrated into the South in the early 1960s. Even his own men feared him.

In May Pitzer and Johnson were shifted to another location for indoctrination purposes. Jackson, who evidently had been judged a hardliner by the Viet Cong because of tough resistance to interrogation after capture, remained with Rowe. The two became concerned when they learned of an ultimatum the Front had delivered to the South Vietnamese government threatening execution of American prisoners should Saigon execute three captured Viet Cong. The memory of Versace and Roraback weighed heavily on the PWs. When an extended dry season drained the canals, limiting fishing, Rowe and Jackson force-fed themselves a dish called *ca mam*, a vile, maggoty mess of decayed fish fermented in brine. Although they had decided that circumstances dictated escaping, they had become too ill to try.

Pitzer and Johnson returned to camp in July. The onset of the rainy season made fresh fish available, but with four Americans to feed again there was not enough to go around. This time it was Jackson who rapidly deteriorated, tottering on the edge of both starvation and sanity. The steady diet of *ca mam* had poisoned his system and caused him to vomit uncontrollably. Only when Mr. Sau authorized vitamins and other medications and a VC medic produced a can of condensed milk and some sugar—the riches of Araby to the desperate prisoners—did Jackson begin to rebound. Rowe attributed Jackson's survival to his simply beating back the resignation instinct and, unlike Tadios, resolving to stay alive. "He was just about ready to go over the edge," Rowe said. "Jackson was the only one who reached that point and came back."[22]

No sooner had Jackson mended than did Rowe again fall ill with violent cramping, fever, nausea, and diarrhea—his intestines hurting so badly it was "as though broken glass was being forced through them." The swelling indicative of beriberi had returned, and even the sulfa tablets administered by the VC passed through so fast he was absorbing nothing. About this time an order to keep the Americans alive apparently reached Mr. Sau, and he had guards plant greens and peppers and forage for chickens. The diet subsequently improved, and so did Rowe's condition. He and the others spent the rest of the summer listening to Radio Hanoi's cant and planning a magnificent resort on the Gulf of Mexico. Rowe committed his ideas and sketches for the "Hacienda del Sol" to a tiny notebook, which he kept for the duration of his captivity and managed to bring out with him.[23]

In late September, Johnson, whose health had been the best in the group over the years, began to suffer coughing spasms, shallow breathing, and bloody stools until his pulse climbed to 125 and he lay close to death. A week's round-the-clock attention, unprecedented amounts of medicine, food supplements like sweet potato and banana soup, and, finally, a decision by the Front to release him along with Pitzer and Jackson, pulled him through the crisis. "If Johnson had been in camp five more days," Rowe reckoned, "he would have died."[24]

The release of Rowe's three comrades in November coincided with an upsurge in the antiwar movement in the United States and followed the massive protest rally in Washington that culminated at the steps of the Pentagon. Not coincidentally, Johnson and Jackson were both black. Pitzer, as a medic, may have been included to help insure that the stricken Johnson survived the arduous trip home.* The VC informed Rowe that his bad attitude, violation of camp regulations, and escape attempts prevented his release, a high-ranking cadre adding in a menacing aside, "Do not think that merely because the war ends that you will go home. You can rest here after the war." In a final humiliation, Rowe was directed to cook a ceremonial supper for his departing

---

* The trio was released in neutral Cambodia to antiwar activist and peace committee representative Tom Hayden, placed on a flight to Prague, and removed from the plane during a stopover in Beirut, where they were officially returned to U.S. custody. Upon arrival in Washington, Johnson was taken to Walter Reed Army Hospital for treatment and a successful recuperation. See *Washington Post* and *Times Herald*, 12-14 Nov 67; OASD(PA) News Release 1094-67, 16 Nov 67; Jackson interv with *Ebony*, Aug 68.

mates. Daunted by the turn of events but still battling, the lieutenant slipped a message to Pitzer for delivery to his parents. At dark, the Americans
exchanged farewells as best they could as the releasees were put in boats for
the journey out of the wilderness and to freedom.[25]

Rowe combated the ensuing loneliness by sparring with indoctrinators
and harboring thoughts of rescue, since he had discussed with Pitzer and
Jackson a plan for an operation back into the area if any of the men were left
behind. His spirits soared when an observation craft circled over the camp,
but then sank when jets swooped in and dropped cluster bombs, one of the
bursts wounding Rowe slightly. The vexed captive concluded that Washington had decided it was more important to knock out the camp than to rescue
a lone American PW.* Rowe did not know that the U.S. Army had in fact
undertaken a number of rescue operations in 1966 and 1967, though with
scant success once the captive had been removed from the vicinity of the
initial engagement.[26]

Christmas 1967 found Rowe singing carols to himself and partaking of
the Viet Cong's version of a special holiday repast—tea and cookies. The
indoctrinator, Mafia, furnished a candle for mass and gave Rowe the gift of
news that Johnson was responding well to medical treatment. On New Year's
Eve, guards and Front cadre from at least two camps assembled to conduct a
program with tape recorder and camera in which Rowe was called on to make
a speech for peace but stopped short of the propaganda message that Mafia
had hoped to extract. His fungus problem worsening—he had no fingernails and only three toenails left—and the solitude making him restive to the
point where he thought he might foolishly strike out at one of the guards, the
prisoner wrote in his diary on 6 January 1968: "Loss of sleep affecting strength,
disposition, morale. Now working on mental buck-up before trouble sets in.
Can't fight on multiple fronts—political is enough; add fatigue, strong homesickness, extreme tiredness of POW life plus the chance of health breakdown
and the picture is not bright. Tonite the buck-up begins, tomorrow a new day,
a new, brighter outlook."[27]

Rowe remained at No-K through all of 1968, surviving a flea infestation
that forced him to shave his head, a conflagration fanned by dry-season winds
that nearly torched the camp, and three nights in irons and without clothes
or netting at the mercy of rampaging mosquitos, the latter episode Rowe
interpreting as "a lesson for the uncooperative American."[28] Worst of all, by

---

* No camps known to hold American prisoners were intentionally attacked by U.S. aircraft,
but it is probable that inadvertent strikes did occur and that PWs were accidentally killed
by U.S. or South Vietnamese strafing. NLF representatives in Paris so stated in 1970, and
enemy prisoners and defectors also reported such deaths. Moreover, surviving captives
reported many near misses and, as in Rowe's case, injuries from such attacks. One PW, civilian Thomas Ragsdale, is believed to have been killed by friendly aircraft fire while being
marched from South Vietnam to North Vietnam in 1968 (see Chapter 21).

Rowe following escape.

autumn he had painted himself into a corner when camp authorities learned from the Front's Central Committee that their charge had been lying all along with his cover story and that the "simple engineer" was in fact a Special Forces officer. (Rowe assumed that someone at home, perhaps an antiwar collaborator, had sent the enemy the incriminating biographical details. More likely, the VC gleaned the information from news accounts appearing in the aftermath of his colleagues' release.) Left unattended while the guards took their meals, the PW discovered a document in their hut indicating he was about to be transferred to higher headquarters. Recognizing the ominousness of the situation, he now prepared for an all-out escape attempt.

In mid-December the VC vacated No-K as U.S. bombing activity in the area intensified. For more than a week the guerrillas slogged through a labyrinth of canals, bivouacking in patches of tall reeds while trying to elude U.S. gunships and advancing ARVN troops. When a pass directly overhead scattered the party, Rowe found himself isolated with a single guard, whom he clubbed unconscious. Moving to a clearing and waving frantically toward a descending helicopter, he benefited from an extraordinary stroke of luck when the commander of the air cavalry group, Maj. David Thompson, seized what he thought was an opportunity to take a Viet Cong prisoner alive. Only when the command ship swept in and lifted the black-clad figure out of the jungle amid a hail of fire from VC in the woods did the helicopter crew realize that it had bagged an American. The date was 31 December 1968, and the recovery ended five years and two months of captivity for Rowe, who entered the Delta a lieutenant and emerged from it, he was soon to learn, a major.[29]

On the 20-minute flight to Ca Mau and safety Rowe downed several cans of C-rations and marveled at the sight of the horizon and "the green prison" below. Upon landing at the airstrip he was greeted excitedly by fellow officers and handed a fatigue jacket with a gleaming major's gold leaf on its collar epaulets. Wearing socks and boots after being barefoot for so long created a strange sensation, as did the spectacle of white-sheeted bunks and the ice cubes in a glass offered him to toast the New Year. The adjustment to freedom was marred only by the appearance of a debriefer who matter-of-factly read him his rights under the Uniform Code of Military Justice. "Five years of developed cynicism washed over me," Rowe recalled, "as I viewed the interrogation procedure through the eyes of a prisoner and saw this debriefing as being as dogmatic as my former tormentors'." Later Rowe would urge that the debriefing process be shortened and made less callous and formal.[30]

There followed medical checks, bathing and shaving opportunities he would never again take for granted, and a visit by the deputy commander of U.S. forces in Vietnam that had Rowe struggling to remember protocol. A quiet flight home was interrupted by wandering thoughts, "like pebbles dropping into my mind,"[31] of America and what his reacclimation would be like. After a round of press conferences he was at last reunited with his parents in McAllen, Texas.

Like many returnees, Rowe would be stalked by further tragedy. After marrying and quitting the Army in 1974 for a stab at politics and a career as a civilian author and lecturer, he rejoined the military in 1980. In April 1989, while serving as a counterinsurgency instructor for the Joint U.S. Military Advisory Group in the Philippines, the former PW, now a colonel, was ambushed and assassinated by suspected left-wing terrorists. Word of Rowe's killing occasioned much sorrow and grief, but also remembrance of his heroic exploits in Vietnam.[32] His death at the hands of Communist guerrillas in a steamy faraway land had a poignant element of déjà vu and added a final ironic footnote to his remarkable saga.

13

PWs in South Vietnam's Heartland, 1965-1967

The U Minh Forest, home to Nick Rowe's group in the Delta for most of their captivity, was only 140 miles southwest of Saigon, but it might as well have been a continent removed, so disconnected was the thick jungle habitat from civilization. More populous but only marginally more hospitable to PWs was South Vietnam's so-called Heartland, the area north of the Delta and south of the Central Highlands (up to about the 12th parallel) that comprised Military Region III of the U.S.-ARVN deployment scheme.

Most of the Americans captured in this zone were held in camps near Tay Ninh or across the border in Cambodia. Because of the proximity of guerrilla operations to Allied bases in the area, PWs were moved frequently to avoid contact with Allied forces, often found themselves the unintended target of Allied artillery salvos, and experienced considerable frustration at being able to see or hear but not communicate their status to friendly forces. The upside of captivity in the Heartland was that food and supplies—stolen from Allied stores or obtained on the black market that flourished in the vicinity of large U.S. military facilities—tended to be more plentiful than elsewhere in the South, although here, too, availability was erratic, depending on the course of the war and rapidly changing tactical and logistical circumstances.[1]

Counting 7 already in captivity at the close of 1964, at least 29 U.S. servicemen and civilians were prisoners of the Viet Cong in this region between January 1965 and December 1967. Additionally, 13 "foreign nationals"—British, South Korean, Japanese, Filipino, and French—were captured or held with the Americans during this period. Of the 42 total, 40 met their fate—execution, death in captivity, escape, or release—by the end of 1967; the other two remained prisoners until the general release in 1973.

In January 1965 Special Forces Sgts. Issac Camacho, Claude McClure, George Smith, and Kenneth Roraback—captive since November 1963—

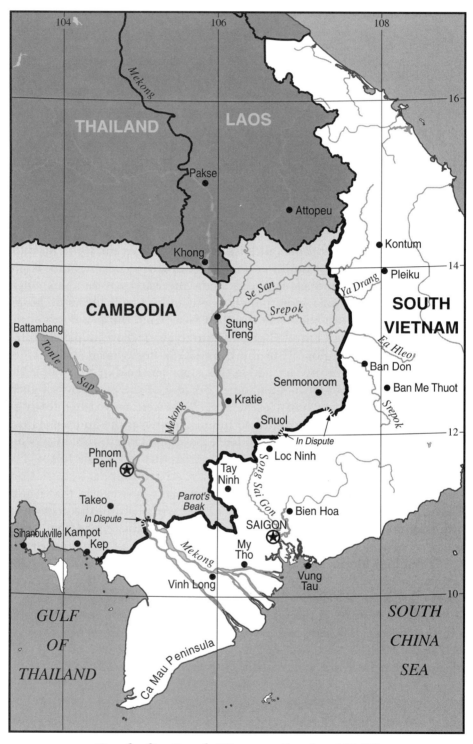

Cambodia-South Vietnam Border (1965)

languished in a well-concealed guerrilla camp northeast of Tay Ninh that they had named "Auschwitz."* Meanwhile, three other Americans—Army Sgt. Harold Bennett, Army PFC Charles Crafts, and Marine Capt. Donald Cook—had been captured east of Saigon between 29 and 31 December 1964. Bennett and Crafts were trapped when the ARVN battalion they were advising was overrun by Viet Cong and abandoned them. Cook, seized in a separate battle near Binh Gia, where he was advising a Government Marine battalion, joined Bennett and Crafts in early January. Toward the end of the month the trio was marched northward in the direction of the Camacho group.[2]

It took the Cook party four months to complete the rendezvous, with layovers at camps the PWs named "San Jose" and "SOB." Cook, who was wounded in the leg at capture and had trouble walking, took a hardline stance from the outset. In February, when he refused to fill out a data card, the VC handcuffed him and locked him in leg stocks for a month as punishment. So little did he speak or respond to his captors that a later releasee doubted the Communists even knew he was a Marine. Bennett was also uncooperative. In February he undertook a hunger strike as a method of resistance, a tactic that infuriated the guards, who were eating the same diet he refused; this brought him three beatings. He and Cook tried to escape in March, but a guard alerted the camp before they had cleared its perimeter. The punishment that followed further weakened Bennett before he was separated, seriously ill, from the group late in May.

Exactly what happened to Bennett remains something of a mystery. Crafts later reported that the sergeant suffered a breakdown from the lack of food and psychological distress that manifested itself in an obsessive turn to religion. Crafts last spotted him on 28 May 1965 when guards were kicking and punching him along the trail to make him move faster. Both Crafts and Cook were later told by VC officers that Bennett had been shot, but Crafts remembered hearing no gunfire at the time of Bennett's disappearance. In June the National Liberation Front announced Bennett's execution in retaliation for the Ky government's execution of Tran Van Dong, a Communist caught attempting to bomb an officers' billet in Saigon. It is uncertain whether Bennett was actually designated for execution to avenge Dong's death or the Viet Cong contrived the rationale to suit their purposes. Circumstances suggest he may well have died *before* Dong, possibly killed by guards in transit—they had come to hate him for his belligerence despite illness and injury—or simply lapsing into a coma and suffering a fatal decline that guards were unable or unwilling to prevent. The Front chose to label the death an execution, according to this explanation, to extract propaganda advantage from the episode, protect its "humane and lenient" image against a charge of murder, and serve warning to the other prisoners.[3]

---

* See Chapter 4.

When Cook and Crafts finally linked up with the Camacho group, the latter were being held at a new camp south of Auschwitz they had dubbed "Carefree" (also called "Paradise" or "Dachau"). The new arrivals approached the Camacho bunch hesitantly at first, suspicious of the relative freedom they saw, their comrades locked in cages only at night and during the day allowed to visit each other and even play cards. Gradually the men exchanged information and set up a notedrop at the camp's well. With a skill and sophistication more characteristic of communication operations among PWs in the North, the prisoners used a medicine-type bottle and an array of whistles and gestures to trade messages. In case of trouble, a lookout hummed the tune "Stormy Weather."[4]

Smith and the others were advised by Prevaricator, a VC functionary who had been assigned to the Camacho group since early 1964, that Cook was "an evil man" who was to be avoided. Shortly after Cook and Crafts arrived, camp officials gathered the other four PWs for a ceremony during which they presented each a large Red Cross parcel that contained candy bars, raisins, cookies, corned beef, coffee, vitamins, and sundry other items, including soap and underwear. The foursome made up packets for Cook and Crafts and conned a guard into delivering them. When the guard was reprimanded for handing the package to Cook, it was apparent at least to Smith that the Marine captain had become a marked man.[5]

The first week in July Army Capt. John Schumann, caught in an ambush on 16 June just above the Mekong River, was brought into camp after a long hike north.* A tall, heavy man, he had been an irritant to guards during the journey, partly because of resistance and partly because his weight caused small footbridges to break along the route, plunging him and his handlers into one stream or canal after another. He and his new mates began to study the sounds of nightly howitzer fire and daily bombing raids. They estimated that no more than 10 miles from Carefree lay friendly forces and freedom. The cannon salvos gave them a direction bearing without which, even after slipping camp, they would have had to wander haphazardly through the jungle and risk starvation or—Camacho's greatest fear—being devoured by tigers. With the benefit of directional guidance, the chance for a successful getaway was measurably enhanced, and suddenly the thought of escape became more appealing.[6]

In decent shape and encouraged further by the imminent return of seasonal rains that would help cover their tracks, Smith and Camacho decided to seize the moment. Camacho worked a crossbar loose in his cage. The men fashioned survival kits from the remnants of the Red Cross parcels. Captain

---

* Evidently the Mekong divided VC areas of responsibility, else he would have joined the Rowe group in the Delta.

Cook was advised of the plan through the dead-drop system and signaled approval. To allay anger over the escape and mitigate likely retaliation against those left behind, Camacho left a letter thanking the VC for good treatment and explaining that the escape was motivated only by the desire to go home. When the rains finally came, late in the evening on 9 July, Smith told Camacho to go it alone since the candle in their cage was out and a guard would be returning to relight it and would discover them missing unless one remained to hand over the lamp. Camacho then removed the loosened bar and, undetected in the darkness, jumped from the cage, made for the perimeter, and within five minutes or so had fled the camp.[7]

As it turned out, about 15 minutes after Camacho had slipped off, a guard walked over to Smith's pen and asked him to pass the lamp out for relighting. Had Smith gone with Camacho, the escape would probably have failed. The guard did not notice Camacho's absence—the sergeant had stuffed his pajamas with his blanket and laid them on his bed—and Smith carried out his part well in the morning, feigning shock at the discovery of his cagemate's disappearance. A furor followed, with the VC racing around like Keystone Cops trying to determine the American's whereabouts and how he had gotten away. "I was sitting there trying to act scared," Smith recalled, but "I wanted to laugh so bad. It was the funniest goddamned thing I'd ever seen." By the time they got organized, Smith reckoned, Camacho had gotten an 8- to 10-hour headstart.[8]

For four days Camacho evaded Viet Cong search patrols. Traveling through dense jungle in an easterly direction, using the sun (to the extent that he could locate it through the thick tree canopy) for orientation in the absence of further artillery soundings, and dodging leeches, VC snares, and occasional village traffic, he reached friendly lines on 13 July, flagging down a Vietnamese medical vehicle that drove him a short distance to a U.S. Special Forces camp. Within a week he was back home in Texas, where, peppered by reporters, he stoutly defended the war effort and criticized protesters. On 4 September the city of El Paso observed a special day in his honor and in a ceremony at Fort Bliss the ex-PW was awarded the Silver and Bronze stars for his accomplishment.[9]

At Carefree, blame for the escape fell mainly on Roraback, owing to his recalcitrance and his seeming seniority, he being older than the others. All the prisoners now were chained around the clock. Schumann, like Camacho somehow holding on to his boots after capture, had them abruptly taken away.*

---

* For some inexplicable reason, perhaps because of injury at the time of capture, a few of the prisoners in the South (besides Schumann and Camacho, 1964 capture Jim Thompson, for example) managed to keep their boots. One of the factors in Smith's decision to stay behind and cover for Camacho rather than vice versa was that the latter possessed boots. Camacho credited the footwear as a key to his success in making it out of the jungle. See Smith, *P.O.W,* 237, 239; Evasion and Escape Memo on Camacho experience, 24.

After several days of heightened security, the VC suddenly announced they were breaking camp and gave the men a minute to roll up their packs. The hasty evacuation indicated to the Americans that Camacho had made good his escape and that the guerrillas, realizing the camp location had been compromised, were pulling up stakes in anticipation of an attack or rescue mission. The party moved west toward Cambodia, the prisoners shackled wrist to wrist, McClure, Roraback, and Smith in one group and Schumann, Crafts, and Cook in another.[10]

The new campsite, reached after a difficult march of about 10 days, was situated near a well-trafficked road and within short range of Allied bombing activity, such that Smith said it seemed they "were right in the middle of a combat zone." Smith named the camp "Baffle" because of its odd location and unfamiliar layout. Their guards had turned markedly hostile after the Camacho incident, and the nearby and constant bombardment, diminishing supplies, and the increasing tempo of the war made them edgier still. Roraback incurred further wrath by ignoring orders not to talk to Cook and then, when scolded, laughing in the face of the camp commander, the dour Oil Can Harry, who had accompanied his charges from Auschwitz to Carefree and now Baffle. Roraback's mocking affront to Harry may have been his final act of defiance. The next evening, 25 September 1965, Prevaricator took Roraback to see the commander; shortly afterwards, guards came and collected the PW's meager gear.

Roraback became another phantom casualty, much the same as Bennett, neither of their bodies ever recovered. Two gunshots in the jungle the morning following Roraback's summons convinced Smith that the Communists had killed the sergeant. Cook counseled that it was a trick to intimidate the prisoners, but they learned nothing more of Roraback's fate during their captivity. They did not know that on 26 September 1965 the Front's "Liberation Radio" announced that Roraback, along with Captain Versace in the Delta,* had been killed that morning in retaliation for Saigon's execution of three Communist partisans.[11]

By the middle of October camp personnel appeared more relaxed and conditions again improved. While Cook and Schumann were paired in a separate cell, the others were able to resume card playing to pass the time, Crafts teaching Smith and McClure to play cribbage since, Smith noted nonchalantly, "there weren't enough people for hearts." In a series of propaganda stunts, all the PWs were trotted out for a meeting with two Cuban journalists and a memorial service for antiwar protester Norman Morrison, who burned himself to death in front of the Pentagon on 2 November. The service for Morrison (and Alice Herz, another pacifist who had immolated herself

* See Chapter 12.

months earlier) was a quiet, respectful ceremony, moving in its own way and occasioning some uncomfortable moments for the prisoners.[12]

Smith and McClure, told that the Front was considering their release as a gesture of appreciation to the gathering peace movement in the United States and abroad, were ordered outside to do calisthenics and given extra food to improve their health and appearance. Their already shaky resolve eroded further by the latest VC overture, over Cook's objections they wrote letters requesting their freedom and declaring their opposition to the war. Release followed soon afterwards, the men escorted on a winding journey through jungle swamps, leech-infested grasslands, and open rice fields until they crossed into Cambodia, where officials took them by car to a hotel in Phnom Penh. Treated to a lavish dinner and hot showers, they were giddy with elation until sobered by a French-language newspaper story of their emancipation that contained mention of Roraback's execution.

Wilfred Burchett, who had interviewed them the previous year, came by to wish them well. Senator Mike Mansfield was coincidentally in town visiting with Prince Sihanouk in the midst of a fact-finding tour for President Johnson. Smith and McClure saw his motorcade from their balcony and wondered why he did not stop by to see them.* At a press conference on 30 November, Smith commented offhandedly about joining the peace movement upon his return to the United States, and both made other ill-considered remarks that prompted the American news media and superiors in Washington to characterize the two men as either turncoats or the victims of brainwashing. On 5 December an officer from the Australian embassy, which represented U.S. interests in Cambodia, placed the ex-PWs aboard a plane for Bangkok, where they were returned to the control of the U.S. Army. At the American base at Korat, Thailand, they were given physical examinations, advised of their legal rights, and allowed to call home before boarding a jet for the Philippines and proceeding on to Okinawa and extensive debriefings with U.S. counterintelligence agents.[13]

On 21 December, on the basis of information supplied by the releasees and the previously repatriated Camacho, Army officials filed misconduct charges against the men, alleging that they had aided the enemy with writings and statements inimical to the United States. Concerned that a court-martial proceeding might be exploited by antiwar interests† and acknowledging the men's

---

* The American government had known for some time of the scheduled release, but even at the last minute U.S. officials were distrustful of Front intentions and reluctant to give the Viet Cong any more propaganda mileage than they had already achieved. See, for example, memo LtCol A. P. Butterfield for SecDefSpAsst John M. Steadman, 29 Nov 65.
† While Smith and McClure were sequestered on Okinawa, frustrated reporters seeking access to them published a series of articles that stirred sympathy for the soldiers stateside, sparking a number of rallies and the creation of a legal defense fund in their behalf.

complete cooperation in the investigation and previous excellent records, the Army in April, in the face of mounting administration and public pressure, decided to drop the inquiry. Shortly afterward it granted Smith and McClure general discharges and, unceremoniously, flew them home. McClure reenlisted in July 1966 but, denied reinstatement of his security clearance and restricted to routine duties, he remained hostage to his tainted record.[14]

Though only a minor episode in the larger prisoner-of-war story, the Smith-McClure contretemps contributed to a reexamination of the Johnson administration's PW policy. In one of his first steps as the government's overall coordinator for PW matters, Averell Harriman emphasized to Secretary of Defense McNamara the prudence of greeting any releasee or escapee with open arms and, except in the most flagrant instances of wrongdoing or outright collaboration, refraining from taking legal action against repatriated prisoners.* Citing specifically the Smith-McClure case, Harriman wrote McNamara in June 1966 that harsh treatment and indictment of returnees gave the appearance of being "unnecessarily heartless" and thus strengthened the propaganda hand of the enemy. Deputy Secretary Cyrus Vance assured Harriman that the Defense Department shared his concern,[15] and, although no new policy guidelines were formally instituted during the course of the war, the heightened sensitivity to the issue resulted in practice in a softer official stance toward questionable PW conduct. Debate over standards of Code of Conduct accountability would continue during and after the war, both in Washington and in Indochina among the PWs themselves, but it is perhaps significant that after mid-1966 no returning serviceman faced prosecution solely for making statements inimical to American interests while a prisoner of war.

With Camacho's escape and Smith's and McClure's release, Charles Crafts, Donald Cook, and John Schumann remained behind in the South Vietnamese heartland, but they were not alone. There followed from 1965 through 1967 a steady stream of new prisoners, both military and civilian. One of the most intriguing additions to the PW ranks in the region was Donald Dawson, a civilian who spent only four months in captivity but whose story is one of the most remarkable for courage and devotion.

Not satisfied with the Army's sketchy account of his brother Lt. Daniel Dawson's presumed death in the crash of his reconnaissance plane in November 1964, Dawson left his job and family in California early in 1965 and journeyed to South Vietnam to find out for himself what had happened. He contacted and questioned crewmembers of his brother's flying unit, then

* See Chapter 10.

checked out reports in the coastal city of Vung Tau that an L-19 had gone down in the vicinity, killing its American pilot and Vietnamese observer. He printed a reward leaflet and persuaded pilots to drop copies over the alleged crash site, and wrote letters to the National Liberation Front requesting information and permission to enter VC territory. He then engaged a local interpreter, a young French-Vietnamese woman named Collette Emberger, to interview a rubber plantation manager who claimed to know the crash location. Although Dawson learned little from these probes, word of the American's presence in Vietnam spread until he had become known to area natives as "Brother of the Pilot."

For the first three months of 1965 Dawson prowled the countryside north and northeast of Saigon distributing his leaflets, seeking new clues to his brother's disappearance, and subjecting himself to miserable living conditions and great danger. Carrying a carbine, two pistols, a knife, and hand grenades, and accompanied by a small, fiercely loyal shepherd dog, Dawson went from village to village on foot, by bus or sampan, sometimes even by helicopter. Several times he walked through Viet Cong roadblocks, trudging past the puzzled insurgents before they had time even to react.

In mid-April he set out from the village of Thai Hung with Emberger and a local Catholic priest. At a hamlet not far upriver the party was stopped by two VC soldiers, who released the priest and took Dawson and Emberger to their commander, a lieutenant. The latter harassed them and shot and killed Dawson's dog when he lunged reflexively at the threat to his master, then marched them blindfolded to a VC camp where Dawson finally received some answers on his brother's fate.* An officer informed Dawson that his brother was in fact dead, killed while making a low pass when ground gunners fired several shots into the aircraft. The officer said that one bullet had passed through the flier's body, and that both he and his observer were buried near the site where the L-19 had crashed and burned.

Depressed by the seeming confirmation of his brother's death and now incarcerated himself, Dawson went through a period of alternate rage and despair. At one point he attempted suicide by ingesting an entire package of pep pills he had been allowed to keep after convincing the VC they were an ulcer medicine. Like so many other, more conventional PWs, he combated stupefying boredom with a vivid imagination, constructing in his mind an ideal commercial fishing boat (he had been a partner in his father's operation) bolt by bolt, plank by plank, then sailing it on fanciful trips to Alaska.

---

* The camp was SOB, the way station named by Bennett, Crafts, and Cook during their layover there on their own march north to the rendezvous with the Camacho group. Their and Dawson's stays overlapped slightly, the three soldiers managing a brief contact with the civilian before departing SOB in mid-May.

Emberger was held in a separate area and, although apparently treated well by the guerrillas, suffered herself from fright and lassitude. Dawson's spirit improved when after two months of confinement to his cage he was permitted outside to clear brush, carry water, and help with other chores. He was contemplating escape when told he was about to be set free.

Awaiting release, Dawson came down with malaria and for more than a week was racked by fever and chill. While recovering, he was visited by a well-dressed man purporting to be an NLF representative who explained that the Front had merely been "detaining" him until it had had a chance to verify his identity. The man handed Dawson a yellow lifesaver vest that he said had been retrieved from his brother's plane. He maintained that everything else had been so badly burned he was unable to produce positive identification or a uniform with a name tag, but he promised that the Front would care for the gravesite and that Dawson could claim the remains after the war. Guards then returned several items that had been confiscated from Dawson at capture, including money, and exchanged pleasant farewells. One, whom Dawson had dubbed "The Thing" for his hideous appearance and diabolical demeanor, even offered a souvenir of a small oil lamp.

The Viet Cong assigned several escorts to guide Dawson and Emberger toward friendly forces. After three days of tramping through the jungle—during one spell having to dodge detection by, ironically, an L-19 similar to the aircraft that Daniel Dawson had flown and that they feared would mistake them for enemy—the pair arrived just outside of Thai Hung, where the adventure had begun. It was 24 August 1965. As their escorts departed and Dawson and Emberger approached the village, local defenders, thinking them VC, opened fire. Dawson coolly told Emberger not to run but just to keep walking, and he started singing at the top of his lungs, "What Can You Do With A Drunken Sailor?" The shooting stopped, whereupon the brash American and his plucky companion safely entered, bringing to a close one of the more daring missions, and bizarre PW chapters, of the war. [16]

Others captured in the Heartland region did not have so extraordinary a tale or as happy an outcome. Gustav Hertz was the first U.S. foreign service officer to fall captive. An administrative adviser for the State Department's Agency for International Development, he was kidnapped in February 1965 while riding a motorbike on the outskirts of Saigon. His story is complex, involving efforts to arrange a prisoner exchange, intercession by Prince Sihanouk of Cambodia, and communications among high-level officials of the American and South Vietnamese governments and the NLF, but its ending was tragic. Two months after his capture, VC radio broadcast a threat to execute Hertz if the Saigon government carried out the death sentence of a Front partisan; in 1967 another Communist broadcast suggested that Hertz had indeed been put to death as an act of reprisal, but did not specify when. Finally Sihanouk notified Hertz's wife that, based on information he received directly from the Front's Central Committee, her husband had not been killed but died of an acute attack of malaria on 24 September 1967. The State Department pursued inquiries for a year, and, learning nothing further, issued a certificate of death in December 1968, while continuing to press for the return of the officer's remains.[17]

During the same week that Hertz was seized, James McLean, an Army medic advising ARVN forces at Duc Thong, also fell into Viet Cong hands. McLean survived at least until October 1965, when he was seen by friendly forces and was the object of a futile rescue effort. Reports that he was sighted later, still captive, exist, but the NLF denied knowledge of him during the final prisoner accounting in 1973. He is presumed to have died in captivity.[18]

On Valentine's Day 1965, William Wallis, a British citizen employed as a security officer by a civil contracting company, was captured together with two Vietnamese sisters, his co-workers, while cruising aboard a motorboat a few miles from Saigon. As Wallis brought the small craft around to return to the capital, VC riflemen exploded the gas tank, forcing the boat to shore. One of the sisters was let go, Wallis and the other woman detained. It is not clear whether the second woman elected or was compelled to stay with the captors, perhaps impressed into service as a translator, but neither she nor Wallis was heard from again. From the released sister's account and other intelligence sources, State Department officials were able to determine the circumstances of the capture and to place Wallis subsequently at a camp in the Tay Ninh region. Unconfirmed but convincing details supplied by a VC defector led U.S. analysts to conclude that the Englishman was killed by the Communists, probably sometime in 1966, after refusing to cooperate with interrogators.[19]

In the same area where Hertz was captured, Joe Dodd, like Wallis an employee of RMK Construction Co., was ambushed while riding his motorbike along a secondary road on 10 October 1965. Dodd managed to escape soon after incarceration, as did two other RMK workers, Henry Hudson and Edwin Jones, who were seized in December. Not so lucky were Air Force Sgts. Samuel Adams, Charles Dusing, and Thomas Moore, captured with Sgt. Jasper Page while returning from a weekend's swimming and relaxing near Vung Tau. The four hired a Vietnamese with a truck to drive them back to their airbase at Tan Son Nhut when they were unable to make military transportation arrangements. A VC patrol grabbed them at a roadblock. Two days later, while guards marched them toward a camp, Page and Adams worked their bonds loose and tried to escape. Page wrested a carbine from one guard, but the weapon jammed when he attempted to fire it. Adams struggled unsuccessfully with another of the guerrillas, failing to get his weapon and scurrying up a trail with VC in pursuit. Page made it back to friendly lines, but the other men were never seen again. At the end of hostilities in 1973, the Front reported that Adams, Dusing, and Moore had all died of "diseases" in December 1965 and lay buried at a location a few miles northeast of the capture site.[20]

On 26 April 1966 Army Spec. Edward Reilly disappeared from his platoon while on patrol northwest of Tay Ninh. When U.S. forces overran a rebel camp later that summer, they discovered Reilly's personal papers among the captured documents. They found as well a Vietnamese notation that the young soldier had been killed following interrogation. In May, two civilian workers for an engineering firm, Robert Monahan, a plumber, and Thomas Scales, a mechanic, were captured by a band of guerrillas southeast of Saigon. In June Vincente Gaza, a mechanic for Air America, and his wife Ofelia were ambushed while riding in a taxi from Saigon in the direction of Vung Tau, in the same general area where Captain Cook, Sergeant Bennett, and PFC Crafts had been caught.* Although the VC treated the Gazas well, Mr. Gaza fell seriously ill as they were hiked through the countryside to join Monahan and Scales in midsummer at a holding area northeast of Saigon and east of Bien Hoa.

Yet two more civilians, Australian Henry Stephenson and American Daniel Niehouse, the latter a salesman for Ford Motor Co., were captured in the fall of 1966 and taken to the same camp that held the Gazas, Scales, and Monahan. While the Vietnamese were planning how to exploit the batch of civilian prisoners, fate unexpectedly and sadly forced their hand. Vincente Gaza's illness took a turn for the worse, and Stephenson suddenly died from unknown causes. The two men were buried as Christmas approached. Hoping to salvage what propaganda capital they could, the Front released Scales, Monahan, and Ofelia Gaza at New Year's 1967. Why Niehouse was not liberated with the others remains a mystery. VC cadre were aware that he had briefly served with the U.S. Army in Vietnam. There is evidence that he was an outspoken complainer who may have simply stretched the VC's patience. Whatever the case, the Communists kept him prisoner at least three months longer. What happened after that is uncertain, but the 1973 NLF list of those who died in captivity reported his death as occurring 12 April 1967.[21]

The release of Monahan, Scales, and Mrs. Gaza yet retention of Niehouse raises the larger question of why the Viet Cong—and the North Vietnamese— seemed to prefer emancipating PWs in groups of three as opposed to one or two or, when the opportunity existed, four or five. Although the release of Smith and McClure late in 1965 was an obvious exception to the pattern, remember that Lieutenant Rowe was left behind when Sergeants Pitzer, Jackson, and Johnson were set free in November 1967, and in most other instances,

---

* A few weeks later four South Korean civilian workmen were also captured in this area, but they were not held with Americans and their eventual fates are unknown.

too, deliverance came in threes. (In North Vietnam all four release incidents involved three prisoners.) Analysts have suggested various explanations for the phenomenon, ranging from pure coincidence to possible historical and religious influences, for example the significance of the number three in Buddhist philosophy (though hardly likely to be venerated by Communists). When asked at Paris in 1973 whether the number was deliberate, North Vietnamese Premier Pham Van Dong replied that it was and that the symbolism should have been manifest. No one has been able to discern Dong's meaning, nor have captured documents revealed any conscious policy. Yet the Communists did little in the way of staging that was not calculated. A logical explanation would be simply that three was an optimum number from the standpoint of having a propaganda impact—enough to warrant an elaborate ceremony and press conference and to attract international attention.

Among the handful of prisoners captured in the Heartland in 1967 were Armando Carreon and Benjamin Calderon, drivers for the RMK construction company; Dewey Holt and Donald Braswell, Army technicians; Army Pvt. McKinley Nolan, who either fell captive or went AWOL southeast of Saigon; and Japanese civilian Masahiko Seko, seized near Can Tho then later released. Prisoners in several camps saw Nolan apparently living with a local woman and working with the VC; though these accounts and subsequent intelligence reports were less than definitive, the Army later judged Nolan to have deserted. Little is known of his whereabouts after 1972. Holt, a civilian, and Braswell, an Army Specialist, were captured near a beach in the Vung Tau area while taking a break from their duty of testing engines on Boston Whaler assault boats. The two anchored their craft offshore at Phuoc Hai and swam in to explore a cluster of empty houses when guerrillas hiding among the rocks took them into custody. The next day they were able to snatch their guards' weapons, shoot the men, and reach safety with the aid of a South Vietnamese paratrooper. The soldier guided them to his post, from which they shortly made it back to their own base. Not so fortunate were Carreon and Calderon. After their ambush, they remained missing for years and were eventually presumed dead.[22]

The prisoner held longest by the Viet Cong, Douglas Ramsey, was captured in the Heartland on 17 January 1966.* A U.S. foreign service officer attached to the Agency for International Development, Ramsey surrendered to VC after vainly attempting to run a guerrilla roadblock near the village center of Trung Lap north of Saigon. He was transporting a shipment of rice

---

*Army Capt. Jim Thompson (see Chapter 4) was in VC custody longer but spent part of his captivity in the North.

and other emergency foodstuffs to refugees in the area and felt certain, he later recalled, that as "an inconsequential State Department-AID type helping out their fellow countrymen in disaster relief and economic development . . . surely they'd let me go." As it turned out, Ramsey would be a Viet Cong prisoner for more than seven years. In a record noteworthy for grit as well as longevity, he would endure as much hardship, disease, and despair as any American in captivity and emerge as a leader among the PWs in the South.[23]

Ramsey's captors hustled him away from the ambush site as mortar rounds from local Government security forces began to fall. The party plunged through paddy and jungle until they reached a hamlet that had recently been leveled in an ARVN "search and destroy" operation. The sight of dazed villagers and smoking ruins both distressed and frightened Ramsey, who now feared retribution at the hands of the distraught residents. The rebels, however, eager to protect their catch, quickly moved him out and marched him northwest toward Tay Ninh and the foothills and rain forest near the Cambodian border that served as a VC sanctuary.

Ramsey settled into his first PW camp the last week in January. For the better part of a year, he was virtually restricted to a small thatch cell with a crude bamboo-slat bed, prostrate there for long periods except for trips to bathe and relieve himself or, occasionally, to perform outdoor work. He existed on rice, parsnips, and a few nuts and beans. "Our meat came in spurts," he remembered,

> which is to say that for months we wouldn't see a scrap of it. Generally speaking, we got less [food] than our captors, not always a lot less, but less in relation to body size and needs, and at times there was enough nutritional variance to have a crucial differential effect on relative health of captives and captors. If they ate well, we managed to get by. If they ate poorly we were malnourished. If they got so little as to become malnourished, we descended to the next level and starved.[24]

The protein deficiency took its toll in the form of hair loss, boils, leg cramps and swelling, impaired night vision, and other symptoms relating to beriberi and scurvy. VC paramedics initially gave him shots for typhoid and smallpox and periodically administered drugs, but the quality and dosage of medications varied widely, as did the competence of the personnel. At that, Ramsey was fortunate in that the camp was located in a headquarters area, so that experienced physicians and nurses regularly passed through.

Although Ramsey was aware of other prisoners in the camp, he did not speak to them until July, when he made contact with Donald Cook and Charles Crafts at a funeral service for John Schumann. The Army captain had succumbed to a variety of ailments, including beriberi, kidney complications, and pneumonia, despite apparently earnest efforts by VC doctors to save him.* The Americans did not talk again until they broke camp three months later, but they managed to slip notes to one another in the interim.

Ramsey was subjected to more interrogation than most civilians, probably because he spoke Vietnamese fluently and because the Viet Cong were convinced he was a CIA agent. When seized he had in his possession a large amount of cash that they suspected was a bankroll for covert activities rather than funds for an AID construction project, as the prisoner maintained. Moreover, American reporters in Saigon filed stories identifying him as a prominent U.S. official and there had been at least one high-level attempt early on to secure his release by offer of a ransom. Ramsey was grilled by an older man dubbed "Grandpa" and a senior cadre nicknamed "Alex," the latter having worked with the Camacho group. Although the VC did not torture him, they terrorized him with threats of execution and tormented him with elaborate atrocity skits that depicted him as a murderer and spy. The combination of fear and guilt, together with his isolation and difficulty sleeping (the result of boils and cramps, and snakes that would wander into his cage at night seeking rats and warmth), drove him almost insane, until late in August, "near hysteria," he summoned the strength to fight back.

Ramsey's coping took many forms. Always a physical fitness devotee—he once climbed California's Mount Whitney in near-record time—he began a rigorous exercise program of calisthenics and running in place, eventually "jogging" the equivalent of seven miles a day. He wrote a statement for the Front's Red Cross that he loaded with telltale cliches to negate any propaganda worth and, for good measure, recorded the message for a radio tape in a parodying tremolo. Finally, he was buoyed by the dawning realization that sustained many a prisoner in both the South and North: that his captors had more to gain by keeping him alive than by killing him. "In the long run," he came to understand, "their grossly inflated view of my importance probably saved me more often than it put me in mortal jeopardy."[25]

By the time he returned from the edge, the Viet Cong had decided to move the captives eastward to evade intensified Allied bombing. The PWs and a contingent of guards broke camp on 28 October 1966 and undertook a two-week trek over some of the roughest terrain in the South, clambering across steep ravines on slippery log bridges and plodding through dense forest heavy

---

* Crafts, who tended to Schumann between May and his death on 7 July and was present when his comrade expired, later said "they gave him everything they had available." Despite his size, Schumann was described by fellow PWs as a man of gentle spirit and quiet courage. Crafts thought the Communists held a special respect for him and perhaps for that reason, according to Crafts, he "received more medical treatment than any of the other POWs." See Crafts case summary attach memo Allen for Berg, 21 Apr 67, 2, and other materials in Schumann file; Smith, *P.O.W.*, 247.

Medal of Honor winner Cook (left), Ramsey.

with humidity and mosquitos. The prisoners now numbered four, Ramsey, Cook, and Crafts having been joined by Sgt. Sammie Womack just prior to the transfer.* The trek was difficult for all the men, but especially Cook, who had contracted malaria on the eve of the move, lost all bowel control, and suffered additionally from night blindness that affected his equilibrium. "By sheer willpower," Ramsey recalled, Cook traversed the march's 150-200 miles. "It was a super-human performance."[26]

Cook's raw courage and adamant resistance had always impressed his fellow PWs. Even the misanthropic Sergeant Smith wrote admiringly in his post-release memoir that Cook was "really hard-nosed. I believe he would have stopped shitting if he had thought 'Charlie' was using it for fertilizer." "If you don't count eating," Smith testified, "Cook was being one hundred percent uncooperative, to the point that he wouldn't tell them his symptoms when he wasn't feeling well. They wanted him to write them down, but he'd refuse to write anything since his capture, even his name. In his view, writing violated the Code of Conduct." Cook paid dearly for his intransigence, receiving less food than the others and spending more time in solitary. Ramsey believed that after Cook survived the forced march, even the VC came to admire him; subsequently they seemed to accord him more respect and better treatment.[27]

---

* Womack, 22, from the small town of Farmville, Virginia, was a squad leader whose infantry unit was ambushed and decimated in a firefight near Bien Hoa. The circumstances surrounding his capture and other aspects of his captivity experience, including Communist attempts at racial exploitation because he was black, are detailed in a case summary attached to memo Allen for Berg, 21 Apr 67.

"The V.C. could not have found a more inhospitable location for a camp," Ramsey later said of the new site. Torrential rain and poor soil prevented cultivation of crops, such that even rice was in short supply and they had to make do with a meager diet of manioc, bamboo shoots, and an occasional rat for protein supplement. When monsoon downpours hit early in 1967, the water table would periodically rise several feet, saturating the campsite for days and flooding the prisoners out of their dugout cells, which had been built underground ostensibly to protect them from Allied bombing raids. The Viet Cong had planned to stay at the location only temporarily, intending to move on to higher elevation, but with B-52 attacks in the area unrelenting, they opted to wait out the monsoon season and ended up remaining in the miserable spot for a year.[28]

Soon after their arrival, Ramsey and Crafts joined Cook in the malaria ranks. Ramsey's case was particularly severe, evolving into the cerebral type that caused convulsions and usually death. Cook's caring attention despite his own illness and a senior cadre's decision to use the guerrillas' limited supply of quinine to try to save the civilian brought Ramsey out of a sinking coma.[29] By January all the men were taking indoctrination, up to six hours a day split into a morning and an afternoon session. Womack later told a debriefer that discipline was light, enforced mainly at night, and that although there was no fence or wire around the camp, the prisoners were warned the area was booby-trapped. The guard force consisted of 10 men who rotated shifts and for the most part were considerate if not friendly. Still, Womack was brutally punished—chained, thrown into a trench, and starved for two days—for refusing to complete an index card, and Crafts, too, reported being placed in "The Hole."[30]

Crafts later stated that Schumann's death had profoundly affected him, leaving him more vulnerable to the enemy's threats—and blandishments—than previously. The VC must have perceived this, as they had worked on Crafts for a statement in August by threatening to kill him and Cook, and now, early in 1967, they informed Crafts that he and Womack were candidates for release but that he would have to persuade the young sergeant to improve his attitude. Neither Crafts nor Womack was sure what the Communists had in mind, except that with the approach of Tet, the liberation of a pair of PWs, one a black, could be expected to garner the VC some propaganda points. Crafts made no attempt to influence Womack, and the two decided simply to act politely and write letters requesting release without criticizing the war effort.[31]

Sometime during the Tet holiday period in February, Crafts and Womack were ushered to a specially constructed hut for a formal release ceremony presided over by a senior official and attended by the entire camp, including

Cook and Ramsey. The release was delayed when Crafts's malaria flared up, but by 16 February they were on their way. As they left, the men carefully studied the area and noted a small clearing that could serve as a drop zone for a rescue operation, but they could not identify enough landmarks along the departure route to find the place ever again. By 23 February they reached a main highway where their escorts put them aboard a civilian bus, which deposited them at a U.S. checkpoint that afternoon.[32]

At considerable risk, Crafts smuggled out with him a letter from Ramsey to his parents and two letters from Cook addressed to his wife and to "Big Sam," the latter meant for U.S. authorities. Because of its bulk, Crafts decided to memorize the letter to Mrs. Cook and convey its contents to the captain's wife upon his return to the United States. The Ramsey letter, dated 13 January 1967, was surprisingly upbeat in describing the state of the PW's health and the conditions of captivity. Whether he sought to reassure his family of his well-being or, as U.S. intelligence analysts suspected, he anticipated that the communication might be intercepted by the enemy, Ramsey put the best possible face on his ordeal.* If the letter did not offer any particular revelations about his personal trials, it did contain a remarkably prescient forecast of the likely futility of the American effort in Southeast Asia. "We have a tiger by the tail and can't let go," Ramsey fretted. He hoped that "our leaders have no illusions about ultimate political victory here and that they do not entertain ambitions going beyond a minimum face-saving roll-back which will permit our withdrawal without undue loss of military prestige." "Anything more," the foreign service officer concluded, "is wishful thinking, and any attempt to achieve it would be to compound past folly with future folly."[33]

For Ramsey and Cook, the release of their fellow prisoners was a bitter-sweet occasion. Although happy for their comrades and comforted by the fact that Crafts and Womack would carry out news of their captivity, they had no expectation for release themselves. They spent the next six months suffering variously from anemia, dysentery, and recurrent attacks of malaria and beriberi. Ramsey's beriberi became so acute his left thigh ballooned to twice

---

* It must be noted, however, that Ramsey took a rather benign view of his experience and of his captors even after he returned home and could freely state his opinion. He believed that in the South the elements were crueler than the enemy, and that captives and captors alike were at the mercy of the jungle's inclemency. "Despite the medically and sometimes ethically horrendous nature of some of the episodes I have experienced," he wrote in 1973, "I don't hold much of a grudge against the VC . . . . [Their] behavior was generally within the range one would expect of civilized people from far more technically advanced societies under equally trying conditions. Perhaps it was a little better than many of us would have displayed if the shoe had been on the other foot." See "The Cruel Years—Two Exclusive Reports," *Nutrition Today*, May/Jun 73, in *American Prisoners of War and Missing in Action in Southeast Asia, 1973*, 231.

its normal size. Cook had briefly regained his strength, such that Crafts remembered him being "strong as a bull" when he last saw him, but he continued to run a low-grade fever from malaria and before long he was again gravely ill. Although the VC had stepped up their care of him, Cook, according to Ramsey, could not keep down any food, until "his abdomen swelled up as if he'd swallowed a basketball."[34]

In September, Army Capt. William Hardy joined the camp. An agricultural development adviser, Hardy was taken prisoner when he had the bad luck to drive his vehicle right into a firefight between Viet Cong forces and an American armored unit. With him was Dang Vu Loat, his interpreter. The rebels held both in a field until darkness, then marched them toward the detention location. Loat was separated and later released. For Hardy, it was the first leg of an odyssey that would not end until 1973—he was the other individual besides Ramsey captured in the Heartland before 1968 who came out in 1973—and would include stays in 10 prison camps as well as at several temporary holding sites.[35]

Late in 1967 the group pulled up stakes again, heading northwest back toward the Cambodian border and the drier climate of the highlands. Hardy, in the best shape of the three PWs, made the trip in 10 days despite having to carry the bulk of the prisoners' equipment. Cook and Ramsey followed at a slower pace, with Ramsey, his swollen limbs causing him intense pain and hampering his ability to climb the steep slopes, finally arriving on 27 December after a month's straggling. When Ramsey rejoined the party, he noticed Cook missing and, inquiring about his whereabouts, was told that the Marine had been taken to "a distant camp." Not until his release in 1973 did Ramsey learn from a VC interpreter that Cook had died along the trail, probably from another malaria seizure, only a week or so after the two were separated.[36]

For years, Cook's heroism was little known outside the tiny band of PWs with him in the Heartland. Sergeant Camacho carried out the first fragmentary reports when he escaped in 1965. When Smith and McClure were released in 1965 and Crafts and Womack in 1967, they added to the legend. Ramsey completed the account at homecoming, sending a letter to the Marine Commandant, General Robert E. Cushman, Jr., on 3 April 1973 attesting Cook's rigid adherence to the Code of Conduct, inspirational leadership, and extraordinary valor even in the face of steadily failing health. The Marine Corps soon drafted recommendations for a high honor for the gallant captain while continuing to list him as missing in action and possibly still a prisoner of war. Despite Ramsey's report of his passing and his inclusion in a died-in-captivity compilation provided by the Communists at war's end (that cited his death as occurring on 8 December 1967), the Department of Defense did not officially remove him from the MIA list until 26 February 1980. Finally, on 16 May of that year, at an impressive ceremony in the interior courtyard of the Pentagon, Donald Cook's widow received her husband's Medal of Honor* from Secretary of the Navy Edward Hidalgo.[37]

The redoubtable Ramsey received no medal, but he somehow managed to survive, along with Hardy, another five years' captivity. Like the Viet Cong themselves, the two were reduced to fugitives trying to elude the incessant pounding of B-52s and strafing of helicopter gunships, as advancing U.S. and ARVN operations forced the guerrillas eventually to seek shelter inside Cambodia. Toward the end of 1967, Cambodia's Prince Sihanouk promised Mrs. John F. Kennedy that he would attempt to intercede with the NLF on Ramsey's behalf. The prince had been advised by the Front's Central Committee that Ramsey was still alive but that "his fate depends on the conduct of the American imperialists and their puppets." That assessment was so much grist for the propaganda mill, but it reflected the bitter truth that American PWs in the Heartland increasingly were threatened as much by the onslaught of their own attacking forces as by any harm the enemy intended for them.[38]

---

* Besides Cook, six other American PWs in Vietnam were awarded the Medal of Honor: Navy Cdr. James Stockdale; Air Force Majs. George Day and Leo Thorsness and Lt. Lance Sijan; and Army Sgt. Jon Cavaiani and Pvt. William Port. Sijan and Port, like Cook, were given the medal posthumously. Thorsness, Cavaiani, and Port earned their medals in combat prior to capture.

14

PWs in the Northern Provinces of the South, 1965-1967

Captivity in the northern provinces of South Vietnam, a region encompassing the Central Highlands, the coastal area north and south of Da Nang, and the mountains just below the Demilitarized Zone, was something of a mixed blessing. As a rule, prisoners here were not moved as frequently as in the Heartland because the Viet Cong were in solid control of the territory and were seldom forced to evacuate due to Allied operations. However, conditions were every bit as primitive as elsewhere in the South and the isolated location of many of the camps contributed to chronic shortages of food and medicine. Moreover, U.S. personnel seized on the northernmost frontier, above Hue and near the Laotian border, were typically hauled soon after capture across the DMZ to North Vietnamese internment centers. The passage from jungle to jail placed them in a marginally healthier if not friendlier environment but effectively closed off the possibility of escape. By 1970, with increasing Allied penetration into Cambodia, PWs everywhere in the northern provinces were being shepherded into North Vietnam.[1]

It was in this region that Old Man of the South Jim Thompson had been captured and Army physician Floyd Kushner spent the most trying period of his captivity. Describing his camp in the mountainous jungle of western Quang Nam Province, Kushner contrasted the rugged beauty of the land from the air, a landscape dotted with "emerald peaks" and "swiftly running creeks and rivers," with the gruesome reality on the ground. "For those who endured, and those who were not so lucky," he wrote following his release, "Quang-Nam was a hideous, muddy, leech and insect-filled, twisted Procrustean bed which all too often became a tomb." Of the 27 American servicemen confined at Kushner's camp, one third succumbed to disease, starvation, or overexposure.[2]

Not all prisoners in the northern provinces fared as badly as Kushner's group. All camps had their share of deaths in captivity, but there were also early releases, successful escape attempts (mainly in the vicinity of Da Nang), and many, including Kushner and Thompson, who survived to be repatriated at homecoming. From 1965 through 1967 the number of PWs in the region was still limited, perhaps two dozen Americans altogether, but even among this group there were sharply contrasting outcomes. Their stories run the gamut from quiet courage and conspicuous heroism to unspeakable tragedy and, for one young Marine, lasting notoriety.

Assigned to protect the American airfield at Da Nang, the military hub of the U.S. northern deployment, the Marine Corps bore the brunt of casualties—and captures—in the region. Between the fall of 1965 and December 1967, 21 Marines were known to have been taken prisoner by the Communists. Six of these—aviators Harlan Chapman, Howard Dunn, John Frederick, Orson Swindle, James Warner, and Edison Miller—were captured in North Vietnam; their experiences are recounted in other chapters. The rest, except for Lance Cpl. Frank Cius, who was apprehended after his helicopter crashed across the border in Laos,* were seized in one or another of the South's northern provinces.[3]

As was the pattern throughout the South, PWs in the northern region fell captive under a wide variety of circumstances. Among the Marines, two were grabbed while enjoying themselves on leave, another two when separated from their squads during night reconnaissance patrols. Several were captured in combat action, one after being wounded, two when their positions were overrun, another in a major battle near Quang Tri. The aforementioned Cius was downed on a remote rescue mission. One man was abducted as he stepped outside a compound gate and another during a routine errand as he was turning his jeep around on a dead-end road. In still two other incidents, one victim was ambushed while driving a convoy truck, another when he escaped from the base brig and wandered into VC territory.

The Marine caught on the dead-end road was PFC Robert Garwood, a 19-year-old motor pool driver who disappeared on 28 September 1965. Although there is evidence he had taken unauthorized leave, Garwood later contended he was responding to an emergency order to pick up an officer at an operational location near Da Nang and bring him back to the base for dispatch home. According to his account, he got lost en route and was stopped at the end of a dirt lane by camouflaged guerrillas, who shot him in the right forearm, dragged him from his jeep, and marched him for 10 days between villages until reaching a small hillside camp perhaps 20 miles from Da Nang.

For six weeks, Garwood lay captive in a crude bamboo cage while nursing his wounds and numerous leech and mosquito bites. He soon contracted

* See Chapter 15.

dysentery and other illnesses and, after a failed escape, was beaten and forced to watch the Russian Roulette-style execution of South Vietnamese prisoners. The multiple ailments and brutal intimidation had him on the defensive almost immediately and he became easy prey for exploitation. An NLF political officer coaxed him into signing a propaganda statement in return for a vague promise of release.* In November he was transferred to a second camp, where he was joined by Army Capt. William Eisenbraun, a Special Forces officer seized in July near Quang Ngai, 50 miles south of Da Nang. The pair observed a group of ARVN PWs undergoing indoctrination, some of them gaining release after demonstrating a sufficiently "progressive" shift in their thinking. (One of these releasees carried Garwood's dog tag out with him, returning it to an American unit.) Garwood and Eisenbraun would spend the next two years together before the captain's death. It was during this period, which included all of 1966 and much of 1967, that Garwood made the alleged accommodations with Viet Cong and North Vietnamese handlers that would form the basis for later charges of collaboration with the enemy.[4]

In the spring of 1966 Garwood and Eisenbraun were moved to another location, high on a mountain, where they were joined by Marine Lance Cpl. Edwin Grissett. Grissett had been captured on 22 January after attacking Viet Cong overwhelmed his outmanned patrol and he failed to reach a helicopter pickup point.[5] A North Vietnamese interpreter the Americans called "Hum" supervised an indoctrination program that had the men reading propaganda literature and listening daily to Radio Hanoi broadcasts in English. The tedious routine was interrupted by an abortive escape attempt by Eisenbraun and Grissett that landed them in leg stocks and led Grissett to accuse Garwood of having tipped the VC to their absence.[†] After a year at this camp, following a damaging B-52 raid in the area, guards marched the three Americans along with ARVN PWs to another site still further from Da Nang. Here Garwood was persuaded to make another propaganda tape and, in exchange for continued cooperation, offered preferred treatment in a hut separate from his mates. Garwood accepted the proposition, he maintained, with the approval of Captain Eisenbraun, who viewed Garwood's possible early repatriation for good behavior as an opportunity to communicate word that both he and Grissett also were alive.

* The anti-American statement was widely circulated—it appeared in published leaflets and was aired on Hanoi radio—and was judged authentic enough for the Marine Corps to change Garwood's status from missing to presumed captured.
[†] Grissett, like Eisenbraun, died while in captivity, so that one has to rely on Garwood's recollection here. Garwood denied any complicity. In *Conversations With the Enemy* (see note 4), he cited growing friction between him and Grissett that became irreconcilable after the escape episode. Unsteady as Garwood was proven to be, there is ample evidence of Grissett's own instability that must have worsened under the stress of captivity. See Grant, *Survivors*, 83, 88.

Garwood   Eisenbraun

The hoped-for release never materialized, and while a disappointed Garwood brooded, the older Eisenbraun's health gradually deteriorated. Hobbling
about camp with a cane and poor eyesight that required him to squint in order
to see (his glasses were lost during capture), Eisenbraun appeared more grizzled
than his 35 years. He was a wreck from the combined effects of malnutrition,
unchecked dysentery, and periodic punishment in the stocks. Still, when he
died, in September 1967, the end came suddenly and stunned his companions.
Grissett reported to Garwood that, according to a VC nurse, the Special Forces
officer succumbed to internal bleeding from broken ribs and a punctured lung
suffered when he fell from his hammock bed. After a brief service, Grissett,
Garwood, and three other recently arrived American prisoners, Army Pvt.
Luis Ortiz-Rivera and Marine Cpls. Jose Agosto-Santos and Robert Sherman,
said the Lord's Prayer and lowered the body, wrapped in bamboo, into a carefully dug grave.*

Garwood later said that the death of the soldierly Eisenbraun, who was
a father figure to him as well as a senior officer, affected him deeply, leaving
him "suicidal" and in a "state of paralysis" from grief and trepidation.[6] Even
given Garwood's tendency to hyperbolize, the event may well have pushed
him over the brink. Confused about his obligations, desperately seeking some

* The fates of Ortiz-Rivera, Agosto-Santos, and Sherman are discussed elsewhere in the chapter.

middle ground between resistance and accommodation, and having already rationalized that cooperation with the enemy was a legitimate means to enhance his chances for survival, the vulnerable private drifted increasingly into a pattern of collusion with his captors.

By 1968, Garwood had apparently adopted the Vietnamese name Nguyen Chien Dau, which could be translated "Nguyen the Fighter," and, at least in the eyes of PWs who crossed his path in the northern camps, had become an out-and-out defector. He lived outside the prisoner compound, fraternized with the guards, wore a Viet Cong uniform, and was seen carrying a weapon on the trail. Moreover, as he became fluent in Vietnamese, he was enlisted by the Communists as an interpreter and eventually functioned as an interrogator and indoctrinator, proselytizing and even occasionally guarding his countrymen.

Some of the surviving witnesses to Garwood's metamorphosis surmised that he had collaborated because the Vietnamese gave him trust and responsibility, engendering a sense of importance and self-esteem that had eluded him in civilian life and that in any case was a powerful lure to a man who had no special rank or status in his own army. They reported his telling them the VC had made him a lieutenant, given him a Christmas gift of a watch, and paid him a stipend from which he deducted "traveling expenses." Although there were those prisoners who harbored bitter resentment and contempt toward him, others were impressed by his friendly if enigmatic behavior, interest in conversation with fellow Westerners, and seeming uncomfortableness in the turncoat role.[7]

In sum, the preponderance of evidence indicates that he did cross over but that his "defection" stemmed more from opportunism than any genuine political or ideological conversion. His biographers say simply that Garwood was "at sea" and "opted for survival." Defense attorneys at his court-martial had psychiatrists testify that he had been traumatized by his captivity and could not appreciate the criminality of his conduct. In a 1981 interview, Garwood attributed his actions to fear, immaturity, and a desperate struggle to stay alive. He said he had no illusions about the moral superiority of the Communists. He knew he was being manipulated: "I was like some damned vegetable or a tree. They didn't give a shit. Every now and then, they'd water me and that was about it."[8]

Although Garwood vigorously denied ever fighting alongside the Viet Cong, over the years rumors circulated about a "white VC" guiding enemy units into combat against American troops. The reported sightings included one incident, in the summer of 1968, where the Marine Corps suspected that Garwood had in fact been wounded and possibly killed. In that instance a

Marine reconnaissance patrol opened fire on an enemy force accompanied by a Caucasian wearing fatigues and brandishing a Chinese AK-47 rifle. In the ensuing battle, the mystery figure was heard calling for help in English after being shot and collapsing into a streambed. The patrol had to disperse but later another U.S. contingent returned to search the area without finding a body or a grave. Several members of the patrol identified Garwood from photographs of captured and missing men. A year later another Marine unit caught in a firefight reported spotting a Caucasian pointing out targets for the enemy, the American company commander believing the individual to be Garwood.[9]

Garwood dropped out of sight after 1969, by that time living in North Vietnam and, according to scattered U.S. intelligence reports, training or studying in Moscow. By his account, he spent the next decade shuttling between Hanoi hospitals and provincial prison camps with relative freedom but little comfort or activity, essentially being kept under wraps by the North Vietnamese while they figured out what to do with him. Garwood grew ever more restive, occupying his days reading and gardening and in the evenings playing cards with his guards. Eventually he worked out an arrangement with a couple of his regular attendants whereby he was able to spend an occasional "night on the town" in Hanoi. It was during one such outing early in 1979 that he managed to pass a note to an English-speaking man, a Finnish economist he overheard in a hotel dining room, informing him that he was an American. After a nervous exchange, Garwood scribbled his name and serial number on the paper and asked the man to notify U.S. authorities that he was alive and wanted to return home. Two months later the North Vietnamese turned him over to the International Red Cross. On 22 March, 14 years after his capture, an ICRC representative placed him aboard an Air France plane that flew him to Bangkok and into the waiting arms of U.S. officials.[10]

Other Marines captured in the northern provinces of South Vietnam never achieved the prominence of Garwood, but if their names remained largely anonymous and their experiences obscure, their ordeals were just as real. Like Garwood, most were young enlistees, "grunts," average guys from ordinary backgrounds suddenly thrust into extraordinary circumstances. Significantly, although Garwood's collaborationist path was atypical, he was only one among several in the bunch who buckled badly and early under pressure, suggesting that as a group they may have been victimized as much by their youth and inexperience as by the South's peculiarly adverse conditions. The dozen or so Marine infantrymen seized in the northern provinces between September 1965 and December 1967 averaged barely 20 years of age,

12 years less than the aviator-officers incarcerated in North Vietnam. For all their raw physical toughness and youthful bravado, their lack of training and discipline, along with the isolation and the dearth of senior leadership and PW organization inherent in the Southern situation, left them especially ill-equipped to deal with the psychological demands of captivity. This is not to say that there were not instances of heroic and intelligent resistance among them, only that, as a group, they tended to be less stable and steadfast and coped less successfully than older, more seasoned hands in both the North and South.

A case in point was Cpl. Richard Burgess. Captured in the northernmost province of South Vietnam on 25 September 1966, Burgess slipped into a severe depression shortly after his internment. He was the sole American held by a dozen or so enemy personnel, and when he was troubled by the guilt that commonly afflicted prisoners after their initial concessions to interrogators, he did not have the advantage of communication with comrades or their peer support (and pressure) to sustain him. Also ill and in pain from an arm wound suffered when apprehended, he became robotic, for weeks refusing to bathe or remove his one uniform, until his keepers finally rendered assistance. His spirits briefly revived, he attempted an escape early in 1967, only to return after reaching the outskirts of the camp and having second thoughts. During the winter and spring of 1967 he was moved in a southwesterly direction through a series of hamlets, along the way worked over by 10 different instructors who elicited from him signed confessions and appeals for clemency.[11] By 8 May, when he was loaded onto a truck for a trip back north, his sanity was again dissolving along with his self-esteem. He was resigned to perishing in the wilderness when he was bolstered by the discovery aboard the vehicle of another American PW, Marine Corps rifleman Alfonso Riate.

Corporal Riate had been captured two weeks earlier as his company launched an assault on an enemy-held hill. At the new location he and Burgess were pressured for more propaganda statements, which they furnished in order to improve their living conditions and chances for escape. The tactic worked. Quartered in a loosely guarded pagoda, by August they were able to tunnel underneath a wall and slip away down a dike system to a canal, which they swam. They then crossed low-lying fields until hitting higher ground, stopping at the top of a hill to rest and treat cuts and leech bites. The first day they avoided search parties, but during the second, as the two hid in bushes, a group of Vietnamese children spotted them and sounded the alarm. Angry guards towed them back to camp, placed them in leg irons and handcuffs, and tied them to the inside of a bamboo cage.

A week later, still in August, they were on the move again, this time hauled along a network of trails across the DMZ and into North Vietnam—

the first PWs from South Vietnam since Jim Thompson to be marched north of the demarcation line.* The exhausting trek took six weeks and brought Riate and Burgess to a camp that would acquire the nickname "Portholes" for the circular vents and windows in the walls of its several buildings. Burgess was deposited in a room next to the guard post, Riate in a three-foot by eight-foot cell at the opposite end. Although drained from the trip, the two Marines had been given adequate food and water and were now convinced that the Vietnamese intended for them to live. Indeed, Riate was developing a certain empathy for his captors that would eventually lead to his own case of questionable conduct and, upon his repatriation in 1973, the filing of charges against him by fellow PWs.

Leonard Budd's captivity migration took a less circuitous route than that of Burgess or Riate, but it landed him in the same place. Corporal Budd was captured in August 1967 near the Marines' northern frontier base at Dong Ha when his vehicle, the third truck in a convoy, was stalled by a guerrilla ambush and he sought cover in a ditch. Walking 10 hours a day, stopping infrequently for water but eating little or no food, his captors marched him a long distance until pictures of Ho Chi Minh in the windows of village homes told him he had crossed the DMZ. Only 21 and with no countrymen for companions, he demonstrated surprising fortitude and composure through twice-daily interrogations. When he failed to obey a command to salute and bow to enemy officer staff, he was sometimes locked into wooden ankle stocks.[12]

Budd's condition began to deteriorate from lack of food and the onset of malaria. Although he was finally issued PW clothing, a blanket, soap, and a towel, he was kept alone in cramped quarters, always restrained by ropes, stocks, or handcuffs. In October he plotted an escape but circumstances never quite allowed him the opening he needed to proceed with the plan. Early in 1968, faint from malnutrition, he traveled with guards on foot and by jeep past the North Vietnamese city of Vinh to a new compound where he spent two months in constant misery. Here, however, he would soon have company—it was the Portholes complex that housed Burgess and Riate as well as other Americans. In time he would also get vital care, which, with the companionship, would enable him to bounce back.

Another Marine, Lance Cpl. Jose Agosto-Santos, entered the PW ranks further south in May 1967. He had been seriously wounded during a firefight in which most of his squad were also wounded or killed. On his first night of captivity, a Vietnamese medical team removed two bullets from his

---

* Thompson reached the North only a month or so before them. The veteran PW spent the middle years much the same as he had the early ones, in pain and in solitary while lugged through a series of small nondescript camps on the northern fringe of the South near the Laotian border.

body, an excruciating procedure as the cutting was done without anesthetics. During his recovery the VC treated him well while interrogating him and attempting to manipulate him with promises of release in return for his cooperation. He was permitted to write a letter to his father in June before being moved to a second location, where he was confined with an Army captive, also Puerto Rican, Luis Ortiz-Rivera, captured six months earlier.

It was in this second camp that Agosto-Santos encountered Garwood, who already appeared to be enjoying a privileged status. Curiously, Garwood's own recollection would be that it was the two Puerto Ricans who seemed to be unduly subservient and amiable toward their captors and who were showered with favoritism as the VC endeavored to exploit their Hispanic identity.[13] Although we have only Garwood's shaky testimony here, his description of their treatment would have been consistent with Communist policy to exploit PW ethnicity in order to sway minorities fighting for the United States in Southeast Asia and recruit sympathetic liberals to the antiwar cause. In any case, in January 1968, just before the Tet offensive, the Viet Cong released Agosto-Santos and Ortiz-Rivera during a ceremony outside a hamlet near the provincial capital of Tam Ky. Whatever concessions the two had made to gain advantages while in custody, upon repatriation they reaffirmed their loyalty to the United States and, after some initial evasiveness, supplied service debriefers with useful information on camp conditions and other prisoners.[14]

The only officer in the group of young Marines captured in the northern provinces during this period, Lt. William Grammar, never had a chance to prove his mettle. His captivity was one of the shortest—and, from all indications, most horrible—on record. Grammar and Army Sgt. Orville Frits were separated from their units and seized by enemy troops during a major engagement northeast of Quang Tri on 20 May 1967. When an ARVN battalion with American advisers drove off the guerrillas that same afternoon, they found the corpses of the two men in a church courtyard, where they had apparently been tortured and murdered and their bodies mutilated. Grammar had been shot in the head at close range; witnesses at the scene noted that his arms were tied behind his back and his throat was cut. Frits had large holes in the palms of his hands, as if he had been fastened to the ground with bamboo stakes; his throat had been slashed, his legs showed both burns and bullet holes, and his back contained numerous stab wounds. Villagers reported that the Viet Cong had executed them just before the Government counterattack.[15]

Four others were spared the test of a prolonged captivity when they were lucky enough to escape soon after imprisonment. On 18 October 1965 Pvts. Joseph North and Walter Hamilton were on leave from the Marine

Marine infantrymen captured in the South's northern provinces. *Clockwise from top left:* Riate, Dodson, Grissett, North, Eckes, Burgess.

installation at Da Nang when, groggy from an evening of drinking and revelry, they were knocked out and abducted by several armed Vietnamese believed to be Viet Cong. During a week's stay in a small hamlet, they were treated adequately until an interrogator threatened to cut off their testicles if they did not respond to questions, whereupon they supplied inconsequential personal and military information. On the night of 27 October, their tenth day in captivity, they took advantage of a commotion in the camp and lax security to flee the hamlet. Fortunately, their detention site was only a few hours from Da Nang and, with the aid of South Vietnamese troops who spotted them before the enemy, they were able to make it back to a Marine checkpoint. North earned a Purple Heart for a wound received during the getaway.[16]

In another successful escape, in the spring of 1966, two Marines captured four days apart just south of Da Nang used their wits and steely determination along with fortuitous circumstance to gain their freedom. On 6 May, Sgt. James Dodson was surveying a road construction project when six Viet Cong approached, overpowered him, and led him away. About the time that Dodson reached the VC confinement area, Cpl. Walter Eckes was returning from a supply run when he encountered three men in ARVN uniforms carrying American weapons who disarmed him, tied him up, and herded him off to a jungle trail. The two PWs met when Eckes joined Dodson and a dozen South Vietnamese prisoners on 12 May in a small camp somewhere southwest of Da Nang. For the next month the Americans were made to read Communist propaganda pamphlets and listen to Radio Hanoi broadcasts in English while they were intermittently quizzed by the guerrillas' leader. The latter took a particular interest in Dodson, perhaps because he was black—casually plying him for information, and dropping the name of Garwood as an American prisoner who had benefited from a cooperative attitude. Neither Dodson nor Eckes complied with the chief's requests and they deflected the overtures adroitly enough that there were no attempts to coerce statements from them.

Although reasonably well treated, the two Marines decided early on to make a break for it at the first opportunity. The chance came on 18 June as they were being marched through the mountains to another camp and their three guards carelessly left their carbines leaning against a tree. As the prisoners snatched the weapons, the startled guards took flight, leaving behind equipment packs with clothes and provisions. Dodson and Eckes donned boots, discarded their black pajamas for green fatigues, and took only a canteen and some hard candy to keep their load at a minimum. Even with the favorable start, they had to overcome punishing lacerations and exhaustion, the result of descending the steep terrain, and a series of predicaments—a brush with quicksand, stampeding water buffalo, and near detection by a VC search party that passed within three feet of them—before they reached a South Vietnamese Army camp on 22 June. The South Vietnamese arranged transport to a nearby airfield, from which they were flown to Da Nang, grateful to be alive and satisfied that they had faithfully upheld the Code.[17]

If providence smiled on some of the young Marines, others were cursed by plain misfortune, especially those who wound up at the camp whose horrors were later documented by Dr. Kushner. Cpl. Robert Sherman was captured on 24 June 1967 when, possibly lured by a passing Vietnamese woman, he strayed outside a compound gate while on guard duty.[18] Sherman arrived at the northern camp that housed Garwood, Grissett, Agosto-Santos, and Ortiz-Rivera in late August. To the other PWs he appeared "defeated and dazed," "passive," and "fatalistic"; prisoners who encountered him subsequently had much the same impression, one saying his eyes "had the glint of a cornered cat." The Idahoan was on his second tour in Vietnam. The first ended abruptly when he was sent home for medical treatment and psychiatric counseling after becoming unhinged at the sight of a buddy's remains while processing bodies at the Da Nang morgue. Judging from his comrades' observations, he was still deeply troubled at the time of his capture and ill prepared to deal with the rigors of captivity. It did not help that the Garwood camp near Tam Ky eventually became the camp associated with Kushner; it was among the most abysmal camps in the South. While there Sherman witnessed the deaths of prisoners from infections, disease, and in one instance as a result of an unsuccessful escape attempt of which he himself had been a part. Following the escape incident he spent two months in leg stocks during which he slipped into acute depression and refused to eat. Verging on insanity, he finally succumbed to malnutrition and malaria in November 1968.*

Sherman's cohort who died in the course of their abortive escape effort was PFC Earl Weatherman. A maverick in and out of scrapes with authorities, the brash 20-year-old was doing a stretch in the Marine Corps brig at Da Nang when he slipped out and took off for Saigon, he told fellow PWs, to locate his Vietnamese girl friend and child. There are several conflicting accounts—the result presumably of different stories he told different prisoners—as to how he came into Viet Cong custody, but he either was captured by or defected to the VC in November 1967. Whichever the case, by the time he turned up at the Garwood-Kushner camp, he evidently was already receiving special treatment, given considerable freedom of movement and other liberties in return for assisting the Communists' propaganda operation. The Marine Corps listed him as a deserter in the hands of the enemy rather than as a prisoner of war, and indeed the consensus among the Americans in camp was that he was a defector much like Garwood. However, Weatherman's degree of complicity is hard to judge. There were those who believed he was simply an inveterate con artist who was now deceiving the VC. John Hubbell in *P.O.W.* portrays him as a "dropout" rather than a "crossover" who mistakenly assumed the Viet Cong would provide him with safe passage out of the country.[19]

The peculiar relationship between Weatherman and his captors, whatever its tenuous basis, soon soured and Weatherman gradually took on the status of a more conventional PW. In April 1968, he, Sherman, and three recent arrivals to the Kushner camp—Army PFC James Daly and Marine Cpls. Joseph Zawtocki and Dennis Hammond—were on a work detail gathering manioc

* In 1985 Sherman's remains, along with those of Army Sgt. Gerasimo Arroyo-Baez, were returned to the United States. They were the first American PW remains recovered from the South. See *Washington Post*, 10 Apr 85.

when Weatherman and Hammond overpowered a lone guard and seized his weapon. The pair slugged the Vietnamese but did not kill him and when he ran away, Sherman, Daly, and Zawtocki decided to return to camp rather than risk getting caught and face harsh reprisal. Weatherman and Hammond opted for escape but were soon apprehended by Montagnard villagers, who had been alerted to the prisoners' disappearance and swarmed after them "howling, yelling, jabbing their spears into the air" in a scene "right out of a Tarzan movie," Daly later recalled. A Montagnard elder placed a gun against Weatherman's face and, after one misfire, blew his head away. Hammond was retrieved by converging Viet Cong and severely beaten and punished by the VC commander; Sherman drew leg stocks for his peripheral involvement in the incident.[20]

In retrospect, the escape attempt, even with its disastrous outcome, made good sense. The chances of the men reaching friendly forces were not high, but had the five stuck together, with some luck and strength of numbers they might have made it. Weatherman died trying but three of the remaining four would perish anyway from disease or starvation. Only Daly, a conscientious objector who had never fired his weapon in combat, would survive to return home.*

Yet another casualty of the Kushner camp was Marine Cpl. Fred Burns, the last Marine to be captured in 1967. Burns was separated from his squad while on patrol Christmas night and seized the next morning while attempting to make his way back to his post near Da Nang. Only 18, he resisted gamely in the early weeks of captivity, refusing to sign a letter protesting United States presence in Vietnam, but once he contracted dysentery he went downhill rapidly. Garwood escorted him into the camp near Tam Ky in March 1968. As Burns became seriously ill, Kushner pleaded with the Vietnamese to allow him to treat the young prisoner, or at least find some medication for him, but, as with others close to death in a camp desperately short on supplies, they refused his requests. Burns became delirious, then died on the day after New Year's 1969.[21]

"Russ" Grissett didn't make it into 1969. The senior PW at the Tam Ky camp (in point of longevity) after Garwood's defection and Eisenbraun's death in 1967, Grissett never fully recovered from the two months spent in leg stocks after his and Eisenbraun's escape attempt. By 1968 he was suffering from severe intestinal and skin problems, his weight down from 190 pounds to 125. Further weakened from a flogging he received for killing a favorite camp cat for food, he developed bronchial pneumonia which, along with starvation, eventually consumed him. Several survivors of the Kushner

---

* The ordeal of the Kushner group during 1968-70 is described in Chapter 21.

camp noted that over time Grissett had simply lost the will to live. Still, at the end, one of them recalled, "Russ went harder than anyone." Grissett died in Kushner's arms around Thanksgiving 1968.[22]

"That he was not a hardened combat veteran or a career-minded officer, but a nineteen-year-old kid one step ahead of the juvenile authorities, certainly made a difference with respect to his appreciation of the code of conduct."[23] Winston Groom and Duncan Spencer's characterization of Robert Garwood could apply as easily to Alfonso Riate, Joseph North, Walter Hamilton, Earl Weatherman, or any number of the young leathernecks captured in the northern provinces between 1965 and 1967. Not only were they irreverent toward the Code of Conduct, but they were often abusive, surly, and contentious toward one another. Petty squabbling and narcissism undermined morale and resistance, exacerbated their sense of isolation, and increased their vulnerability. With so much mistrust and dissension within their own ranks, it was no wonder that among them, as well as among other young servicemen captured in the South over the years, there would be a higher incidence of capitulation, collaboration, or—just as insidious in terms of its effect on morale—the perception or insinuation of collaboration, than occurred among the more mature and cohesive aviator-officer PWs in the North.

The enemy's Tet 1968 offensive brought a large influx of new PWs into the South's northern camps, including many more Army personnel, among them a batch of roguish noncoms and green youngsters with many of the same qualities, and vulnerabilities, as their Marine precursors. Snaring only a few Special Forces strays like Thompson and Eisenbraun before 1968,* the northern frontier would claim dozens more soldier PWs after Tet, so that, increasingly, Army prisoners would be dominating the captivity rolls in the region and writing their own checkered record there. But that is getting ahead of our story.

---

* Five members of an Army infantry unit were captured in the same firefight in July 1967: Sgts. Cordine McMurray and Martin Frank and Specialists Nathan Henry, Stanley Newell, and Richard Perricone. With WO David Sooter and Pvt. Joe DeLong, they were held at a camp inside the Cambodian border near the intersection of Cambodia, Laos, and South Vietnam. All survived to homecoming except for DeLong, who was killed in November 1967 during a failed escape attempt.

15

Laos in the Middle Years:
Live and Vanished PWs

What the *New York Times* referred to as the "twilight war" continued in Laos through the 1960s, the backwater kingdom remaining a secondary theater in the struggle against Asian Communists but regaining importance as a strategic corridor through which North Vietnamese cadre and supplies flowed into the South. So vital had the Laotian panhandle become as an infiltration route that by 1968 some analysts were again calling it a "key" to the outcome of the contest in Southeast Asia and U.S. MACV Commander General William Westmoreland undertook planning, even as he was unsuccessful in pressing Washington for authority, to conduct ground operations to destroy enemy access to the area.[1]

The U.S. government persisted in denying military involvement in Laos beyond routine reconnaissance flights and training and supply activities to bolster anticommunist forces. To enhance credibility, officials eventually resorted to the term "armed reconnaissance" to clarify the nature of the air program. It was no secret, however, that by 1965 both Air Force and Navy planes were flying bombing missions in an effort to interdict guerrilla movement along the so-called Ho Chi Minh Trail and that the numbers of advisory and support personnel assigned to Laos were increasing as well. Volunteer pilots, sometimes outfitted in civilian garb, flew highly classified raids under such code names as "Yankee Team" and "Steve Canyon," while Army special-operations teams carved airstrips out of the jungle. The CIA, too, had its people in Laos, using both officers and private contractors to ferry ammunition to rightist troops, provide other forms of paramilitary assistance, and cultivate the native population. Commenting on the conspicuous U.S. presence in the country despite efforts at concealment, one reporter noted in June 1968 that restaurants along the Mekong River were "crowded with husky young Americans who, as a local resident puts it, 'aren't in the Peace Corps' . . . ." Only years later, with the publication of insider

277

accounts like British journalist Christopher Robbins's 1987 *The Ravens: The Men Who Flew in America's Secret War in Laos*, did the full extent of United States involvement there become more evident.[2]

The unpublicized air campaign in Laos claimed scores of American fliers but produced few known PWs. On the one hand, a relatively high percentage of downed airmen were rescued on the ground in Laos: unlike in North Vietnam, Laos's sparse population and proximity to search and rescue teams operating out of airfields in South Vietnam and Thailand offered good odds on recovering fliers who survived their shootdowns.* On the other hand, among those who were not rescued, most became MIA statistics, their fate remaining a mystery owing to the dearth of official or even third-party contacts with the Pathet Lao and the absence of any released prisoners from Laos (after 1962) who might have provided information on the living as well as the dead unaccounted. Only when Navy Lt. Dieter Dengler escaped in 1966 and Navy Seaman Douglas Hegdahl was freed by North Vietnam in 1969, the latter briefing U.S. authorities on the existence of transferred Laotian PWs in Hanoi's prisons, was there confirmation of Communist capture of Americans in Laos, and then only a handful.

Most likely, the majority of missing aviators simply did not survive their parachute drops, perishing upon impact with the thick jungle canopy or sharp karst ridges or from resulting injuries. "Even if you are healthy in the chute," George Coker, a North Vietnamese-held PW familiar with Laos, testified after the war, "when you finally land you've got to penetrate those trees . . . and then you've got to fight that karst . . . . That stuff can be so sheer that . . . it will actually peel you like a grater." Others who were in good condition on the ground but could not be located by rescue teams likely contracted disease or infections, which, left untreated and worsened by a scarcity of food and water, might have consumed them after a few days of wandering in the Laotian wilderness—unable to reach friend or even foe, who perhaps would have at least dispensed water or minimal first aid. "The thing that gave you protection from the enemy," Coker noted, "is now the enemy itself, because now if we can't rescue you immediately, if we can't find you and get you out of there, you are stranded, isolated in the boondocks." To be sure, there were the horror stories of atrocities committed by Laotian villagers and soldiers against downed American fliers: in one instance, an Air Force pilot had allegedly been mutilated by his captors, "virtually skinned alive," to convince a second captive

---

* According to a 1976 House report, 61 percent of downed airmen returned alive from Laos, as opposed to 45 percent from North Vietnam. The figure for South Vietnam, where airborne rescue forces could most speedily be deployed and a generally friendly populace could be counted on to aid and protect fallen pilots, was roughly 70 percent. See *Americans Missing in Southeast Asia*, Final Report of House Select Committee on Missing Persons in Southeast Asia (13 Dec 76), 153.

to call for a rescue on his survival radio as the guerrillas waited in ambush for the search plane. Nonetheless, Coker argued persuasively, a Laotian shoot-down typically fell victim to the hostile environment rather than the enemy. "Laos killed him," Coker concluded; "it just gobbled him up."[3]

Despite a preponderance of such evidence to the effect that natural causes were sufficient to explain the disappearance of scores of U.S. airmen, and, for that matter, dozens of other service personnel and civilians in Laos, the resolution of the Laotian MIA question would remain one of the more controversial and enduring issues of the Indochina conflict. It seemed implausible, even to many who shared the view of Laos as a no-man's-land, that only 9 out of over 300 U.S. personnel listed in 1973 as having been lost in Laos turned up on the capture rolls among those released by the Communists at homecoming. The large number of personnel that remained unaccounted for, along with the covert nature of U.S. operations in Laos, fueled speculation that American officials were withholding information on the status of the Laotian casualties, either to cover CIA tracks or to protect the continuing national security interests in the country. Charges ranged from a conspiracy of silence to outright obstruction and deceit, with some critics accusing the government of betraying and abandoning men whom officials knew to be at one time alive in captivity.

In fact, Defense Department spokesmen themselves raised concerns as early as 1966 about the credibility and release of casualty data from Laos. "We are faced with a serious problem in connection with reporting U.S. casualties suffered in operations in and over Laos," a worried Assistant Secretary of Defense for Public Affairs Arthur Sylvester wrote Secretary McNamara in July.

> What is at stake now is the credibility of the Department of Defense and of the Administration as a whole. We have been accused recently of not telling the whole story with respect to all our Southeast Asia combat casualties, and we cannot truthfully deny such accusations. To date, no one of note has questioned this matter but we cannot hope to stay clear of the problem indefinitely. I have discussed this matter at length with the key members of my office and we are all agreed that we must face up to it now or be subjected to great censure if some enterprising journalist or politician digs into it.

Regarding possible prisoners of war, a memo circulated within DoD's Office of International Security Affairs early in 1968 urging that more pressure be put on the Pathet Lao, through the Soviet Union or some other intermediary, to identify and release any American held captive in Laos. Toward that end, Navy Capt. John Thornton recommended "a change in our past policy of seeking to maintain the image of Laotian neutrality and protecting the credibility" of claims of limited intervention. "The plight of American POW's in Laos," declared the clearly

Hrdlicka (left) and Shelton, missing in Laos.

frustrated officer, "can no longer be relegated to an obscure position. Though the number may be small the principle is large . . . . More definitive steps must be taken to help them."[4]

Although the Johnson administration opted to dig in its heels on the sensitive matter of public disclosure, there is no evidence—Thornton's restlessness notwithstanding—to indicate that it was not trying actively and earnestly to ascertain the status of the MIAs or to recover those who might still be alive and in Pathet Lao custody. Thornton's impatience reflected growing anxiety through the mid-60s over the fate of U.S. PWs *generally*, including those in North and South Vietnam.* PW numbers were difficult to validate everywhere, but, whereas in Vietnam investigators at least had concrete leads supplied by conventional intelligence channels, freed prisoners, and the enemy's own prolific propaganda, in Laos they had mostly conjecture, rumor, and the sketchiest of details to go on.

The presumption among informed sources, even before the Hegdahl revelations, was that some of the Laos MIAs had indeed been captured. Dengler brought out word of Duane Martin's and Eugene DeBruin's imprisonment, though Martin died on the trail during the Dengler escape and DeBruin, who was thought to have been recaptured during the same incident, was never heard from again.† A photo of Air Force Capt. David Hrdlicka, who bailed out over

* See Chapter 10.
† See Chapter 3.

Laos in May 1965, appeared in the Hanoi press about a year later with an accompanying statement indicating he was still alive, yet at no time afterwards did the Communists concede he was being held prisoner. Radio contact was made with Air Force Capt. Charles Shelton after his F-101 went down in Laos in April 1965; the Pentagon notified Shelton's wife that her husband had ejected safely, and a villager who witnessed the crash observed him being led away by Pathet Lao troops, but, except for sporadic reports that placed him in both Laos and North Vietnam, he, too, vanished. Two months after Shelton's presumed capture, U.S. Ambassador to Laos William Sullivan cabled Washington that an American PW thought to be either Shelton or Hrdlicka had been rescued by friendly agents, but the information proved to be incorrect. Although analysts believed Shelton died in captivity from malaria or dysentery, for years following homecoming, as a symbol to suggest that the U.S. government was not closing the door on the possibility that PWs might still be alive in Southeast Asia, the missing captain, alone among the 2,500 American servicemen unaccounted for at war's end, remained officially listed as a prisoner of war.[5]

As with everything else about Laos, the captivity experience there must be reconstructed from spotty information and limited sources. Although many men who were assumed to be prisoners, notably Hrdlicka and Shelton, and others known to be prisoners, for example Martin, DeBruin, and Army Capt. Walter Moon, never returned to convey their experiences, more than a dozen military and civilian PWs in Laos did survive to relate their stories. Five of these—Army PWs Lawrence Bailey, Roger Ballenger, and Edward Shore, Navy PW John McMorrow, and civilian Grant Wolfkill—were released in August 1962. Dengler escaped to freedom in July 1966; Navy pilot Charles Klusmann, in August 1964.* Although there were no returnees between Dengler and the nine, mostly post-1968, captures repatriated at homecoming, there were still others, such as Jim Thompson, who were counted on Vietnam casualty lists but who spent considerable time in Laos as well and thus could speak authoritatively on life in the Laotian camps.

What then from this patchy record can one conclude about captivity conditions in Laos? To a man, those who were held in both Laos and Vietnam judged Laotian internment to be both physically and psychologically the equal of the worst-case situations in Vietnam. The same karst ridges, steep-sided valleys, and roadless wilderness that victimized shootdowns on the run in Laos also plagued captured PWs, who were hauled along mountain trails in poor shape and with typically scarcer edible food and potable water than was available in even the

---

* All of these early cases are discussed in Chapter 3.

remotest reaches of Vietnam. So primitive were Laotian sanitation standards and so severe the water problem in particular that, to those transferred to North Vietnam, Hanoi's jails seemed like hotels by comparison. Laotian survivors, Coker remarked in his post-mortem, "said that the big trouble was lack of water. Laos is dry, especially if you are up in the high ground. Absolutely dry." Early captives such as Bailey and Klusmann evidently were given ample amounts of food and water and in some instances were treated surprisingly well, receiving even medicines and cigarettes on occasion, but, as happened in Vietnam, with the intensification of U.S. bombing in the middle years, captives and captors alike gradually experienced more hardships. Toward the end of Dengler's confinement in the summer of 1966, drought, disease, and shortages of food claimed five Lao guards and had the PWs foraging for rats and insects in their quarters.[6]

Of the Pathet Lao's reputation for savage handling of prisoners, doubtlessly the atrocity tales were exaggerated, though summary executions of men dangling from trees in their parachutes or too weak to travel with the guerrillas is not difficult to imagine given the brutish environment. Coker challenged the notion of wholesale executions by the Laotians but acknowledged that "this idea of being shot upon capture in Laos seemed to be more prevalent than it was in North Vietnam." It was probably not mere coincidence that the nine Laos captures who returned at homecoming had either been seized by North Vietnamese or come under their control soon afterwards and thus spent little or no time at the mercy of the less disciplined and unpredictable Lao.[7]

Prison accommodations in Laos resembled those in South Vietnam's Delta and hinterlands, in both countries the Communists stashing their charges in makeshift huts, cages, or cave cells between frequent moves. As in the South, American PWs in Laos were so few and so scattered that they often had to endure their ordeal alone, without comradeship. Significantly, even the group transferred in the later years to Hanoi—the so-called "Lulus" (Legendary Union of Laotian Unfortunates)—were kept sequestered in an isolated corner of the PW compound, denied mail privileges and visits with other prisoners at a time when conditions in the North were improving for their compatriots. The Lulus had good reason to suspect that the North Vietnamese were holding them as bargaining or propaganda chips, possibly to embarrass the American government in any final accounting. Because they had knowledge of North Vietnamese activity in Laos and thus could implicate North Vietnam itself in violations of Laotian neutrality, their worst fear was that they might not be released at all, Hanoi refusing to admit that they were even in custody.[8]

The secrecy on both sides that surrounded their status made a harrowing captivity all the more anxious. If the American prisoners in Vietnam were in a legal limbo because the United States had not formally declared war against the North, the PWs in Laos were in even greater jeopardy since Washington denied even authorizing their activities. The Laotians could maintain with more cogency than the North Vietnamese that their captives were mercenaries or intruders who had no claim to PW protections under international law. Moreover, the clandestine cloak that U.S. officials placed over the air war in Laos, with servicemen sometimes flying out of uniform or assigned to embassy slots in Vientiane for cover purposes, reinforced the Pathet Lao contention that they were intelligence agents or political operatives rather than professional military. "Like the North Vietnamese, we weren't supposed to be here," one prisoner described their predicament.[9] The lack of public disclosure and official recognition increased their vulnerability and sense of isolation.

That we know as much as we do about conditions in Laos in the middle years can be attributed in large measure to a civilian prisoner who spent 1965-68 there and in nearby locations just over the North Vietnam border. Ernest Brace survived barbarous mistreatment and decimating illness over an eight-year period (the last five in prisons in and around Hanoi) to become one of the most seasoned and respected PWs among all the Americans captured in Southeast Asia. He was the longest-held civilian prisoner of war and the longest-held survivor, civilian or military, to return from Laos. His story, related at length in post-homecoming debriefings and congressional testimony and in 1988 in an intimate memoir, is one of the more riveting captivity chronicles of the war and one of the few that shed light on the Laotian experience.[10]

Brace's incredible adventure commenced on 21 May 1965. "On that date," his debriefer gushed admiringly in 1973, "began what is sure to be heralded as the most unusual prisoner of war tenure spent by any American."[11] A pilot employed by Bird and Son, a private airline flying supply missions in Laos and Thailand under contract to the U.S. Agency for International Development, Brace was taken prisoner when his aircraft was trapped on a runway recently seized by Communist troops. He had flown his Swiss Porter plane from Thailand on a series of stops in Laos delivering rice and salt and ferrying four passengers, among them Thai Special Forces Sgt. Chi Charn Harnavee and a pair of Royal Lao soldiers. As Brace landed at the small airfield at Boum Lao, about 75 miles northwest of the ancient capital city of Luang Prabang in northern Laos, his plane was hit by grenades and rifle fire that prevented him from turning around and taking off again. The hail of bullets shattered his windshield and fuel tanks and wounded the wife of one of the Lao soldiers, who himself was killed when he tried to escape the crippled craft. Brace, Harnavee, and the other Lao soldier surrendered to the ambushers, who turned out to be uniformed North Vietnamese Army regulars. Brace managed to radio a mayday message before stepping out of the cockpit.

Left: Ernie Brace, longest-held civilian and Laos survivor. *Right*: Thai Sergeant Harnavee, to become a valued friend of American PWs in Hanoi.

While the injured woman took refuge in a nearby village, the captives were tied to trees in a canopied clearing that served as a base of operations for the North Vietnamese and their Pathet Lao allies in the area. At nightfall the trio witnessed guards dragging a teenage youth to a log and lopping off his little finger with a machete, punishment for having helped build the American airstrip at Boum Lao. Before the boy was released, Sergeant Harnavee passed him the prisoners' names in the hope that information about their capture might reach friendly forces. Brace's mayday transmission had been heard, as soon after the ambush incident several U.S. planes circled the Porter's wreckage, but Brace feared that search crews would assume the dead Lao's body to be his and abandon their efforts, which indeed appeared to be the case.

Bound loosely that first evening, Brace wasted no time making his first of several escape attempts, a bid that gained him only a few feet before guards spotted him and retied him more securely. The prisoners spent three days in the Boum Lao area before being moved north to Muong Hoc, an old French army camp with some of its barracks still intact, and then to Muong Sai, a Pathet Lao stronghold. Along the way friendly villagers treated boils that had developed under the men's fuel-soaked clothes, sheltered them after a day's march through a drenching rain, and gave them food. Brace took advantage of their pausing at a Buddhist temple that was observing a local festival in which one of the ceremonies required the natives to tie money on strings as an offering for a good growing season. Still having Thai money in his pocket, Brace wrote his and Harnavee's names on one of the notes and hung the money from a string, again hoping to communicate word that he was alive.

At Muong Sai they were quizzed by a monk fluent in English and a Laotian officer, the latter accusing Brace of being a spy for the CIA and threatening to execute him. When Brace agreed to write answers to a set of fairly innocuous questions of a personal and political nature, the firing squad unloaded their weapons. During the stay at Muong Sai they were allowed to bathe for the first time since capture and were attended by a physician who drained and bandaged their wounds. Now clad in black pajamas, their clothes and possessions having been removed and inventoried, Brace and Harnavee, minus the other Lao prisoner, were herded north into the jungle again on 31 May.

Over the next week, as the captives noticed increasing numbers of enemy troops with North Vietnamese insignia and passed through an array of checkpoints and sizable base camps, one containing a fully equipped field hospital, Brace realized they were headed in the direction of North Vietnam. On 6 June he made his second escape attempt while spending the night in the communal hut of a small village. Before dawn he was able to free his hands and feet and leave the hut in order to relieve himself in nearby bushes. Seeing no sentries, he tried to slip away, but was observed by a villager who awoke soldiers with his screams. Brace decided to run for it, charging a few hundred meters down a trail before diving into a ravine thick with vegetation, which he hid under. For two hours troops searched the area in vain until they finally discovered him. They fired into the ground around him as a warning, then dragged him from his hiding place, beat him with bamboo poles, and slapped and kicked him until they broke his nose and loosened his teeth. Brace probably averted yet more serious injury by feigning unconsciousness.

After several more days of uneventful travel, the small party reached Muong Lao, a Laotian community on the North Vietnam border and a key crossroads en route to Hanoi. Here Brace saw his first motor vehicles since he left Thailand and for the first time the prisoners were kept overnight in actual confinement cells, albeit a crude dugout type. Muong Lao was a hotbed of joint North Vietnamese-Pathet Lao activity and an apparent rendezvous point for PW transfers. Placed in the custody of a new unit, Harnavee and Brace were marched and then driven east a short distance into North Vietnam, stopping around midnight on 12 June just west of the historic site of Dien Bien Phu. Brace called the spot *Doi Sai*, Laotian for "Mosquito Mountain." It was to be their home for almost a year.

The prisoners were placed in two small dirt-floored cages, their mobility hampered by the cramped quarters and by a neck rope secured to one side of the cage; at night their hands and feet were tied also. Neither allowed to exercise nor given the opportunity to work, they had to contend as much with boredom as discomfort, but, aside from their constricted confinement and an occasional hostile guard, their treatment was humane. Brace remembered receiving adequate food, primarily sticky rice and bamboo shoots, with some meat when it was available, usually two or three times a month; still, his six-foot frame carried no more than 150 pounds when he arrived at Doi Sai ("I was having difficulty keeping my pants up")[12] and his weight would continue to drop. The men were let outside their cages twice daily to relieve themselves, given shaves and haircuts periodically, and provided water for bathing. Once every six weeks or so they were permitted to wash in a large stream nearby.

On 4 July 1965 a pair of visitors whom Brace believed to be North Vietnamese intelligence officers gave the PW his first formal interrogation. They asked Brace if he recognized the names of several other American prisoners, mentioning specifically Alvarez, Shumaker, "Bloot," Vohden, and Storz. Brace knew the first two, but not the others.* Evidently working from a report supplied by the monk in Muong Sai, the inquisitors pursued the spy allegation. Satisfied with Brace's answers and after delivering a dissertation on the Vietnamese victory over the French, the senior interrogator authorized a mosquito net for the examinee and granted him a request to write his family, though the letter was never mailed. Encouraged by these concessions, Brace asked to be put with the other Americans but was told his "situation was different," one of the first indications he had that as a Laotian capture his status would remain separate from that of countrymen seized in Vietnam. The older man warned him against escaping and offered some hope for release in the example of Lieutenant Klusmann, who, he insisted, did not escape but rather gained his freedom after a deal was struck. The interrogators departed early the next morning, the last significant English-speaking contact the American pilot would have for more than three years.

Brace spent the rest of 1965 in unsplendid isolation, pestered less by the enemy than by swarms of mosquitos (not as tormenting after his receipt of a net), rats that nested in the thatch of his cage and the snakes that hunted them, intense cold weather, and multiple ailments including ringworm, mouth ulcers, and intestinal disorders. To sustain his morale, he contemplated escape despite the interrogator's admonition, devising a program in which he allotted points for various circumstances—so many for heavy rain or a dark night, so many for unattentive guards, etc. He determined to make his break when the point total reached 20. He never quite achieved the necessary figure, although he faithfully did his calculations every evening. To pass the time he used a shard of bamboo

* "Bloot" may have been a reference to DeBruin, or Navy Lt. Phil Butler, captured in April 1965, or possibly civilian pilot Alan Blewett, who, like Brace, had flown for Bird and Son in Laos. Blewett had been presumed killed in a crash in July 1962, but the "Bloot" mention raises the question of whether he survived the incident and, at least briefly, may have been a PW.

to carve bits of sandstone he found outside his cage. His likenesses of people and animals were good enough that the Vietnamese would steal the figures while he was at the latrine. Seeing in their thievery an opportunity, he scratched his name and date on each piece, hoping that if the soldiers were later captured or killed, friendly troops might discover and inspect the carvings.

By February 1966, with U.S. air activity zeroing in on a truck-repair facility near the Mosquito Mountain camp, guards were distracted enough to embolden Brace to implement his escape plan. Gradually loosening the bars on his cage and waiting for the monsoonal rains that would help cover his flight, Brace made his break during a violent storm in the late afternoon of 17 April. For two days he trekked through sharp bramble patches and tall elephant grass, skirting villages and beaten paths to avoid detection, existing on wild tomatoes and berries while grabbing snatches of sleep. On the third day he located some yellow banana leaves and laid them out in a field in the form of a distress signal, the letter K. His body by now deserting him, dehydration and fatigue setting in, on the fourth day he entered a village looking for food and water. Instead he found a soldier, who recaptured him and, with reinforcements, returned him to Doi Sai.

Once again, Brace was punished severely, spreadeagled against barbed wire and flogged with split bamboo poles from neck to ankles so that when he was cut down and deposited in his cage he had deep lacerations on his back, legs, and torso. Further, he was secured now with tight leg stocks that pressed painfully against his swollen limbs and an iron neck hoop that prevented him from lifting his head. In anguish but undaunted, the prisoner fashioned a saw from strands of yarn (the remnants of his socks) and the quartz sand from his cage floor. Slowly, for days on end, he used the makeshift blade to cut a groove in the iron collar. Before he could saw through, or be caught in this latest indiscretion, a truck pulled into camp the night of 13 May, and guards removed the neck iron and hauled Brace aboard the vehicle. Inside the truck was Sergeant Harnavee. The two exchanged smiles as they drove off with a squad of soldiers for another canyon camp some two hours away. Brace took advantage of the darkness and his handlers' momentary inattention to heave the iron hoop, left on the seat beside him, down the road.

No sooner was he incarcerated at the new site, which he referred to simply as "Doi Sai No. 2," than did Brace prepare to break out again. For six weeks he collected bits of wire, bamboo, and other odds and ends to enable him to unscrew the bolt on his cage door. He then waited for the right conditions, a steady rain on the night of 17 August, to slip away. He climbed a hill behind the cage and had almost reached the top when a log collapsed, pitching him down the slope and into the underbrush below. The noise alerted sentries, who quickly recaptured him.

This time the punishment was fiendish. An officer ordered guards to place Brace upright in a hole and fill it with dirt up to his chin. The prisoner remained there for seven days, losing all feeling in his body and nearly his senses, too, as he was fed only two cups of soup the entire week. He learned to tilt his head so as to catch rainwater in his beard, then lick it into his mouth to quench his thirst. Local chickens solved one problem by pecking at the insects crawling around his head. By the time he was extricated on 25 August he was mud-encrusted, suffering from kidney dysfunction, and partially paralyzed except for spasms of excruciating pain when guards extended his arms and legs. Almost a month would pass before he would regain the use of his limbs and normal body functions.*

Brace and Harnavee spent the next year in a mindless rut of sweeping their cages and silently watching soldiers come and go. To preserve his faculties Brace took to solving mathematical problems in his head, reconstructing portions of his life, and fantasizing. "The calendar became an obsession," he recalled. When a Russian aircraft dropped supplies at New Year's, the prisoners each received a blanket, Brace converting his into a jacket that served him well during the cold winter nights. "I had always thought there were no seasons in the jungle," Brace wrote after his release. "Living in a bamboo cage was teaching me that there definitely was a delineation." In April 1967, first Harnavee and then Brace were moved from the hillside camp to another on the other side of Dien Bien Phu. Looking down on the famous valley and noticing "the pastoral scene of rice paddies and quiet villages," Brace "found it hard to picture it as a battleground where thousands of men had died in just a few historic weeks in 1954."[13]

Dien Bien Phu almost claimed Brace as well. In September the dexterous prisoner was up to his usual tricks, this time devising bamboo picks to loosen his ropes at night. When a guard on a routine check shined a flashlight into the captive's cage and saw his hands untied, he beat the PW viciously, one ferocious kick to the head knocking him unconscious and, as it turned out, paralyzing and nearly killing him. Over the next two months, Brace gradually lost the use of his right leg, then his left, then all motor coordination until he could not perform even the simplest of tasks and lost control of his bowels and kidneys. His keepers saw he was ill but offered no assistance as his cage became a foul mess of urine, excrement, and vomit. On 10 December, his son's birthday, he tried to strangle himself with his neck rope, succeeding in passing out but not dying. Brace went through that entire winter without a bath or a change of clothes but somehow summoned the resolve to recover. He began a conditioning program that by the end of February had him flexing his hands and regaining bowel control. In March 1968 a replacement unit arrived at the camp, washed the

---

* In an interview with Kiley, Brace suggested as one lesson learned that, if you are going to be buried upright, you should lean backward while dirt is being shoveled in because it will be easier to breathe later.

prisoner, cleaned his cage, and sheared his matted beard and hair. For Brace, the nadir of his captivity experience was behind him.*

Ernie Brace owed his survival to his own indomitable will and to a strong constitution. In Laos one had to have both, and some luck as well, to come out alive. Brace was no ordinary "civilian." He had been a decorated Marine pilot in Korea at age 21. Moreover, as his debriefer noted in 1973, by occupational circumstance he had "lived, eaten and slept" with Laotian tribesmen prior to his capture and was not unaccustomed to the rugged environment: he "did not go from white sheets and hot meals to the field captive situation." Dengler, Klusmann, and others who made it out may not have been as familiar with the territory, but they, too, had what Brace's debriefer called a "high adapt-ability coefficient." Dengler's group used vines for dental floss and stored extra food in bamboo tubes; prior to their 1966 escape they saved their urine to loosen the support posts of their stockade.[14]

Marine Lance Cpl. Frank Cius learned about Laos's special challenges during the summer of 1967. Cius was a gunner aboard a helicopter forced down by enemy fire while attempting to remove a battered contingent of South Vietnamese and American troops near Laos's border with South Vietnam. In the ensuing assault, an Army sergeant and three Marines, including the pilot, Capt. Stephen Hanson, and the copilot, Lt. John Gardner, were killed, and Cius and Army Sgt. Ronald Dexter were shortly taken prisoner. By the end of July, Dexter was dead of complications from a hepatitis-like illness and Cius was in the midst of a long journey north to Hanoi. Cius's Lulu status consigned him to almost two years of continued solitary confinement, much of it in darkness.[15]

No American PW had a stronger will or constitution, or suffered a crueler fate, than Air Force Lt. Lance Sijan, a back-seater in a disabled F-4 that crashed in Laos on 9 November 1967. The plane's pilot, Lt. Col. John Armstrong, was presumed killed in the wreckage although his body was never recovered. Sijan managed to bail out at a low level and, despite multiple traumatic injuries, including a compound leg fracture, mangled hand, and concussion, evaded capture for 46 days before North Vietnamese soldiers found him by the side of a dirt road on Christmas morning.[16]

Like Cius, Sijan was one of several airmen who went down along the Laos-Vietnam border and whose names have appeared under both Laos and North Vietnam (in Cius's case, South Vietnam) on U.S. casualty lists, sometimes for reasons of political sensitivity but often because of the difficulty in establishing the precise crash and/or capture location. If terrain was any clue, Sijan almost

* Brace's, and Harnavee's, later years in captivity are discussed in subsequent chapters.

Sijan

certainly landed in Laos. During his six-week evasion he dragged his broken leg over an extensive area of jagged karst and experienced shock, dehydration, and extreme weight loss from lack of food and water as well as from his untreated injuries. Once incarcerated, although crippled and emaciated—the flesh of his buttocks worn to his hipbones from crawling for miles along the karst on his back—he knocked out a guard with a single chop to the head and had made it back into the jungle when he was recaptured after several hours.

Sijan's exploits might have gone unnoted had he not been taken to a holding area near Vinh in North Vietnam, where, around New Year's Day 1968, he joined recent Air Force shootdowns Lt. Col. Robert Craner and Capt. Guy Gruters. The pair overheard their fellow officer being tortured for information and between screams responding only with his name, rank, and service number. Gruters knew Sijan from their stay at the Air Force Academy, where the lieutenant had been a strapping 220-pound football player, but he did not recognize him when the three men boarded a truck for Hanoi. By now semi-lucid and incontinent, a green pus oozing from a hole in his badly infected leg, Sijan recounted his evasion ordeal and asked his comrades for help exercising so he could escape again. Placed in the same cell with the delirious PW at Hoa Lo, Craner and Gruters desperately tried to save him, but their devoted efforts and the captors' belated medical attention could not revive him and in the dank January chill he contracted pneumonia, which dealt a final blow. Removed from his cell on 21 January, Sijan, according to the Vietnamese, died the next day in a military hospital. For his invincible courage and extraordinary dedication to the Code of Conduct, in March 1976 he became the first graduate of the Air Force Academy to be awarded the Medal of Honor.

Sijan's heroic acts did not need any embellishment, but Malcolm McConnell's overwrought 1985 narrative, *Into the Mouth of the Cat*, practically canonized the fallen aviator.* With the likes of Sijan, Brace, and Dengler among Laos's internees and given the air of intrigue and mystery associated with Laos itself, it was perhaps inevitable that Laotian captivity in general would acquire a certain mythological aura. The Lulus would themselves contribute to the mystique with their name and by forming a kind of brotherhood, borne of necessity owing to their sequestration, after they arrived in Hanoi. Some of them would later depict the North Vietnamese prisons as a dramatic improvement over bondage on the Ho Chi Minh Trail. When Brace eventually entered the Hilton in October 1968 he marveled at the sight on his plate: "My God . . . it's bread." Reading his memoir, one gets the impression of a prisoner coming in from the cold, rejoining civilization, as his jeep passed through Hanoi's paved streets and approached Hoa Lo.[17]

Surely it made a difference having a solid roof over your head and having comrades nearby even if you were kept isolated. The differences were real, not mythical. But they could be deceiving. A steady diet of moldy bread was scarcely more palatable than one of weevily rice. Sijan's losing battle with respiratory problems pointed up Hoa Lo's own inclement climate. Brace happened to arrive in Hanoi when the atrocities of the middle years were giving way to an extended bombing pause, so that his sanguine turn may have been as much a product of a change of pace as a change of scenery; had he arrived a year earlier he might have blanched at what he saw. For sheer terror, the random beatings and capricious cruelty that characterized captivity on the trail, however severe and frightening in themselves, hardly surpassed the programmed torture inflicted in the Northern jails.

The Laos transfers soon learned that in exchanging cages for concrete cells they were not exactly trading purgatory for paradise. In the end, of course, comparisons are moot. In the PW experience in Southeast Asia there was enough grief and suffering everywhere to entitle all survivors to bragging rights. Still, if numbers were any indication, with over 95 percent of U.S. "missing" in Laos never heard from again, those who emerged safely from the clutches of the shadow war could be forgiven a special sense of accomplishment.

---

* Although the book was marred by excesses of sentiment, McConnell provided an absorbing description of rescue and recovery operations in Laos, relating at length the daring and repeated but ultimately abortive efforts to retrieve Sijan prior to his capture.

16

Higher Stakes: Little Vegas at the Hilton

By February 1967, with the closing of the odious Briarpatch camp, the resumption of secret negotiations that promised a possible early settlement of the war, and the onset of Tet, the festive Vietnamese New Year celebration, the vicious cycle of on-again, off-again terror in the Northern prisons had entered a relaxed phase. Near the end of January, half the Briarpatch men were blindfolded, tied, and loaded onto a bus for the 35-mile trip to Hanoi, where they were placed at the Zoo. On 1 February, the remaining Briarpatch PWs were given a final quiz in which the camp commander asked them to list personal articles they had lost when captured, which some of the prisoners construed to be a hopeful sign of impending repatriation. The next day, they, too, were bused to Hanoi.

To make room for the first contingent of Briarpatch prisoners, the Vietnamese moved 22 Americans from the Zoo to a previously unused compound in the northeast corner of the Hilton. The second group from Briarpatch, numbering 32, were taken directly to the refurbished facility when they arrived in Hanoi about a week later. The new complex, consisting of several buildings ringing a courtyard, had been reconstructed from open bays into about 60 rooms of which 40 were cells, the rest military offices and chambers. One of the transfers from the Zoo, Air Force Capt. Dave Hatcher, dubbed the place "Little Vegas" after the Nevada resort well-known to fighter pilots for its proximity to Nellis Air Force Base.

Not only did the "Vegas" tag stick, but individual cellblocks within the compound soon acquired the nicknames of casinos. The largest, with about 15 rooms, became "Thunderbird." Adjacent to Thunderbird on the west end was a building with three large cells and a utility room that sometimes doubled as a medical station; it became "Golden Nugget." Southeast of Nugget was a similar building that bore the name "Riviera." Along the east

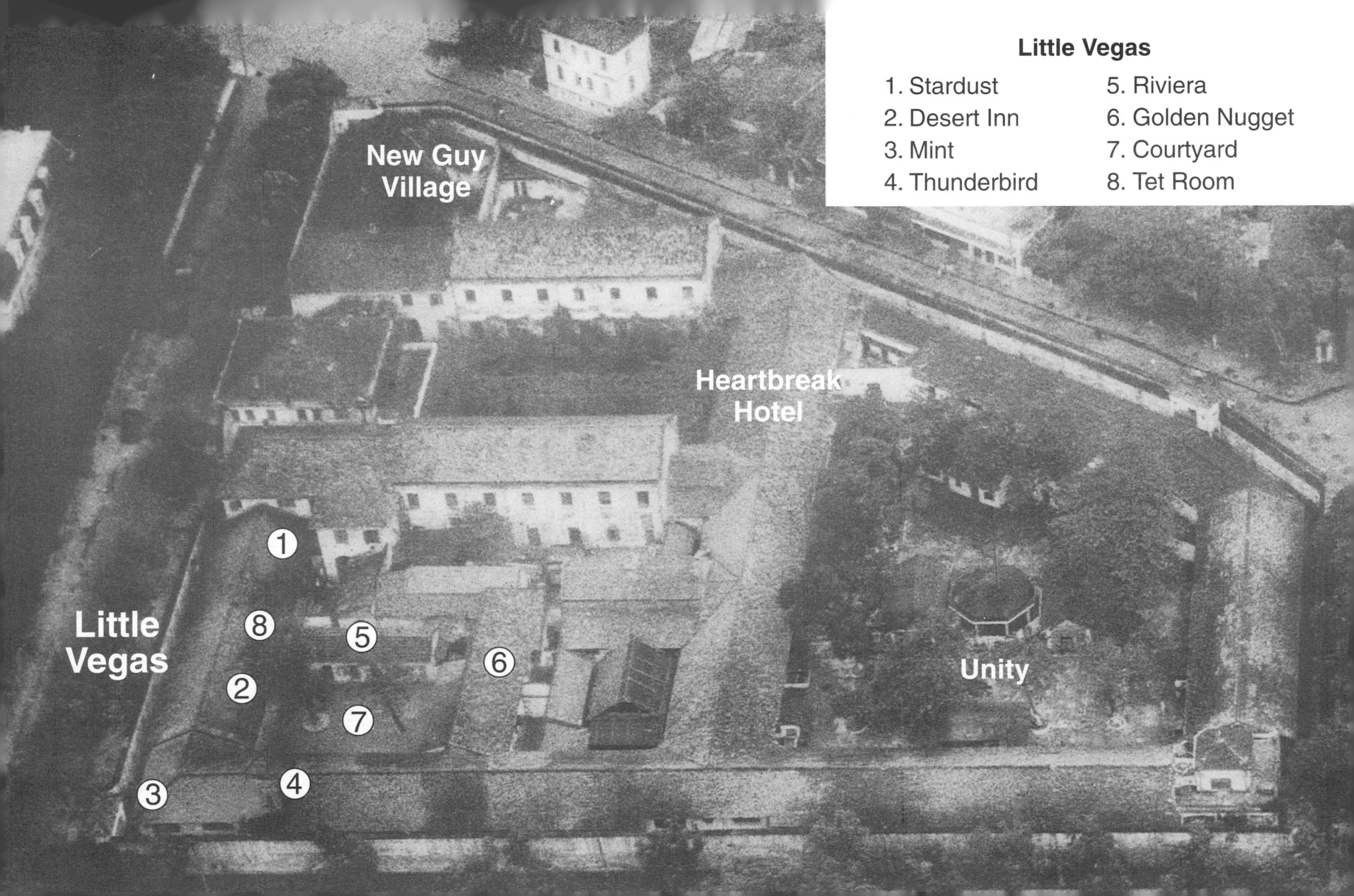

Little Vegas

1. Stardust
2. Desert Inn
3. Mint
4. Thunderbird
5. Riviera
6. Golden Nugget
7. Courtyard
8. Tet Room

Unity

Heartbreak Hotel

New Guy Village

Little Vegas

① ⑧ ② ③ ⑤ ⑦ ④ ⑥

side of Vegas were three cellblocks christened, north to south, "The Mint," a three-cell maximum-security area; "Desert Inn," an eight-cell section; and "Stardust," a seven-cell "bad attitude" section separated from Desert Inn by a large barren chamber that the prisoners would call "the Tet room." A shed with a dozen back-to-back bath stalls occupied the center of the courtyard.

For reasons not entirely clear, the Vietnamese decided to send to Vegas most of the Zoo's senior officers, a collection of Navy commanders and Air Force lieutenant colonels that included Stockdale, Denton, Jenkins, Mulligan, Rutledge, Lamar, and Franke.* (Overall PW senior Robinson Risner remained in isolation in another part of the Hilton.) More puzzling still was the decision to corral the Zoo's seniors at Vegas and then disperse them among the younger men who came over from Briarpatch. Mulligan was among several prisoners who theorized that the captor had decided to gather all the troublemakers, both seniors and juniors, in one location,[1] perhaps to limit their pernicious influence to their own ranks and in any case to keep them from "contaminating" the new arrivals entering the system through Hoa Lo's main receiving stations, Heartbreak Hotel and New Guy Village.

To discourage collaboration among the new prison mates, the enemy took elaborate steps to stymie communication in Vegas, constructing cellblocks so that no two cells faced one another and no two cells shared a common wall. Using dead space or narrow corridors to separate adjacent rooms, the Vietnamese sought to preclude the wall-tapping that they had come to realize was the PWs' prime communication mode. Vegas's labyrinthine design, however, was no match for the ingenuity of its tenants, who used the floor or common outer walls for tapping and drinking cups pressed to the ear to amplify the sound. "The investment of a year's construction," Stockdale later wrote, "was about to be canceled out . . . . We all had outside walls, and in minutes, we were tapping 'round the bend' . . . ." Jerry Coffee recalled that at siesta time, when the prisoners took advantage of their guards' napping, there was so much tapping that Vegas "sounded like a cabinet factory," such "that it was sometimes difficult to maintain your own communications link." Mulligan, in cell 6 of Desert Inn, using his fist, managed to thump the tap code through the air space separating his cell from Jim Lamar's, the two men learning from Dave Hatcher, who had a window view of PWs moving through the courtyard, the identities of Vegas's select company.[2]

It took the group quartered in Stardust "about ten minutes," according to Stockdale, to establish communications. Joining Stockdale there were Denton, Jenkins, Sam Johnson, recent shootdown Air Force Maj. Hubert "Bud"

---

* The Navy learned that Franke was a prisoner about this time. He had been reported killed in action when his aircraft was shot down in August 1965 (see Chapter 6). His family in San Diego had already held funeral services for him when they were informed he was still alive.

Flesher, and young Navy Lt. George Coker. "Sounds carried so well," said Denton, "that Stockdale could lie on his bunk in his cell across from me and send messages by thumping on his chest in code." Capitalizing on initial disorganization among the guard force and clearing procedures that enabled the prisoners to track guard movements and signal safe times to communicate, the Stardust bunch found that they could convey information by simply talking under their cell doors. The other buildings developed their own system of lookouts and warning techniques, so that soon messages were being relayed through voice contact and hand signals as well as by the safer but more cumbersome tapping. Nor was there any impediment to inter-cellblock communication, as dishwashers and bathers using the courtyard's stalls exchanged words or notes and men assigned cleaning chores in common areas pounded waste buckets or swept brooms in tap-code sequences.[3]

Communication activity on such a large scale, however clever and guarded, could not have gone unnoticed by the Vietnamese. That it was tolerated for several months was an indication of the generally permissive atmosphere that prevailed throughout the system over the remainder of the winter and into early spring. Interrogators at Vegas pestered prisoners with attitude checks but the sessions were low-key and punishment for resisters was minimal. Brazen communicators Denton and Mulligan were closeted in the Mint's tiny cells, each one roughly the size of a bed, but, except for a brief period in irons, escaped further reprisal. Indeed, they continued to converse while at the Mint, tapping to each other and contacting newcomers Navy Lt. (j.g.) Michael Cronin and Air Force Capt. Julius Jayroe. Although Vegas's sheltering walls apparently afforded little relief from the bitter winter cold—Mulligan still had uncontrollable shivers and remembered pacing the floor with a blanket wrapped over his head, looking like "a medieval monk . . . reciting his daily prayers"—in other respects morale picked up as a result of the leniency and overall improvement in living conditions.[4]

By most accounts, the food at Vegas, including maize and greens and extra rations of rice, was more plentiful and of a somewhat better quality than it had been at Briarpatch or the Zoo. (In retrospect, the Vietnamese may have been fattening up the PWs for another round of propaganda exploitation.) This is not to say there were not the usual complaints about the inedibility and monotony of meals, including grumbling over the absence of bread, normally a staple in the city prisons but in short supply early in 1967. As always, the diet would fluctuate according to the changing seasonal and political climates, both of which affected availability of meats and vegetables.[5]

Vegas's cells ranged in size from the Mint's cubbyholes to the fairly roomy compartments at Golden Nugget and Riviera. The majority were small and snug, with as many as four individuals typically jammed into a nine-foot-square space with two double bunks; leg stocks attached to the beds were a grim reminder of the ever-present threat of persecution. For those who had spent months in isolation, however, the claustrophobic conditions were a welcome tradeoff for the company of comrades. Ralph Gaither, recovering from a hellish final month at Briarpatch, happily shared a cramped cell in Thunderbird with Bill Shankel, Dave Wheat, and Tom Collins. Howie Rutledge savored the irony of being paired with George McKnight, as the Vietnamese had joined two of the more roguish hardliners, each after a long stay in solitary: "Both of us were incorrigible . . . . For eighteen months I had experienced only snatches of covert conversation with anyone. He, too, had suffered under silence. The result was hilarious. We talked nonstop for three days and nights." Accommodations at the new prison had one other redeeming feature: they were, at least for a time, clean, walls having been white-washed and bunks freshly cemented during the renovation process.[6]

On the whole, sanitary conditions at Vegas initially were much improved over what the prisoners had experienced previously. Besides having relatively clean berths, the men could wash most mornings at the central bath area and dump waste buckets into one of several crude toilets located around the compound. Sinks adjacent to the toilets provided running water for rinsing the buckets and filling cooking pots. A medic in Golden Nugget dispensed aspirin, diarrhea tablets, vitamins, and, occasionally, out-of-date penicillin and tetracycline. He even provided epsom salts to a few of the prisoners afflicted with the painful, burning "Briarpatch feet."* When conditions began to deteriorate, of course, medicine, like baths and food, would be used as a device to induce PW compliance.[7]

The latest lull was therapy enough to a number of men who had never rebounded from the previous fall's abuses and who were desperately in need of a breather. A case in point was Larry Chesley. The Air Force lieutenant, downed in April 1966 in the same incident in which Sam Johnson was captured, had been beaten and tortured both at Hilton's Heartbreak and at Briarpatch. By the time he arrived at Vegas, his weight had dropped to 100 pounds (from 160) and his feet were so inflamed from beriberi that he was sleeping less than an hour a day and, despite the freezing temperatures, could not bear to have a blanket on them. His roommate, Jim Ray—the two had transferred together from Briarpatch—finally called for a doctor, incurring the wrath of guards and spending two weeks in shackles for his insistent appeals for help for his friend. In March the pair were moved from Desert Inn into Golden Nugget's sick bay, where Chesley received vitamins and extra food until he began to recuperate.[8]

With Risner kept incommunicado and Denton under wraps at the Mint, Stockdale willingly assumed the leadership mantle at Vegas. Moved

---

* See Chapter 11.

into Thunderbird after a week or so in Stardust, the senior used his central location, the favorable communication setup, and his freedom from isolation to firmly take command. When the Vietnamese installed a loudspeaker system and directed Al Brudno to read excerpts from Harrison Salisbury's critical reports of American bombing, the Air Force PW, in a performance modeled on Bob Lilly's and Dick Bolstad's garbled rendition of the "news" at Briarpatch in 1966,* resorted to mispronunciations and exaggerated phrasing to make a mockery of Salisbury's commentary. Brudno, an exceptionally bright officer who had commanded his ROTC detachment at the Massachusetts Institute of Technology and who, according to Chesley, had hopes of becoming an astronaut, skillfully outwitted the captor while providing fellow prisoners with hours of entertainment. Nonetheless, Stockdale was not amused. While admiring Brudno's cleverness and judging the effort effective, he was concerned about the precedent, worrying that PWs less able than Brudno might not be so successful at the tactic. To discourage such freelancing, he put out an order that the men were to take a week in leg irons before agreeing to talk on the camp radio.[9]

Stockdale's "radio" instruction reflected his penchant for finding a middle ground between doctrinaire obedience to the Code of Conduct and a principled yet tenable standard of resistance. His "abhorrence for directives that 'can't be followed,'" said Hervey Stockman, "set the framework for his guidelines." As Stockdale later explained: "Effective resistance was not built so much on desperate goal-line stands, heroic displays of high thresholds of pain . . ., as on unified, timely, persistent, committed" guidance that all the prisoners could abide by and that would send clear signals to the Vietnamese as well.

> Men of goodwill of the sort that inhabited those dungeons, faced with a torture system that made them write, recite, and do things they would never think of doing in a life of freedom, wanted above all else to enter a society of peers that had rules putting some criteria of right and wrong into their lives. Authority was not something that had to be imposed from the top; to be led, to obey fair and universal orders within the capability of all, was a right that this community of Americans demanded. A life of perfection was for them out of the question, but they all elected to take pain in a unified resistance program, to fight back against degradation. To tell them "Do the best you can and decide for yourself how to resist" was an insult. They demanded to be told exactly what to take torture for. They saw that it was only on that basis that life for them could be made to make sense, that their self-esteem could be maintained, and that they could sleep with a clear conscience at night.[10]

---

* See Chapter 9.

Stockdale formulated a set of policies during this period early in 1967 that amplified and supplemented the previous instructions of Denton and Risner. In summary form it was conveyed by the acronym BACK US:

B — Bowing. Do not bow in public, either under camera surveillance or where nonprison observers were present.

A — Air. Stay off the air. Make no broadcasts or recordings.

C — Crimes. Admit to no "crimes," avoiding use of the word in coerced confessions.

K — Kiss. Do not kiss the Vietnamese goodbye, meaning show no gratitude, upon release.

US — Unity over Self.

Meeting the needs for both compassion and discipline and carrying the personal signature of a respected senior, Stockdale's policy guidance lifted morale at Vegas as much as any of the improvements in the men's physical circumstances. Of more far-reaching significance, it would become a moral-legal compass for prisoner conduct for the remainder of the war, and not just at Vegas but throughout the PW ranks. As luck would have it, a shortage of space at Hanoi's satellite prisons, caused partly by the closing of Briarpatch, increasingly required the Vietnamese to use Vegas as a holding point for new captures between their initial shakedown at Heartbreak or New Guy and assignment to an outlying camp. "That population in transit through Las Vegas in the spring of 1967," Stockdale later noted the importance of the time and place, "provided a unique courier service for the dissemination of standardized orders all over the North Vietnamese prison system."[11]

Hanoi had almost no spring in 1967. The climate changed from cold drizzle to witheringly humid midsummer heat within the span of a couple of weeks. The PW situation turned just as quickly. By April the latest peace initiative had collapsed. President Johnson ordered the resumption of intensive bombing, which now sent U.S. planes into the teeth of antiaircraft defenses that the Vietnamese had strengthened during the pause. In the next few months U.S. losses both on the ground in the South and in the air over the North rose sharply. By year's end the capture count would almost double that of the previous 12 months, with more Americans being taken prisoner in 1967 than in any other year of the war. Mulligan had memorized the names of 170 PWs in the North as of late March.* [12] A busy rest of the

---

* Mulligan's figure was consistent with the State Department's tabulation as of 3 April of "128 confirmed" and "50 suspected" U.S. captives in the North, all aviators. See *Washington Post and Times Herald*, 4 Apr 67.

year would test his memory as well as his sanity, as the intensification of the war brought not only a multiplying of the PW population but also Hanoi's most vicious crackdown yet.

The first sign at Vegas of the renewal of strong-arm tactics was the sudden strict enforcement of communication regulations. The prisoners' success at solving the compound's communications obstacles, aided by lax policing of their activities, had resulted by March in a network that was operating almost with impunity and so efficiently that Stockdale thought it "indestructible."[13] To shut down the system, beginning in April prison officials brought in additional guards and turnkeys and instituted a policy of absolute silence. PWs were ordered to sit upright and immobile in their cells, which were inspected regularly for scrap paper or bits of charcoal, soap, and other materials that could be fashioned into pencils or crayons. Guards prowled the corridors listening for tapping or whispered conversation. Offenders were dealt with swiftly, subjected to stocks and cuffs, prolonged kneeling or sitting, and ropes; repeaters like Denton and Mulligan now risked savage reprisal. Also, to disrupt Vegas's organization as well as communication channels, jailers continuously shuffled the prisoners—"so often," Gaither recalled, "that later we would talk of playing musical rooms." The communications purge would combine with other coercive programs through the summer, all of them relying increasingly on torture as an instrument of enforcement and control.[14]

Gaither discovered that the rules had changed when he was moved out of Thunderbird to another cellblock on 21 May and, with new roommate Mike Cronin, was "caught cold" in the bath stalls attempting to school a couple of novices in the art of the tap code. He and Cronin, the latter himself a captive only since January, were bound hand and foot for five days in a twisted, bent-over position that prevented sleep and caused excruciating pain. As the perceived instigator, Gaither spent an additional 10 days in the position, tormented by mosquitos, fatigue, and incessant pain until finally freed and allowed to shower and shave. As bad as his Briarpatch experience had been, the Navy lieutenant later rated this incident, which caused nerve damage to his legs and left his ankles permanently scarred, the worst of his entire captivity.[15]

Phil Butler, another Briarpatch veteran, was nabbed in May while discussing resistance with a nearby prisoner. He was beaten until his clothes were shredded and splattered with blood, then placed in solitary where his wrist was cuffed to his ankle for a week. For a suspected violation, Mulligan was clamped in stocks so tight his bowels gave out and his mind was reduced to "putty." Replacing Mulligan and Denton at the Mint in late May were Jerry Coffee and Howie Rutledge, the latter getting a new partner after a month living with McKnight. In his memoir Coffee would refer to Rutledge as a "compulsive communicator,"* but in fact they both were and they paid dearly for their efforts. The two spent weeks in shackles, Rutledge developing a severe heat rash over the summer from the 100-degree temperatures. The rash blistered and then turned into boils that enveloped his body, including his nose, ears, and hair, and almost drove him insane until a medic gave him some sulfa pills.[16]

The third man at the Mint during Coffee's and Rutledge's tenure there was Nels Tanner. Balding and stocky, described by Denton as "stolid, quiet, strong morally and physically, and unrelenting toward his captors," the unassuming Navy lieutenant commander had become a minor celebrity among his fellow PWs after only a few months in custody. Seized in October 1966 with backseater Ross Terry when their F-4 went down over the North, Tanner was credited with one of the most famous ruses of the war. He and Terry had been tortured mercilessly for propaganda statements almost immediately upon capture until Tanner suggested they "confess" that fellow carrier pilots Lt. Cdr. Ben Casey and Lt. Clark Kent had been court-martialed for refusing to fly their missions. Not only did the Vietnamese excitedly accept the claim, but they then had the fliers repeat the story in a televised interview with a Japanese journalist. Only when excerpts of the interview circulated to the outside world, to howls of amusement, did Hanoi realize its blunder.[†] With several prominent prison officials, including Cat and Rabbit, losing face as a consequence, Tanner became a marked man. Transferred from the Zoo to Vegas in mid-April and winding up at the Mint, he endured a record 123 consecutive days in irons.[17]

21 May 1967 appears to have been the date of a wholesale reshuffling at Vegas in which all or most of the PWs there found themselves with new cellmates and at new locations. "It was a hot night late in May," Stockdale

---

* Of Rutledge's communication skills, Sam Johnson later wrote: "We dubbed him 'the Great Communicator.' Nothing stopped Howie . . . . Not only was he a fearless communicator, but he also seemed able to discern and identify sounds that the rest of us never even heard. It was uncanny. He could hear footsteps on a dirt path or the concrete hallway of the cellblock and tell whether they belonged to a friend or foe. We all learned to identify the sounds of our compatriots—the way they walked was distinctive—but Howie was the master. He could almost read our minds by listening to our footsteps outside his cell door" (*Captive Warriors*, 103).

† Coffee and Stockdale among other PWs supposed that American leftists read a transcript of the interview or some other reference to the Casey-Kent confession in a socialist magazine and alerted the Vietnamese to the hoax. However, Western news sources had also gotten wind of the incident, and it was widely reported, including mention in a *Time* article in April 1967, so that officials in Hanoi hardly had to rely on Communist sympathizers to advise them of the deception.

recalled, "when lots of moving started around the camp. . . . The 'mixing' of youth and age had been inexplicably ended, and age with age and youth with youth was the general pattern now . . . ." Besides Gaither's move out of Thunderbird and the switch that had Coffee and Rutledge supplanting Denton and Mulligan at the Mint, Stockdale was transferred two doors down in Thunderbird to a cell with his former Heartbreak comrade Jim Lamar; Marine Capt. Orson Swindle was deposited in Desert Inn with a trio of intransigents, McKnight, Ron Storz, and Wes Schierman;* and Denton and Mulligan were reunited in an eight-foot by four-foot room in Stardust.[18]

In part the rearrangement was precipitated by the capture on 19 May, Ho Chi Minh's birthday, of six Navy aviators for whom space had to be found at the Hilton. Having to face the usual intimidating interrogation preliminaries at Heartbreak and then being thrown into Vegas in the midst of the communications purge there, these unfortunates (and others seized that summer) had one of the roughest initiations of any PW class. With U.S. planes attacking ever closer to Hanoi and pounding vital facilities elsewhere in the North, the Vietnamese wasted no time putting their new prizes under the gun, working them over for the next day's bombing targets and for other tactical and operational information. "Interrogations for tactical intelligence increased markedly in mid-1967," Michael Murray noted in his Code of Conduct study. As the enemy improved collection methods for acquiring U.S. aircraft manuals, unit rosters, and other materials and as the captor also became more familiar with U.S. targeting techniques, Murray observed, interrogators were able to grill American prisoners for more specific details and ask more penetrating questions. The 19 May shootdowns were among the first to be so intensively quizzed.[19]

Navy Lt. Cdr. Eugene "Red" McDaniel was captured when his A-6 was struck by a SAM while on a raid over Van Dien, a truck repair center south of Hanoi the fliers called "Little Detroit." The plane's bombardier-navigator, Lt. James Patterson, apparently bailed out safely but died sometime afterwards. McDaniel, ejecting at 550 knots, near the speed of sound, smashed his left knee on evacuation and crushed two vertebrae during a sprawling descent in which he tore his chute and landed in the top of a high tree on the steep slope of a mountainside. Jerking to a halt 40 feet off the ground, "like a block of cement in an elevator shaft," he suffered the back injury when he unsnagged the chute and plunged to the jungle floor. Before rescue helicopters could reach him he was seized by a group of armed peasants who turned him over to authorities.[20]

---

* Swindle had firmly established his own resistance credentials during a brutal 39-day trip to Hanoi from his capture site near the DMZ. See Hubbell, *P.O.W.*, 276.

About dawn the third day of his captivity, a Sunday, McDaniel arrived at the Hilton following a truck ride in which people along the route were allowed to enter the vehicle and kick and abuse him. Thrown into a windowless cell and warned not to try communicating, he was immediately pressed for targeting data and information on the Navy's new Walleye missile. Four times in two days he was tortured in the ropes. Dehydrated and sweating rivulets, he bit his shoulder to transfer the pain and slammed his head to draw blood in an effort to moisten his lips. Finally interrogators brought him a small bowl of water, just enough to keep him alive and conscious so that they could continue. To gain a respite he fabricated a bombing target and fed them a phony story that he flew the A-1 Skyraider, a low-tech craft used for rescue missions (of the type that retrieved Dieter Dengler in Laos) whose characteristics were not highly classified. They did not necessarily believe him, but there were the other "Black Friday" shootdowns to get to.

Other Navy fliers taken prisoner on 19 May included Lts. (j.g.) Gareth Anderson, William Metzger, and Charles Plumb and Lt. Cdrs. William Stark and Kay Russell. Each underwent his own baptism of torture. Plumb was placed in an apparatus consisting of manacles, bars, and electric wire torn from a light fixture and used as rope. "I was a human pretzel," he wrote in his memoir, "a teacup with arms for the handle and the rest of my distorted body for the bowl." Kicked about the head and face while strung in this position, he remembered "staring at the floor and seeing my tears drop into pools of blood coming from my nose."[21]

Metzger especially was in bad shape. McDaniel joined him in the Tet room and found him lying naked on the floor, pus draining from huge open wounds on his arms and a deep gash in his thigh where a two-pound piece of shrapnel had penetrated. The other leg was broken and the stench from the untended wounds was such that the Vietnamese burned incense sticks to counter the smell. So convinced were they of his imminent death that they bothered neither to treat nor to clothe him. McDaniel recalled how he and the younger man looked at each other "as if we were each seeing an apparition. Metzger later was to tell me that when I walked in I looked like a man sixty-five years old, with boils all over my body, a dangling right hand, left leg dragging from the knee, and stooped over from my torture in the ropes." Were it not for McDaniel's and other comrades' ministrations—scrounging cloths to bandage him, keeping rats at bay, and pleading for medical attention for him—the critically ill Metzger would have likely succumbed.[22]

The Vietnamese must have been using the Tet room as an infirmary of sorts during this period. Celled with McDaniel and Metzger there were fellow Navy pilot Anderson, suffering from a broken eardrum and a leg badly infected from irons, and a pair of Air Force PWs, Thomas Sterling

Newcomers stashed at Vegas. *Top, from left:* Milligan, Metzger, Anderson; *middle,* Russell, McDaniel, Sterling; *bottom,* Day, Fuller, Lawrence.

and Joseph Milligan. Sterling, a graying 42-year-old major, had two broken legs, one a compound fracture. The enemy had worked him over for a propaganda tape before treating the shattered limbs; what passed for surgery had left his feet angled outward by several degrees, so that he hobbled about penguin-like when he tried to walk. Milligan, a young lieutenant engulfed in flames when he ejected from his F-4 northeast of Hanoi, was treated decently by locals at first, receiving ointment for his burns and liniment for a damaged knee. Upon reaching New Guy Village, however, he was trussed into ropes and metal bars much like the others, and by the time he entered Tet, he, too, was a mess.[23]

Although their government's intensified bombing campaign promised to hasten the war's end and in that respect boosted the prisoners' morale, in many ways it complicated their immediate predicament. The steady flow of new shootdowns into the Hilton strained Vegas's facilities and contributed to supply shortages and a general worsening of conditions. Rob Doremus, who had come over with the Briarpatch group in February, noticed the supply situation deteriorating in late May, with water and cigarettes scarcer and food quality poorer. Doremus attributed the slippage less to willful neglect than to the overcrowding and logistic problems caused by the bombing escalation. The rupture of city water mains left Hoa Lo without running water. Crippled transportation infrastructure and fuel shortages interrupted food deliveries. To restore water at Vegas, workers, with the help of the prisoners, dug three wells in the courtyard, but because the holes were so shallow and were contaminated with runoff from the toilet area, the effect was tantamount to drinking and bathing out of a sewer. By late summer, the makeshift water supply was less "running" than "crawling"—with stinking impurities, worms, and other vermin. After only a few short months of operation, the newly renovated compound was acquiring the same air of decay and squalor that characterized the older prisons.[24]

The hardships affected the Vietnamese as well and, along with the bombings' physical devastation, put the captives' handlers on edge just as the crackdown moved into full swing. Presiding over the punishment at Vegas were Cat and Frenchy, with some new faces joining familiar enforcers Bug, Pigeye, Rat, and Big Ugh. Two new interrogators were promptly dubbed "Hack" (for his chronic cough) and "Kid," the latter also known as "Squint." In charge of Desert Inn was a junior officer the PWs called variously "Greasy" (for his slick style), "Maggot" (for his unpleasantness), and "Flea" or "Fly" (for his diminutive size); a heavy drinker, he turned from smooth operator to sadist as he became more alcoholic. Denton was impressed by a tall turnkey the Americans named "Abe," whose Lincolnesque visage belied a malicious temperament.[25]

Many of the veteran PWs who spent the summer of 1967 at Vegas consider that time the most harrowing stretch they experienced—matching, and for some exceeding, the misery and brutality of the post-Hanoi March round of terror at Briarpatch and the Zoo. Hervey Stockman later cited Vegas's communications purge as having "few equals in ferocity." Bob Shumaker, who as the second-longest-held PW in the North spent eight years in captivity, reflected on that summer at Vegas as "the worst for me." When the Vietnamese discovered Stockdale's policy guidance, they introduced a version of "Make Your Choice" that had resisters shrieking in agony all hours of the night. Shumaker recalled "praying for death on a number of occasions, and finding myself a little envious of my buddies who had been killed."[26]

Although there is no evidence of any outright executions at Vegas in 1967, at least one prisoner appears to have died from mistreatment. Norm Schmidt was last seen by his Desert Inn companions being led off to interrogation one day in late August; from their own anxious encounters with Greasy, cellmates Shumaker, Harry Jenkins, and Air Force Capt. Louis Makowski concluded that Schmidt had angered the unpredictable officer and suffered a fatal beating.*[27] Others narrowly survived. Forced to kneel for hours in the hot sun in cuffs and irons, Denton contracted a high fever that left him incoherent and at one point convinced he was not going to make it. Shumaker, who had attempted suicide at Briarpatch, almost had his death wish fulfilled when he refused to participate in the filming of a propaganda movie and was subjected to a horrible session in the ropes. A team of five guards hoisted him until his head nearly touched his feet and then, to silence his screaming, shoved a rag on a steel rod into his mouth.

---

* While Schmidt may have been the only fatality at Vegas, there were other casualties among the American prisoners during this period that attested to how precarious the captivity situation was becoming generally. Air Force Maj. Ward Dodge, seized on 5 July, died a week later in a North Vietnamese prison of unknown causes. Of the 21 U.S. servicemen who became PWs during the two-week interval 17-31 May, 8 would die in captivity, including 3 Navy fliers—James Griffin, Jack Walters, and Homer Smith—who perished in another section of Hoa Lo, probably Heartbreak, within a day or two of their capture (whether from untreated shootdown injuries or abuse is not known). A fourth Navy aviator from this group, Ronald Dodge, was seen in a photo after capture but Hanoi never acknowledged holding him; a fifth, Kenneth Cameron, hung on until the fall of 1970, when he disappeared after being taken to a hospital. In the South, Marines William Grammar and Orville Frits were apparently murdered shortly after capture on 20 May (see Chapter 14). On 15 June the Viet Cong announced that civilian PW Gustav Hertz had been executed in an act of reprisal, though he is believed to have died sometime later from malaria (see Chapter 13). A story in *Look* on 25 July headlined "Are U.S. Prisoners Mistreated?" only hinted at the magnitude of the unfolding tragedy.

Although he recovered from near-suffocation, the incident damaged his throat and resulted in difficulty swallowing that would persist even after his return in 1973.[28]

The so-called "Stockdale purge" claimed still more victims. Beginning in August prison officials pressured Vegas's beleaguered occupants into exposing the leadership and revealing details about the chain of command and other aspects of the PW organization. Stockdale later recounted the bravery and suffering of several of his disciples who resisted:

> Dan Glenn* was tortured and in irons two months, interrogated mercilessly, and never let anything crucial escape his lips. Nels Tanner, on his one hundred and twenty-third day in leg irons in the Mint, was caught at communications, tortured, and made to reveal before movie cameras the content and meaning of my orders. Ron Storz was buttonholed and told to come across with information on me, and his response was to take the pen they asked him to write it with and jam it nearly through his left arm. He carried a big scar from that the rest of his short life. Marine Warrant Officer John Frederick was kept blindfolded in leg irons for a month while Rabbit tried to make him reveal "Stockdale's connection with the CIA." He knew no details and kept silent.

Jerry Coffee, Tanner's neighbor at the Mint, remembered that he and Howie Rutledge "prayed for Nels" when it became apparent that Rabbit was finally going to settle the score for the "Ben Casey-Clark Kent" embarrassment. Turned over to Pigeye, Tanner was wrapped in the nylon straps that the Vietnamese had been stripping from the Americans' gear upon capture and increasingly using instead of rope; stronger than plain rope, the nylon rigging quickly transformed Tanner into a flailing "ball of pain" until he agreed to implicate Stockdale. A week later Coffee went through much the same routine.[29]

Storz, a key cog in the PW network and one of the few men to have close contact with both Stockdale and Risner (he would shortly get to know Denton well also), was visited by Greasy on the evening of 21 August. Already brutalized many times for his refusal to cooperate, he was now gagged, locked in stocks, and cinched in rope. When his Desert Inn roommates McKnight, Schierman, and Swindle protested, they, too, were manhandled—one guard stomping on McKnight's stomach as the PW choked on a towel that had been stuffed down his throat. The foursome was then dragged off to the bath area, strung up in separate stalls, and beaten savagely throughout the night. The next morning they were forced to indict

* See note 11.

Stockdale in taped and written statements. When Swindle balked, he was told to comply "or be fed the contents of his waste bucket." Storz, more dead than alive after the overnight mauling, was tossed in the Tet room to recuperate. There he communicated to Air Force Capts. Barry Bridger and Thomas Sima (within earshot in corner cells at Desert Inn and Stardust) that guards had broken several of his ribs and hurt him badly but that he had divulged nothing of consequence.* [30]

It was only a matter of time before the Vietnamese got around to Stockdale himself. In June the PW leader had engaged Cat in a contest of wills over taping a statement for the camp radio and appearing before an assemblage of Communist filmmakers and correspondents. When he frustrated the superintendent's plans, Greasy, Pigeye, and an assortment of other henchmen ran him through the gauntlet, leaving him close to sunstroke on one occasion and close to losing his arms on another; in the latter instance, Bug finally ordered a release of ratchet cuffs that had been notched "well beyond the point where mere blood stoppage took place." In between punishments Stockdale issued a new order, "No repent, no repay," in response to Cat's proposal that the Americans show contrition by helping clean up debris at sites damaged by bombs ("for every shovel of dirt moved," Stockdale thought, "there would be five cameras there"). August found the senior isolated at the Mint and the Vietnamese executing a "Ted Williams shift" by vacating the Vegas court when he went to the wash area: "in almost a childish way," his debriefer later noted, they were daring him to communicate and thus get caught "red-handed" in a conspiracy violation.

The showdown came in September. With shrapnel from nearby bombing strikes regularly falling on the compound, Hanoi's water system now barely functioning, and the electrical system faltering, Stockdale believed the North Vietnamese were becoming "unglued" and the prison system "peaked up to a pose of seething rage." When a lookout witnessed him about to tap to Sam Johnson, he was hauled out of Vegas to the Knobby Room in New Guy Village. Johnson had been told at quiz that they were going to make a "domestic animal" out of the senior. Stockdale later said he felt "like Jesus about to go on the cross." For three weeks he was alternately interrogated and tortured for the names of his principal lieutenants and other information about the chain of command. His mending left leg reinjured by a session in the ropes, the continual pressure of a blindfold (removed

---

* Two of Storz's three Desert Inn cellmates, Schierman and Swindle, never saw him again, as after they became separated their and their companion's paths never crossed again before Storz died in captivity. The "pen" incident to which Stockdale refers above occurred when Storz was removed from the Tet room and celled next to Stockdale in yet another attempt to get him to inform on the senior.

only at mealtime) threatening to damage his eyes, a pus-filled crotch torment-ing him even when he was not being worked over, he tried to buy time by giving Cat a list of *all* the prisoners:

> Finally, . . . at a point where I was afraid I was about to spill my guts, I told them to give me a pencil and paper and let me be alone and I would give them my "central committee." I came up with a long-shot solution: I wrote down the name of every pris-oner on my list (except Risner, of course, who was stashed back in the cellblock around the corner from me there in New Guy Village . . .). I gave them a list of 212 American names, in (as best I could figure) rank order . . . . I held it up and said, "This is our organization. It is a lineal responsibility list. It is like a snake you can't kill—the head will always grow back: Take me out and Denton will take over; take Denton out and Jenkins will fill in."

At length Greasy extracted more specifics and an apology, but Stock-dale succeeded in obscuring the identities of key juniors like Tanner and Storz, "the young Turks" who were the nuts and bolts of the organization "buried down in the pack on the seniority list." Unable even to use his waste-can because he was not allowed outside to empty it, the Navy captain* had been reduced to "a blind, crippled animal, shitting on the floor," but the organization—and the prostrate leader's charisma—were still intact.[31]

Although the communications crackdown continued unabated through the summer and into the fall, undeterred operators even at the height of the terror managed to keep tap and note channels open. Stockdale recalled how during a low period some unknown fellow prisoner, pretending to shake his bath rag dry, snapped in unmistakable code "GBUJS" for "God bless you, Jim Stockdale." Air Force Capt. John Fer, whom Mulligan remem-bered as having "an encyclopedic memory," operated a wire service of sorts, getting colleagues up to date on national and world events occurring prior to his February shootdown.† During a brief stay with Shumaker, Jenkins, and Makowski in Desert Inn, Mulligan "marveled at their ingenuity" in evading detection. The PWs had broken off a long piece of wire mesh from their window, coiled it, and secreted it in a crack. To communicate, they straightened the wire and slid it through a rat hole and across the open

---

* Before shunted to New Guy, Stockdale had received word of his promotion from recent capture Navy Cdr. William Lawrence, who arrived at Vegas in July.
† Fer benefited from the appearance of poor health. Upon ejecting from his crippled bomber he suffered wind blast damage that blinded him temporarily and left his eyes extremely bloodshot. He played upon the condition to gain tolerable treatment after early torture though his deception was nearly exposed in later years.

space that separated their cell from the one next door, then guided the wire through a rat hole in the adjacent cell. While Makowski did calisthenics to block the view of the guard sitting in the hallway, Jenkins squatted on their waste bucket and manipulated the wire in code, managing in this way to network covertly with both adjoining cells.[32]

With the end of the Stockdale purge, a little more than a month after it began, the struggle at Vegas entered yet another phase. Stockdale was "lugged" back to the compound around 1 October and reunited with Jim Lamar in Riviera. Lamar, who had been tortured to reveal Stockdale's alleged "CIA ties" and, according to the senior, had done a "masterful job" of hedging, advised his comrade of recent additions to the prison roster. As it turned out, more important than the list of new arrivals would be the abrupt departure in late October of several key Vegas veterans, including the most prominent seniors. Having failed to dismantle Vegas's organization with the Stockdale purge, the Vietnamese decided to remove Stockdale altogether, along with the others they believed to be ringleaders—Denton, Mulligan, Jenkins, Rutledge, Johnson, Shumaker, Storz, and Tanner—and isolate them at another location.* [33]

The loss of the leadership dealt a serious setback to both organization and communication activities at Vegas and weakened the level and quality of resistance there generally. A fall 1967 arrival reported that when deposited in his cell in Thunderbird the silence was such that he "could hear a pin drop." "Men who lived in the building at this time would tell me later that they continually talked under the doors," he recalled, but "I must have experienced temporary deafness . . . for I never heard an American voice in five weeks." With no familiar seniors left in the loop, the old problem of determining who was SRO resurfaced. As one of the prisoners observed: "Some POWs weren't sure of the date they had received their last promotions, and many of us from the academies had made rank simultaneously. Had we been free, we could have checked our lineal numbers in the *Blue Book* to settle the controversy; but since we did not have access to it we agreed to assign seniority in these cases by alphabetical order of last names."[34]

Eventually Vegas's communication and organization networks were rebuilt, though the system would never operate as efficiently as it had under Stockdale that spring. Hervey Stockman noted that "despite the fragmented PW organization and communications in Las Vegas during the 1968-69 time frame, there were outstanding examples of cell block

---

* The transfer of this group (and McKnight and Coker, who joined them under different circumstances) to a special facility called "Alcatraz" is discussed in Chapter 17. Stockdale remarked: "The lineup was in fact my leadership team at Las Vegas, in spite of my attempts to protect such standout juniors as Shumaker, Tanner, Storz, and Johnson" (*In Love and War*, 278).

leadership." Stockman cited several "Navy 05s with good command background who were captured in the summer of 1967" (among them Bill Lawrence and Mel Moore, the latter actually seized in March) and conscientiously filled the vacuum created by Stockdale's departure. Nonetheless, resistance after October 1967 was organized around individual cellblocks rather than coordinated camp-wide, and it waxed and waned markedly in relation to how effectively the Vietnamese were able to inhibit communication. In a camp history of Vegas, the authors, former PWs there, found that "communications improved again in the spring and summer of 1968 only to weaken again in the face of renewed V pressures against it in the fall and winter of that year." In one incident in the fall of 1968 the prisoners were ordered to carry their belongings into the courtyard, where they were blindfolded, stripped, and searched for unauthorized articles. Even in the most accessible periods there were those PWs who never received the tap code and thus never truly entered the system; during the rebuilding period at Vegas there were many, the authors of the Vegas study wrote, who for want of timely contact "existed in unnecessary isolation unaware of a PW organization and its strength-giving properties."[35]

Of course, for some men the matter of a strong centralized leadership was a moot issue. Ultimately, in the crucible of the torture rooms, the PW had to go against the captor one-on-one—and it was in these lonely sessions and supremely personal trials that the true stalwarts rose to the occasion. Vegas had no lack of extraordinary individual performances during the winter of 1967-68 and over the course of 1968, even at times of organizational disarray.

Gaither and Cronin returned to Vegas in October 1967 after "summering" at a nearby camp, arriving the same day that the Stockdale group was evicted. "Life went on with the same pattern of the past," Gaither mused, "the same guards, the same regulations, the same punishment. Many was the time I heard a man cry out in the night for mercy . . . . Torture was always just around the corner, and it was a constant ominous cloud." The two cellmates exchanged Christmas presents with neighbors Bob Peel and Orson Swindle through a drainage hole that connected their rooms: a die made from bread scraps was swapped for a poem scribbled on toilet paper. Early in 1968 Gaither took repeated abuse before consenting to memorize and regurgitate the pages of a propaganda booklet.

Coffee, Franke, and Lamar were others who carried on gamely amid diminished contacts and plunging morale. Coffee roomed with Larry Chesley in Stardust between October 1967 and November 1968. The pair, Coffee recounted in his memoir *Beyond Survival*, had contrasting styles but similar dedication:

Chesley had an interesting philosophy about dealing with the V in interrogations. Most of us felt that a strict military bearing—straight and proper—was the most effective way to deal with an interrogator, to at least elicit his respect as a fellow military officer. Chesley, on the other hand, consciously tried to present himself as the most pitiful, disheveled, unpromising resource for Communist exploitation that he possibly could. Relatively slight of build and with thinning hair, he'd shuffle off to be quizzed in rumpled clothes as if he were about to collapse in a heap. He didn't escape the torture any more than the rest of us, but the V probably enjoyed hammering him less than those of us who puffed out our chests from the quiz stool. We all had to be actors at one time or another, and this was Larry's act. Of all the mice in this cat-and-mouse game, he may have been among the cleverest. Beneath the surface of our differing styles and our bullheaded debates, we grew to love and appreciate each other immensely.

Like Gaither and Cronin, they relied increasingly on religious faith to sustain them through what Coffee characterized as "weeks of mundane routine punctuated by purges and pressures." Chesley remembered 1968 as "probably my most spiritual year in prison."[36]

In December 1967 Navy Cdr. Robert Byron Fuller faced the rope torture for the second time since his capture in July. Fuller suffered two dislocated shoulders and multiple fractures upon ejection from his aircraft. In spite of the extensive injuries, interrogators at Heartbreak had administered both ropes and ratchet cuffs to pry loose tactical and technical information on his carrier's capabilities. The pilot had barely recovered from this first excruciating session* than he was subjected to a second extortion session at the Mint. Refusing to provide more than name, rank, and serial number, he was told he would never see his family again. He resisted until the rope application reseparated his right shoulder. Redeposited in the Mint, he would remain in solitary for more than two years—one 05 who had little opportunity to lead but who set a magnificent example for the few men who knew what he had gone through.[37]

"He has to be one of the toughest men alive," an admiring comrade and fellow PW survivor said of Air Force Maj. (by then Col.) George "Bud" Day a few months after homecoming. Day achieved lasting distinction among the American prisoners in North Vietnam before arriving at Vegas, indeed before ever setting foot in Hanoi. Following his shootdown and capture in the jungle north of the DMZ on 26 August 1967, he had managed to escape and evade the enemy for two weeks despite crippling injuries

---

* John Hubbell attributes Fuller's survival to the efforts of Air Force Maj. Dewey Waddell, who bathed and comforted his fellow aviator until they were split up in October.

and having to live off berries and uncooked frog; the only American prisoner to escape from the North, he had crossed the demilitarized zone and was within two miles of a U.S. Marine outpost when shot and recaptured.

Transported back to the North, Day took extreme torture both en route to Hanoi and on entering the Hilton around the time of Stockdale's transfer. When pressed for the names of pilots in his unit, he responded with the likes of Charles Lindbergh, Billy Mitchell, Wylie Post, and Will Rogers. "Had I known of the severe consequences of Nels' [Nels Tanner's] deceit," he later quipped, "no doubt I would have opted for less glamorous personalities like Jones, Brown and Smith." For his remarkable escape feat and continued maximum resistance over the next five years, at Vegas and elsewhere, Day would be awarded the Medal of Honor. Unfortunately, Vegas's communication restraints and his own poor condition—his mangled right arm was encased in a clumsy cast and his left hand was virtually useless as well—prevented him from learning the tap code while there and limited his contact to Thunderbird cellmate Norris Overly.* Only after Day left Vegas at the close of 1967 did he gain the physical mobility and communication access that would enable him to have wider influence.[38]

In June 1968 Robbie Risner reemerged in Vegas after a lengthy exile on the Heartbreak-New Guy side of Hoa Lo that had him so isolated that many prisoners who had seen or been with him earlier wondered if he was still alive. Unremitting threats and torture had forced him finally to produce incriminating propaganda tapes and statements. The mental anguish of having to cope with overwhelming guilt and suffering in prolonged solitude, exacerbated by unbearable pain from recurring kidney stones (the result of water deprivation), left him, by his own estimate, close to a nervous as well as a physical breakdown. Between March and July 1967 Air Force Lt. Ronald Mastin shared a cell with him, providing desperately needed companionship, but by summer Risner was on his own again and reeling from more torture. Suspended in nylon straps, he remembered his proficient handler pressing his shoulders behind his head until he resembled "a ship's prow." A "jumbo" iron was clamped on his left leg and cuffs pinched his wrists so tightly they bit into bone, causing his right wrist and fingers to swell like balloons from infection. "I did not think an arm

---

* Overly was an Air Force major seized on 11 September. Ailing himself with a large cyst on his tailbone, he had also taken considerable punishment en route to Hanoi. Day had an ambivalent attitude toward Overly, appreciating his kindness and assistance that helped nurse him back to health but critical of Overly's willingness to cooperate, which he believed contributed to the pilot's early release. See Chapter 18.

could swell that much and keep from bursting," he recalled. Worst of all, the Vietnamese boarded his windows and left his cell darkened for 10 months. Experiencing panic attacks and fits of crying and screaming that he attempted to keep from guards by burying his face in a blanket to muffle the sounds, by the time he left New Guy for Vegas he was "like a man hanging on to a cliff by his fingernails."* [39]

"Robbie lost battles—as we all would," Jerry Coffee later wrote, "but he never lost the war." No sooner had Risner been moved into Golden Nugget than he tried to make contact by passing notes to PW dishwashers through leftover food. Close surveillance apprehended him in November and he was soon back in straps, though now his handler made sure to tuck his sleeve between his skin and the sharp nylon in an effort, Risner supposed, to avoid the telltale scarring that might later supply evidence of prisoner mistreatment. He spent the next year rotating between the Hilton's torture rooms and secluded spots in Vegas at Riviera and the Mint, all the while removed from the PW mainstream and prevented from exercising senior responsibilities. Fellow Air Force 05 Gordon Larson believed that Risner underwent "more pressure, more degradation, more torture, more humiliation and more isolation" than anyone. "The NVN put him in a class by himself fearing his potential as a leader and organizer . . . . [They] never allowed him to remain in a position where he could control the situation"— at Vegas or elsewhere. [40]

Significantly, so muddled was Vegas's PW organization by mid-1968 that the highest-ranking PW (after Col. Edward Burdett, who died in captivity), Air Force Col. John Flynn, was housed in Desert Inn that summer without either Flynn or others nearby realizing his status. Moreover, during 1968 and 1969 there were three other Air Force 06s in Vegas or in close proximity in Heartbreak—Norman Gaddis, James Bean, and David Winn— who remained completely apart from the PW command structure. Gaddis would spend three years in cell 5 of Heartbreak, during which time no American contacted or responded to him. Flynn, according to Hervey Stockman, "chose to keep his exposure minimal in those days," the SRO explaining that he opted for a low profile out of a "deep concern at the time that any opportunity or excuse he gave the Vietnamese for punishment and torture would make him vulnerable to questions on highly sensitive subjects which at that point had not been addressed by the interrogators." Herein, Stockman agreed, "lies a real dilemma for senior officers, who by virtue of their rank alone, are

---

* Risner's memoir *The Passing of the Night* takes its title from this extended period of unlit solitary.

regarded by the enemy as privy to a variety of valuable classified material." Jon Reynolds later speculated that the Air Force colonels' apparent disengagement may have stemmed from simple ignorance of established communication procedures and techniques owing to their having missed the key formative years and then never acquired proper initiation. Some of the juniors were more critical, one of them later relating exasperating efforts to reach the quartet: "We went out of our way, taking far greater risks than should have been necessary. At times it seemed that George McKnight was going to batter down the wall in an attempt to communicate with them while we emptied our buckets in the latrine next to their room."

Stockman believed that Vegas's hobbled organization contributed to the seniors' predicament: "Was it worth it to actively involve oneself in communications and organization which in those days appeared tenuous and not particularly productive?" The four did remain outside the main PW network until much later, and so here was another instance where potential leadership in the post-Stockdale era at Vegas was nullified.[41]

When Stockdale returned to Vegas in May 1969 after an absence of 18 months, he found the camp organization so emasculated and the communication system so throttled that he scarcely recognized the place. "What the hell has happened to American spirit in this place?" he thought. "What American is running this camp? It seems like we are going backward; our hard-won gains, our unity, our sense of responsibility for each other, are slipping away in a vacuum of zero leadership." "Life in Las Vegas," he concluded, "was clearly without central American authority," an impression that was confirmed by Air Force PWs Will Forby and Tom Curtis, who remembered the signature of his crippled gait (hence the code name "Chester," after the gimpy character on the TV show "Gunsmoke") from their stay together in Thunderbird and who got him back "on the wire" in June. Forby informed him there was no camp-wide organization and that a "bird colonel" had been present among them for over a year (presumably Flynn) but was still incommunicado. "The real shocker" for Stockdale occurred when the camp radio transmitted a dialogue between two self-acknowledged American senior officers, "Bob" and "Ed," in which they talked freely and seemingly under no duress about the illegality of the war.* [42]

---

* The hour-long tape was just as startling and distressing to those prisoners who had been at Vegas all along. "Larry, can you believe this shit?" Coffee asked Chesley incredulously (*Beyond Survival*, 223). "The Bob and Ed Show," as it was cynically called by American PWs who heard the broadcast throughout North Vietnam, was the product of Navy Cdr. Robert

Stockdale's judgment was probably too harsh, no doubt colored by his own sacrificial experience during the interim he was away from the compound, as well as by a communications purge in April 1969 that removed the ingenious Mel Moore.* The cumulative grind of two years of unrelenting pressure had taken its toll on the resistance at Vegas, as indeed, we shall see, at every other prison in North Vietnam during this period. By 1969 Vegas's tenants were more in a survival than a resistance mode. Even if Stockdale and the original leadership had not been transferred in the fall of 1967, the system would have likely encountered similar problems, with discretion increasingly becoming the better part of valor. Even at some compromise to the Code of Conduct, reason and good sense called for lying low, waiting it out, until conditions improved. The resistance had not shut down entirely—Bob's and Ed's uncoerced confessions were an anomaly, Fuller's and Day's heroics were more typical—but as an organized and coordinated front it could not be sustained indefinitely under the assault of successive purges and recurring torture.

Stockdale, ever the pragmatist, conceded as much when, upon rejoining the communication net, he reissued his policy guidance with a new instruction advising prudence: "Get off the hook as soon as you can." He lamented the concession, but it was plain to him "that since he had counted at least 19 or 20 different voices on the Vegas radio" during the summer of 1969 "this broken floodgate could not be instantly repaired . . . [and] nothing else appeared practical." The next year would bring a remarkable turnabout, but for now all bets were off at Vegas as to when the suffering would ease, much less end. Early in his captivity Stockdale had reckoned that the war—and the PWs' incarceration—would last maybe five years. Steadily it dawned on him that this initial estimate "was but an optimistic pipe dream." With the enemy holding all the trumps at the Hilton casino, seniors and juniors alike played what cards they had, wagering for the long haul and with no illusion that the odds would change any time soon.[43]

Schweitzer and Marine Lt. Col. Edison Miller. Roommates at Desert Inn, they appeared to some prisoners to have cut a deal with the enemy in return for preferential treatment. For the continuing controversy surrounding them, see Chapters 20 and 25.
* Moore had managed to contact Colonel Winn, who was unaware of the tap code, by constructing a stick out of bits of bamboo and sliding it across the hallway between his cell and Winn's, then maneuvering it through a small hole in the door of Winn's cell. Suspicious at first, Winn eventually tugged on the stick, which quickly disappeared and then returned with a note giving him the tap code, the names of the buildings in the compound, and an explanation of how PW communications worked. Winn was thus the first 06 in the communication system. A few days later, when Moore passed a message to SRO Bill Lawrence about Winn's rank and location, Lawrence sent Winn a short note that read "At your service," confirming that Winn was among fine people in that oppressive place. (Kiley interv with Winn.)

17

Dirty Bird and Alcatraz: Special Arrangements for Hostages and Hardliners

Risner's comment about his state in late 1967 and early 1968, that he was hanging on to a cliff by his fingernails, was an apt description of the PW plight everywhere in North Vietnam at the height of the middle years. The seamless web of malaise, terror, and misery that appeared, at least to Stockdale, to paralyze the resistance at Vegas afflicted, in whole or in part, all the camps between 1967 and 1969. Larry Guarino faced 1967 thinking, "It's got to be better—it can't continue this way."[1] But he was wrong. The only change was the introduction of several new installations to accommodate the burgeoning prisoner population. To the Heartbreak and New Guy sections of Hanoi's main downtown prison, Vegas had already been added, and to the Zoo and Briarpatch other satellite compounds around and outside Hanoi were now added. Some were merely auxiliary facilities designed to provide more cell space; others, however, appeared to have special functions. In the latter category, two camps that opened in Hanoi in 1967-68 had limited capacity but served a sufficiently important purpose to warrant their activation. Dubbed "Dirty Bird" and "Alcatraz" by their American occupants, they were the latest euphemisms to denote a captivity experience that had gone from inhumane to inhuman.

Between June and October 1967 the North Vietnamese confined more than 30 U.S. PWs in the vicinity of the Yen Phu thermal power plant in northern Hanoi. The Yen Phu complex consisted of a series of buildings covering more than five city blocks and included, besides the main facility, machine shops, warehouses, an underground factory or assembly plant, a school, a small market, and a medical station. The site was located near the government district, some distance from the industrial-commercial and residential centers of the city. The Vietnamese, recognizing that it was a relatively isolated and hence vulnerable target, began moving prisoners into the area on 18 June—the same day that Secretary McNamara asked his staff to prepare the lengthy study of United States involvement in Indochina that came to be known, after Daniel Ellsberg leaked it to the *New York Times* in 1971, as the *Pentagon Papers*.

Although the Communists would deny it, their conspicuous display and virtual announcement of the PWs' presence at the power plant evidenced a transparent attempt to use the prisoners as hostages to discourage U.S. bombing of the facility. A collateral benefit may have been to reassure frightened workers at the complex and other citizens in the neighborhood that they were safe from air attack. Through calculated disclosures to visiting journalists and diplomats, local placard publicity, and exhibiting the captives in full view of civilians—all sharp departures from their normal practice—the Vietnamese could be certain the PWs' presence would be reported to the U.S. government. And indeed, by 4 July U.S. intelligence had verified that American prisoners of war were jailed at the site.[2]

Because of Yen Phu's sprawling size and diverse physical features and the staggered rotation in which prisoners were sent there, it acquired an assortment of names depending on when the detainees arrived and where on the grounds they were quartered. This wide variation in nomenclature and circumstances would later result in numerous discrepancies in reminiscences and debriefings that would be difficult to reconcile. The PWs themselves probably encountered more confusion in comparing notes with comrades on this camp than on any other, frequently assigning different names even to the same area within the complex. Such confusion occasionally had serious consequences. In order for the resistance to operate and communication to work, prisoners had to know not only who was confined but also where each was held; effective networking required everyone to employ identical terms of reference, or information could be inaccurate or irrelevant. What for the historian could prove a nuisance, for the PW could be a dangerous misunderstanding.

The earliest arrivals to Yen Phu occupied an eight-cell section adjacent to the power plant along Pham Hong Thai Street near Yen Ninh Street. Finding the place filthy, littered with debris, and covered by a layer of black dust, they soon named it "Dirty Bird." The building apparently had housed some of the plant's workers before being converted to a prison, as it contained appurtenances for cooking and washing and the cells, a relatively spacious 15 feet square, could previously have been crude apartments. At the east end were a quiz room and latrine. On the west side were a storeroom,

Thermal Power Plant

Dirty Bird Annex held one group of prisoners at the power plant.

a small bath stall, and a pair of large coal bins that explained the blanket of dust.

When a similar eight-cell prison opened about a month later a few hundred feet west of Dirty Bird, it was filled with several Vegas refugees and two men who were shifted from the first cellblock. Those fresh from Vegas called their new jail variously "Doghouse," because they assumed it was a punishment spot; "Foundry," because of an incessant, piledriver-like pounding at a nearby building; "Army Post," as it was christened by the Navy's Ralph Gaither; or simply "Power Plant" or "TPP." The pair from Dirty Bird, however, linked the name of the new set of cells to that of their previous jail, calling it "Dirty Bird Annex," or "Dirty Bird West," or "Section B, Dirty Bird." No consensus was reached on a single designation for the second section, and so when the prisoners from the two Dirty Bird locations were dispersed to other camps, they carried with them several names that had in common only a location next to the thermal power plant. Although the confusion would be addressed to some extent in 1971 when the Americans were brought together in large groups and, with freer communication, were able to sort through their experiences, it was never entirely resolved—the inconsistencies relating to time frames and activities within the respective cellblocks surviving even in postwar accounts.[3]

Less confusion surrounded a separate part of the power plant complex where yet a third batch of prisoners was kept. On a triangular tract north of the main entrance to the plant the Vietnamese constructed another make-shift cellblock from a cluster of offices and storerooms that once had housed a school but more recently was used as an administrative and support depot. Finding stacks of Chinese and Vietnamese textbooks as well as chalkboards and student desks stored in the area, the prisoners promptly called the compound "The School." That name would be used by most of the men incarcerated there, although Yen Phu Avenue's surface rails, which ran adjacent to the tract, gave rise to an alternate name, "Trolley Tracks." The School was open from 8 August to 25 October and held from 3 to 18 PWs over that period in a maximum of seven cells.

For sheer dreariness the Dirty Bird installations were a match for any camp in North Vietnam. Besides the debris strewn about and the proximity of the coal sheds, the entire power plant and surrounding neighborhood had been painted a drab gray to throw off the color-sensitive U.S. homing missiles. Jerry Coffee, who spent part of the summer and early fall there in between stays at Vegas, remembered the air being choked with coal dust "so thick that it collected on bare shoulders like black dandruff." The dim cells had their windows bricked shut, preventing any ventilation and making the summertime heat unbearable. Except during punishment periods, the dehydrated prisoners were let outside daily to escape their ovens. Some were able to pull themselves up and peer over the eight-foot wall that girded the complex. The vista over the wall was almost as grim as the view on the inside: barricades closing off the road to traffic, extensive damage from the spring air raids, and boarded buildings across the street, abandoned except for an occasional drifter.[4]

Although the men transferred to Dirty Bird surmised they were sent there for correction purposes, treatment itself was no worse and generally better than at Vegas and elsewhere. The prisoners were usually in solitary, often in irons and handcuffs, and guards enforced the prohibition on communication, but there was no torture and interrogations were limited to attitude checks and lectures on the war. A doctor dubbed "Oops" and two nurses, the battle-ax "Flo Nightingale" and the young and gentle "Nurse Jane," were allowed to administer medical care, Nurse Jane tending the severe heat rash and badly infected ingrown toenail of Tom Collins. Offsetting the comparatively benign treatment were horrible living conditions, the grimy physical environment and sealed rooms exacerbated by infrequent bathing and, even by PW standards, terrible food. The officious Louie the Rat managed the two cellblocks, supervising half a dozen subordinates, among them the toothsome "Bucky Beaver," the husky "Jack Armstrong," the self-important "Dude," and an unctuous duo Coffee referred to as "Swish" and "Mouth."

It soon became clear to the inmates that Dirty Bird and its annex were no ordinary prisons. In July, guards led puzzled PWs out hidden back doors to a waiting jeep, transported them along city streets, then reentered the power plant through the front gate amid a contrived loud commotion. On at least one occasion the prisoners were merely driven around the block. At other times the Vietnamese took the Americans outside the prison to perform menial and perfunctory work on public avenues—sweeping, shoveling dirt, or holding the rope of a grazing cow. In one instance, they were organized into a water detail, marched along a meandering route that took them onto a major boulevard trafficked by hundreds of civilians, including foreigners, and then returned to their cells. "The more 'going and coming fire drills' staged by the authorities," Coffee concluded, "the more obvious it would be that Americans were being imprisoned here." The exercises were probably intended, too, to suggest there were more PWs housed at the power plant than was actually the case, thus adding more weight to the "hostage" issue and concern to any U.S. decision to bomb the complex. What Coffee termed "this Chaplinesque drama" continued for the several months that Dirty Bird and Dirty Bird West were open.[5]

The hostage charade did not deter U.S. strikes on the target. The plant was attacked regularly after 13 August, with apparently no casualties and conflicting reports on the extent of damage to the power facility and PW cellblocks. Coffee told Louie at one point, "You can remember in the last raid the power plant was hit but our cells were not hit. Our pilots are always very, very accurate." He was bluffing, of course, and admitted privately that they had been lucky so far: "In the lethal crossfire of SAM 2s plus triple-A and light arms fire that saturates the sky over this entire end of the city, in spite of their intentions the guys were doing damn well just to hit the city block that the power plant was on, let alone to miss our little prison enclave." As a precaution, the Vietnamese moved the prisoner-hostages to more protected areas within their buildings and, at the School, to an underground shelter.[6]

Dirty Bird's roster was a random mix of veterans and recent shoot-downs with no seeming common denominator to their selection or length of stay. The first group included 1965 capture Collins and 1967 captures Julius Jayroe, Gareth Anderson, Jack Van Loan, Joseph Milligan (Van Loan's backseater), Edward Mechenbier, Kevin McManus, Read Mecleary, David Gray, and Gary Thornton. Air Force Lieutenants Mechenbier and McManus had just been seized on 14 June after ejecting from their stricken plane. McManus, who was in the better condition of the two, had been run, literally, for more than four hours through seven villages as soldiers displayed their catch en route to Hanoi; the two Americans spent one night pinioned in a corner of a hut, tormented by captors who, among other harassments, tossed rats at them. After the ordeal in the countryside and the abuses they encountered upon reaching the Hilton, they found Dirty Bird a welcome relief.[7] Collins, Jayroe, Anderson, Milligan, Gray, and Thornton had been at Vegas. Several of the men had either come from or would soon wind up at yet another new camp, "Plantation," that will be discussed in the next chapter.

After the departure of the initial group, most of the new arrivals to the power plant in July were celled at Dirty Bird West. This contingent included a half dozen naval aviators, among them Lt. (j.g.) David Rehmann, whose post-capture photograph showing him, obviously injured, being prodded down a crowded street, became internationally famous as a symbol of the American PWs and MIAs. Also in this bunch were Vegas transfers Paul Galanti, Ralph Gaither, Mike Cronin, and Marines John Frederick and Orson Swindle, joined by Navy colleague Thornton, a holdover from the original group who now vacated Dirty Bird for Dirty Bird West. Remaining at the power plant through the summer, Thornton wondered why he was staying put when almost everyone else was being transferred.

The decision to send the likes of Gaither and Cronin to the power plant gave some credence to the notion that the hostage installation doubled as a punishment facility. The dispatch of other hardliners to the camp in July and August further supported this view. Swindle was soon followed by his ornery Vegas cellmates McKnight and Schierman. Allegedly for an infraction of the rules, Bob Peel, one of the longest-held PWs, was consigned to Dirty Bird West on 7 July and was kept isolated and in irons for almost his entire stay there. 1965 shootdowns and tough resisters Jon Reynolds and Bob Jeffrey logged time at Dirty Bird West that summer between terms at Vegas. McKnight, Schierman, Reynolds, and Jeffrey returned to Vegas on 15 August, but the first two moved back to the power plant 10 days later. Some of the shuttling no doubt had to do with the Vietnamese concocting a sense of activity around the plant, but there may also have been reasons relating to punishment or to the attempt to disrupt the communication network at Vegas.

As the summer wore on, the hostage-prisoners endured the stifling heat, sickening food, and ubiquitous filth. All were plagued by dehydration, boils, infections, and diarrhea. Periodically Rabbit or one of his minions turned up to deliver a propaganda lecture, sometimes with a film as well. Questioned by the prisoners about the policy of jailing captives so close to an obvious target, Rabbit denied that there was any connection. In the meantime the Vietnamese parked a large tank truck in the street outside the complex, as technicians released chemicals through pressurized nozzles to generate a thick smokescreen over the plant, presumably to conceal the site from attacking U.S. planes. Judging from Gaither's reaction to the air raids, the tactic had little success: "Our bombers poured out their loads with terrifying regularity . . . . There were some horrendous explosions. Each time I heard the bombers coming I dived under the bed. The building shook, windows rattled, shutters were blown from their hinges, plaster rained down from the ceiling like white hail."[8]

Late summer brought another mix of grizzled veterans and relative newcomers to Dirty Bird. Air Force Capt. Thomas Storey had been shot down in January on a mountainside near Thai Nguyen, north of Hanoi. Despite a compressed fracture of the back and a damaged right knee suffered during ejection, he evaded capture and hid in a cave for five days before searchers found him. His subsequent experience followed the standard 1967 pattern: once in Hanoi, intensive interrogation and torture at Heartbreak; cursory medical treatment (a nurse examined his leg in an auditorium filled with curious onlookers and photographers, smeared iodine over a bruise, but did nothing for the serious back and knee injuries); then a series of inexplicable "musical chairs"-style moves between compounds. At Vegas Storey got a break when placed with an old Air Force acquaintance and "favorite back-seater," Capt. John Clark, who had gone down in March and been captured immediately upon landing in a cornfield.* The two shared a room in Thunderbird and Desert Inn and came over to Dirty Bird West together on 6 August.[9]

Older hands ticketed for the power plant about the same time as Storey and Clark included Jerry Driscoll, Larry Chesley (ill again, now with pneumonia), Jim Ray, Willis Forby, Tom Curtis,[†] Al Brudno, and Bill Tschudy. A week later, when Jerry Coffee arrived with John Heilig, Driscoll was hauled back to Vegas. On 23 August, most of those still remaining in the Dirty Bird area moved three-fourths of a mile south to the School, a shift possibly prompted by U.S. air strikes closing in on the target. A near miss two days earlier, Coffee remembered, had "caused quite a stir."[10]

The School was marginally cleaner than Dirty Bird. More important from the standpoint of prisoners who saw the power plant's low walls and unconventional arrangements as an invitation to escape, it was even less secure in that its cells had wooden bars. Of course, once outside the grounds, there remained the matter of how to make good on the flight from Hanoi without being noticed, especially since the School bordered a major street. Nonetheless, the healthier PWs entertained the possibility. Coffee and Storey were among those who hatched plans. If nothing else, the escape aspiration was good for morale and it kept the mind active. Coffee said he "occupied his time trying to walk like a Vietnamese" so that he wouldn't be detected once he went over the wall.[11]

The Vietnamese may have been on the same wavelength. They assigned 20 personnel to supervise the School, never leaving the Americans unguarded. In charge was a junior officer the prisoners called "Snake." Still bent on exposing the PWs to the populace, officials had the men return to the main power plant building to retrieve water and coal for the School on highly visible errands. Almost daily they scheduled cleanup details before large groups of children who gathered at the south gate of the complex. When an order came down in September to renovate the cellblock kitchen, guards escorted the prisoners in search of old brick, lumber, and roof tile, again on a circuitous route that took them in full view of civilians. Once the kitchen was ready, the PWs anticipated an improvement in their food, then with chagrin recognized the camp cook as a former nemesis from the wretched Briarpatch.[12]

---

* Clark saw his pilot, Capt. Edwin Goodrich, parachute into a nearby patch of jungle, then heard what sounded like pistol shots. Aboard the truck that took him to Hanoi he noticed his crewmate's blood-stained chute, confirming his worst fears.
† Curtis's and Forby's captivity experiences frequently overlapped, beginning with Curtis's capture on a mission to rescue Forby. The two fell into Vietnamese custody the same day, 20 September 1965.

When the inevitable escape attempt came, it occurred not at the School but at Dirty Bird, where George McKnight remained stashed even as most of his comrades at the power plant had been removed to the newer installation. Why McKnight stayed behind is not clear, although he may have been singled out as a problem case. A fellow PW mentioned him along with Swindle, Schierman, Rod Knutson, and Fred Flom as among those the Vietnamese had it in for—"all masters of the fuck-you look." At any rate, in September he was joined by George Coker, a staunch resister at both the Zoo and Vegas whom Jim Stockdale likened to the actor Jimmy Cagney in appearance and manner. A wrestler during his college days at Rutgers, Coker was a feisty bantam who once responded to a cohort's question as to how tall he was, "Two inches taller than Napoleon." The square-built Navy lieutenant was a perfect accomplice for the lanky Air Force captain— 10 years McKnight's junior but matching his courage and determination.[13]

The two were kept isolated and shackled, each with a wrist cuffed to one ankle, until McKnight managed to unlock his constraint with a wire and made contact with Coker. When Coker discovered how to wriggle the wire to free himself, the pair rendezvoused almost daily following the noon-time prisoner check, taking advantage of the guards' normal half-hour siesta to review the layout of the power plant and discuss escape plans. It was Coker who first broached the subject. As a trained navigator with many missions over Hanoi, he knew from the location of the nearby Doumer Bridge the proximity of the Yen Phu complex to the Red River and the currents and confluences of the waterway that could take them to where friendly forces operated in the Gulf of Tonkin. Furthermore, while at the Zoo he had learned from Jerry Denton how to pry loose the locking mechanism on his cell door,[14] which was similar to that at Dirty Bird. McKnight thought they could get over the wall at Dirty Bird, but beyond that, as John Hubbell wrote, "the scheme struck him as harebrained—a couple of Caucasians swimming sixty-odd miles along a heavily trafficked river through one of the world's most densely populated regions, then somehow stealing a boat and sailing off to good-guy country." Implausible as it seemed, they decided to go for it, and set the date for 12 October 1967.[15]

That evening, after rigging their bunks with spare clothing and other odds and ends to make them appear occupied* and slipping their cell door locks, the two prisoners made their break. They climbed over a wall, dropped onto the street, and, crawling through the shadows, followed a route to the riverbank that had been carefully mapped by McKnight during his chores outside the compound. They found the Doumer Bridge illuminated

---

* To accustom the guards to the lumpy forms on their bedslabs, the PWs had been sleeping under blankets despite the heat.

with the torches of welders repairing bomb damage but managed to scramble unnoticed to the river's edge. Stripping down to their underwear, they secured themselves with a rope fashioned from their pajama drawstrings (augmented by an extended piece stolen from a prison clothesline), then buried their clothing and waded into the water. The scheme called for them to swim at night and hide during the day. After three or four nights they expected to reach the river's mouth, overpower the crew of a sailboat or small fishing boat, and flag down a vessel from the U.S. Navy's Seventh Fleet. Figuring on an eight-day adventure, they would drink polluted river water as necessary and eat anything edible they could find.

Strong swimmers, Coker and McKnight traversed some 15 miles that first night, but that was as far as they got. Jinxed by a bright dawn and trouble finding cover on a bare open bank, they were spotted early the next morning, Friday the 13th as it happened, by an old woman and young man fishing along the shore. Soon they were surrounded by armed peasants and turned over to soldiers. The two spent a few days in irons at Hoa Lo before being returned to Dirty Bird. To their surprise they were not tortured, perhaps because McKnight leveled with interrogators, telling them that they had both expected to die in prison from the poor conditions and mistreatment and that escape was an honorable if desperate choice. They, and their colleagues back at the power plant, may have been spared retribution, too, because of no evidence of concerted PW organization and complicity in the escape effort: no escape committee, no SRO to approve or disapprove the plan, and no cellmates upon whom the wrath of the authorities would fall.[16] (McKnight had confided only in his former cellmate and trusted comrade Swindle, so that someone would have knowledge in case he and Coker died in the attempt.)

Sometime around the middle of October, Ralph Gaither recalled, security suddenly increased at the School. "We did not know what had happened," he wrote in his memoir, "but we suspected that someone had made a break. It was obvious that something had shook them up. High-ranking officers were walking around our camp, a sure sign that something had made them nervous." Coffee noted that anxious guards applied leg irons to the prisoners overnight and outfitted cell doors with reinforced bolts. A perturbed Rat accused Coffee and Heilig of communicating and separated the two. The PWs at the School counted heads and assumed that missing Al Brudno was the fugitive responsible for the agitation, but Brudno was too ill to have tried escape—he had merely been temporarily sent to Dirty Bird for a propaganda taping.[17]

Within two weeks of the Coker-McKnight escape, all the power plant prisons were closed. Perhaps the North Vietnamese, recognizing that the hostage gambit was not working, had planned to shut them down anyway, or perhaps the escape convinced them to return the prisoners to more conventional and secure lockups. In either case, on 25 October all those remaining at the School and Dirty Bird were moved back to Hoa Lo, most of them deposited in Vegas. The program of exploiting the PWs for hostage purposes was over, an odd and ultimately failed experiment that added a brief but eventful chapter to the captivity story. As for Coker and McKnight, their comrades eventually learned of their tale. As the news spread from camp to camp, it lifted spirits and earned the pair the enduring respect of their fellow prisoners. It also persuaded the Vietnamese to include the two transgressors among the group of incorrigibles for whom they had designed a special camp at the Ministry of Defense. And thus it was that George McKnight and George Coker joined the Alcatraz Gang.

The same day that the Vietnamese ceased PW operations at the power plant, 25 October 1967, they opened a new camp closer to downtown that was even smaller and more narrowly conceived. "Alcatraz," as it came to be called by the proud coterie incarcerated there, was established specifically to house a select group of hardliners whom the Vietnamese wished to remove from Vegas and keep isolated.* Located about a mile from Hoa Lo, in a courtyard behind Hanoi's Ministry of National Defense, it held the same 11 prisoners for the better part of two years, the 9 leaders who came over from Vegas—Jim Stockdale, Jerry Denton, Jim Mulligan, Harry Jenkins, Howie Rutledge, Sam Johnson, Bob Shumaker, Ron Storz, and Nels Tanner—and Coker and McKnight.

Jenkins, Shumaker, and Mulligan were among the first to arrive. After exchanging hurried good-byes with Desert Inn roommate Lou Makowski, they were blindfolded and loaded into vehicles for the short 10-minute drive to the new destination. "I looked at my cramped surroundings and went into a state of shock," Mulligan later wrote. "I had a premonition that things had suddenly turned very bad for me. If anything, this initial feeling was a massive underestimate." Denton, too, reached Alcatraz on 25 October, finding the cells comparable to the crablike quarters he and Mulligan had occupied at the Mint, but the Mint was a temporary sentence and Alcatraz promised to be long-term. Denton described his compartment as consisting of a standing area four feet square and a raised pallet the length of a man's body that had a nail protruding where the right shoulder blade would touch when sleeping. Stockdale described his cell as "just a little bit

* See Chapter 16.

bigger than those in the Mint—maybe nine feet long and less than four feet wide. The difference was that this one had no bunk—just a raised portion of concrete floor where one spread out to sleep."[18]

Alcatraz—Shumaker is credited with the name—was as close to a dungeon as any prison in North Vietnam. Not only were the cells tiny, but they were also sunken, with earthen walls and no windows, the only ventilation coming from a few small pencil-size holes in a steel plate above the door and a recessed space below the door. A dim bulb, "ten watts or less" by Denton's reckoning, provided the only light. "At last we knew the truth about that old refrigerator joke," Rutledge mused. "When the guards closed the door, the light really did go out." Inside there was mostly darkness and silence. Outside there was filth and stench. Lining the courtyard were two buildings, a long, low one that contained 10 cells and, at a right angle to it, a second, smaller one that had 3. In one corner was a pigpen and not far from the bath area was an open cesspool.[19]

The Defense Ministry compound had once been used by the French to quarantine their most feared political opponents, sequestering them close at hand where they could keep an eye on them. It was now being employed as a camp for those whom the Vietnamese perceived to be among the most influential and refractory Americans—a veritable rogues' gallery from their standpoint. In the first eight cells in the main building, in order, went Rutledge, Jenkins, Johnson, Shumaker, Storz, Tanner, Coker, and McKnight. Cell 9 served as a storage room and guard shack. The enterprising Denton was kept isolated even among these diehards in cell 10 in the southwest corner. In the shorter building were placed Mulligan in cell 11 and Stockdale in cell 13, with cell 12 between them kept vacant. Denton later offered profiles of the distinguished lineup:

> Howie Rutledge had killed a man with his pistol during his capture when the man had charged him with a weapon. Rutledge despised the North Vietnamese and didn't try to hide it. He was extremely clever at communicating and paid for it. . . . His retentive memory and quick mind helped make him a superior leader, but mainly it was his indomitable will that made him a marked man.
>
> Harry Jenkins, in the cell next to Rutledge, was famous for his daring raids off the carrier *Oriskany*. Skipper of an attack squadron, he had got a good deal of publicity for his exploits before he was shot down and had had more than his share of torture and mistreatment. A tall, rangy man with prominent ears and beetle brows, he had the best sense of humor of anyone at Alcatraz.*

---

* With his prominent features and skinny frame, the well-liked, good-natured Jenkins was often the butt of humor as well. Some of the PWs affectionately referred to him as "Ichabod."

Alcatraz

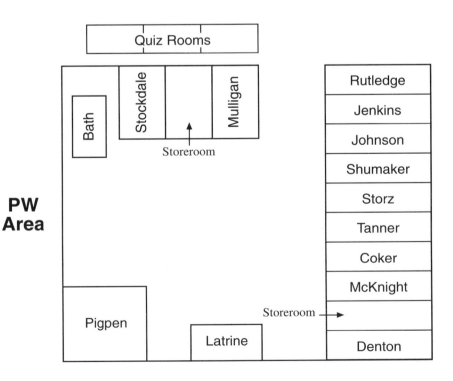

| Quiz Rooms | | | |

PW Area

| Bath | Stockdale | Storeroom ↑ | Mulligan |

| Rutledge |
| Jenkins |
| Johnson |
| Shumaker |
| Storz |
| Tanner |
| Coker |
| McKnight |
| Storeroom → |
| Denton |

| Pigpen | Latrine |

Sam Johnson looked like a Texas cowboy, and in fact he was from Texas. He was a strong resister and a good trooper despite a badly twisted arm which he could barely use. He exerted a steadying influence on everyone around him.

Bob Shumaker was in a class by himself. The sandy-haired Californian was a temperamental genius who was slicker than anyone at inventing new ways to communicate. He was so slick in fact that the Vietnamese seldom caught him, but they could tell by the patterns of communication that he was foxing them. An athletic ex-boxer, Shumaker had missed the astronaut program only because of some lymph nodes near his ear.

Ron Storz was a tall, gangly New Yorker with long arms and legs, prominent ears, and a permanently mournful expression.* He showed early that he would be one of the toughest. Once he refused to put his heels together during a quiz at the Office and the guards practically shredded his body with a metal rod. At Little Vegas he would pass notes containing the tap code to new shootdowns by slipping them in their rice while he was picking up his own food from the chow rack. He was constantly homesick and, unlike most prisoners, was pessimistic about the war. He knew it would last for many years, and didn't believe he would survive.

Nelson [sic] Tanner had made the North Vietnamese a laughing-stock [with the Ben Casey-Clark Kent story], and they never forgave him . . . . The overeager enemy had publicized the biography, and the resultant horse laughs had made them furious. Tanner set the record for consecutive days (123) in irons.

Young, baby-faced George Coker† was just too tough for the North Vietnamese to handle. Strong-minded and doctrinaire, he was scrupulous in his attitude toward them and simply wouldn't talk to them. His advice to new shootdowns was: "Look them in the eye and say No!" He wrote good poetry, was an excellent bridge and chess player, and was strictly moral in everything he did. He had engineered an escape with McKnight, which undoubtedly earned him some points toward Alcatraz, but my guess is that he would have been there anyway because of his resistance.

George McKnight, a slim 6-footer, had been a boxer in college. He had intense eyes deeply set in a long, lean face. He was a brave man who, in my judgment, was among the top five resisters in prison. When he wasn't planning an escape, he was thinking up new ways to foil the enemy. He, Stockdale, Rutledge, Risner, and I each spent more than four years in solitary. Ernie Brace, a civilian

---

* Denton's pen portrait does not do Storz justice. By most accounts he was quite handsome. Alvarez wrote that "he had the build of a classical Greek statue" (*Chained Eagle*, 258).
† Denton and Stockdale were plebes at the Naval Academy the year Coker was born. See Stockdale, *In Love and War*, 403.

pilot . . ., was the only other American prisoner to achieve that dubious distinction.*

Jim Mulligan, a six-foot Irishman, had . . . demonstrated time and again his willingness to sacrifice himself for others, and was always a vital force in the resistance. His constant good humor and his ability to laugh in their faces was a tremendous irritant to the North Vietnamese.

Jim Stockdale, who had been the air wing commander aboard the *Oriskany*, was considered a "high-grade criminal" by the North Vietnamese, and his "BACK U.S." program had frightened them. To add insult, he had once given the BS signal during a filmed confession and the signal had got through . . . . From his central location . . . [in] the Hilton, he had run a vigorous, successful resistance operation until the "BACK U.S." program had been traced to him . . . . Because he had led the prisoners at Vegas so well, he had become the No. 1 target. He was the senior officer at Alcatraz and in command.

The "eleven of us had truly reached the bottom of the Hanoi barrel," Stockdale observed. "We all had pedigrees of which we were proud . . . . We would be Brer Rabbits in the briar patch."[20]

The first several months at Alcatraz turned out to be less severe than the 11 "archcriminals" anticipated. The jailers enforced strict discipline and rigid isolation, but, as at Dirty Bird, punishment stopped short of torture and interrogation was relatively innocuous. The men were terrorized less by the Vietnamese than by the sound of exploding bombs from their own aircraft. "Some of the targets must have been very close to Alcatraz," Mulligan recalled, because their force "blew concussion waves that hammered my cell door . . . . The raids were close enough that Rat came and instructed each of us to sit in the corner with our heads in our hands and covered by our blanket." Mulligan for one was not so much afraid as thrilled at the "show"— "I cheered the Yanks on as if I were rooting at a football game"—and he allowed himself the hope that the pressure "would help bring a quick settlement to the war."[21]

Most onerous were the heavy U-shaped irons shackled to their ankles and worn 15 or more hours a day except at Tet and Christmas. Weighing 10 to 20 pounds and connected by a sliding bar, the restraints were a major impediment to sleeping and even the most perfunctory moving about. The discomfort was compounded by careless guards who distributed the wrong set or put them on backwards so that they rested against the PWs' shin

---

* Excluding Viet Cong captive Jim Thompson, who logged the most solitary time of all in a series of jungle camps in the South and North. At least one other in this category omitted by Denton was later capture Army Lt. Col. Benjamin Purcell.

bones. In the former instance, Denton remembered that "each prisoner had his own set . . . to which he had become accustomed, and the guards would frequently mix them up. There would be howls of anger until the prisoner got his proper set." By December 1967, turnkeys merely shoved the irons under the cell doors in the evening, then peeped in to watch the men lock themselves up for the night. In time a few prisoners learned how to click their padlocks without actually securing them. When it worked the ploy brought welcome relief.[22]

Although treatment was surprisingly mild those first few months, the living conditions confirmed Mulligan's presentiment. The tiny cells, lack of ventilation, solitude, and minimal time outdoors fostered excruciating claustrophobia and boredom as well as disease. The irons were locked in place each evening about 5:00 p.m. and not unfastened until morning when the prisoners were taken individually to the latrine area to dump their waste buckets and, when scarce water was available, to wash. Food consisted of pumpkin or cabbage soup, sometimes with a piece of pig fat floating in it. The lack of protein and poor sanitation left the PWs vulnerable to the usual infections, parasites, and diarrhea. Typical was the incident described in Rutledge's memoir where Jenkins awoke one night with what he thought was a piece of string in his mouth that turned out to be a six-inch worm. The men did receive a ration of two or three cigarettes daily, which they greeted eagerly as a means to mask their hunger or punctuate the routine.[23]

The combination of "isolation and deprivation," Johnson commented in his memoir, posed a "supreme test of our sanity and strength." Although in the beginning there was no overt torture, "the solitary confinement and the prison conditions were, themselves, torture." With no incoming prisoners to pump for information on the progress of the war or stateside developments, the men existed in "a virtual vacuum," made worse, said Johnson, by the guards being "meticulous about not allowing us to see each other. They were obsessive about trying to make each man believe he was here alone." Committed to the task was a large force of some two dozen personnel commanded by an army officer who, in Stockdale's words, "looked like the nickname we assigned to him, 'Slopehead.'" Rat was second-in-command, and such veterans as Mickey Mouse, Rabbit, and Frenchy appeared at various intervals. The Vietnamese always had at least one armed guard on patrol of the small courtyard and sometimes two. Counting part-timers and auxiliary help, all told there were about three Vietnamese for each American PW, an unusually high ratio that underscored the notoriety of Alcatraz's tenants.[24]

As so often happened in even the most closely supervised camps, however, segregation did not prevent communication. By peering underneath

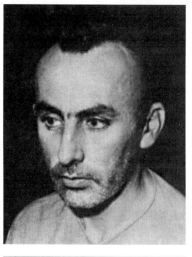

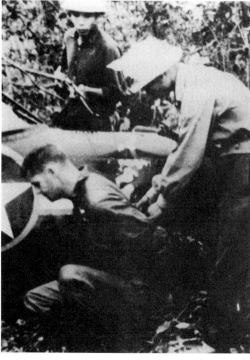

Alcatraz hardliners. *Top, from left*: Mulligan, Rutledge, Jenkins; *middle,* Coker, McKnight, Tanner; *bottom,* Storz, Johnson.

doors or through cracks, the prisoners soon learned who and how many were present. "I had to figure out some way to get a window on this world to which I was condemned," Johnson wrote of his determination to gain access to his mates. "I had to see beyond these walls. The tiny cracks in the wooden door of my cell beckoned me like sirens, but they were too small to offer more than a skinny shaft of light." Johnson used his mealtime spoon to pick away at the rotting wood until he had carved out an observation port that enabled him to see the comings and goings in the courtyard. Others contrived their own devices to fill the vacuum. They were all expert communicators and, as Hervey Stockman has pointed out, tapping between cells at Alcatraz was facilitated by the common walls. Between the two of them, Mulligan and Stockdale had identified five of their comrades the first day. After a couple of weeks the two buildings were linked when Stockdale and Tanner devised a flash version of the tap code and transmitted messages by moving a hand along the floor beneath their cell doors and interrupting the light; Tanner, the middle man in the longer cellblock, then tapped to either side of his building, a painstaking effort that Denton said required great courage and patience on the part of Tanner "but it worked."[25]

Because of the guard omnipresence, voice contact would be rare at Alcatraz. "Except in a few highly unusual instances," John Hubbell notes, "none of the prisoners was to hear another American voice during their long Alcatraz confinement." But there was no lack of other options. Besides tapping and flashing, they scraped their wastecans and swept brooms in code. Shumaker was considered an artist at sweeping, such that the men looked forward to those days when he drew the cleanup duty. He sent messages "with every swish of the broom," one of his correspondents recalled. "In a short time, we began to think of Shumaker as our news anchor." Each man gave him bits of information, which he circulated as he swept. It was at Alcatraz that Denton refined his "vocal" tap code into a versatile system that plugged assorted coughs, sniffs, and wheezes into the tap matrix. With everyone, including guards, suffering from colds and allergies, such sounds were not especially suspicious.[26]

Transmitters identified themselves with single-letter signatures. Mulligan, Jenkins, Tanner, McKnight, Coker, Denton, and Stockdale each used the first letter of his last name. So as not to duplicate Stockdale's sign-off, Ron Storz adopted "R" and Bob Shumaker took "B"; Sam Johnson, junior to Jenkins, chose "L," and Howie Rutledge selected "H," though he could have insisted on "R" because he outranked Storz. The group also had signature tunes they would whistle in certain emergencies, each prisoner picking a song related to his home state. Thus Shumaker's was "The Pennsylvania Polka" and Tanner's "The Tennessee Waltz." "Mulligan requested a waiver on the state-song idea," Stockdale later quipped. "He wanted 'When

Irish Eyes Are Smiling.' We let him have it." The critical clearing function
was accomplished by several methods, one being to pool a little water under
the cell door, then watch it from the proper angle to detect the reflection of
any approaching guard. Denton felt that the Vietnamese knew communication was going on but initially chose to overlook it much of the time,
never suspecting the extent and sophistication of the system. "Never have I
seen such universal sensitivity to sound . . . ," Stockdale marveled. "With a
quiet throat clear, I could summon Nels and immediately see his finger under
his door, ready to receive my message." Given their reputation as both troublemakers and communication virtuosos, it is not surprising that Mulligan
found the Alcatraz gang to be "the most proficient and aggressive comm[uni-
cations] men that I knew of in the entire POW community."[27]

With the onset of winter that first year, insulation became as worrisome
a concern as ventilation. Their earthen bunkers had tin roofs that afforded
little protection from the raw chill. "We were cold and hungry all the time,"
Johnson wrote, their emaciated bodies battered by the freezing temperatures.
Christmas brought no relief from the weather but conferred the usual ephemeral holiday dispensations: a special supper, release from irons for the night,
letters from home for some,* broadcasted carols, and incongruous gifts of
chocolates and candies accompanied without fail by "humane and lenient"
proclamations. Shumaker was even allowed to make chessboards for the men
from small scraps of coarse paper. Although Rat instructed them to play only
against themselves, he knew full well, Denton related, that "we would tap our
knuckles and fingers raw playing the game with each other." When Rutledge sardonically requested "a cup of coffee and a bus ticket to Saigon,"
Rat drew the line on the holiday privileges. An unintended bonus resulted
from the Christmas relaxation when Mulligan was permitted to attend a
Catholic mass at another prison and passed word to Jerry Coffee of the
Alcatraz eleven's whereabouts.[28]

1968 began uneventfully, the prisoners continuing to do more languish-
ing than hard punishment. A dismal, rainy January and February "drifted
past," as Denton described the atmosphere. "The drizzle and chill were constant,
and sometimes a storm would fill the cement gutter and cold, dirty water
would flood into the cells," carrying all manner of dead vermin. There were
sporadic cat-and-mouse contests where the PWs courted trouble and Slopehead or Rat administered a well-chosen object lesson. Communication
violations typically drew around-the-clock irons for 10 days, though at least

* Mulligan was elated to receive a letter with photographs from his wife Louise. Although
10 months old, not only did the missive bring cherished news of his family but in it Louise
described her trip to "visit mutual friends" in Washington, confirming that she had received
the PW's Christmas 1966 letter and had gotten it to the proper Navy authorities.

one of the men, Jenkins, spent 85. Stockdale fenced repeatedly with prison staff, taking full-time irons that further damaged his bad leg. The group celebrated Easter early. Having no knowledge that the holy day fell on 14 April that year, they decided on the fourth Sunday in March for their observance. Denton composed a three-part poem and circulated one stanza daily for Holy Thursday, Good Friday, and Holy Saturday. The prisoners scraped their approval each morning while cleaning wastecans.[29]

In April the Vietnamese resumed regular quizzes, Rat and a large-toothed guard named "Marty Mouthful" pressing the men to complete biographical questionnaires similar to those most of the PWs had been forced to fill out previously. When the prisoners resisted, they were made to roll up their trousers and remain in a kneeling position. When knees became so bloodied or swollen that kneeling was no longer possible, guards locked on double leg irons and compelled the prisoners to stand erect until they succumbed. Some lasted 24 hours in this punishment, others less. McKnight held out more than two days, then gave Stockdale a "thumbs up" as he passed the senior's cell. Mulligan, by now lacking "the physical strength of a wet noodle," prayed as he knelt and passed out before complying.[30]

As they took their lumps, the PWs heard on the newly installed camp radio about the first prisoner release in the North,* the revelation precipitating a protracted internal debate among them over the propriety of PWs accepting early release and how to counter the so-called "Fink Release Program." Stockdale promulgated a policy, eventually transmitted to the other camps, that entailed procrastination until the prisoner could ascertain the conditions of the release (whether to the United States or to some other country, whether other prisoners were involved, what propaganda advantage the enemy might gain, etc.) and seek permission for the repatriation from his senior officer.[31]

By late spring unrelenting sun and humidity once again converted the unventilated cells to "steam closets." In Mulligan's metaphor, refrigerators became ovens. Johnson remarked that "the tin roofs overhead served as solar conductors and radiated heat that broiled us in our cells . . . . Suffocation seemed a very real possibility." Denton added, "We crept to our cell doors and sucked like animals for air . . . ." When temperatures reached what seemed "130 degrees or more," Mulligan stopped eating. When others did, too, Denton asked to see Rat and "congratulated" him on the clever, hands-off torture program whereby the prisoners were being put to a slow death by heat. Fazed by the possibility of losing the captives on his watch, Rat had workers unbolt the steel plates over the cell doors, remove grills from

* See Chapter 18.

building windows, and lay straw and vines on the roofs to screen the sun. Denton's deft lobbying eased the crisis, bringing the men welcome light as well as air, but the group's condition remained precarious.[32]

In July Rat was replaced by an officer known as "Slick" or "Soft Soap Fairy," a smart, polished high-ranking deputy in his thirties who spoke English exceptionally well and whose nicknames derived from both an effeminate appearance and con-artist reputation. From Hanoi Hannah's broadcasts the prisoners learned of the assassinations of Robert Kennedy and Martin Luther King and of the nominations of Richard Nixon and someone named Agnew to run against Senators Humphrey and Muskie. They were now getting news fragments but the filtered content was hardly encouraging, as their countrymen were having their own awful summer. On the 4th of July, guards served a larger than usual meal because, according to Slick, the American people had rejected Lyndon Johnson's war. On 2 September, the North Vietnamese national day, the prisoners had another good feed. Slick surprised the men with an announcement that they would have daily 10-minute exercise and bath periods outdoors. On 9 September, the third anniversary of his shootdown, Stockdale was accorded "the most meaningful citation I've ever received," a chain message swished out in sequence by his 10 comrades at the morning bucket scrub: "Here's to CAG* for three great years. We love you. We are with you to the end."[33]

The desultory summer ended abruptly with the reassignment of Slick and promotion of the harder-edged Mickey Mouse to take his place. Denton felt certain the personnel move portended a change in their treatment, "a change for the worse," and indeed, in the fall what had amounted to a year's "sabbatical" came to a close and the Alcatraz gang entered a new phase of outright torture that matched their worst days at Hoa Lo. In mid-December a communications purge claimed McKnight and Denton, who were severely beaten and left tied in excruciating positions until they produced propaganda statements. More torture followed after Christmas, the men marched individually to one of three quiz rooms at the east end of the courtyard. The pretext was always a communication infraction or some other transgression—Rutledge was hounded over the old incident of having shot a Vietnamese at capture—but the objective was plainly to manufacture more propaganda to play to an increasingly disenchanted U.S. electorate. Nixon's election, several of the PWs thought, may have given that strategy new urgency. In any case, at length the 11 hard-nosed prisoners all capitulated, though they strove to blunt the effect of the coerced confessions with insertions of telltale

---

* Navy acronym for Commander, Air Group. Designating the CO of the flying squadrons aboard a carrier, the term conveyed great respect, and many of the PWs in Hanoi referred to Stockdale simply as "CAG."

gibberish. One, for example, interjected the line, "Such famous men as the great Latin American humanitarian S.P. de Gonzalez were against the war in Vietnam." (Spoken on tape, the name sounded like "Speedy Gonzalez.")[34]

The renewal of the torture campaign reached a flash point shortly after midnight on 24 January 1969. Jenkins, seized with terrible cramps from an attack of intestinal worms, began yelling for help, the other prisoners soon joining him in a spontaneous protest. When guards ordered the men back to bed, Stockdale sent a message through the flash-and-tap network for a two-day hunger strike. The Vietnamese responded with medication for Jenkins but blamed Stockdale for the "Alcatraz riot" and moved the senior back to Hoa Lo and its dreaded room 18 for a "sustained and vicious" period of correction. Stockdale had been in horrible shape when he arrived at Alcatraz—Mulligan thought he had aged 20 years in the last year alone and "now looked like a man in his late sixties"—and the two-month stay in the Hilton's correction chamber added more scars to his collection. Johnson wrote, "Only months later would we learn the nightmare dimensions of his torture." Within 20 minutes of entering room 18, Stockdale recalled, "Pigeye had me roped and screaming for mercy."[35]

Stockdale was convinced that officials at the Hilton were after him to make a movie for PW consumption in which he advised junior officers to cooperate with the captors. To defeat the plan, he tried fasting, then disfigured himself by chopping his hair and scalp with a razor and, when the Vietnamese requisitioned a hat, pounding his face with a stool and against the wall until he was unfit to be photographed or filmed. The fasting reduced his weight to below 120 pounds but did not work because he found it necessary to indulge himself with a few morsels of stowed bread in the middle of the night and because, unlike Mulligan, for example, he could not faint even after days of complete denial.* The use of "puke balls," scraps of laundry soap that enabled him to retch on cue, stalled his antagonists for a time. But the best counterextortion technique proved to be the self-defacement. Painful as it was—he had to "freshen" his bruises with his fists to keep his eyelids swollen and cheekbones mashed—it allowed him to regain some measure of control from his tormentors.[36]

Stockdale spent the remainder of 1969 at Hoa Lo, moving into room 5 off the Heartbreak courtyard in March and over to Vegas in May. (Why the Vietnamese decided to return him to Vegas, where he could cause potentially

---

* The fasting technique had saved Mulligan on several occasions when he was able to pass out and jailers would have to carry him back to his cell. Unfortunately, "this device was not physiologically available to Captain Stockdale although he practiced it several times in attempting to develop the ability to lose consciousness . . . . Stockdale's body reaction was such that he could not faint and was still able to do 10 to 15 pushups after 7 days without food" (Stockdale file).

more trouble, instead of Alcatraz is not clear.) Back at Alcatraz, with Denton now senior and the band down to 10, Mickey Mouse alternately baited and bludgeoned the men for amnesty pleas and yet another, "blue book" version of the autobiographical resume. Denton, "by example and guidance," an admirer later wrote, led the prisoners in a tenacious delaying action, which bought some time but also harsh reprisals. Enforcers introduced a bamboo switch that intensified beatings and added new wrinkles to the rope torture. Shumaker, whose knees had ballooned to the "size of a large grapefruit" from the previous spring's kneeling punishment, ran a gauntlet of ropes, irons, and belts. Johnson had his jaw and skull smashed by the rifle barrels of a squad of female soldiers who set upon him like a pack of mad dogs. Tanner was stripped naked, thrown on the concrete deck outside the quiz room, and flogged savagely. One by one, they were again broken. Finally, in late summer, the pace slackened and treatment gradually improved.[37]

At one time or another most of the Alcatraz group were on the verge of losing their grip, but all, save one, survived the ordeal. Ron Storz had been among the bravest and most aggressive American PWs anywhere in the North—Stockdale extolled him as "our spark plug, our hero"—but, highly emotional, given to fatalism, and plagued by homesickness, he was also regarded as among the most vulnerable. Storz was well into the fifth year of his captivity in the summer of 1969. Mentally and physically wrecked by successive rounds of torture and traumatized by a belief that in submitting to his captors he had failed his country and comrades, he had been on the brink of collapse even before entering Alcatraz. While at Alcatraz, Stockdale remembered, Storz's "swagger and friendly grin slowly evolved into a stumbling shuffle and a vacant stare." He impressed his mates as increasingly self-destructive and irrational, fasting even when inappropriate and on one occasion slashing his wrists with a razor after complying with torturers' demands. A blood transfusion, Johnson remarked, "saved his life, but there was little that could be done to save his spirit. . . . In the summer of 1969 we knew we were losing him."

Storz's weight dropped from 175 pounds to perhaps 100 until his gaunt frame looked "wraith-like." As they became aware of his plight, the Vietnamese gave him a bible and a deck of cards in an effort to distract him and began to feed him intravenously. Mulligan at one point commanded him to eat. But it was to no avail. "We all did what we could for him," said Stockdale, "but we all saw a man disintegrate before our eyes." Storz was left behind when the rest of the group departed Alcatraz at the end of the year. The Vietnamese were "embarrassed about his condition and didn't want the other prisoners to see him," Denton concluded. The Air Force captain who had played such an integral role in the formative years of the resistance was never heard from after December 1969, when Mulligan last made contact with him. His demise was one of the great tragedies of the PW story, deeply felt by all his fellow prisoners and especially by those who witnessed his desperate struggle. North Vietnam later informed the U.S. government that Storz lapsed into a coma and died in a military hospital in April 1970.[38]

The remaining nine members of the Alcatraz Gang huddled through a quiet final season of uncertainty, benefiting from the general mellowing that followed the death of the North Vietnamese leader Ho Chi Minh.* Frenchy, who had just replaced Slopehead as the camp commander, ordered the PWs to pack up on 9 December. Minus Storz, the gang wound up where their roller-coaster ride had begun more than two years earlier—back in Vegas. Coker and McKnight were sent to the Mint and the others assigned solo quarters in Stardust. (Stockdale was in Thunderbird when they arrived.) To Denton, the roomier and airier Vegas suddenly seemed luxurious. He was deposited in cell 6 at Stardust, which "after Alcatraz . . . was like the presidential suite."[39]

Alcatraz stayed open another six months with a skeleton crew to accommodate Storz and two other prisoners who were also deemed "problem" cases.† They were believed to be the last Americans to occupy the prison.‡ Denton and the other original "Alkies," as their elite fraternity came to be called, did not realize how long a stretch they had yet ahead. Some of them mistook their release from Alcatraz as a harbinger of their imminent release from captivity and were dismayed to discover that they had merely come full circle back to Vegas. "We dared to hope that the nightmare was ending and that we were going home," Rutledge wrote of his disappointment.[40]

Nonetheless, if they were not going home, they had at least emerged from what in retrospect would be for most of them the darkest abyss of their captivity. For all of Vegas's own loathsome conditions and reign of terror, Johnson observed, "the shadow of death [there] did not seem quite so smothering." Alcatraz, "with its tomb-like cells and dugout earthen walls, had seemed a silent, constant death threat." Looking back on the experience in 1976, Denton related that "Alcatraz meant solitude, filth, hunger, and despair—and many other things that even now the ten survivors are sometimes reluctant to talk about." If it had been a "badge of honor," as the senior put it, to be admitted to Alcatraz—"each man had earned his way in"—the archcriminals had burnished their reputations still more by making their way out of what Denton termed "this final horror."[41]

---

* See Chapter 22.
† See Chapter 23.
‡ With the possible exception of one prisoner seized in the South, PFC Jon Sweeney (see Chapter 21), who evidently was detained there for five weeks in July and August 1970 prior to his repatriation. See "Prisoner of War Camps in North Vietnam," DIA rpt, Nov 72, 51.

18

Plantation: Exhibitions and Early Releases

The middle years 1967-69 were an ultimate testing time not only for the American prisoners of war but also for the U.S. commitment to rescue Southeast Asia from communism. Mounting body counts, increasing skepticism about the wisdom of United States military involvement in the Indochinese conflict, and consuming problems at home steadily eroded what had always been a thin base of domestic support for the U.S. action. Continuing sharp internal debate within the Johnson and then Nixon administration between those advocating more massive use of airpower and those urging a diplomatic solution produced a series of tentative on-again, off-again bombing campaigns that convinced the enemy—and many of the PWs*—of Washington's lack of resolve. The psychological victory gained by the North Vietnamese through the Tet offensive during the first half of 1968 placed U.S. "hawks" further on the defensive. In what had come down to a test of political will rather than military might, Hanoi was clearly prevailing, and the Communists wasted no opportunity to exploit both the demoralized PWs and a divided and defeatist-minded American public to cement their advantage.

Such was the context in which the North Vietnamese established yet a third new PW camp in these years, one devoted specifically to the production and dissemination of propaganda. Opened in the spring of 1967, shortly before Dirty Bird, this camp was located on the outskirts of downtown Hanoi a few blocks south of the power plant and virtually across the street from the Alcatraz compound at the Ministry of Defense. (The smaller Alcatraz shared the same kitchen and much the same personnel.) Situated on a tree-lined two acres, it had formerly been the home of the colonial mayor of Hanoi. After

* See Chapter 20.

340

the French left, the property's once stately grounds and large mansion-style house went unmaintained, so that by the time the American prisoners arrived the house was crumbling and the estate was in general disrepair. The faded grandeur of the place inspired the nickname "Plantation," although the prisoners referred to the site by a number of other names as well, among them "Country Club," "Funny Farm," "Holiday Inn," and "The Citadel," the last for its proximity to the defense ministry building. The Vietnamese converted a portion of the facility into a Potemkin village of sanitized cells, garden patches, and scrubbed corridors that would serve as a showplace for displaying the captives to visiting delegations and conducting photo sessions and other propaganda activities.

At the center of the trapezoidal tract was the main residence, which the prisoners called the "Big House" or "French House." Bud Day, who spent January to April 1968 at the camp, described it as a "pretentious old two-and-a-half story Georgian building, garnished with ornate frieze work, and sprawling, elaborate porches . . . . Although it had been an elegant building in its time, it was in the typical state of decay, needing paint and care. In the light of day it was seedy, dowdy, and unattractive." The lower floor of the Big House was used for interviews and interrogations and contained the camp radio room; the upper floor housed prison staff and administrative offices. Russian magazines lying about and pinups of Russian women on the mansion's walls suggested that it may have recently been occupied by Soviet personnel.

The PWs lived in the surrounding outbuildings that once contained servants' quarters and utilities. The principal cellblock, with 14 or 15 cells, was in a long, low shed appropriately dubbed the "Warehouse." Other structures were called "Gunshed," for the artillery piece outside its entrance (7 cells); "Corn Crib" (3 cells); and "Movie House" (1 cell and an auditorium that doubled as a staff recreation hall and PW assembly area for propaganda movies, church services, and the like). The size of the cells varied from 6 feet by 10 feet to 14 feet by 24 feet; holding from one to five men, they were spacious even by Vegas standards. Most comfortable were the three cells that comprised the "Show Room," the area featured in the propaganda events. Although the camp was ringed with a brick wall that was topped with barbed wire and broken glass and all cell windows were boarded or shuttered, Day noted that it "lacked the chilling, fearful look of the Hilton."[1]

The first arrivals at the Plantation, in early June 1967, were a group of eight who came over from Vegas. After just a month or so, six of those would be transferred to Dirty Bird, but not before helping construction workers ready the camp with extensive cleanup and repair of the buildings and grounds. Included in that first contingent was Tom Collins, a Mississippian who was credited with originating the camp nickname. Plantation's population steadily increased as improvements were made, including the installation of bath and

1. Big House   4. Warehouse
2. Show Room   5. Corn Crib
3. Gunshed   6. Movie House

Plantation

Guard walking PWs outside the Warehouse.

kitchen facilities, until it reached a peak strength of 52 or 53 inmates in January 1968—most of them recent shootdowns and young fliers who did not yet show the permanent scars of sustained torture and had not yet been "corrupted" by the resistance organization, and hence were prime candidates for propaganda display.

As one would expect in a "show" camp, carrots predominated over sticks in the treatment of the captives. There was little physical abuse, at least initially, rather mostly soft-sell efforts to modify attitudes through indoctrination quizzes, visits to historic sites or to view local bomb damage, and exposure to antiwar literature. Though exercise was limited after the initial cleanup and preparation of the property for its new function, the prisoners did get outside to make coal balls for the kitchen fire, dump waste buckets, and use the bath stalls two or three times a week. As in the other Northern compounds, summer water shortages curtailed bathing. Food was not appreciably better than at the Hilton—at least one occupant judged it worse—nor was ventilation or sanitation any better in the worst of the cells, at the Gunshed. In actuality, except for the showcase cells, conditions were not much improved over those at Hoa Lo, even if the latter's fortress-like ambiance did seem more forbidding.[2]

Presiding over the new camp were a cadre of high-level prison officials—Cat himself made occasional supervisory calls—who, consistent with the standard Communist practice, represented both the military and political sides of the party. Slopehead and Slick, or Soft Soap Fairy, in charge of military and political affairs respectively at Alcatraz,* appear to have held the same positions concurrently at Plantation. Slopehead, sometimes called "Stoneface,"† oversaw camp construction and management, while Slick ran the interrogations and supervised the propaganda campaign. Rabbit and Bug turned up from time to time. Subordinates, many of whom were new faces, included Chihuahua, Smiley, Boo Boo, Chico (probably the same guard referred to as "Marty Mouthful" at Alcatraz and as "Prick" elsewhere), Ajax (a cleanliness nut whom some PWs may have confused with "Rat"), Frankenstein, Bucky Beaver, Eel, Fubar,‡ Lt. Fuzz (a young interpreter), and Brutus.

By most accounts, the key figure at Plantation was Slick. The Americans regarded him, with both admiration and wariness, as one of the most effective operatives in the whole prison system. Pleasant, soft-spoken, his obvious intelligence enhanced by his excellent English, he was far more subtle, and plausible, than the droning, parroting indoctrinators to whom the prisoners had become

---

* See Chapter 17.
† The two appear to be one and the same, but there is at least one personnel roster compiled by the returning PWs that lists them separately. In either case, this Stoneface was a senior officer, different from the turnkey of that name mentioned earlier.
‡ "Fubar" was an old military acronym meaning "fucked up beyond all recognition (or repair)." It was applied to a number of maladroit guards in the North Vietnamese prisons, one of them at Plantation.

accustomed. Brushing his longish hair back from his eyes in a way that is characteristically Vietnamese but appeared effeminate to the Americans, he would expound on world conditions or Vietnamese life, then slip in a seemingly innocent question or innocuous request. Because of his considerable education, fine English, good clothes, and graceful demeanor, the prisoners assumed he came from a background of wealth and privilege, an impression buttressed by his sometimes being trailed by two handsomely dressed young children. It was precisely his refined manner and engaging style that made him a dangerous adversary.[3]

The spring of 1967 had been a busy season for Hanoi's propaganda directors even prior to the activation of the Plantation camp. In one of the most dramatic incidents of the psywar, on 6 March the North Vietnamese had forced Dick Stratton to appear at a press conference in which they first played an extracted taped confession, then escorted the PW onstage to bow before a swarm of television and movie cameras. Tortured repeatedly since his capture in January,* Stratton had paid a steep price for his taunting defiance, suffering from multiple wounds and recurrent sickness, but his still husky build and "imperialist" swagger continued to make him a prize candidate for the spotlight. With the Vietnamese apparently bent on both exploiting and humiliating him, the aviator decided this time to hedge his resistance with a maneuver that outwardly complied with the enemy's command but in such robotic fashion that it left the hosts nonplused and the assemblage of reporters shaken. Zombie-like, standing rigidly and glassy-eyed in his striped prison pajamas, he bowed mechanically and expressionless before the cameras as though drugged or brainwashed. The resulting pictures, in stark black and white, were published worldwide, accompanied by stories in *Life* and *Time* referring to the "Pavlovian" and "Orwellian" overtones of the exhibition. The Communists received a public relations black eye as damaging as the effect of the Hanoi March.[4]

Possibly to repair the harm done by the Stratton incident, the Vietnamese had relatively healthy-looking Air Force PWs Maj. Jack Bomar and Lt. Joseph Crecca meet with a trio of Russell Tribunal representatives on 16 March, presumably to assure the visitors that the prisoners were being treated humanely. Hanoi also distributed an alleged recording by Stratton in which the American denied that he had been brainwashed or subjected to pressure.† In another blunder, however, on 6 May, officials paraded three

---

* See Chapter 11.
† Stratton actually was reprising his "Manchurian candidate" performance, mouthing monotone, programmatic responses to a reporter's questions about his condition: "Get enough to eat . . . . In the camp I can listen to the radio Voice of Vietnam . . . . We get the medical care we need." He repeated the same replies no matter the queries. The tape was edited to convey the impression that Stratton was fit and clear-thinking. See Blakey, *Prisoner at War*, 145-46; "U.S. Prisoner Said to Deny Pressure by Hanoi," *NY Times*, 17 Apr 67.

fliers—Air Force Lt. Cols. James Hughes and Gordon Larson and Lt. James Shively—through the streets of the capital a day after their capture and then presented the shellshocked men, visibly injured (Hughes had suffered serious burns, and Larson had multiple fractures) and under duress, before another press gathering. The U.S. State Department, which had expressed grave concerns over the Stratton matter and had demanded then that Hanoi allow the Red Cross to examine the captives, renewed its charges of mistreatment.[5]

No doubt the strong U.S. reaction and the widespread revulsion internationally to the heavy-handed propaganda spectacles gave impetus to the decision to institute a gentler program, in a more benign setting, at the Plantation. It was not mere coincidence that Stratton, Crecca, Hughes, Larson, and Shively—along with other prisoners whose identities were known to the world through propaganda tapings or news releases, such as Dave Hatcher, Paul Galanti, and Dave Rehmann—turned up at the Plantation and soon began appearing in carefully orchestrated poses. In the case of Stratton, one would have assumed that the troublesome PW had outlasted his usefulness, but Cat or someone else in authority must have judged that his celebrity, however notorious from their standpoint, enhanced his psywar value. For Stratton and the others, the name recognition would be a double-edged sword: it may have guaranteed their survival, but it also marked them for regular exploitation.

The first significant use of the show camp occurred in late June and early July when an East German film company visited North Vietnam to make a propaganda movie contrasting the destruction wrought by the American bombing with the Communists' benevolent treatment of the undeserving captives. Dividing the filming between the Plantation and the Zoo,* the East Germans depicted the PWs in staged capture scenes, interviewed 10 of them, and portrayed others with brooms sweeping immaculate rooms or shovels digging shelters to protect themselves from ongoing U.S. air raids. Guards hid behind posts and corners just out of camera range while the crew filmed the men showering, exercising, reading, or receiving food. The PWs managed to sabotage some of the shooting—Galanti, placed on a bed in one of the sanitized cells, glowered and pointed his hands downward with middle fingers extended—but the end product, professionally edited, technically proficient, turned out to be more sophisticated and persuasive than most such efforts. Running some four hours, shown on East German television over four nights and later, in an abbreviated one-hour version, in the United States, *Pilots in Pajamas*, as the documentary was called, would become one of the major propaganda coups of the war.[6]

* Scores of prisoners were enlisted for the production. Even Colonel Risner, on stash at the Hilton, was dragged before the cameras. "To make me look relaxed," Risner related in his memoir, "they gave me some hors d'oeuvres, a bottle of soda pop, and offered me chewing gum." See *Passing of the Night*, 164.

The success of the East German enterprise was followed up with other films and videotaping sessions. Although the North Vietnamese utilized all the prisons that spring and summer in the intensive drive for propaganda materials—they even operated a separate movie studio in Hanoi*—over the next two years the Plantation increasingly became the hub of the political warfare activity. It was here that Risner met with American writer Mary McCarthy; that correspondents from East Germany, Czechoslovakia, Hungary, Japan, Cuba, France, and other countries typically conducted their interviews and shot their footage; and that most of the American antiwar activists touring Vietnam got their first exposure to "prison conditions" in the North, little realizing the controlled and contrived nature of their perspective.

By mid-July more than two dozen Americans had taken up "permanent" residence at the camp. From Dirty Bird came Joe Milligan, Jack Van Loan, Read Mecleary, Gary Anderson, Kevin McManus, and Ed Mechenbier. From the Zoo arrived Stratton and a young Navy apprentice seaman, Douglas Hegdahl, who would become as much a thorn in the side of the enemy as Stratton. In the advance group from Vegas that had helped renovate the camp, Galanti, Julius Jayroe, Gary Thornton, and David Gray moved on to the power plant, but Dave Hatcher and Charles Plumb remained, joined by Bill Stark and Kay Russell. Arvin Chauncey, Ron Webb, Mike McCuistion, Dick Vogel, Bob Wideman, and Larson were fresh May-June shootdowns who had barely had their initiation at Heartbreak before they found themselves at Plantation. Chauncey had been interrogated by Chinese soldiers on his first day as a PW, and despite having his arms bound he had escaped from the Vietnamese during a rainstorm the second night. Like many in this group who clearly had "bad attitudes," he did not last a year at Plantation.

Hegdahl was perhaps the most intriguing member of the bunch. In his 1990 captivity account, Geoffrey Norman rated him "in many ways, the most extraordinary POW in North Vietnam." John Hubbell went so far as to call him "one of the most remarkable characters in American military annals." The subject of such acclaim was a self-effacing, unprepossessing 19-year-old South Dakotan who had been in the Navy less than six months when he was captured in the predawn hours of 6 April 1967. The youngest U.S. prisoner seized in the North, Hegdahl, according to Hubbell, prior to joining the service had never "been east of his uncle's Dairy Queen stand in Glenwood, Minnesota, or west of his aunt's house in Phoenix, Arizona." On the morning of his capture, he was serving as an ammunition handler below deck on the

---

* Outfitted with a false beard, Jerry Coffee while at Vegas was taken there and forced to portray an American adviser leading ARVN soldiers across terrain that looked like the Mekong Delta. Bob Shumaker remembered being hauled to "an old movie colony . . ., where an elaborate set complete with makeup personnel, actors and extras were waiting." This was the incident in which the Vietnamese nearly killed Shumaker when he resisted (see Chapter 16, note 28).

guided missile cruiser USS *Canberra* in the Gulf of Tonkin. Eager to witness a night bombardment, he went topside without authorization and was knocked overboard by the concussion of the ship's giant guns. A powerful swimmer, he stayed afloat for several hours before being picked up by North Vietnamese fishermen and turned over to militiamen. The *Canberra* reversed course when his absence was discovered, but failed to locate him. A memorial service was held aboard the cruiser even as he was being trucked to Hoa Lo.[7]

Hegdahl's explanation to interrogators in Hanoi that he had fallen off a ship seemed so preposterous that the enemy first suspected him of being a commando who concocted the tale in order to conceal his real mission as a spy. After several days of being grilled and slapped around, he convinced officials that he was in fact what he appeared to be: not a special agent, not a pilot, not even an officer, but an enlisted man and raw recruit privy to no military secrets and one of the smallest fry they had caught. There was nothing puny about Hegdahl's size: he was over six feet tall and weighed 225 pounds at high school graduation. When the prison staff began treating him as an oafish, ignorant country boy, he played the bumpkin role to the hilt; having lost his glasses in the incident at sea, he even had trouble seeing. "In actuality," Jerry Coffee later wrote, "Doug Hegdahl was dumb like a fox." Because guard personnel viewed him as insignificant and unthreatening, they indulged him more than their more accomplished charges, and he was able to capitalize on the disarming facade to gain extra communication opportunities and time outdoors—in the process becoming a valuable reconnaissance asset in the PW resistance network.[8]

Hegdahl and Stratton came over from the Zoo together in June after brief stays at the suburban prison; Hegdahl had been there only a month, Stratton since late January. Soon after their arrival at the Plantation, they were trotted out to meet with American peace coalition leader David Dellinger and to participate in the shooting of *Pilots in Pajamas*.[9] After a period in solitary, they became roommates. There could hardly have seemed a less compatible couple—the one a provincial farm kid and untested sailor just out of boot camp, the other a macho, well-traveled and-educated (Georgetown and Stanford) officer and aviator. Despite the cultural gulf and rank and age gaps, they took an instant liking to each other, Hegdahl in awe of the cocky commander and Stratton impressed by the youngster's courage and cleverness. Although, as Stratton's biographer Scott Blakey notes, there remained some military correctness in their relationship,[10] the pair would bond in an unusual friendship that was mutually respectful and beneficial and that had important consequences for their comrades as well. Over time each would have a significant impact on the course of events at the show camp and on the captivity experience generally.

Perhaps foreshadowing the special plans the Vietnamese had for the two, they were initially placed in one of the high-ceilinged show cells. Hegdahl remembered entering the room on 11 July and spotting the pilot looking "like he needed a shave, which was kind of normal for Stratton." "He is from the air and you are from the sea, and now you live together," Cat told them. "One of the smallest light bulbs in the history of electric power," wrote Blakey, illuminated the words "Clean & Neat" painted over Stratton's bunk, a remnant of the East German filming. The dim light, foul waste buckets that sufficed for toilets, creeping cobwebs, and smell of urine from guards relieving themselves nearby betrayed how quickly even the camp's best quarters could revert to form between propaganda productions.[11]

In August 1967 the cellmates' spartan conditions inexplicably improved, as did their diet. They suddenly received three meals a day, the standard fare of watery pumpkin soup and moldy bread supplemented with meat and french fries. They were taken on "sightseeing" trips around the capital to visit parks, museums, a hospital, and a "state store," now dressed in green coveralls, Hegdahl recalled, "so the local populace would think they were members of a delegation and not captured Americans." When they were given physicals and extra doses of indoctrination, Stratton became convinced something was up, that they were being groomed for early release. In his case, he figured, it made sense for the Vietnamese to unload an embarrassment and trouble-maker; by returning him sound and healthy, the Communists could refute once and for all the lingering brainwashing charges. As for Hegdahl, the repatriation of the "poor defective peasant" would generate additional favorable publicity and restore some credibility to their "humane and lenient" assertions. With guards doling out more food and allowing them outside for sun every day, Geoffrey Norman observed, it was "almost as though they were being fattened and tanned in order to make a good impression."[12]

Both prisoners believed the release plans were part of a general policy thrust and that there were other PWs going through the same "preparation ritual," Hegdahl citing Air Force officers Shively, Loren Torkelson, and Robert Abbott (the latter two captured in late April) as being "on the band-wagon" about the same time. Indeed, the Vietnamese seemed increasingly willing to play the "early release" hole card for propaganda benefit. In the South, the Viet Cong had let go a pair of Army enlistees in February and were shortly to release three sergeants also.* Hanoi appeared ready to follow suit with selected prisoners in the North, using the Plantation as the base for the release operation.

Not about to become the first American officer to go home under such circumstances, Stratton resolved to outmaneuver the "Hansel and Gretel routine," but he ordered an equally reluctant Hegdahl to accept release if it were offered him. Among the sailor's many surprising skills, an uncanny

---

* See Chapters 12 and 13.

Unlikely duo Stratton (top) and Hegdahl. *Right:* At work at the Plantation (Hegdahl in foreground).

memory enabled him to recite the Gettysburg Address forward and backward and to retain not only the names and shootdown dates of captives but also the names of their family members and hometowns and innumerable other bits of information. Stratton judged him the perfect courier to deliver to Washington, unbeknownst to the enemy, a comprehensive list of the Americans in custody at the Plantation and updates on the status of hundreds of others they had learned about.[13]

On 20 August Stratton and Hegdahl were separated. As "a little obedience test" Cat asked the aviator to copy in his own handwriting material that PWs at the Zoo had penned under pressure. When he refused he was ushered to a room in back of the Warehouse, arriving as a guard was unscrewing the light bulb. For seven weeks he battled rats, roaches, and an existential loneliness in complete darkness, his "black bubble" finally pierced by the tapping of Jack Van Loan, who "soothed" him back to sanity with news and "time hacks" on the hour, as he had lost track of day and night. After the punishment episode, the Viets' obsession with Stratton seemed to wane. He continued to participate in the Plantation's media outings, but with less fanfare and a lowered profile. The PW surmised that Cat had had a change of heart, declined to spar further with him on the release matter, and simply began to lose interest in him. "I think," Stratton later reflected, "they had decided it was the end of the road for the bowing incident, that they had protested too much and it was getting them into deeper kimchee and they had gotten all of the mileage they could get out of me."[14]

Stratton would remain a controversial figure even among his fellow prisoners. Despite the scars attesting to his courage and conviction and his unhesitating rejection of the enemy's repatriation overture, there were those men who questioned his conduct and commitment to the Code. The 6 March "confession" that preceded the famous bow, broadcast throughout the camps, became a sore point for hardliners like Denton; Stratton maintained that he had attempted to "screw up the tape" with mispronunciations and a halting delivery, but what survived after several retakes was a convincing denunciation of and abject apology for the dropping of U.S. ordnance, including napalm and phosphorus bombs, on innocent civilians. If the confession seemed excessively compliant, the bow itself some viewed as obsequious and dishonorable, even if it was a calculated and successful ploy. In essence, the controversy over Stratton's behavior epitomized the larger philosophical debate that pitted the hardliners and "strict constructionists" against the advocates of accommodation and a more pragmatic, flexible approach to resistance. Where the one group regarded Stratton's actions as expedient and corrosive, the other perceived them as resourceful and sensible. There is no question that he was highly regarded among those who knew him well at the Plantation—men like Hegdahl and Van Loan—who considered his leadership and performance to be exemplary.* Eventually he won over most of the doubters, who granted that, whatever liberties he took with the Code, he suffered as much or more than most. Significantly, as late as 1970, when most of the Americans were playing out the string under relaxed conditions, he absorbed a brutal beating for ignoring a Vietnamese command. Although, as one observer noted, he would never "completely shake" the March 1967 confession, his stance in fact was not far from Stockdale's and would be consistent with that later approved by a postwar review committee on the Code of Conduct.[15]

Hegdahl, meanwhile, struggled with his own ethical dilemma, how to obey Stratton's order that he accept early release and not compromise his own strong commitment to abide by the Code. After he and Stratton split up, he spent time in solitary, then moved in with Joe Crecca for most of September. During the fall he met with two more delegations, one headed by Tom Hayden and the other representing the Women's Strike for Peace. After a month, he and Crecca were separated when they were caught communicating with the

---

* See, for example, Navy Lt. Robert Frishman's comments at his post-release news briefing, 2 Sep 69, transcript in OSD Hist, 5-6; Lt. Cdr. John McCain's estimate in "How the POW's Fought Back," *U.S. News & World Report*, 14 May 73, 52f; and Norman, *Bouncing Back*, 85-86.

men in an adjoining cell, but not before Crecca passed on the names of more
PWs. Apparently Hegdahl was being evaluated during this period, along with
others being "auditioned" for possible release, and he made the worst of his
chances—giving Hayden the finger, refusing to write an amnesty request to
Ho Chi Minh, and throwing away the extra food proferred him. The Vietnamese were never sure whether his actions stemmed from belligerency or sheer
stupidity. While they pondered what to do with the "dense" enlistee, others
on "release row" were moved ahead of him.[16]

Although they often seemed to be at center stage of the Plantation's propaganda pageant, Stratton and Hegdahl had plenty of company. The paths
between the outbuildings and the Big House were worn thin from regular
visits to the mansion's interview and interrogation rooms by virtually all of
the camp's occupants. As Hegdahl was leaving the session with the Women's
Strike for Peace group, he spotted Larry Carrigan, an Air Force Phantom pilot
captured only 18 days earlier, on the way in. In August American correspondent
David Schoenbrun and his wife arrived in Hanoi* with lotion from Mrs.
James Hughes to treat her husband's burn injury. (Pictures of Hughes's pro-
cessional through the capital with Larson and Shively in May had been widely
circulated, as had reports of his condition.) The Schoenbruns met with release
candidates Shively, Torkelson, and Abbott, then Hegdahl, before seeing
Hughes, who had been trucked in from Vegas for the occasion. It was about
this time, too, that Risner was brought in to the Big House from the Hilton
to chat with Mary McCarthy.[17]

Notwithstanding the opportunity for refreshments and contact with
the outside world, sometimes with a countryman, most of the PWs dreaded
the appointments with the delegations. It placed them in a familiar position
of having to make a Hobson's choice between shame and sanctions. "Of all
the indignities we were forced to undergo," Risner later remarked, "I guess I
resented meeting the foreign delegations more than any other." If the pressure
to appear before such groups was great, so was the lure—not merely cookies
and conversation, but the chance to get a message or a picture to an anxious
family. The Schoenbruns promised to carry out a letter and tape recording
from Hughes for his wife. With Vietnamese monitors hovering nearby (the
Schoenbruns later professed to feeling "uneasy about the whole set-up"), Hughes
stammered through a statement expressing remorse for any harm caused the

---

* The Schoenbruns had invited Ho Chi Minh to dinner in 1946 when David was a young
reporter covering negotiations in Paris between the Communists and the French after World
War II. Twenty-one years later Schoenbrun recalled the engagement in a letter to Ho asking
permission to visit Hanoi. It is not clear to what extent the connection may have facilitated Vietnamese approval, but the request was granted within weeks while other journalists
waited for visas in vain for months. See Schoenbrun, *Vietnam: How We Got In, How to Get
Out*, 177-80.

North Vietnamese propaganda strategy switched from featuring the American prisoners in humbling or humiliating poses (*clockwise from bottom left,* Stratton, Hughes, Rehmann) to staging scenes of lenient and humane treatment *(facing page)*.

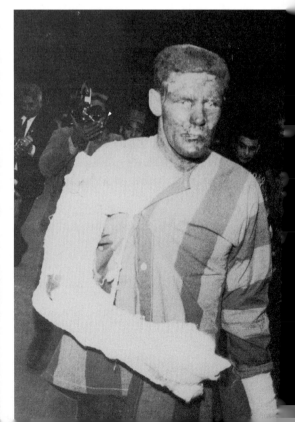

CLEAN.NEAT

Plantation sideshows.
Clockwise from top left:
Carrigan (left) and Baker
feeding birds; Galanti
under "Clean & Neat"
sign; Shively (left) and
Abbott carrying trays
laden with food; Shively
and Crecca playing pool.

Vietnamese people and hope that his wife would work to end the war. The Schoenbruns, moved by the emotional encounter with the stooped, haggard, plainly anguished colonel—few of the interviewees were in such bad shape— at least made sure the prisoner's message was delivered. There were many instances where such promises went unfulfilled, as when a tape done by Hegdahl and handed to Tom Hayden never reached his parents.[18]

In the Hegdahl case, officials may well have seized the tape from Hayden prior to his departure owing to displeasure with the sailor's performance. In general, for all their elaborate preparations and coaching, the hosts were seldom satisfied with the outcome of the staged sessions. Even the successful East German tour had not been free of snags, Galanti's finger-flashing haunting the Vietnamese for months when copies of an unretouched photograph of the gesture turned up in the West. (The picture appeared on the cover of *Life* on 20 October, but with the PW's hands delicately air-brushed. "One of my relatives thought my fingers had been cut off," Galanti later learned.)[19] Frustration over the pace of the propaganda campaign may have contributed to one of the rare incidents where a Plantation internee was tortured, when Larry Carrigan was practically drawn and quartered for a subpar perfor- mance before the Women's Strike for Peace members.

Carrigan had already cheated death by the time he followed Hegdahl in to meet with the women's delegation. Shot down in the vicinity of two other pilots, Air Force Capts. Charles Lane and Ronald Sittner, whose bodies were never recovered, Carrigan had weathered a close call at capture when a Vietnam- ese boy grabbed his .38 pistol, aimed it at him, and pulled the trigger twice. A guard, fortunately, had unloaded the gun moments earlier. After enduring a punishing initial interrogation at Hoa Lo, he entered Plantation with cell- mate and senior Air Force Maj. Elmo Baker, yet another 23 August casualty. Carrigan agreed to meet with the women, three Americans, in return for their carrying a letter home to his family. Baker advised him that he saw nothing wrong with the arrangement so long as the letter contained no antiwar refer- ences that could be exploited by the enemy.

Not only did the aviator not admit to or apologize for bombing civilians, he vigorously defended the U.S. strikes, telling the delegates that aircrews had specific orders to avoid civilian areas and were disciplined for straying from strictly military targets. A flustered and furious Cat pulled the plug on the meeting, hustled Carrigan back to his room, and the next day had the prisoner returned to the Hilton for correction. After being beaten with fists and sticks, he was subjected to an excruciating, gallows-like version of the rope torture, whereby he was hoisted onto a ceiling hook and then had a supporting stool kicked out from under him. Carrigan dangled in blinding pain, the ligaments in his shoulders stretched to tearing, until he was brought to his feet—only to have the sequence repeated. When finally unharnessed, he was dragged back to Plantation and left in leg irons, cursing the visitors whom he held responsible for his ordeal and vowing never again to be set up that way.[20]

Cat seemed genuinely vexed by Carrigan's behavior. Doubtlessly the commissar and his psywar staff counted on a low level of resistance from the PWs at the Plantation. After all, those ticketed to the propaganda factory had been hand-picked and carefully screened—chosen in most instances for their suspected pliability or vulnerability or simple youth and inexperience. The unconventional prison was looked upon by the captors, and by captives at other locations, as "a patsy camp," Stratton later allowed.[21] Moreover, even if the Plantation's occupants were inclined to mount a strong resistance, there were numerous obstacles to any organized effort. The absence of high-ranking seniors or captivity-seasoned juniors created a conspicuous leadership vacuum. Networking and communications were hampered by the newcomers' unfamiliarity with PW policies and signaling techniques and by a sprawling physical layout that, as at the Zoo, segregated prisoners over several buildings.[22] And there was no camp that had a more inherently divisive atmosphere, with easy opportunities for, and rampant speculation about, prisoner capitulation or outright collaboration, especially involving those men being considered for early release.

If for these reasons resistance did not exactly flourish at the show camp, it nonetheless was present, and not merely in the individual freelance defiance of the type waged by Galanti and Carrigan. That it existed eventually on a large scale may be attributed to the determined efforts of an array of both ranking officers and subordinates to surmount the Plantation's organizational challenges and instill some semblance of unity and coordination among the inmates incarcerated there. Stratton, as the first senior at the camp, deserves credit for much of the spadework. Shrugging off any peer criticism that dogged him in the wake of the bowing contretemps, he took advantage of Cat's ignoring him during the fall to provide crucial guidance to his younger comrades, imparting rules and regulations he had acquired at Hoa Lo and the Zoo. "[The other prisoners] needed me," he recalled. "I was one of their main strengths. I had a wealth of information others didn't have about the prison system and what the V. were doing." Stratton reminded them of their duty and obligations but, preaching what he practiced, counseled reasonableness and common sense in dealing with the captors. The consummate "lone ranger," who could be as arrogant toward shipmates as he was towards the enemy, became a steadying bellwether, unshirkingly embracing the leadership responsibility, perhaps as a chance for redemption. Winning the confidence of the men with his knowledge and savvy—admirers said "he had a gift for making chicken salad out of chicken shit"—he capably filled a big void.[23]

For a considerable period that Stratton functioned as the nominal SRO at Plantation, there was actually an officer senior to him, an Air Force lieutenant colonel, who was present but because of poor health and other circumstances had been prevented from taking command. Hervey Stockman entered the camp in September three months after going down with his co-pilot Ron Webb while flying escort on a bombing raid north of Hanoi. A veteran pilot who had flown P-51 Mustangs over Europe during World War II and had been a pioneer in the dangerous U-2 high-altitude reconnaissance program in the 1950s—he made the first U-2 overflight of the Soviet Union—at the time of his capture he had more than 60 missions behind him in Southeast Asia and was flying a last sortie before a scheduled leave to meet his wife in Japan. Stockman's aircraft collided with another Phantom from a sister squadron on the same mission, forcing him and Webb to eject as their crippled plane crashed. The pair were captured separately* and trucked 40 miles to Hoa Lo, where they underwent an immediate and vicious shakedown for target information. Stockman came out of the session delirious, with grotesquely swollen arms and legs, a broken cheekbone, and a silver-dollar-sized hole in his spine that became gangrenous with infection.[24]

Webb was soon shuffled off to Plantation but Stockman stayed the summer in the Hilton's Vegas section, where he might have perished but for the intervention of cellmate Jim Hughes. Hughes, of course, was in a terrible state himself, with head injuries in addition to the burns that had prompted the Schoenbrun visit with medication from his wife. But Stockman was worse still, only intermittently coherent, raving in French about previous Air Force assignments, and pushed closer to death by an allergic reaction to penicillin the Vietnamese had dispensed in an attempt to save him. Hughes nursed his stricken comrade back from the edge, aided by the decent medic the prisoners call "Tonto." The latter halted the penicillin treatment, excised the diseased area in Stockman's back, and gave the PW vitamin injections and a powdery compound Hughes thought to be sulfa to control the infection. Gradually Stockman improved.[25]

Possibly because of their feeble condition, which limited any threat they posed, Stockman and Hughes, both 05s, were among the few seniors of that rank the Vietnamese moved to the Plantation. For almost two months after their arrival, the Vietnamese appear to have kept them out of contact with the other prisoners. Only after they were shifted in the fall from an isolated corner

---

* Only several hundred yards apart when taken into custody, they would not see each other again until reunited in cell 7 of Camp Unity in December 1970. The two men in the other aircraft were killed in the collision.

cell in the Gunshed to a more central location at the Warehouse were they able to get out their identities and receive PW policies and communication instruction (as they had been separated from comrades at Vegas as well). One of the Plantation's juniors remembered seeing two new guys "who were really torn up. Multiple scars showed that bamboo stakes had impaled their feet [an unwarranted assumption as it turned out], and their macabre bodies seemed close to starvation . . . . Some of us took terrifying risks to open communications with these men. If they left clothing on the line, we clipped notes inside a shirt-sleeve. If they went out to bathe or to dump their *bo's*, we shouted, 'Name! Name!'" When Stockman and Hughes failed to respond, partly out of apprehensiveness and partly from unaccustomedness, the juniors persisted until contact was finally made.[26]

Stockman, senior to Hughes by date of rank, learned he was SRO in November, yet deferred to the incumbent Stratton while he continued to recuperate. Hughes, apparently, was either too infirm himself or too compromised by his "delegation" activity to take over. Explaining his delay in assuming command, Stockman later said "he was inhibited rather significantly by his own shame at being broken and to a greater degree by the problems of his roommate, who was deeply involved with extricating himself from Vietnamese exploitation and did not want his plight known to his fellow prisoners . . . ." Whatever the reasons for the 05s' taking a back seat, Stratton was still effectively exercising authority, and was still recognized by most of the men as the camp leader, into 1968. Despite an inauspicious debut caused largely by illness and injury, Stockman eventually accepted the leadership reins and, according to Charles Plumb, "took charge with enthusiasm and competence."[27]

No organized resistance could have been achieved at the Plantation without finding a way around the communication hurdles. As usual, "like vines reaching for the light,"[28] the prisoners persevered and ultimately prevailed in their obsession to reach one another. For most of 1967 the Vietnamese were able to keep PW contacts to a minimum by dividing the prisoners among the compound's several facilities and setting aside empty cells within a building as "circuit-breakers." However, as more men arrived with knowledge of the tap code and as space shortages elsewhere required officials to fill the Plantation's cellblocks, it became ever more difficult for the enemy to prevent communication links. Lightly staffed compared with other camps, the Plantation was normally attended by 20 to 30 guards, with only a quarter on duty at any given time,[29] so that the Vietnamese would be hard pressed to tighten surveillance once the communication gates were opened.

The five-stall bath area in the southeast corner of the camp offered a convenient clearinghouse for messages. Stratton used Hegdahl as a mailman, the sailor's simpleton guise lulling guards into allowing him to roam the grounds, supposedly on errands, at long stretches with little supervision; not only did Hegdahl pass notes back and forth, but he scrounged food, cigarettes, writing implements, and other supplies and while ostensibly cleaning, dispatched news in code with the sweeps of his broom. From his command post in cell 1 of the Warehouse, Stratton relied on Arv Chauncey, an expert tapper—a later cellmate described him as having "great ears and fine hands"—to relay his directives; when Chauncey's knuckles became raw from pounding the wall, the PW switched to a nail, which he handled like a telegraph key.[30]

When Stockman took over from Stratton, he benefited from having four neighbors—Anderson, Milligan, McManus, and Mechenbier—who had been assigned dishwashing duty by the Vietnamese and thus, like Hegdahl, enjoyed enhanced mobility and access. Like Hegdahl, they acted as messengers, identified newcomers, and reported on any unusual activity. The quartet informed Stockman that he was SRO and that Larson (another 05), and not Hughes, was next in seniority. Stockman subsequently named Larson Operations Officer; Stratton, North End SRO and Senior Naval Officer; and Van Loan, jailed in an optimum location at the south end of the Warehouse, South End SRO and Communications Officer. The dishwashers, who codenamed themselves "The Rogues" and their commander "Tiger," were an invaluable source of intelligence to which Stockman later acknowledged a great debt.[31]

Two other juniors who merit recognition for helping to shred or at least shrink the Plantation's communication barriers are Plumb and Mecleary. Classmates at the Naval Academy, they were holed up at opposite ends of the Warehouse. Almost from the moment they arrived at the show camp in July they undertook to link the cellblock with tap and note systems. Plumb was especially adept at scavenging and fashioning writing instruments. Devising such tools had always been a challenge to aspiring correspondents. Stockdale mentioned using "a variety of crayons ranging from toothpaste to 'rat turds'" to return notes at Vegas. For ink Plumb resorted to ashes, medicine, or berries, depending on what was available. "Paint scraped from door frames and mixed with saliva was another concoction," Plumb related in his memoir. "We used our own blood if we had nothing else, but generally found it illegible after it dried." For pens Plumb said they either walked off with ones at interrogation or fabricated them from feathers, metal shards, and other trash. Van Loan, who roomed with Mecleary, marveled at receiving a Plumb message in red ink that had been put together with purloined mercurochrome and sharpened bamboo slivers.[32]

As Plumb observed, delivery of notes was as complicated as composing them. In one procedure, to signal a note drop at the *bo* dump, the PW leaving his cell to empty his waste bucket and planning to deposit a note would carry the pail in his left hand; upon retrieving the note and returning to his cell, the recipient would signify receipt by carrying the pail in his right hand. Each prisoner had a "mailbox." Plumb's was a small hole between bricks concealed by a rock, Van Loan's a nook behind a rafter. Depending on how closely they were being watched, a week or 10 days could elapse before a transaction was completed.[33]

As the leaders proceeded, fitfully but tenaciously, to organize the Plantation and extend a communications net over the camp, a concerted resistance gradually emerged. Van Loan estimated that it was not until the spring of 1968 that the entire prison was linked up, but there were signs of a stiffening camp-wide posture throughout the previous fall. Carrigan and Baker met with Tom Hayden's group in October, but thereafter refused to see other delegations and rebuffed Slick's efforts to have them tape statements. Crecca refused to write any more pages of a propaganda-infused history Slick had been pressing him for; he so impressed Hegdahl during their stay together that the sailor counted the Air Force lieutenant as one of his chief inspirations along with Stratton. Hegdahl and Carrigan both eluded propaganda traps at Christmas. While taping reminiscences of past holidays, the enlistee was asked incidentally to comment on whether Stratton was "tortured" and responded obliquely, using the enemy's own prescribed jargon, that he was not "but he did receive some resolute and severe punishment." Carrigan spoiled a camera session at a holiday service by making obscene gestures until guards removed him.[34]

In *Bouncing Back* Geoffrey Norman focuses on a handful of officers at the Plantation who to his mind exemplified both the tribulations and the toughness of the PWs there and elsewhere during this trying period. Navy Lt. Cdr. Hugh Allen Stafford, Air Force Maj. Robert Sawhill, and Air Force Capt. Thomas Parrott were all captured at the height of the air war in August 1967. Stafford, Norman's central figure, broke his arm, collarbone, and ribs when his A-4 was downed by a SAM over Haiphong. Seized after radioing his squadron leader, "Sorry boss, . . . I'll see you after the war," the aviator sat for three days on a stool without water in the Hilton's Knobby Room, its green walls a "pale, sickly shade" that reminded him of "pea soup or bile." On the fourth day at the Hilton Stafford was introduced to the ropes. Hysterical with pain and thirst, to gain relief he finally blurted out a spate of rambling answers to an interrogator's questions. Believing he had violated the Code of Conduct, he tried to hang himself from his pajamas, but the makeshift noose failed to work. In September he, Sawhill, and Parrott—the latter two also taking gruesome punishment at Hoa Lo—became roommates at the show camp. In late fall Stafford and Sawhill, minus Parrott, moved in with Stratton and Chauncey, who taught the pair the tap matrix. In time Stafford, despite being unable to raise his crippled arm, became a spark plug in the resistance and a deputy of sorts to Stratton during their year together in Warehouse One.* Curiously, when the Vietnamese moved Stafford again, they placed him in a cell with Stratton's other protege, Hegdahl, who would later cite the Air Force PW as a third influential mentor (with Stratton and Crecca).[35]

The end of 1967 brought two more key additions to the growing resistance at the Plantation. Bud Day arrived from Vegas in mid-December and, although not yet having the use of his arms, picked up where he left off, refusing outright to meet with visitors and displaying contempt for the captor at every turn. Bug told him they were prepared to let both of his arms rot until they had to be amputated.[36] Why the "bad attitude" case was sent to the Plantation is puzzling, unless the space crunch system-wide was becoming so acute that the Vietnamese found their options increasingly limited. Easier to explain was the appearance of a second December transfer, Navy Lt. Cdr. John S. McCain III.

McCain had been taken prisoner on the afternoon of 26 October when his A-4 had one of its wings shattered by a missile and he was forced to bail out upside down at a high speed. The awkward ejection broke his right leg, his right arm in three places, and his left arm, and tore his helmet off and knocked him unconscious. He nearly died when he descended into a lake in the middle of Hanoi and the weight of his survival gear dragged him to the bottom. After coming to and twice kicking himself to the surface, then sinking again, he somehow activated his life preserver and floated to the top, only to be bashed and bayoneted by an enraged mob until soldiers finally intervened and loaded him onto a truck for prison. "No American reached Hoa Lo in worse physical condition than McCain," John Hubbell wrote. He was carried on a stretcher into the Vegas section where, despite the trauma of his wounds, he was worked over for military information by Pigeye and Big Ugh. Nauseous, semiconscious, his right knee "the size, shape and color of a football," he was taken to a hospital soon after the Vietnamese learned he was the son of four-star Admiral John S. McCain, Jr., the commander-in-chief of U.S. naval forces in Europe. The captors judged the "crown prince" a prize worth saving and a natural for the Plantation's propaganda stagings once he was well enough to be taken there.[37]

---

* For the last six months, after Sawhill and Chauncey were reassigned to the Zoo, Stafford and Stratton roomed alone. Norman has an interesting section on their relationship, describing them as "temperamentally very different men," Stafford a high-strung extrovert, Stratton more introspective, cerebral, and given to brooding. "Without realizing it," Norman writes, "each man [matched] his strengths to the other's needs . . . . If Stratton was the professor in their cell, then Stafford was the raconteur." See *Bouncing Back*, ch 9 (quotes 131, 132, 135).

The admiral's son did not get to the Plantation until just before Christmas. He spent all of November and most of December in a filthy, dank hospital room guarded by a 16-year-old who was supposed to feed him but who ended up eating most of the food. Although McCain received blood and plasma, he was not washed once in six weeks and endured an agonizing two hours writhing on a crude bed while a doctor tried to set the bones in his right arm without the use of an anesthetic. Finally the attendant settled for wrapping him in a body cast. Eventually the Vietnamese operated on his bad leg and outfitted him with another large cast, but the hospital stay was notable mainly for a parade of visitors, including Minister of Defense General Vo Nguyen Giap, who wanted a glimpse of the prominent hostage.*

Still dangerously weak and feverish, McCain was transported to the Plantation by ambulance and put in a cell shared by Day and Norris Overly, the Air Force major who had tended to Day at Hoa Lo† and then accompanied him to the show camp. Having devotedly nursed Day out of danger, Overly presumably was now expected to do the same for the newcomer. Only 31 but with a shock of prematurely gray hair, McCain impressed Day as "a white-haired skeleton" when he was brought in, his damaged limbs showing faint movement and his arm sticking out of "an immense body cast . . . like a broomstick arm protruding from a snowman." His head and body were cloaked with sweat and grime, food particles clung to his face and hair, and he could neither wash nor relieve himself without assistance. Overly remembered he "appeared to be 'damn near dead.'" The major cleaned, fed, and cared for him, along with Day, until both rebounded substantially during the winter of 1967-68. Day could understand why the Vietnamese would want to nourish the admiral's son back to health but he grew suspicious when guards began to lavish extra attention on all three of them, at one point delivering 57 bananas to their room on consecutive days.‡ The reason became clear when in early February 1968 officials suddenly removed Overly, apparently tapping him to replace Hegdahl as part of the first early release group in the North.[38]

* Cat advised McCain that the repair of his leg was contingent on a filmed interview with a French television correspondent in which the American was expected to say that he was getting humane and lenient treatment and hoped the war would be over soon. When McCain hedged, the newsman, although a Communist, "helped him out of a difficult spot" by telling the impatient Vietnamese that the tepid statement was satisfactory. McCain's wife later visited the Frenchman in Paris and he gave her a copy of the film, which was shown on television in the United States in February 1968. See McCain, "How the POW's Fought Back," 48. A copy of the interview exists in the DIA PW archive.
† See Chapter 16.
‡ The bananas were tiny by American standards, each perhaps the length of an index finger, but they were a banquet nonetheless. Why 57? The PWs speculated that Cat or whoever placed the order may have been showing off, assuming the Americans would recognize a reference to Heinz's "57 varieties."

Above: Plantation seniors, left to right, Stockman, Larson, Guy. *Below:* Key contributors, clockwise from top left, Stafford (note the withered left arm), McCain, Van Loan, Plumb, Chauncey.

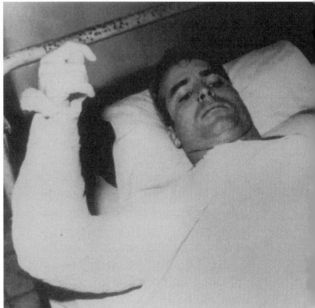

When Day departed the Plantation in the spring as the result of a camp-wide shakeup, McCain was left in solitary, where he remained for the next two years. Although his room was a decent size, approximately ten feet square, it had no windows, only slight ventilation from a pair of four-inch holes in the ceiling, and a perpetual dimness alleviated by a small bulb burning overhead. The Vietnamese made no demands on him until his first summer there when, around the time his father was named commander-in-chief of U.S. Forces in the Pacific, Cat prodded him to accept early release, an occurrence that would have handed Hanoi an exquisitely timed propaganda victory. McCain begged off despite being plagued by severe dysentery, continuing weight loss, and residual pain from his injuries that in the opinion of the SRO qualified him to be the only man sick enough to legitimately accept release on Hanoi's terms. Cat made the PW pay for denying them their coup, singling him out for what was probably the harshest sustained persecution of any prisoner at the Plantation, lasting over a year, including an episode in September 1968 when over a span of four days his left arm was rebroken, he was trussed in ropes, and he was beaten "every two to three hours" until he signed a confession of criminal wrongdoing and apology.[39]

That statement was about all they got out of the "crown prince." He fended off pressure to meet with the delegations. He diverted interrogators with useless information, once listing the offensive line of the Green Bay Packers as the members of his squadron. "McCain had an uncommon ability to endure abuse and [bounce] back from it again and again," Norman observed. He was "an inventive resister, one of the very best at screwing up the propaganda broadcasts. The other POWs considered him a master at garbling the syntax of the camp news." Day later cited McCain's "hair-trigger mind" and "a fantastic will to live."[40]

McCain's resilience was all the more remarkable given his long stay in solitary. Although he knew the tap code, he had little opportunity to use it until civilian PW Ernie Brace turned up in an adjacent cell in October 1968. Brace, just arrived from a lengthy confinement in a series of camps near Laos,* had not spoken with an American in three and a half years and credited his Navy neighbor—the two using their wall "like a confessional booth"—with bringing him "back into the world of reality." McCain himself would later credit another neighbor and communicant, Air Force PW Bob Craner, with helping him through some of his roughest moments.† McCain's wounds would never completely heal—PWs released in 1969 reported seeing him with a

---

* See Chapter 15. Brace made a brief stop at the Hilton, just long enough for processing at the main prison, before being trucked over to Plantation.
† Craner and Guy Gruters, who also wound up at Plantation, entered the show camp soon after their futile effort to save Lance Sijan at Hoa Lo. See Chapter 15.

pronounced limp and using a crutch, and at homecoming his right arm was two inches shorter than his left—but the admiral's son survived to become, in spite of his lameness and relative isolation, a principal player in the Plantation's resistance operation.[41]

If it had been any other camp, the captor would have likely countered the spreading rebelliousness at the Plantation with a ferocious general crackdown on communication and other PW activities. But the camp's peculiar status as a showplace for visitors limited the actions that the Vietnamese could take to restore control. Although they sporadically resorted to brute physical force, as with McCain and Carrigan,* officials could not institute a camp-wide reign of terror at Plantation without subverting the very purpose for which the facility was established. Instead they relied on more subtle psychological means to undermine PW organization and solidarity, preying on the group's inexperience and exploiting the prison's Potemkin character to maximum advantage. In a kind of shell game intended to fuel both suspicion and confusion, they moved prisoners in and out of cells and rotated men between the show rooms and the other lockups, the latter practice especially raising questions among the residents as to who was getting preferential treatment and why. To sow dissension further, they allowed some individuals writing privileges, usually those whose identities as PWs were already known, while denying a man's cellmates the same indulgence. In October 1967, for example, Plumb was summoned to the Big House for welcome news that he could write home, but his joy was tempered by the concern that his companions would be resentful. It did not matter that his letter, containing a poem to his wife, was so heavily censored that when mailed it bore only a vague resemblance to his original composition.[42]

By spring 1968 it became clear to Cat that the hands-off approach was not working and that unchecked resistance at the Plantation threatened to ruin the high-stakes propaganda program. Deciding on more drastic measures, the prison superintendent rounded up a dozen or so known or suspected troublemakers—Day, Plumb, Mecleary, Van Loan, Chauncey, Sawhill, and Stockman's "dishwashers" among them—and had them deported to the Zoo, where they could more easily be monitored and "corrected."[43] The strategy seemed to pay off. The loss of key communicators, combined with stricter

---

* Plumb was another who got mauled. He reported twice being spreadeagled on the ground and whipped with a fan belt, but the "common punishment," he said, was for guards to force violators to their knees and beat them about the face with open hands, much preferred "because it left only welts and bruises" whereas the fan belt left permanent foot-long scars (*I'm No Hero*, 152).

enforcement of communication regulations, throttled the PW network over the late spring and summer, such that when Stockman was returned to Vegas in May, three weeks went by before his second-in-command, Swede Larson, was aware that he was now in charge. Larson managed to issue a few directives before the Vietnamese, as they had done to Stockman initially, stashed him in an isolated spot in the Gunshed.[44]

Sometime in July, with Larson still incommunicado, recent arrival Air Force Lt. Col. Theodore Guy assumed the helm. Guy had gone down near the border in Laos in March and been captured after a shootout in which he killed two North Vietnamese soldiers. One of the PWs described him as "a real tough nut," lean and mean, "sort of short, maybe five foot eight, thin, with a lantern jaw and brown hair neatly combed and parted." (It would not stay that way, of course. He did not receive a comb until 1971; by then his hair was "long and unkempt.") Guy believed that Larson was senior to him by about a month, but the issue became moot when the latter remained sequestered, "jailed in a section of the camp where it became impossible to contact him for guidance." Guy only slowly gained communication access himself, no easy feat with the Vietnamese keeping rooms vacant on his right and left. Operating under the code name "Fox,"* he passed policies by tap and note that held the 44 men (by the SRO's count) now at the Plantation to a somewhat more rigid standard of conduct than had his predecessors. As invariably happened, he would relax his stance over time to allow for the captives' unusual circumstances, but his stern demeanor contrasted sharply with the more laid-back style of Stockman and Stratton.[45]

The most troublesome problem Guy inherited was the "early release" matter. Although Stratton, Hegdahl, McCain, and a number of other prime prospects courted by the Vietnamese had summarily rejected the repatriation proposition and were successful in either repulsing or stalling the enemy's solicitations, there were comrades—weaker of will or body, or simply insensitive to the principle involved—who were proving to be more susceptible to the offer. Their staged liberation, leaders on both sides knew, not only would give an immense boost to Hanoi's propaganda campaign but also would have a profoundly unsettling impact internally on prisoner morale and cohesion. Stratton had encouraged Hegdahl alone to accept early release, but he was concerned enough about the implications of the practice generally that he

---

* Guy went by other designations as well. A. J. Myers's history of Plantation has him as "Dry Fly," and at a later point he was known as "Hawk." As with Stratton's dual names, "Beak" (for his generous nose) and "Wizard" or "Whiz" (for his canniness), signatures were periodically changed to keep the enemy guessing. See Myers, *Vietnam POW Camp Histories*, vol 1, 273; Grant, *Survivors*, 303; Blakey, *Prisoner at War*, 237; Hubbell, *P.O.W.*, 506-07. On occasion the PWs themselves lost track of the seniors' calling cards; in a case of mistaken identity that cost Ron Webb, see ". . . But 'Whiz' Was Not Webb," in Rowan, *They Wouldn't Let Us Die*, 87-88.

and his communication partners had made frantic attempts to contact the other parole candidates and get them to quit the bandwagon. The scramble to reach them was complicated by the fact that toward the end of 1967 the Vietnamese had soundproofed the show rooms with blobs of cement, and by the time Stratton, at great exertion and risk, made contact with one of the individuals in the bath stalls, his stabs at both persuading and ordering the man not to cave in fell on deaf ears.[46]

Stratton's worst fears were realized when on 16 February 1968, coinciding with the Tet offensive, the enemy released three of the Plantation PWs into the custody of peace activists Daniel Berrigan and Howard Zinn.* The three were Air Force Capt. Jon Black, a fall 1967 shootdown whose conduct, regarded by companions as craven and selfish, alienated fellow prisoners as it must have endeared him to the captor (Black had been the object of Stratton's unavailing bath-stall appeal); Navy Ensign David Matheny, a 24-year-old pilot whose greenness and worry about an untended infection left him easy prey for Cat's coaxing; and Overly, who had taken Hegdahl's place when the latter continued to balk. The inclusion of Overly struck Stockman as "intriguing," given his ministrations to fervent resisters Day and McCain. Overly maintained he had made no special concessions to gain his freedom, but Stoneface mentioned to his cellmates that the major had shown a "good attitude" and Day himself was skeptical of Overly's toughness. It is possible he was chosen merely because he was in reasonably good health and the Vietnamese may have thought the McCain connection would yield publicity dividends. At a congressional hearing in 1971 Overly attributed his selection to a confluence of factors: He "hadn't been there very long, and therefore couldn't tell the whole story . . . . I was in relatively good physical condition. I had been in a cell with two men who had received medical aid, therefore I could honestly come home and say in all truthfulness I saw medical aid being administered."†[47]

The Vietnamese gave the trio a red-carpet sendoff, handing them over to their pacifist escorts in front of a pack of foreign newsmen, party officials, and distinguished guests as a battery of cameras and taping devices recorded the

---

* Berrigan, a Jesuit priest, and Zinn, a professor of history and government at Boston University, were recruited as emissaries by David Dellinger and the National Mobilization Committee to End the War in Vietnam, which had been approached by the Vietnamese to act as an intermediary. The envoys got into a bitter dispute with U.S. officials over whether the servicemen would fly home on commercial or military aircraft. On the complex negotiations leading up to the release and then the altercation over departure and homecoming arrangements, see Project CHECO Report, 15 Mar 69, chs 3, 4; Zinn, "The Petty Route Home," *Nation*, 1 Apr 68, 431-37. A file of newspaper clips, cables, and other materials pertaining to the incident is in OSD Hist.
† Overly would strenuously defend his captivity conduct and acceptance of release against insinuations that he had been derelict or disloyal. See memo Overly for ATC/DP, nd [1974], sub: Correction of Officer Effectiveness Report.

proceedings. Their mates were tipped off to the timing of the event when Hegdahl saw a prepared news bulletin and Arv Chauncey (who had not yet left for the Zoo) was told that morning to sweep the courtyard "cleaner than usual." Many of the men who had a view of the Big House were able to watch a portion of the program through cracks in their cell walls or under their doors. The rest, as well as colleagues in other prisons, would hear broadcasts of the ceremonies and follow-up press conference on camp radios over the next several days, including taped statements of contrition the parolees were required to make as a condition of their release. Over the long haul the releases would benefit those left behind, as Hegdahl had managed to pass Matheny a large chunk of his PW name bank (the ensign memorized at least 70 of them before Hegdahl was removed for Overly), which would be conveyed to sources in Washington upon the group's repatriation.* The immediate effect, however, was a devastating blow to PW morale, at the Plantation and throughout the system.[48]

At Plantation, the releasees were referred to as "M-O-B" or "Mob," an acronym for the first letters of their last names. Contempt for the trio was mingled with envy and testy debate over whether they had actually violated the Code of Conduct, which explicitly forbade "parole" but was vague on the broader issue of selective release. Most of their fellow prisoners believed they had transgressed. Alcatraz's small band of hardliners was "shocked" to hear the farewell messages, Stockdale recalled, and decided that the men had clearly broken faith and ranks and accepted what amounted to a grant of amnesty in exchange for collaboration. The Alcatraz Gang labeled the tactic the "Fink Release Program" and denounced its beneficiaries as "slimies," terms that would soon gather currency at the other camps. Denton later commented that "some in Alcatraz would have happily cut the throats of the speakers." Others were more charitable. As Jerry Coffee, in Vegas at the time of the release in February 1968, opined:

> My reflection on that event probably mirrored those of every other man in Stardust. I envisioned myself going home, the reunion with my family, and an end to the mental and physical abuse and the mind-crumbling harassment. Yet we knew these men were disgraced . . . . And surely no amount of rationalization on their part could obscure this fact from them. What bittersweet return awaited them,

* To his credit, the alleged "black sheep" Captain Black also made a significant contribution on his return, providing information on the Heartbreak section of the Hilton and sketching from memory an aerial view of the Plantation that enabled intelligence analysts to pinpoint its location and salient features on maps. Black, with Overly and Matheny, helped the Defense Intelligence Agency compile a substantially updated and more accurate profile of "Prisoner of War Detention Installations in the Hanoi Area," AP-365-6-1-68-INT, May 68.

the boundless joy and relief of reunion overshadowed by the thoughts of comrades in arms left fermenting in the Communist prison of North Vietnam. But I might have faced the choice myself. Had I been standing at the airport in my newly tailored clothes, suitcase in hand, and certain release waiting with but a signature on a letter of amnesty to go—literally, perhaps a life-and-death decision—would I have been able to resist the short-term relief for the long-term peace of mind and self-esteem? I was glad it hadn't come to that. It would have been a different dimension of torture.[49]

Parenthetically, it bears noting that as the prisoners heatedly debated the "early release" issue behind bars, officials at the Pentagon were also grappling with its ethical and practical ramifications.* The Air Force argued (as Overly did) that if a man refused release it might anger the enemy and result in reprisals that would worsen the lot of the captives. In a stance that Stockdale would question, DoD's PW Policy Committee eventually declared that early release was permissible as long as it had the approval of the SRO and was transacted under "honorable" conditions. Overly may have believed he was acting in good conscience and consistent with the Code of Conduct, but by this standard, since he, Black, and Matheny had proceeded without consulting a senior officer and, in order to obtain their freedom, had made statements that gave propaganda aid to the enemy, it could be fairly maintained that they had breached the Code. In their defense, however, it must be said that determination of and access to the SRO at Plantation was no easy matter, and as to what constituted the scope of "honorable" conditions, there would remain considerable ambiguity—and SRO latitude—on that crucial point. Even where there would be good communication and access to seniors, the "early release" question was seldom a case of "black and white," rather a thicket of difficult choices. As late as 1970 it would still be a thorny problem for service conferees back home[†] and a contentious issue in the camps, though the Alcatraz group's and other PWs' knee-jerk recriminations and blanket indictments in the aftermath of the first release would give way to qualitative judgments based on an individual's health, his overall performance in captivity, and the specific circumstances under which he departed.[50]

---

* As they had, albeit involving a fundamentally different situation, when Sergeants Smith and McClure were released from the South in 1965. See Chapter 13.

† The seizure of the U.S.S. *Pueblo* by North Korean forces in January 1968 and subsequent 11-month detention of its 82-man crew gave the PW Policy Committee another batch of Code of Conduct issues to ponder, some of which overlapped those pertaining to prisoner conduct in Vietnam. See Davis, *The U.S. Government and American PWs in Southeast Asia*, ch 8 (ms); Murray, "Historical Analysis and Critical Appraisal of the Code of Conduct," ch 4.

In the weeks following Mob's release, Plantation's fractured leadership pre-occupied itself not with their homeward-bound comrades' guilt or innocence but with damage-control measures to limit fallout. Whatever the moral or legal culpability of Matheny, Overly, and Black, the seniors recognized that a dangerous precedent had been set, that an important line had been crossed for the first time in the North, and that once the agitation and rancor had subsided the potentially more serious outcome would be that others would take the bait. As Stockman later wrote, "Once prisoners knew that the Vietnamese promises of amnesty were not completely empty, there remained for some the pervasive thought that somehow, by some slight adjustment in prisoner-captor relationships, though not by a sell-out to the enemy, they might be identified for release . . . ."[51] The threat to senior authority, PW unity, and the whole culture of military discipline was manifest.

To keep wavering individuals focused, Stockman issued clearer orders instructing that early release was to be accepted "only in order of shootdown with sick and wounded first." To bolster morale he delineated roles and responsibilities down to the major and lieutenant commander ranks and made sure that all services were properly represented in the refined chain of command. Further, he overruled Stratton when the latter continued to press his belief that Hegdahl would be a more valuable asset for the PWs back in Washington. Stratton, for his part, transmitted a steady patter of messages exhorting the captives to pull together and put the release episode behind them. Norman credits Stratton (although by now Stockman was firmly in command and by his own account originated the order) with getting through to a new group that had been moved into the show rooms and directing them, "before they had been fully compromised," to reject any "deal" from the enemy.[52]

By the time Guy took over, the Plantation PWs were still trying to shake off the effects of the February releases as well as bounce back from Cat's springtime housecleaning that stripped the resistance of many of its strongest members. Guy had barely arrived at the camp when the North Vietnamese were in the process of staging a second release. Although evidently two of the three slated to be included in this group were "rescued" by Stockman's and Stratton's prodding, a third, Air Force Maj. James Low, ignored orders and was packing for home—along with a pair of replacements for the other two, recent captures Air Force Maj. Fred Thompson and Air Force Capt. Joe Carpenter.

Low, a Korean War ace with a reputation as a nonconformist,* had been captured in December 1967, Carpenter and Thompson in February and

* According to Larry Guarino, "In Korea, he was noted for breaking flight integrity to go off on his own in search of a MiG kill. He was a very capable man, but his lack of flight discipline very nearly got him court-martialed" (Guarino, A POW's Story, 158).

August 1968 releasees, *left to right,* Thompson, Low, and Carpenter at staged press conference.

March 1968. Their experiences were similar: initial grilling at Heartbreak (Low was the only one subjected to torture), early transfer to Plantation, and intensive indoctrination prior to their repatriation. All received favored treatment at the show camp, but, kept under tight wraps, they may not have realized how privileged it was. Moreover, except for Low, whom Stockman had specifically instructed to "alter his conduct," it is possible they did not receive the SRO's policy messages. All denied any wrongdoing, believing they had been chosen at random and not because of any special pleadings or concessions. Of Low, Hegdahl, who roomed with him for several months, later said the officer was "perfectly candid": he "did not like the Vietnamese, he did not relish captivity, and he would speedily quit Hanoi if he could." In a replay of the February scenario, the three were run through a gauntlet of farewell ceremonies, tapings, and press conferences before being delivered to an American pacifist delegation on 18 July. Whether last-minute transportation snags intruded, as the Vietnamese professed, or Hanoi was intent on prolonging the occasion for propaganda mileage, the actual release did not occur until two weeks later, on 2 August, when the party was finally permitted to board an aircraft to begin the trip to the United States.[53]

The latest releases, although less stunning, triggered another wave of tension and malaise as word spread through the camps. Now at the Zoo,

Bud Day heard the tapes on the radio and reacted with a mixture of disgust and sadness, ashamed that the three were all Air Force officers. Guy remembered seeing Plantation inmates shuffling by his cell "with heads hung low." To stop the hemorrhaging of morale and discipline, Guy took Stockman's edict one step further: no one was to go home regardless of their condition (with the possible exception of McCain) or shootdown date. If they could not leave together and honorably, Guy felt, "we would all stay if it took another twenty-five years." The senior was fortunate to have a solid nucleus of resisters still around after the spring-summer purge—besides Stratton, there were Stafford, Hegdahl, Crecca, McCain, Craner, Webb, and Baker among others—who remained steadfast through all the tumult. Brace joined the network in October and soon became an active link despite Vietnamese efforts to keep a lid on their "Laotian" captive, whose status was still unknown to Washington or his family. Cat consigned him to solitary and gave him minimal opportunities to communicate, but he made the most of his proximity to McCain, what few exercise and bath minutes he had, and a chance contact with Hegdahl that would later result in getting word out about the fate of PWs who had been seized in Laos. Others who made contributions to reviving spirits and organization at the Plantation during this period were Navy Lt. Cdr. Collins Haines and Lt. (j.g.) Thomas Hall and Air Force Lts. Melvin Pollack and Herbert Ringsdorf.[54]

Except for Brace, the prisoners were allowed to congregate for a Christmas 1968 meal and program that was filmed by a Japanese camera crew. The presence of the Japanese and other photographers prevented the Vietnamese from clamping down on communication and, with PW contingents from other camps being trucked in to the Plantation's Movie House for the occasion, a spate of information was exchanged while guards looked on helplessly. The Communists scored propaganda points by extracting from a dozen or so of the men declarations of gratitude for the holiday generosity, but not without some nettlesome upstaging by a defiant McCain and clever scene-stealing by Stratton and Stafford, the latter pair filmed "dutifully using their middle finger" to dip paste from a jar while decorating the room with posters. In another poster stunt the next month, a group of prisoners, instructed to draw Tet New Year's greetings for visiting delegations, prepared obscene signs using altered Vietnamese expressions that wound up prominently displayed on the walls of the Big House.[55]

1969 started out calmly enough, with the organization again jelling and communication humming. Guy recalled that "as 1969 began we had made a good deal of progress." A communications committee established new drop locations and assigned a new set of code names: McCain was "Crip"; Hegdahl,

"Mug"; Brace, "Stol," the acronym for the short-takeoff aircraft he had flown before going down in Laos. "The POWs and their captors coexisted in sullen harmony," Norman described the mood. The prisoners "were careful not to be too blatant [when tapping or signaling], and the guards no longer tried very hard to catch them." In May, however, a dramatic escape attempt from the Zoo* ignited a system-wide inquisition in which, Blakey writes, "every camp was shaken down, every cell inspected, almost every prisoner beaten or questioned," and painstakingly built PW networks destroyed. Although the repercussions were less severe at the show camp than elsewhere, Stafford, Webb, and McCain were among those furiously worked over for communication information and escape plans. When guards discovered note-passing holes between Stafford's and Webb's cells, the two were brutally beaten until Webb's wrists were broken and Stafford was forced to divulge details on the chain of command, dissembling as best he could. Brace, who had become increasingly "reckless," grabbing "snatches of conversation" whenever men on dishwashing duty passed his room, was surprised he was spared. He concluded his suspected CIA connection may have "worked to my advantage in Hanoi, where my interrogators spoke of the agency with a mixture of awe, hatred, and fear."† By summer the senior's identity was out, and Guy himself was dragged into a punishment session, where he was flogged across the back with a rubber hose.[56]

Even the ostensibly innocuous Hegdahl appeared to be on thin ice that summer. Unburdened by Stockman's order from having to show a good attitude for early release purposes and perhaps tiring of the simpleton role, for the better part of a year he had seemingly been intent on blowing his cover. In August 1968, shortly after the release of the Low group, the Vietnamese had outfitted the seaman with a sailor's blouse and dungarees and driven him to a beach area to reenact his capture for the benefit of photographers. Hegdahl botched the production by grinning, waving—Hubbell portrays him "striding ashore as though he were MacArthur returning to the Philippines"—then overpowering the guard-actors until, after several takes, some of which required him to change into a flight suit and helmet, the director canceled the shooting. He spent the fall and winter in solitary, attending Christmas services at the Movie House but having no roommate until Stafford joined him in February.

---

* See Chapter 22.
† In fact, Brace had few interrogations and virtually no indoctrination at Plantation, or, for that matter, at subsequent confinement sites in North Vietnam. Although he had been treated harshly in the jungle, the North Vietnamese for the most part left him alone once he reached Hanoi. One source remarked, his "encounters with interrogation at the Plantation were few in number and limited in scope . . . . One gets the distinct feeling that the North Vietnamese were unsure of exactly what to do with Mr. Brace." No doubt Brace's civilian status, unique among PWs in the North, was also a factor in his cautious handling.

When Stafford and Webb were caught communicating he was quizzed and reprimanded but got off with only minor punishment. He had been trying Cat's patience for so long that the Vietnamese may well have finally given up on him as an early release candidate but for the perseverance of Stratton. The latter persuaded Guy to order him home, and this time Hegdahl, depleted from a hunger strike and the long stretch in solitary, willingly consented. According to Blakey:

> . . . Stratton, using his reserve supply of Irish wit, cajoling, and arm-twisting, had pressed his case; he wanted Hegdahl out, he wanted Hegdahl's names and information out, and that was that. Guy finally relented. And Hegdahl, again under direct orders and still recovering from his self-imposed fast, was less adamant about opposing release. He himself was convinced now that he had a mission, and believed he could do as much good outside Vietnam as he could do inside the Plantation.[57]

On 4 July 1969 Hegdahl was brought to the Big House with Navy Lt. (j.g.) Robert Frishman and Air Force Capt. Wesley Rumble. Frishman and Rumble had been captive for 22 and 16 months respectively, most of that time at the Plantation, where they had met with Italian journalist Oriana Fallaci and other correspondents. Cat now served the men a tray of food with tea and beer and notified them that they would be freed if they cooperated. Hegdahl, of course, had Guy's blessing. The two officers did not, but, unlike the previous releasees, they were suffering from extreme weight loss and serious shootdown injuries, Rumble in a body cast with a bad back and Frishman with a shattered arm minus an elbow. Why the Vietnamese broke with policy and selected the two injured men for repatriation is not clear, although they may have been responding to increasingly vocal U.S. concerns about wounded PWs: pictures of an emaciated Hegdahl and Frishman had been among those circulated by a foreign news service and were brandished by Secretary of Defense Melvin Laird before Communist negotiators in Paris earlier in the year. On 4 August, after a month of fattening up, sunning, and indoctrination tours, the three prisoners were turned over to an American peace delegation headed in this instance by Rennie Davis, top coordinator for the National Mobilization Committee to End the War in Vietnam. Cat hauled in Colonel Risner to participate in the taping of goodbyes, along with three other PWs who were interviewed by the pacifist escorts, Air Force Maj. Roger Ingvalson, Air Force Capt. Anthony Andrews, and Navy Lt. Edwin Miller. (Asked about the quality of the food, Risner quipped, though the joke may have been lost on the antiwar zealots, that he hoped to get recipes for some of the dishes before his own release.)* In a parting shot, Hegdahl butchered his scripted farewell speech and then, as the ceremonies concluded amid smiles and applause, "edged over to the camp commander's desk and stole his cigarette holder."[58]

Once back in the United States, Frishman and Hegdahl appeared at a press conference at Bethesda Naval Hospital (Rumble, in the worst shape of the three, was convalescing at an Air Force hospital in California) and talked openly about their experience and that of their comrades. Discounting their initial post-release comments, which had been conveyed to the press by the escort delegation, as coerced and contrived, Frishman refuted Hanoi's claims that the PWs were being treated humanely. Over the next several months he would elaborate on the prisoners' ordeal in a series of newspaper interviews and an article for *Reader's Digest*. Hegdahl was visited in the hospital by Alice Stratton just as he was about to begin a debriefing session with a representative from Naval Intelligence. The PW wife "sat ashen and still in the chair," the debriefer scribbling away, as Hegdahl related in detail the commander's torture and humiliation, including a full explanation of the bowing incident. All three of the returnees proved to be fountains of intelligence, with Rumble's roster of names turning out to be even more fine-tuned than Hegdahl's. "It was decided that Rumble's list of names was the more accurate," Blakey notes, "and it was his that was used as the 'official' list. Hegdahl's phenomenal memory was used as the cross-check and further picked over for an incredible array of information."[59]

The unmuzzling of the 1969 returnees was part of a calculated campaign by the Nixon administration, begun in May, to "go public" with the concern over the plight of the American prisoners. Until 1969 it had been the general policy of the U.S. government to refrain from direct charges of PW mistreatment—except in blatant cases like the Hanoi March and Stratton episode—both for lack of documentable evidence and fear that public denunciations would provoke retribution. With increasing indications, however, that captives were being tortured and abused, and under mounting pressure from the families of prisoners to take more assertive action, the administration decided to spotlight the issue; Secretary Laird and other officials steadily challenged North Vietnamese conduct through the spring and summer.[†] After it trotted

---

* Risner continued to be exploited mercilessly, periodically turning up at the Plantation on a temporary basis, as if to furnish window dressing for special events. The *New York Times* cited a 1969 interview he had with a Cuban reporter that must have taken place at the show camp, as the Cuban, in an article in which he "quoted" Risner extensively, described the prisoners "watering fruit trees, pruning plants and feeding pigeons." See "Cuban Says 11 U.S. Fliers Held by Hanoi Are Well," *NY Times*, 3 May 69.
† On the evolution of the "Go Public" campaign, see Davis, *The U.S. Government and American PWs in Southeast Asia*, ch 11 (ms).

out Frishman and Hegdahl to meet reporters in Bethesda, the Pentagon had them travel around the country to confer with the wives and parents of captives to offer the families assurances and news. Getting the story out became a personal crusade for Hegdahl. Upon accepting an honorable discharge he toured the nation as a private citizen, discussing the prisoner issue with PW relatives and anyone who would listen, at one point journeying to Paris to petition the North Vietnamese embassy for information and permission to return to Hanoi with a Red Cross inspection team.* Later, in a turnabout that, had they known, would have surely made his patronizing captors wince, he was hired as a civilian instructor by the Navy's survival training school.[60]

Soon after Hegdahl, Frishman, and Rumble left the Plantation, the prisoners there witnessed an appreciable improvement in their conditions. Myopically, they attributed the amelioration to the release, assuming that Hegdahl in particular had exposed their neglect to officials at home and that the ensuing media coverage, headlining their story, had compelled the Vietnamese to upgrade treatment.[61] Certainly Hegdahl's and Frishman's revelations helped their cause, lending credibility to the charges of Communist abuse[†] and galvanizing the administration's still evolving "Go Public" campaign. There is also evidence that the Vietnamese were cognizant of the reaction to the Bethesda press conference in the United States, Brace later mentioning that "the NVN in talking with LCDR McCain indicated that there was substantial feedback through the media on the data disclosed by the released group."[62] However, the Vietnamese had probably already recognized that their "humane and lenient" protestations were engendering more skepticism than sympathy—why else the decision to release wounded men in this third group—and that it was time for a fundamental reassessment lest even their supporters became skittish over continuing reports of brutality. Moreover, in accounting for the transformation that took place after September 1969, not only at the Plantation but throughout the prison system, a far more salient event was the death of Ho Chi Minh, the same day as the Bethesda briefing, a development that made possible the institution of a new regime with fresh policies.[‡]

---

* Hegdahl's trips were financed by H. Ross Perot, the wealthy Dallas businessman whose passionate interest in the PWs was manifested by tireless, sometimes extravagant efforts on their behalf (see Davis, ch 11), including an attempt to fly a planeload of humanitarian supplies for the prisoners into Hanoi in 1969. While in Paris, Hegdahl stayed briefly at the Hilton before moving to a more modest room at a small pensione because the Hilton's poshness—and even its name—made him uncomfortable.

† Antiwar spokesmen were quick to dismiss the charges as either exaggerated or fabricated, part of a plot by the administration to discredit the peace movement and mobilize popular support for the war. See Lewy, *America in Vietnam*, 336-37. One of the more cogent dissents, critical of U.S. motives in the handling of the releasees, was Jon M. Van Dyke, "Were They Tortured?," *Nation*, 6 Oct 69, 334-35.

‡ See Chapter 22.

The Plantation apparently became a casualty of that new regime. Whether its long-running show had lost its credibility or simply was becoming too familiar to be effective, in the fall of 1969 Hanoi's political department decided to close down operations there and move the propaganda activities, on a less grandiose scale, to the Zoo. (As we shall see in the next chapter, the Zoo was one of the more notorious facilities of the middle years. Its reincarnation as a show camp after 1970 was a bittersweet epilogue for those who had survived its excesses in the mid- and late 1960s.) Brace, McCain, Guy, and Larson departed the Plantation in early December, trucked over to Vegas together in the same vehicle, blindfolded and cuffed but able to tap their names to each other with their feet—until one of them started tapping on a guard's foot. A number of the other mainstays also found themselves at Hoa Lo by year's end.

Plantation officially closed in July 1970, its remaining occupants dispersed to the Zoo and elsewhere. As they were being evacuated the inmates were told that the reason for the shutdown was a severe water shortage, but the diminished PW population and the recent absence of filmmakers and visitors were evidence enough that the once bustling camp was past its prime. The prison would reopen late in 1970 for an anticlimactic last act, under far different circumstances and with none of its earlier pretensions.[63]

How successful was the Plantation program? Even granted its frequent clumsiness, mixed results, and abrupt termination, the propaganda pageant achieved much of what Hanoi had hoped to accomplish. The prisoners registered occasional victories and draws, but these were minor and fleeting compared to the substantial political gains Hanoi reaped from the weekly ushering of dignitaries and reporters through the camp, worldwide dissemination of *Pilots in Pajamas* and other film and photo "documentaries," and ballyhooed early releases.

The PWs themselves judged the enterprise a frustrating success. Ho "applied his most creative energies to employing . . . American PWs to tell his story," Sam Johnson later lamented in a general comment that had special relevance to the Plantation. "He danced us across the stage of world opinion and presented the world with the best orchestrated propaganda show this century has beheld." So disturbed were Navy and Air Force officials by the manipulation of U.S. PWs at the phony press conferences that in 1968 the services made curriculum changes at their survival training centers to give more attention to the hazards of such exhibitions. But as long as the peace emissaries, wittingly or not, collaborated in that manipulation there was little the prisoners could do. Even those less ideologically disposed than the

Dellingers and Haydens accepted too literally what they were shown or what they heard. "I found it almost impossible to believe that American peace envoys and antiwar activists could be so naive," Johnson said. "Although history lay on the page in front of them and contradicted Hanoi's claims, they refused to see it. . . . They returned home with reports of prisoners dressed in clean clothes, sitting at tables heavy with fresh fruit." And, until Frishman and Hegdahl gave compelling testimony to the contrary, the peace travelers' whitewashes, and the equally impressionable observations of lavishly courted journalists, were the only versions of the captivity experience available to the public in firsthand accounts.[64]

Contrasting the seemingly benign treatment of the American PWs at the Plantation with the destruction wrought by U.S. bombing, such "eye-witness" accounts gave corroborative weight to Hanoi's assertion of moral superiority just as the antiwar movement was cresting in the United States and abroad. It was no accident that Plantation's prime coincided with the surging of war-related unrest in New York and Washington. Opponents of the U.S. involvement increasingly resorted to confrontation after 1967, with peaceful protests and rallies giving way to violent clashes between police and demonstrators, sabotage against military labs and induction centers, seizures of administration buildings on college campuses, and marches on the Pentagon. The North Vietnamese designed the Plantation's propaganda pitches to sway both the prisoners and their countrymen, but the show clearly played better back home. Even as indoctrination efforts were "failing miserably" to convert the prisoners to the Communists' point of view, Johnson fumed, they were "working splendidly" in America.[65]

Except for the damaging fallout from the final one, the early releases especially proved an effective tool in the propaganda campaign. They demoralized the remaining prisoners, enhanced the political influence and stature of the pacifist intermediaries who secured the releasees' freedom, and polished the enemy's image in a series of high-profile mediagenic displays that assured maximum publicity. Like Plantation's other stagings, they were intended to exploit the deepening divisions over the war within both the American society and government, and to that end they were masterfully timed—the first occurring at a pivotal juncture in the progress of the war (during the Tet 1968 offensive) and the second and third at around the July 4 holiday and in the midst of deadlocked peace talks.* [66] To the extent that Hanoi could control the psywar, it could control the political and ultimately the military

* Predicting the timing of the releases and evaluating the strategy behind them became a favorite exercise among Pentagon and State Department analysts. An example is Intelligence Note 921, State Dept Bureau of Intelligence and Research, 27 Nov 68, sub: Will Hanoi Release More US POW's?

outcome of the contest as well. And, of course, that is exactly what happened, as in the aftermath of Tet the Communists essentially translated a military defeat into a psychological and political triumph that fundamentally altered the strategic calculus for the duration of the war.

Plantation's early releases also had the unfortunate effect of tarnishing the reputation of the men held there, and not just those who accepted the ticket home. Especially after a later batch of Plantation misconduct cases came to light, involving a completely different group of Army and Marine enlisted men captured during and after Tet and incarcerated there after 1970,* by association all of the camp's occupants came to be perceived as somehow lacking guts or staying power and indeed assigned to the show camp in the first place because the Vietnamese presumed them to be exploitable. For a long time even after homecoming a certain stigma clung to them like tar, many of their comrades regarding them with barely veiled contempt and attributing Hanoi's propaganda successes at the camp to their weakness rather than in spite of their resistance.

In truth Plantation's PWs were no more all lambs than the "Briarpatch gang" were all lions. As a group they may well have been more exploitable because the Vietnamese tended to send younger and earlier shootdowns there, but the likes of Stratton and Day were assigned there also despite the enemy being well aware of their cussedness from previous encounters. The camp had its share of callow and brittle members, but it also could claim numerous instances of individual heroics and an often resourceful resistance under adverse organizational circumstances. "Some of our toughest, most gutsy people were in that camp," Day remembered. Citing Van Loan, Plumb, and Hegdahl in particular, Stratton noted that Plantation "had its hard-liners and its soft-liners and an over-all mix of personalities . . . just like the other prisons."[67]

Similarly, Plantation was never the "easy" or "patsy" camp that some PWs at other, more unpleasant locations imagined. Confinement there may have been less threatening and less onerous than elsewhere, but it was not without its own deprivations and suffering: shivering or sweltering in dim, windowless compartments, even the show rooms lacking insulation against the fierce seasonal extremes of temperature; the chronic water shortage that sometimes meant a month between baths; a monotonous, insufficient diet that at one stretch had inmates eating only soup for 180 consecutive days; and always what John Hubbell called "the Niagara of propaganda" that "washed endlessly" over them. Fred Thompson, one of the *indulged* releasees, complained after his return home that the floor of his cell "was covered with

* See Chapter 25.

paraffin from petroleum spills, and it smelled like an old storage bin." Of the shaving routine, Thompson said: "Now and then a guard would hand you a razor in the bathing room. There were no mirrors, though, and when you were about the tenth guy to use it, you'd just as soon not because it would be more of a self-sacrifice than a shave."[68]

For those jailed at Plantation, then, the nicknames "Country Club" and "Holiday Inn" were never intended to be anything but mocking sarcasms. The PWs there experienced their own captivity rites of passage, even if in most cases they were milder. If Stratton's conclusion that "what was supposed to be a patsy camp ended up falling flat on its face"[69] was overly self-congratulatory, it is also true that he and his mates had nothing to be ashamed of and that, on the whole, the performance of the prisoners at the show camp matched that of the men undergoing their own separate tests elsewhere in North Vietnam.

19

The Zoo, 1967-1969: The Cuban Program
and Other Atrocities

I f there was another relatively less brutal camp in terms of torture during
the middle years besides Plantation, it was Camp Hope. Located approximately
20 miles northwest of Hanoi near the town of Son Tay, Hope was no show
camp, rather a nondescript walled compound that had existed for some time
and appeared to be reactivated on short notice. The Vietnamese resorted to
it to alleviate the space crunch in the capital's jails, but it served also as a
means to thin the veteran ranks and further decimate the PW organization
at the Hilton. Opened in May 1968 with 20 transfers from Vegas, it never
housed more than 55 men. In terms of actual physical conditions, it was one
of the most dismal and ill-provided of all the camps in the North, with rats
rampant, cells filthy, and food and ventilation terrible even by the usual
standards; not as distant or as primitive as Briarpatch, it nonetheless suffered
from some of that isolated camp's logistical problems, with meat and medicine
especially in short supply. A number of PWs were brutalized; however, as at
the Plantation, many occupants of Hope were spared the excesses of Alcatraz
and Hoa Lo.

Render Crayton was senior among the first arrivals, a group that included Al Brunstrom, Chuck Boyd, Rob Doremus, Jerry Driscoll, Fred Flom,
Dan Glenn, Bob Jeffrey, Ron Mastin, and Jon Reynolds. The Vegas transfers found the camp's buildings crumbling, their beds nearly devoured by
termites, the garden areas overgrown, and no working plumbing or electrical fixtures. Cleanup and additional construction brought improvements
but conditions would remain among the worst of any of the confinement
sites. Initially the prisoners were all placed in a small-cell area known as
the "Opium Den," but as the camp's population more than doubled by

autumn* the men were moved into larger spaces in buildings dubbed the "Cat House" and "Beer Hall." The new setup, with as many as eight in a room, offered unprecedented opportunities for companionship and communication and no doubt contributed to the name "Hope." "What a Thanksgiving that was," Ralph Gaither recalled that interval of joyous fellowship they shared in the fall of 1968.

The Vietnamese steadily imposed stricter discipline at Hope. A new officer the PWs called "Bushy" commanded the camp, assisted at first by Greasy, who accompanied the original contingent of prisoners from Vegas, and then Louie the Rat, who had been in charge at Dirty Bird but operated in a subordinate role here. Jim Warner and Ken Fisher were forced to make tapes. Crayton and Gaither cited Swindle, Schierman, Dunn, Alcorn, and Jayroe as taking heavy punishment for "bad attitudes" and others suffering humiliations and health problems. Through 1969 treatment toughened and the PWs, perhaps abandoning hope, took to calling the camp Son Tay for the village nearby. Still, whatever its own challenges and disappointments, the austere satellite facility represented an oasis of relief compared to what was transpiring at another suburban prison closer to Hanoi.[1]

From its inception in the summer of 1965, the Zoo had had a reputation as a "bad treatment" camp, on a par with Briarpatch and the nastier aspects of Hoa Lo, with which, owing to its nearness to the city, it frequently shared personnel and programs. It had always had an abundance of "headbutters," any number of whom would have qualified for Alcatraz had there been more room there. The onrushing collision course between the PW resistance and the enemy's countervailing torture and exploitation made it an especially dangerous place in the middle years.

At the start of 1967 some 120 U.S. PWs (and a few Thai prisoners as well) occupied the large rectangular complex near Cu Loc on the southwestern edge of the capital, jailed in a dozen separate buildings upon which they had conferred assorted barnyard and other colorful names. The easing of their treatment during and following the Tet holiday was offset by the loss of most of their senior members when a score of ranking officers were deported en masse to Vegas in February,[†] a move the Vietnamese would later regret

* Vegas sent 17 more PWs in July and another 15 in November. Among the familiar names: Larry Chesley, Tom Collins, Mike Cronin, John Frederick, Ralph Gaither, David Gray, Julius Jayroe, Jim Ray, Wes Schierman, Orson Swindle, Gary Thornton, and Bill Tschudy. Some new faces, all 1967 captures: Marine Capt. James Warner and Air Force officers Ben Pollard, Kenneth Fisher, and Leon Ellis. For whatever reason, many of those selected for Hope had previously spent time at Briarpatch.
† See Chapter 16.

but which in the meantime left a leadership vacuum and ruptured organization at the Zoo.[2]

Filling the cells vacated by the seniors' exodus was a veteran group that came over from Briarpatch: Larry Guarino, Ron Byrne, Everett Alvarez, Rod Knutson, Ed Davis, Bob Peel, Bob Lilly, Dick Bolstad, Porter Halyburton, Paul Kari, John McKamey, Tom Barrett, Kile Berg, Skip Brunhaver, Jerry Singleton, Jim Bell, Arthur Burer, George Hall, Jim Hivner, and Dan Doughty. These joined a slew of solid holdovers—Ray Vohden, Bob Purcell, Wendy Rivers, Ray Merritt, Norm McDaniel, Norlan Daughtrey, Quincy Collins, Dick Keirn, Duffy Hutton, Jim Kasler, Ron Bliss, A. J. Myers, John Borling, Ross Terry, Larry Spencer, Ed Hubbard, Tom Pyle, and Jim Young among others—to leave an imposing lineup at the Zoo. Additionally, although they would be transferred out during the year, Dick Stratton, Jerry Coffee, Joe Crecca, Al Brunstrom, and Nels Tanner spent the first part of 1967 at the Zoo. Hence, the PW community there had no lack of quality or continuity. Nonetheless, the departure of the likes of Denton, Jenkins, Mulligan, and Rutledge left gaping holes in the camp's chain of command and large shoes to fill.

The leadership loss was critical at a camp where the captor had a sizable presence and firm grip. During 1967 there were as many enemy personnel as prisoners quartered at the complex, although only a portion of them were assigned to duty there. Lump was the chief political officer in residence throughout the middle period, supplanting Fox, who would return in 1969. A previously obscure major, named "Cochise" for his chiseled features, was military commander. Spot and Dum Dum, known here also as "Marion the Librarian" for his supervision of the camp's reading materials, continued as key lieutenants. Bud Day, who came to the Zoo from the Plantation in 1968, remembered Dum Dum also as the "Goat" because of his resemblance to "a nanny goat wearing glasses." "Dum-Dum's English was atrocious," Day recalled, "and he was angered when we didn't understand him. Like the Bug,* he relied on the 'icepick between the eye' technique, pure and simple terror." Guarino despised Dum Dum "above all the others," saying he was the one Vietnamese he truly hated. John Dramesi knew him by yet another name, "Colt 45," for the revolver habitually strapped to his side.

Auxiliary staff included a quartet of new interrogators: "Captain Midnight," who enjoyed extended quizzes that sometimes lasted late into the night; "Joe Louis" (also "Garuba"), a slow-witted flunky held in low esteem by fellow officers and facially a look-alike of the American boxing champion; the tiny and repugnant "Elf"; and "Weasel," a name bestowed at one time or

---

* See Chapter 11.

another on at least four North Vietnamese, here on one who bore a physical resemblance to the animal and who had a surprising if exaggerated knowledge of naval tactics and weapons (the latter earning him the alternate nickname "ONI," for Office of Naval Intelligence). Finally, there were a particularly vicious set of guards who worked the Zoo: the burly thugs "Lantern Jaw" (a.k.a. "Death") and "Slugger" (or "Slug"); the whip-relishing "Cedric"; and the squinty "Magoo" (he was also known during this period as "Billy the Kid" and "Eliot Ness"), who was so unstable that a number of the PWs were convinced he was on drugs.[3]

As U.S. planes carried out new bombing attacks over the North in the spring of 1967, brutality returned to the Zoo like a deadly cancer after remission. As had happened at Vegas, the institution of a "modified," more comprehensive and stringent set of rules for the prisoners signaled the end of the Tet timeout. Twice-daily room searches, stepped-up quiz and indoctrination schedules, and the ever-increasing pressure for propaganda statements raised the anxiety level for captive and captor alike. Around Easter, Guarino saw Dum Dum for the first time in about a year and noticed that "the change in his appearance was remarkable. He was thinner, black circles rimmed his eyes, and his complexion was sallow. He was a nervous wreck, and we surmised that the incessant bombing near Hanoi had made its mark on him. He was terrified, and we figured he was more likely to use us as his kicking post than ever before." When Guarino, exercising by running in place, was accused by the camp medic of communicating by pounding his feet on the floor, Dum Dum lowered the boom, clamping the major in leg irons and ratchet handcuffs for the next 10 days. Under the threat of harsh reprisal, McKamey and several others were made to rewrite earlier confessions. Roommates Alvarez, Barrett, and Berg were all punished when the latter gave "the wrong answer" to a question at quiz. Fred Cherry, who joined Guarino and Byrne in cell 1 at the Barn, continued to take abuse despite a shoulder that, in Guarino's words, "had no muscle tissue left and looked like a wire clothes hanger."[4]

With Plantation not fully operational until the summer of 1967, the Zoo remained a prolific propaganda factory that spring, the men noticing a "new twist" in the program that was to become standard procedure at the show camp: prior to meeting delegations they were now being methodically drilled with select questions and approved answers that not coincidentally turned out to be scripts for the sessions. In April some 30 prisoners were filmed being interviewed by the British journalist Felix Greene and other Communist minions who followed the script to the letter. Clips of Greene's interview with Maj. James Hiteshew and Lt. Herbert Ringsdorf appeared on the CBS Evening News on 18 July. Others were recruited for the East Germans' *Pilots in Pajamas* production that was shot mainly at Plantation. The pressure to appear in the staged events and to perform satisfactorily was greater at the Zoo than at the Plantation, where bruises and scars were kept to a minimum for cosmetic purposes. Targeted inmates often saw Cat lurking in the background, lifting a cigarette carefully from his silver case and inserting it into his polished holder, never striking a prisoner but always nearby as push came to shove.[5]

The summer of 1967 was awful throughout Southeast Asia, and one of the hottest and driest on record in Vietnam. The combined cruelty of treatment and climate made those months as severe a survival test as any the prisoners would endure. At the Zoo the discomfort was exacerbated when workers sealed cracks in doors and windows and constructed walls around buildings to prevent communication. September 1966 capture Air Force Lt. John Nasmyth recalled that "the sweat rolling off the top of my head and the back of my neck rotted two great big holes" in the blanket he used as a pillow. With everyone suffering from heat rash, boils, and peeling skin, Nasmyth knew "what it feels like to be in a leper colony." Wendy Rivers counted 40 boils on the body of Ray Merritt, including 8 of "one to one and one half inches in diameter" on his head. The heat rash alone could be disabling, the surface itching and spasms of burning pain driving some men to the edge of sanity. Food rations were enough to sustain life but not health, the diet consisting of a little pumpkin soup twice a day, rice laced with impurities, and occasional smidgens of pork fat and an unidentifiable dark meat paste. Jim Bell remembered the water from the Zoo's well looking like the dirty runoff from an American street, but the PWs had no choice except to drink it.[6]

Petty harassments added to the misery. Guards would bring soup bowls to the 10 rooms forming the Pool Hall and begin collecting the first bowl just after serving the tenth. With the soup deliberately overheated, the prisoners burned their tongues and mouths rushing to finish the scalding meal. Even at the height of the summer, with temperatures reaching 120 degrees, the PWs were required to wear long clothes while sitting on their plank beds listening to "educational" broadcasts. Magoo beat those who did not pay attention, fold their bedding properly, or stay under their bunks during air raids. Guarino was made to shave off his mustache. "Quiz Kids," junior noncoms given interrogation opportunities to help them improve their English, became a pestering nuisance. One of the trainees, named "B. O. Plenty" by the Americans after the comic-strip character, so infuriated Maj. Donald Burns that he provoked Plenty into summoning Dum Dum. Burns, an F-4 Phantom pilot seized in December 1966, and Maj. Dewey Waddell, who moved to the Zoo after nursing Commander Fuller at Vegas,* both paid a heavy price for embarrassing the quiz kid.[7]

* See Chapter 16.

Manacles were favored over ropes that summer at the Zoo. Navy Lt. Cdr. Richard Mullen had become something of an authority on them from an extended bout in the restraints earlier at Hoa Lo. Relating after homecoming how they nearly destroyed his wrists, he explained:

> When you get those manacles on, I guess animal instinct sort of takes over. It reminds me of a wild animal caught in a trap. If he can, he will chew a paw off to release himself from that trap. You are really in the same sort of situation. The pain . . . is so excruciating you are constantly working your wrists so that, hopefully, you can even make your hands shrink to try to slip out of those darn things. You are always working them. Well, what you are doing is just cutting your wrists to shreds.

Mullen's wrists became so badly infected the Vietnamese packed them with sulfa powder and bandaged them, but others were left to lie in their own urine and feces, their wounds festering with no care and no benefit of fresh air or sunlight. Pool Hall SRO Jim Kasler was ratcheted in cuffs for a month around the clock except for 15 minutes at mealtimes. He and Air Force Capt. John Brodak had been rooming together at the Zoo since December 1966; Kasler's bad leg, helped by an "operation" in April and Brodak's attentiveness, finally mended to the point where the Vietnamese felt safe again in assaulting him. Brodak, too, was beaten regularly that summer, on one occasion forced with Kasler to sift excrement for rice to be fed to the hogs that the captors raised at the compound. Kasler told a *Time* reporter after the war how Magoo would come into their cell about twice a week and clobber them "for no cause, just open the door, come in and knock us around."[8]

The post-Tet crackdown and the new barriers erected between cellblocks complicated but did not curtail communications among the prisoners. For a couple of months after the departure of the seniors in February the communications net, according to Stratton, "was all screwed up," the "lunatics [the Vietnamese]. . . firmly in control of the asylum for the moment." But a major intercamp shuffle in May spread word that Guarino was again overall SRO; operating under the code name "Prince,"* he was able to establish contact with other building chiefs from his stall in the Barn. The Briarpatch bunch that came over in the February exchange added a cohesive and skilled unit of communicators who helped to get others up to speed. Communication remained "snatchy" and hazardous, but it "improved daily" during the spring,

* Guarino also liked to use "YKB" for "Yankee Boss," as distinct from the "GKB" used in tap parlance to identify the "gook boss." See Guarino, *A POW's Story*, 190.

Mullen remembering "talking walls, hand signals, coughs, [and] scrapes," which he described as both "lifelines" for the ailing and lonely and "news networks communicating instructions, policies, and the trivia that passed for major events." On the use of coughing to convey messages, Nasmyth recalled, "The whole damn camp sounded like it had TB."[9]

As usual there were certain key individuals whose creativity and risk-taking kept the channels open when they threatened to close. Nasmyth cited Dick Bolstad for introducing the sweeping technique to the Zoo. Guarino would credit Dan Doughty with spending "literally hundreds of hours lying on the floor, peeking under the door to make sure the hall was clear of guards." Alvarez referred to James Connell as "a uniquely brave Navy lieutenant" who while holed up in a "dark sweat box" of a cell in solitary confinement at the Gatehouse, near the camp's main entrance, "was like a sentry, keeping a watchful eye on all movements in and out of the Zoo." "His window on the world," Alvarez noted in his memoir, "was through a peephole in the door and, higher up, through the single ventilation space no bigger than a regular brick. Despite these handicaps, he triumphed as the self-appointed nerve center of our communications network . . . ." Ed Davis later confirmed Connell's central role, saying that a feigned disability—he had faked the incapacitation of his hands in order to avoid writing propaganda statements—lulled the Vietnamese into putting him in a less secure cell that gave him "the widest field of vision in the camp." Alvarez remembered Connell relying on the sign language alphabet the PWs used when in visual contact with one another, and Davis heard him tapping "as fast as a telegraph" on other occasions. Another colleague said, "He had a remarkable memory. We could pass to him as many as twenty-eight to thirty messages a day by brooms, hand signals, and even coughs whenever we came anywhere near his building. And he would remember them all. In turn, he would pass this information on through notes he placed under his toilet bowl . . . ." Guarino would laud him as "my worldwide connection." It was fortunate that Connell's heroics as the linchpin of the Zoo's communication system would become known through the acknowledgements of grateful comrades, since he would not survive captivity to tell his own story.[10]

Although by 1967 the Vietnamese were familiar with the tap code and its many variations and by late spring had begun again to enforce communication prohibitions, their efforts to stifle the contacts produced mounting frustration that culminated during the summer in a concerted purge similar to what occurred about the same time at Vegas. The inquisition began in July at the Office and did not end until it reached the Garage in October, the enemy isolating and torturing selected PWs in each building until they surrendered details of the organization or confessed guilt. Like Kasler (code-named "Baron") at Pool Hall, Pigsty SRO Maj. Albert Runyan ("Jason") was subjected to 30 days in manacles. Rivers was fingered as a ringleader and for a week received daily a half-dozen slaps to the side of his head "as hard as the guard could hit," the blows on the last day administered with a clenched fist and breaking the aviator's jaw. A prisoner knew it was his turn when a "small caravan" of guards arrived at his building and he heard a key clattering in his lock.[11]

Some of the worst pounding was reserved for Guarino and his deputy, Ron Byrne. Already 43 years old when captured, almost grounded by ulcers and other medical problems, entering his third year of incarceration in the summer of 1967, Guarino was not among the halest of the PWs, but what he lacked in physical strength he made up for in fortitude. He was a realist who encouraged the prisoners to maintain a low profile, not recklessly antagonize their keepers, and concede useless information to interrogators, believing, for instance, "there was no point in being tortured for telling the price of our tennis rackets," an "icebreaker" question asked of some new shootdowns. Yet he could not refrain from tweaking the Vietnamese himself, letting his mustache grow back "just to test them, to see if I could get away with it." Over the span of the captivity experience he would take as much torture as anyone. In a postwar interview Bud Day called him "a very tough guy" who "set the example continually." Later Day would go so far as to declare him "the greatest hero" of them all in terms of the sheer amount of punishment he endured "at the helm of a hard camp longer than any other officer in the system." Of Byrne, who combined strong religious faith with a stalwart sense of duty and honor, Guarino would write, "It was a fantastic stroke of good luck for me to get him as a cell mate."[12]

The two leaders got their comeuppance in August. Hauled off to the "Hut" (most of the PWs knew it as the "Gym"), a small building in the southeast corner of the camp, they were locked in cuffs and irons for a month during which they were beaten by day and attacked by hordes of mosquitos at night. Going 16 days without sleep, battered until their faces were blue, out of their minds from pain and fatigue, the partners were briefly separated, Guarino trussed in ropes and threatened with a pistol to his head that Dum Dum promised to shoot if the senior did not admit to crimes. When the Vietnamese put the barrel to his mouth, Guarino muttered, "Please, do me a favor, will you?" Byrne also spent time in the ropes before they were thrown back together, then separated again. The daily beatings stopped in November but Guarino would remain clamped in leg irons at night for another six months, the shackles not removed until April 1968.[13]

The communications purge was effective in putting Guarino, Byrne, and the building SROs out of commission for several months. In the meantime new faces turned up at the Zoo—on both sides of the bars. In late August prisoners noticed a tall Caucasian getting out of a chauffered car and being warmly embraced by Lump, the mystery man shortly to launch his own personal reign of terror and to become one of the archvillains of the captivity story. Among the Americans, newcomers to the camp in 1967 included Air Force Capt. Joseph Abbott, shot down the same day as and not far from Lt. Robert Abbott (both were flying F-105s out of Thailand), the latter winding up at Plantation;* 40-year-old Air Force Capt. Konrad Trautman; Navy Lt. David Rollins, blasted out of the sky 10 days after his thirty-sixth birthday; Lt. Cdr. Charles Everett Southwick, downed with Rollins while flying a Navy F-4B off the USS *Kitty Hawk* on a flak suppression mission (Alvarez spotted him for the first time on his way to quiz and blurted to his roommate Barrett, "Holy smokes, Tom . . . . That was Ev Southwick!"); Air Force Lt. Michael Kerr, celled with Norm McDaniel, who later praised him as "an ebullient character" and "great company"; and two Air Force majors seized in September, Bobby Bagley and John Stavast. All these men would make important contributions. Rollins survived a low-level ejection and fractured back to become one of the prison system's most versatile members. Bagley would incur numerous injuries, including two broken jaws and paralyzed hands, as a result of determined resistance, and would become famous over the years among Zoo PWs (he remained at the camp through the summer of 1970) for his covert Bibles, written at great risk using powdered tile, rough toilet paper, ashes, spit, and bits of bread and wood. Stavast and Trautman would become much admired seniors.[14]

With the Zoo's capacity again stretched to the limit by the fall of 1967,[†] some of the new arrivals were jailed in an adjunct section of the complex that soon acquired the name "Zoo Annex." The Annex was located at the southwest end of the main compound and, although sharing a common wall with the Zoo, was so distinct in character and so segregated physically

---

* See Chapter 18. The U.S. PW roster contained four Abbotts altogether, the others being Air Force Capt. Wilfred, also at the Zoo (see Chapter 11), and Navy Cdr. John, who disappeared soon after being taken prisoner in 1966 (see Chapter 8, esp. note 25). The three Air Force officers with the same last name created some confusion among PW recorders charged with keeping a count of the captives. Joe Abbott was the father of seven young children, including a son born just a week before the aviator departed for Vietnam. In the absence of a definitive finding as to his fate, he was listed as missing in action until two and a half years after his capture, when his family learned he was alive.

† The Pentagon's POW-MIA staff, which would exceed 100 persons by the spring of 1968, worked overtime as the shootdown toll for 1967 approached record proportions. Two dozen fliers fell into enemy hands in August and again in October. The Defense Department's evolving organization and actions pertaining to the PW situation are discussed in memo ASD(ISA) Paul C. Warnke for DepSecDef, 7 Mar 68, sub: Report on the PW Problem; ltr Warnke to SecAF Harold Brown, 3 May 68.

and administratively that most PWs considered it a separate camp. Opened on 19 October, it contained its own quiz rooms and auxiliary facilities and a cluster of cellblock buildings that surrounded a drainage pond which the Americans unaffectionately dubbed "Lake Fester." Each of the cellblock structures was partitioned into two large rooms that measured 17 feet by 20 feet and held four to nine prisoners. Aside from providing additional space, the new section enabled the Vietnamese to isolate another batch of junior PWs. Its first tenants included 24 juniors from Vegas and 6 from the Zoo. For most of its existence, even as its population doubled, it would house officers of the rank of 03 or below.[15]

Except for those unlucky enough to become the first victims of Lump's Caucasian guest, the fall of 1967 and the following winter passed relatively uneventfully at both the Zoo and Zoo Annex. Food continued to be both scarce and repulsive. Even the Christmas dinner was not as tasty as usual and the holiday in general, Rivers recalled, was "a rather dismal affair," not as special as in previous years. Rivers, Merritt, and Hutton visited a room with a "scraggly old Christmas tree with a few lights on it." Spot was drunk when they arrived, offered each of them a cigarette and a cup of coffee, then told them the coming year would be worse if they did not improve their attitudes. At the Annex roommates Bill Shankel, Dave Wheat, Hayden Lockhart, and Barry Bridger refused Dum Dum's invitation to pray at a makeshift altar. In January cookies and milk were distributed to the most malnourished and ailing PWs, a concession to how desperate the food situation had become, with substantial weight loss evident even among many of the captor personnel.[16]

The juniors at the Annex enjoyed comparatively mild treatment during this period, with heavy indoctrination but light interrogation and daily activity outdoors on trash and gardening details. The camp commander was a young officer the PWs knew as "Chester" or "Sweetpea";* he was a rarity among the system's higher-ups—a soft touch and a reluctant inquisitor—though he was backed by a prickly staff and a malicious pair of guards. Although many of the newcomers were as yet ignorant of or unskilled in the tap code, such expertise was unnecessary where a half dozen or more men occupied the same compartment and did not have to penetrate walls in order to make contact. Still, inter-building communication suffered as a result of their inexperience and the ability of the

* He may have been the same man, also called "Snake," who supervised the School section at the power plant prison complex. See Chapter 17.

1967 Zoo tenants. *Top, from left:* Trautman, Connell, Mullen; *middle,* Southwick, Merritt, Bagley; *bottom,* Burns, Waddell, Doughty.

Vietnamese to restrict the movements of the individual groups and visibility between cellblocks, so that camp-wide communication and organization was virtually nonexistent at the Annex until well into 1968. The enemy's attempts to disrupt organization through a "Room Responsible" program—whereby a man in each cell was appointed (with no relationship to rank) to deal directly with prison authorities—proved unsuccessful,* but for a spell further complicated the PWs' determination of their chain of command. For the few occupants of the Annex with sophisticated communication skills and aware of the quality of the resistance organization elsewhere, it was a frustrating time. Red McDaniel, for example, who had learned the tap code from Ralph Gaither and Mike Cronin at Vegas and been among those transferred to the Annex in October, quickly became exasperated while trying to link up with a nearby group of novices.[17]

Communication and organization, at both the Zoo and Annex, benefited from another room shakeup in March and April 1968 that brought Guarino to the Pool Hall and scattered the other men about in a way that helped disperse news and information along with tap methods. Ed Davis shared a cell at the Annex with eight other lieutenants—Jerry Singleton, Rod Knutson, Martin Neuens, Burton Campbell, Fred Baldock, Brad Smith, Mike Lane, and Bernard Talley. Shankel's foursome joined Al Lurie, John Fer, Phil Butler, Tom Sima, and Scotty Morgan in another building. By May McDaniel, Stavast, and most of the Annex's few officers of even middle rank (among them Ed Martin, Charles Tyler, and Peter Schoeffel) had moved over to the Zoo while a number of younger lieutenant commanders, including John McKamey, switched places with them. The comings and goings left Captain Trautman in charge of 71 PWs at the Annex, a position he would hold for more than two years under the code name "Fat Chance," after a character in the "Smilin' Jack" comic strip.[18]

Trautman succeeded Stavast as Annex SRO after a cumbersome checking and cross-checking of the names, ranks, and shootdown dates of the camp's residents, a protracted process that left some men still in the dark as to who was commander. Orders were disseminated by inmates working the cleanup details, who, gradually gaining more mobility, uttered, tapped, or swept messages as they walked the courtyard and labored outside cells. In a fateful decision, the senior authorized the formation of an escape committee. When guards demanded that the prisoners dig foxholes in the

---

* Early in 1968 the Vietnamese initiated a similar plan, called the "Junior Liaison Officer" program, to undermine and muddle the status of ranking officers at the Zoo. It also failed. See Chapter 7, note 26; Myers, *Vietnam POW Camp Histories*, vol 1, 146-47. Sources differ as to when the JLO policy was inaugurated, some stating 1968 but others pointing to 1971. Most likely the latter instance was a refinement or recurrence.

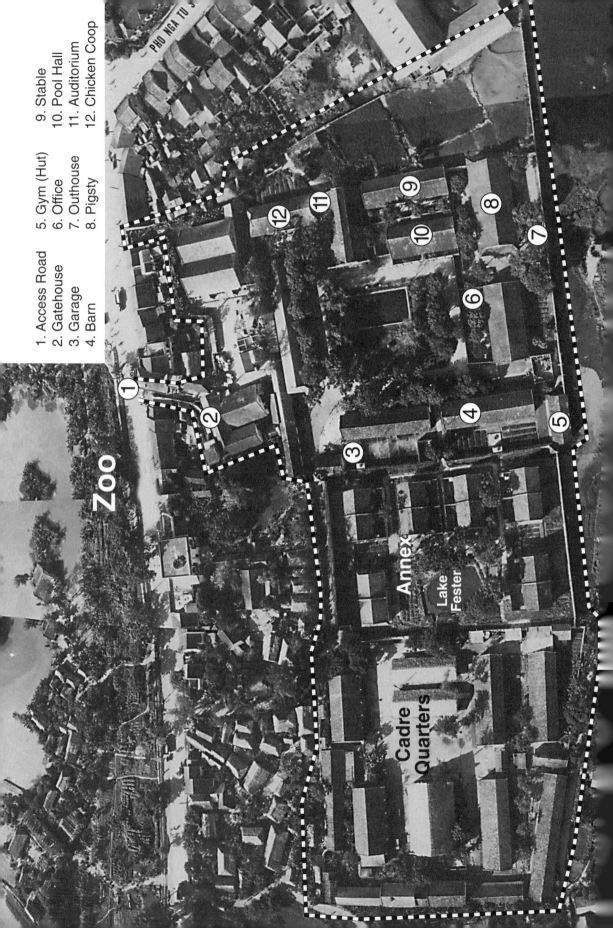

1. Access Road
2. Gatehouse
3. Garage
4. Barn
5. Gym (Hut)
6. Office
7. Outhouse
8. Pigsty
9. Stable
10. Pool Hall
11. Auditorium
12. Chicken Coop

Zoo

Annex

Lake Fester

Cadre Quarters

PHO NGA TU SO

courtyard, Trautman instructed the men not to comply; a potentially disastrous confrontation was averted when Chester let the matter drop. The Annex community slowly developed more effective communication between cellblocks and by the end of 1968 cell 5 had even managed to establish a temporary link with the Garage cellblock on the other side of the wall in the Zoo.[19]

At the Zoo Guarino could not imagine why the Vietnamese had released him from irons only to put him "right back into circulation and in an excellent position to communicate policy." "We didn't know what to think," the senior later wrote of the spring 1968 turnabout, "but it was a good move for all of the POWs, and we made the most of it." The night he was deposited in the Pool Hall, which had the best internal communication arrangements of any of the camp's cellblocks, "the building was rocking; the communications going on between the walls was unbelievable." The network was bolstered by the arrival, nearly concurrently with Guarino's resumption of command, of a band of "reactionaries" from the Plantation who had been deemed too ornery for the show camp. The group included Bud Day, Charles Plumb, Jack Van Loan, Arv Chauncey, Bob Sawhill, Bob Wideman, Dewey Smith, Kay Russell, Bill Stark, Kevin McManus, and Ed Mechenbier. McManus and Mechenbier were soon up to their old tricks, pulling dishwasher duty and using their central access, as they had at Plantation, to serve as a message clearinghouse. Day became Barn SRO, briefed through the wall by Jim Kasler, who was now stashed there in solitary. So efficient was the communications system, Day recalled, "we were able to find out in the afternoon what the mornings' quizzes had been about." Still, direct inter-cellblock communication continued to be hampered by the wide spacing and narrow sight lines between buildings. Barn-Office linkups, for example, depended on the precarious maneuvers of a man standing on another's shoulders and waving his fingers in code through a four-by-four-inch hole.[20]

Phil Butler described the enemy's attitude at the Annex through 1968 as "indifferent," and to a certain extent it is true that life for most of the prisoners at both the Annex and the Zoo during 1968 did become somewhat more tolerable. But the absence of rampant terror and torture should not be mistaken for a condition of "benign neglect." Gross mistreatment may have been the exception rather than the rule at the Zoo complex during this period—limited, as we shall see, to a score of special cases—but that hardly placed the others outside of the ring or out of jeopardy. "The threat of violence never diminished," Alvarez said. "It was always there, whether open and undisguised or indirect and roundabout." "For an insignificant, trumped-up violation," Day, Sawhill, and Chauncey spent the end of April—three of their first four days at the

Zoo—on their knees* until they got Lump's message, in Day's words, that "You are new guys! This is a tough camp. You better shape up!" Day described his turnkey as "a spindly, vicious animal, with a permanent sneer" and a propensity for kicking and slapping. "Goldie," a mincing and menacing homosexual with gold-capped teeth, replaced Dum Dum sometime during 1968 with no discernible letup in meanness, one hatchet man succeeding another. By contrast, a disarmingly relaxed and casual interrogator appeared on the scene in 1968 who immediately got the PWs' attention and respect, even as he proved to be trouble. "Stag" (Smarter Than the Average Gook)— handsome, confident, bright—had impressed Jim Lamar at Vegas earlier in the year as "one of the more dangerous interrogators of all the V I met . . . the joker I'd have to really be on guard against." Making the rounds at the Zoo, the low-key officer interviewed Alvarez, Plumb, Wideman, Myers (who bestowed the nickname), David Everson, Leo Thorsness, and George McSwain among others; when they were subsequently roughed up, more than one concluded that Stag had marked them for exploitation or correction.[21]

If 1968 was unexpectedly kind to some of the Americans confined at the Cu Loc complex, it was hideously cruel to others. Indeed, a possible explanation for the apparent "indifference" that some captives perceived on the part of the Zoo's administrators at this time was that a majority of the PWs at the suburban camp may have gotten a bit of a breather while officials were preoccupied with the torture and manipulation of a small "control group" of their comrades. These unfortunates became the subjects of an unusually intensive and prolonged operation that monopolized the camp's torture apparatus for much of the year and that came to be known among the prisoners as the "Cuban program."

Air Force Capt. Donald Waltman, an F-105 pilot seized in September 1966 and quartered at the Zoo for most of his captivity, was the first American prisoner to meet "Fidel." The date was 20 August 1967. Waltman was escorted to interrogation by a guard who told him he was about to be quizzed by "camp authorities." With Lump were two foreigners—a principal interrogator in his thirties who stood over six feet tall and weighed about 180

* Day felt that the kneeling torture "was probably the most painful and insidious long-term . . . that could be applied." "The sensitive human knee," he observed in his memoir, "when in contact with rough, bare concrete for a long period of time, generates great pain. The best comparison is that of driving a long nail under the kneecap. In addition to this pain was the pain of holding myself rigidly upright with my hands in the air. If you have any doubts about this, try kneeling on a broomstick with your hands in the air for fifteen or twenty minutes" (*Return With Honor*, 141).

pounds, and an older, shorter, slimmer man—both with light complexions and able to speak precise idiomatic English. As Waltman answered their questions cautiously, he wondered about their nationality, whether they might be Italian or perhaps from an Eastern European country like Romania or Hungary. Because they had a Spanish accent and an intimate knowledge of Central America, the PWs decided they were Latin American, probably Cubans, although they never identified themselves.* The older man became known as "Chico," and a third confederate who would arrive later, a large mustachioed aide to the other two, was nicknamed "Pancho." Waltman returned to his cell after the brief encounter, puzzled by and uneasy about the foreigners' role but not yet alarmed.[22]

The PWs were used to meeting with foreign visitors, but not Caucasians participating in an interrogation capacity and being driven around camp in a chauffered sedan. Even Lump normally rode a bicycle. Guarino when he learned of their presence "wondered what this portended, but put it out of my mind." Another 1966 Air Force capture and Zoo veteran, Capt. Glendon Perkins, tracked the Cubans' visits from a perch in solitary confinement. He initially assumed they were iron-curtain newsmen or a Western antiwar delegation, then became concerned when the same green Russian-style automobile entered the Zoo night after night to deliver Fidel and Chico to a darkened shack in the corner of the camp that was lit up only for the two hours they were there. Alvarez and Barrett got a glimpse of the strangers from their cell in the Auditorium. For two weeks they had collected litter, cut grass, and spruced up flower beds in anticipation of "the arrival of a Vietnamese big shot" or Red Cross inspector. When the sedan pulled up to a rousing reception at headquarters, a scene repeated the next day at the same twilight hour, and in the driver's seat sat a Vietnamese *officer*, they realized these were no ordinary VIPs.[23]

By September Alvarez found himself at quiz seated before Lump and the newcomers. The taller man of the two Caucasians wore a white shirt, pressed blue trousers, and pointy-toed European-style shoes; with straight jet-black hair, penetrating eyes, and an intimidating bearing, he reminded the aviator of the movie star Anthony Quinn. The smaller sidekick—having gray streaks in his brown hair, more even-tempered, and obviously a subordinate—was less threatening, and indeed over the next year Chico would regularly play the "nice guy" to Fidel's bully. As Alvarez puffed nervously on a cigarette, Fidel pumped him for routine biographical information and lectured him on discrimination in the United States and Yankee imperialism,

* During their stay Quincy Collins and Glendon Perkins read a report in a propaganda magazine about the visit of a Cuban friendship delegation to Vietnam headed by a Maj. Cacillio Moss and guessed that Moss may have been Fidel's real name.

specifically mentioning Cuba as a target of U.S. exploitation. When the session ended, Lump ordered guards to move Alvarez to the "Chicken Coop," a small facility adjacent to the headquarters building, for further handling. As Alvarez heard the ominous rattle of leg irons outside the interrogation room, Fidel appeared to overrule the camp commander and told the PW he could return to the cell he shared with Barrett. That was essentially the last contact Alvarez had with the visitors, but it was only the beginning of a nightmarish year for Barrett, who was selected a few days later to join Waltman, Perkins, and seven others as the first batch of subjects for the Cuban program.[24]

Alvarez may have been passed over because of his fluency in Spanish or, as he and some others surmised, the Vietnamese may have considered him "their own." Why the other 10 were chosen remains a matter of conjecture. All had been tortured previously. Perkins would be coerced into playing the organ during Christmas 1967 while photographers snapped pictures of a staged religious service. He was still bothered by burns received when he ejected on the same mission that resulted in Norm McDaniel's capture. Despite two broken arms Norlan Daughtrey had taken heavy punishment, as had Larry Spencer. Jack Bomar was hobbled by multiple injuries incurred when an EB-66 aircraft carrying him, John Fer, and a third PW, Lt. John Davies, went down in February; soon after capture, in a demoralizing sequel to the Stratton incident, he was duped into meeting with agents of Lord Russell's Tribunal.* The senior in the bunch, Ray Vohden, was perhaps in the worst shape of all—on crutches and with three inches of his shinbone lost to a serious shootdown injury and the "amateur carpentry" of Vietnamese medical personnel. The three remaining members were Ed Hubbard, yet another casualty of the McDaniel flight; Air Force Capt. David Duart, an F-105 pilot seized in February two weeks after Bomar; and Allen Carpenter, a Zoo prisoner since November 1966.[25]

Any notion that the Cuban operation was an early release program was dismissed by the poor condition of many of the men and the treatment that followed, which would cripple them further. On the other hand, their vulnerability made them sitting ducks for other exploitation purposes. Bomar and Hubbard believed they were picked because of their background as navigators on the EB-66, a plane whose electronics, capable of locating the SAM sites and communication centers vital to the North's antiaircraft defenses, would have been of keen interest to enemy interrogators. Some analysts later suspected that the Vietnamese had enlisted the Cubans to produce early releases but of the brainwashed "Manchurian candidate" type.

---

* See Chapter 18. On Stratton's recollection of Bomar, see Blakey, *Prisoner at War*, 148-49, 151.

The prevailing opinion among the subjects themselves was that they had simply been chosen at random, either to give the Cubans training as intelligence officers or as experimental fodder for testing new domination techniques. A profile of the group supports the "random" conclusion. The 10 included both strong and moderate resisters and a cross-section of ranks and personalities, with 3 of the men Navy and 7 Air Force. (For a second batch of victims in 1968 Fidel would actually draw one PW from each of the Zoo's cellblocks, lending further credence to the "sampling" theory.)[26]

From outward appearances, Alvarez was convinced of Fidel's eminence, the Cuban's air of authority buttressed by his physical dominance. Alvarez remembered him tramping cockily about the camp, "looking over the buildings like some lordly overseer." He "towered over the short, spindly Vietnamese, making them look like a tribe of lowly pygmies. And when he lounged on Lumpy's porch, sipping tea with the camp's top administrative officers, Fidel looked to all intents and purposes like Gulliver in an oriental Lilliput." In fact, Fidel's and the other Cubans' curious relationship to Lump and their Vietnamese hosts was not all that clear, with considerable debate among the affected prisoners as to whether the Cubans were trainers or trainees. All that was certain as the Americans compared notes in the four cells in the Stable where they were gathered was that they were trapped in a new program that could only spell trouble. As Vohden confided to cellmates Bomar and Duart, "I think we're in deep shit."[27]

Harsh treatment began soon after the 10 prisoners were established at the Stable. For eight days, except for interrogation and meals, the men were locked in irons, an excruciating punishment for those with sensitive flesh wounds or healing fractures. Magoo had evidently been instructed to drub them periodically, serve their food cold (Fidel became upset upon learning this was customary), and eliminate the cigarette ration. For quizzes they were removed to the execrable confines of the Auditorium or Shed (the aforementioned "darkened shack," opposite the Gatehouse), but asked mostly innocuous questions. What did the prisoners think of world affairs? Did they like Mexican food? Did they like classical music? With Daughtrey Fidel discussed the Hungarian Revolution of 1956. With Bomar he talked of the United Fruit Company's exploitation of Latin America. With others he examined the question of German reunification. Incidents here and there confirmed the Cuban connection. Duart noticed Chico write the word "squadron" one day in the Spanish manner—*esquadron*—and Perkins was asked by a Vietnamese guard whether he would *Bao cau Khu Bah*, meaning "surrender to Cuba."[28]

Fidel gradually raised the level of physical violence, but kept the prisoners off balance by alternating hard sell and soft sell, sometimes switching roles with Chico, and leavening temper with humor. To add to the uncertainty, he subjected cellmates to sharply contrasting treatment and would order one beaten viciously while the other was forced to watch. Thus Bomar looked on helplessly as Fidel brutalized a writhing Vohden, and Daughtrey was dragged in to see a bloodied, semiconscious Hubbard. Fidel seemed to have a special animosity toward Hubbard, whom he kept in leg irons through mid-December and pummeled unmercifully, holding the flier's head between his knees while he pounded on his back. The Cuban threatened to break Waltman's fingers one at a time and terrorized Perkins over three months with bashings that busted an eardrum and left him dazed and incontinent. With Carpenter, Fidel took a milder approach, scheduling the young aviator for a meeting in late October with a visiting delegation from Bulgaria, but not before having him witness an object lesson or two on the price of resistance.

The goal appeared to be compliance, pure and simple, and in this respect the Cuban program resembled the "Make Your Choice" program instituted by the North Vietnamese in the summer of 1966. If there was a key difference it was that the Cubans relied on a more controlled and orchestrated mingling of physical torture and psychological pressure, suggesting that theirs was a more consciously experimental program with an emphasis as much on assessing the efficacy of tactics as on realizing results. Fidel had Bomar make a metaphorical choice between a cigarette case, representing cooperation and security, and a flimsy matchbox that he would either crush or push off the edge of a table to signify the PW's fate if he did not submit. When Bomar refused to play the game, the Cuban applied torture cuffs to his wrists and strapped him in ropes until Bomar howled in agony. Finally, when Bomar still refused to "surrender," a guard squeezed his throat to the point of almost crushing his windpipe, "and that," the PW recalled, "sort of speeded up my capitulation."[29]

As the days grew shorter in the autumn of 1967, so did Fidel's patience. Methodicalness increasingly gave way to caprice and expediency. The Cuban took to kicking the prisoners with his paratrooper boots, introduced the fan belt to the repertoire, and, said Bomar, "loved direct hits to the face." With a couple of the stiffer resisters he used the water torture, gagging their mouths and pouring water into their nostrils. By Christmas all 10 PWs had been broken. Only then did Fidel relax the pressure. Over the holidays he dispensed extra cigarettes, distributed toothbrushes and sandals, allowed the men rare mail privileges, and permitted them to work outdoors cleaning the camp pool and digging fish ponds. Following weeks of torture and deprivation, the exercise and freedom were all the more intoxicating, and the prisoners imbibed the sweeteners gratefully even as they knew they were being manipulated. As a reminder of Fidel's unpredictability, Waltman was severely beaten the day after Christmas, such that a fortnight later he still bore traces of the bruises and swelling.[30]

With the recruitment of three more subjects after the first of the year, the Cuban program entered a second phase. Air Force Capt. Earl Cobeil and Navy Lts. (j.g.) Charles Rice and Earl Lewis had been seized in October and November 1967 and were brought to the Zoo from Hoa Lo in January. It seems possible, given activity at the Plantation during this period and North Vietnam's growing interest in releasing select American PWs early, that the intention was to groom these more recent captures for repatriation. As junior officers on whom no visible damage had yet been inflicted, they were ideal candidates. In Cobeil especially, Fidel got more than he bargained for. When his "conditioning" program failed to achieve the desired results, the Cuban reacted with a fury that produced one of the most heinous and tragic atrocity cases in the Northern PW experience.

All three new prisoners decided to feign mental illness as a means to resist exploitation. The ploy staved off Fidel briefly, but by the middle of February he was extracting concessions from all but Cobeil. To demonstrate Rice's submission, Fidel handed him a cigar at the end of interrogations and required him to smoke it, a humiliating certification of his "progress," as he returned to his cell. Cobeil, however, refused to make even the minor concessions that might have saved him. The captain had suffered a head injury when shot down and at least one PW felt that his "mental stability was already marginal" when he arrived at the Zoo. Waltman wrote that "he had apparently been pushed to the point of a mental breakdown at 'Heartbreak' and when he came to the 'Zoo' he was no longer rational," walking and acting "like a 'Zombie.'" Whatever Cobeil's psychological state upon engaging Fidel, it is unlikely any captive would have survived the assault that followed.

Fidel beat Cobeil day after day, convinced that the prisoner was faking insanity even as cellmates Rice and Lewis worried that he was indeed losing his mind. He began to distrust the other Americans, accused them of being Russian spies, and muttered incoherently. Fidel had him put in solitary, which no doubt worsened his condition. In a torture session of unspeakable horror on 21 May 1968, he was trussed in ropes overnight and mauled for 24 hours straight for declining to bow. A couple of days later Daughtrey and Bomar overheard the sickening sounds of a terrible beating nearby. An enraged Fidel emerged from the commotion, spotted the PWs, and shouted: "We've got a fucker that's faking! Nobody's gonna fake and get away with it! . . . I'm gonna teach you all a lesson. . . . I'm gonna break this guy in a million pieces! He's gonna eat, he's gonna bow, he's gonna work, he's gonna do everything we say! He's gonna surrender, just like all of you surrendered!"

John Hubbell describes the scene as the Cuban led the limp, senseless Cobeil into Bomar's cell:

> The man could barely walk; he shuffled slowly, painfully. His clothes were torn to shreds. He was bleeding everywhere, terribly swollen, and a dirty, yellowish black and purple from head to toe. The man's head was down; he made no attempt to look at anyone. . . . Bomar introduced himself, offering his hand. The man did not react. He stood unmoving, his head down. Fidel smashed a fist into the man's face, driving him against the wall. Then he was brought to the center of the room and made to get down onto his knees. Screaming in rage, Fidel took a length of black rubber hose from a guard and lashed it as hard as he could into the man's face. The prisoner did not react; he did not cry out or even blink an eye. His failure to react seemed to fuel Fidel's rage and again he whipped the rubber hose across the man's face.
>
> Bomar was nearly physically ill at what he saw happening, and at his helplessness to stop it. Again and again and again, a dozen times, Fidel smashed the man's face with the hose. Not once did the fearsome abuse elicit the slightest response from the prisoner. . . .
>
> Bomar helped the battered prisoner to a bath stall. In the stall was a concrete tank containing some dirty water, and a pail. Bomar had some soap. He got the man undressed and found that he had been through much more than the day's beatings. His body was ripped and torn everywhere; hell cuffs appeared almost to have severed the wrists, strap marks still wound around the arms all the way to the shoulders, slivers of bamboo were embedded in the bloodied shins and there were what appeared to be tread marks from the hose across the chest, back, and legs.[31]

Comrades pleaded with Fidel to halt Cobeil's persecution, insisting that the captain was not faking and was in desperate need of medical attention. Fidel moved him in with Bomar's group, who tried to feed him through clenched teeth and coax him back to sanity. The catatonic prisoner continued to infuriate the Cuban, who, incensed by Cobeil's unresponsiveness, banged him around some more before finally having him transferred to a hospital for what the PWs were told were electric shock treatments.[32] In the meantime Fidel concentrated on another half dozen subjects whom he had collected for the second phase of the program in February and March 1968 and who were assembled at the Pigsty. The latest additions were Ron Bliss, Bud Flesher, Mike Kerr, Wendy Rivers, Peter Schoeffel, and Navy Lt. Cdr. Paul Schulz, the latter captured only a couple months earlier. Jim Kasler would join them during the summer, so that—counting Cobeil, Rice, and Lewis—this second-phase increment would involve 10 men also.

"Cuban" subjects. *Top, from left:* Waltman, Cobeil, Rivers; *middle,* Duart, Bomar, Hubbard; *bottom,* Perkins, Kasler, Schoeffel.

For the most part, the second group was kept separate from the first group (although they occasionally spotted each other on work details), and both groups were isolated from the rest of the camp (though the other prisoners at the Zoo received enough glimpses and snatches of gossip to know that some of their colleagues were living under very different arrangements). As the Cubans focused on the new contingent, they spent correspondingly less time with the original one, whose members remained quartered at the Stable. Fidel occupied the original group with a set of "educational" projects that had them building an oven to bake bread, carving wooden toys, and raising fish in the ponds they had excavated.[33] Why he attached so much importance to these diversions is another mystery, except that the alternation of relaxation with brutality fit the usual pattern. He was not yet finished with the first group, just putting them on the sidelines while he brought in a fresh unit. Sometime in the spring the third Cuban, Pancho, arrived to bolster the program. A fourth man, whom Perkins believed to be "a technician of some sort," was seen from time to time handling microphones and speakers and may have been accompanied by a woman whose Spanish accent was heard on the camp radio during this period.[34]

Ron Bliss met Fidel on Valentine's Day. Guards shoved him into a room containing a table, low stool, and other furnishings hidden by a curtain rigged along the table top. When the curtain opened, he saw Fidel glaring at him across the table. A largely uneventful "get acquainted" session ended with Bliss being led to a rear area of the Pigsty, where he was joined by the veteran Rivers. Rivers had been through some of the worst of times, including the 1966 Hanoi March. Somewhat superstitious, he had persuaded his wife to leave a lipstick impression on a cabin pipe in his living quarters aboard the carrier *Coral Sea*, an impression he always kissed on his way up to the flight deck before launching on a mission. Always, that is, except on the day he was captured, when he was scrambled for a mission without time to stop in the cabin. He still mused about that coincidence and another that had the Hanoi March falling on his thirty-eighth birthday. To the cell with Bliss, he brought a positive spirit and seasoned judgment that helped both of them go mostly unscathed through a series of interrogations that lasted into July. They warded off Fidel's advances with tact and candor, and, for whatever reason, the Cuban chose not to hammer them to the point of total abject surrender.[35] On the whole, the second phase proved gentler than the first, with less intensive interrogation and less sustained punishment, though the extreme cases of Cobeil and Kasler refuted any notion that Fidel may have been mellowing.

Cobeil returned from the hospital just as the early summer weather turned warm and humid. He was no better for the hospital treatment, and he had several serious infections. "Slasher," the Zoo's paramedic,* lanced Cobeil's boils to drain them, leaving it to his cellmates (he was reinstated with the Bomar group at the Stable) to tend the open wounds. Hubbard and Spencer sprinkled them with sulfa powder from a couple of pills they had squirreled away for an emergency, while the PWs, Spencer especially, who would become the closest to Cobeil, took turns caring for him around the clock. Amazingly, the boils spread to everyone but Spencer. Bomar developed 44, one of which caused blood poisoning in his hand and arm. Hubbard contracted 200 and was in unrelieved agony but somehow summoned the strength to care for himself as well as devotedly assist Cobeil.[36]

The summer of 1968 was as rainy as 1967's was dry. Flood conditions almost required an evacuation of the prison. The steady demise of Cobeil continued when guards enforced the bowing regulation and showed up at the invalid's cell 39 times in a single day, demanding bows both when they entered and when they left. Seventy-eight times that day alone Cobeil was slugged and whipped for not complying. After an indiscreet remark by Bomar, prisoners from both the Stable and Pigsty, one by one, were lashed with a fan belt as they knelt in front of a crowd of camp workers. On 25 June, for a communication violation guards beat everyone again, showing no mercy for Daughtrey's broken arms.[37]

Kasler entered the picture in July. The Air Force major had already endured almost two years of constant suffering from either illness or torture, most recently when Spot supervised a session in the Auditorium that combined cuffs and ropes in an effort to force him before a delegation.† The strong, silent type—Guarino called him "the poor man's Gary Cooper" for his lean six-foot frame and soft-spoken demeanor—he would take pain to the point of passing out before giving the enemy the satisfaction of hearing him scream for relief. The session with Spot was murderous, including a garroting in the ropes and shellacking as he was made to kneel on his damaged leg. But nothing prepared him for the 11 appointments he had with Fidel in July and August, among the worst sieges of torture any American withstood in Hanoi.[38]

Kasler knew of Fidel through the communication network. He did not come face to face with him until 3 July, when the Cuban roared into his cell and as a calling card smashed the heel of his boot into the PW's chest.

---

* It is unclear whether this was the same Zoo medic whom Bud Day and others referred to as "Ben Casey." See Day, *Return With Honor*, 188.

† The occasion was the supposed downing of the 2,000th U.S. airplane over North Vietnam. The actual number in mid-1968 was well under 1,000, including helicopters, but the Vietnamese continued to inflate figures and celebrate phony anniversaries, issuing postage stamps, for example, to commemorate the hyped events. The Defense Intelligence Agency has a framed set of these stamps.

Ostensibly Lump handed Kasler to the Cubans to get him to appear before Spot's delegation, but Fidel had bragged to one of the prisoners six months earlier that he looked forward to locking horns with a warrior of Kasler's reputation, so the assignment may have been planned or solicited all along.[39] In any case, Fidel welcomed the challenge of breaking a hardliner who had defied some of Hanoi's toughest extortionists. Over the course of two months he employed every weapon in his arsenal, from flattery to fan belt, to conquer the American. He deprived Kasler of water, wired his thumbs together, and flogged him until his "buttocks, lower back, and legs hung in shreds."[40] During one barbaric stretch he turned Cedric loose for three days with a rubber whip. By the time Fidel wrung Kasler's token compliance and called off the savagery, the PW was in a semi-coma and bleeding profusely with a ruptured eardrum, fractured rib, his face swollen and teeth broken so that he could not open his mouth, and his leg re-injured from attackers repeatedly kicking it.

Had the Cuban program not wound down toward the end of the summer, Kasler might well have gone the route of Cobeil. As it was, he nearly lost his leg and took months to recover his spirit and strength. For weathering the ordeal with his mind and honor intact, in Guarino's judgment the ace fighter pilot should have received the Medal of Honor. In August the prisoner was moved from the Auditorium to a cell in the Pigsty. In a final exchange Fidel tossed his prostrate victim a pack of Viceroy cigarettes and a package of Juicy Fruit gum, probably pilfered from Red Cross bundles, and ordered him to take them. When Kasler declined, Fidel threatened to resume the punishment and the prisoner acceded.

While Fidel pulverized Kasler, Cobeil's situation turned even grimmer. Another stay in the hospital improved him slightly but then he retreated into his shell again, cursing and spitting at his mates as they attempted to help him. Caring for him became increasingly demanding and frustrating. It required a team of men to restrain him in order to feed him, as he was certain they were trying to poison him. Bud Day refers in his memoirs to the contortionist maneuvers of a trio known as "Choker, Stoker, and Poker" who crammed food into him as he squirmed and flailed.[41] To protect him from further reprisals for refusing to bow, his comrades dragged him to his feet when a guard entered and used a wrestling hold to force his head downward. They contacted Guarino for permission to seek early release for Cobeil. The senior approved the request and ordered Daughtrey, who was known to need treatment for his injured arms, to escort Cobeil home should the opportunity arise. (Guarino also authorized early release for a number of other Zoo PWs with serious problems, but these were precisely the individuals the Vietnamese did not want to spotlight. Neither Cobeil nor any of the others on Guarino's list made it out at this time.)[42]

Hubbell points to dissension among the cellmates as "some of the men, sick and weary themselves, reached the end of their patience with their deranged compatriot." Guarino later acknowledged there were "violent arguments" over what to do. "You'd think that the . . . situation would have drawn the group together, but it didn't." One side argued that they were no longer able to nurse him and that they had no choice but to give him up to the Vietnamese for hoped-for proper psychiatric care. Bomar worried that if they lost custody of him they would never see him again. Spencer and Hubbard volunteered to move into a separate room with Cobeil to ease the burden on the others, but the Vietnamese rejected the offer.[43] Incredibly, Cobeil lasted two more years, a pathetic figure shunted between prison and hospital, shuttered in solitary for a spell, until he disappeared for good in the fall of 1970, a casualty of both Fidel's excesses and his own demons.*

If, as some of the PWs suspected and U.S. personnel stationed in Hanoi in the mid-1990s concluded, the Cubans had begun to wear out their welcome by the summer of 1968, the Cobeil disaster may have hastened their departure. The Vietnamese may well have been shocked by what happened to the young prisoner in Fidel's hands. There were signs that summer that guests and hosts were becoming disenchanted with one another. Fidel was drinking heavily and, according to Alvarez, losing enthusiasm and roaming the camp "sluggishly, like a castrated bull." Except for his personal supervision of Kasler, he relinquished more responsibility to his young Vietnamese assistants. He may have been disappointed that none of his conquests were selected for early release, while satisfaction with the progress of that program at the Plantation may have given the Vietnamese second thoughts about Fidel's "Manchurian candidate" approach. With President Johnson stepping aside and the American press conceding U.S. defeat after the Tet offensive, the Vietnamese may have decided they no longer needed Fidel, or perhaps the operation had simply run its scheduled course and the Cubans were due to leave anyway. Fidel had first shown up in August 1967 and, as Kasler reflected in a homecoming interview, he may have just been completing a "one-year tour."[44]

On 15 August Kasler observed Fidel and another Cuban, probably Chico, at what in retrospect was possibly a going-away party thrown by camp

---

* Spencer visited Cobeil in a hospital ward late in 1968. According to a report by Ron Bliss, Cobeil did not appear to recognize the PW and was "totally unaware of his surroundings," but his weight had stabilized and the impression was that the Vietnamese were trying to keep him alive. Bliss noticed guards walking the prisoner past the Auditorium into cell 7 of the Barn about the beginning of September 1969. Later that month he was transferred to the Zoo Annex, where he spent several months before winding up in a cell at Hoa Lo with two other terminal cases. See Chapter 23.

officials. Kasler held his breath for days, hoping that his nemesis was in fact gone.[45] News from other buildings tapped through the walls of the Pigsty seemed to confirm they had left. Guards let word slip that indicated they had pulled out. The green sedan ceased delivering the foreigners to the compound. The "Cuban" interregnum was over.

The many unanswered questions surrounding the Cuban affair would never be fully resolved. Speculation over the men's identities, origins, mission, and relationship to the Vietnamese would occupy the PWs and Pentagon analysts for years to come.* Fidel remained an enigma to the end. Much of the fascination and controversy that he stirred, then and in post-mortem evaluations, stemmed from the incongruities in his behavior that stamped him a sadistic tyrant one moment and a quixotic, at times amiable party functionary the next. Was he a Jekyll-Hyde madman, or were his mood and tactical swings all carefully calculated to keep his prey on edge? Was his dwelling on Cobeil and Kasler a mark of depravity or forbearance (he had the opportunity to destroy them all)? Was the seeming obsession with the two fliers merely an efficient if grisly way to make his point by (not unlike Cat) targeting one or two individuals for special abuse? There were those participants in the Cuban program who later depicted him as less sadistic and sinister than commonly supposed, maintaining that he treated them no worse and sometimes better than the Vietnamese had.† Certainly there were intervals, as when they were allowed to communicate freely and get valuable time outdoors, when some of the participants understandably might have acquired that perspective. But then the other boot would drop and the PWs would be reminded of Fidel's ferocity and cruelty.

On balance, surely the Cuban visit brought no relief to the Americans. Fidel "inflicted unbelievable pain and damage to us," Bomar related years later. To the prison system's "shop of horrors" (Sam Johnson's phrase), he either contributed or helped institutionalize such innovations as the fan belt, "kiddie quizzes," and "blue book" autobiographies. When he left, the Vietnamese distributed his prisoners around the Zoo so that the details of his mayhem, especially the butchery of Cobeil and Kasler, soon became well

---

* DIA, CIA, and FBI investigators joined in an exhaustive manhunt for the presumed Cubans that continued after the war. Analysts studied stacks of photographs, biographical sketches, and leads relating to Cuban activity in North Vietnam during 1967-68 without establishing positive identification. Intelligence sources counted more than 2,000 Cubans serving in various capacities in the North during that period. See Operation Homecoming Debriefing Summary, AF Intelligence, 23 Mar 73, attach, 4-5. One of the Zoo's Cuban operatives was placed at another outlying camp (Farnsworth) as late as December 1969.
† See Naval Center for Prisoner of War Studies, "The Cuban Program," nd (probably 1973), 7-9. This report cites Rice and Carpenter (significantly, among the program's lesser victims) as among those who had a more tolerant view of Fidel.

known. In this respect his most lasting legacy was as a magnet for the collective rage of the growing number of American PWs at the Zoo and beyond who would come to associate him with the worst evils of the Communist regime.[46]

The subjects of the Cuban program melted back into a Zoo population that approached 200 by the fall of 1968. With no large-scale moves from either the main compound or the Annex since the spring, the PW community at Cu Loc acquired a stability and continuity that elevated the level of organization and communication throughout the complex. The prisoners managed even to hold a mock presidential election in which they registered their disgust with the Democrats' "no-win" Indochina policy, Day reporting that 17 of 18 tenants in the Barn and 16 of 18 in the Garage voted for Richard Nixon. They were angry at the announcement a week before the election that President Johnson had ordered a stop to all bombing over the North. The Vietnamese heralded LBJ's decision on the camp radio, which also carried praise for Hubert Humphrey and aspects of the Democratic platform. Sam Johnson, at Alcatraz that fall, later recalled how newscasters in the North "gushed" over Humphrey and how Nixon's victory made the Communists uneasy.[47]

Through autumn groups of inmates were taken to Hanoi's war museum, visiting the displays at night after hours. The fact that the visits were not being filmed or photographed for propaganda consumption was construed as a positive sign by the men, as was the fingerprinting and issuance of ID cards in November to occupants of the Annex. Coinciding with the resumption of peace talks in Paris, the "processing" activity gave optimists reason to believe they were being readied for release. Day discerned "a little easing of pressure on us in the late fall. It was clear that they were trying to mend their fences with the POWs, yet stay in full control in case . . . [the peace negotiations] fell apart."[48]

At Christmas, Norm McDaniel, Mike Kerr, and Quincy Collins were required to conduct a musical program that put them in touch with comrades at the Plantation.* From their position in the choir, the trio flashed signals apprising the congregants, who had been gathered from other camps, of the status of the Zoo and the existence of the Annex. For the first time many of the Zoo's residents received holiday packages from home. (Even Cobeil was handed a parcel. It included pictures of his family that

---

* See Chapter 18. The musically gifted Collins was a perennial choice for the Christmas show. Guarino said he "could sing, dance, recite comical monologues, and play a number of instruments" (*A POW's Story*, 49).

his cellmates hoped would revive him, but, according to various accounts, the prisoner either tore them up or flung them across the room.) The Vietnamese attempted to extort statements of good treatment in return for delivering the Christmas mail, then relented when many of the prisoners refused to sign the formatted receipt.[49]

Although morale plunged with the realization that the Paris talks— and the PWs—were going nowhere, oversight of the camp remained lax and treatment relatively lenient into the new year. Dick Bolstad estimated that conditions for those Americans at the Zoo early in 1969 "were probably the best they had experienced up to that point." The diet improved significantly for about a month—with meat, fresh fish, potatoes, and roasted peanuts on the menu—before deteriorating again. Several of the men visited a dentist. The prisoners were able to bathe daily and some who suffered from fungus problems were even allowed to keep small bottles of iodine in their cells. Still, Bolstad was quick to add, "all was not completely rosy." The thud of the fan belt and rattling of irons were still in evidence, the Auditorium pens still regularly occupied. Day had gotten a holiday reprieve from a kneeling sentence by faking a kidney stone attack, but Goldie soon had him back in punishment. Others, too, were paying the penalty for real or alleged offenses. Johnson detected officials in Hanoi responding to the political transition in the United States with a shift of their own, hoping to accelerate U.S. withdrawal by eliciting increased propaganda footage and statements from the PWs.[50]

The first hint of another general crackdown occurred in April, when Guarino ordered the prisoners not to cooperate in the production of a new set of autobiographies. The Vietnamese had prepared a more elaborate 20- to 30-page questionnaire with lined spaces for answers. Bound between blue covers, the so-called "blue book" had appeared at other camps previously but not yet at the Zoo, except as an element of the Cuban program. The SRO feared that the heftier resumes would make the PWs more vulnerable to future exploitation. At the Annex Trautman decided to authorize compliance after reasonable resistance as long as no new information was supplied. Guarino, initially at least, urged his men at the main compound to resist and the result was the first torture many had had in months.[51]

An irony here early in 1969 was that while Cobeil's certifiable insanity had been challenged by Fidel, actual "fakers" at the Zoo were resorting to all manner of shenanigans to get off the hook and occasionally succeeding. Besides Day's sporadic kidney stone ruse, John Fer and Paul Kari feigned blindness, Connell the problem with his hands, and George McSwain his own version of a nervous breakdown. McSwain, in the words of Charlie Plumb, was "a tough hombre" who "still bore street-fight scars," rode with the motorcycle gang "Hell's Angels" in his younger days, and "rebelled against anything that resembled authority." A cohort remarked that no one "hated the Gooks worse." For all his belligerence he tried to bluff his way out of the blue book requirement. Curled up in a ball and refusing to eat or wash—Plumb said he perfected the charade by watching Cobeil—he was so convincing that for a time he even fooled comrades, before the unraveling of his hoax almost got him killed.[52]

McSwain got trapped, as did the others, by a dramatic turn of events in May that shattered the equilibrium at the Zoo and that made no concessions to illness or injury. As his buddy John Nasmyth noted, "Unfortunately for George, he picked the wrong time to go crazy."[53] The escape of two prisoners from the Annex during the night of 10 May, although they were apprehended, triggered a fierce reaction that engulfed the entire prison system in a final spasm of terror and torture. Lasting through the summer, the violent backlash would dwarf the scale and sweep of previous purges and bring the Extortion Era at the Zoo and elsewhere to an explosive climax.

20

Coping: The Daily Grind

To a man, the American prisoners of war would rate their introspective moments, the time between visits to the torture room, as often just as trying and terrifying as the torture sessions themselves. Brooding over their predicament and fate, the separation from family and country, doubts about their own standard of conduct and staying power could be as paralyzing and painful as the lash of the whip or constriction of the ropes. Feelings of loneliness, guilt, and despair could become as unbearable as physical persecution itself. Even boredom and idleness, the long unbroken spells of numbing inactivity that might seem to have been a blessing in the violence-filled middle years, could take on their own hellish quality without tactics or a strategy to combat them. In all these respects, battling one's own demons and the sheer mental duress of captivity posed as great a challenge to survival as withstanding the harshest physical punishment. Elemental, day-to-day coping became a supreme test in itself, one that, as Stockdale noted, brought out "the very best and the very worst" in the PWs.[1]

Once the initial culture shock of the captivity situation—the "Alice into the rabbit hole" sensation—wore off, the seized prisoner had to come to grips with the realization that his incarceration in this remote gulag could last for years and indeed that he might never return. As the likelihood of an early end to the war dimmed by 1967, the captives struggled to prepare themselves psychologically for the long haul. The prospect was not an easy one to contemplate. In January 1967 Jim Mulligan "had a sickening premonition" that the war "was stuck on . . . dead center. My gut feeling told me that I'd be a POW for a helluva long time . . . ." Besides a fear of dying in such a purgatory, there was, especially among the younger men, the dread of wasting their prime years. Geoffrey Norman writes in *Bouncing Back*: "Some were fathers of children they'd never seen, husbands of women they had lived with for only a few weeks. It seemed increasingly possible—probable, even—that they would be middle aged or older before they left Vietnam." That they had so little control over their destiny, that their fate could be determined by a random event or fickle individual, Stockdale found most disturbing. "Chance and continual uncertainty," he jotted in his memoir, "are the ultimate destabilizers." Denton figured he had "about a one-in-four chance of coming out alive, and about a one-in-fifty chance of coming out sane enough to live a normal life."[2]

Time on their hands allowed creeping doubts to become obsessions. Mulligan, preoccupied with thoughts of old age and mortality, knew he was "mentally thrashing" himself. He imagined himself the last leaf on a tree and mused, "If I . . . get out of this place I'll never have to go through old age again because I've already lived it." Rallying his spirit one day at Alcatraz, he tapped to Stockdale a warning that the PWs should be on guard against infantile regression. The SRO confirmed that there were men who had lost bladder control and were wetting beds, not specifying whether the problem was physical or psychological. Even daydreams became the stuff of nightmares. Stockdale remembered "one afternoon seeing one of my fellow floor-dwellers, a beetle, on its back being eaten alive by ants. The poor thing was helpless because it couldn't get its feet under it, and it was being slowly lugged toward the doorsill, still moving while the ants were all over it, eating holes in it. I felt just like that beetle . . . ." Paul Galanti and Allen Brady were among a handful of prisoners who were convinced they had been drugged, so vivid were hallucinations they experienced, though analysts later suggested such heightened perceptions could have been induced by stress and sleep deprivation alone.[3]

Some men deflected self-absorption with anger—at the enemy, at the "politicians" in Washington, at antiwar zealots like Jane Fonda and Tom Hayden whose perceived collaborationism more than one prisoner would never forget or forgive. On the pacifists' obtuseness, Ernie Brace recalled the visit to Vietnam of folk singer Pete Seeger: "He was running around singing songs about how grand and glorious the Vietnamese people were, and at the same time I was pulling a worm out of my roommate's rear." Judging from their splenetic post-homecoming comments on the conduct of the war, the captives must have stewed plenty over the unconventional strategy that had placed them in harm's way without a clear set of objectives and with crippling restrictions on their operations. Even prior to his shootdown Mulligan chafed at an air war that "was falling flat on its ass." Sam Johnson later poured out his frustration over American pilots wasting their firepower, their airplanes, and themselves against "junk targets." "The bombings," he bristled, "left hundreds of elephants dead on the jungle floor, but Ho Chi Minh's forces continued to thrive."[4]

The flow of antiwar rhetoric on the camps' radios, quoting prominent United States congressmen and respected journalists no less than the crusading celebrities, caused as much consternation as resentment. Some of the prisoners told their interrogators that such open criticism of the U.S. commitment was one of the virtues of a free society, but privately the growing chorus of dissent left them shaken and bewildered; the increasing evidence of their country's lack of resolve added to their unease. Stockdale worried about "getting left stranded high and dry" by an administration in retreat. As he was about to vacate Vegas for Alcatraz in October 1967, "it was clear, even to one whose only contact with the world was aural, that the bombing raids that were finally doing the job late that summer had dropped off. No longer did the siren scream all day. No longer were the Riviera doors being blown open by concussion." Thinking "the bottom was dropping out," Stockdale was afraid the whole enterprise, along with the PWs, was about to be sacrificed to some dubious moral imperative ("Those conscience-stricken pissants who ran our government had suddenly 'got religion,'" he cursed in his memoir) or to shifting political and diplomatic agendas.[5]

If there was contempt for the policymakers and for the fainthearted among their compatriots, there was also sadness and concern over the reports of America's political and social turmoil. Johnson "listened in horror" as Hanoi broadcast news of racial clashes, student demonstrations, and mob confrontations with police outside the Democratic national convention in Chicago. "It sounded as if our country was aflame with anarchy, hatred, and violence." The group at Alcatraz were walked through a room with a photo display of U.S. national guardsmen wielding clubs and spraying tear gas against student rioters. "I could not drag my eyes away from the awful scenes," Johnson later reminisced. "I felt my chest tighten. What was really happening back home? I recalled the blurred and faded Civil War photos in history books—images of Americans fighting Americans. Could it be happening again? I returned to my cell feeling appalled and forlorn." It did not help that in the wake of the Tet offensive, which they did not know had been militarily inconclusive, the enemy's spirits soared in seeming contraposition to the sinking mood at home. "In the five years and seven months that I spent in North Vietnam, I never saw their spirits so high," Bud Day said of the Communists' morale in the spring of 1968.[6]

Stockdale's and the other seniors' guidance and the intermittent communication opportunities with mates helped to keep the prisoners focused, but what Johnson termed "our sojourn in hell" almost always ultimately led inward and became intensely personal. Nearly every PW spent time in solitary

confinement,* stripped of the usual support mechanisms and left, sometimes in darkness and shackles, to his own devices. Scott Blakey tells of Dick
Stratton's experience in his "black bubble" at Plantation in August 1967
when, on the verge of "striking out," he was revived by "the sweet sounds of
the tap code, the sheer symphony of a hand thumping against a wall." Fortunately, as happened with Stratton, solitary did not always entail complete
isolation, as the "solo" prisoner could still be within range of a communicator
in a nearby cell.† Nevertheless, rare was the individual in solitary who did
not have a version of what Stockdale called "the melting experience," where
"you come to realize that under the gun, you must grow or fail . . . grow
or die." In *Captive Warriors* Johnson tells of fighting off recurrent bouts of
depression and insanity, in more than one instance seeing what Stockdale
characterized as "the bottom of the barrel coming up to meet you." Wedged
into a tiny cell at Vegas's Mint in the summer of 1967, "surrounded by
the stench of death," Johnson recalled "the present was unbearable and the
future almost unthinkable." He learned at the Zoo earlier that year that
"sometimes the spirit can override the body, and from somewhere deep
inside, from a hidden spring, comes fresh strength for the moment." A defining moment for Stockdale occurred at Alcatraz on Christmas night 1968
when, as the loudspeaker outside his cell played a nostalgic recording of the
song "Till" by pianist Roger Williams, a guard handed him a letter from his
wife with the wrenching news that his mother had died. He bade farewell to
her in a haze of memories, then "stood there in my leg irons and wept."[7]

Were it not for the PWs' repeated and movingly graphic testimony to
religious experiences while in prison, it might seem a cliché to say that many
of the men relied on the power of faith to pull them through. There is virtually no personal account in the Vietnam PW literature that does not
contain some reference to a transforming spiritual episode. "Those not subjected to the prisoner-of-war experience may have trouble understanding
how real was the presence of God to most of us," Denton later explained.
"If we had had rosary beads, we would have snapped them until they
wore out," said Guarino. In solitary especially, PWs rediscovered religious

---

* After-action estimates indicated that 94 percent of the PWs spent some time in solitary,
usually immediately following capture and in special punishment or extortion situations; 40
percent spent at least six months, half of these longer than a year; and 10 percent were alone
for over two years. Mulligan spent 42 months companionless; a half dozen, including Stockdale,
Denton, and Risner, more than four years. See Vohden, "Stress and the Viet Nam P.O.W.," 11;
Myers, *Vietnam POW Camp Histories*, vol 2, 152-53.
† Even a prisoner beyond the range of the tap code and living in a darkened chamber could
be dropped a note through his air vent or under his door in the form of a knotted thread that
could be "read" like Braille. Coffee disclosed this and another unusual technique to reach
inaccessible PWs in *Beyond Survival*, 142.

connections that had either lapsed or become too casual: Charlie Plumb devoted two hours to meditation and prayer in the morning and again in the evening; Howie Rutledge painstakingly struggled to recall verses of scripture and hymns from his childhood. Those with access to communication held Sunday church services, whistling or humming the Lord's Prayer and reciting psalms as circumstances permitted. They closed tapped conversations with the sign-off GBU for "God bless you," hid and secretly exchanged makeshift crosses and Bibles, and said grace over the scraps that passed for meals. Those who had been practicing Christians, for example Larry Chesley, Kay Russell, Tom Barrett, Ralph Gaither,* Ron Byrne, and Norm and Red McDaniel, helped others with mass and other observances. As Byrne had succored Guarino through their ordeal at the Zoo, Red McDaniel shared his strong religious belief with the gravely injured Bill Metzger at Vegas, and Harry Jenkins's patient coaching enabled Rutledge to reconstruct the sacred passages that had long ago faded from memory. Captivity sometimes made for interesting interdenominational pairings, as when the Mormon Larry Chesley exchanged thoughts on the gospel with his Catholic cellmate Jerry Coffee.[8]

This is not to say that every PW had a "leap of faith" or underwent a deathbed conversion while in prison. In his memoir *In the Presence of Mine Enemies*, Rutledge recounted how he and George McKnight, two "tough guys" who prior to their imprisonment had not been particularly reverent, traded prayers and renounced swearing during their time together at Vegas. "Don't misunderstand," Rutledge elaborated. "We weren't two fully-developed saints sitting dispassionately through the day discussing theology. There probably wasn't a thimbleful of serious theology between us. We just knew that without our faith in God, without our common belief that He was with us, we could not have made it through." At a National War College seminar in 1988 top-ranking PW senior Col. John Flynn, by then a retired lieutenant general, allowed that there were atheists among them who "also did well" and that love of country, family, and their fellow prisoners were equally powerful sustaining and inspirational forces. In his postwar writings Stockdale, too, while not denying the value of prayer, would cite the importance of more secular "ethical and moral guideposts," including adherence to the Code of Conduct, pride of heritage, and self-esteem, as sources of strength and conviction. What was crucial to the PWs' survival in Stockdale's estimation, more than any sudden epiphany, was a

---

* Of Gaither, a comrade wrote: "He was such a religious fanatic, I used to call him 'the Preacher.' Sundays he gave full-fledged sermons, and I mean you thought you were listening to a hellfire Baptist with a Charlton Heston voice. Gator could quote the Bible better than the Pope, and he did and did and did" (Nasmyth, *2355 Days*, 190).

philosophy or mindset—be it religion or patriotism or "simply a question of doing their jobs"—that emerged from the melting experience and that stayed with them and could deliver them through continuing crises.[9]

Stockdale and others also pointed to the stabilizing effect of a daily routine, of which prayer was but one ritual. In a comment that had application beyond the case of solitary confinement, Stockdale wrote in 1978: ". . . When a person is alone in a cell and sees the door open only once or twice a day for a bowl of soup, he realizes after a period of weeks in isolation and darkness that he has to build some sort of ritual into his life if he wants to avoid becoming an animal." For those unfettered and physically up to it, exercise became another one of those rituals. Even in the pinched quarters at Vegas's Mint or in Alcatraz's pits, where there might be only three or four square feet of open floor space, ambulatory prisoners initiated a walking or running-in-place regimen in an effort to keep fit and pass time. Some days Johnson walked at least five miles in the small space between the bed slab and the door of his compartment at Alcatraz. Mulligan began each day "running at least 2000 counts on my left foot." For Rob Doremus, "pacing was a very large part of the day." Those in better shape or with the luxury of more room, as at the Plantation, did both "jogging" and calisthenics. The athletic Ted Guy followed a rigorous schedule of alternating brisk walking in a circle around his cell with a series of push-ups, half of them with one arm, until he "built up two and a half inches on my chest." Those accustomed to lifting weights used the only equipment available, curling waste buckets filled with excrement.[10]

For many, of course, a simple pushup or situp was excruciating. Johnson was cheered when his damaged shoulders healed to the point where he could do three consecutive pushups. When Mulligan's torn shoulder muscles did not permit pushups, he turned to knee bends and other leg flexes. Typical was the case of Plumb, whose "body ached" and who "lay day after day not wanting to move" until he realized both his mind and body were on the verge of atrophy. "Very slowly, I tried a sit-up," he recalled. "After a half hour of agony, I completed my maneuver until my fingers touched my knees. I wrenched my hands and stretched my toes." As pus exuded from an ulcerated wound, he cried. "But I could not let myself quit and within two months I accomplished my first real sit-up." Coffee had trouble walking, as he had to "keep my torso fairly immobile as I continued to hug my injured arm to my body." Still, inching his way along his small cell, he managed "three short steps in each direction with a cramped, sideways turn at each end" until at length he traversed three miles. As he "swung and bobbed through my daily journey to nowhere," he developed an appreciation for the zoo inhabitants who pace "restlessly back and forth on a well-worn path in their cages, . . . establishing an invariable rhythm between the barriers that defined their pitifully scant horizons." Coffee "vowed never again to add to their indignity by standing there, gawking, as they expressed their deepest stirrings."[11]

Although the majority of the PWs credited exercise with helping them both physically and psychologically,* some believed its benefits were mixed at best. When Stratton was senior at Plantation he was convinced that physical exertion would aggravate injuries and burn precious calories, exhausting what little energy men on starvation rations had in reserve. Plumb suggested that Guy may have imagined he was becoming more muscular, as some of the men were only losing weight and seeing more muscle definition. Moreover, exercising could result in punishment, as the sounds of grunts and shuffling feet could violate noise regulations. Only as treatment and the condition of the captives improved after 1969 did strenuous exercise programs become commonplace. Late in the captivity, prisoners reported calisthenic counts in the thousands and engaged in competitions that matched roommates and whole cellblocks. Fred Baldock claimed 4,400 situps at one stretch. In a contest between neighboring cells at the Zoo Mike Brazelton reached 3,000 situps before he had to quit when, according to John Nasmyth, his tailbone came through his emaciated hide and he started bleeding. At the time they were released, by Plumb's calculation "the push-up record peaked at 1500 and the sit-up challenge was over 10,000!" Both Plumb and Nasmyth marveled at the gymnastic feats of Barry Bridger, who could walk on his palms and do 27 handstands at a clip.[12]

Incongruous as it may seem, in bad times as well as good, except in the most gruesome cases and bleakest hours, the prisoners were able to leaven solemnity with humor. Much of it was of the gallows type, but it helped to defuse tension and chase depression. "Maintaining a sense of humor," said Norm McDaniel, "kept most of us from getting lost in self-pity." In the words of another observer, it "gave the POWs a way to take back a crucial part of their identity, to put on the irreverent and defiant face that fighter pilots have always tried to show the world." Often the jokes were at the expense of the Vietnamese—the fractured pronunciations of Ho Chi Minh and other Communist leaders, the identification of American popular culture icons like John Wayne and Clark Kent as fellow aviators, the derisive nicknames they hung on nemeses such as Magoo and Mickey Mouse, the many ruses

---

* Civilian captive Douglas Ramsey, for instance, who could barely stand erect in his bamboo cage in the South, attributed his survival to a "compulsive neurosis vis-à-vis exercise." See the section on Ramsey in Chapter 13 and the sidebar "Life Under Viet Cong: Crude Bamboo Cages," *U.S. News & World Report*, 26 Mar 73. In a postwar survey of prisoners in the North, 76 percent felt that exercising had a positive effect on their morale and 14 percent that it was "essential to well-being" (Bernasconi et al, "Morale and Human Endurance," 171).

and pranks that embarrassed and humiliated the unsuspecting enemy on tape and film. PWs at the Plantation mocked the bowing requirement by genuflecting at "trees, buildings, dogs, pigs, chickens and other things in the yard," one of the occupants there recalled. And when guards would try to learn some basic English, the PWs substituted obscenities (in the manner that Kile Berg taught "I'm queer") for simple words like "Hello." Such mischief was cathartic as well as diverting. Coffee remembered that each man would develop "his own unique signature sneeze," using expletives such as "Rat shit!" or "Fuck Ho!" Thus:

> A man could gin up a good healthy sneeze and practically shout out his pent-up anger, contempt, and frustration. The guards never seemed to regard this practice for what it really was—insults really— and it would afford us some small pleasure in putting something over on them on a continuing basis. Strangely enough, it would become comforting to hear these expletives throughout the day and night; sort of a humorous little reminder that the family was all there, and things were normal; dismal as ever, but normal.[13]

To prisoners craving order and predictability in the anxious middle years, the very timetable for exercise, prayer, and other activities mattered a great deal. Echoing Stockdale, debriefing officer Charles Redman reported in 1973 how "the prison cell may take on a womb-like aspect wherein the PW attempts to establish a daily routine and thus attains a degree of security . . . , with any disruption of routine becoming a threat . . . ." Another post-war study noted how "each individual would establish his own routine and eventually knew what time it was at any point of the day by whatever event he was doing. If the routine was broken for any reason during the day, it was very upsetting for some PWs." Early release Joe Carpenter described as "amazing how the routine became habit forming." When he was moved to a new camp that was out of earshot of the church bells that in the city served as a clock for the PWs, "although I had no way of telling the exact time . . . I always felt that I knew the actual time of day within a few minutes."[14]

The prison schedule itself did not change much over the years: wakeup at 6:00 a.m., morning meal between 10:00 and 11:00 a.m., afternoon meal from 3:00 to 5:00 p.m., bedtime at 9:00 p.m.; minor fluctuations occurred depending on the camp and the season. Trips to quiz and indoctrination and holiday indulgences punctuated the routine only slightly. Cigarettes continued to be distributed three times daily, although guards spitefully would often withhold matches, forcing the Americans to devise other means to light up.* The noon siesta became the appointed hour for PW com-munication—Johnson said they looked forward to it "the way school kids anticipate recess." Gongs signaled and controlled their movements, raising them from their bedslabs in the morning, lowering them back in the evening, and directing them through their paces during the day. The toll-ing helped some to tell the time but was one repetition the PWs loathed. At Dirty Bird Tom Collins found the peculiar sound disturbing, a constant haunting reminder of their captivity. One change they welcomed was a switch, sometime in 1968, to a new standard uniform, a solid navy blue or black that replaced the hideous red-striped pajamas.[15]

If routine offered a comforting familiarity and regularity, for many it also had an oppressive downside, accentuating the problem of boredom. The undeviating sameness of the schedule fostered its own malaise, and required its own coping mechanisms. As noted previously, Denton came to greet quizzes with relief, and others periodically risked propaganda exploit-ation with visits to museums and participation in media events just to get a break from the monotony. Through the years, concocting diversions to alleviate the tedium and fill the endless empty hours became ever more challenging. Nasmyth observed that the days took an eternity while the years passed relatively swiftly. Gaither agreed: "Time functioned in that inversely logarithmic manner. If a man could make the minute, he could make the year. We did not even try to face the years, only the minutes." Hence, Doug Hegdahl explained, "the smallest little thing became the big-gest event. Dick [Stratton] had coined the term 'Events.' Everything was an Event. Eating was an Event. Smoking your three cigarettes a day [was] three Events." "The idea," especially in solitary, Hegdahl said, "was, when you were doing something you thought only of that action, e.g. when you were smok-ing a cigarette you did not daydream about some other event, you concen-trated on the cigarette."[16]

Such "creative inactivity" was unnatural to an enterprising, action-oriented group of pilots—Risner and Day told a magazine editor after the war that "learning how to waste time skillfully is 180 degrees opposite to what we have been used to"—but it proved to be yet another source of salvation. Red McDaniel made a small ball from Metzger's leftover bandages and with his one good hand tossed it up in the air again and again, counting "five

* Red McDaniel said they "managed to beat the no-match business" by using a lit cigarette to kindle a "punk" of toilet paper, which they kept burning as long as they could. A more effective solution was to steal matches during interrogation sessions. Nasmyth and his cell-mates, Jim Pirie in particular, became so adept at it "we had a real match-thievery ring going on." See McDaniel, *Before Honor*, 94; Nasmyth, *2355 Days*, 90-91; Plumb, *I'm No Hero*, 182-85. Plumb noted that cigarettes, even once lighted, did not burn long due to the mediocre quality of Vietnamese tobacco, holes in the paper, and damp conditions.

thousand catches within a few days as I tried to make this pastime fill the void . . . ." Carpenter whiled away much of his time at Plantation "just watching shadows move across the floor." He "missed them . . . on cloudy days as that was just one less thing to do." Gazing at the colonies of insects, lizards, and other creatures that shared their cells, a favorite distraction among the earliest American denizens of Hoa Lo (see Chapter 7), became more addictive over time as the captives began to relate to the creatures and as the increasingly restrictive confinement of the middle years shrank their visible universe. Even the menace presented by rodents and other vermin became secondary to the spectacle they provided. Tracking and feeding flies to a single spider kept one prisoner busy for two weeks. Coffee's memoir contains a chapter titled "Kinship With All Life" in which he reminisces in intimate detail about the mating habits and other characteristics of the chameleon-like gecko. The aviator paid special homage to a fledgling sparrow named "Charlie" who was "rescued from oblivion" and adopted by a group of PWs in Stardust.[17]

For the prisoner in solitary or with few visual or aural outlets, no diversion could go a longer way than spinning one's memory. By 1968 and 1969, long-term PWs had reconstructed whole chapters of their lives with the precision of diarists and were retrieving moments and details so trivial and distant their vivid recall astonished them. As Denton sifted through the events of his youth, he would "laugh to myself over some childhood prank, or weep over some nostalgic reminiscence. I remembered a toy airplane I had received on my third birthday and tried to bury myself in the swirling, pleasant memory." Mulligan flashed back to 1928 and a drive past an Indian cemetery with his grandparents at age two. Day by day at Alcatraz he slowly put together the pieces "to the puzzle of my life." Bill Lawrence was amazed at "how many names out of my first-grade class I could resurrect." Over the period of his captivity he "relived" his life "in minute detail three times." Guy was one of those who had never had the time or inclination to reflect on his upbringing. "As my intestines slowly mended," he later wrote, "I realized my troubles had just begun. The walls started closing in. Boredom and inactivity could prove as deadly as a bullet . . . . I went through the alphabet and tried to remember all the boys' names that began with each letter, then did the same with girls. I tried to recall every detail I could about people I'd known with those names." When that project was completed he tried to recall the tunes and lyrics of songs he used to play with his musician father. "I kept up the exercise my entire imprisonment. It took me two years to get 'C'est si bon' down perfectly."[18]

"My memory had never worked so well," Stockdale confessed. "I could bring up details from my childhood that were inaccessible in the clutter of conversational life." Explaining how he, Mulligan, Hegdahl, and the others could become so proficient at keeping PW lists in their heads, McCain commented that it was easy "when you don't have anything else to think about, no outside distractions." Plumb reported that one sports enthusiast, Galand Kramer, "memorized the names of over 750 baseball players, and after that list became tiresome he memorized it in reverse." Jack Fellowes replayed whole ball games and reproduced team rosters, including "the entire lineup for both teams in the 1946 World Series." Stumped by the name of the New York Giants quarterback who replaced the injured Y. A. Tittle, Fellowes puzzled over it for three years, fruitlessly seeking help from comrades over the communications system, until the name Earl Morrall finally came to him. Red McDaniel was luckier: roommate Dwight Sullivan was able to fill him in on the second baseman for the 1950 Philadelphia Phillies Whiz Kid team.[19]

Eventually the memory well ran dry. Plumb had undertaken "to recall every incident in my life. I tried to envision every course I had ever taken at school, every movie I'd seen, every birthday, every person I'd met. Nine hundred hours later, I reached the last pages of my life story." He then exchanged stories with cellmate Kay Russell. They discussed "every song, every television program, every sport, the war, history, geography, religious doctrines, philosophies, everything, until there was almost nothing original left for us to share. At that point, our minds were scraped clean, and silence saturated the room for hours at a time." During such lulls imagination would have to take over and the men would embark on fantasy trips or adventures, practice invisible pianos and guitars, design construction projects or financial schemes that took on ever more elaborate accretions over the years.* "I built five houses in my imagination during my seven years in North Vietnam," Rutledge wrote after the war. "Carefully I selected the site, then negotiated with its owner for purchase. Personally, I cleared the ground, dug the foundations, laid the cement, put up the walls, shingled the roof, and landscaped the property. After I had carefully furnished the home, I sold it, took my profit, and began the entire process once again." Bob Shumaker spent 12 to 14 hours a day building and rearranging his dream house: "I'd buy all the lumber and materials and everything for it . . . . I knew how many bricks were in it; how much it weighed; the square footage . . . ." Danny Glenn planned his residence down to the location of joists and studs and the exact gauge of the electric wire. Plumb remembered being awakened by Glenn in the middle of the night for his opinion on "paneling that family room downstairs."[20]

---

* See Chapter 7 on some of these early enterprises, including Kile Berg's airport negotiations, Doremus's car restorations, and Mulligan's investment fund.

Geoffrey Norman distinguished between "idle daydreaming and disciplined fantasizing." The construction projects were of the latter type, as were Al Stafford's boating activities. Stafford would not only imagine himself sailing, but "would decide where the wind was coming from and how strong it should be. He would visualize the boat he was sailing. How was it rigged? What sort of sail did it carry? . . . How much water did it draw?" Using hypothetical checkpoints and keeping a logbook, "at the end of an hour or two of sailing" he "could taste the salt on his lips and feel the sun on his skin." In another instance a man would play golf two hours a day on a course he knew intimately hole by hole. "During his golf game," said Norman, "his cellmates would leave him alone. It was easy to know that he was playing because he would be sitting on his sleeping pallet, in something like the lotus position, with his eyes closed and his lips moving, just slightly, as he talked himself through the round. Then, after a couple of hours, he would open his eyes and begin to stretch, as if to relieve the tension." Such serious make-believe not only consumed large chunks of time, but could also be self-improving and brought the fantasizers into touch with "a world of almost tangible reality." Of course, Norman added, however productive and effective the escapes, they were "still no substitute for the real thing. When it was too hot and he was too dispirited even to fantasize successfully, Stafford wondered when he would see blue water and feel the wind again. Or, in his worst moments, if he ever would."[21]

Many of the captured aviators had engineering backgrounds, and if some occupied themselves blueprinting or building imaginary houses, others mulled mathematical problems. Stockdale counted "one of the greatest gifts I ever received in prison" the formula for expanding exponential numbers that he got from Shumaker while at Alcatraz. "I became the world's greatest authority on the exponential curve," he proclaimed. Mulligan, according to Denton, "ran a mental computer. Once he passed the word that at 8:24 a.m. on Sunday, 5 percent of the week was gone. Now and then, when someone was trying to communicate with him, he'd flash, 'Call me later, I'm working on something.'" During his long stay in solitary, Risner, who had never much liked math, combated recurring panic by "running" up to 25 miles a day and solving square root and fractional problems with lessons he had learned from Ron Mastin. "Math became something like a personal friend" to Risner and others fumbling in the dark without pencil or paper but still possessing sharp and retentive minds.[22]

For those with more of a humanities leaning, poetry and literature offered similar refuge. Air Force Capt. Norman Wells, who as a boy would memorize a poem each year to recite at his family's Thanksgiving reunions, passed one verse a day of ballads like Noyes's "The Highwayman" through the walls of his cell at the Zoo. Coffee cited the poetry of Rudyard Kipling as having special appeal to the captives' taste for adventure and sense of duty. Air Force Maj. David Burroughs, who had a graduate degree in literature, was an expert on Ernest Hemingway and quoted passages from the author's novels and short stories to appreciative comrades at both the Zoo and Vegas. Some men studied languages, using stolen toilet paper and ink made from cigarette ashes to compile dictionaries. Lt. Cdr. Claude Clower returned home with a 2,000-word Spanish dictionary he copied in minute writing and hid in a bar of soap. Another PW pilfered English and French editions of the same magazine from a camp "library" during an indoctrination session and by comparing texts learned the meaning of some 3,000 French words. The champion linguist may have been Bob Craner, who could speak French, Spanish, and German and toward the end of the war would pick up some Russian from 1968 capture Marine Capt. Lawrence Friese.[23]

The resident intellectual at the Zoo was A. J. Myers, a tall, bearish man with a professorial bent, wide-ranging knowledge, and a penchant for collecting obscure vocabulary. The ankle he crushed upon ejection had never healed and he became a familiar figure hobbling about on crutches and dispensing his esoteric glossaries. Nasmyth described him as "a big ugly guy with four teeth missing in front" but "a dandy roommate . . . extremely smart, a real intellect . . . . Somehow he'd gotten hold of a pencil stub and reams of toilet paper on which he'd copied several thousand words . . . . He had a virtual pile of paper wadded up, stuck in his pants." Myers was a frequent visitor to interrogation and Nasmyth could only imagine his frustration as "the poor guy spent hours listening to gooks who could hardly speak English."* Mentors like Myers found a receptive audience in a PW community that was uncommonly literate—74 percent of the captives in the North had four or more years of college and another 22 percent had some college.† After 1970, in the two or three years prior to their release, the PWs would be in a better position to organize camp-wide "classes" of instruction and study, but in the middle years such educational endeavors, like all prisoner activity, was hamstrung by the relative isolation of the men and the danger of communicating. One development that facilitated foreign language translation considerably was the use of the drinking cup to talk

---

* After the war Myers would coordinate one of the most thorough and valuable surveys of the American PW experience in Vietnam.

† As English professor and PW chronicler Craig Howes put it, "Hanoi was the Harvard of POW camps." Gaither boasted that "almost to a man, the IQ level was 135 or more. Almost to a man, the education level was bachelor degree or better." See Howes, *Voices of the Vietnam POWs*, 7; Gaither, *With God in a P.O.W. Camp*, 119.

through the wall, which a postwar study deemed "a major breakthrough . . . because PWs could hear a word pronounced and much more information could be passed in a shorter time."[24]

For all their genuine interest in academics and self-improvement, it would be a patent exaggeration to depict the prisoners' conversational moments as dominated by discussions of Faulkner and quantum mechanics. Where men huddled in the same cell or contacted others through the walls, the purpose was usually to offer solace or encouragement, or share news and information. And where they sought diversion, the patter would gravitate naturally to more mundane subjects such as sports, movies, and women. During the period of relatively lax supervision at the Plantation and Zoo prior to the Dramesi escape (see Chapter 22), each camp's communication system, in between transmissions of organizational guidance and condition updates, bristled with locker-room banter. Red McDaniel remembered his group at the Zoo "taking polls as to the most beautiful movie star—I voted for Rhonda Fleming, but Liz Taylor won. The athlete of the century turned out to be Jim Thorpe, though I voted for Joe Di Maggio. The man of the century was Winston Churchill, far and away. The poll showed Adolf Hitler to be the one who had made the biggest impact on history in the twentieth century."

In the Plantation's Warehouse, Al Stafford, Ben Ringsdorf, and Jim Shively swapped ridiculous puns and rearranged proverbs in nonsensical yarns they called "Aesop's feebles." In one instance, according to Norman,

> Stafford reworked the aphorism "A penny saved is a penny earned" from *Poor Richard's Almanac*. He invented a character named Benny for his story—this was especially good, since Benny could be Ben Ringsdorf himself. Then he had Benny shave all the hair on his body. At the conclusion of the story, Benny is struck by lightning and reduced to ashes, which are put in a small jar.
>
> The story took days to tell. Finally, at the end, Stafford asked through the small hole, "And you know what the lesson of that story is?"
>
> Ringsdorf thought a moment, but he was stumped.
>
> "No."
>
> "Well, it just goes to show that a Benny shaved is a Benny urned."

"As in some old, preliterate society," Norman observed, "storytelling became an important art." Jack Van Loan and Air Force Capt. William Austin narrated scenes from *Gone with the Wind* and *The Caine Mutiny*, while others recapitulated popular television shows. *Dr. Zhivago* became a favorite "film" at the Plantation. Over the years it and other classics like *Tom Jones* would have their plots and dialogue embellished so that several versions became available.[25]

Although on the whole the prisoners probably talked—and fantasized—more about food than sex, there were those macho types who enjoyed trading tales of gallivanting escapades and amorous conquests. "A lot of the guys," especially the bachelors, Coffee wrote, "regaled the rest of us with their sexual exploits." "Conversations about sex were predictably coarse, at first, just like back in the squadron," Norman noted, but there were also heart-to-heart talks about wives and relationships and sensitive unburdenings of pent-up desires and longings for physical affection. Belying the chauvinistic references to women in the memoirs of Alvarez, Denton, Dramesi, Guarino, and others, impotency and fading masculinity were gnawing worries to men for whom the subject of females became "increasingly abstract." Postwar accounts freely confess to occasional masturbation and titillation at the sight of Vietnamese water girls and other female prison personnel, but in fact the combination of resignation and enervation caused most of the PWs to lose both interest and drive. "Women certainly were a topic with us," said Doremus, "but it was something we just kind of put out of our minds." Brace told an interviewer that one of the captives, Jim Bedinger, "lived with me longer than he lived with his wife before he was captured . . . . You get to know each other extremely intimately, as far as everything in your background goes. But, as for discussions of sex, I'd say that matter was rather insignificant. We had other things on our minds . . . ."[26]

While some men refrained from patting or embracing cellmates for fear of homosexuality, there were many cases of remarkable tenderness. Coffee conceded they were "wary of excessive touching—even though we may have longed for it—because of what it could conceivably lead to in such emotionally harrowing circumstances." But the guardedness did not prevent him and others from stroking and massaging comrades who were hurting. In *Beyond Survival* Coffee has a poignant recollection of one such instance:

> When Dave Rehmann and I shared a cell in late '69 and early '70, he suffered interminably from asthma attacks. His pain and anxiety over his badly disfigured arm which had been shattered on ejection would have been enough, but the asthma exacted an even higher toll. He sat up sometimes through entire nights sucking for air, muscles exhausted and sweating profusely. There was little that could be done without medication, but frequently I'd massage his neck and shoulders to relieve the tenseness, to help him relax, and perhaps at least to doze. I had felt no qualms about this tenderness toward my cellmate.

Although homecoming brought scattered reports and rumors of homosexual behavior, the returning prisoners, both Northern and Southern, were almost unanimous in their comments for the record in maintaining that they knew of no such activity and that it was virtually precluded by the strong cultural prohibition in the military and by the fact that most cells contained more than two men.*[27]

Where there was communication, there was also game-playing, albeit with awkward constraints and a few new wrinkles and rules. Individuals found ingenious ways to assemble crude game boards and decks of cards and then to approximate play. The manufacture of chess sets and checker-boards evolved impressively over the years from the days when Gaither and Byrne employed rocks and straw. Plumb related the method for making backgammon, beginning by laminating layers of toilet paper with a glue synthesized from leftover rice: "Six or eight of these layers made a very tough cardboard and an excellent acey-ducey board for backgammon. We needed checkers, and so we pinched out the soft center of a bread loaf, poured water on it, kneaded it to form nickle-sized wafers. We colored one team's checkers with red brick dust. Ashes were rubbed into the others to make black." For dice they mixed bread with water and allowed the cubes to harden, then punched holes with a wire or nail and filled them with a scavenged tincture or toothpaste to form the numbers. Nasmyth anointed Dick Bolstad "the master poker chip and dice maker in POW history." His chips were "perfectly round, perfectly decorated, perfectly colored and hard as a rock." To keep the bread-laden chips out of the clutches of rodents, Bolstad "found some secret ingredient to mix in with his chips which kept the rats away. This discovery kept his chips tops in quality."

No recreational improvisation was more challenging than devising a way to play cards. Describing how the men managed to play bridge, Norman wrote:

> It took some resourcefulness to get a rubber going in prison, when all four players were in different, and not always adjacent, cells. But the players had time to come up with the necessary solutions.
>
> First, you needed cards. The Vietnamese were not handing any out. (They were included in Red Cross and other packages sent to the POWs but were not distributed until very late in the war.) So the POWs had to make them.
>
> Toilet paper was available. A quill could be made from broom straw, ink from ashes and water. The cards were made small so they could be easily concealed.

---

* By contrast, several of the returnees mentioned evidence of homosexual conduct among the Vietnamese soldiers and guards, though allegations of it being "rampant" were probably exaggerated or else there would likely have been some molestation of the Americans. Only one PW claimed he had been raped by a Vietnamese.

Next came the fundamental problem of how to play the game. The men who decided to make up a bridge foursome would arrange their cards in the same order. Then the instructions for shuffling would be tapped through each wall. Sometimes these instructions would be relayed by a man who did not play bridge but was willing to help keep the game going and do a little tapping to pass the time.

CUT DECK TEN CARDS DEEP.
CUT LARGE PILE FIFTEEN CARDS DEEP.
PLACE THIRD ON FIRST PILE.

And so on until the deck was shuffled. Then every man would deal four hands, pick up the one that was his, and begin the bidding. Once the bidding was complete, the dummy hand would be turned over. The other hands would remain face down, and as a card was played, the man making the play would tap the card and its place in the original pile so that the other players could find it without looking at the other cards in the hand. It would have been easy to cheat without being caught but also, under the circumstances, utterly pointless. A hand of bridge that might take ten minutes to play under normal conditions could last for two or three weeks when every play had to be tapped through several walls.

As with other aspects of communication and items of contraband, the exposure of PW games and game equipment could entail serious penalties and punishment, a sanction that did not always make the amusement reward worth the risk. Yet even at closely monitored Alcatraz, the shut-ins there were undeterred. The Vietnamese briefly overlooked Shumaker's chessboards* before the Alkies, according to Denton, voluntarily turned them in. They continued to use their tap virtuosity to play "Five Questions," a quiz game that required them to supply, for example, the names of five fish that can live in both fresh and salt water. Some of the answers would be contested and checked after homecoming. Denton later sent Jenkins $100 and Stockdale $200 "for bets I had lost."[28]

Between the simulated games, the mental gymnastics, prayer and calisthenics, insect-gazing, and snatches of communication, some of the prisoners killed time so successfully that some days they found themselves "overbooked." Coffee reminisced in 1990: "Sometimes with all the tapping and clearing, along with my own prayer and exercise time, working on my French vocabulary, POW roster and other memory lists, memorizing and composing poetry, and planning projects for the future at home again, I'd frequently go to sleep at night thinking, Hell, I didn't get done everything

---

* See Chapter 17.

I'd wanted to do today." Coffee may have forgotten how *infrequent* such days were, or else he was hyperbolizing for effect. More typical was Al Lurie's comment on how limited their horizons were and how painful "going down memory lane" could be, especially visualizing his wife and children: "My mind just cut off that circuit . . . . That was the way I was most vulnerable, the way I could be hurt the easiest." Despite all manner of contrived diversions and "creative inactivity," there was scarcely a man who did not experience prolonged periods of feckless stagnation. Red McDaniel cited "the long Sunday afternoons or the hours after four every day [following the evening meal] that got to us the most—those hours when time hung heavy and we hunted for things to do." For all their stratagems to banish it, boredom, said Plumb, "visited us like a bill collector." Still, to the extent they could keep it at bay, stay alert and active, and make each day purposeful, the greater hold they had on sanity and survival.[29]

In prison, as outside it, necessity became the mother of invention. From writing and communication paraphernalia to matches and toilet paper, clocks and calendars, Bibles and gameboards, the PWs, using ingenuity and the scant materials available to them, improvised as needed. Just as they had to invent pastimes to divert and distract, so they had to find ways to stay warm, keep clean, and ward off disease.

It helped to have so many bright minds with an engineering aptitude. David (Jack) Rollins utilized his background as a mechanic and metalsmith* to fashion tools and knives and then build everything from pens to stoves. Dubbed "Mr. Fix-It" by his Zoo mates, the Navy lieutenant was especially proficient at crafting needles, which the prisoners used to both embroider American flags and patch clothes. Rollins later explained his technique:

> I managed to acquire some copper wire. Once I took a section right out of the Vietnamese electrical system and another time from the public address system. I would break off a piece of wire about an inch and a half long and grind it down on the concrete until it was sharpened to a point. Then I'd take a small nail and sharpen it to a point and drill a little hole through the end of the wire needle. I must have made approximately 100 needles. Some of the men wore them as lapel pins when we were released. . . . I got to a point where I could make a needle in a couple of hours. I had a really good nail and could get a needle polished up and ready to use during a nap period with no problem at all.

* As an enlisted man Rollins repaired aircraft for over a decade before being commissioned an officer in 1960.

At the Plantation another expert needlemaker and talented gadgeteer was 1967 capture Tom Hall, who chiseled sewing needles out of fish bones and produced a mousetrap from scrounged pieces of metal and string and an empty tin can. When comrades could muster neither the skill nor the spare parts to build their own traps, he advised them to filch some of the red-hot bell-shaped peppers the Vietnamese ate with their rations and stuff ratholes with the peppers, which even the rats could not ingest—effectively plugging the holes. Nasmyth swore that Ralph Gaither could "make anything," could "make something out of nothing . . . . When we needed to drill a hole through a wall from one cell to the next for communication purposes, Gator made the drill. He made drills from pieces of wire better than you can buy at the hardware store. His drills buzzed, they were that fast; it took them only twenty minutes to get through three feet of concrete." When Nasmyth asked, "Hey, Ralph, I want to drill through two bricks, what should I use?," the aviator replied, "Use a Gaither Number Four." When rooming with Mark Ruhling, the last man captured before the November 1968 bombing halt, Gaither designed a mouthpiece for Ruhling from wet bread dough that was "better than the two-hundred-fifty-dollar one the doctor made back home!"[30]

The most innovative of all of the PW handymen may have been Plumb. An inveterate tinkerer, ham radio operator, and Annapolis graduate with a degree in engineering and interest in electronics, Plumb turned his cells first at Plantation and then the Zoo into veritable workshops. Not only was he a wizard at fabricating writing implements,* but he developed a dozen or more "homemade" devices and methods for telling time and temperature, determining weight, and in other ways gaining control over "a completely foreign environment." While staring at the ceiling he "stumbled on to" a rudimentary thermometer, a light bulb dangling from a twisted cord. As the temperature rose, he noticed that the cord would expand and straighten, causing the bulb to revolve slightly; as the temperature fell, the cord contracted. "It was only necessary for us to put a mark on the bulb and to graduate the hairline shadow it cast on the floor," Plumb recalled. He nearly put together a radio from a collection of smuggled parts—wires, spools, tin foil, waxed paper, razor blades, and nails—before the Vietnamese discovered the device as he was about to package the components.[31]

Plumb's temperature takings confirmed what was palpable, that Hanoi's climate was one of extremes. Coffee told a debriefer that "the beginning of a new winter would have one longing for the summer and vice versa." Sam Johnson had lived most of his life in Texas and Georgia but Vietnam's heat

* See Chapter 18.

Making the best of it. *Top, from left:* handymen Hall and Rollins, medic Warner; *middle,* prayer leader Norm McDaniel, chipmaker Bolstad, situp champ Brazelton; *bottom,* jailhouse scholars Myers, Craner, and Burroughs.

and humidity, he declared after his return to the United States, "were unlike any I had ever known. The air was like a damp blanket too heavy to shed." During the May-September monsoon season, temperatures could rise above 110 degrees, with precipitation averaging 10 inches per month. Although torrential downpours could turn the camps into quagmires, many prisoners welcomed the rain: it cooled them, increased water supplies, and, according to Guarino, caused the Vietnamese to ease up on interrogations "because the guards didn't like to get wet taking the POWs back and forth." On steamy midsummer days the men fanned themselves with pieces of cardboard or the lid from their waste buckets. "If you sat perfectly still all day long with a fan . . . and learned to fan yourself with just the tiniest of movements," Nasmyth related, "you could stay almost dry. But if you should do any exertion such as get up to pee in the bucket, when you sit down you're soaked. You lie on your back after doing something and your eye sockets fill up with sweat." So that the perspiration would not burn their eyes at night, PWs in the habit of sleeping on their backs learned to sleep on their stomachs.[32]

As noted previously, many of the Northern captives dreaded winters more than summers. Though temperatures in Hanoi seldom dipped below freezing, North Vietnam's chill was unusually penetrating because of the high humidity. Having to bathe in cold water with "little tea towels" for drying forced a choice, as one sufferer remarked, "between B. O. and pneumonia." In a generous moment an enemy commander suggested a remedy: "Exercise before you take bath. Start low on body and wash up very slowly. Wet feet, then knees, then legs, until you get chest area. No direct dousing." Plumb and others "discovered that the guy knew what he was talking about." Eventually the PWs came up with their own methods to combat the cold, ranging from experimentation with layered clothing at the Zoo during the inclement winter of 1966-67* to improvising hats at the Plantation. Using a bamboo needle, Plumb knitted from rags a cap replete with ear flaps.[33]

"Housekeeping," Norman observed, "was humdrum stuff for men accustomed to flying supersonic fighters and turning their dirty uniforms over to a laundry run by enlisted men." But housekeeping and elementary hygiene were as crucial as they were challenging in so inherently unsanitary and unhealthy an environment. The prisoners ate from metal dishes that rusted and were licked by rats and other vermin when left outside cells overnight. PW dishwasher assignees, having to make do without hot water and with one bar of lye soap per month for each building, tried as best they could to sanitize cleaning and handling, including separating and isolating the cups and utensils of those with serious illnesses. Hall's mousetraps and peppers

---

* See Chapter 11.

helped alleviate the rodent nuisance at the relatively clean Plantation, but, as a postwar study on PW living conditions noted, "after sundown, rats and mice literally took over North Vietnam," and in the dirtier prisons they foraged in droves. Ants and flies were also abundant, but in warm weather mosquitos were the most irritating pests, swarming by the thousands and spurring "room kill" contests that could dispatch over 300 in a single day. Denton complained about spiders as big as tarantulas, but they proved to be a boon when their cobwebs caught batches of the mosquitos.[34]

Odors were a ubiquitous problem. Waste buckets were emptied daily but, with cellmates sharing them and a water-heavy rice diet causing frequent urination, they regularly overflowed, especially in winter owing to reduced perspiration. Dysentery spoiled clothes and bedding, which were washed only occasionally. "Clothing odors were a fact of life," Chesley reported, "and towel odors in particular were unspeakably bad." With bathing itself sporadic, usually three times a week during the middle years and less in punishment cases or during extortion periods, the stink was unrelenting and overwhelming. Describing the waste odor that was perhaps worst at Briarpatch but common to all the PW jails, Alvarez wrote:

> The stench was with us all the time. We had long since accepted as normal having to sit a few feet away from each other when one of us had a bowel movement, which was often because we always seemed to come down with diarrhea. There was never enough water to wash the odor off our hands. And though we took daily turns dumping the bucket and swishing the inside with sticks and straw brushes at the well near the bottom of a hill, they never supplied us with any disinfectant. As the tin buckets were not replaced, they developed a hard coating of crap that no amount of cleaning could remove. Though it was the source of the interminable smell, we had to live with the bucket in our sealed quarters day in and day out.

The prisoners scoured the buckets with rotten fruit, but to little benefit. The noxious odors remained one of their most intractable annoyances. Some were able to put the smells out of their minds, others could not. "I tried my best to be blasé," said Plumb, "but I never became accustomed to an open *bo*."[35]

The PWs had more success in overcoming initial difficulties in using their crude toilets. The buckets had jagged edges that made squatting in the usual fashion hazardous. The solution, which Norman credited to Hall at Plantation but which was practiced earlier at Briarpatch,* was for the prisoner to place his rubber sandals between his buttocks and the bucket

---

*Berg introduced the technique to Alvarez there after he had picked it up from another prisoner either at Briarpatch or the Zoo. See Chapter 11.

before sitting. Plumb devoted a page of his memoir to the evolution of toilet technique:

> Of course we had no porcelain seat to sit on, and the rim of the bucket was uncomfortable. Some guys used what we called the cantilever method, holding themselves a few inches above the *bo*. The one drawback to this method was that it caused a splash factor of 7 or 8 . . . and some were left in worse shape than if they had sat down. To solve this problem, many would put a layer of toilet paper over the top of the liquid, reducing the splash factor to about 0.5 . . . .
>
> We could always tell who used the cantilever method because when he stood up he was generally unblemished. But for sitters, it was different. They would return with perfect twelve-inch bucket imprints around their "cheeks."
>
> Some ingenious fellow took pains to balance his sandals on either side of the bucket; he could sit on them and relax in comfort. When he got up, however, he was branded with bright-red footprints.[36]

Shaving also presented dilemmas. The combination of inferior and worn blades and heavy beards made the once-weekly affair a test that required its own strategies. The question for cellmates, as Plumb framed the problem, was, "should the guy with the heavy beard shave first because he was the toughest to shave? Or should the guy with a light beard shave first because he wouldn't dull the blade?" The absence of mirrors caused some roommates to "play barber," especially where tortured prisoners had lost sensitivity in their hands. PWs also used the razors to shear hair because of the infrequency of haircuts. After 1969 both schedules and implements would improve, and Rollins recalled that during his last year of captivity, as one of the camp barbers, he "became quite good with a razor cut."[37]

An ablution missed by the Americans perhaps even more than regular bathing and shaving was brushing their teeth. New captives were usually issued a toothbrush and toothpaste, but these would have to last for months, with the toothpaste running out and brush handles breaking and bristles flattening until the brushes became useless. Mulligan remembered how during his stay at the Zoo "my teeth felt like they had hair on them. I rinsed my mouth with tea and constantly tried to massage my gums and teeth with my forefinger but this did little to relieve the discomfort that I was feeling." To augment the flimsy brushes prisoners made toothpicks from wood and bone splinters and dental floss from blanket threads and bits of clothing. Beginning in 1969 some PWs briefly were permitted to keep toothpaste sent them in packages from home, but in December 1970 the Vietnamese confiscated the American-made items. The local product, named *Bac Ha*, had "a peculiar soapy taste," said Mulligan, "that in a free competitive market would have caused it to be a flop, but there in Hanoi it had no competition and was infinitely better than nothing at all."[38]

Dental troubles were common, the result not only of inadequate care but also injuries from beatings, a lack of vitamins and minerals, and teeth chipping from stones and other foreign objects in their food. Some men cleaned their teeth so obsessively with the deteriorated bristles or ersatz toothpicks, perhaps as a way to consume idle hours, that they damaged gums in the process. Many a returned PW, especially those seized later in the war who escaped the worst torture, would cite prolonged toothache as the source of their greatest physical distress in captivity. "Willing to try anything" to gain relief from broken and impacted teeth, Nasmyth took the advice of Jim Warner, who had been a pre-med student and driven an ambulance while in college and, by Nasmyth's estimate, "had read every medical book he could get his hands on . . . [and] was the closest thing there was to a doctor in North Vietnam."* On Warner's recommendation, Nasmyth put a pinch of hoarded tobacco between his lip and gum and got "instant relief" from the aspirin-like effect.[39]

With regard to the dental miseries, a postwar analysis concluded that "self-care or care by other POWs was widely practiced and, as a result of ingenuity and common sense, many minor ailments and injuries were reasonably well alleviated." The same could be said of other medical and health problems as well. The prisoners lanced boils with razors and needles, made mud casts and wood splints for broken bones, applied pig fat to chapped or cracked lips, gargled with salt (when available) for sore throat, nibbled on charcoal (salvaged from dump piles and fire pits) to check diarrhea and flu, even sipped kerosene from lanterns when the guards' attention was diverted in order to kill intestinal worms. To heal cankerous wounds or burns incurred on shootdown, they allowed flies to lay eggs on the decaying skin, the newly hatched maggots cleaning the infection as they dined on the putrescence. For bandages they used vines or mosquito netting; for antiseptics, toothpaste and even urine, which on passing is sterile. Some of the makeshift remedies came from family medical lore, some from survivalist training, others from intuition and sheer desperation. One man with a deviated septum solved his breathing problem at night by sleeping with a finger propping his nostril open. An individual plagued by hemorrhoids stood on his head for several hours a day. Besides Warner, comrades singled out Doremus and Sgts. Art Black and Art Cormier for their paramedic assistance.[40]

---

*Nasmyth also extolled Warner's storytelling ability, naming him "the undisputed Academy Award-winning movie raconteur . . . . His timing, emphasis, and fierce blue eyes said as much as the words. He drew crowds talking about his mom and dad or the time he baby-sat a boa constrictor" (2355 Days, 167).

For many ailments there was neither cure nor relief, only the will to endure. Stockdale tried easing his crotch rot—the result of not having been permitted to bathe for the first eight months of his confinement— by alternately wearing his pus-caked pajama pants frontward and back- ward, but the horrible itching continued unabated. Almost every cellblock had someone suffering from asthma, including captives who had no pre- vious history of serious allergies. Red McDaniel speculated that men were smoking cigarettes who either had quit or abstained prior to captivity, induced by boredom, nerves, or the belief (evidently held by the Ameri- cans and the Vietnamese alike) that nicotine, in the short run at least, was more palliative than harmful. Besides the aforementioned Rehmann, Wes Schierman was another with an acute respiratory problem, nearly dying one damp winter at Son Tay when, Gaither said, "the phlegm built up to the point that he had to sit up through the night to keep from smothering. . . . The sound of his gasping filled us with terror because of our helplessness. . . . Wes' trouble recurred every winter after that. During each summer, knowing what probably lay ahead of him, he exercised to build up his strength to get him through the next winter. All of us had tremendous respect for that man. He fought hard for his life, and he won." Those worried about cancer from excessive smoking devised filters from pieces of straw and bamboo, but these were about as effective as the fabricated trusses made out of old clothing that hernia victims employed. And of course there was no remedy for the handful of PWs who wore glasses, which were confiscated at capture, or for those whose eyesight deteriorated while in prison.* Chesley later estimated that half of the prisoners required glasses after they returned home.[41]

In reviewing post-homecoming reports one finds considerable dis- agreement among the PWs as to both the availability and quality of medical care furnished by the enemy. Consistent with other aspects of the captivity, it seems clear that medical treatment was generally stinting and perfunctory during the early and middle years, more frequent and earnest later on, but to some extent it was erratic and unpredictable throughout, subject to shifts in both handlers' attitudes and official policy. Stratton felt that prison authori- ties approved treatment for those PWs who were being groomed for early release or other propaganda events or who would have otherwise died, or to reward good behavior.

> There was no such thing as preventive medicine except in rare cases
> or when they thought, over the years, we might be going home.
> One time they thought they had a cholera epidemic and we were

---

* When Coffee complained of eye problems, he was taken to a hospital for an eye examination that turned out to be a propaganda photo session. He later received fish oil for his eyes, but it had no effect.

> inoculated; I remember getting [inoculated] that first year when they
> thought the peace marches in San Francisco and New York were
> going to win the war for them. They ran around giving people shots.
> [The stuff in the hypo] was mucky-looking, like something they'd
> picked out of a mud puddle. The interrogator said it was four
> shots in one. The [medic] came through and inoculated the whole
> cellblock. He used the same needle; he never cleaned it.

In fact there were occasions unrelated to propaganda concerns, behavior manipulation, or *in extremis* conditions where the Vietnamese administered care, even performing intermittent physical examinations, although the latter may have been token exercises primarily to satisfy the International Red Cross. Stratton himself had a tooth extracted, albeit by a "dentist" who was also the camp butcher and veterinarian and who used Czechoslovakian novocaine that "was two years old when they got it." Most of the Northern camps had either a nurse or a medic as well as a doctor who rotated among the sites, tending to both the prison staff and the PWs at each location. The prisoners, more often after 1969 but earlier as well, were periodically given vitamin shots for beriberi, sulfa tablets for dysentery, or antibiotics such as penicillin when there were ample supplies and when disease threatened the camp population. The drugs appeared to be mostly of Eastern European origin, were typically outdated, and were given in seemingly indiscriminate dosages, but there is no reason to suppose prescriptions or therapies were any different for Vietnamese personnel than for the Americans. Robert Frishman reported that iodine was dispensed for a time at the Plantation for ringworm until guards discovered the PWs were using the tincture to write notes.[42]

Frishman and Wesley Rumble both gave debriefers extensive and somewhat conflicting assessments of the level of PW medical care upon their early release in August 1969, underscoring how divergent individual appraisals could be depending on one's perspective and experience. Day referred in his memoir to a "low-caliber corpsman who could not have diagnosed daylight" and almost every returnee had a medical horror story to rival Stratton's. On the other hand, Vietnamese medical incompetence and neglect may have been exaggerated based on post-repatriation health evaluations that revealed a not insignificant number of cases where enemy practitioners displayed marked attentiveness and surprising skill; these included the setting of fractures with steel pins and at least two successful appendectomies.*

---

* A sampling: eye surgery on Lynn Guenther; repair of Wilfred Abbott's broken leg and Terry Geloneck's broken and dislocated shoulder; treatment of Douglas Peterson's multiple fractures; and intravenous feeding of Thomas Klomann during a period he was semiconscious. See Berg, "Medical Aspects of Captivity and Repatriation," 98. It is noteworthy, however, that most of these cases occurred late in the war.

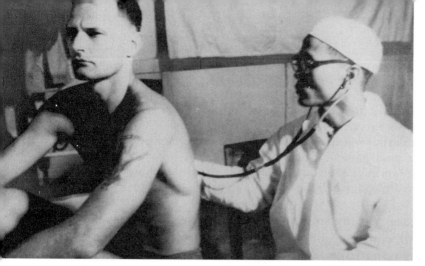

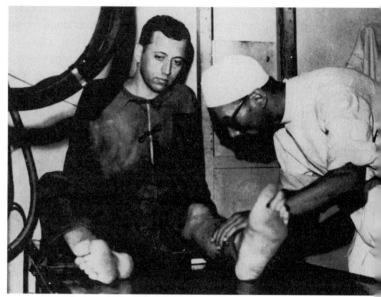

Navy Lts. Bradley Smith (top) and Robert Fant (right) undergoing medical checkups; Kasler (below) on hospital cart. The North Vietnamese mingled propaganda displays with real treatment.

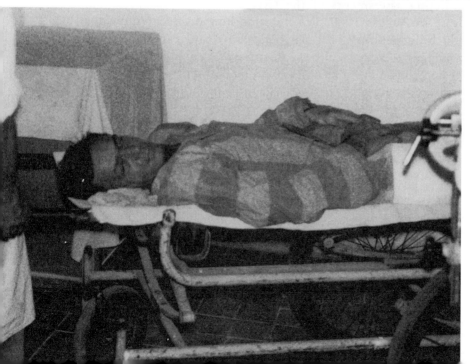

McDaniel said the men did not see a real dentist until 1971, but Wendy Rivers related having a tooth pulled in 1967 by a female Army major who claimed to have graduated from a Paris dental school. Rivers told a debriefer it "was an almost painless operation" and "there were no photographers there for propaganda purposes." Elmo Baker reported good treatment for a broken femur, including proper anesthetic and post-operative care. SRO John Flynn acknowledged at a press conference on his return that the North Vietnamese "had done a very professional job" repairing injuries to both his legs. Frishman, who prior to joining the Navy had been enrolled in a dentistry program at the University of California, had "a major orthopedic procedure" performed in which a Hanoi surgeon reconstructed his mangled elbow; doctors at Bethesda Naval Hospital grudgingly praised the technique, one allowing "he didn't get Fifth Avenue treatment, but he recovered."[43]

Moreover, however primitive enemy medical care was by American standards and however uneven, belated, and sometimes counterproductive was its application, the captor's medical intervention doubtlessly did in some instances save lives. George Coker testified to how vulnerable the PWs were to the ravages of shootdown injuries, a tropical climate, and "zero hygiene," so that "the least little scratch" could lead to a softball-size infection. Coker was convinced he would have died if the North Vietnamese had not transported him to a hospital to have his grossly infected leg drained and medicated. Hervey Stockman likely would have succumbed to gangrene without the ministrations of the medic "Tonto."* Mulligan and Kasler were others who, for all the *mis*treatment inflicted on them, probably owed their survival to haphazard but vital treatment at a critical juncture. At Alcatraz, consumed by high fever from a kidney infection, Mulligan was resuscitated by "fifteen large white pills" and a special diet of bouillon. Navy Lt. Cdr. Dale Osborne, a 1968 capture whose body was riddled with shrapnel when his Skyhawk cockpit took a direct hit from an antiaircraft shell, almost certainly would not have made it back without medical care for massive leg, arm, and head injuries.† Like Stockman, Mulligan, and Kasler, Osborne received crucial assistance from a cellmate, in this case Lt. Cdr. Brian Woods (seized five days before Osborne), but in the end he owed his life to Vietnamese personnel who removed the shrapnel and repaired and bandaged his shattered limbs.[44]

* See Chapter 18.
† Guarino wrote: "The fragments ripped some of the muscles of his left leg from ankle to thigh —he was loaded with steel splinters, and his right forearm was destroyed. In the several weeks it took to get to Hanoi, Dale was nearly buried a couple of times by Vietnamese who thought he was dead. He woke up in the nick of time each time" (*A POW's Story*, 295).

The fact that the enemy released no amputees among the fallen aviators was construed by some as an indication that the Vietnamese preferred to let the most gravely ill prisoners die rather than return them maimed, but a less sinister explanation might be simply that they were able to mend or stabilize those threatened with the loss of a limb. Debunker Bruce Franklin overstated both the enemy's willingness and ability when he asserted, "The miracle is that despite its overwhelming problems, North Vietnam was willing and able to provide enough of its pitiful medical resources to preserve the lives of hundreds of men captured while devastating their country,"[45] but on balance Hanoi may not have received enough credit for its medical care record especially in the later stages of the captivity. Of course, the availability and quality of care under the Viet Cong in the South was a different story altogether, with far more limited supplies of both medicines and dietary supplements, inferior or nonexistent facilities in a guerrilla environment, and generally more adverse circumstances for captor and captive alike.*

Ironically, one of the major "coping" tests for the Americans held in the North involved not relations with the enemy but interaction between and amongst themselves. What Ray Vohden referred to as "interpersonal relationships" accounted for a surprising amount of stress in those PWs with cellmates. Although being united with a fellow countryman invariably brought joy initially, the honeymoon could quickly fade under the duress of claustrophobic conditions and too much time on their hands. As Chesley put it: "It would be an unreasoning idealization to suggest that all was constantly sweetness and light . . . . In the cramped and physically unpleasant conditions it was easy to get irritated with each other when men were tired, when they were hungry, when they didn't have anything to do."[46]

Living together in such close quarters magnified annoying habits and idiosyncracies. "Absurdly simple things grated on our nerves and soured our dispositions," said Plumb. Red McDaniel confessed that "just the way a man burped" bothered him, or the way he walked, "the peculiarities of his movements, the same hitch in his stride." Snoring could be particularly irksome; at the Plantation, Mike McCuistion would throw his sandal at Bob Wideman to register his displeasure. Among exercisers, "pacers" sometimes ran into "circlers." Other peeves: hacking coughs, grinding teeth, loquaciousness, cigarette smoke, body odors, sloppy urinaters. When rooming in a space the size of "a bus station rental locker," John Fer noted, something as inconsequential as the way one brushed teeth or folded clothes caused flare-ups that left cellmates cross for days. Bob Craner had a reputation as

* See Chapters 4 and 12.

a loner,* but his comment after the war that "solo is preferable to living with one other man" was likely shared by others who, after the thrill of companionship wore off, would have willingly traded the benefit of overly familiar company for some privacy.[47]

The same homogeneity that boosted morale and camaraderie among the officer-aviators who dominated the Northern PW rolls also fostered rivalry and competition. Stubborn differences of opinion on trivial matters erupted into raging debates. Fer observed that quarrels over whether Casey Stengel or Yogi Berra managed the New York Mets or whether dark glasses were necessary in order to hunt pheasants never got resolved because there were no reference books on hand to settle the issue. Vohden cited the example of two men who "argued continuously for 3 days over what the food bought at a ball park that comes in a soft bun and is eaten with mustard and relish is called. They never agreed whether it was a frankfurter, weiner [sic] or hot dog." Even the best of friends locked horns. Chesley and Coffee bickered over the definition of "bountiful." Guarino confided that he and Byrne "became hypercritical of everything the other one did: how he ate, sat, folded his blankets, or tapped the wall." At Alcatraz, Johnson remembered "tension among the Alkies soared to a dangerous level . . . . The games we had made up to keep us stimulated and united became small battlefields." Denton complained about a "garrulous" Rutledge and recalled "violent arguments that on occasion nearly resulted in blows. We would soon get over it, but in other cells, long-standing grudges developed and there were some slugging incidents." A prisoner held by the Viet Cong who experienced both confinement milieus chalked up the advantage to the South in this respect: "In the jungle, arguments could be avoided by simply getting up and walking away. But in a small cell there was no place to go."[48]

More substantive disagreements occurred with regard to how faithfully men were adhering to the Code of Conduct and, indeed, what exactly the Code required of them. Disagreements developed about such things as whether to bow to minor prison workers like the "Gungas" (water girls) and whether to resist by bowing less than the required 90 degrees. Service pride sometimes colored perception. Don Heiliger told Dramesi that the "Navy types" with whom he roomed initially "had a different attitude about this whole thing," implying they were too complacent; Navy hardliners would say the same of less driven Air Force mates. Contrary interpretations of the Code, Marine PW Howard Dunn attested, "created greater schisms among the prisoners . . . than their captors ever could have hoped to achieve." The acrimonious debate over the issue of early release at the Plantation[†] paled next to the

---

* Guarino characterized him as "a very intelligent person" who disdained small talk and "wasn't easy to get close to" (*A POW's Story*, 291).
† See Chapter 18.

problem posed by those who appeared to be guilty of outright misconduct if not active collaboration, especially where the issue divided cellmates.[49]

No case caused more anguish or bitterness than that of Navy Cdr. Robert Schweitzer and Marine Lt. Col. Edison Miller, whose seemingly uncoerced antiwar tapings had stunned compatriots at Vegas and who had become notorious throughout the PW community as their "Bob and Ed Show" was carried on camp radio all over the North. Miller had gone down in the same plane as Jim Warner in October 1967. Warner remembered him as a first-rate pilot with a zeal for combat but an independent sort who, once he recovered from extensive injuries, thought nothing about stating his frankly critical views of the U.S. involvement, or having them broadcast. When Warner was transferred to the new camp at Son Tay in the summer of 1968, Miller was joined at Desert Inn by Schweitzer and later by Navy Cdr. Walter Eugene "Gene" Wilber. Schweitzer eventually recanted and made his way back into the fold, though some colleagues would never forgive him and would continue to associate him with Miller and Wilber as renegade seniors who had embraced their indoctrinators' concept of the war and were disseminating it in return for favorable treatment. Feelings toward Miller and Wilber, whose judgment, Coffee suggested, may have been impaired by a partial stroke and remorse at having lost his crewman, ranged from incredulity to utter disgust. Toward the end of the war, when they became increasingly isolated and alienated even erstwhile defenders, their conduct engendered such hatred that most of the resistance fraternity would call for their court-martial.*[50]

Mail was another bone of contention. Between 1966 and 1968 only a smattering of letters from and to the PWs were delivered. A portion of these were carried in and out of Vietnam by pacifist intermediaries,† but in other instances accounting for why some prisoners received mail and others did not became a guessing game among comrades that sometimes took on a cynical edge. It was natural to assume that inmates who were getting mail were somehow cooperating and those who were not were being punished

---

* See Chapter 25.
† Believing that some channel was better than no channel, U.S. authorities looked the other way while correspondence-toting Communist sympathizers and antiwar activists traveled to and from Southeast Asia in violation of passport restrictions. Additionally, the U.S. government relaxed postal regulations to permit the direct transmittal of mail between families and prisoners. Such encouragement brought meager results, as the exchange of a letter or package between a prisoner and his family remained a major event through the middle years, even at holiday time. All 22 parcels shipped to American prisoners in Hanoi during Christmas 1966, and 451 of 465 at Christmas 1967, were returned bearing a rejection stamp by the North Vietnamese post office. (Of the 14 unaccounted for from the 1967 batch, none apparently reached its intended recipient. They may have gotten lost or been confiscated by the enemy.) On U.S. policy and arrangements regarding PW mail, see Davis, *The U.S. Government and American PWs in Southeast Asia*, ch 6 (ms). Mail statistics, including records covering PWs in the South, are in scattered compilations in OSD Hist.

for their bad attitude—except that the evidence often did not fit the pattern. There seemed no rhyme or reason, for example, why Mulligan received correspondence and fellow Alcatraz bitter-enders Jenkins and Rutledge did not. Clearly the North Vietnamese brandished the mail privilege as a carrot, but in fact there were few takers and where Hanoi granted permission it may have been simply to sow confusion and dissension or to score propaganda points for its "humane and lenient" campaign. Significantly, the "writers" were almost always individuals who had previously been identified to the world outside Vietnam as captives. As Plumb came to discern:

> Prior to spring 1970 some of the fellows still had never received or been allowed to send mail. We could never figure out how the selection was made. It wasn't based on good behavior—some of the fellows who seemed to be camp favorites weren't writing. On the contrary, some of the most defiant men sent letters. They left their leg irons, prepared their messages, and returned again to solitary. We finally surmised that the opportunity to write was given to verified POWs who had been publicized by Vietnamese propaganda.

Such understanding did not soften the hurt of seeing a neighbor buoyed by receipt of a letter or parcel from home, even when he eagerly shared the contents. (Of course the news did not always turn out to be good, as when Stockdale learned of his mother's death or Alvarez detected his wife's growing estrangement.) Resentments and jealousies inevitably arose over the issue until the Vietnamese expanded the privilege to most of the PWs after 1969.*[51]

Aside from normal personality clashes between introverts and extroverts, "Oscars" and "Felixes," and otherwise conflicting temperaments, friction stemmed also from differences of age, rank, and branch of service. Coker grew weary of Denton's "incessant" tap transmittals at Alcatraz and balked at relaying the veteran's communications until Stockdale interceded and set him straight. A pair of Air Force officers, Jack Bomar and Dave Duart, sparred over who was in charge of their cell: Bomar technically outranked Duart, but the latter was a pilot who resisted taking orders from a navigator and, according to Guarino, "gave in grudgingly to Bomar's authority." A similar tension existed between Navy pilot George McSwain and his senior radar intercept officer Dick Ratzlaff.† There was also the awkward case where newly downed junior officers found themselves under the command of seniors who had been the subjects of a "how to get yourself bagged" briefing and whose professional judgment they might now be reluctant

---

* A large number of prisoners received mail and packages for the first time at Christmas 1968 and regularly after October 1969, though correspondence continued to be censored and the contents of packages confiscated or stolen. See Chapter 22.
† Nasmyth refereed this one. See *2355 Days*, 117. On disputes relating to legitimate questions of command authority where seniority was difficult to determine, see Chapter 7.

to accept. The "generation gap" between younger and older captives in the North became more prominent as the war progressed and as later shoot-downs tended to be younger and of lower rank to begin with. As they witnessed the arrival of a fresh flock of prisoners in the summer of 1972, Mulligan and his grizzled pals "were thunderstruck. They seemed so young and had so much long hair, sideburns, beards and mustaches." Not only had service regulations pertaining to hair style changed in the interim, but so had the culture itself, so that to many of the newcomers the veteran seniors seemed strait-laced and hidebound even beyond their years.[52]

What held most of the petty peeves and simmering conflicts in check during the middle years was the transcendent need, recognized on all sides, for unity in the face of the enemy's systematic exploitation and torture. As the prisoners' treatment would become more relaxed, so would their sense of urgency regarding solidarity; unity would suffer, as well as discipline and obedience, especially after the PWs were consolidated into large rooms late in the captivity and senior officers had to deal with both the widening generation gap and increasing challenges to the Code of Conduct in a more permissive atmosphere.* At times the intramural clashes would become so fractious the Vietnamese would say, "We will let you kill each other!" But in the end even the most finicky and cantankerous men learned patience and tolerance. Navy Cdr. Kenneth Coskey, a 1968 capture, tried to explain the nature of the accommodation to an interviewer after the war: "You say: 'He picks his nose, but maybe I scratch my ass.' You learn tolerance. You learn a *lot* of tolerance."[53]

Learning to get along with a cellmate, like everything else about being a prisoner of war in Southeast Asia, required adaptability. Dunn, speaking primarily of the PWs in the North, noted how well prepared the predominantly college-educated and career-oriented officers were, rating them

> vastly superior to any group of prisoners in any previous conflict in which the United States has engaged. . . . Their extensive military experience required little or no adaptation to the strict discipline required in a prisoner of war environment. The majority were aviators or personnel who had received similar high-risk, specialized training which required and cultivated self-confidence and imagination. . . . Most had attended some form of survival, evasion, resistance to interrogation, and escape (SERE) course; and while no course can ever prepare an individual completely for becoming a prisoner of war, SERE training aided the prisoners in recognizing the importance of discipline, leadership, and cohesiveness in the prisoner of war environment.[54]

* See Chapter 25.

These much vaunted advantages of training and maturity notwithstanding, the returning PWs themselves were the first to admit that their SERE courses and impressive professional and educational credentials were of limited benefit in a captivity situation that in terms of longevity alone was without precedent. By 1969, the early captures were the longest held prisoners of war in American history, and much more than proficiency, their fate depended on qualities of resiliency and durability for which fancy resumes were no guide to or guarantor of success.

Long-term physiological stress itself hampered the coping capability. Natural and cumulative metabolic changes in the prisoners—scaly skin, rotted teeth, failing eyesight, plummeting weight—affected mental outlook as much as scars inflicted by abuse. Coffee "watched with curious resignation" as owing to diet deficiencies his fingernails became less than half their previous thickness. Chesley lost 60 pounds in three to four months; others saw their waist measurements shrink from a 36 to a 31. Being hungry, Chesley later vented, "doesn't mean just going without food for two or three days. It means going for days and weeks and months seeing your body deteriorate, feeling yourself become steadily weaker . . . . It cannot be described—only experienced." Men developed curvatures of the spine and callouses on pressure points and buttocks sleeping on beds of concrete or warped boards with only a thin rice mat for a mattress. Unusual was the torso that was not encrusted with sores and scabs. McDaniel said it was "a blessing in disguise" that they didn't have mirrors "because we could not see our gaunt, haggard faces."[55]

Jay Jensen wrote in his memoir *Six Years in Hell* that what he missed most while a prisoner was "a soft bed, a hot shower, and a toilet seat." Each man had his own priorities and compulsions, and therefore vulnerabilities. Some obsessed on their injuries, others on the filth around them, others on hunger. Navy PW Robert Naughton observed in a postwar "motivational" assessment that "some men crave water even before their parachutes deliver them to earth, and several sweltering days without washing, plus involuntary immersion in rice paddy water with a human excrement additive, produce an almost maniacal desire for a bath." Hegdahl recalled how he and Stratton "talked about our lives and our families, but the subject almost always eventually got around to food. . . . I always thought of chocolate milk, thought that it would be great to have chocolate milk. Dick used to talk about clams and having clambakes." John Flynn would later joke that new arrivals thought they were getting rye bread "until they saw the rye seeds begin to move"; eating and digesting their vermin-infested rations became its own form of torture for many of the prisoners. Alvarez remembered how during the winter at Briarpatch "the last meal of the day frequently came when it was already dark . . . and while we ate we could hear the telltale crunch as our teeth bit through the hard outer coverings of live roaches." There were those who could not eat or keep down such fodder even when it meant staying alive. And there were those who managed to adapt, Nasmyth and fellow "garbage men" Will Gideon, Jim Warner, and Ed Davis making the most of "grease" sandwiches and Plumb and others finally tasting the "flotsam" in their "murky soup." Reflecting on the "grotesque hunk of hog" floating in his soup bowl, Plumb said that "within a couple of months our starving bodies superseded our sensitivity. We certainly needed protein, and the lard might help fill the gaps between our ribs. After six months—what the heck?—down the hatch went pig bristles and all."*[56]

As some men "shut down" and became passive or numb in captivity, others discovered that deprivation actually sharpened their senses. Alvarez remarked that with little to touch or feel and with vision often restricted to looking through cracks and shutters, their other senses became more acute. Thus men in isolation could identify a passing prisoner or guard from his body odor or the sound of his walk. (After the war Navy Lt. Joseph Mobley, a 1968 capture, maintained he could "feel the effect of an aspirin [and] smell a bar of Dial soap at 400 yards.") Plumb scratched out a keyboard on his bunk and practiced chords until he could "actually hear the notes in my mind." Solitude also enhanced memory but it could drive a man insane unless he found a way to expand his world. During his stay in solitary Rutledge related to the hero of Edgar Allan Poe's "The Pit and the Pendulum":

> Poe's hero saw the walls slowly moving toward him, threatening to crush him to death. In Heartbreak Hotel I realized Poe's walls may not have moved at all. It is something in one's head that moves to crush him. I had the best of survival training in the navy, and it got me through that first long day of interrogation. But after that I was alone, and no survival training can prepare a man for years of solitary confinement. What sustains a man in prison is something that he has going for him inside his heart and head— something that happened, or did not happen—back in childhood in the home and church and school. Nobody can teach you to survive the brutality of being alone. At first you panic. You want to cry out. You fight back waves of fear. You want to die, to confess, to do anything to get out of that ever-shrinking world. Then, gradually a plan of defense takes shape. Being alone is another kind of war, but slowly I learned that it, too, can be won. Like a blind man who is forced to develop other senses to replace his useless eyes,

* PWs in the South ate almost exclusively rice at long stretches, the monotony alone destroying their appetites. Lieutenant Rowe reported on the experience of his group in the Delta: "We found that we had to eat the equivalent of a one-quart pan of cooked rice each meal in order to maintain our strength. . . . You reach a point with this rice diet where you're actually vomiting. It's all mental. It's completely mental. But . . . it takes mental resolve to continue to eat until finally you get it to stay down" (Rowe interv in *Southeast Asia Survival Journal*, Apr 72, 45-50).

a man in solitary confinement must quit regretting what he cannot do and build a new life around what he can do.[57]

Whether deposited in solitary or with roommates, some were able to build that "new life" and some were not. Some died because of injuries that would not heal; others died, or suffered terribly, because they lost what McDaniel called "the war inside." Nasmyth wrote that "the POWs who were captured in my era, 1965 through 1968, all went a little crazy after a while." Risner had his uncontrollable panic attacks. Stockdale became philosophical to the point of stoicism. Guarino tried hypnosis to cure severe headaches. There was one prisoner, Air Force Lt. Gerald Venanzi, who wheeled around his cell on an imaginary motorcycle in a pantomime so elaborate and realistic that neither the enemy nor his own comrades were sure whether he was play-acting or had gone mad. Almost all of the captives who were subjected to the crucible of the middle years experienced depression, nightmares, and a crisis of the spirit at some juncture. But most of them also, through one coping mechanism or another, were able to endure what Stockdale termed "the melting experience" and regain control of their destiny, even if it meant continuing to cling to the edge and conquering one day at a time until things improved.[58]

The last stanza of William Ernest Henley's "Invictus" was a Stockdale favorite and an injunction that many of the American prisoners came to know and recite:

> It matters not how strait the gate,
> How charged with punishments the scroll,
> I am the master of my fate;
> I am the captain of my soul.

It remained for Guarino to speak for those less lucky or less capable of such mastery. Jim Kasler had raised the question with him as to why some of their mates "hung tough" and some caved in, and Guarino responded:

> It had been in my thoughts since I was first captured, when I had reason soon after to question my own level of courage and my determination to resist the enemy. But for the Grace of God, there could have been many more of us in the prisons who flunked the test. We all knew men whose abilities, both physical and mental, in holding the line against the Vietnamese were disappointing. The majority of us were able to endure to a point where the Vietnamese backed off long enough for us to recover our faculties, and then we managed to bounce back against them. But some of us could not endure, and I think people must withhold judgment of men who have undergone such strenuous tests, because he who has not weathered the storm can never know the true nature of the cataclysm and the harm it works.[59]

21

PWs in the South, 1968-1971:
Bondage and Vagabondage

Until 1968, the number of Americans seized in South Vietnam had never topped 25 in a given year, and the list from year to year had expanded only incrementally. Indeed, at the close of 1967, of some 100 U.S. personnel known to have been taken prisoner in the South since 1961, there were only 25 still in captivity, including 2, Robert Garwood and McKinley Nolan, who were thought to have "crossed over" to the enemy. The rest had either died, escaped, or been released.

The 23 (not counting Garwood and Nolan) still incarcerated were widely scattered. Five (Jim Thompson, Richard Burgess, Alfonso Riate, Leonard Budd, and Army Special Forces Sgt. Carroll Flora) had been moved north of the DMZ. Two, Nick Rowe and Army Pvt. King Rayford, were being held by themselves in isolated camps in the South, Rowe to escape at the end of 1968.* Seven, the most prominent of whom was Army doctor Floyd Kushner, were hidden in a patch of dense forest around Tam Ky. Another seven (the McMurray group mentioned at the end of Chapter 14, plus civilian Robert Grzyb) were confined at or were en route to a camp in northern Cambodia near where Cambodia converged with South Vietnam and Laos. And two, civilian Douglas Ramsey and Army Capt. William Hardy, survived at a temporary camp northeast of Tay Ninh along the South Vietnam-Cambodia border.

The Tet offensive tripled their numbers within a four-week span. Between 30 January and 26 February 1968, the Communists in the South acquired more than 50 new U.S. prisoners, almost half of them civilians. The rest of 1968 and subsequent years would bring significant accretions also but nothing on the order of the Tet windfall. Yet even as their ranks swelled, the

* See Chapter 12.

"Southern" PWs' treatment and circumstances did not measurably change. If the story of the prisoners in the North featured slammers, torture, and heroic resistance, the Southern ordeal continued to be dominated by forced marches, casual brutality, and extreme neglect and deprivation. Gradually, as more of the Southern PWs were herded north, the two experiences would intersect and merge at about the time that conditions improved generally, but for most of the Tet captives that was still two or three long years off.

In the weeks leading up to Tet, Viet Cong and North Vietnamese Army troops were busy throughout South Vietnam and in the sanctuary and staging areas inside Laos and Cambodia preparing for the massive Communist assault. In the North, thousands of NVA regulars were setting up positions and stockpiling supplies for the soon to be launched siege of Khe Sanh, a Marine stronghold on Highway 9 in western Quang Tri province, just six miles from the Laotian border and astride a major NVA infiltration route into the South. In the course of the buildup a number of Americans fell into enemy hands even before the attacks had begun.

The first American captured in the South in 1968, Army Pvt. Roger Anderson, was luckier than most. Anderson was seized on 3 January while serving as a perimeter sentry near My Tho. His captivity lasted only nine days, as a U.S. helicopter crew picked him up after strafing the sampan in which he was traveling and killing or scattering his guards. Three other Americans would be captured in early January and make their way back to freedom after a brief captivity. Army Sgt. Lee Brewer, captured on 7 January, escaped the following day. Marine Lance Cpl. Steven Nelson and his buddy Pvt. Michael Roha were also captured on 7 January when their platoon was overrun. Taking advantage of lax supervision during siesta, they slipped out of camp two weeks later and spent a scary night in the jungle before happening upon a Marine compound nearby. In like fashion, another dozen Army and Marine PWs would manage to escape from flimsy detention facilities in the South through the remainder of 1968 and 1969, in almost every instance within days, at most a few weeks, of their capture.[1]

Less fortunate were Army WO Frank Anton and his Huey gunship crew that went down on 5 January on a fire support mission in an area south of Da Nang known as "Happy Valley." Anton's co-pilot, WO Frank Carson, somehow eluded capture and made it back to friendly lines, but Anton, his crew chief, Spec. 4 Robert Lewis, and his door gunner, PFC James Pfister, were caught in the rice paddies where they had tumbled out of the crippled helicopter. They, too, would make it back to friendly lines, but not until 1973.

The crash of Anton's chopper was followed by the capture of eight more Army personnel in the same vicinity, four of them soldiers from the battalion he had been covering and who subsequently conducted a sweep of the area in an effort to locate the downed crew. The four, who stumbled into a Viet Cong ambush on 8 January, were First Sgt. Richard Williams, seriously wounded in the hand; Pvt. Francis Cannon, also seriously wounded by mortar shrapnel in the back and neck; PFC David Harker, suffering from a bayonet wound in the side received while struggling with his captors; and PFC James Strickland. During their trek westward into the mountains they were marched over rough terrain while bound with heavy wire that aggravated their injuries. Harker later described their first encounter with a VC medic:

> A medic showed up to look at Williams' and Cannon's wounds. Williams' fingers were intact, but the top of his right hand had been torn away, leaving a bloody thicket of bone splinters. The VC's field medical technique was typical of what we were to see; he turned his head, held his nose, and poured alcohol on their wounds. It wasn't enough. The wounds of both had begun to turn gangrenous. They insisted on eating separate from Strictland [sic] and me so as not to spoil our appetites. Blowflies had laid eggs in Cannon's back wound. Maggots fell out as he walked.

After a week on the trail, during which they slept in an underground cave and were interrogated at a hut in the jungle, the four prisoners met up with Anton, Pfister, and Lewis.[2]

Meanwhile, the day after the Harker quartet had been seized, troops from a second company of the same battalion entered the battlefield. They, too, were hit hard, taking many casualties, including four more members who fell into Communist hands—PFCs James Daly, Richard Rehe, and Derri Sykes and Spec. 4 Willie Watkins. The badly wounded Sykes and Rehe, the latter shot twice in the chest, lasted less than 48 hours, adding two more names to the growing list of Americans who would die in captivity in the South. Daly and Watkins would spend the next two months tramping through a succession of villages with extended stays in two camps where they received decent treatment and instant indoctrination.[3]

The Anton group, now numbering seven, arrived at a makeshift PW compound on 17 January. It was the mountain camp where Capt. William Eisenbraun had perished, where Garwood was earning notoriety as a turncoat, and where six other Americans were already confined: Captain Kushner, who had entered the camp in early January after spending the first month of his captivity on the move, the lone American with a group of about 10 ARVN prisoners; Jose Agosto-Santos and Luis Ortiz-Rivera, a Marine corporal and Army private who were released the day after Anton's group came; and Marine PWs Edwin Grissett, Robert Sherman, and Earl Weatherman.* Two days after the departure of Agosto-Santos and Ortiz-Rivera, the American prisoners, now numbering 11, were packed up and hiked northwest to a second location about six hours away. Here they would remain for over a year, joined at intervals by Daly and Watkins, 1967 capture Fred Burns, and a half dozen other PWs seized in the region; for many of them, it would be their final resting place.[4]

Twenty-three U.S. civilians, along with several Allied civilian personnel, were taken prisoner in the South during Tet.[5] The first of these was Michael Benge, an adviser with the Agency for International Development. Benge was abducted on 28 January in the Central Highlands while driving around Ban Me Thuot, where he worked, to check on the status of other Americans living in the area. A former Marine fluent in Vietnamese and several Montagnard dialects, he had been in Vietnam since 1962 and had been adopted by a Montagnard tribe and even given a tribal name. Suspected of being a CIA agent by his captors, he was hauled northward along the Cambodia border, joined after a few days by two other Americans captured at the onset of Tet—Henry Blood, a 53-year-old missionary, and Betty Ann Olsen, a 33-year-old nurse serving in the leprosarium at Ban Me Thuot. The three wandered on a seemingly pointless journey, going from one temporary camp to another as their Communist keepers, North Vietnamese Army regulars, evaded ARVN patrols and U.S. spotter planes. Chained together, exposed to the elements with little protection from either the weather or leeches and other jungle scourges, drawing little nourishment from miniscule portions of rice and manioc, before long they all were beset with serious illness. In the spring Benge was stricken with a case of malaria that left him delirious and intermittently blind for over a month before it finally subsided.[6]

By June, both Blood and Olsen also had malaria, and Blood developed skin ulcers. The paltry diet had resulted in scurvy, causing their teeth to loosen and their gums to bleed. Blood, a man of great courage and will whose age placed him at a disadvantage, contracted pneumonia and steadily weakened. He died in July, the NVA taking no pains to save him. Benge and Olsen continued on their meandering trek, crossing into Cambodia and

---

* The release of Agosto-Santos and Ortiz-Rivera and experiences of the Marine noncoms— all 1967 captures—are discussed in Chapter 14. Agosto-Santos and Ortiz-Rivera were let go by the Viet Cong about the same time that Hanoi released three U.S. aviators in the North (see Chapter 18), both actions coming on the eve of Tet and hence possibly diversions or propaganda enhancements related to the offensive.

then doubling back east toward Ban Me Thuot, their ordeal exacerbated by monsoonal rains and infestations of lice and leeches. Olsen lasted until September. Severely anemic, her hair now white and coming out in hand-fuls, her legs hideously swollen and cramping with symptoms of beriberi, her body devastated from dysentery, the young woman died as bravely as any soldier. Benge, racked with dysentery and beriberi himself, later said "the death of those two wonderful people, Betty and Hank, created in me an iron will to live . . . . Each morning I'd look at the sunrise and see it as a signal of success." By October he was in Cambodia again, this time headed north-ward toward a military base camp where he would stay for a year and get better food and care.[7]

Given the heavy infiltration of enemy forces around Saigon and the intensity of the fighting there especially in the early days of Tet, it is some-what surprising that only five civilians were seized in that area during the Communist offensive. AID officials Richard Utecht and Norman Brookens were grabbed near the airfield at Tan Son Nhut on 4 February when three armed Viet Cong gunmen commandeered their jeep. The pair were hustled off and moved northwest toward Tay Ninh and the Cambodian border. At one stop they linked up with Australian businessman Charles Hyland and a third American civilian, James Rollins, the latter a construction company employee captured in a Saigon suburb on 5 February. Hyland was soon separated from the Americans and would be released in late November. In March the other three settled into a camp where, secured in tiger cages and with chains padlocked to their ankles, they languished for four dismal months before moving on again. In the summer they would be united with a fourth American civilian taken during Tet, English teacher Michael Kjome, as well as other U.S. prisoners captured in the Saigon region during 1968.[8]

Far to the north, the Tet assault fell with a special fury on Hue, the ancient capital of Vietnam which became the scene of the worst bloodbath of the war as the Viet Cong and North Vietnamese troops slaughtered thousands of anti-Communist soldiers and civilians. In his vivid account of this episode, Stanley Karnow described the wholesale arrest and murder of foreigners assumed to be associated with the South Vietnamese regime:

> Captured in the home of Vietnamese friends, Stephen Miller of the U.S. Information Service was shot in a field behind a Catho-lic seminary. Dr. Horst Günther Krainick, a German physician teaching at the local medical school, was seized with his wife and two other German doctors, and their bodies were found in a shallow pit. Despite their instructions to spare the French, the Com-munists arrested two Benedictine missionaries, shot one of them, and buried the other alive.

By the time South Vietnamese troops and U.S. Marines liberated the city in fierce fighting at the end of February, the Communists had taken into custody three dozen American and third-country prisoners, including a large batch of civilians. Among them was Foreign Service Officer Philip Manhard, who by virtue of his State Department grade would become the senior American PW of the entire war, technically outranking even the several Air Force colonels in Hanoi.* The 46-year-old Manhard had served as an intelligence officer in the Marines in World War II and Korea, where he participated in the interrogation of Chinese PWs. Although he had had vast experience in Asia and spoke both Japanese and Chinese, he was newly arrived in Vietnam when in the early hours of 31 January he was roused from his sleep by the sound of small arms fire erupting around his villa. Before they could be reached by a rescue force from the MACV compound in Hue, he and four employees of the construction company Pacific Architects and Engineers—Richard Spaulding, Russell Page, Alexander Henderson, and Cloden Adkins—wound up in VC hands. The Americans were interrogated for information on the MACV defenses, then herded out of the city in a southwesterly direction, joined on the trail by Eugene Weaver, a CIA employee whose capture had been filmed by the NVA and was later shown on a CBS evening news broadcast.[9]

Army Sgt. Donald Rander was also awakened by the early morning shelling that signaled the start of the attack on Hue. Grabbing flak jackets and weapons, he and the other members of his detachment billeted in the same house—Capt. Theodore Gostas, Sgts. Robert Hayhurst, Edward Dierling, and Ronald Patterson, and Cpl. Gary Wolk—huddled on the second floor for the rest of the night, slipping downstairs to destroy classified documents. At dawn, low on ammunition and with enemy mortar rounds exploding around them, the group crept next door to a building occupied by four civilian employees of the Defense Department: Lawrence Stark, Lewis Meyer, Everett Siddons, and an unidentified colleague. All that day and into the next night the beleaguered Americans held out as the Communists peppered the house with rockets and gunfire that killed Wolk and Patterson. "It was like Custer's last stand the next morning," Rander recalled. "All the North Vietnamese in the world seemed to be outside the door." As they surrendered on 1 February, Stark concealed a grenade on his person, determined to take some of the enemy with him if the captors began killing the prisoners. When it was clear that the men were being prepared for movement, Stark handed over the grenade to a shocked guard.[10]

---

* Manhard's status in relation to his military compatriots became an issue when he was later incarcerated with an Army officer. See p. 559. On the chain of command dilemma posed by high-ranking civilian PWs, see Chapter 7.

The group was dragged through the streets of the city, dodging the local fighting, to Manhard's vacated villa, where they spent the night stuffed in a small shower stall. The next morning, two more civilian prisoners, Robert Olsen and Thomas Rushton, joined them. That evening, minus Siddons, who was left behind with foot injuries (he was rescued by American infantrymen when they retook the town), they headed out. Gostas, Rander, Hayhurst, and Dierling, all working in military intelligence, collaborated on a cover story to explain their civilian clothing and identification. They agreed that they would portray themselves as Army civilians whose job it was to conduct personnel security investigations on Vietnamese applying for employment with the U.S. government. The pose, at least for a time, may have succeeded. Although it hardly won them any deferential treatment, it may have saved them from the harsher punishment meted out to CIA agent Weaver after he was recognized by a VC he had once interrogated. Weaver, along with Manhard, Spaulding, Page, Henderson, and Adkins, were already at a place the prisoners would later nickname "Camp Runamuck 1" when the Rander group arrived on or about 4 February. Over the next two weeks they would be joined by 13 other PWs captured in the battle for Hue.

On 6 February, Marc Cayer, a Canadian, and Gary Daves entered Runamuck. Both had been working as teachers for International Voluntary Services (IVS). On 7 February, another group of seven checked in. Five of them, Marine Lt. James DiBernardo, Army Sgts. John Anderson, Donat Gouin, and Harry Ettmueller, and Marine Cpl. John Deering—all assigned to the Armed Forces Vietnam Network TV station in Hue—had been captured on 5 February after a running battle in which several of their comrades had been killed and the five prisoners had all been wounded, Anderson seriously with shrapnel wounds in the chest and hand. West of Hue the five had linked up with Marine WO Solomon Godwin, an intelligence specialist, and Thomas Ragsdale, a civilian employee of the U.S. government, neither of whom would survive captivity.* Others to turn up at the camp were Charles Willis, civilian manager of Voice of America operations in Vietnam, and his Filipino assistant, radio engineer Candido "Pop" Badua. Arriving together and housed apart from the other prisoners were two American women, Dr. Marjorie Nelson, a Quaker affiliated with IVS, and Sandra Johnson, an IVS teacher whom Nelson had been visiting in Hue.[11]

---

* Godwin, like Weaver before him, tried to conceal his status as an intelligence officer only to be identified shortly after arriving at Runamuck 1. He and Weaver were separated from the others and held at another site outside Hue until the summer when they were moved out. On 25 July, as they were being marched to a permanent camp in North Vietnam, Godwin, malnourished and with acutely infected feet, died and was buried along the trail. Weaver continued on to the North, to begin years of solitary confinement and brutal treatment.

In heavy forest on a mountainside near Phu Bai, Camp Runamuck 1 appeared to the prisoners to be a way station for NVA troops as well as a collection point for PWs seized in and around Hue. Except for the two women, the prisoners were shoved into a 20- to 30-foot-long bunker that had been carved into the mountain and covered with a bamboo and thatch roof. More than 20 PWs were crammed into the dark and dirty hole, sleeping in shifts because there was not enough room for them all to lie down at once. Unlike the strict routine they would later encounter in the Northern camps, activities and schedules at Runamuck were just that—disorganized and erratic. There were no set eating or wake up times, sporadic interrogation mainly for autobiographical data, and no attempts at indoctrination in the brief period they were there. Meager rations were limited to debris-laden rice.

On 19 February, after a couple weeks' stay, the Hue PWs and their captors broke camp, leaving behind Page, Rushton, Gostas, and Anderson, who were judged too ill to travel. (These four would stay at Runamuck until 10 March and would link up with their comrades in April at a site in North Vietnam.) The rest began the arduous trek north. Walking barefoot (some tried wrapping rags around their feet) through mud and over rocks, they were beset by leeches, stalked by a menacing tiger, and had to sleep on the ground, sometimes in the rain, without blankets. Left untied as they traversed a narrow, twisting portion of the trail, the prisoners saw an easy opportunity to escape, and two of them who were in the best shape, Hayhurst and Dierling, seized it. On the morning of 23 February, the pair slipped away unnoticed and backtracked until they found a stream and then a road that led them to a Marine artillery camp and freedom—the only prisoners in the Hue bunch captured during Tet who managed to escape.* Under tightened security the group then divided for a week, taking two separate routes, before reuniting in early March at a site they would call "Camp Runamuck 2." Along the way they picked up Army WO Michael O'Connor, captured after his helicopter was downed by ground fire, and bade farewell to Dr. Nelson and Sandra Johnson, whom the North Vietnamese had decided to release in a "humanitarian" gesture.[12]

After a week at the new camp they were off again, this time leaving behind Ettmueller, Rander, Gouin, Deering, and Manhard, all suffering from their wounds or from badly bruised and bleeding feet. (Like the foursome

---

* One PW captured south of Da Nang during Tet, Marine Cpl. William Tallaferro, seized on 6 February, successfully escaped after a week in custody. Although he had been seriously wounded in the capture incident and had one of his fingers amputated (without aid of anesthetic) at a crude NVA field hospital, he managed to crawl away from his captors when he was left unattended. Reaching Highway 1, he flagged down a passing Marine truck with the help of an ARVN soldier. From documents Tallaferro had on him when he returned to friendly hands, there is the possibility that the NVA allowed him to escape to deliver a propaganda message.

left at Runamuck 1, they would rejoin their fellow prisoners in April in North Vietnam.) On 16 March tragedy struck at a temporary camp the PWs subsequently named "Death Mountain." That afternoon, perhaps attracted by the smoke from cooking fires, an American jet attacked their hillside location with bombs and rockets. Pandemonium ensued, with the prisoners and guards alike dashing for cover. Afterwards, Henderson found Tom Ragsdale crushed to death by a tossed boulder. The next morning guards allowed the prisoners to bury their comrade in a shallow grave. His body was recovered by U.S. forces the following year when they came upon a wooden cross that had been left to mark the spot.[13]

The bottom of Death Mountain turned out to be a major Communist supply depot and checkpoint for traffic entering and exiting North Vietnam. Resuming the journey north by truck on a circuitous route that took them briefly into Laos, they wound up on 25 March at their first camp inside North Vietnam, still in the jungle but by now 90 miles north of the DMZ and 20 miles inland from the coast not far from the city of Vinh. The Americans would call the place Bao Cao (see p. 90) or, owing to the shape of its cell-block windows, "Portholes." Already there were "Old Man of the South" Jim Thompson and Marines Burgess, Riate, and Budd.* The two clusters of Hue captives who had been left at the Runamuck sites rendezvoused with the others the second week in April.[14] Other Americans seized in the northern tier of the South would soon be corralled there as well.

On 7 February, as the Hue prisoners were being assembled at Camp Runamuck 1, the U.S. Special Forces camp at Lang Vei on the Laotian border west of Khe Sanh fell after a vicious assault that saw, for the first time in the war in the South, the NVA use tanks. The camp, garrisoned by several hundred Montagnard irregulars and elements of a Royal Lao battalion and supervised by a team of U.S. Army green berets, suffered hundreds of casualties as it was overrun. Along with numerous Lao and Montagnard soldiers, three Americans—SFC Harvey Brande, S/Sgt. Dennis Thompson, and Spec. William McMurry—were captured.[15]

Brande, one of the most heroic prisoners of the war, almost did not survive the first few days of his captivity. Serving his third tour in Vietnam, he was severely wounded in the chest and both legs by bullets and grenade shrapnel during the attack on the outpost. As he was about to be executed by a young NVA captain, he received a reprieve when an older officer appeared and ordered him moved, with Laotian and Montagnard prisoners, to a temporary camp in a jungle clearing inside Laos. For a week

* See Chapter 14.

he lay in a bamboo hut hurt and bleeding, forcing himself to crawl to the small stream that ran through the camp, where he attempted to wash out his wounds, which had become infected. At one point Brande saw 40 Lao prisoners stripped and led off to be killed.

Soon he was joined by Thompson, who had been collared with a group of the Montagnards as they awaited evacuation from Lang Vei. On a par with Brande as among the strongest resisters in the PW ranks, North or South, Thompson had been horribly beaten by his captors after repeatedly trying to escape en route to the camp. He had been brutally interrogated, bashed until unconscious, and, like Brande, saved from execution only by the intercession of a senior officer who was aware of the official policy to keep the Americans alive as sources of propaganda and negotiating leverage.

On 18 February, the courageous pair, despite their injuries and more than a week with virtually no food, made yet another escape try. For seven days, they evaded the thousands of enemy soldiers swarming over the area and headed back to Lang Vei, hoping that the camp had been reoccupied, or, at least, that they could pick up some food and survival gear. Thompson ignored orders of the barely ambulatory Brande to leave him and make it back on his own, in the end hauling Brande through the dense jungle piggyback-style. They were within a mile of Lang Vei when they were recaptured.

Ushered north along the Ho Chi Minh Trail, Brande carried in a hammock and the escape artist Thompson now bound at the wrists, around the end of February they linked up with Army Spec. John Young. Young was a fellow member of the Special Forces unit at Lang Vei who had been seized on 31 January near the camp while leading a small group of Lao soldiers on a reconnaissance patrol. He experienced a harrowing initiation when an NVA interrogator pulled and kicked his bullet-shattered leg and threatened him with death in an effort to get him to reveal information on Lang Vei's defenses. To give the threats credibility, the Vietnamese shot two wounded Lao prisoners in the head as the American watched.*

At another temporary camp Brande, Thompson, and Young joined McMurry, himself seriously wounded, and an 18-year-old Marine, Ronald Ridgeway, captured near Khe Sanh on 25 February.† The irrepressible

---

* Young would later be associated with a coterie of enlisted PWs captured in the South who issued antiwar statements while incarcerated in the North and were accused of collaboration by PWs in the Northern prisons. He later denied having divulged any information on Lang Vei that the enemy did not already have, although the successful attack on the outpost a week after his capture inevitably raised suspicions that he had compromised its position. Despite the terrifying interrogation, Young traced his second thoughts about the war to the generally good treatment, including decent food and medical attention, he alleged he received during this period. See Grant, *Survivors*, 200-11.

† Ridgeway was thought by the Marine Corps to have died in an ambush. He was listed as "killed in action" until 1973, when, just prior to homecoming, authorities learned he was alive.

Thompson, handcuffed and locked into leg stocks, was at it again. Using a bamboo tube issued to prisoners in stocks to draw off their urine, he managed to pry open his constraints and break out, only to be detected as he was sneaking away. Guards almost beat him to death, leaving him to lie in a rat-infested hut for the next 10 days. Toward the end of March, the band of five headed out, crossing a leveled area of jungle inside North Vietnam that Young recalled "looked like the moon." Sometimes on foot, sometimes by truck—all the while Thompson's upper body and arms trussed "mummylike" in heavy rope—a fortnight's journey landed them in the middle of April at the Portholes camp where the Hue PWs awaited their fate.[16] Still other prisoners captured in the northern provinces during Tet and the ensuing months joined them there.

One was Lt. Col. Benjamin Purcell, deputy commander of the U.S. Army logistical support headquarters at Da Nang. Purcell would later make two of the most ingenious escape attempts from the North and would spend most of his five-year captivity in solitary confinement. On 8 February he and five other passengers went down in a fiery helicopter crash after the chopper was hit by ground fire near Quang Tri. Also on board were crewmembers Joseph Rose, Roy Ziegler, Robert Chenoweth, Michael Lenker, and James George. All were quickly rounded up except for Ziegler, who managed for a time to evade capture. When George, whose eyes were swollen shut from severe burns that covered his face and hands, could not go on, guards motioned him to sit and prodded the rest of the prisoners up the trail. Purcell heard a shot. He and the others never saw George again. Bare feet raw with cuts and bruises, the remaining captives on 11 February reached a small bivouac area, where they stayed four days and underwent their first serious interrogation. Purcell passed his fortieth birthday squatting in a hole, put there for refusing to answer questions.[17]

On 16 February the group went on to another camp where they were to spend a month. His feet by now "a solid mass of blisters," Purcell arrived in a blanket rigged as a stretcher and carried by ARVN prisoners. (The colonel's rank and a sympathetic opposite number may have won him some privileges here. In a rare instance of medical aid being furnished in such circumstances, a medic dusted his feet with a white powder, wrapped them in gauze, and injected a hypodermic into his rib cage to relieve pressure from cracked ribs.) Waiting at this camp was King Rayford, the lone American held by a band of guerrillas in a series of jungle hideouts since his capture in July 1967. Two days after they reached the site, Ziegler was reunited with his comrades and promptly tried to escape again, this time with Rayford. After slipping out of their hutch and wandering around in circles all night, they were apprehended the next day only a few hundred yards away.

Singled out for punishment, Ziegler was thrown in a hole for a week and placed on half rations.[18]

On 16 March, the party advanced north, first on foot and then in trucks. On the way they linked up with Gostas and other Hue captives who had lingered behind the main contingent, finally crossing over into North Vietnam and reaching the camp near Vinh in April.

On 28 March, as the Purcell bunch was being herded up the Ho Chi Minh Trail, Marine Capts. Paul Montague and Bruce Archer were seized after their helicopter was shot down southwest of their base at Phu Bai. For several agonizing weeks, adhering to the "big four," they endured savage beatings and a version of the rope torture before an interrogator they named "Spike" extracted some false information and a worthless propaganda statement from them. En route to Bao Cao they encountered Army Spec. Michael Branch, who had been brutalized by the same sadistic interrogator who had tortured them. The two Marines arrived at Portholes in the middle of June (Branch would turn up there in mid-August), deposited in the same building with Jim Thompson, Rose, Ziegler, and DiBernardo and O'Connor from among the earlier Tet catches.[19]

All through the spring and into the summer, new prisoners continued to appear at the camp. Air Force Capt. Edward Leonard, a search and rescue pilot, had been shot down over southern Laos on 31 May. Marine Sgt. Abel Kavanaugh and PFC Robert Helle, captured on 24 April near Phu Bai after being inadvertently left behind by the helicopters that lifted the rest of their unit back to their base camp, arrived in mid-July, both sick with malaria and dysentery they had contracted on their three-month trek north. Army PFC John Sparks had been captured in a separate incident on the same day as Helle and Kavanaugh. Spec. Bill Baird, with severe foot injuries that necessitated the amputation of several toes, entered the camp in mid-August, around the same time as Branch.[20]

Lacking a perimeter fence and other customary infrastructure of a traditional prison camp, Bao Cao was still a far more formal and regimented PW facility than existed anywhere in the South. It had been used as a semi-permanent detention center since September 1967 and was expanded to accommodate the influx of captives transported from the South in the aftermath of Tet. The prisoners occupied a half dozen specially constructed wooden cellblock buildings interspersed among the thatched huts and sheds of a sprawling North Vietnamese village. Upon arrival they were segregated into three groups: civilians (including a few military, like Rander and Gostas, whose civilian pose continued to mask their military intelligence identities), junior enlisted personnel, and finally senior enlisted personnel and officers. The civilian group was housed in an area the prisoners would

More than 50 Americans were seized in the South during Tet. Among them: *top, from left,* Green Berets (Dennis) Thompson and Brande, escape artist Ben Purcell; *middle,* Army sergeant Rander, Marines Archer and Deering; *bottom,* missionaries Blood and Olsen, Foreign Service Officer Manhard.

call "Duc's Camp" for the turnkey who had responsibility for that section. The junior enlisted personnel inhabited a similar cellblock area, called "Minh's Camp," separated from the civilian area by a canal-like stream that ran through the camp. Further away, on a knoll surrounded by grassy fields and outside of the village complex proper, was the officers' area. Captured South Vietnamese military personnel and their Lao and Montagnard allies who had been traveling with U.S. and third-country PWs were detained at a location west of Bao Cao and were never again seen or heard from by the other prisoners.[21]

The cellblock buildings, consisting of sturdy timber walls and thatched roofs and each about 30 feet long, contained a series of tiny individual cells that looked like chicken coops. Typically 3 feet wide, 6 feet high, and 6 feet long, many of the compartments amounted to little more than the tiger cages the men had occupied in the jungle. Still, to Jim Thompson, a living skeleton after four years of starvation and mistreatment, they were huge compared to the 2 by 2 by 5 temporary enclosure he had been stashed in for the first several months after his arrival at Bao Cao the previous fall.[22] The doors to the cells were made of heavy lumber and secured with both a bar and padlock. Inside, the cells were bare except for a wooden leg stock, into which recalcitrants were locked at night as punishment. The prisoners received a standard issue of clothing along with a towel, toothbrush, metal bowl, and blanket. For sleeping there was not so much as a slab to lie on; a thin woven mat was all that separated them from the hard plank floor. Ventilation was virtually nonexistent, especially in those cellblocks that were dug into the earth, with only about two feet of the wall above ground.*

Movements of the inmates were strictly regulated, each activity announced by a gong made out of a large-caliber shell casing. Following a 6:00 a.m. awakening, each man was let out of his cell, one at a time, to wash at the stream and go to the latrine, a foul-smelling hole, swarming with flies, dug by the prisoners near their cellblocks. Although there were no fences, security was tight, with barbed wire in spots and armed guards constantly in attendance. After washing, the men were returned to their cells or led away for interrogation or work details. At 10:00 a.m. they received a meager breakfast of a little rice and dried vegetables, after which each prisoner might smoke one of the two cigarettes allotted each day. The meal ritual was repeated in the afternoon at 4:00 p.m. In short, the routine closely resembled the regimen followed in the more urban Northern camps, only in a more rustic setting that conferred even fewer amenities. To the trail-weary

---

* According to one source (Stark), the small circular "portholes" would be drilled into the doors and some outside walls in response to complaints from civilian PWs about the stifling heat.

Southern PWs, their world now had shelter and more predictability but also more onerous discipline and the heightened recognition of the permanence of their prisoner-of-war status. Purcell "realized with a sense of despair, we were now somewhere in the countryside of North Vietnam. That was very significant to me. All the time we were in South Vietnam there was always the hope, no matter how dim, that we might encounter an American patrol. But there were no American ground troops in North Vietnam, so even that remote hope was now denied."[23]

Whether out of overzealousness or insecurity, the young and inexperienced guards at the border camp not only demanded strict obedience but were fanatical about requiring outward signs of respect from the prisoners, insisting on their bowing at every turn and that their every communication begin with the Vietnamese phrase *Bao Cao* for "please" or "may I." (Hence the name by which the place was known to most of the Americans incarcerated there.) Their keepers' gawky demeanor, fractured English, and signature physical features evoked the usual array of irreverent nicknames: Goldtooth, Pugnose, Slaphappy, Many Sticks, Not My Friend, Goofy, Dumbo, Toy Soldier. "Chet and Dave" were christened by DiBernardo, the pair somehow reminding him of the famous news team of Huntley and Brinkley. One particularly fiendish guard earned the sobriquet "Little Hitler."

The degree of interrogation and mistreatment to which the prisoners were subjected varied. Some, especially the lower-ranking enlisted personnel and the civilians who managed to convince their captors they were not CIA agents, were questioned only infrequently and were not exposed to torture. Others didn't fare so well. Phil Manhard, treated more harshly than any other civilian, was suspended by a rope tied under his arms, his feet dangling off the ground, for over 15 hours. Sergeant Rander, his cover story as a civilian unraveling, was interrogated repeatedly and forced to stand or kneel at attention for hours on end. Rander had kept his story going by glancing at the notes on his interrogators' tables, which he read upside down—a talent he acquired as a kid riding the New York subways. Anxious to keep secret his knowledge of classified operations in the South, the sergeant let Dumbo draw unclassified information out of him slowly, lying and fabricating names whenever he thought he could get away with it—a tactic that many a Navy and Air Force PW had tried and discovered to be dangerous when confronted with a skillful interrogator. "Dumbo" was a highly intelligent officer fluent in English—he earned his nickname from his oversized ears, not any lack of mental acuity—and Rander paid the price.[24]

The two incorrigible Special Forces NCOs from Lang Vei invited especially rough handling. Brande, confined with Young in a "dispensary" shed during the early months of his stay at Bao Cao,* was starved, clubbed, and tortured, one of the perpetrators taking delight in inserting bamboo slivers three or four inches deep into his wounds. Dennis Thompson was saddled with extra loads on supply details and more than once seemed on the verge of being killed by guards enraged by his insolence. On one occasion, he and Arturo Balagot, a second Filipino civilian (in addition to Badua) captured in Hue, were led off to dig a grave and then forced to stand in front as shots from a firing squad rang out from behind them. Another time Thompson was blindfolded, marched to a field, and told he was about to be executed.[25] At the other extreme, some of the junior enlisted prisoners fell prey to soft-sell indoctrination efforts. During the summer they were removed from their one-man coops in the enlisted cellblock to a bamboo hut nearby, where they were allowed to mix freely and received decent food and treatment. The group, headed by Riate, who was appointed "room commander" by the North Vietnamese, composed antiwar poetry and even an antiwar song they performed on a guitar for their captors. With Young, several of this bunch, including Riate, Chenoweth, and Kavanaugh, would later form the "Peace Committee."[†]

Bao Cao's expansion was short-lived. On 3 July, even as they were bringing in new prisoners, the North Vietnamese packed up 14 of the camp's civilian and 4 of its military occupants (Purcell, Jim Thompson, Gostas, and Rander) and moved them to a location further north, a penitentiary-type facility near Bang Liet about five miles southwest of Hanoi. "Skid Row," one of several names by which it came to be known, would be their home for the next three and a half years. By late August 1968 officials evidently had decided to shut down the PW operation at Bao Cao altogether, transferring the remaining prisoners to a place the Americans called "Farnsworth," near the town of Duong Ke about 18 miles southwest of Hanoi.[26] The shifts represented the first of several incremental movements over the next two to three years whereby the regime in Hanoi sought to tighten its claim and grip on the "Southern" captures, intent not only on herding them into the North but then consolidating them in camps in and around the capital.

The PWs in custody in the far northern reaches of the South could be moved fairly expeditiously across the border and then closer to Hanoi. But

---

* Brande and Young, neither of whom could yet walk, were the only prisoners not kept in the cellblock buildings. John Hubbell noted that "an intense hatred was to develop between the invalid twosome," the one hard-nosed and defiant, the other oblivious to the Code of Conduct and having doubts about the legitimacy of the U.S. involvement. See Hubbell, *P.O.W.*, 411-12, and Grant, *Survivors*, 271-72, for two quite different versions of their conduct at Bao Cao. Brande would be one of Young's principal accusers after the war.
† See Chapter 25.

for those captured further to the south, the journey was greatly complicated by logistical and health problems that made the trek that much more arduous and dangerous. As a rule, the farther south a man fell into captivity, the greater the delay as well as more protracted the march north. The Kushner group, holed up well below Hue, would not be moved into North Vietnam until 1971. Those held in northeastern Cambodia made their way across the DMZ in two migrations in late 1969 and early 1970. Prisoners captured in Military Region III between the Central Highlands and the Mekong Delta (including those seized near Saigon during Tet) would be held in the South throughout their captivity, gradually coalescing into two main groups (the "Schrump Group" and the "Ramsey Group," so-named after the senior member of each band). These men were interned in a series of camps along the Cambodian border with Tay Ninh and Phuoc Long provinces, periodically traveling further west into Cambodia in response to increasing Allied pressure on the border sanctuary areas; they were united in a camp near Kratie, Cambodia, early in 1973 and ultimately released as a single group at Loc Ninh. Finally, for the few captives held either singly or in small groups in the Delta region south of the Mekong River, the trip north was never really a viable option. Only one American, Army Capt. Robert White, captured in November 1969, was released from this area at the end of the war.* The rest died in captivity, were released early, or, like Lieutenant Rowe, managed to escape.[27]

As the Tet offensive slackened and was finally repulsed with the retaking of Hue from the Communists in late February, the number of Americans captured in South Vietnam dropped sharply. Fewer than one-third of the more than 100 Americans seized in the South during 1968 fell into enemy hands after 1 March. Of these, the eight captured in the northern provinces during March, April, and May (Archer, Montague, Branch, Helle, Kavanaugh, Sparks, Baird, and Air Force Lt. Col. Theodore Guy†) were moved into North Vietnam shortly after incarceration, all except Guy joining the prisoners from Hue at Bao Cao. Six of the 1968 captures from the post-Tet period would escape after a brief captivity,‡ five would join the Kushner camp in the Tam Ky area, two would be held at the camp on the Indochinese tri-border, and the remainder were scattered through the

---

* White spent his entire captivity in the Delta's swamps. Navy Lt. Cdr. John Graf ejected safely with him when their surveillance plane was hit by ground fire, but White lost track of his partner soon after the pair was carted off and he never saw Graf again.
† Guy became a PW after having to bail out of his F-4 west of Khe Sanh. He was taken to Hanoi and held with pilots shot down in the North (see Chapter 18). In the spring of 1970 he would link up with prisoners from the South at Farnsworth and spend the rest of his captivity with them.
‡ Spec. 5 Donald Martin, USA; Spec. 5 William Taylor, USA; Cpl. Frank Iodice, USMC; Sgt. Albert Potter, USMC; Maj. Richard Risner, USMC; and Sgt. Buddy Wright, USA.

lower half of the South, most of them ending up with Major Schrump in the Tay Ninh region.

The Kushner Camp

The Kushner group spent all of 1968 and the start of 1969 at their second location (cited as Camp Bravo in debriefs) in the complex of camp-sites around Tam Ky that we have referred to collectively as "the Kushner camp." To the 11 prisoners mentioned previously* were added Daly, Watkins, and Burns in March 1968, along with two more recent captures, Marine Cpls. Dennis Hammond and Joseph Zawtocki.[†] In April came Army Spec. Isiah McMillan and Sgt. Thomas Davis; in May, Army Pvt. William Port; and, over the next several months into 1969, Marine Pvt. Fred Elbert[‡] and Army Pvts. Gustav Mehrer and Coy Tinsley. Port was in by far the worst shape, a grenade blast leaving him partially blind and with severe injuries to his head, toes, and arms.[§] Owing more to harsh conditions, chiefly starvation, than abusive treatment, seven of Bravo's occupants died during the 15 months Kushner was there.[28]

David Harker, who would survive, later painted this description of Bravo, situated along a creek bank blanketed by thick forest:

> . . . The compound was surrounded by a bamboo fence. The enclosure was surprisingly small, about thirty meters long and ten or fifteen meters wide. . . . The lower portions of the bank were lined with poisonous punji stakes. Anyone trying to escape by jumping over the rear fence would be impaled . . . .
>
> The surrounding area was impenetrable forest and jungle— ferns, vines, bamboo thickets, wild banana trees, hardwoods, and other tropical exotica. The jungle floor was covered with thick brush and rising ferns. Above that grew broadleaf trees of middling height, and above that giant hardwoods rose a hundred feet or more and spread their branches to interlock. The effect was that of a triple canopy which closed out the bright tropic sun and left a damp twilight of perpetual gloom.

At first the men lived together in a single grass hutch, sleeping on a bamboo platform that ran the length of the small structure. "The platform," Harker recalled, "was six feet wide and stood three feet off the ground. This was our

---

* See pp. 448-49.
† Hammond and Zawtocki were present only a month when they participated in the aborted escape attempt that cost Earl Weatherman his life. See Chapter 14.
‡ Quiet and peculiarly detached, Elbert went by an alias and for most of his captivity was known even to his fellow PWs as John Peter Johnson. See Grant, *Survivors*, 245-46.
§ Port received the Medal of Honor for shielding comrades from the explosion.

communal bed. Between the platform and the outer wall was a walking space three feet wide. At the end of the walkway was a dirt hole braced with several rocks: our kitchen. A small hole dug in the ground at the farther end of the compound was our latrine, and dried banana leaves were our paper." Eventually they spread into a second hutch that offered more room, but any hope for improvement was dashed by diminishing supplies of food and hammering monsoons that turned the camp into a bog. Before the rains came, workers built a classroom with bamboo benches that, but for the subject matter, might have resembled an early schoolhouse on the American frontier. The prisoners took an intensive two-week indoctrination course taught by an instructor who supposedly had taught Garwood to speak Vietnamese.[29]

At Garwood's trial, Kushner testified to their desperate state during the fall of 1968 and the succeeding winter:

> Well, from September until January six men died, most of them in my arms, and we—our ration was very low. We were eating approximately three coffee cups of vermin-infested rice per day, with some fish sauce. We had a terrible skin disease that was keeping people up all night. It was itching. It was causing a lot of psychological anguish as well as physical anguish. We were horribly malnourished. People had malaria and dysentery, so that they were perhaps defecating many, many times a day, fifty or sixty times a day, could not make it to the latrine so that the prison yard was littered with human excrement. It was the rainy season. It was cold and miserable, and in general just a very horrible—I don't know the words that can describe how bad these times were.

Of the itching alone, the physician told a crowd of reporters upon his return home that he could not overemphasize the effect it had on them: "For eight months I couldn't bend my fingers more than 10 degrees. I recall very, very vividly ten or eleven POW's lying on a crowded bed . . . screaming and asking God or someone to take their life so this itching would stop." His own suffering compounded by the bitter frustration of his not being able to treat his dying comrades, he was "on the edge of insanity."* A leadership vacuum further depleted morale. As Anton later admitted,

> At the beginning Kushner, Williams, and myself got together and discussed what we should do. The person who led the camp had to be physically strong. None of us was. We decided to try to use our influence as a group. We made no attempt to create a military organization. The VC warned us individually several times that if

---

* Complicating matters, Kushner's glasses had been broken in the capture incident and he had trouble seeing. At one point he apparently used Fred Burns's pair, which had not been confiscated.

we did we would be punished. Moreover, we weren't sure of our legal rights in the matter. Kushner was a captain but a doctor and therefore a noncombatant. I was a warrant officer, a pilot with no command responsibility. Williams was a first sergeant but wounded.

Williams, who had won the Silver Star in Korea, initially commanded respect, but, at 41, was soon overmatched as his hand injury became gangrenous and both his health and spirit rapidly deteriorated. By default, noncoms Watkins and Davis, physically the most able, emerged as decisionmakers.[30]

The absence of leadership and organization was exacerbated by friction among the PWs stemming from the usual personality clashes and from social and cultural differences between the officers and enlisted members of the group. Racial tensions, which the Vietnamese readily exploited, also contributed to the strained relations. Five of the prisoners—Watkins, Davis, Daly, Lewis, and McMillan—were black, and their handlers plied them with extra indoctrination, for a while segregating them in a separate third building. The dissension affected attitudes toward the enemy and toward one another and, as reflected in the survivors' postwar accounts, resulted in widely divergent and highly personal assessments of individual treatment and performance. Kushner himself emerges as either a caring hero or a shirking wimp depending on the beholder. During indoctrination classes where the men were expected to "criticize" one another, swipes at comrades did not always have to be coaxed and on occasion became gratuitously mean. There is no question that conditions were horrible, but it is also clear that the bad blood between them worsened their plight and lessened their chances.* [31]

Watching their compatriots perish one by one, as if by plague, brought them closer. McMillan said the divisiveness lasted "till people started dying like hell." Cannon and Williams succumbed the same week in September 1968 from the ravages of beriberi-induced edema and their untreated wounds. Port, Sherman, and Grissett died within days of one another on or about Thanksgiving; Burns, at the beginning of the new year. About 1 May 1969 the survivors were moved to another location (Charlie), where they stayed through the middle of December with no appreciable change in the routine or circumstances, save for once again living under one roof and having to venture further on work details to gather manioc. The precious

---

* Craig Howes challenges the argument, implicit in Hubbell's *P.O.W.*, that the Kushner PWs failed in part because they "lacked the senior Hanoi POWs' strength, intelligence, and discipline." Downplaying the leadership and unity factors that he believes were exaggerated in the Northern camps, he raises an intriguing point: "How would the Alcatraz POWs have fared in the Kushner camp? The official story implicitly argues that they would have survived with their honor and military bearing intact, but we cannot know. Similarly, one can only wonder how many of the Kushner POW casualties . . . would have survived if they had gone right to Hanoi." See *Voices of the Vietnam POWs*, 98-101, 210-17 (98, 217, quotes).

Kushner (top left) with other members of his group. *Top, from left:* Harker, McMillan; *middle,* Zawtocki, Davis, Port; *bottom,* Williams, Anton, Watkins. Zawtocki, Port, and Williams were among seven U.S. servicemen who died in the Kushner camp.

tuber provided starch to supplement their rice diet, and the stronger among them, used much like slave labor, were hiked for miles through rain and heat on day-long expeditions to obtain it. "It is doubtful," Kushner later observed, "that the calories derived from the fruits of such an ordeal equaled those expended in the effort." Nonetheless, it contributed to their fragile subsistence and when it was not available, in part due to U.S.-directed defoliation activity, they and their captors had to fall back on bare roots and leaves to fill the void.[32]

The stay at Charlie was notable mostly for comings and goings. Shortly after they arrived, they spotted a group of Caucasians being led into the camp. They were West German nurses, Knights of Malta volunteers who had been working in local hospitals in the South and were abducted while on an outing near Da Nang. One had died on the trail and now four were being housed in a newly constructed hutch. Despite their youth (the oldest was 28) and good treatment, the jungle quickly demolished them. Tall, strapping Georg Bartsch and Hindrika Kortmann became gravely ill with malaria and, weakened by dysentery and malnutrition, died within the span of a week in July. Monika Schwinn and Bernhard Diehl departed the camp in September, destined to encounter other American PWs as they traveled their own route north to Hanoi and release in 1973.* In November 1969 the Vietnamese released Strickland, Watkins, and Tinsley in time for a major antiwar demonstration in the United States. "Why the VC had chosen Strictland [sic] and Watkins," Harker reasoned,

> was not difficult to figure out. They had worked hard and kept their noses clean. The VC liked them. As a black and a white they provided a racial balance. And both were in fairly good physical shape. The choice of the Tennessean [Tinsley] was more subtle. We always thought that if a release came, Joe Zawtocki would be included. He was a hard worker, had a personality the VC liked, and had served time as a squad leader along with Watkins and Strickland [sic]. But Zawtocki had become very ill in the summer of '69. The National Liberation Front's public image would not have been helped to release someone who looked like he just walked out of Dachau.
>
> The Tennessean, on the other hand, had received relatively good medical attention, showing the lenient and humane treatment of the Front. Besides, Dr. Kushner told them he thought the Tennessean had contracted serum hepatitus [sic]. I think they were worried

* Schwinn would become the only Caucasian woman held by the North Vietnamese. The story of her and Diehl's survival, told firsthand in *We Came to Help* (New York: Harcourt Brace, 1973), is an epic in itself. The book is especially interesting for the Germans' impressions of Garwood and, later, Phil Manhard.

about another prisoner dying. As we later learned, Hanoi had begun to improve the treatment of POWs held in the north around this time, probably because of world interest in them. The policy undoubtedly was passed down to the VC.

Perhaps no one was more disappointed at not being included among the releasees than Garwood, who later suggested that he had hoped his collaboration might earn him a pass home. Seldom seen since escorting the Germans into the camp in the spring, the mysterious deserter would part with the group for good before they reached their next location (Delta) the third week in December.[33]

Zawtocki was the next to expire, on Christmas Eve as Radio Hanoi played carols on the compound's scratchy transistor. Another winter passed, in Daly's words, with "the same supply runs, same classes, same storytelling bull sessions at night, same hopes that maybe something great would happen in Paris." Although the prisoners benefited from the improvement in treatment that was occurring everywhere by 1970, food became even scarcer as a result of constant shelling in the area that excited both hope and terror. In February the group, now numbering 12,* got a new mate with the arrival of Marine Cpl. Jose Anzaldua, seized during a nearby operation that almost uncovered the camp. By the end of March they were down to a dozen again with the death, on St. Patrick's Day,† of Hammond. The rugged PW, who had survived savage punishment following the April 1968 escape failure, steadily declined from the effects of protein deficiency and dysentery until his heart gave out.[34]

As the guerrilla encampments in the Tam Ky region increasingly became a target for Allied air strikes, the captors decided sometime in 1970 to move the Kushner prisoners into the North. Although they were not out of the woods yet, either literally or figuratively, by February 1971 they were on their way north via Laos and the Ho Chi Minh Trail. A two-month journey by foot, truck, and finally rail from Vinh brought them to Hanoi on 1 April. When they removed their blindfolds they found themselves inside a walled courtyard with low-slung structures that reminded Daly of a motel. It was the Plantation. Here they would encounter less freedom and more discipline

* Anton, Daly, Davis, Elbert, Hammond, Harker, Kushner, Lewis, McMillan, Mehrer, Pfister, and a peripheral figure named "Long" who creeps into Kushner's and others' narratives but is never fully identified. By a process of elimination one can only surmise he was Army Spec. Julius Long, who was captured in the South in May 1968.
† Anyone looking for sad ironies could find them in the tragic coincidence of death and holidays that seemed to stalk the Kushner group: besides Hammond, the would-be escapee Weatherman on April Fool's Day, the several who died close to Thanksgiving or New Year's Day, and Zawtocki on Christmas Eve.

(much of it from the new demands of a functioning PW organization) than they had been accustomed to in the jungle, but also cleaner clothes, loaves of bread, and bath facilities. "After South Vietnam," Daly reckoned, "you couldn't put a price on things like these."[35]

Camp 101/102

"Camp 101," as the prisoners named it, straddled the tri-border with Cambodia and Laos, just inside Cambodia and due west of the South Vietnamese city of Kontum. Six U.S. soldiers—Warrant Officer Sooter, Sergeants McMurray and Frank, and Specialists Henry, Newell, and Perricone—had been caged there since July 1967,* joined in December by civilian Robert Grzyb, a former serviceman who was unemployed and in trouble with local authorities at the time he was abducted by Viet Cong north of Pleiku. In May 1968, two weeks after he was captured in a skirmish in which his radio operator was killed, Capt. Stephen Leopold entered the camp. By then the group had moved to a larger compound nearby, which took the name "102."[36]

Michael Benge[†] and Army PFC Peter Drabic arrived in the fall of 1968, and four more Army captives—Don MacPhail, Gail Kerns, William Smith, and Thomas Horio—during 1969. Benge judged the conditions good, but only by comparison with the tortuous trek that had claimed fellow civilians Blood and Olsen. The stockaded facility was a well-organized Communist base camp that had doctors and a hospital, from which the PWs periodically benefited. Still, they subsisted on scraps of food and were locked in cagelike compartments all day except for a brief morning exercise session and to go to the latrine. Grzyb died in October 1968 of complications from malaria and malnutrition. The others endured a year to a year and a half at the permanent location before hitting the trail again—this time the Ho Chi Minh Trail—in November 1969.

The 102 group, augmented by several recent captures, journeyed north in two contingents that reached the outskirts of Hanoi at the close of 1969 and in April 1970. The grueling trip, mostly by foot, and the return to a "catch-as-catch-can" diet caused a recurrence of Benge's beriberi symptoms. Benge and Horio stayed behind at a rest stop until they were well enough to continue with the second group. Smith either died or was killed in transit. By April altogether 23 Americans had made the passage from the Cambodian camp to North Vietnam, winding up at Farnsworth beside the Bao Cao PWs who had been there since 1968.[37]

---

* See p. 276n.
† See pp. 449-50.

The Schrump Group

The mountainous region west of Saigon in the area of the Parrot's Beak was not much kinder to prisoners of war than was the Tam Ky area that wasted the Kushner group. At the start of 1968 four U.S. servicemen—Roraback, Cook, Bennett, and Schumann—had already perished in the wilderness along the Cambodian border in the vicinity of Tay Ninh.* In the aftermath of Tet another batch of Americans were being collected there and organized into two distinct groups that would remain largely separated until late in the war.

The group that would take its name from Army Maj. Raymond Schrump originated with the capture of Spec. Thomas Vanputten on 11 February 1968. For three weeks Vanputten was shuffled from one Viet Cong outpost to another, threatened with death if he did not respond to questions and subjected at each stop to indoctrination and a crudely staged mock trial. At one camp he met Mike Kjome, the teacher seized near Saigon during the Communist drive. In May the two linked up with a pair of Army advisers, Lt. John Dunn and PFC James Ray, who had been caught two months earlier in an ambush while accompanying an ARVN unit. Dunn, a military intelligence officer, was lucky that one of his captors had taken his brass MI insignia as a souvenir so that he was able to conceal his identity. Still, he underwent a brutal interrogation during which he was forced to kneel at attention, beaten when he refused to answer, deprived of food and water for several days, and told he was about to be executed. The prisoners' treatment relaxed during a mostly uneventful summer when, in September, they were marched off to another camp. Here they would join Major Schrump and other of their countrymen.[38]

Schrump is a significant if unheralded principal in the prisoner-of-war story in the South. At the time of his capture on 23 May 1968 he had been a dedicated and successful officer who had twice served as a sergeant in Korea before graduating from Officers Candidate School and qualifying for Special Forces. He had had experience as a team commander in Ethiopia and was serving in a training capacity in Okinawa when he volunteered to work as an adviser with the South Vietnamese in Tay Ninh Province. From January to May 1968 he struggled to organize and prepare local forces to defend their own territory from marauding Viet Cong. Contending not only with the local militia's lack of discipline but also with government leaders in the district whom he found corrupt and incompetent, Schrump was not entirely surprised when the Viet Cong overran the area in May. He was seized after being shot while rushing to the aid of a wounded soldier.[39]

---

* See Chapter 13.

For two weeks Schrump's captors moved him along trails in the direction of the Cambodian border before turning him over in early June to intelligence personnel for extensive interrogation. Although he was not tortured and in fact received care and treatment that saved his damaged arm and possibly his life, he soon realized the long odds of surviving the indefinite jungle captivity that lay ahead, an odyssey that would wind through more than a dozen camps, half of them in Cambodia. Like others confined in the South, he would endure serious illness, exhausting marches, bombardment by his own forces, and fear and depression without the benefit of the numbers and organization that sustained the PW resistance in the North. And as a senior officer he had a duty to lead and motivate the other prisoners with him, including managing the problems and welfare of civilian PWs. Schrump had to, and by all accounts did, summon the wherewithal to inspire others to survive when attending to his own survival was challenge enough.

On 19 July at his second camp (Bravo) Schrump got his first companions. At dawn he heard a commotion and American voices that turned out to be those of civilians Dick Utecht, Norm Brookens, and Jim Rollins. The three men were gaunt and haggard from their five months together since their capture during Tet,* Rollins already having lost over 30 pounds. The newcomers brought more than companionship. They were good men to be with in difficult times. Utecht had served as an engineer in Special Forces units with Schrump before retiring and taking a post with AID, and Brookens was a veteran also. Their resiliency was quickly tested. Early in August, after an observation plane spotted the camp and called in an air strike, the four had to scamper with their handlers to another site (Charlie) an hour away.

The stay at Charlie lasted slightly over a month before they were on the move again, joined briefly along the trail by PFC Felix Neco-Quinones, a diesel mechanic whose truck convoy had been ambushed on 16 July close to the spot where Captain Schumann had been captured in 1965. (Guards led Neco-Quinones away before the group reached their next camp, Delta, inside Cambodia. He would rejoin them a year and a half later.) Dunn, Ray, Vanputten, and Kjome were already at Delta when the group arrived. For the six months the prisoners were there they lived and slept in hammocks about 10 meters apart in a semicircle watched over by a centrally located guard. Although kept chained and incommunicado much of the time, they were allowed to exercise and to bathe once a week in a nearby stream. There was no formal indoctrination, just occasional

* See p. 450.

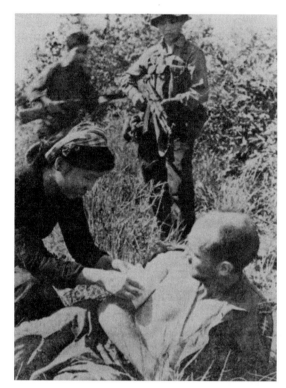

Schrump at capture; civilians
Utecht (top) and Brookens.

discussions with "Joker," the captors' commander (called "Chief Smirk" by Vanputten for the habitual twisted smile on his face), some propaganda pamphlets they were given to read, and the nightly airing of English-language broadcasts from Radio Hanoi, whose reach seemed to know no bounds. Gradually a set of routines and arrangements developed that would become more or less standard for most of their captivity.

Some of the guards treated the PWs humanely (one in fact crossed over to the government side in 1969 carrying a photo of Schrump with him), but there was nothing benign about their shelterless existence. Although the camp was located within range of an American artillery base and there were almost daily overflights of the site by U.S. aircraft, the place remained undetected due to effective camouflaging, heavy woods, and brush so thick that the prisoners sometimes could only catch glimpses of their fellow captives. Kjome, whom the Vietnamese suspected of having CIA ties, was singled out for abuse, constantly threatened by execution until, by year's end, he was verging on a total breakdown. Vanputten could hear him sobbing at night. Perhaps believing it was a matter of time before the others would falter as well, the young soldier planned an escape when he noticed guards becoming careless. On 29 March 1969 he slipped away after having his irons unlocked to go bathe, then deliberately took a northerly route away from the area containing the U.S. base, figuring correctly that the VC would search for him in the opposite direction. Miraculously, after 18 days of evading search parties, nibbling on raw lizards and fruit peels left by feeding monkeys, and frantically waving to passing aircraft overhead, he was sighted and picked up by a friendly helicopter.[*][40]

Within hours after Vanputten's escape from Delta, the captors hurriedly packed their equipment and hauled the seven remaining prisoners along the border to another holding place 10 miles to the north. At this next camp (Echo), the Vietnamese took more precautions, stashing the PWs in belowground cages (hence the Americans' nickname for the place, "Monkey Cages") and in general tightening security. They spent a year here during which Schrump would experience some of the blackest days of his captivity and tragedy would befall PFC Ray. Confinement had been especially difficult for Ray, who twice had tried to escape. As he became more agitated, guards treated him roughly until, in heavy chains, he attacked one and made a desperate break for freedom. Quickly he was subdued and dragged away, the other prisoners never to see him again.[†] Accused of collusion, Schrump and Dunn were locked in their bunkers for a month. Menaced by snakes and insects and decimated by infections and beriberi, Schrump lost 50 to 60 pounds and was nearly out of his mind when he broke and wrote a propaganda statement for indoctrinators.

In the spring of 1970 the Schrump group underwent a major reshuffling when the two officers were separated from the four civilians[‡] and acquired 11 new mates, all of them fellow Army personnel seized in Military Region III. One of them was Neco-Quinones, whom they had passed in 1968 en route to Delta. Another, Ferdinand Rodriquez, Dunn had known briefly at another camp before he joined Schrump. The others were Walter Ferguson, Bobby Johnson, John Sexton, Gary Guggenberger, Frederick Crowson, Richard

---

[*] His first words to the pilot: "I love you! I love you! . . . . I've escaped from the enemy. Give me something to eat." Upon devouring a meal of warm root beer, fruit cocktail, and chicken with noodles at a field hospital north of Saigon, he exclaimed, "I have never tasted such delicious food in all my life."

[†] Ray is assumed to have died soon afterwards. One prisoner reported seeing him lying in a hammock at a different camp, apparently dead, around the beginning of November 1969. Although the Viet Cong listed him as among those who died in captivity, his would be one of the cases cited by critics of the Pentagon's casualty accounting. See Cawthorne, *The Bamboo Cage*, 74.

[‡] Utecht, Brookens, Rollins, and Kjome were hiked northeast to the Ramsey Camp to be consolidated with the several civilians there. See p. 475.

Springman, WOs Daniel Maslowski and Michael Varnado, and Capt. Robert Young. Varnado, a wounded helicopter pilot, was detached from the others, supposedly to receive medical attention, but he never reappeared and is presumed to have died in captivity. Ferguson is believed to have died in the summer of 1970 after being shot during an escape attempt. After a long illness Captain Young would succumb to a severe stomach disorder in September 1972, just months before his comrades were freed.[41]

The reconstituted group spent 1970 and 1971 relentlessly on the run, going back and forth between Echo and other locations and plunging deeper into Cambodia in order to avoid advancing Allied operations. At one point, the PWs were so near to American forces that they heard artillery crews yelling to each other. The close proximity probably encouraged Ferguson's escape try as well as others by Johnson and Sexton, also unsuccessful although they survived. Sexton, in fact, in a rare prisoner exchange was released in October 1971, stumbling dazed into an Allied camp with a map furnished by his keepers.[42] Two more additions in 1971, WO James Hestand and civilian Richard Waldhaus, would bring to 11 the number under Schrump's command who finally made it out of Cambodia in 1973.

The Ramsey Group

Doug Ramsey, entering his third year in captivity in January 1968, and Army Capt. William Hardy, a PW since June 1967, learned about the Tet offensive from the exultant reaction of their Viet Cong guards to news of the fighting on the camp radio. The pair had just been moved to yet another desolate patch of jungle in the mountains along the Cambodian border north of Tay Ninh, some distance northeast of where the Schrump group was beginning to form. Perhaps anticipating a surge of new prisoners, the VC enlisted the men to help clear the wilderness site, but Ramsey's legs, horribly swollen from successive marches and the effects of beriberi, left him incapacitated, and Hardy shouldered the burden for both of them. The two were kept apart much of the time, Ramsey sleeping in a thatched cage and Hardy in the open in a hammock with one foot chained to a tree. Over a period of 10 months Ramsey's health recovered and then deteriorated again.[43]

By November increasing air activity forced another series of evacuations, causing the small party to scramble from one side of the mountain to the other. Swarms of mosquitos greeted them at each new bivouac. At one location they stayed almost a year, joined by three civilian workers seized near Saigon in February 1969—John Fritz, James Newingham, and Tanos Kalil. All three were ill, probably with typhoid, and late in June Kalil died, reportedly of kidney failure. Four months later, with the bombing so intense their bunkers were disintegrating around them, the band crossed into Cambodia. There, in April 1970, their numbers doubled when Brookens, Utecht, Rollins, and Kjome—the four civilian transferees from the Schrump group—suddenly turned up in camp.

As was the case with PWs throughout the border region, the summer of 1970 found Ramsey and his cohorts in a no-man's-land dodging mortar rounds and fleeing what were once safe guerrilla havens. Ramsey's debriefer later recorded one of many harrowing moments as the party tried to ford a river and came under a fusillade of rocket and artillery fire:

> . . . The group remained pinned down until nightfall. The V.C. tied themselves in pairs with the POWs and forced the prisoners to cross a roaring torrent of water. They were burdened down with packs and held in their hands various belongings. Ramsey still wonders how they made the treacherous crossing in the black of night. All lights were doused or shaded. It was difficult to find footing on the uneven river bed. The fast-flowing river added to their problems but somehow they managed to grapple their way to the other side.

Climbing ever steeper terrain under a hot sun, in high humidity, and with dwindling food, both captors and captives verged on collapse when they encamped for several weeks on a hillside where they killed and feasted on an elephant. Contaminated water and resulting diarrhea added to the PWs' misery, along with the growing hostility of their stressed guards. To keep Utecht, who was older than the others, moving, one of the Viet Cong put a rope around his neck and pulled him "like a milk cow." At one point Utecht had to be revived by Ramsey with mouth-to-mouth resuscitation. Newingham, who had played football and run track in college, also foundered, able to continue only after Hardy and Fritz helped restore his breathing and carried his pack.[44]

That none of the group (after Kalil) died under these circumstances is amazing, though at intervals each came close, with the emotionally unraveling Kjome probably the sickest of them all and Brookens also terribly ill at one stretch. Ramsey said they ate "every variety of animal, from field mouse to elephant," and at one meal believed they were dining on Brookens's remains when they hadn't seen him for a few days and noticed a chunk of wrist in their rations. (To their relief, the "tidbit" showed no trace of their friend's tattoo. It turned out to be the hand of a large ape.) As they pushed deeper into the jungle that Ramsey thought "must be the ancestral home of the anopheles mosquito," malaria combined with malnutrition to overwhelm even the strongest among them, but they somehow survived this nadir of their captivity.[45]

Late in 1970 conditions began to improve when the caravan settled into a permanent camp 30 miles inside Cambodia and their Viet Cong

Viet Cong release, *left to right*, Smith, Jones, and Brigham.

handlers were gradually replaced by North Vietnamese personnel. The change-over, including a new commander, introduced more food and medicines and a team of English-speaking interpreters who may have been installed for train-ing purposes. Hardy, who was black, found indoctrination sessions increas-ingly pitched to race, but partnered unswervingly and effectively with Ramsey, whom the Vietnamese had come to recognize as the group's spokesman. Although Ramsey communicated their common concerns, the eight captives were kept so isolated it was some time before they realized a new member had joined them. Army Spec. Keith Albert, who had passed through a num-ber of temporary camps since his capture in May 1970, arrived in February 1971. The nine men stayed at the permanent location until April 1972.[46]

What proved to be the next to last leg of their journey ended up being one of the most difficult due to oppressive heat and a water shortage that left the Americans dangerously dehydrated and Ramsey "ready to drink out of a mud hole." At last it rained and the prisoners "guzzled" the runoff from the plastic sheets that now covered their bamboo "cells."[47] Near Kratie on the Mekong River they put in to an abandoned military camp where they remained into 1973 and linked up with Schrump's band in January. The two groups were released together a month later inside South Vietnam.

Between the release of Agosto-Santos and Ortiz-Rivera in January 1968 and Sergeant Sexton of the Schrump group in October 1971, the National

Liberation Front freed 10 other American PWs in South Vietnam. All of these releases were U.S. Army personnel and all occurred in 1969, when the NLF stepped up its bid for broader international acceptance as the position of the South Vietnamese government continued to erode. Besides the three November 1969 releases from the Kushner group already noted (Strickland, Watkins, and Tinsley), the Communists freed three (Donald Smith, Thomas Jones, and James Brigham) on 1 January,* one (Kenneth Gregory) on 30 May, one (Jesse Harris) on 20 October, and two (Michael Peterson and Vernon Shepard) on 10 December. Additionally, five U.S. servicemen seized by the Viet Cong in Cambodia were turned over to Cambodian authorities and released after short internments: Earl Gurnsey was let go on 6 January 1969, and four other Army personnel—John Fisher, Querin Herlik, Laird Osburn, and Robert Pryor—on 12 March. Brigham died two weeks after returning to U.S. custody. The Vietnamese insisted that he had been repatriated in good health and accused the United States of murdering the enlisted man because he was black and might rouse black opposition to the war. U.S. officials indicated that Brigham died from an infection resulting from a head wound that had been improperly treated while he was a prisoner.[48]

Gregory's was an interesting case. There was confusion initially as to whether he had been released or escaped. Gregory maintained he had participated in a "practice" release but managed to extricate himself and get away before having to make the requisite antiwar statements at a planned formal ceremony. He was eventually officially classified as an early release, but for a time the Pentagon chose to discredit the NLF's "humane and lenient" explanation and characterized the episode as an escape. An even stranger case was that of PFC Jon Sweeney, captured in February 1969 in the hills west of Hue and shown on some PW rosters as a 1970 releasee. Sweeney became separated from his Marine unit after an altercation with his company commander and wound up in Communist custody. He was taken to Hanoi where he made propaganda tapes for the North Vietnamese before they inexplicably released him via Moscow to Sweden. The Marine Corps considered him

---

* The three had ties to the Schrump group, Jones having been captured in the same incident with Bobby Johnson and he and the other two briefly encamping with some of the Schrump members along the way. Their emancipation took place in an open field near Tay Ninh in an unprecedented arrangement wherein U.S. and Viet Cong military representatives met face to face under cease-fire conditions. A score of newsmen from both sides witnessed the ceremony. Intelligence analysts in Washington had predicted that the Front, eager to bolster both its image and the prospect of recognition and direct negotiation by the United States, would resort to some such gesture to coincide with the NLF's 20 December anniversary date or the inauguration of President-elect Nixon. See *NY Times*, 20 Dec 68; *Washington Post*, 26-31 Dec 68, 2 Jan 69; Intelligence Note 921, DirINR to SecState, 27 Nov 68, sub: Will Hanoi Release More US POW's?

a defector rather than an early release. Upon returning voluntarily to the United States in August 1970 he was court-martialed on desertion and collaboration charges but acquitted, mainly for lack of corroborating evidence.[49]

Because the prisoner population in the South was more fragmented and transient, and therefore more difficult to track, there would be more so-called "discrepancy" cases involving PWs in South Vietnam than in North Vietnam. Among those Americans lost in the South between 1968 and 1971 there are many whose status, either as PWs or MIAs, remains uncertain owing to inconclusive information or, as with Sweeney, the absence of corroborating sources. Several of these individuals—Graf, Ray, Varnado, Ferguson—have already been mentioned. Others include Army Spec. Philip Terrill and Sgt. James Salley, both reported as having been alive when seized in March 1971 before they disappeared. Salley turned up on the Viet Cong's "died in captivity" list, but Terrill's name was missing; neither body was ever recovered. PFC Donald Sparks was thought to have died in an ambush of his platoon near Chu Lai in June 1969. When a search patrol could not locate his body and a year later letters in his handwriting were found on a slain Viet Cong soldier, hope flickered that he might still be a prisoner, but his final fate also remains a mystery.[50]

All told there are still over a thousand Americans listed as missing and unaccounted for in South Vietnam. Undoubtedly the great majority of those died or were killed before ever entering captivity, but exactly how many lost their lives while bound on a lonely trail or caged in an uninhabited outpost—victims of the peculiar blend of bondage and vagabondage that was the Southern PW's lot—will likely never be known.

22

1969: A Watershed Year in the North

For the veteran PWs jailed in the North, the more than 300 downed U.S. airmen who entered captivity before or during the middle years and lived to return home in 1973, 1969 was the pivotal year of their experience. At the start of that last year of the torture era, although they faced varying degrees of abuse and suffering depending on their specific confinement location, none but the most determined optimists among them could yet see light at the end of the tunnel. But in a year of momentous happenings—within months there was the inauguration of a new U.S. president and the landing of a man on the moon—1969 proved also to be a turning point for the war and for the fortunes of the American prisoners. By year's end a series of developments in Washington and in Paris and, most significantly, the death of Ho Chi Minh in Hanoi, substantially improved both the PWs' treatment and their prospects, though not before another season of horror once more tested the Northerners' strength and sanity.

To be sure, 1969 did not begin particularly auspiciously for the captured aviators, any more than for their compatriots imprisoned in the South. Alcatraz and Hoa Lo were in the throes of renewed terror; the Plantation and Zoo, in the midst of a jittery intermission. At the latter two camps there were encouraging signs that President Johnson's pre-election suspension of bombing over North Vietnam had at least softened the captor's disposition; at the Plantation especially, as Geoffrey Norman has noted, by spring "the level of fear had dropped almost to manageable proportions."[1] However, if there was any chance that the turbulent middle years would exit gently, it ended with the ill-advised action of a brash comrade who had grown impatient waiting for a break in their situation. The disastrous escape attempt of Air Force Capt. John Dramesi and a cellmate in May resulted in

479

a final wave of havoc and brutality that again pushed many of the Northern PWs to the brink.

To many of his colleagues at the Zoo, where he had been one of the last occupants to move to the Annex from the main compound during the 1968 shuffle, Dramesi was an accident waiting to happen. The son of a boxer, a star wrestler in high school,* and a scrapper since his childhood in South Philadelphia, he was a fearless, abrasive type whose rigid commitment to the Code of Conduct and open contempt for those with any less zealousness aroused in his peers both respect and resentment. In a review of Dramesi's memoir *Code of Honor*, Joe Dunn observed that "many POWs admired Dramesi's strength and courage [but] others considered him immature, selfish, and intolerant, and they believed that his activities were counterproductive." Dick Stratton, no shrinking violet himself, thought him "a gadfly who irritated others with his exalted standards and superior will power," and roommate Alton Meyer called him "a medal-hungry gloryhound in combat who cared for nothing except how to become a hero." He had already tried escaping once, a week after his capture in April 1967 on the way to Hanoi, and by the time he arrived at the Annex in the summer of 1968 he was hellbent on trying again.[2]

Dramesi's maverick ways would generate controversy throughout his tenure as a prisoner. To those who placed unity and obedience to the chain of command above doctrinaire adherence to the Code, says Craig Howes, he was "a suicidal renegade"; he in turn condemned the "hypocritical sheep" who followed the seniors' orders even when it might have meant compromising personal honor and duty. The issue became joined in 1968-69 at the Zoo over the clause in Article III of the Code that required PWs to "make every effort to escape." Dramesi construed the requirement literally, but senior officers at the Zoo and elsewhere were inclined to apply the discretionary standard that had informed decisions on the "early release" question and other troubling aspects of the Code. Even the most by-the-book seniors were reluctant to sanction escape attempts where there were hopeless odds or where failure (or success) could have serious consequences for those left behind. Risner's initial guidance had counseled that no one should try "without outside help," such as a friendly guard, safe house, or some other contact, though Denton later opined that Risner would have agreed with him "that God is our outside help."[3]

As Coker and McKnight had discovered in their flight from Dirty Bird, what made the undertaking so difficult was not so much breaking out of prison as accomplishing a successful getaway. Red McDaniel and

---

* He went on to wrestle at Rutgers, a decade earlier than another PW—and escape aspirant—George Coker.

Bill Austin contemplated giving it a try at one point, McDaniel recalling their reservations:

> . . . Even if we did make it out of the compound, the people in Hanoi were dedicated to tracking down any foreigners and were promised $1,500 by the government for every American flyer they caught. It would be tough trying to get through that kind of "police force." What's more, the average North Vietnamese is about five feet two inches tall, with black hair, yellow-skinned, slant-eyed. How would I, at six feet three inches, now about 160 pounds, with red hair, fair-skinned, and round-eyed, fit into that population if I tried to use its traffic patterns to get to the sea?
>
> And there was another problem, that of environment—the miles of jungle, the thick, cruel bush that a man would have to negotiate to get out. To illustrate the nature of the land we were living in, Bill Austin killed a poisonous snake in our room one night, and in the morning when we emptied our toilet bowls, we hung it up on the fence. We watched that snake periodically through the door peephole, and in three hours it had been completely devoured by insects. Nothing was left of it—nothing. We knew the same thing could happen to us if we tried to make it 110 miles to the sea.
>
> For all that, we still spent time thinking up ways to break out of the prison itself. Austin and I managed, after weeks of labor, to get the inner metal doors off their hinges. It really would have been no problem to walk straight out the door if we wanted to. And then one night in the room next to us, where Captain Konrad Trautman and three others lived, the guard had forgotten to lock the door altogether. That was a rare occasion, but it happened, and the men there thought all night of that unlocked door. In the morning Traut-man pounded out the message to us that the door had been open all night and then added, "But where to next?"
>
> That about summed it up. If we did get out, where to then? . . .

Larry Guarino, in command of the main compound, concurred. "The possibilities of an escape of an obvious westerner, out of the city of Hanoi, toward the west into Laos, in our physical condition, with the lack of available clothing and footgear, made the chance of success a big fat zero," he concluded. "Nor could I visualize heading east toward the Gulf of Tonkin. Caucasians would stick out like sore thumbs among hundreds of thousands of Asians." He believed that "any escape attempt was gallant, but, all things considered, also foolhardy."[4]

Dramesi spent much of the summer of 1968 brainstorming the notion with roommates, all fellow Air Force captains, Bill Baugh, Mike McCuistion, Lauren Lengyel, Don Heiliger, Al Meyer, Wallace Newcomb, Glenn Wilson, and Ed Atterberry. After some initial excitement, none had much enthusiasm for the idea. Meyer had a bum leg; Baugh, a badly damaged eye incurred during ejection that impaired his depth perception. The others were able but not particularly willing, either put off by Dramesi's aggressive personality or inhibited by the same long-shot circumstances that discouraged McDaniel and Austin. At length only Atterberry elected to join him.[5]

To his credit, it must be said that there was more to Dramesi than sheer bravado. He was as meticulous as he was bold. The effort did not fail for lack of planning or preparation. And to his cohorts' credit, although Dramesi's memoir would treat them ungraciously, for the most part they cooperated with and assisted him despite their misgivings and their concern about reprisals against those left behind. While they debated the wisdom of the enterprise and any ethical obligation they had to follow him,* they helped him collect bits of string, wire, bamboo, and metal that could be used for tools or weapons and donated scraps of food toward a cache of provisions. Over several months the supplies were secreted in an attic space above the cell, along with a stash of straw, thread, and cloth that Dramesi and Atterberry accumulated in order to weave costumes that would resemble civilian attire. The fabricated outfits included "surgical masks," of the sort worn by Vietnamese to prevent the spread of disease, which the escapees hoped would conceal their facial features; conical hats made from the rice straw of their sleeping mats; black garments fashioned from their prison garb; and sandals. For props the pair managed to steal a couple of baskets and a bamboo shoulder pole, standard peasant carrying gear. To complete the disguise, Dramesi acquired some brown iodine pills and, after saving a portion to use to purify water along the escape route, ground and mixed the rest with a paste of brick dust and water to produce a skin coloring that closely matched the locals' complexion.

The plan called for departing on a moonless and rainy night when they could not easily be spotted and the rain would cover the sound of their movements. Dramesi decided a Saturday night would be best since guards would be lax, the citizenry would be inside socializing, and with workers in from the fields on Sunday they would be able to travel across the countryside more freely. They would climb through a pre-cut trapdoor in the ceiling, assemble their disguises and equipment, and get out onto the roof by removing and then replacing some loosened tiles. Then, lowering themselves to the ground, they would run through the shadows, scale the 10-foot outside wall, and be gone. Atterberry, who had been a telephone lineman before joining the Air Force, was expected to play a key role in dismantling

---

* For a time Dramesi was not only the escape ringleader but also the senior man in his room by date of rank, until a policy clarification basing seniority on date of rank at time of shoot-down put Wilson in charge.

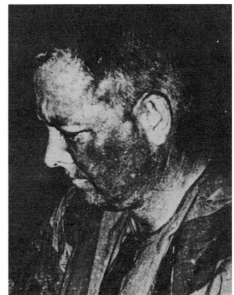

Dramesi   Atterberry

the barbed wire and shorting the electrical wiring atop the wall, the latter calculated to plunge the north side of the camp into darkness. Since a storm alone frequently blew the lights, the power outage would not cause undue commotion. To prepare themselves physically, Dramesi and Atterberry exercised in their cell, jogging in small circles for a mile and a half each day.

As he organized the plot, Dramesi sought approval from Annex SRO Trautman, who instinctively opposed it as too dangerous but did not feel he could flatly deny a dedicated man the opportunity to try to escape. Grudgingly Trautman gave room 6's "escape committee" the go-ahead with their preparations, but attached conditions relating to time, consensus, and other constraints. Dramesi, who had been itching and ready to go since the fall, grew increasingly restive while the SRO issued new requirements and scrubbed the plan until after Christmas. The onset of winter further postponed any action. By spring, still without Trautman's formal approval, the escapees worked through some final details and began a countdown waiting for suitable weather. In the late afternoon of 10 May, as darkness approached and the sky clouded over, with thunder and lightning on the horizon, Dramesi had a mate hoist him into the attic to consult with Trautman in the adjacent crawl space. Trautman reiterated his objections, refused to give his blessing, but still could not bring himself to order the PW to cancel. In the end it was Dramesi's decision and he told the SRO unhesitatingly, "We're going tonight."[6]

At approximately 6:00 p.m. Dramesi and Atterberry were boosted into the attic to begin donning their costumes and coating their faces. By 9:00 p.m., judging the moment right, they climbed onto the roof, and minutes later, after a frantic dash between buildings, were over the wall. By sunup Dramesi estimated they had traveled four or five miles when they noticed armed patrols searching nearby fields. Soldiers discovered them hiding in a bramble thicket next to an abandoned churchyard. Whether it was a rope left on the roof, loosened tiles that fell to the ground, tracks in the mud, or a simple headcount at dawn that gave them away is not clear,* but by noon, blindfolded and in handcuffs and with their paraphernalia in tow, they were returned to the Zoo. Unlike the 1967 Dirty Bird escape, this one had all the earmarks of a well planned and coordinated effort, with every indication that the conspirators had not acted alone. Beginning with the escapees and then rapidly moving from room 6 to other cells in the Annex, then throughout the Zoo and, over the ensuing weeks and months, to other camps as well, prison authorities conducted a sweeping inquisition and crackdown that, for the scope and intensity of the reprisals, was the most violent episode of the captivity.

Both to punish Dramesi and to extract information from him on who ordered or assisted him in the escape, the Vietnamese went at him for 38 days straight. In the Zoo's Auditorium he was flogged with a fan belt, walloped about the face with roundhouse swings, strapped in extreme positions in the ropes, and forcibly kept awake. Moved to Hoa Lo's room 18, familiar to Dramesi from a previous torture session, he was placed in heavy irons that soon bore into his flesh as Bug had him tape and write. Strung in the ropes more than 15 times, fed only two small pieces of bread and two cups of water each day, having to sit in his own filth ("my little stool was my living room, my bedroom, and my bathroom"), the PW eventually broke but protected the identities and involvement of his accomplices as best he could. That the Vietnamese relented at all may have been the result of Atterberry's death in a separate torture chamber close enough to Dramesi's so that he could hear his partner's screams.† 7

---

* Another advantage of leaving Saturday night was that on Sunday morning guards normally arrived later than usual and did not take the PWs outside their rooms to bathe, so that the prisoners could mill about in such a way that a casually glancing turnkey might not realize two men were missing. On this morning, however, a guard must have detected something peculiar, as the camp wakeup occurred at 5:00 a.m., even earlier than on weekdays. For various explanations of what could have gone wrong, see "U.S. Aircrew Members Escape from Permanent Detention Facilities," 44-45; Kiley interv with Baugh; Plumb, *I'm No Hero*, 222.
† Atterberry evidently replaced Stockdale in room 5, across the courtyard from room 18, when the latter returned to Vegas. The Vietnamese later said the flier died on 18 May—eight days after the breakout—from the effects of a virus and pneumonia; even if true, any sickness must have been incidental to his suffering. One inmate would report that the escapees' disciplining while at the Zoo was so savage the shrieks could be heard the equivalent of two blocks away.

Within hours of the pair's recapture, prison personnel removed the other members of the Annex's "escape committee" and grilled them one at a time. Over the next two weeks they were tortured for information and apologies. After a siege of punishment at the Hilton, Trautman was returned to the Zoo, where he remained in isolation and manacles for the next five months. The Annex's other room seniors also underwent extended interrogation and torture before being thrown together in cell 8 on half rations and in leg irons. The clamp on communications became total and absolute, with wall and ceiling vents sealed, room checks doubled, and severe beatings inflicted for the slightest infractions—procedures that would soon be instituted elsewhere also.[8]

Ironically, except for the escapees themselves, the harshest reprisals fell on the Zoo occupants on the other side of the wall from the Annex. Because that was where most of the camp's senior officers were held and where the PW communication and organization hubs were thought to be, the Vietnamese assumed the escape plot must have been hatched there. In fact, not only had the Zoo's ranking officers not masterminded the scheme but they had not even been aware of it, since Trautman for security reasons had not relayed any word of the plan to them. Consequently, when, as Plumb put it, "all hell broke loose," they faced their interrogators without a common cover story and so as they fumbled for answers they got caught in lies and inconsistencies that then became the basis for further punishment. As one after-action study concluded, while it was understandable that the prisoners in the main compound were not informed of the plan (given the Annex's self-contained features and Trautman's concern for secrecy), the omission "proved to be very costly," as many of the Zoo PWs were brutally tortured to give information about an escape of which they knew nothing.*[9]

Depending on which account one reads, the terror at the main compound commenced either immediately on Sunday 11 May or the next day. Shortly after a jeep drove through the camp's front gate with Dramesi and Atterberry in the back seat, prisoners learned something was amiss through a grapevine of hand flashes and note drops before the communication channels were shut down. By Monday afternoon men were being pulled out of their cells and marched to either the headquarters building or the Auditorium. In the days following, prison officials inspected every cell and implemented an array of draconian security measures, including confiscation

* Trautman may have supposed that this was a case where ignorance was bliss, but, as A. J. Myers later observed: "The idea that the less a man knows the less he can tell is only half of it. As the post-escape purge demonstrated, the less a man knew, the more he made up. This buys time for the escapee, while the captor cross-checks stories, but it's disaster for those who stay behind. There is no way one can corroborate the other's story. Had the escapees not been captured before the Zoo purge began, there might well have been far more than one death" ("POW Doctrine for Survival With Honor," 30).

of nonessential materials, sealing of vents and shutters, and banning of exercise. Over the course of the next two months, at least two dozen Zoo prisoners were beaten severely and dozens of others dragged off for questioning, the building SROs in particular wrung for information about the organization within their cellblocks. One man was hung from the ceiling by his arms and subjected to electric shocks from an auto battery. As guard staff plugged light and air holes, they eliminated not only communication but ventilation as well, sending summer room temperatures soaring. Around-the-clock quizzes cracked both the communication and organization networks, until the only way the PWs could chart the progress of the purge was to track the direction of the victims' cries as teams of torturers proceeded from one group to another.[10]

The activity at the Zoo was supervised by an unfamiliar older officer whom the Americans called "Buzzard," a watery-eyed, hook-nosed fiend with wisps of gray hair who apparently replaced Cochise as camp commander after the escape. Rabbit, Lump, Spot, and Goldie took turns as the chief hatchetmen, assisted by extra personnel brought in for the headhunting. By the end of June, when the violence peaked, the grimly efficient fan belt had emerged as the instrument of choice. The rubber belts, in John Hubbell's phrase, "literally flayed the hides off" the victims. "The procedure was to require the prisoner to drop his trousers and to lie on the floor, spread-eagled on his stomach. Two guards stood a distance away, each in a different corner of the room, each holding a rubber whip." In alternating charges the floggers would lash the prisoner's buttocks and thighs with such ferocity that Bud Day likened the barbarity to a scene "out of the days of Mongol Hordes." Day chronicled his ordeal in a chapter of his memoir entitled "Crucifixion." Guarino, reflecting on the sheep-to-slaughter aspect, would make comparisons to the Nazi death camps: "People all over the world are still wondering why the Jews going into the gas chambers went quietly. I believe that each of them hoped that a last minute miracle, or change of heart, would come about just in time to save his life. Some POWs had the same kind of futile hope about the retribution over the escape attempt."[11]

Guarino entered the Auditorium on 12 June and spent the next three weeks there and in the Chicken Coop being whipped, clubbed, or forced to kneel for hours until his knees "were puffed up like two rotten jelly doughnuts, and felt like they were stuffed with broken razor blades." The goon squad did not come for Day until 16 July, but wasted no time, shoving him into cuffs and manacles and keeping him on either his stomach or knees for four consecutive days. "It was torture in perpetual motion," said Day. "I was to be beaten and questioned all day, then forced to kneel all night. It was the sentry's job to keep me awake at night and on my knees, to soften me up for the whip beaters during the day." The aviator stopped counting at 300 blows. He earned a brief respite by giving Goldie the names of several fictitious PW committees ("I eventually gave him a committee for every function performed by every army since the conquests of the Caesars—intelligence, supply, military police, medical, morale, historical, and many others") before the torture was resumed. Into August he was still taking lashes, although at a slackening rate.[12]

By most accounts no one at the Zoo absorbed more punishment than Red McDaniel. He, Al Runyan, and Ken Fleenor were caught in the eye of the storm when the Vietnamese discovered that their cell in the Zoo's Garage was the primary information link to the Annex. Over a period of two weeks McDaniel received approximately 700 lashes, suffering 38 open wounds during one session alone. In between he was slapped in the face with a hard sandal, given electric shock, bound in irons, and hoisted in ropes, at one point left dangling hideously with a compound fracture of the arm, the interrogation continuing while a guard attempted to put the protruding bone back into place.[13]

McDaniel endured much of what he called his "darkest hour" in silence, in part in an effort to protect the Zoo's key point man in the communication system, J. J. Connell, whose disability ploy* left him little room to maneuver once the going got rough. Others, too, had tried to protect the young lieutenant, but in the end it was to no avail. Connell's activities inevitably were exposed during the sweep and he was beaten unmercifully. Guarino would contrast Connell's mistake in trying to maintain his ruse even after discovered with George McSwain's wise decision to come clean with the Vietnamese once his insanity pose was revealed. John Nasmyth recalled: "A bunch of guards were sent for George. They hung him up over a pole like a tiger, tying his hands and feet over the pole. Then they hauled him out to the torture room and whipped him, kind of like they whipped Colbiel† until he died." Guarino said "the gooks pounded the pee out of George for a month" until "he decided he was on a wrong tack and altered his course. That's the only reason he is alive today."[14]

As the summer wore on, the crackdown spread to the prisons in downtown Hanoi, although the PWs there were in the dark as to why treatment was worsening again. Webb, Stafford, McCain, and Guy were among those hammered at the Plantation.‡ At Hoa Lo, the by now "infamous" Bug, who had brought some of the most heroic PWs to their knees (Day and Risner among them) and who oversaw the humiliation of Stratton and last days of Lance Sijan, had even freer rein than usual. Stratton later described the

* See Chapter 19.
† A reference to Earl Cobeil. See Chapter 19.
‡ See Chapter 18.

round, diminutive officer, who seemed to assume steadily more importance through the middle years, as "the most miserable and lowest of all
creatures. He was given the name of an insect because he was, in fact, an
insect; a madman as far as I'm concerned." Stockdale, who had been in
and out of torture most of the year but had been enjoying a relatively mild
"summer interlude," found himself back at the Mint in August for a return
engagement with Bug. When guards discovered that Stockdale was somehow still in communication through what must have been an intricate
note-drop system, the senior realized "they had the drawstrings of a web
that would suck dozens of my old friends and many I had never communicated with into complicity. All my friends would first go into the ropes.
In turn, third parties would be involved, and then *they* would be put in
the ropes. I was about to be the cause of another Las Vegas purge with all
the grief and death that this was likely to entail."[15]

At the start of September Stockdale was taken to a tiny cell near
Hoa Lo's kitchen area; infested with cobwebs and layered with dust, it
"appeared to have been locked up for years." He named this new "black
hole" of a punishment pit, which he would be the first American to
occupy, "Calcutta." He lay there for three or four days before being
removed to room 18, where Bug had him kneel on his one good knee
while slashing him across the face with a fan belt. Ready to die or at least
"make them think that I was ready to die" rather than divulge the details
of the note-drop scheme, that night Stockdale managed to break a window pane and with the glass shards chopped his wrists. He had passed out
in a pool of blood when guards entered and frantically summoned a medic,
who washed and bandaged his arms. On 12 September the senior was moved
back to Calcutta and left alone to allow his wounds to heal. In retrospect
Stockdale believed that the shifting mood after Ho's death the first week in
September and the increasing pressures being exerted on behalf of the PWs
in Paris probably saved him. The whole process was at a "crossroads," he told
a debriefer in 1973, "so it didn't help matters at all to have me laid out on
the slab there with self-inflicted wounds."[16]

At camps further away from Hanoi, whether owing to fallout from
the Dramesi-Atterberry escape or simply the scorching July and August
heat, the atmosphere became more combustible there, too, that summer of
1969. At Son Tay officials stepped up inspections and punished prisoners
when guards found suspicious marks around cell windows, though security remained lax enough that a group of the PWs began planning how to
establish contact for a search-and-rescue effort against the camp. Orson
Swindle had one of his worst experiences at Son Tay around this time.
At Farnsworth, which housed some 30 prisoners who had come up from

the South,* the senior officers especially were watched closely, either on "death row," a series of one-room structures about 100 feet apart, or in the "Drum," a square building so-called because of acoustics that scarcely allowed one to "breathe without being heard by a guard stationed in the hallway." A sadistic interrogator known as "Cheese" † enjoyed poking and squeezing the eyeballs of his subjects, torturing Captain Leonard and three other men for six weeks with such cruelties along with beatings and sleep deprivation. By different means—drinking urine, hanging, or chewing the veins of their wrists—the four unsuccessfully attempted suicide before Cheese finally relented.[17]

By fall the far-ranging purge had pretty much run its course, though the aftereffects, in terms of heightened surveillance, crippled PW organizations, residual tensions, and continuing harassment, were still discernible almost a year later in some of the camps. So traumatic had been the overall experience that even when escape became a more feasible option late in the captivity, the prisoners were still haunted by the catastrophic consequences of the Dramesi-Atterberry attempt. One Zoo inmate recalled that after the incident "we didn't think much about escape—not that it would be impossible but that the aftermath for the remaining prisoners would be too horrible." In fact, there would continue to be escape planning—the ethical dilemma posed by Dramesi and the Code of Conduct was never truly resolved—but what one post-mortem referred to as "the conservative legacy" of the affair would temper all such deliberations for the duration of the captivity, at least among those SROs and other PWs who had been through the summer of 1969.[18]

As for Dramesi, having survived the captor's retribution, he would have to confront the censure and ostracism of comrades who blamed him for much of their suffering and Atterberry's death. Even in the euphoria of homecoming there would still be those PWs who harbored bitter resentment toward him. Atterberry's was a truly tragic case, for if he had held on just a few months longer he would have found *real* light at the end of the tunnel, not in the chimerical lure of escape but in the dawn of a new era in the captivity story.

Without access to North Vietnamese archives, the historian can not know for sure why exactly the treatment of the American prisoners in the

---

* See Chapter 21. The camp was also known as "D-1," which was the marking on the first building the prisoners saw when they entered. "Farnsworth" allegedly took its name from a monicker the Americans attached to one of its Vietnamese officers.
† Myers, *Vietnam POW Camp Histories*, vol 1, 479, has "Dum Dum," the Zoo's notorious interrogator, turning up as the chief political officer at Farnsworth. He and "Cheese," the name given him by the prisoners who arrived from the South, may have been the same person.

Northern jails improved so markedly beginning in the fall of 1969. Who or what was responsible for the transformation, whether it was the product of a sudden decision or an ongoing reappraisal that the Dramesi-Atterberry furor had interrupted, remains a matter of considerable speculation, among the former PWs as well as analysts who have tried to explain the phenomenon.

What is known is that there were many forces at work during this period, both internal and external, that would have made a reversal of the enemy's prisoner policy understandable. Those factors already mentioned —Vietnamese concern over the deteriorating condition of many of the hostages, the death of Atterberry and destruction of Cobeil from beatings, the steady consciousness-raising of the PW issue both in the United States and abroad since the Hanoi March of 1966, the boost given the awareness effort by the launching of the "Go Public" campaign by the Nixon administration earlier in 1969, the impact of the Frishman-Hegdahl press conference in early September, the death of Ho that same day*—all no doubt figured prominently in Hanoi's reassessment. Larry Chesley would later single out an International Red Cross conference in Istanbul in September as a key, and others would point broadly to the influence of the extended bombing pause and progress of the talks in Paris, but the Red Cross had had a frustrating lack of success in swaying the North Vietnamese previously and the winds of war and peace seemed no less fickle this season than the last.

What probably occurred was a conjunction of circumstances and events all of which contributed in some degree to what Stockdale had characterized as a "crossroads." When he briefed the Joint Chiefs of Staff in 1973, Guarino offered the opinion that 70 percent of the change was the result of public pressure, while also crediting the prisoners' own resistance in discouraging further use of the PWs for propaganda purposes. Hubbell cited "two major factors: the death of Ho Chi Minh; and, by the time of the dictator's demise, the enormous and growing concern in the United States over the fate of those American fighting men who had fallen into Hanoi's hands." On the latter point, had the PWs been released in the summer of 1969 as part of a war settlement, Operation Homecoming would have presented a far more somber scene, the American people likely to have been outraged at the pitiable procession of returnees staggering or being carried out of the repatriation aircraft.[19]

---

* The North Vietnamese president died the morning of 3 September Hanoi time (2 September in Washington). Because of the time zone differential and confusion owing to a delay in the announcement, contemporary reports and even subsequent accounts sometimes give the date as 2 September or 4 September.

Certainly, even if the policy shift had been evolving, Ho's passing was a milestone event and an opportunity for a more thoroughgoing break with the past. Hervey Stockman suggested that the leader's death may have unlocked the stalemate in Paris as well as paralysis within the North Vietnamese government. "Suddenly, almost without any advanced notice," Stockman observed, the atmosphere changed. "What bearing his death had on the change in the prisons' climates which became so apparent in October 1969 is unknown, but the coincidence is worth noting." Stockman may have exaggerated the instantaneousness as well as the depth of the change, but the relevance of the connection is inescapable. "The speed with which Ho's political heirs moved to improve life for the prisoners seemed to indicate some degree of understanding that the old regime's policies had been counterproductive," Hubbell wrote. Alvarez remembered officials wearing black arm bands as "mournful music filtered out of the squawk boxes . . . but none of us got over-excited." The mere "absence of Ho" occasioned no expectation of "a quick breakthrough," Alvarez recalled. Still, soon there was "a lot less brutality—and larger bowls of rice."[20]

The pace and extent of improvement varied from camp to camp but the conclusion reached in a 1974 Air Force debriefing summary was essentially correct in stating that "the era of heavy torture and poor treatment was replaced with an environment of lighter punishment, better food, and generally improved living conditions." By year's end most prisoners were getting a third meal daily, extra blankets and clothing, and double the usual allotment of cigarettes. The third meal was a "breakfast" of toasted bread, sometimes sugared, with a half cup of milk added later on. Gradually, canned meat and fish were also introduced, as was a more flavorful soup, thickened with a flouring agent and served with noodles and more vegetables. Although Ken Coskey would say that he and roommates Carl Crumpler and Byron Fuller "decided that the kitchen did not know what was going on in Paris," other veterans who thought they had learned to gauge the political climate by the quality and amount of their rations, felt the diet upgrade was one of the first and surest signs of a significant turnaround.*[21]

Reinforcing that impression was a general relaxation of regulations. The Vietnamese reduced the bowing requirement to a nod of the head, within a

---

* Of course, "gastro-political" calculations had proven to be less than axiomatic. Guarino wrote: "After months of starvation and torture, any slight improvement in treatment made my mind go wild. . . . Just getting a smidgen of decent food became a major 'indicator.' The first time they brought me a small saucer of steamed cauliflower with some lumpy tomatoes on it, I just knew (again) that the war had to be over! They wouldn't be giving me such delicious food if it wasn't! The cauliflower was cooked exactly the way Evy made it— a little garlic, black pepper, and a splash of tomato. To this day, whenever I peek into a pot on the kitchen stove and see cauliflower I say, 'The war's over, Evy!'" (A POW's Story, 139). The incident occurred in 1967.

year dropping it altogether. They continued to prohibit communication but transgressors encountered looser monitoring and lesser penalties. PWs who had been in solitary or isolation for months or years suddenly received cellmates. Risner's long sequestration ended in late November when Colonel Larson, himself confined alone at the Plantation for 18 months in an unventilated cell, joined him in a room at Hoa Lo. Stockdale emerged from Calcutta in the fall and, after another spell at the Mint, was placed in Thunderbird, where he was celled with an American for the first time in over two years.* As the pressure to tape and write propaganda eased, the prisoners gained more outdoor exercise time and other privileges without having to make concessions in return. Sam Johnson went so far as to suggest that "the Vietnamese appeared to be trying to accommodate and without saying it . . . were bending closer and closer to adherence to the Geneva Convention," even limiting punishment to the 30 days prescribed under the Geneva agreement.[22]

The summer's unbroken overcast seemed to be lifting almost everywhere that fall. At Son Tay workers unboarded windows and tore down walls to give the prisoners more ventilation and space. Rob Doremus remembered that "somehow things just changed. There was nothing we could put our finger on at first but there were little signs of something in the air." Jim Warner, who had had a particularly difficult stretch, was told by a Vietnamese officer claiming to be a general that a new order was being installed. At Plantation, Ted Guy's flogging abruptly ceased the day Ho died, and John McCain, to his amazement, found guards removing the transom over his door nightly to let in the breeze. Dramesi was still in solitary at the Hilton when he heard the somber music and a 21-gun salute signaling Ho's burial. By November he was released from his irons periodically to shower, wash clothes, sun, and exercise. In early December a guard took off the irons for good and escorted him over to Vegas, where he joined fellow escape artists Coker and McKnight (just transferred from Alcatraz) in the Mint's three maximum-security cells. Eyeing the tiny compartment, Dramesi thought he "was going from bad to worse," but the reality was that he—and his mates—had come a remarkably long way in a few months.[23]

Nowhere were the PWs breathing easier than at the Zoo, which had taken the brunt of the summer violence and where Ho's passing had produced an edgy uncertainty as to whether treatment would improve or regress. "It was a dicey prospect," Guarino worried, and "we knew we'd just have to sweat it out." By 18 October "all of our questions are answered,"

* Stockdale's companion was Jim Hughes, whose erratic behavior created new problems for the senior naval officer. See Stockdale, *In Love and War*, 360, 392-95; Stockman, "Authority, Leadership, Organization," 25; Bedinger, "Prisoner-of-War Organization in Hanoi," 12-13.

Nasmyth noted in his post-captivity journal. "The food ration is doubled, the cigarette ration becomes a real ration, something you can count on, and guards no longer have the authority to do anything they want . . . . Now we can tell a guard to get fucked, and he has to get permission from an officer before he belts us." At the Pool Hall, Jim Kasler was moved into a larger cell with Ray Vohden and Jim Bell. To Red McDaniel's surprise at the Pigsty, the captors dismantled the wall dividing the cellblock and a solicitous Rabbit asked what could be done "to make the camp look more presentable." The knocking down of partitions and unbricking of windows helped to reestablish communication, so that details about the status of Connell and Cobeil and the ordeals of McDaniel, Kasler, Day, Fred Cherry, and other sufferers filtered throughout the compound.[24]

Day had been one of the last of the Zoo "heavies" to undergo torture. The policy reversal came within a month or so of his near-fatal "crucifixion," and the rapid decompression jolted him. Still in irons, he did a double take as he spotted a clump of moss roses planted in the bath area on his way there to wash the blood stains out of his clothes. Handed a package from home by Rabbit, he trembled: "For a moment, I thought that my brain had become disconnected from my ears." A new, clean blue blanket hanging on the Pool Hall clothesline "looked unreal," as must have seemed the "strange item," a foot-high round wicker basket (dubbed a "cobra" or "Easter" basket by the PWs), that arrived in October and soon became a fixture in cells throughout the prison system. Brightly colored, lined with cloth, and with a layer of rice straw for insulation, the lidded object with a small jug inside was a tea caddy of sorts, designed to keep their drinking water hot during the winter.[25]

"Night had turned to day!," Denton exclaimed, recalling his sense of joy at what had transpired at Alcatraz following Ho's funeral, which took place only a few blocks from the downtown prison. For some time after the solemn proceedings, grief-stricken guards at the facility appeared dazed and red-eyed from crying.* When the mourning subsided, Denton said, "our jailers had changed along with our circumstances." Free to step outside his cell without shackles or a guard's rifle poking him, Johnson ventured across the Alcatraz courtyard "with long, luxurious strides." He "stood and stretched for a moment, and then began walking and swinging my arms, exulting in the sense of freedom." For a day at least they shaved with water that attendants had heated and ladled into a basin for them. Then came

---

* PWs at locations inside and outside the city reported hearing nonstop tributes to the departed leader on camp radios and uncontrollable sobbing among their handlers. At his camp in the mountains of South Vietnam, Floyd Kushner remembered guerrilla captors, including collaborator Robert Garwood, wearing black ribbons. See Groom and Spencer, *Conversations With the Enemy*, 381.

bread for breakfast, blankets and tea baskets, and, most welcome of all, only perfunctory warnings when caught communicating. The improvements came too late to save Ron Storz, who was left behind when on 9 December the Vietnamese moved the Alcatraz group back to Vegas.* Nonetheless, the closing of the dungeon-like prison and return of its hardline occupants to the mainstream PW community was a fitting symbol of the passing of the old regime and end to the Extortion Era.[26]

Another unmistakable signal was the demotion of Cat, the confident, durable superintendent of prisons since the beginning of the war who became commander at Hoa Lo sometime in the early fall. When he informed Stockdale of his new position, the senior was stunned: it was as if "a four-star admiral" had told him that "he was now the skipper of a destroyer!" Evidently a scapegoat for, in any case a casualty of, the past mistreatment of the prisoners, the major had lost a star along with being relieved of overall command responsibilities, and now skulked about the Hilton humbled and conciliatory. Denton noticed "the arrogance and sparkle were definitely gone. He appeared tired and distraught, and a nervous tic had developed over one eye." After the spring of 1970 no American prisoner ever saw him again. "This devious, immaculate man with his careful English who held all power over all POWs," Scott Blakey wrote, "simply vanished."[27]

Thanksgiving through Christmas had always been an emotional season for the American prisoners in Southeast Asia, a time for marking calendars and taking stock. For those captives in the North who had weathered the watershed year, 1969's holidays had more meaning than most. In a year of wild fluctuations there was still much bewilderment and trepidation; the holiday mood was more prayerful than festive. Some of the men were too sick or exhausted to appreciate the change in their treatment. Through a crack in the door separating their cells, Day viewed the "demoralizing sight" of Guarino, "pathetically thin, bearing huge kneeling holes on his knees and feet, massive iron burns on his Achilles tendons, and enormous black circles under his eyes." With severe headaches and a worsening stomach ailment, Guarino spent much of the holiday season lying on his bunk in misery. But there were also those daring to speculate again about release, and, as Day remarked, "even the super pessimists began to find a certain amount of helium in their balloons."[28]

Another boost came when mail and packages arrived in unprecedented numbers. Almost all the prisoners received letters from home that Christmas,

† See Chapter 17.

and, with a few exceptions, were allowed to write home as well, albeit with restrictions on length and content. Some of the letters from family members contained news of promotions or peace negotiations, obfuscated to get by the censors. Nasmyth explained the methodology:

> "The gold leaves have turned to silver," simply meant someone had been promoted from major to lieutenant colonel.
> "There's a new eagle in our tree" tells the letter recipient he's now a full colonel.
> One wife used the first letter in each word as her code.
> "Please always remember I still think about loving kisses sweetheart. So eager remain I over ur safety."
> Extract the first letter and you have—"Paris talks serious."

Others included photographs that also harbored messages. Holding a crude magnifying glass up to a picture with a bumper sticker in the background revealed the National League of Families manifesto "Hanoi Release the Prisoners." Packages that previously had been stripped of most items now were received laden with vitamins, playing cards, and checkerboards.* Most telling was the sharp increase in the number of letters written by prisoners that actually got delivered. A 1971 statistical survey indicated that in all the years prior to 1969 PW families had received a total of 620 letters from 103 prisoners. "During the next 11 months," a subsequent analysis showed, "the number climbed to 940 from 294 writers, most of the additional 320 letters being written in November and December. Of those, 191 came from new writers, whose fate for the most part had remained unknown to their families."[29]

Veteran PWs at the Zoo judged the Christmas Day 1969 dinner— served from a porch table piled high with turkey, beef, rolls, candy, and beer—the best meal they had eaten in captivity. A major inter-camp move on 10 December in which 11 prisoners were transferred from Son Tay to sites nearer Hanoi may have been at least in part an effort by the captor to enable Catholic prisoners to attend Christmas mass at services in the city. (Ten of the eleven transfers were Catholic, and the men who took their place, trucked in from Vegas and Plantation, were all Protestants except

---

* By contrast, prison officials had emptied the Christmas 1968 parcels of much of their contents. Guarino commented: "We saw them running around with vacuum bottles of hot water. Rabbit suddenly gained weight. We POWs bitched among ourselves continuously about theft, but I think that by 1970, the V had finally quit stealing stuff from them" (*A POW's Story*, 184). On the rifling of the 1968 packages, see also Alvarez and Pitch, *Chained Eagle*, 193. An inventory check at repatriation comparing a list of items his family sent Lt. Mark Gartley with a list of those he received suggested the Vietnamese were still withholding if not pocketing gifts, medications, and toiletries even after 1970.

for one the Vietnamese did not know was Catholic.) While previous holidays had brought similar privileges and indulgences, and while even these favors were accompanied by the propaganda trappings of posters and cameras and "gook VIPs" making the rounds, the atmosphere this time seemed distinctly different—less heavy-handed, less transparently phony and more genuinely humane. Those participating in the Protestant ceremony at Son Tay reported only "a couple of comments that had political overtones." Wendy Rivers recalled for the first time seeing a movie in the Zoo's Auditorium where the building wasn't darkened and strung with blankets to prevent prisoner contacts.[30]

His first night back at Hoa Lo Sam Johnson pondered the significance of all that had occurred in the recent months. For the trip from Alcatraz "the Vietnamese had not bothered to try to confuse us by taking a circuitous route through the city. It seemed it did not matter any more if we knew our whereabouts." Fretting over the status of Storz and hoarse from whispered conversation, he finally went to bed. "As I lay down on the wooden bunk in my cell that night, emotionally exhausted from the excitement and drained after the long hours of communicating," he confided, "I breathed a prayer of thanksgiving." Though "still an ocean removed from home and Texas, . . . my legs were free of the awful heavy irons. I felt calm and, for the first time in more than three and a half years, I was almost happy."[31]

23

The "Good Guy Era": The Northern Prisons, 1970

Old Man of the North Everett Alvarez had not entered a real bathroom in more than five years when in the winter of early 1970 a guard led him to a lavatory inside the Hanoi War Museum. A group of Zoo PWs had been jeeped into the city for one of their periodic visits when the Navy lieutenant felt the need to relieve himself.

> . . . I stood and looked at the urinal and regular seated toilet with amazement, unused to anything but the crude jagged-edged slop bucket I had used for so long. Who would have thought that squatting on a toilet seat could induce such a feeling of comfort and well-being!
>
> But then, as I went to wash up, I saw the mirror. It had been five-and-a-half years since last I saw my face. I approached like a man entranced, as if transfixed by the image of my own face growing larger with each step forward. My God! Could that be me! Delicately, as if afraid my skin might crumble, I touched my stubbly cheeks and felt my chin and then my eyes. I dragged my fingers over the furrowed lines. Something inside of me recoiled from the image in the mirror. Good God! I looked so old! With shock and astonishment I saw the flecks of gray in my hair. I could not believe it. I was only thirty-two but the man in the mirror did not look a day younger than forty.

The revelations of a more relaxed captivity were not always kind.[1]

What some of the prisoners would refer to as "the big change" eventually materialized throughout the prison system, but it unfolded by fits and starts and unevenly from camp to camp. The end to atrocities, in any case, did not mean an end to hard times. However genuine and arresting the improvement in the PWs' treatment and conditions after the fall of 1969, there were still anxious moments and bad days ahead, including relapses in the captor's behavior, more suffering (and deaths) from injuries and disease, and the continuing routine mental and physical challenges of what remained a spartan captivity. Blakey noted that "prisoners were not tortured; still, the threat was always there. For most of the prisoners, resistance remained a primary function and a high-risk endeavor."[2] And as the Vietnamese became less menacing, personal and philosophical differences within the Americans' own ranks suddenly loomed larger, posing threats to command, organization, and morale that in their own way became just as serious as those posed from without by the enemy.

All of these crosscurrents were evident during a period of transition following the 1969 turnabout, an interval of a year or so that sometimes takes the name "Good Guy Era" from the "follow-on . . . soft-sell" nature of the Viets' post-Ho exploitation attempts.[3]

The Zoo, the most volatile of the Northern camps during 1969, was among the quietest during 1970. Erstwhile enforcer Rabbit took on the duties of a veritable recreation director, supervising music and art programs and operating a ping-pong and reading room that alternated between the Auditorium and headquarters building. For both captor and captive, such activities offered more than mere diversion. The contest may have become more benign, but the cat-and-mouse game was still on. The prisoners used these opportunities to communicate and plan; the Vietnamese tried to exploit them to produce film footage and artwork to impress a still skeptical public that the PWs were indeed being treated well.* "Though we were no longer being physically abused," Guarino said, "they didn't stop pressuring and browbeating us to produce something to make them look good to the outside world." Those pressures were now "mostly verbal—reasoning, convincing, and hinting of possible restrictions"—but they also included what some of the nonparticipants thought to be special dispensations—candy, more mail, extra baths—so that the programs caused some dissension, which further served the Viets' purpose.[4]

Rabbit himself had undergone a marked change, as full of himself as ever but without the vicious streak and by turns bored, preoccupied, and, like his mentor Cat, philosophical. To the extent there was a villain at the Zoo in 1970 it may have been Elf, who threw Bill Shankel and Dave Wheat in summer sweatboxes, albeit with a water supply, for minor infractions. For

* Paintings and drawings from the Zoo and Son Tay turned up at exhibits in Moscow and in Paris during the peace talks there. See Day, *Return With Honor*, 179; "Memories of Divided Families," *Life*, 4 Dec 70, 37.

the most part, however, guards took a hands-off approach. Guarino remarked that "the Vietnamese, imbued with Asian patience, take a long time to make changes," but "the treatment *was* changing." By midyear a bothersome roommate "had replaced Rabbit and Dum Dum as my chief mental tormenter." In August workers installed basketball backboards and volleyball nets and began distributing checkers, chess sets, and Bibles. Alvarez noted the irony of guards correcting prisoners who, out of habit, continued to bow.[5]

In a series of moves over the summer, all 61 occupants of the Annex and several dozen from the main compound were sent to a new camp at Dan Hoi.* (Red McDaniel, who departed with a group in September, recalled the rough bus ride, with blankets covering the windows and the men handcuffed to the seats and "stuffed into that vehicle like animals. Oddly enough, it was done in the usual style . . ., keeping us from seeing anything of the outside and as little as possible of each other.") The closing of the Annex and other transfers left 68 PWs at the camp, which was now organized into several enclaves of 10 to 20 prisoners. Although the groups were segregated by a labyrinth of walls and screens that in effect formed separate compounds, within each there was what Alvarez termed an "open-door policy," whereby members could freely mingle inside or outside their building, wash anytime, and play basketball together. Alvarez wound up at a much enlarged Pigsty in which four big rooms housed a total of 20 men: with Alvarez were Dick Keirn, Jerry Coffee, Norm McDaniel, Norman Wells, Harold Johnson, Dick Ratzlaff, Mike Lane, Mike Brazelton, Tom Browning, John Borling, Robert Woods, John Davies, Read Mecleary, Art Cormier, Bill Robinson, Art Black, Gary Sigler, Harold Monlux, and David Carey. At the Barn, John Nasmyth joined A. J. Myers, Jim Pirie, Fred Baldock, Ed Martin, Will Gideon, and Paul Brown.

Balancing the newfound liberties were persistent reminders of their subjugation: lockups on Sundays and during siesta when guards were not on duty to prevent contacts between buildings; intermittent interrogation and indoctrination chats; and the ever-present cameramen and photographers who were becoming more in evidence as the remodeled camp increasingly took on the character of the Potemkin-like Plantation. The PWs knew they were being set up for propaganda display but offered only token resistance so long as they had assurances (not completely true as it turned out) that all the buildings were receiving the same treatment and that the cameras were therefore recording an accurate picture.[6]

As Christmas 1970 approached, the remaining Americans at the Zoo nourished the hope, no longer unreasonable, that it might be their last

* See p. 504.

yuletide in captivity. Christmas Day was observed with the customary special meal and religious rites along with a delivery of holiday packages from home. Then suddenly on the evening of 26 December, the camp closed. Inspection teams showed up to give the prisoners physicals and a change of clothing before transporting them to Hoa Lo. Alvarez later wrote of his vexation "when at short notice they herded us into trucks and drove us over quiet roads into the bustle of the capital. We entered the familiar double gates which clanged shut with a ringing echo, and drove over the bumpy brick path and through more metallic-sounding gates before coming to a halt in the courtyard. I was back in the Hanoi Hilton."[7]

Visions of their being assembled for pre-release processing were soon overtaken by dread that the torture regime was about to be restored. Neither was the case. They were brought to the downtown prison for the same reason that PWs at other jails outside the city were being moved into Hanoi —as a security measure in the wake of a U.S. commando raid on the Son Tay camp in late November. That rescue effort foundered when intelligence sources failed to detect that the Son Tay prisoners had been transferred a few months earlier, but the operation's near success* convinced the Vietnamese to abandon the outlying camps and collect their hostages at the Hilton. For some of the Zoo PWs, that Christmas turned out to be not even their last one at the suburban camp. The Cu Loc complex was close enough to Hanoi for officials to feel safe reopening it in 1971, when Alvarez and some of the other Zoo veterans moved back there.

Larry Chesley remembered that as 1970 dawned at Son Tay, increased rations "shortened the hunger pangs of the night. Getting outside every three or four days for an hour or two at a time gave us a little more fresh air and sunshine. Spurred particularly by the vitamins in the packages from home which the North Vietnamese were now allowing us to receive, our health began to pick up generally." During its last months, Son Tay underwent considerable renovation, perhaps indicating that the Vietnamese had not planned to vacate the site. A newly constructed building the prisoners

---

* The strike force was able to penetrate deep into North Vietnamese airspace, land helicopters at the site, overwhelm defenders, and return safely without losing a single man. The searchers may have killed as many as two dozen or more of the enemy, but could not find any of the Americans, who had been withdrawn to another location in July. A large folder of material relating to the Son Tay raid, both its intelligence and operational aspects as well as the subsequent debate over its merits, is in OSD Hist "Son Tay" file. For a summary of the circumstances and significance of the raid that is drawn from these sources, see Davis, *The U.S. Government and American PWs in Southeast Asia*, ch 12 (ms). The fullest and best written unclassified account is Benjamin F. Schemmer, *The Raid*.

"The big change" at the Zoo, 1970. *Above:* Fall basketball (notice the PWs' weight gain following improvement of diet). *Below:* Norm McDaniel leading carols at Christmas service.

christened the "Stag Bar" became an activity center with a ping-pong table and a small library; for a brief period the PWs were permitted to play volleyball on a court they put up in the middle of the compound. Other significant improvements included expansion of the bath area and installation of a water storage facility, the latter intended to alleviate chronic shortages.[8]

As at the Zoo, however, for every two steps forward, the captor took one step backward. Chesley said, "It was as if the prison authorities were reluctant to relinquish entirely their 'right' to control by force and physical violence. They had to keep reminding us that they had the big guns." The new section of the camp contained a play room but also an interrogation room. By some accounts guards immediately took over the recreation facilities for their own use. When Air Force Lt. Richard Brenneman climbed the volleyball pole to gain a look over the compound wall, he was beaten and locked in a shack for 30 days. Ben Pollard was hauled off to the Cat House for a month for angering the camp commander. Wes Schierman continued to suffer from asthma, the winter of 1970 one of his worst, yet pleas from his mates for assistance were again ignored.[9]

Son Tay's seniors fared especially poorly during the transition following Ho's death. On Christmas Eve 1969 Render Crayton was isolated in the Cat House, then, when caught communicating, placed in a 4' x 6' x 5' cell called the "Bat Cave" that had neither windows nor lights. He spent the next three months in this dark coop, unable even to straighten up, before being moved again to a small cell under the guard tower. Now incommunicado, Crayton relinquished command to Howard Dunn, who is credited with establishing a code of resistance policies at Son Tay under the acronym "Blades."* Dunn was SRO for only a short time before both he and Crayton, with Pollard, were shipped to Hoa Lo on 22 June, whereupon Claude Clower took charge. Despite the leadership disruptions, right up to their evacuation the PWs continued to transmit data on camp routine and security to U.S. intelligence sources, using covert methods to signal reconnaissance aircraft that regularly flew over the area.[10]

Clower had been senior less than a month when Son Tay was shut down. All 52 prisoners were packed up and sent to a brand new camp at Dan Hoi, a refurbished barracks and communications complex located 10 miles west of Hanoi, about midway between Son Tay and the capital. Although it is possible the Americans were moved because the Vietnamese either suspected U.S. preparations for a rescue operation against Son Tay or believed the isolated site was vulnerable to such a strike, it is more likely the transfer occurred because the camp remained in poor condition even after the spring renovation. By comparison Dan Hoi, which soon acquired

---

* **B**itch constantly about necessities, **l**uxuries bitch about occasionally, **a**bsurdities debunk, **d**iscourage propaganda, **e**veryone participates, **s**elect what is to be bitched about individually.

Son Tay

Added in late 1969 or early 1970
(do not appear in the earlier photograph)

Outhouse

Stag
Bar

Beer
Hall

Opium
Den

Well

Cat
House

Bath
House

the nickname "Faith," contained freshly whitewashed rooms, individual beds, and, all in all, the best conditions American prisoners encountered anywhere during any period of the captivity.[11]

The Dan Hoi facility was actually six compounds in one, each with its own stone and stucco cellblock, guard tower, courtyard, latrine, and bathhouse. Occupants estimated that if all six compounds had been filled, the camp would have held about 320 captives. Because of the size of the place and the extensive planning obviously involved in its conversion, analysts have theorized that the North Vietnamese meant to gather all of the U.S. prisoners there eventually.* On the heels of the 52 men from Son Tay, who arrived on 14 July, came 25 from the Zoo and 31 from the Plantation on 29 July; the 61 from the Zoo Annex on 20 and 24 August; and another bunch from the Zoo on 30 September. Two of the six compounds never opened, and the camp population would top off at about 220.[12]

The same "open door" arrangements instituted at the Zoo about this time were introduced here as well but on a larger scale and phased in gradually. The long cellblock buildings each contained five roomy cells that held from 8 to 20 prisoners apiece. Each compound also had two solitary confinement cells, but they were rarely used, as guards were apparently under orders to avoid confrontations and refrained from even corporal punishment. Although turnkeys supervised all activities, they went about their duties nonchalantly, "looking bored" and allowing prisoners to communicate and even exchange mail. Chesley, who came over with the Son Tay contingent, mentioned in his memoir that his cellblock set aside a section in their small courtyard for sunbathers, allocating the space on a rotating basis. Red McDaniel found the freer access exhilarating: "Now we could meet prisoners out in the courtyard. No longer did we have to stick to that peephole in the door to see out and try to identify someone across the walkway. It was enjoyable to move from one man to another; if I didn't like the conversation in one place I could move on."[13]

Ralph Gaither, another who came over from Son Tay, would declare his quarters at Dan Hoi "the best I had while in prison" and his treatment there "the closest we ever came to humane treatment under the Geneva Agreements. For the first time in almost five years I got more food than I could eat—soup, bread, a lot more meat." The men received fruit, oranges and bananas, every other day. Many received their first letters and pictures from home while at Faith. Medical treatment improved noticeably, with "an honest attempt . . . to provide comfort as well as to maintain life," including relief for asthma and sulfa to combat diarrhea. Dysentery remained

---

* The 320 figure did roughly correspond to the total number of U.S. PWs believed to be in custody in the North in the summer of 1970.

a serious problem, however. According to one source, flies were present in far greater numbers at Faith than at any other camp, perhaps because of the large population and hence number of latrine buckets. Although there was now plenty of soap available from stateside packages and hygiene in general improved through more frequent washing, the incidence of disease remained high, partly because colds and flu spread more rapidly as contacts between the prisoners increased.[14]

Although the PWs at Dan Hoi were given a long leash—after some negotiation, camp officials even permitted SROs to establish rosters for details such as sweeping and dishwashing—even in this relatively idyllic spot, vestiges of the earlier captivity environment inevitably surfaced. The guard towers, barbed wire, and 16-foot-high walls were manifestation enough of their continuing predicament. For insulting one of his keepers, Gaither was briefly thrown into solitary, the 10 days spent in the small, dark chamber nonetheless "child's play" compared to his torture at Briarpatch and Vegas. Although the "hammer was off," Shankel and seven other men in his cell who had come over from the Zoo—Jerry Singleton, Rod Knutson, Burt Campbell, Bernard Talley, Jerry Driscoll, George McSwain, and Porter Halyburton—had to be careful not to push guards too far. The bowing requirement may have been dropped, but the prisoners were still subjected to petty harassments and indignities, for example forbidden to walk on a porch in front of their cells and having to say "Good morning" to certain of their handlers. Even as some of the Vietnamese officers became friendlier and more considerate, they were not ready to accord their American counterparts full respect: when the seniors attempted to exchange hand salutes with their ranking opposites in order to gain recognition of the PWs' military organization, the Vietnamese refused to respond.[15]

Fear and depression were in retreat, but, like dysentery and disease, hardly conquered. McDaniel was still nagged by injuries and hounded by worry. "On into 1970 and the late fall of that year," he would reminisce, ". . . I had never fully recovered from my wounds received in torture . . . . I still sweated when I heard the key in the lock, still feared being called up again for the quiz, the ropes, the leg irons. I lay tense at times, waiting. And I prayed often that it would not come again, that the change in treatment meant we were getting closer to the end of our time. More and more I was thinking of home and family as the nights seemed longer, the days dragged, and it seemed it would never end." McDaniel added that the eternal "hope-mongering" and the length of their imprisonment were wearing them down. Congregating in larger groups had its obvious benefits but "it also compounded our discipline problems. As the treatment got better, our discipline seemed to vanish. It was the old story about adversity drawing us closer, prosperity making us independent and more selfish." Another source recalled that "personal conflicts . . . which had been submerged for years" now erupted in earnest, though they were still "generally low key and not serious."[16]

If the potential for fraternal tiffs increased in Dan Hoi's populous compounds, so did the opportunities for organization and collaboration, whether for amusement or resistance purposes. Geoffrey Norman, who tracked the PWs who came to Faith from the Plantation, noted that "it was no longer necessary to tap each hand of bridge laboriously through a sequence of walls. Now the men played—with real cards from packages sent by families —for hours, forming partnerships, setting up tournaments, and establishing a system for awarding Hanoi master points. Exercise sessions were organized and records kept. And someone had the idea of forming a toast-masters' club, in which each man would speak for exactly five minutes on some topic. This led, inevitably, to educational programs." Car buffs Tom Hall and Joe Crecca taught Al Stafford automobile mechanics. Joe Milligan, who had grown up on a farm in New Jersey and then gone on to agriculture school, instructed a group in dairy farming and animal husbandry. The study groups at Dan Hoi, on subjects ranging from French and Spanish to history and real estate, became the basis for many of the organized classes and seminars that would make up the more elaborate "Hanoi University" at Hoa Lo during the last couple years of the war.* On the resistance front, the escape-minded prisoners from Son Tay used the more permissive arrangements to explore new breakout possibilities, including the construction of a tunnel.[17]

During the night of 20 November (21 November in North Vietnam) the Americans at Dan Hoi were aroused by the sound of gunfire in the distance and flashes of light to the west in the vicinity of Son Tay. Alvarez later pointed out the irony of the former Son Tay prisoners witnessing the raid that had been undertaken to free them, "seeing the explosive flashes light up the dark sky and hearing the U.S. fighter cover scream right over" the camp to which they had been transferred. The "luckless" captives, reduced to spectators, "had come tantalizingly close to being rescued." It would be months before the Dan Hoi PWs would learn the full significance of the nocturnal disturbance,† but some were already surmising that the commotion was a rescue effort, when, within a couple days of the incident, "heavily armed and visibly nervous" guards hurriedly packed men and belongings. At dusk

---

* See Chapter 24.
† In the weeks that followed, Vietnamese personnel would let slip that a "commando raid" had occurred but made no mention of a rescue mission. See Watkins and Redman, "Captivity in Southeast Asia," 20-21.

Dan Hoi

PW Detention Area Legend

1. 16. 18. Latrines
2. PWs from Zoo Annex
3. PWs from Zoo
4. 15. Unfinished Compounds
5. 7. 8. 13. 14. Ponds
6. Storage Building
9. 11. Support Buildings
10. Water Tank
12. Administration Building
17. PWs from Son Tay
19. PWs from Plantation

—w— Wall
■ Guardtower
⊣⊢ Gate/Entrance
☉ Earth-covered Bomb Shelter

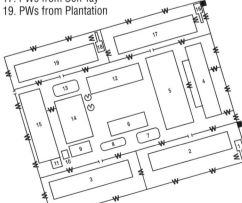

on 24 November, Gaither remembered they were washing and stacking dishes when the Vietnamese dashed in and told them they were leaving. "Within two hours, or three at the most, we loaded everything onto the trucks—clotheslines, dishes, buckets, everything."[18]

Like those rounded up at the Zoo a few weeks later in December, the Dan Hoi prisoners were moved en masse into the safer confines of Hanoi and Hoa Lo. The respective compound groups were kept intact, each corralled into one large, multi-sectioned room. John McKamey's group, for instance, had 57 men in a 20-foot by 60-foot area. The cells, smelling of urine and infested with bedbugs, had recently been used. Because the PWs had seen Vietnamese prisoners standing outside Dan Hoi as they boarded the trucks for the trip into the city, the Americans assumed they were trading places with ARVN and possibly some civilian prisoners who had been incarcerated at the Hilton. In any case, Dan Hoi was never occupied by Americans again, the experiment of collecting the U.S. prisoners at a model camp in the countryside abandoned after only four and a half months.[19]

Conditions at Hoa Lo, at least in terms of the physical environment, improved only marginally through 1970. Those who arrived from the Zoo or Son Tay, and certainly the gleaming Dan Hoi, were typically dismayed when they entered the stygian fortress in which most of them had undergone their captivity baptism. Howie Rutledge, who should have been overjoyed at vacating Alcatraz, could scarcely contain his disillusionment as "the iron doors of Las Vegas swung open to receive us once again." To Rutledge,

> Everything seemed the same. The place was as bleak and cold and filthy as ever. The waters of the Sands still ran thick with sewage, alive with parasites of every description. Men were still crowded into cells not big enough for animals, and the pigs still slopped in troughs around the Mint . . . .
>
> It was like repeating a bad dream. Would it all begin again, the long interrogations, the threats, the torture? Had nothing changed?

As he walked outside his cell the morning after his return, it appeared to Sam Johnson "as if time had stood still," from the familiar odor of the bucket-dumping area and the dirty water that dribbled from the tiny shower stalls to "the same bar of lye soap that never lathered." Wendy Rivers observed that "the small rooms of the Thunderbird were quite a contrast to the improving conditions at the Zoo." Rob Doremus, who had been the only one of the Christmas 1969 transfers from Son Tay to wind up at Hoa Lo, was disappointed "not to be 'welcomed' at the Hilton with at least some sort of food. Luckily, I had brought my evening snack in my duffle and was able to gnaw on a crust of french type bread before sleeping, once again in the cells with the leg irons." Still, Doremus went on, "I felt that I had come full cycle and there was an air of looseness in this old French period prison that enriched my hopes that my trek had, if not been a good one, was not bad either." And Rutledge realized "little by little . . . that something had changed at Las Vegas. There were no agonizing cries in the night from torture rooms. There were no fresh rope burns, no new broken bones. Physical torture had ended, or so it seemed. The rumor spread. Hope mounted."[20]

Gradually through 1970, as a result of the several camp closings and the general trend toward consolidation, Hoa Lo reclaimed center stage in the captivity drama. The return of Rutledge and his Alcatraz mates in December 1969 coincided with the year-end shift of a dozen other PWs from the Zoo, Son Tay, and Plantation to the main prison. Five who came over from the Zoo—Rivers, Kasler, Daughtrey, Schoeffel, and Anderson —were placed in Thunderbird, along with Doremus. Ernie Brace and John McCain, from the Plantation, were nearby in the Golden Nugget. Seven of the nine "Alkies"—Denton, Mulligan, Rutledge, Jenkins, Johnson, Shumaker, and Tanner—filled Stardust, with Coker and McKnight assigned to the Mint. With the likes of Stockdale, Risner, Bill Lawrence, and the 06s Flynn, Bean, Gaddis, and Winn already in residence and other seniors like Crayton, Dunn, Guy, Guarino, and Day (the latter pair were brought in from the Zoo in June) turning up through 1970, virtually all the high-ranking officers in the PW organization were ensconced at Hoa Lo even before the influx from Dan Hoi.

Most of the approximately 80 prisoners at Hoa Lo at the start of 1970 were housed in Vegas, with only a handful "outside the strip" on the Heartbreak-New Guy side of the prison. Despite the persistence of horrible living conditions, even the unhappiest conceded that there were many reasons to be thankful. By February, all the Alcatraz gang had roommates except Johnson, who inexplicably remained in solitary. Rutledge and Jenkins had an emotional reunion. The two aviators had not been more than 30 feet apart all during their four years in prison and, said Rutledge, "we knew each other intimately through our covert communication efforts," but to shake his friend's hand and see him face to face "was something else." Doremus was delighted to find mirrors installed in the bath area. They were now shaving three times a week and with a half-decent blade. Hot water was sometimes available for those who had received packages of instant coffee from home. For recreation each cell was allocated time in the Tet room, where a ping-pong table was set up, some cells also having access to a small billiard table in the east end of Riviera. Denton and Mulligan remembered a particularly bright and pleasant English-speaking turnkey, a tall man with a large Adam's apple whom they called "Ichabod."[21]

Trouble still lurked at every turn. For every good-natured Ichabod there was an unregenerate Bug or Big Ugh waiting for a misstep. Bug's roving patrols may have been leashed but they were still capable of inflicting misery. And even as Cat's influence and vigor steadily declined (Denton said "his tic got worse, he lost weight, and his hands began to shake," and Mulligan thought "Cat must have a terminal illness"), the commandant had a hard time letting go. During the first half of 1970 as many as a half dozen prominent targets, including Denton, Stockdale, McCain, and Lawrence, did time in Calcutta. McCain, Stockdale, Guy, and Dramesi were among those who were pressed to see delegations or tape political statements. Routine interrogations and attitude checks also continued, though Rivers was struck by the addition of a new question to the drill: "What would you say if you were told you're going to be released?"[22]

Hardships, too, remained a daily occurrence. Despite more frequent and much improved medical attention, the men continued to suffer from serious health problems. According to Rutledge, three-fourths of the prisoners came down with high fever and dysentery from a flu epidemic that swept Hanoi in February. Denton was among those who finally received treatment for abscessed teeth that had caused them great pain. Denton was operated on by a sure-handed dentist and also had a tumor removed from his chest by a surgeon who did an excellent job and left only a faint scar. Guy, confined in solitary since coming over from the Plantation in December, was lonely and depressed, thinking constantly about his wife and three sons. As he struggled with the offer of permission to write his family if he agreed to read over the camp radio, "one side of my head turned snow white," he recalled. "The white hair eventually fell out and I was half bald till it grew back its normal brown color." The solo Johnson drifted back into despondency, unable to eat or sleep, his six-foot two-inch frame down to 125 pounds.[23]

The overarching problem confronting the Hoa Lo prisoners at the start of 1970 was their own lack of organization. Despite the presence of so many seniors, the usual command channels were either blocked or blurred, a legacy of the successive purges of the Vegas leadership between 1967 and 1969 and then the crackdown following the Dramesi-Atterberry incident. Discipline and organization had never truly recovered after the transfer of Stockdale and his core group to Alcatraz in October 1967. Although Stockdale had been back for the better part of a year, banishments to the

Mint and Calcutta and a balky roommate* had kept him on the sidelines. Risner and the 06s were still incommunicado in Heartbreak or New Guy. The errant 05s Miller, Wilber, and Schweitzer were gushing propaganda over the radio in exchange, or so it appeared, for being allowed, among other privileges, to take meals outside their cells at Desert Inn. And what structure remained at Vegas was fragmented and failing despite the best efforts of Lawrence, Byron Fuller, and those left to run the place under very difficult circumstances. Communication itself was so throttled that many of the long-term prisoners at the Hilton did not even know that Ho had died or that the torture policy had been scrapped and there was nothing terrible to fear anymore by refusing to cooperate with the Vietnamese. Hervey Stockman, who had been at Hoa Lo since mid-1968, later said he did not learn of the "no torture" policy until August 1970 and only then stopped reading news tapes on the camp radio.[24]

Upon his arrival from Alcatraz, Denton stepped into the void. He began by issuing "no more reading or writing" instructions, his fellow Alkies helping him pass the word on Hanoi's moderation. Using the traditional tap methods and note drops to overcome continuing communication obstacles, they determined to get everyone "on line."[†] Slowly a revived communications system took shape, and with it came improved organization, discipline, and morale. With the names of Plantation PWs he picked up from McCain and other new faces he now counted at Vegas, Mulligan expanded his memory bank to over 300 captives. Prisoners who, except for censored mail and snatches of select news heard over Radio Hanoi, had not had a U.S. or world news update in two years (the 1968 bombing halt over the North sharply reduced not only the numbers of captured airmen entering the Northern jails but also the flow of current information the newcomers brought) suddenly got up to speed through the presence and tenacity of Jim Bedinger, a recent shootdown from Laos who had been moved into the Golden Nugget. With Ernie Brace,[‡]

---

* See p. 492n.

† Dramesi, ever the maverick, surprised Johnson with his ignorance of the tap code and reluctance to learn it. Johnson found him "an enigma. He had one thing only on his mind: escape. Maybe he believed that learning to communicate in this place was a concession to the reality that he was here for the duration of the war. I never figured it out. The code was complicated, but with practice it could be learned, yet Dramesi wouldn't practice" (*Captive Warriors*, 218).

‡ Brace was mated with Bedinger in the number 3 cell; McCain and Air Force Lt. Col. John Finlay were two doors down in number 1. Brace described Bedinger's flustered reaction upon meeting the veteran PW, who by now looked twice his age: "Though he later learned that I was only thirty-eight, Bedinger thought I was an old man. My gray-streaked hair and grizzled stubble beard, with a gaunt face whose eyes seemed lost in their deep black sockets, gave him this impression. My legs were so infirm that I virtually staggered into the room. When I smiled in greeting to the young aviator, Bedinger noticed several teeth missing in front . . . . 'My God,' thought the twenty-three-year-old Navy officer, 'he looks like the Count of Monte Cristo'" (*A Code to Keep*, 191-92).

the junior-grade lieutenant, an enterprising redhead whom Risner called "a ball of fire," published on strips of toilet paper daily editions of the *Vegas Gambler* that informed comrades of the lunar landing ("U.S. made jump like cow, July 69, two sat down"), the Six Day War in the Middle East, and other important events. Despite the quarantining of the prisoners from Laos, the location of the Golden Nugget beside the common washroom facilities enabled Brace and Bedinger to "deliver" the newspaper from cellblock to cellblock. Brace said their room became "the hub of a communications wheel, and we found ourselves relaying, as well as initiating, many messages from one unit to another."[25]

Toward the end of April, Denton, sensing that their keepers had "lost their teeth" and "can't bite us any more," ordered a partial fast to protest the retention of Johnson, Doremus, and Guy in solitary and the special treatment accorded Miller, Wilber, and Schweitzer. Whether because of or in spite of the week-long action, in the weeks following authorities transferred Coker, McKnight, and Dramesi from the Mint to Stardust and addressed the solitary issue.* Believing Stockdale to be the instigator of the strike, the Vietnamese threw him back in the Mint and then Calcutta again, but the senior greeted this latest reprisal with "immense relief" since it freed him of his nettlesome roommate. By midsummer both Stockdale and Johnson were reunited with their Alcatraz mates in Stardust. Johnson, who had been in continuous solitary for three years, was allowed to stop at Denton's and Mulligan's cell on the way to joining Shumaker and Tanner. "When the door opened," he recalled, "two pairs of skinny arms grabbed me and pulled me into the cell. We hugged and pounded each other on bony backs, and my whole body shook with sobs I had tried to hold back." Denton remembered his joy at the sight of Stockdale among them: "In all the years of our prison association he had been little more than a fleeting glimpse, a tap on the wall, a voice under the door. Now he was there with us."[26]

For his part, Stockdale was impressed by what Denton had accomplished. He would tell a debriefer that the wall of Stardust "sounded something like the Merrill, Lynch, Pierce, Fenner and Smith Office in Palo Alto with all the teletypes going. The program was in full swing . . . . The camp was

---

* Opinions diverge on whether the protest made matters better or worse. Mulligan judged it successful in that "it rocked the Vegas camp sufficiently to get rid of Cat and get Sam out of solo, and forced new shuffles that were to our benefit" (*Hanoi Commitment*, 225). Others didn't like the order and questioned its impact. Rivers deemed it "ineffective." Franke maintained it was counterproductive. Guarino, who heard about the fast after he arrived from the Zoo, thought it was another case of Denton's ardor overtaking his common sense (*A POW's Story*, 260). Brace contended the fasting achieved "very little and . . . caused some unnecessary grief." See also Dramesi, *Code of Honor*, 181; Larson, *Autobiography*, 44–45.

. . . back on the rails." Guards banged on doors to keep the men quiet and left up bamboo screens to inhibit contacts but to little avail. Where PWs were on the radio, it was to take aim at Senators "Halfbright" and "May Govern." Mulligan's springtime boast that "except for the three finks living in the Desert Inn," Bug's propaganda effort was producing "zero" may have been a bit premature in April but by July was close to the mark.[27]

Still, there remained an element of confusion relating to command. When Guarino moved into the Riviera in June, he wondered why Denton was in charge:

> Jim Stockdale was somewhere in Vegas and so were Dave Winn, Norm Gaddis, Jim Bean, and Jack Flynn, all of whom outranked Denton, and since they all *did* outrank Denton, I wanted to know what the hell was going on in the camp. The people I asked told me that "Stockdale was hurt and 'gun-shy,' and a fellow he lived with tried to blow the whistle on him." I was told the other four colonels said "they felt out of touch." Maybe they were, but the guys felt "Denton is the only guy with the balls to take over."

In fact, Stockdale, who was senior to Denton "by a mere matter of class standing . . . a few numbers in the book," had willingly deferred to his colleague until he was able to recuperate and was sure he was "off the hook."* By his own admission and several other recollections, he was still reeling from the many months in and out of limbo. As he emerged from Calcutta in July he confessed to being "lonesome, hot, demoralized . . ., and coming to the end of my string again." His nerves were shot and he "was starting to have little crying jags." "The serene strength that had characterized him when I first met him was gone," Johnson observed. "In its place was fear and such absolute sadness that it was almost a physical presence in the cell." After a couple weeks, however, Johnson noticed him "squaring his shoulders," "the crisp, solid commander's stance" returning. Soon he "took his place on the wall," his thinking again concentrated and the fire back in his eyes. "The only thing that bothered me," Johnson said, "was that he resumed his old habit of consistently beating me at chess."[28]

Autumn brought some new wrinkles, most of them welcome: expanded visitation privileges between cells; extension of the "dining out" option to others besides the trio in Desert Inn; smoked fish on occasion; and a batch

---

* As Stockdale noted, the two had "swapped off leadership" before, when Stockdale was "boxed in" at the Zoo and then received the baton back when he was in a better position at Vegas in 1967. "Jerry and I all the time we were there [in Vietnam]," he explained the relationship, "ran what we called the blue and the gold system. This was named after the submarine procedure of blue and gold crews. I would trust Jerry Denton with my wallet and my wife, and vice versa I am sure."

of new guards, many of them able to speak English. In October a half dozen seniors, all of them 05s—Jim Lamar, Bill Franke, Vern Ligon, Jim Mehl, Leo Profilet, and John Finlay—were farmed out to the Zoo, then returned after an uneventful month of "fireside chats" and gentle prodding by interlocuters; why they were sent is not clear, except that the Vietnamese may still have hoped to indoctrinate or in some way exploit a senior group for propaganda purposes. As at the other camps, as the pressure eased, boredom and impatience among the PWs mounted, with one another as well as the enemy. Memoir accounts of this period reveal numerous tensions —subliminal and overt—between Denton and Stratton,* Dramesi and Guarino, and even comrades as close as Denton, Mulligan, and Rutledge. The three fought over cribbage, pool, and ping-pong, as "the games had become the biggest things in our daily life." Shumaker, alternately testy and depressed as he approached his sixth year in captivity, grumbled about communication indiscretions and perceived slights. Mulligan wrote that "flare-ups of temper, unnecessary arguments about inconsequential events, and little irritations brought on open verbal hostility. Like it or not, we were getting cabin fever."[29]

Stockdale felt well enough to assume command the first week in November but within days had to pass the baton again, this time to Risner, who had just been moved into Thunderbird after a year on stash with Larson in room 18 outside New Guy. No sooner had Risner established control than the leadership switched once more, Lt. Col. Ligon taking the helm as Risner was about to circulate his first set of directives. Ligon, who had been kept isolated in various spots in Vegas since his November 1967 capture (during most of 1970 he was with Stockman in Desert Inn), knew little about the PW organization or communication techniques until his October stay at the Zoo, when the other transfers filled him in. Evidently he realized only then that he was the ranking 05 among all those in the system,[†] whereupon, under the code name "Squire," he took over from Risner on his return to Hoa Lo. The title of Risner's memoir chapter "Who Is In Command?" epitomized the seniority muddlement during this interval, when Risner wrote "there were four SROs in a matter of a few days. Needless to say, there were a lot of code names going around and quite a bit of confusion." The "musical chairs" would not be complete until the missing 06s finally surfaced in December and Colonel Flynn succeeded Risner.[30]

---

* Stratton moved to Hoa Lo when Plantation closed that summer. For his ongoing problems with Denton, see Chapter 18, note 15.
† Risner had been promoted to colonel in 1965 while in captivity, less than three months after his shootdown, but in the PW chain of command he remained a lieutenant colonel until 1971, when the rules were modified. Ligon, who had attained lieutenant colonel in 1958 (before Risner) was thus senior to Risner by shootdown date of rank.

Just before Christmas the few men still being held in the Heartbreak section joined their comrades in Vegas. Flynn, Bean, Gaddis, and Winn had been in Vegas since June, when, still secluded, they replaced Coker, McKnight, and Dramesi in the Mint. With the arrival of Risner and Larson in early November, that left only three Americans on the Heartbreak-New Guy side of the prison: Bud Day and Jack Fellowes, deposited there when they arrived from the Zoo in June, and Ben Pollard, who entered from Son Tay, also in June. Day remembered the fall of 1970 as "a banner time," as he and Fellowes received and wrote their first letters. "I had great difficulty reading since I had not read anything for three years," Day recalled. "In addition, my facial injuries and time's erosion of my sight made it difficult." Like the PWs in Vegas, they got larger portions of more edible food, including "huge servings of soy bean cake," supplemented by packages from home, which were delivered "highly pilfered, but good. Amazing tongue-appealing delicacies . . . toffee candy, dried apricots, chocolate pudding, and canned meat." "Almost as enjoyable as the package items," Day added, "were the package smells. Nothing in the world smells as good as American products." Best of all, they had the satisfaction of standing up to Bug and others who "still acted and talked as tough as in the old days" but whose "fangs had been pulled."[31]

The excitement of Day, Fellowes, and Pollard at joining the large company in Vegas in late December was tempered by the awareness that three seriously ill compatriots they had spotted in Heartbreak during the summer were now nowhere to be found and had seemingly disappeared from the system. Fidel victim Earl Cobeil, Navy Cdr. Kenneth Cameron, and J. J. Connell languished for months at Heartbreak within range of the other three but too physically and mentally impaired to effectively interact with their mates or one another. The insane Cobeil had never recovered from the Cubans' torture. Pollard saw him pacing the courtyard in silence, vacantly looking up at the birds in the sky, acting like a "2 or 3 year old child." Cameron, one of the flock of Navy fliers seized in May 1967, had been confined in solitary his entire captivity. Day described him as "a tall man with a large, rawboned frame and a ruggedly handsome face" and with a resistance posture as "tough as shoe leather," but the extended isolation and repeated beatings caused him to become morbid and then completely unhinged, to the point where he would neither eat nor bathe. By September 1970 Cameron's weight had dropped almost in half (the Vietnamese were now giving him extra food, bananas, and sweet milk, but he seemed intent on starving himself), he had not washed in over a year, he was sleeping on the concrete floor, and Pollard said he and Day "realized that we had an unbalanced man on our hands." Connell was a casualty of the Zoo purge following the Dramesi-Atterberry escape. With Cameron, he had been moved into the Hilton after spending the first half of 1970 at the shuttered Alcatraz. He, too, was eating and bathing erratically, acting paranoid, and resisting efforts by both the Vietnamese and the Day trio to resuscitate them.[32]

In early or mid-October—Day's and Pollard's accounts differ—Cameron, Cobeil, and Connell were removed to a hospital, Connell after reporting chest pains. None of the three were seen again.* Along with Storz and Atterberry, they were three for whom the "Good Guy Era" came too late. Day and Pollard later wondered why they and Fellowes had been placed in Heartbreak and if they had narrowly escaped a similar fate. Pollard theorized that "in 1970 the V decided to put the prisoners who had mental problems in 'Heartbreak Hotel' and certainly . . . [Connell, Cameron, and Cobeil] gave indications of mental disorder. As for the rest of us, we feel that the Camp Commander at 'Son Tay' and the 'Zoo' decided to get rid of the POWs causing them great difficulties by saying we were crazy, and thus we ended up in 'Heartbreak.'"

Significantly, when a North Vietnamese official met with United States representatives in Paris in December and handed over a "complete" roster of U.S. prisoners of war being held in the North, the Heartbreak occupants were among the few names of those later known to be PWs who were omitted from the list.[†][33]

Farnsworth and Skid Row, the two camps in the North that housed prisoners up from the South, remained somewhat outside the experience of the other Northern camps through 1970. Perhaps because the implementation of torture and terror had never been as orchestrated or as systematic here as at Hoa Lo or the Zoo, so the post-1969 improvements at these camps were less discernible, too.

Since its opening in August 1968, Farnsworth had been a strict and abusive place where officers and enlisted were kept mostly segregated but shared a miserable existence. By the time a group of 20 PWs arrived from Cambodia on Christmas Day 1969, bringing the number of Americans at the prison to 53, the harshest treatment had abated but the reprobate Cheese was still in

---

* According to the Vietnamese, Cameron died on 4 October, Cobeil lived until 5 November, and Connell passed away on 14 January 1971. Connell's death was attributed to a damaged liver and collapsed cardial artery.

† The list, which did not include those captured in South Vietnam or Laos, contained 339 names, an additional 20 PWs said to have died in captivity, plus 9 who were previously released. See footnote (1) to "American Prisoners of War and Missing in Action in Southeast Asia (as of February 28, 1971)."

charge and conditions remained abysmal. In small, windowless rooms painted black, the officers were forced to sit up in their beds all day, taking meager meals and seldom allowed to step outside except to visit the latrine. When Ted Guy showed up in June,* he found half the PWs still in solitary and interrogations and regulations still much in evidence. "We were getting only two meals a day, roughly half the food I'd received in Hanoi, and were down to two cigarettes," he recalled.[34]

The enlisted at Farnsworth on the whole were treated better—they were kept in larger groups and were getting regular exercise and recreation time by 1970—but Hubbell draws a picture of divisiveness and mistrust within their ranks based on individuals' attitudes toward the enemy and the war. Tensions and suspicions sown during an itinerant captivity in the jungle ripened in the permanent quarters at Farnsworth. Dennis Thompson was described by Hubbell as having been "kept in the dark so long that his eyes were going bad. His teeth were loosening and falling out. His hair, once thick and black, came out by the handfuls whenever he ran his fingers through it." Thompson cited Captains Leonard, Montague, and Archer and Cpl. John Deering as others who were "getting the shaft" for their hardline resistance, while some of their comrades were getting off easy for cooperating. By one account several "diehard" Marine enlisted were ready to kill an Army cellmate suspected of informing on them. The rifts would harden but conditions finally improved after Thanksgiving 1970, when the Son Tay raid caused the Vietnamese to close the camp and bus the entire group, officers and enlisted, into town to the Plantation.[35]

Skid Row owed its name to the filth and disrepair it accumulated over many years as a sporadically utilized civilian penitentiary. In operation as a PW brig since July 1968, the run-down facility was located a few miles south of Hanoi, not far from the Zoo. It initially contained 15 Americans and 3 foreign nationals, most of whom had been captured in and around Hue during the 1968 Tet offensive and subsequently transported north. Fourteen in the group were civilians,† who occupied cells formerly inhabited by local convicts. (Upon arrival the Americans saw signs some local prisoners were still being lodged there as well as ARVN PWs.) The four U.S. servicemen transferred from the South, all Army, were Lt. Col. Ben Purcell, Capts. Jim Thompson and Theodore Gostas, and Sgt. Donald

* Guy came over from Hoa Lo in the shuffle following the Vegas fast. His unusual captivity route, rotating between the "Northern" and "Southern" PW groups, may have resulted from his capture on the North Vietnam-Laos border and prison authorities identifying him with both clusters.
† Some sources list 15: Philip Manhard, Richard Spaulding, Russell Page, Alexander Henderson, Cloden Adkins, Lawrence Stark, Lewis Meyer, Robert Olsen, Thomas Rushton, Eugene Weaver, Marc Cayer, Gary Daves, Charles Willis, Candido Badua, and Arturo Balagot. However, one of these, probably Weaver, entered somewhat later than the others.

Farnsworth

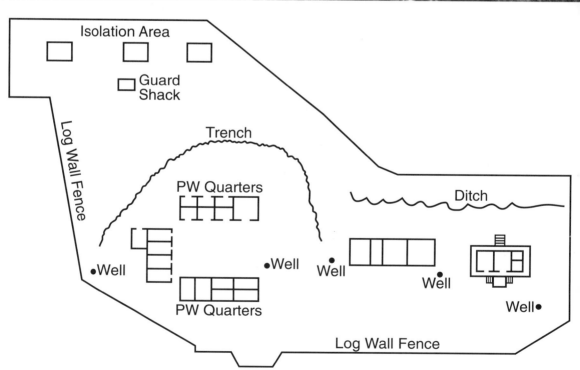

Isolation Area

Guard Shack

Log Wall Fence

Trench

PW Quarters

Ditch

•Well

•Well

Well

Well

Well

PW Quarters

Log Wall Fence

Rander. One Marine captured in Laos, Frank Cius,* moved in from the Hilton in March 1969. In the spring of 1970, two more civilians arrived; they were Bernhard Diehl and Monika Schwinn, the German nurses who had crossed paths with the Kushner camp near Tam Ky in 1969.† Also by 1970 at least one other American military PW had spent time at the camp. Air Force Maj. Kenneth Hughey, a July 1967 shootdown, stopped at Skid Row in between stays at the Plantation and Zoo. When he carried word to the Zoo about the existence of the prison, it became known to the North's Air Force and Navy PWs as "Camp Hughey." The "Skid Row" moniker would be attached by a later group of PWs sent to the place as a punishment measure in 1971. By then it had come to be regarded as a sort of penal colony for men who were not behaving at Hoa Lo.[36]

The interior of the concrete-walled complex was divided into several compounds and one major cellblock into which the PWs were placed initially one to a room. Peeling paint, broken plaster and tiles, strewn rubbish, and the absence of electricity or toilets attested to both its age and neglect. Yet Purcell found his wood-slatted bed and sanitation bucket "a real convenience" compared to his previous experience at Bao Cao. Obviously, comparisons were relative. Day, who did a stretch at Skid Row in 1971, after just getting used to a degree of comfort at the Hilton, implied the place was a comedown from Hoa Lo, a "mud hole" that was "indescribably dirty." Charles Willis, kept in solitary his first nine months, described a "dungeon-like cell" with boards to sleep on, a ragged mosquito net, little ventilation or light, and a heavy padlocked door.[37]

Although treatment appears to have been better than at Farnsworth—there was no equal of Cheese here, at least in the handling of the prisoners from the South—the solitary arrangements and the inability to communicate through the thick-walled cells produced the usual coping problems—and solutions. Willis made friends with a family of lizards and occupied his mind working quadratic equations and building imaginary houses. Schwinn first constructed real "houses" from bits of wood and tile, then built imaginary hotels and hospitals and furnished them with special objects obtained on expeditions to far-off destinations. During 1969 most of the original group were given roommates and moved into larger cells in a separate compound. When Thompson joined Willis and two other civilians, Lawrence Stark and Lewis Meyer, in a four-man cell in late March 1969 it was the first time since his capture in March 1964, except for a brief exchange with Purcell on the trail north, that the Old Man of the South had been in a position to see and talk to a countryman.[38]

* See Chapter 15.
† See Chapter 21 on the capture and earlier confinement of the Purcell group and the German couple, as well as the other civilians.

Skid Row

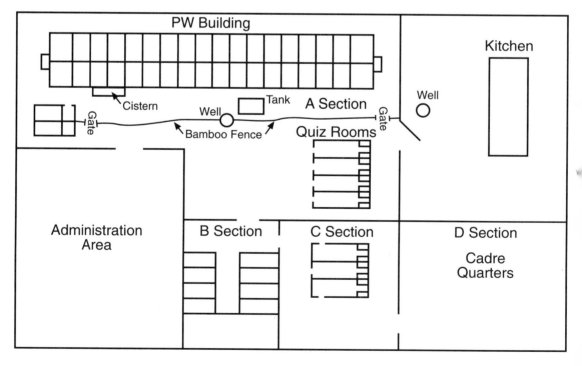

PW Building

Kitchen

Cistern

Tank

A Section

Well

Well

Gate

Bamboo Fence

Gate

Quiz Rooms

Administration
Area

B Section

C Section

D Section

Cadre
Quarters

If there was no torture,* there were few of the privileges and amenities that were beginning to turn up in the other Northern camps. The food was decent, the Southern captives getting their first taste of meat, bread, and hot water, but the menu remained grindingly monotonous, a meal of cabbage, bread, and water served 50 times in January 1970. None of the Southerners was allowed to write home. Interrogation and indoctrination, even if low-key, were more frequent than elsewhere during this period. Besides Skid Row and Hughey, the prison went by a third name, "K-77," for the number stamped on a mimeographed propaganda news sheet that was printed in English and distributed to the inmates.[39]

Aside from Thompson, Purcell was probably the most notable resident at Skid Row in 1970. For refusing to make any apologies or confessions, the senior officer was still stuck in solitary in December 1969 when he tried his first of two escape attempts. For three months he had plied a home-made drill and chisel that he molded from wire, a flattened nail, and morsels of bread to bore 200 holes around the door panel of his cell and then slip it from its frame. The bread crumbs were useful, too, for keeping a "watch-chicken" nearby to warn him of approaching guards and also for refilling the holes as he worked, as he mixed the bread with toothpaste and soot to form a gray paste roughly the color of the door. On the night of 7 December, Pearl Harbor Day, he removed the panel, crawled through the space, and crept to an area where the outside wall was only eight feet high, then slung a crude ladder made from canvas strips and clambered to freedom. Having replaced the panel and evaded guards without detection, he hoped to reach Hanoi and seek asylum at the French consulate. "The trick, of course," Purcell recognized, "would be to get to the consulate without being caught. I obviously wouldn't be able to blend in with the people . . . . But I hoped that if I turned my uniform inside out so that the prison stripes wouldn't show and if I spoke only French, I might get away with it." He may have, had he not lost his bearing and wasted precious hours of darkness walking in the wrong direction. By daybreak he was on his way into the city, managing to hitch a ride on the back of a bicycle, but his luck ran out when the cyclist, whether to ask directions or to turn him in, stopped at a police station and his identity was uncovered.[40]

Had Purcell's escape misadventure occurred six months earlier under the old regime, there is no telling what punishment might have befallen him. As it turned out, he spent only two weeks in leg stocks and suffered mainly a bad cold by being left in the drafty room without a blanket. Undeterred by the mild disciplining, he would try to escape from another camp two years later.

---

* Thompson referred to one instance where Gostas was "tortured" during an interrogation session but there is no evidence it was anything more than a beating, as happened to Cius after he slammed his cell door on a guard's fingers.

24

Unity, Chaos, and the
"Fourth Allied POW Wing"

W hen the PWs at the suburban camps at Dan Hoi (Faith) and Cu Loc
(Zoo) were herded into the city late in 1970, they found themselves
in a section of Hoa Lo none had seen before. It was a separate compound on
the northwest side of the prison that contained seven large open-bay cells
ringing the perimeter in roughly a U-shape and three detached smaller cellblocks, two of those with individual rooms and the third an open bay. The
area had been used previously to house ARVN PWs and as many as 600 to
800 indigenous civilian prisoners, including women and children, who, evidence suggests, were transferred to Dan Hoi and elsewhere to create space
for the Americans.[1]

Prisoners already at Hoa Lo later reported an "explosion" of construction activity and prisoner movement beginning the last week in November,
a time frame that would have coincided with the Son Tay raid and the
decision by the North Vietnamese to move all their American hostages into
Hanoi. Ben Pollard, at this point still in Heartbreak, which enabled him
to hear and observe much of the commotion, recalled seeing lines of
shackled Vietnamese departing the prison through the main courtyard while
laborers strung portable lights and hauled in rolls of matting and wire in
preparation for the newcomers. The 200-plus in the Dan Hoi contingent
were the first American PWs to be moved into the new section, during the
evening of 24 November. The group from the Zoo entered the day after
Christmas. In between, on Christmas night, the several dozen Hoa Lo
residents who had been quartered in Vegas were led through a connecting
corridor after thorough body searches and inspection of their cells to insure

they were not bringing impermissible items.* By year's end, then, over 340 U.S. prisoners of war—all of those captured in the North and known to be still alive—were gathered in one location. It was the first time all the aviators had been together in a single camp. They called the place "Unity."[2]

"Pandemonium" is a word that appears often in the PWs' postwar reminiscences to describe both the confusion and high emotion that accompanied their consolidation in Unity, the excitement heightened by the holiday season and a buzz of rumors about the U.S. attack on Son Tay. Like classmates discovering long lost or forgotten pals at a college reunion, comrades exchanged embraces and stories as they circulated and staked out places for their bedding. "There was so much hugging and handshaking going on," Guarino wrote, "I had to sit down and patiently wait my turn." "Names, faces and voices all came together," said Risner. Dramesi noted that "it was amazing how different people looked. Some ended up being shorter than expected. Some people turned out to be older. It was always different, looking at a person in full view rather than seeing him through a crack in a wall." They were still divided into separate rooms, but in each of the large chambers dozens of men milled about laughing, crying, and speculating as to what it all meant. "For years it had taken as much as twenty-four hours to get a message around that crowd and twenty-four hours to get the answer back," Rutledge penned in his memoir. "Men had risked and suffered much to communicate a sentence in a day. Now, suddenly, we were face-to-face. Everybody wanted to talk to everybody else simultaneously."[3]

Not everyone whom mates hoped to find could be located—Storz, Cameron, Connell, and the other so-called "Lonely Hearts" who had dropped out of sight over the years remained sorely missing—but typical was the reunion of Jack Fellowes and George Coker, who had not known of each other's whereabouts since separated four days after their capture incident in 1966. One of the more interesting collections of prisoners surfaced in a corner of the compound in one of the smaller buildings that the PWs gave the numerical designation "0" (Zero). Here in separate two- and three-man cells were lodged the four Air Force full colonels, four Americans captured in Laos, three Thais, and a South Vietnamese Air Force lieutenant. The Laotian

* All the transfers, including those from Dan Hoi and the Zoo, went through similar examinations, which Stockdale and several others considered the most thorough they had the whole time they were prisoners. The checks were conducted by what appeared to be specially trained intelligence personnel. They ordered the PWs to strip, employed flashlights to examine ears, nails, armpits, and orifices, and even melted bars of soap in their search for contraband. Although much of the PWs' Christmas packages and other items from home were seized in the shakedown, and some hidden materials were uncovered, no one was seriously punished.

captives were a fascinating story in themselves. Ernie Brace and Jim Bed-inger had been joined at Hoa Lo by Maj. Walter Stischer and Lt. Stephen Long in November 1970. The quartet had been spotted by other Ameri-cans in Vegas in December, and by the time they were moved into Unity their isolation and denial of mail privileges had already earned them the label "Legendary Union of Laotian Unfortunates" (Lulus). The Thai trio included Chi Charn Harnavee, the Special Forces sergeant who had been seized with Brace in Laos and who had become a trusted member of the PW community since arriving in Hanoi.* The South Vietnamese pilot, Nguyen Quoc Dat, the Americans called "Max." Regarded by Denton as a "genius" and "secret weapon" for his quick mind and ability to translate the guards' conversations, he, too, would come to command great respect.[4]

If there was unity, there was also chaos. It is important to remember that the conditions the men had left—at the Zoo, especially Dan Hoi, and even Vegas—had become tolerable, stable, and even relatively comfortable by the close of 1970. By comparison, the hurriedly reshuffled compound that the aviators inherited from a rabble of poorly tended civilian and political prisoners was dirty, crowded, and disorganized. The seven peri-meter open-bay compartments each accommodated 40 to 60 occupants in a roughly 20-foot by 60-foot space. An elevated concrete platform in the middle of each room allowed only two feet per man as they slept shoulder to shoulder. In the center of the compound was an octagonal structure that housed a block of showers. Among the lockup facilities were a maze of latrines, quiz rooms, and medical and storage areas. Hastily erected bam-boo fences separated each building and its outdoor space from another. It might have been a cozy setup had several hundred prisoners not had to share it, at that only a third the number that had preceded them in that part of Hoa Lo.

In cell 6, within two days of their arrival at Unity, John Nasmyth's group from the Zoo went from 4 to 11 to 35 members. Another clutch of Zoo veterans landed in one of the smaller cellblocks, named "Buckeye" after senior Dick Keirn's home state of Ohio; Alvarez was among a score of men who slept on two long concrete shelves on opposite walls, with a narrow walking space in between. Forty-five PWs from Vegas settled into cell 7, sharing a 55-gallon-drum latrine and eight urinal buckets. The latrine consisted of a raised cement slab, walled to give privacy, into which were

* When Brace and Harnavee were brought to Hanoi from their jungle camp on the Laotian border in 1968, Brace was jailed at the Plantation and Harnavee at the Hilton. There and at the Zoo Harnavee was used by the captors to carry food to the American PWs and perform other errands; in the process he became a cherished friend of Stockdale among others. To Mulligan, he was "the most magnificent looking Asian I had ever seen," possessed of a "huge muscular body" that the Vietnamese worked "like a pack horse" (*Hanoi Commitment*, 228).

cut holes that drained into an outside ditch. Although the arrangement must have been an improvement over the toting of rusty, excrement-filled waste-cans back and forth to the dump, Sam Johnson would have a keen memory of the cold and damp concrete and "the smell that rose up from the holes" to burn his nostrils.[5]

The Dan Hoi PWs were stuffed into cells 1 through 4 in the same groups that had shared space together at the prior camp. A. J. Myers's history of Unity surveys the early problems caused by the overcrowding and the "internal rules" the Dan Hoi arrivals developed to cope with the situation.

> Cell 1 was smaller than most of the others, and with fifty-seven men, there was only nineteen inches of sleeping space per man on the central platform. The twelve men sleeping in the aisles had a luxurious thirty-six inches. It was almost impossible to roll over at night without bumping the man on either side, and sleeping on concrete makes for much tossing and turning. Thus, some had the problem of getting their rest. This led to complaints against those who wanted to stay up late and talk.
>
> The V had a regulation that everyone must go to bed at 9:00 PM, but with all the mosquito nets hung up, it was possible to stay up and chat without being seen by the guard. The first rule was to reduce talking to a whisper after 9:30, but it is difficult to whisper without disturbing others who are less than two feet away. Also, those who stayed up usually told stories or jokes and laughter was hard to control. Finally, it was necessary to enforce a rule of complete silence after 9:30.
>
> Then there were those who did not appreciate others walking on their sleeping mats, or spilling ashes or food on the mats, or leaving water in a cup which was invariably kicked over. There was no simple solution to this problem because there was no good place to store the cup and when the water bucket was set out for the guard in the morning it was often a long wait before more water arrived. More rules were made.

Still other measures related to exercise time and how to coordinate exercise with bathing in order to minimize the odor of 57 sweating bodies. Finally, there was the matter of what to do with damp clothes, a problem that was magnified on rainy days:

> Many tried hanging damp clothes on the line that ran down the center of the cell which was used for tying up the mosquito nets. The line was soon overloaded and pulled out of the wall. This produced a new rule—no more damp clothes on the centerline. Some tried hanging clothes on lines which ran along the wall (also used for tying up the nets), but the people sleeping in the aisle objected to having wet clothes dripping on their mats. Final rule—no wet clothes inside.[6]

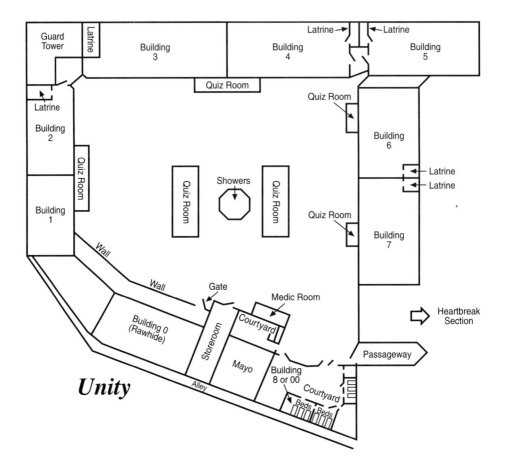

Out of both instinct and necessity, no sooner had new cellmates got-ten acquainted than they began organizing. Nasmyth recalled that over the first few days "it was organize, organize, organize. I think we organized a committee in charge of organization. We split ourselves into four equal groups, one in charge of serving food, one in charge of . . . keeping the cell clean, one in charge of keeping an eye on the gooks while we communi-cated for several hours each day, and the fourth was off. The groups rotated jobs each week." Beyond attending to basic housekeeping chores, there was a need to establish a chain of command within each cell and between cells and to coordinate security and communication procedures. Each of the large cells eventually took on the semblance of a squadron, with an SRO, an execu-tive or operations officer, several flight teams each under its own commander, and some special designations such as a chaplain or medical officer.[7]

The leadership ladder that had had so many missing rungs at Vegas in 1970 gradually got filled in the first month at Unity, but not without con-tinuing gaps and obstacles. Colonel Flynn had made contact and had been messaging since December; he had clearly identified himself as the senior-ranking officer among all the PWs, but, with the other Air Force "bulls" Bean, Gaddis, and Winn, he remained isolated in building Zero after the move to Unity. Using Brace's Lulus as a conduit,* Flynn, operating under the code name "Sky" (later "Ace"), was able to transmit and receive messages to and from the rest of the camp. However, because communication remained, as Stockdale put it, "marginal and sporadic" under this arrangement, with Flynn's concurrence cell 7, where most of the other seniors were located, assumed management of the system on a day-to-day basis. Flynn remained in the loop during this period in January and February 1971, but effectively delegated control to the experienced and more accessible veterans on the other side of the compound.[8]

The ranking seniors in cell 7, sometimes referred to as the "four wise men," were, in order of rank, Ligon, Risner, Stockdale, and Denton. With Flynn's handoff of authority, Ligon became SRO and Risner Deputy for Operations; Stockdale was given responsibility for Plans and Policy and Denton was put in charge of Current Operations. Cellmate Hervey Stockman later conceded that initially there was some reluctance among hardliners to accept Ligon (or Flynn, for that matter) because they had not previously been in the mainstream of the resistance and had even demonstrated, some believed, a seeming unwillingness to accept command until the pressure was off. "If there was any discontent regarding the man in charge," Stockman said of the mixed reception Ligon received, "it came from a small group of 'hard line resistors,' who gave Squire low grades on past leadership performance. These grumblings were no different than those heard at many a change of command throughout military history and quickly subsided." In time both Ligon and Flynn erased doubts about their ability. Detractors eventually learned that Flynn in fact had been brutally tortured upon capture and had stood up to tremendous pressure, possibly surviving only because of the daily care he had received from Navy Lt. (j.g.) Timothy Sullivan, one of the very youngest aviators in captivity, who had been his single cellmate for several critical months. Of Ligon, Stockdale would say he was a "fine man of great maturity who took the bull by the horns."[9]

One of the first tasks of the leadership was the sorting out of names and compilation of a comprehensive, accurate list of confirmed PWs in Unity. This was accomplished speedily under the direction of Rutledge, with Brace keeping a running tally for Flynn. The primary objective then became to standardize and update resistance policies and communication methods

* As dishwashers for the cellblock, the Lulus had access to a central washroom that linked them to the other prisoners, much as had been the case when they functioned as a hub at Vegas.

and abbreviations that had proliferated over many years, with different instructions and corollaries having been issued at different camps under various senior officers. Although Stockdale's BACK US guidance* had been widely disseminated since 1967, the leadership seized the existing opportunity to insure that all the men were operating under the same current understanding of the Code of Conduct. With respect to communication procedures, uniformity and secrecy were still important because, as Stockman noted, "prison authorities continued to forbid communications between buildings and refused to acknowledge any sort of prisoner organization. As a result communications and organization remained covert until the final release elements were organized in February 1973."[10]

Achieving a conformity of behavior became imperative for another reason. With the relaxation of captor regulations and a heightened sense of safety as a result of their numbers, many of the prisoners felt free to pursue their own "self-expression" with no thought to the effect of their actions on the collective interest. Hoping to repair or enhance their reputations as resisters, or perhaps to restore self-esteem, some engaged in displays of bravado that were needlessly provocative and potentially counterproductive. Others, Stockdale observed, were "bent on venting their spleen after years of abuse and misery." Stockman wrote that in the new "laissez-faire" environment, there were men "indulging themselves by allowing their tempers to flare at camp personnel for actions which only weeks before would either have been ignored or accepted in silence." Denton chided those prisoners, "including many who had laid low during the tough years," who were suddenly taking an uncooperative stance toward guards and commanding officers alike: "Like the Children of Israel, we were having trouble with our own people as we neared the Promised Land and the frustrations created by years of imprisonment and torture surfaced."[11]

As they struggled to codify "unified" and "controlled" responses to deal with the captor, the leadership had not only to meld the behavior of men "of all emotional stripes," in the phrase of Stockdale's debriefer, but also to wrestle with the "philosophical" question of what should be the nature of the resistance at this point. "We had meetings among the senior people to decide what our new relationship with the Vietnamese should be," Guarino related in his memoir. "There were varying, and sometimes very opposite, opinions of what we should be doing. Many of us were spoiling for a fight. . . . Others wanted to coast for a while and take a 'wait and see' attitude." Brace recalled, "Some messages from the squad bays suggested that the resistance be hard-core, that guards be harassed and massive escape plans devised.

---

* See Chapter 16.

Others argued that the war's end was probably very near, and that the best policy was to keep a low profile." Stockdale cited the alternatives as "whether to hit the Vietnamese head on or to ease into position." The senior remembered getting a query from cell 6 asking what their "posture" should be and replying, "Our basic posture will be one of oblique envelopment." The word came back immediately from 6, he told his debriefer, "Are you shitting me? Orson (Swindle) can't even spell it." There were also the ongoing disputes over escape and early release policy. In one instance, Alvarez's companions proposed that the SRO seek or, should the occasion arise, at least permit his release on the grounds that he was in his seventh year of captivity. The complexity of the issues and chaos of the circumstances presented the leadership with decisions and communication challenges as daunting as those encountered during much darker times.[12]

While the "wise men" debated amongst themselves and consulted with their troops over what course the resistance should take, the policymaking process was overtaken by events. Incidents erupted all over the compound as guards and prisoners tested each other's resolve under the new arrangements. There was an argument, for example, over bathing routine, the Vietnamese requiring the PWs to shower with their shorts on and some of the PWs preferring—and attempting—to bathe in the nude. The conflict was defused when Bug erected a bamboo fence outside the showers so that any defiance remained screened from onlooking guards, allowing them to save face. (The greater friction here occurred within the bathers' ranks between intransigents who wanted to "rock the boat" and others who saw no purpose in stirring a tempest over such a trivial issue.) Other running battles locked cell 5 in a fight with authorities over making coal balls and cell 4 in a standoff with an overbearing turnkey who refused to count heads until the men were in their proper places. Since outbursts of singing and other clashes at Christmas and New Year's, prison officials had reinstituted prohibitions against loud noise and large gatherings; although such rules were largely ignored and usually went unenforced, they fed the tensions, producing a minor crackdown that sent a couple of offenders back to Heartbreak for brief stints in solitary.[13]

The Vietnamese in fact showed surprising restraint during this "feeling out" period. Guarino conceded:

> Our living together in cell blocks was a trying experience for the turnkeys in charge. At first, they were strongly influenced by the Bug and anticipated the worst. Then, with the passing of time, they eased off and appeared to be taking the new conditions in stride. They were carefully selected people who were comparatively decent to us and very dutiful when it came to delivery of food, water, and

most necessities. Even when we gave them excuses to come down hard on us, they showed a surprising degree of self-control and avoided making mountains out of molehills.

What churned the atmosphere was the continuing refusal by the enemy to accord the Americans the full rights and recognition of prisoners of war. Although Jim Lamar and Bill Franke had had a conversation with a Communist official at Christmas 1970 when the enemy for the first time alluded to them as "POWs," the captives were still being branded as "criminals," and there was enough recidivism in the pilfering of packages* and hectoring by incorrigibles to supply constant reminders of past grievances and humiliations. On the American side, the combination of rising expectations and past memories made an early showdown inevitable, even as cooler heads on both sides conscientiously sought to avoid one. "The confrontation that busted everything wide open," as Risner described the incident, was a clash over the holding of church services.[14]

Despite the ban on organized meetings, the prisoners in cell 7 had continued to conduct a service on Sundays that was part patriotic and part religious, where the men would say the pledge of allegiance, recite psalms, pray, and sing. "The Communists could accept our milling around a cellblock and talking to each other in private conversations," Stockdale said, "but for a single American to stand before a group and lead a prayer, or for a trio to stand before the group and sing a hymn—was a provocative act." Bug had made known his displeasure, but rather than comply, the leadership decided to "go to the wall" on an issue they believed was compelling enough and for which there was overwhelming support. "They had thrown down the gauntlet; we would pick it up," Stockdale remarked. "Even if our new life of ease was at stake, so be it." And so on Sunday morning, 7 February 1971, with Ligon advising Bug in advance of their intent to proceed with the program despite warnings of retaliation, the prisoners in cell 7 assembled for a service led on this day by Risner, Rutledge, and Coker. The turnkeys Hawk and Ichabod interrupted but could not halt the proceedings and when the service was completed, an incensed Bug had the Risner trio pulled out for disciplining. At this point Bud Day began singing "The Star-Spangled Banner," the others joining in with such force and volume that before long

* The prisoners were still smarting from the Christmas inspection that robbed them of valued personal items, which were never returned. Moreover, after a year of relaxation, late in 1970 the Vietnamese again tightened their policy on the handling of packages, no longer allowing items from home, with the exception of coffee, to be stored in cells. "After the PW signed for the package, the V kept control of the package and handed out articles daily on a request basis," a procedure that encouraged thievery and manipulation (Bernasconi et al, "Living Conditions," 179-80).

the other cells around the compound responded in unison. Later that afternoon, as Risner, Rutledge, and Coker awaited their fate in Heartbreak, their comrades renewed the protest, launching into a chorus of "God Bless America," followed by other anthems and popular songs. Then Guarino barked: "This is building number seven, number seven, number seven, this is building number seven, where the hell is six?," the chant picked up by the other cells in turn until the whole camp reverberated like "a stadium cheering section."[15]

The so-called "church riot" was not quelled until Bug summoned a platoon of helmeted reinforcements with tear gas and fixed bayonets to quiet the PWs and restore order. Over the next week, Risner, Rutledge, and Coker remained in Heartbreak while cell 7's ranking officers—Ligon, Stockdale, Denton, Jenkins, Mulligan, Stockman, Lamar, Finlay, and Schoeffel—were interrogated and one by one marched off to building Zero. Ligon and Stockdale were hitched together in the same small bunk in a single set of leg irons for 38 days, learning to maneuver deftly with a shared waste bucket and bed pan while scarcely able to move. Jenkins and Mulligan endured a similar ordeal. Said Mulligan: "Each day one of us was allowed out of stocks to empty our personal convenience buckets. We alternated this privilege as it meant we could get some movement for our bodies. They let us bathe once a week. This meant we were free to move for about fifteen or twenty minutes. The remainder of the time was spent flat on our backs."

More challenges from the other prisoners kept tensions high. A two-day fast unsettled a number of the PWs* as well as their adversaries. An observance on 11 February to mark the start of Bob Shumaker's sixth year as a PW triggered another faceoff, as did the posting of a rough version of the Geneva Convention Articles. When Hawk seized the mock document, Jim Hughes became furious and began yelling obscenities about Ho Chi Minh.† After several more days of sparring, a "truce" was finally negotiated. In the end, the Vietnamese agreed to permit the church services but with restrictions pertaining to length, numbers, and noise and with the requirement that a text of each week's program be submitted in advance. In practice both sides acquiesced in something short of that, and the crisis passed.[16]

---

* The running debate on the efficacy of fasting still aroused strong feelings in some quarters. In this latest instance, see Dramesi, *Code of Honor*, 211-12; Guarino, *A POW's Story*, 285; Day, *Return With Honor*, 202; Nasmyth, *Hanoi Release John Nasmyth*, 235-36.

† The outburst from the loner startled his colleagues as much as his jailers and got him the worst thrashing any American received at Unity. See Dramesi, *Code of Honor*, 218-19 (the account is colored by the author's disdain for some of his cellmates, whom he scolds for being unsympathetic to Hughes's plight); Guarino, *A POW's Story*, 285-86; Myers, *Vietnam POW Camp Histories*, vol 1, 413; Day, *Return With Honor*, 208-09.

Although ephemeral and seemingly inconsequential, the church service confrontation was significant in several respects. It established a still shifting but mutually recognized line in the sand by which both captor and captives put each other on notice as to what henceforth would be tolerated. For the PWs it furnished an occasion to reaffirm their solidarity at a time when increased freedom was testing their unity. On a purely emotional level, it provided a much needed catharsis that enabled many victims of the middle years' suffering to discharge long pent-up rage. Of the pep-rally-like cheering, Denton commented that "the entire camp was blowing out the frustrations of years with a simple schoolboy exercise."[17] Most important, the incident led to the corralling of the dozen seniormost PW officers in one building, thereby banding and strengthening the leadership as never before as the prisoners entered the last phase of the captivity.

By March 1971, building Zero, now going by the code name "Rawhide," was "loaded with brass," in Risner's words. Risner and Rutledge were sent there after the timeout in Heartbreak, and shortly the remaining 05s from cell 7 who were not already there followed, so that for the first time all the 06s and 05s were "under one roof." Stockman wrote of the "mass of talent" that Flynn now had close by: "The movement of the 05s to Bldg 0 provided Sky with the collective expertise of Abe, Chester, Wildcat and a wealth of experience in the other 05s—men who had served as cell block SROs, communicators, hard line resistors as well as others who had pursued a more pliant line with their captors." In placing the "bulls" with the other seniors, Stockdale noted, the Communists had given the PW leadership an unusual opportunity, one it wasted no time exploiting.[18]

Flynn especially rose to the occasion during this crucial juncture. Described by Mulligan as "a large, strong man who gave the physical appearance that he had played in the line for the Chicago Bears," he was also "one of the most mature, compassionate and understanding" men Mulligan had met in all his years in the military, "a dedicated leader whose personal stability brought a great deal of sanity into an insane environment." Presented with a range of views and advice on how aggressively to frame the resistance, Flynn steered a middle course between pragmatism and principle —much as Stockdale had done at Vegas in 1967—that won broad approval. An admiring Stockman said that "Sky first charmed, and then, as quickly, gained the respect of all for his wisdom and judgment . . . . In retrospect Sky's isolation from the PW mainstream may well have been a great asset . . . because it permitted him to judge the alternatives presented him more objectively than they might have been considered by either Abe, Chester or Wildcat." Although Stockdale later maintained that Flynn

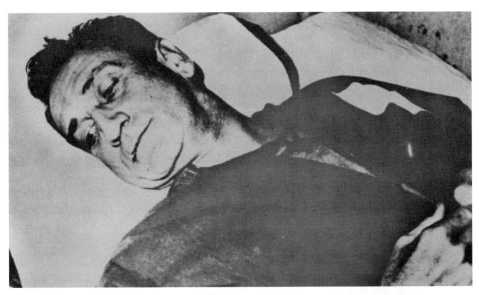

Top: Colonel Flynn, highest-ranking U.S. military PW in Southeast Asia.
Bottom: Other ranking seniors, left to right, Winn, Gaddis, and Ligon.

more or less adhered to the parameters set by the "wise men," Stockman recalled "numerous incidents of emotional advocacy by these and
other seniors that were examined by Sky and then gently but firmly either
altered or vetoed."[19]

In a series of policy statements code-named "Plums" and issued over
the next several months,* Flynn promulgated instructions on command,

---

* According to Alvarez, the word "Plums" was chosen to throw off the Vietnamese: "Occasionally
they succeeded in intercepting our communications. What we needed was a red herring of a
word, something so baffling and irrelevant to our captivity that it would not compromise
us if overheard" (*Chained Eagle*, 235). Five Plums were issued between March and June 1971,
a sixth in the fall, and a seventh in 1972.

resistance, and early release that were more detailed than previous directives but held to much the same commonsense approach to the Code of Conduct. On the one hand, Flynn called for "working with the camp authorities for the improved welfare of all" and ignoring "petty annoyances"; on the other hand, he made clear that there were certain standards that would not be breached and that any flexibility or freelancing was to be subordinated to the need for unity and discipline. On the matter of early release, there were to be "no deals" (no dramatics, no early releases, no appearances for propaganda, no luggage, and no civilian suits).* With regard to command authority, Flynn added a significant new tenet stipulating that any officer whose conduct or emotional stability was deemed unsatisfactory would be relieved.† At the same time, however, he specified that any such action "should be based solely on present and not past performance, and on fact, not hearsay." The qualification was important from a morale standpoint in cleaning the slate for certain individuals who owing to weakness or circumstance may have made some mistakes. With what amounted to a grant of amnesty to those who had strayed beyond the pale, Flynn was both urging his men to forgive and serving notice that backbiting would not be tolerated. "It is neither American nor Christian to nag a repentant sinner," the policy stated. The goal, according to the organization's new motto, was "Return With Honor."[20]

The massing of the prisoners and centralization of the leadership gave Flynn a degree of command and control that had never before been possible. To formalize his authority the SRO created the "4th Allied POW Wing," maintaining and expanding the hierarchy of squadron and flight commanders that had already begun to take shape in the large cells at Unity.‡ Having sighted Risner's name on a promotion list before his own capture, Flynn departed from the traditional policy of determining seniority by shootdown date of rank and designated Risner as his deputy. The 06s and 05s in Rawhide comprised the "headquarters staff," with Stockdale and Denton heading up Operations and others assigned Intelligence, Plans, etc. Anticipating that the enemy might attempt to purge or

---

* Jerry Coffee's homecoming account shows "no appearances"; Stockdale's has "no amnesty."
† Flynn invoked this rule in four instances, one a case of emotional instability and three involving Code of Conduct violations or a failure to carry out orders. The four individuals are identified by Lamar in AF Special Report No 72, sub: Relief of Command, 12 Mar 73.
‡ Stockdale later insisted that the fancy name was actually a publicity contrivance after the fact and that Flynn merely ratified, with some refinements, the existing organization. While not detracting from Flynn's accomplishment in "duplicating as nearly as possible the military structure that people were used to at home," he suggests the action was evolutionary and not as dramatic as has been popularly supposed. See Stockdale file; Melson and Arnold, *The War That Would Not End*, 222n; Solis, *Trial by Fire*, 219n. The "4th" derived from "the fourth war of the century," said Guarino (*A POW's Story*, 287); "Allied" signified the inclusion of Thai and Vietnamese comrades.

isolate the leadership group, Flynn designated cell 7, now commanded by Guarino, as the alternate headquarters. Finally, beyond cementing the organizational structure, Flynn, in Stockman's estimation, deserves credit for effecting a series of administrative changes designed to "reorient prisoner attitudes" back toward a conventional military mindset. By delegating squadron and flight leaders the responsibility for evaluation reports, awards, and decorations and otherwise enhancing their authority and responsibility, Flynn encouraged the restoration of norms of military behavior and procedure* that had eroded in the prison environment despite the best efforts to preserve them.[21]

The command center was no lap of luxury. Rawhide was a fairly miserable place that spring even after those in irons had the fetters removed. There were three or four men in each of 12 seven-foot by seven-foot cells intended for two occupants, so that some of the seniors slept on the floor. Jenkins lived with Stockdale, Denton, and Rutledge; Mulligan, with Bill Lawrence, Charles Gillespie, and Verlyne Daniels. Poor ventilation made the rooms hot and stuffy, and a leaky roof made them wet also until Jenkins improvised a Rube Goldberg-style drainage system that had both colleagues and guards gaping in awe. Although the Lulus had been moved† to make room for the additional seniors from cell 7, the Thais and Max (Dat) remained an integral part of the operation. Denton would laud the Asians as "brave men" who "taught us many lessons," including new communication skills:

> There was a broom in each cell, and Dat showed us how to pull bamboo strips from the brooms, tie them together with threads, and make long poles with which to pass notes across the passageway running the length of the cellblock.
>
> Until Dat's intervention, we had been using stolen pieces of lead and burnt matches for notes, but the product was of poor quality. Dat told us how to mix ashes from pieces of burnt bamboo with

---

* To cite one example: The three Air Force enlisted men at Unity, Art Cormier, Bill Robinson, and Art Black, had been granted battlefield commissions by their commander at the Zoo. When Dick Keirn requested that Flynn honor the commissions, the SRO concurred but also had the men go through an officers training course to certify their achievement.

† Immediately following the church riot, Brace, Bedinger, Stischer, and Long were taken from their cells in the middle of the night and trucked out of Hanoi to a distant camp they called "Lulu's Hideaway," which they later discovered to be Briarpatch (see Chapter 11). The "hideaway" tag betrayed their persisting fear that the Vietnamese might never release them because of the PWs' firsthand knowledge of the enemy's presence in Laos. The concern was reinforced when they were soon joined by another American seized in Laos in February, Air Force Maj. Norbert Gotner. The stay at Briarpatch lasted until July 1971, when they were moved back into Hanoi and deposited at the Plantation. Brace discusses the Briarpatch sojourn, which turned out to be not so bad (a plague of bedbugs was offset by surprisingly good food and considerable freedom) in *A Code to Keep*, ch 29.

shavings from our brown soap and produce what amounted to a
black crayon. The mixtures had to be in exact amounts, and Dat
provided a perfect formula. He also stole a long metal bar about
three-eighths of an inch in diameter which he passed to us. We
used it to bore holes in the wall through which we could pass
notes. This innovation turned Building Zero into a communications
headquarters.[22]

Marveling at the sophistication of the organization and communications network they had soon assembled, Denton worried that they were
overloading with a "flood of to-from-subject memos which sometimes
included numbered paragraphs and sub-paragraphs as the instructions and
policies grew more complicated. I had nine staff men working for me alone
as we developed a hierarchy, and I became swamped with paperwork.
Actually, we were all used to command and were sharks cruising for responsibility." So well-oiled had the machinery become by May that when Flynn,
Winn, and Gaddis were abruptly moved out after the SRO wrote a letter
to the prison commander protesting their conditions, the headquarters continued functioning unimpaired. The colonels were stowed in room 18's
vacant torture chamber on the south side of Heartbreak, where they were
not molested but were again isolated, command of the Wing thus passing to
Risner for an extended period.* [23]

Indicative of the degree to which the tables had turned by the spring of
1971 was Dramesi's reflection on how "things have really changed . . .; the
prisoners now harass the guards." Any number of PW "projects" were going
on in the aftermath of the church riot, some of them undertaken by individual cells with particular peeves to redress, others manifesting the new
capacity for concerted action. Cell 6 had lost four of its leaders—Cdrs. Ned
Shuman, Ed Martin, Collins Haines, and Ted Kopfman—to Heartbreak when
they refused to abide by the new terms set for the church services. In response
the next ranking senior, Ron Byrne, ordered a "stare" program whereby inmates
gave guards dirty looks, murmured under their breath, and acted menacing
enough to make their handlers distinctly uncomfortable.[24] Over in cell 7,
Coker, McKnight, and Dramesi formed the core of an escape committee that
at one time or another also included Kasler and Day and whose link to the
seniors in Rawhide was Stockman. While Guarino and others who had
been through the Dramesi-Atterberry reprisals at the Zoo registered strong
reservations (Guarino told Bill Franke: "I don't think it's wise to put Scorpio [Dramesi] back in the escape business . . . . I don't want to go through

* The fourth 06, Bean, remained behind in Rawhide. Why the Vietnamese ignored him is not
clear, except that they may have been aware of his being outside the circle of influence. One
of the four officers censured by Flynn (see p. 534n), he faded increasingly into the background.
Day drew a scathing portrait of him in *Return With Honor*, 234-35.

that bullshit again!"), plans proceeded with Flynn's blessing, as a network of designated "Stockholders" took to developing a campwide strategy.*

The centralization of authority also gave impetus to a campaign initiated in January 1971 by a group of junior officers (Stockdale and Guarino credited John McCain with the idea, Myers traced it to a group in cell 3) who determined to use the letter-writing privilege as a weapon against the captor. Since Communist officials had come to value the prisoners' outgoing mail—they were now allowing each man one letter a month—as demonstration of the regime's humaneness, any slowdown or stoppage of the PW correspondence, in the captives' thinking, could become an effective instrument of pressure. The so-called "letter moratorium," whereby the prisoners refused to write home, or, more accurately, wrote letters voicing complaints (thereby assuring they would never pass censorship), had several objectives: to obtain better conditions at Unity; to force the Vietnamese both to reform their censorship policy and to deliver letters and packages to intended recipients who were still being denied them; to promote solidarity; and to embarrass the enemy in the propaganda war by calling attention to the suddenly reduced flow of mail out of Hanoi, a seeming regression to past practices. By March the program, now backed by the leadership and coordinated in a more systematic fashion, spread throughout the camp. Although it was kept voluntary in recognition of the vital importance some men attached to even the censored contacts with family, most of the prisoners participated in the project. How successful it was is difficult to gauge, some prisoners believing it contributed to improvements at Unity that occurred over the summer, others considering it disruptive and a waste of energy.[†] Lasting about six months, the moratorium ended with the approach of Christmas and the desire of the men to resume the correspondence home in time for the holidays.[25]

Finding that they were losing face as well as control, prison administrators took a series of steps through the spring and summer to regain the upper

---

* The escape debate—whether to try or not—occupied hours of frequently acrimonious discussion, with Dramesi and Guarino at the center of the contention. Flynn issued no Plum on escape, so complex was the question. See Dramesi, *Code of Honor*, 197-202, 224-31; Guarino, *A POW's Story*, 286-87, 290, 292-93; Johnson and Winebrenner, *Captive Warriors*, 250-51; "U.S. Aircrew Members Escape from Permanent Detention Facilities," 48-49.

† Of course they had no way of knowing what impact the action had in Washington and Paris. Both analysts and families noticed a conspicuous dropoff in the volume of letters received from the PWs especially during the middle months of 1971, when (between May and October) a total of only 170 letters, as compared with 1,300 letters for a like period the previous year, were delivered. The disturbing pattern raised concerns and demands for an explanation that U.S. officials, even after discovering the reason, were able to play to advantage. See, for example, "U.S. Repeats Claim that Hanoi Curtailed Mail from Prisoners," Baltimore *Sun*, 12 Nov 71. The effect of the moratorium on the home front and on negotiations in Paris is treated in Davis, *The U.S. Government and American PWs in Southeast Asia*, ch 17 (ms).

hand. Besides continuing to detain seniors and troublemakers in Heart-break, the captors instituted a version of an earlier program whereby they attempted to wreck the PW chain of command by placing junior officers in charge of cells and designating them the sole intermediaries in cell contacts with jailers. The "Junior Officer Liaison" (JOL) program had no more success than the previous "Room Responsible" plan.[26] At some point Viet-namese authorities decided, too, that sending agitators to the "woodshed" at Heartbreak was insufficient and that housecleaning on a larger scale was necessary. Whether or not Day was correct in his conclusion that Hughes's defamation of Ho "was the straw that broke the camel's back,"[27] two days after the colonel's whipping, on 19 March, guards rounded up a bunch of men, many of them with long records as instigators, and shipped them out to Skid Row.

Included in the group of 36 were the likes of Day, McCain, Fellowes, Shuman, Haines, Swindle, and Warner. Red McDaniel observed that the 19 pulled from his cell had been active in the "stare" project. Guarino thought those tabbed were selected at random and that the Vietnamese were merely employing "scare tactics" to keep the PWs guessing and on edge. Haines and a half dozen others were moved back in May. The rest of the exiles, given the sobriquet "Hell's Angels" by their comrades at Unity, spent about six months at the punishment camp in a compound separate from the prisoners who had been captured in the South.* Placed under the supervision of old-regime holdovers Soft Soap Fairy and Straps and Bars, they were pressed for information on the Wing organization and letter moratorium. Although subjected to stiff interrogations, "some slapping around," and sessions in irons, the men were not tortured, and the most serious problem they encountered was an outbreak of hepatitis. In August they were returned to Hoa Lo for about six weeks as a result of heavy rains that threatened to flood the suburban facility. About 20 of those still judged to be "bad attitude" cases were sent back to Skid Row for a final month before returning to Unity for good the first week in November.[28]

Periodically through 1971 there would be other shuffles within Unity or between Unity and camps outside the city, the Vietnamese sticking to their basic strategy of keeping the bulk of the prisoners in Hanoi but making an occasional transfer to a satellite facility for some special purpose—hiding the Lulus, taking suspected ringleaders out of circulation, etc. Skid Row, for example, received a second batch of PWs from Unity late in the year; Guarino, Rivers, Haines (the second time around for him), Schweitzer, Dunn, and Webb spent the last two weeks in December there, ostensibly

---

* See Chapter 23; Myers, *Vietnam POW Camp Histories*, vol 1, 457.

for refusing to clean vegetables but more likely because a guard found their names printed on an organization chart. Over several months beginning in September dispatchers shuttled 40 to 50 prisoners between Unity and the Zoo, which was reopened after being empty most of the year. The reactivation of the Zoo, spruced up with the help of the first group of transfers, gave the Communists a benign location once again to which to bring journalists and other foreign visitors seeking a window on the treatment of the PWs. The extra capacity the camp furnished also gave the captor a place to sequester new shootdowns, who with the resumption of U.S. bombing raids late in 1971 were entering the system in significant numbers for the first time in three years.[29]

In late September or early October, Stockdale, Denton, Jenkins, Rutledge, Mulligan, and Hughes were moved from Rawhide to another small building within Unity where they were reunited with Flynn, Gaddis, and Winn, the 06s just returned from Heartbreak South. By constructing a tall fence outside their patch of a courtyard and in effect creating a prison within a prison, the Vietnamese no doubt thought they had found another way to isolate the leaders. However, with the aid again of the resourceful Asians, who swept notes between Rawhide and the seniors' new quarters while performing cleaning chores, Flynn and his top staff were soon in touch with Risner and the other 05s. The new command post, referred to in PW accounts as building 8 or 00 (to distinguish it from building 0), at first took the call sign "Utah," then, after a security compromise, "Blue." So crafty were the message codes developed by Rutledge and Jenkins, and so extensive the communication links forged previously by 0 over the summer, that by fall Mulligan was of the opinion the Wing was functioning "almost as efficiently as the normal administration facilities available back home."[30]

Despite the sequestrations, flashes of regression, and simmering tensions through 1971, at no point did either conditions or treatment revert to anything approaching the old days. Stockdale told his debriefer that with the PWs' move en masse into Unity in December 1970 the terms of captivity were fundamentally altered even beyond the major improvements following Ho's death. "From that December day 1970 until the day we were released we lived in a world that was as different from that in which we had lived before as day and night. We still had guards. We still had communications problems. I spent a few weeks in irons as did several others, and all that jazz. But it was really a different emotional and environmental situation." Even the uncomfortable spring in Rawhide, Stockdale said, was a comparative "piece of cake . . . a big picnic." "By April Fools' Day, 1971," he jotted in his memoir, the last vestiges of the extortionist gulag had "receded into the mist," replaced by "a regime of simple straightforward detention."[31]

Amid all the jousting and posturing, the summer of 1971 saw significant improvements in the physical well-being of the Unity residents. Ceiling fans were installed in the camp's large cells in June and offered much relief especially during the long hot evenings. With the addition of sweet milk to the breakfast ration, starch cube supplements, and tastier fare and more generous portions in general, prisoners were beginning to see weight increases for the first time. Jack Rollins noted wryly that "when I started to pick up weight, my shape changed. I had been size 34 waist when I went to Viet Nam, but now I needed size 36." Greater strength and freedom also expanded their exercise options, making possible more ambitious programs, including running laps around the crowded yard. Mulligan remembered the hobbled Stockdale "running lickety-split like a man on a peg leg."[32]

Life in building 8 that fall brought much contentment to Mulligan, even as his group of nine seniors were physically removed from the hundreds of comrades in the main compound.

> Jenkins, Rutledge and I slept in one cell that connected directly with Stockdale, Denton and Hughes. The six of us were always together whenever we were locked in the cell. Directly opposite us the Vee had put Flynn, Gaddis and Winn in one cell. We could talk directly from our cells to their cell and we were always in direct open communication with each other. Between us was a corner room where the Vietnamese installed a crude wooden table and a couple of benches. The nine of us ate our meals together in this room.
>
> Our daily routine was quite standard. Each morning the guard would let the nine of us out of our respective cells. We would get hot water and a light snack for breakfast. Then we took turns bathing and washing our clothes after our exercises were completed. We stayed in the courtyard all morning until after we had eaten our noon meal. Then as siesta time came we were locked into our respective cells.
>
> After siesta we had more outside time, until after the late afternoon meal was completed, when we would again be locked in for the night. Compared to our previous existence it was like living in a country club.

Rutledge gushed that for the first time in six years he had a cell with an open window—"there were bars, but it was a window"—and in the courtyard area he could feel the sunshine on his face. The Vietnamese even took to sterilizing the group's dishes and utensils, although sanitation remained a dicey proposition with so many bodies at Unity and the prison's facilities so primitive.[33]

By most accounts medical treatment, too, improved through 1971, the camp management setting aside a special room the prisoners dubbed "Mayo" where staff attended to the sickest cases. Despite injections to ward off beriberi and hepatitis and the benefits of more exercise, vitamins, and calories, the men remained vulnerable to a host of chronic and often painful afflictions. Mulligan's season of content at Blue was interrupted by an excruciating attack of kidney stones. A pinkeye epidemic spread throughout the camp in June, leaving many prisoners, and guards, in discomfort for weeks; according to Guarino, the Vietnamese blamed the conjunctivitis on the U.S. Air Force's defoliation spraying and said the whole country was suffering from it. Guarino was so bothered by headaches he had cellmate and "amateur hypnotist" Laird Guttersen work at relaxing him. Mulligan's kidney problem eventually cleared up, but Alvarez worried about an untreated darkish skin growth on the chest of roommate Dick Ratzlaff that indeed turned out to be a melanoma. Also of concern to mates was the condition of Render Crayton, who had been picking at his food and declining even sweeteners like bananas and a sugared bean soup until friends feared he had become anorexic. Although he insisted he was all right, the balding six-footer was (he would learn in 1973) suffering from an intestinal blockage that would affect his digestion. He hung tough even as his health deteriorated.[34]

Time healed most of the worst physical wounds but took an unrelenting psychological toll. The average PW at Unity in 1971, according to a contemporary survey, was an 04 about 39 years old, a father of three, with 45 months in confinement that included 6 to 12 months in solitary. A black joke among the prisoners had the PW becoming so conditioned to captivity that when he returned home he would "tap out messages to his wife instead of talking, or at best whispering so the guard would not hear; this followed by a display of urinating in the wastebasket in the dining room instead of using the toilet. Of course, he would steal everything he could get his hands on and display his prowess at hiding everything he stole as well as being an inveterate pack rat." Long-termers like Guarino and Shumaker were most prone to fits of depression. "By November of '71, like many others," wrote Guarino, "I was at low ebb, and particularly victimized by my own frustration over the length of our captivity, with no end in sight." It was not a case of just "being squirrely," Rob Doremus told Stephen Rowan. "We were losing our sense of time and we were getting stale. Everything that we talked about would be circa 1965 or before, because that was when we were 'alive.' If somebody new came in and started talking about an Oldsmobile Toronado, why I just couldn't picture that car. The more the years went on, the longer the time hung heavy, because we didn't know what was going on, and we thought we'd never be able to catch up." When newcomer Maj. Leland

Hildebrand arrived at the Zoo in December, he had "a sense of the world having stopped for a number of PWs."

Letters from home filled them in on what they were missing but were a two-edged sword. Guarino, discovering he was a grandfather for the third time, rued the loss of so many irretrievable moments. He could think of his 18-year-old son only "as a quiet ninety-pounder. Could he really be a married man? With twins?" Of Shumaker, one of his roommates at Unity, Guarino recalled:

> . . . Bob's wife had just had their first child when he shoved off on his last cruise. He got letters from home as regularly as most of us did, and occasionally they contained snapshots of his wife and son. The most recent photos of them were taken at Disneyland in California. The boy was now about seven and an absolute replica of Bob—like he was punched out with a Shumaker cookie press. Bob's wife stood there on the bridge leading into the park wearing a very short skirt, which was very much in style, but we, locked away from the world for seven years, were not aware of that. The first day, showing the pictures around, Bob was okay, but then the impact of the passage of time set in. The fact that he barely knew his wife and son, and was missing so much in their lives, really hit him.

Likewise Sam Johnson had to "force myself not to become morose" as he thought of his children—his high school son who had grown to manhood and his two teenage daughters: "Gini was eighteen and I had already missed the firsts that are so important to a young girl—her first date, her first prom, her first corsage. Would I be home in time to be a part of Beverly's giggling teenage years? Was there a chance I would be there for her first date? Her first lead in the school play? I wondered if there was any way the gaps in their lives could be filled. Could the gaps in my own life ever be filled?"[35]

Whether their wives would be waiting for them and what would be the nature of their resumed relationship became regular grist for locker-room pundits and nervous husbands. The latter became more anxious as the likelihood of their eventual safe release increased. Some already knew or suspected the answers. Plumb remarked sardonically that the postal agents would selectively withhold mail but they "never made us wait for 'Dear Johns.'" Two years of enigmatic silence in which his wife had not responded to his several letters ended on Christmas Day 1971 when Alvarez learned in a letter from his mother that Tangee had left him.* When a follow-up

---

* The same day Risner was handed a letter telling him of his mother's death. Nasmyth agreed with Plumb: "One almost sure way to get a letter was if it contained bad news" (*Hanoi Release John Nasmyth*, 244).

letter in January informed him that she had remarried, all the PW's "carefully orchestrated defenses collapsed." Tangee had been "much more than a loved one": she had been for Alvarez "the light at the end of the tunnel," "a mooring" that had anchored his hopes for the future. Others, too, faced the same uncertainty. When Guarino and Kasler received packages from home loaded with delicacies, and Rivers seemed to be getting "the bare minimum treatment," Kasler muttered, "There's no way [Rivers's] wife is still out there waiting for him." Alvarez was consoled by roommates Jerry Coffee and Dave Carey, the latter himself having gone through a period of "agonizing speculation" until he confirmed that the reason letters from his parents were signed only "Love, Mom" was that his father had died in 1969.[36]

Morale took roller coaster turns, soaring when details of the Son Tay raid finally became known through smuggled inserts in packages, plummeting when Hanoi Hannah reported a stall in the peace talks and the tightening of the Communists' grip in the South. Returnees from the Zoo brought back more uncensored news through their contacts with the crop of recent shootdowns. As with the receipt of mail from home, what they heard was not always reassuring. Revelations that the prisoners were not forgotten and that both their government and a galvanized public were pressing hard to secure their freedom thrilled them, but the "bad news" was that the peace-at-any-price activists had seized the agenda. "Miniskirts, double-knits, square-toed shoes, wide neckties, long collars, and long hair were greeted with mixed surprise and dismay," Day recalled his group's reaction when several mates returned from a stint at the Zoo with "a wealth of news from the States." Stratton was shocked by the latest photographs of his shaggy-haired sons, venting to a cellmate, "Do you think there are any barbers left in Palo Alto?"[37]

In every cell there were men who by nature were optimists or pessimists. Day prided himself on a positive attitude and the ability to fight off nostalgia and self-pity; the mercurial Johnson was all over the emotional map, up one month, down the next; Shumaker was close to running on empty by 1972. Day's roommates "ranged from the most extreme optimist to some of the most incredibly pessimistic people I have had the misfortune to live with . . . . Some men were instant crowd dissolvers. As soon as one of them approached a group, it departed for other places." Day granted that although the signs were pointing in the right direction, "there was still no evidence that we were going to do anything but cool our heels for an indeterminate period of time." The optimists, he conceded, had repeatedly been on the losing side of bets: "Every speculation of the past—this bombing halt, that negotiation, the 1968 elections on which so many hopes had ridden, the Paris Peace Conference, every major subject on which the POW had hung an optimistic . . . 'go home' date"—had proved to be delusional. And lest anyone forget how fragile was Unity's equilibrium, more than one veteran cautioned (and Day himself recognized) that, with Bug their "den mother" and so many old-regime factotums still on the scene, it would not take much for their safe haven to evaporate altogether.[38]

In the meantime they fell back on the same coping mechanisms that had taken them this far. Day noted "there was little that could be manufactured, stolen, or created that we did not have." The prisoners made cakes from bread dough and mixes they collected from packages, one masterpiece iced with the Marine Corps globe and anchor to celebrate the service's birthday. Dramesi stitched an American flag using red, white, and blue remnants of a towel, handkerchief, and other materials and a piece of copper wire for a needle; Norlan Daughtrey contributed the red stripes from a set of underwear his wife mailed him; threads from a yellow blanket supplied the gold border. "Happiness is a pair of glasses," exulted Day after lifting a pair of spectacles from a table at quiz. The "great glasses robbery" won him many friends among the prematurely aging aviators whose weakening vision and dimly lit cells left them straining to make out writing and pictures from home. (Day later learned that his wife had mailed him nine pairs of glasses during his imprisonment, none of which he received.)[39]

The large cells became beehives of nonstop activity: high-stake poker games (debts payable upon release), chess and bridge tournaments, walkers getting their exercise while dodging men doing handstands or practicing golf swings, scribblers working on correspondence or communication notes. Although the captors had confiscated all American-made playing cards and other games as part of their security sweep, they allowed each room a deck of Vietnamese cards and a Russian-made chess set. Using Bolstad's quality chips, cell 6's inmates kept a running tally of their daily poker game, a serious enterprise in which Nasmyth, who happened to be bookkeeper, won over three thousand dollars. (The tallier, who had an understandable interest in keeping the record intact, scored the results on a piece of cigarette paper that he wadded up and stuck in his ear when an inspection loomed.) Day "progressed from a rotten bridge player to a lousy one." Kasler had few peers at chess. Cell 7 converted its center platform into a dance floor, McKnight demonstrating the jitterbug and other steps in anticipation of the "dancing in the streets" that would greet them at homecoming. McCain scanned the tableau of activities and personalities lining his room and pronounced the place a "madhouse."[40]

Every cell had its raconteurs and resident experts. Swede Larson expounded for hours on the science of raising chickens for profit, a subject that had been his form of "mental therapy" through long isolation and about which he had stored huge funds of data and information in his head. Mike Brazelton was one of several talented "movie tellers" at Unity. One group of participants recounted that "hardly a night passed in these large cells without some form of entertainment being provided by someone," a narration, a travelogue, in some cases elaborate skits replete with costume changes and staging. "Dusk was 'show time,'" Plumb remembered, and by 1972 "'low-cost' productions, lasting about fifteen minutes in 1967, became full-blown spectaculars." Most cells had a toastmasters' club that was meant to be both diverting and instructional. When speeches became polemical as well— Guarino accused Dramesi of using the dais as a "personal forum" for his hardline notions—the activity could cause considerable intramural friction as well as get members in hot water with the prison monitors. (Coincidentally or not, most of the group exiled to Skid Row in December belonged to cell 7's toastmasters' fraternity.)[41]

If shows and talkfests occupied the evenings, study—where light and eyesight permitted—consumed whole mornings and afternoons. The informal study groups begun at Dan Hoi evolved into a full-fledged "university" in Unity. An eclectic "curriculum" included history, political science, mathematics, literature, at least four foreign languages (Spanish, French, German, and Russian), and numerous "electives" ranging from music and art appreciation to skiing, beekeeping, and diesel maintenance. In one cell Guy Gruters taught higher math, David Luna (a 1967 capture) taught Spanish, and Jim Shively lectured on international relations. In another, Ben Pollard (a former member of the faculty at the Air Force Academy) taught thermodynamics and Dick Stratton government and American history. History buff Bill Lawrence offered a seminar on the Civil War. Jay Jensen taught classes in "business, banking, accounting, family budget, speech, scouting, and religion." Even Max, the South Vietnamese pilot, got into the act—as a French professor. Among the electives with high "enrollments" were a course given by Rollins on meat cutting (as an enlisted man the instructor had moonlighted as a butcher); music workshops in which Joe Crecca whistled the classics and Bill Butler used his pupils as musical notes, lining them up to sing chords and keys; and, perhaps the most incongruous, a wine appreciation class headed by Ed Mechenbier, who took his charges on "tours" of wine-producing regions and gathered them, "like gentlemen dressed for an evening in Paris," in the corner of his large room for "tastings."* [42]

Of Unity's elaborate educational system, Geoffrey Norman wrote: "As in any college, complaints about overwork, scheduling conflicts, and exams

---

* Although these tastings were imaginary, from time to time the PWs were actually able to manufacture wine from assorted fruits and vegetables that they fermented in water and, when they had it, sugar. See Plumb, *I'm No Hero*, 204.

that came up on the same day were brought to the dean.* Men struggling with difficult material would ask for extra tutoring. It was, in all the essential ways, a real school. Certainly learning was taken seriously, and the appetite for knowledge was great." Although there were no textbooks or library, there was no shortage of willing instructors with advanced degrees, fluency in languages, and impressive expertise. Still, questions and disputes of facts— a historical date, the gender of a French noun—arose where, for lack of an almanac or dictionary, the issue had to be settled on the basis of what came to be called "Hanoi facts," which amounted to educated guesses. Wrote Norman:

> They improvised, as always. Often, a third party would be called in to settle questions of fact. The communications net could be used to find a man in another room with the credentials to settle the matter. WHAT IS ACTUAL DATE OF BATTLE OF FUCKING WATERLOO would be tapped urgently through the wall while a course in European history waited for the answer. With five hundred men as a resource, someone often did know the answer, could supply the missing information so that the course could proceed. But sometimes the men had to settle for what they came to call Hanoi facts. Foreign-language idioms and the gender of nouns, especially, were settled by this technique. "Okay, men, we cannot establish for sure whether your French automobile is a boy or a girl, but as long as we're here in Hanoi, it is going to be a boy. When you get home and take your sweetie to Paris, ask the concierge."

The greatest handicap to learning was the limited supply until 1972 of basic equipment—pens and pencils, paper, chalk, blackboards, and the like —although the prisoners often managed with ersatz writing implements and toilet paper pads. Toward the end of the war the Vietnamese made available pens, copy books, and even a few reference volumes.[43]

In explaining the importance of academics to the PWs, Norman observed that "in all this activity there was release and purpose," a way to combat apathy that was more than sheer escapism. Focusing on young Air Force Lt. Michael Burns, only 22 when he was shot down in July 1968, Norman ventured that Burns did not want to come out of prison a "Rip Van Winkle. He would have a world of catching up to do, but at least he would learn what he could while he was here, keep his mind as sharp as possible and his body fit." And so Burns "took the wine appreciation course and memorized the vintages that he thought he would like to drink when he got home. He took Crecca's course in

---

* Most of the cells had a designated "education officer."

classical music . . . . He memorized Shakespearean sonnets and the details of the battle of Thermopylae. He sang in the glee club." In all these pursuits and even in such simple acts as washing their own clothes and adding a personal touch to their prison uniform,* indulgences that Unity permitted many of the PWs for the first time, Burns and his comrades were now doing more than merely coping and passing time. In the words of Doremus, "Each of us was trying to recapture our status as human beings."[44]

At Christmas 1971, cell 2's McCain, Swindle, Fer, Hivner, and Waggoner starred in a "Hanoi Players" production of Dickens's holiday classic, with Scrooge "meaner than a barrel of snakes" and Tiny Tim and Bob Cratchit "more pathetic than ever." In other rooms hefty Marine pilot Jerry Marvel portrayed Santa Claus and cellmates drew names and swapped gifts—fishing tackle, Stan Getz jazz albums, a set of Samuel Eliot Morison's history of the U.S. Navy in World War II—that they hoped some day to exchange for real. In building 8, Mulligan received a letter from his wife Louise with a picture that showed how much she had deteriorated since their separation. "She had fought the good fight for many years but now she was reaching the end of the rope," he reflected. "She needs me just as I need her. Somehow I've got to get home before it's too late."[45]

---

* For sartorial idiosyncracy, no one surpassed Jack Finlay, who "wore his prison black pajama top over white long johns, white wool socks, his gook rubber thongs, and a muffler he had fashioned from scraps of old clothes. A pipe in his teeth completed the jaunty look" (Guarino, *A POW's Story*, 277).

25

Detours: Dissension and Dispersion

Nothing turned out to be easy for the American prisoners in Southeast Asia, not even playing out the string. While their fate remained tethered to stalemated negotiations a continent away in Paris, their numbers were again increasing—during 1972, over 100 new shootdowns would enter the system—they were again being moved, often without logic or explanation, as in a shell game, between camps, and the tight comradeship that had sustained them through the hard times was dissolving here and there into cliques and recriminations. As the Vietnamese picked their spots to assert control and as the PWs picked theirs to score punches and settle accounts (in some instances, with one another), the last year of the captivity was not without its own flash points and its share of both triumphs and tribulations.

If Camp Unity was marked by chaos, it was also marred by dissension. Despite Flynn and the senior cadre's overall success in maintaining discipline and solidarity, the Fourth Allied POW Wing from the beginning was buffeted by policy rifts, personal feuds, and challenges to the leadership that produced a steady undercurrent of tension. Arguments over resistance tactics (fasting, escape, the letter moratorium), personality conflicts, and quarrels over simple housekeeping rules ("bedtime and toilet duty," in Craig Howes's phrase)[1] undermined unity and eroded esprit de corps even as the PW organization was structurally stronger than it had ever been before.

The large, teeming open-bay cells at Unity posed special problems for the men in charge of the rooms. Cellblock commanders, Stockman observed, "were no longer remote leaders known only by their communications. Now they suddenly had a twenty-four-hour-a-day visibility to those they commanded." "The command situation," Norman noted, was as difficult as could be imagined, straining all the forms, patterns, and traditions of military leadership. The demands were harder under these circumstances; the rewards, the perks, meager to nonexistent. In the first place, military leadership generally works its way through a long chain of command, descending one rank at a time, until the men at the bottom of the chain and those at the top view each other from a distance, if at all. The commanding officer lives in separate quarters, generally more spacious and comfortable than those occupied by the men in his command. He is alone and aloof. He has aides and adjutants, and his remoteness makes the relationship easier on everyone.

When Norman's protagonist Al Stafford took over one of the "Big Rooms," he "slept nose to feet with the men in his command. Lacking a private office, when he needed to talk to someone alone, he used the latrine, a small, foul, walled-off space at one end of the room where conversations were kept short and to the point."[2]

Some men who had been commanders in the smaller camps had to adjust to their junior status among the 05s and 06s. "Not being in command," Day recalled, "was an awkward position for me, for Guarino,* for Render Crayton, Bill Lawrence, and other ex-commanders." "Stafford's greatest obstacle," wrote Norman, "was the fact that all the officers in his room were of middle rank—air force captains and navy lieutenants, for the most part—and many were junior to Stafford by only a matter of months or weeks." The grinding captivity had made "even the best of Stafford's subordinates" disagreeable and, now that the pressure from the enemy was off, not happy about taking orders on how to behave and what time to go to bed from someone barely senior to them. To some of the rank and file, the Plums seemed officious in the new circumstances, the letter moratorium and other concerted actions a nuisance. The lieutenants in Nasmyth's group seemed to gripe about every instruction that came down the line. "Since most of us have only been POWs for four or five years, I guess the Heavies (the high-ranking prisoners) decided we needed a little guidance," Nasmyth wrote sarcastically in his memoir. Risner conceded that for those who "had been resisting the Vietnamese on an individual basis for so long" and had only recently gained some measure of freedom from a tyranny of regulations, "it was difficult to come into a room with forty-seven Americans, with a command set up, directives and certain restrictions."[3]

* Guarino headed room 7 until he relinquished command to Bob Schweitzer in November 1971, an especially awkward transition because of Schweitzer's identification with the outcasts Ed Miller and Gene Wilber (see p. 440). Guarino discusses the changeover in *A POW's Story*, 306.

Although the early congestion at Unity eased following the reopening of the Zoo in the fall of 1971 and the opening of a new facility near the Chinese border in May 1972 (see p. 555), the cluttered bays in the packed compound continued to sow discord. Bob Craner would later recount how in room 1 there was "continuing bedlam," as walkers bumped into one another and those scrambling to relieve themselves had to "fight the traffic" to get to the latrine. Ralph Gaither noted that when the smokers had their daily ration doubled to six cigarettes, it was "an added pleasantry for them, an added burden to us nonsmokers." Ray Vohden was one of those who "seemed always to have a cigarette," his hacking cough becoming as annoying as the fumes.[4]

Philosophical disagreements grew constant and were unyielding. Validating Churchill's definition of fanatics, a fringe among the hardliners changed neither their minds nor the subject on the issue of prisoner conduct, continuing to preach resistance at every turn and sniping at the pragmatists for their relaxed stance toward the captor. Dramesi and Guarino clashed repeatedly over a series of relatively minor points, including how deferentially to "greet" their guards and whether Dramesi's flag should go up on the cell wall, an action that Guarino regarded as a sure provocation and disallowed. The showdown between the pair came over the escape issue, which Guarino worried was dividing their cellblock, keeping everyone on edge, and heading toward "a calamitous conclusion." "If [Dramesi] was allowed to continue unchecked," Guarino thought, "he would be a serious threat to the well-being of the rest of us in the cell block, and perhaps the whole camp." When Dramesi overstepped the bounds with challenges to Guarino's authority, the major gave the lieutenant a public dressing-down that had the effect of discrediting the maverick's latest effort. Shortly the escape committee was disbanded and the preparations halted.[5]

The escape planning did not end there, nor did the debate. In fact, the incorrigible Dramesi was soon "back in business" with a new committee formed with Jim Kasler and Ted Kopfman and going under the name "Tiger." In the spring of 1972 Tiger became the backup for another operation, identified as "Mole," that was organized by a separate group of prisoners who had been formulating a "tunnel" scheme (as opposed to Tiger's "over the wall" plan) since their days together at Son Tay and then Dan Hoi. Dave Hatcher, Jim Ray, Bob Jeffrey, and Navy Lt. Wilson Key hoped to tunnel out of room 3 on the north side of the compound and rendezvous with preplaced U.S. contacts at designated pickup points. The escapees intended to use their language skills to pose as German civilians who spoke French and were employed in a technical assistance program in Hanoi. Flynn appointed John McKamey as project officer to keep the Wing

Commander apprised of the plan's progress. In the end, both Tiger and Mole were canceled owing to the transfer of some of the participants out of Hoa Lo, substantial opposition from prisoners concerned about reprisals, and, chiefly, the decision by Flynn that the chances for success were minimal. Guarino concluded that the SRO's "success proviso . . . was a wise one" that "broke the tension in the camp . . . . The escape program was not as beneficial to morale as it might have been. Instead, it became the greatest threat ever to the command structure and the POW organization itself."[6]

In truth, for all the havoc Dramesi wreaked, the greater threat to unity came not from the bitter-enders but from the wave of new arrivals, fresh shootdowns, that entered the camps in 1972.* There developed a generational split between the so-called "old guys," most of whom were captured between 1965 and the bombing suspension of November 1968, and the "new guys" seized after the resumption of bombing in December 1971. It was not simply a case of the new guys being younger, although that alone created a significant gap. Guarino celebrated his fiftieth birthday in April. Alvarez remembered when

> one day, some of the veteran POWs climbed up a partition between the rooms and looked over at the new shootdowns. In the course of the conversation one of the oldtimers told them I was also being held in the Hanoi Hilton. "Apparently I was a household word because many of the newcomers asked to see me. Somewhat reluctantly, I climbed up and looked over. What I saw was astonishing. Everyone looked so young! Many of them looked like they were scarcely out of high school! I knew that most of them were majors, captains and lieutenant commanders but it was hard to reconcile these ranks with their open, boyish faces. Dressed in shorts, they stared up at me. A wave of awed silence fell upon them. No one said anything but I could detect from their expressions that I had become something of a freakish legend. After all, the period of my captivity spanned the entire length of this undeclared war. I was a living link all the way back to that murky encounter in the Gulf of Tonkin.

Besides the age differential, there was also the matter of the newcomers not having experienced the horrors of the middle years and hence having no appreciation for the importance of self-imposed discipline and the value of collective action and organization in the PW environment. More cynical

---

* Official casualty reports initially showed 114 U.S. military personnel captured during the last year of the war, all but a dozen of them aviators, but that figure increased some after homecoming and has fluctuated over the years according to both changes in accounting nomenclature and the resolution of discrepancy cases. In *Voices of the Vietnam POWs*, 5, Howes cites a total of 130 American servicemen taken into custody in 1972, the bulk of them, 44, in December.

about the cause they were fighting for as a result of their exposure to the antiwar politics and protests of the late sixties, the later shootdowns also had been introduced to a more flexible construction of the Code of Conduct through the services' handling of the *Pueblo* incident and changes in survival training. For all these reasons, the "new guys" found the PW "patriarchy" overly dogmatic, bureaucratic, and even self-promoting in the sense that it seemed to be perpetuating and glorifying a heroic model that had no particular relevance to the newcomers' experience.[7]

Certainly some of the new captures held to the same high standards as their predecessors. A 1991 Marine Corps study cited the example of Capt. William Angus, who was shot down over the North in June 1972 and subjected to a brutal interrogation, "with the same results as with earlier prisoners: despair and guilt for going beyond the 'big four' . . . ." Nonetheless it is probably accurate to say that as a group the younger men possessed a distinctly different set of attitudes about resistance, duty, and conformity. Old guy Leo Thorsness stated flatly that they "were not hardcore resisters," though one wonders how he could tell when there was scant opportunity for them to prove their mettle. *New York Times* correspondent Steven Roberts reported at homecoming that while "most of the oldtimers kept aloof from the guards, . . . some of the younger men developed friendship with them," and whereas "most of the oldtimers . . . were jubilant when the B-52's raided Hanoi [at Christmas 1972] . . . some of the younger men said that they were merely scared." Tendentious authors like Howes and reporters such as Roberts (Seymour Hersh was another) who focused on the departures from what Howes termed "the official story," i.e., the dominant theme in the memoir literature of a monolithic experience and an ironclad PW brotherhood, have perhaps made too much of the old guys vs. new guys split. However, the prisoners themselves were very much aware of the gap in their age and experience, and the division surely caused further strains in a once again burgeoning PW community.[8]

Norman wrote that "the price of unity was resentment."[9] In most cases the conflicts at Unity, as elsewhere, even the uglier episodes such as the Dramesi-Guarino confrontation, were contained and resolved short of mutiny or open revolt. In a few isolated instances, however, there were deeper schisms and total breaks with the organization that went beyond resentment and defied resolution. One of these cases, as we shall see, occurred at the Plantation and involved several enlisted men. The other one of consequence occurred, or at least came to a head, at Unity and involved the longstanding black sheep Ed Miller and Gene Wilber.

Miller and Wilber were two "old guys"—pre-1969 captures—who had more in common with the "new guys" than with their contemporaries.

The pair spent the fall of 1970 at the Zoo with Bob Schweitzer, Roger Ingvalson, Mark Gartley, Marine Lt. Paul Brown, and Navy Lt. William Mayhew. When the group moved into Unity in December 1970 they were placed in building 8, the same secluded cellblock from which Flynn and his headquarters staff would later run the PW organization. Known to the rest of the compound as the "Outer Seven," they remained out of touch with the other Americans at Unity, who knew Miller and Wilber (and Schweitzer) from their propaganda tapings that had continued even after the coercion threat had receded. When building 8's juniors, under the code name "Roadrunners," finally made contact with Dick Keirn's group in building 9,* there followed a period of turmoil within 8 when Miller and Wilber rejected any association with the Wing, derisively referred to the Plums as "prunes," and collaborated on a July 4 antiwar message that was broadcast to U.S. troops in the South. The "deviationists," as Jim Mulligan called them, were adamant about their right to criticize a military action they considered illegitimate and insisted they had taped and written the antiwar statements as a matter of principle and not to curry favor with the captor. As Howes commented of Wilber, he was "practicing civil dis-obedience in Hanoi—but against the POW command." Several participants in the February 1971 church riot recalled the protest chant stopping at the Roadrunners' building.

By the summer of 1971, after further communication contact with Wing members, Schweitzer had disassociated himself from the other two seniors in the building and he and the four junior officers were accepted into the organization. The PW command persisted in efforts to bring the two pariahs around but to no avail. Risner made repeated overtures to them urging them to desist and offering them "a chance to rejoin the team." Finally ordered to comply with the Code and end their cooperation with the Vietnamese or face disciplining, they hedged, asserting again that the war was immoral and the U.S. involvement illegal and that as a matter of conscience (Wilber later cited the Nuremberg trials) they should be allowed to exercise their free speech. On 11 August Risner, who had been coordinating the "dialogue" with them, relieved the pair of command of the Roadrunner group, effectively stripping them of rank, and placed Schweitzer in charge. In late September the prison authority returned the entire "Outer Seven" to the Zoo, where Miller and Wilber would continue to enrage comrades. John Hubbell noted the irony of the situation, as when Flynn and the other ranking seniors occupied their empty cells, "Building 8, recently notorious as a nesting place for collaborators, now took on a reverential aspect."[10]

* Building 9 later became "Mayo," the camp infirmary, when Keirn's group was transferred to the reactivated Zoo in September 1971.

*   *

If, as Norman concluded, "it was not always a happy band of brothers in Hoa Lo,"[11] if the name Camp Unity had become more a symbol than a reality by 1972, it was also true that a strong organization remained intact through all the internal skirmishing. If the PW ranks were not welded solid, there was no mistaking a basic cohesion, rapport, and respect that characterized relations among the vast majority of the prisoners. And for all the distractions and dangers spawned by the dissension, there was no forgetting (save for Miller, Wilber, and a handful of other heretics) that the real opponent remained the Vietnamese.

By 1972 physical abuse had become rare, though Winn was beaten and thrown in the punishment cell Calcutta for six weeks. Besides Angus's rough interrogation, in April Navy Lt. Michael Christian, a spirited resister with a "record of conflict" with the enemy, was beaten severely after cheering a bombing raid over Hanoi that may have hit too close for the jailers' comfort. Stockdale's observation that "all we had to do was act like normal prisoners and take a little crap . . . once in a while" was essentially correct, but Bud Day reminded that there was "a delicate balance to maintain," the goal being to "avoid any hard confrontations . . . without giving the enemy anything or accepting any unnecessary humiliation." The wail of air raid sirens outside their windows underscored their vulnerability even as the springtime bombardment, the first over the capital since March 1968, gave many satisfaction. The possibility of a vengeful populace storming the city prison or mass executions in the event of a U.S. rescue attempt prompted a group of inmates to form a "disaster control" committee.[12]

The shuffling of prisoners to Skid Row and the Zoo did nothing to weaken the organization. The transfers out of Unity carried the Plums, extending the organization's reach beyond Hanoi. Both policies and procedures, including the determination of seniority, were refined on a continuing basis,* the

---

* Stockdale described the new seniority policy implemented in mid-1972: "The way to determine the relative seniority of any two prisoners was to refer to their relative seniority on the date of the first of the two shot down. The best way to look at this is to take any two men, one shot down in July and one in April. The first step to decide who is senior is to examine the situation between them that existed in April. Then after that normal career progression is assumed. Normal career progression is a good term when you are working with one service, but with Navy, Marine Corps, and Air Force it becomes a little bit nebulous." Despite the "more predictable" Navy promotion system and the complexities of the Air Force system, "things really were not too much out of line between the services." If there was evidence to indicate that something other than normal career progression had occurred, such as a sighting of a promotion on a personnel roster by a later captive, then Colonel Flynn as Wing Commander would arbitrate. (In such fashion, Flynn intervened on Risner's behalf in 1971. The procedure was formalized here in 1972.) See File 719.

seniors in Blue in constant consultation and readily able to communicate their instructions despite ongoing surveillance by guards. New prisoners, those who were not whisked to the Zoo soon after shootdown, ended up mostly in buildings 5 and 6 after the original occupants had been moved elsewhere. The newcomers' SRO, Air Force Lt. Col. Joseph Kittinger, a noted high-altitude balloonist, led a tough group who Stockdale and Day surmised were in Unity instead of the Zoo because the Vietnamese judged them poor candidates for the Zoo's propaganda operation.[13]

One of the biggest moves of the entire captivity occurred in the middle of May when prison authorities sent about half of the Unity PWs, 210 men, north to a new maximum security facility only nine miles from the Chinese border. The prisoners were told they were being moved for their own protection, because of the stepped-up air activity over and around Hanoi. A more plausible reason may have been the captor's interest in again having a cache of the aviators stashed at a location outside the capital's environs should U.S. forces invade the city or carry out a commando operation on Hoa Lo. (This, of course, would have amounted to a reversal of the enemy's policy instituted in the wake of the Son Tay raid, but the renewed U.S. offensive may have caused officials to have second thoughts about putting all their prizes in one basket.) A convoy of 16 trucks took two days to get to the remote site, arriving on 15 May. Set in a small valley in a pretty, mountainous region near Cao Bang, the camp soon acquired the name "Dogpatch."[14]

All the transfers to Dogpatch (the Vietnamese called the place Loung Lang) were junior officers, most of them 02s and 03s. Upon their arrival they found a dozen stone and concrete bomb-resistant buildings surrounded on the east side by a brick wall and on the west side by a karst ridge and barbed wire. The compound was heavily camouflaged, the roofs of the buildings painted black and strewn with bushes and vines. Although recently constructed, the detention facilities were, by most accounts, colder, damper, and darker than Hoa Lo. With narrow slits for windows and thick walls and ceilings, the cellblocks, each containing from 8 to 20 prisoners, were miasmal. Chesley later wrote that "this camp had just about all the qualities of a dungeon except that it was not underground." Plumb remembered that with no electricity and the sun going behind the mountains by late afternoon, they spent 14 hours in the dark each day. Nasmyth declared that compared with Dogpatch, "the Hanoi Hilton was like a *real* Hilton."[15]

Gradually conditions improved. Guards brought in kerosene lamps to light the cells in the evenings. To combat the cold—the PWs had become accustomed to the temperatures in downtown Hanoi—the Vietnamese

Majors Stavast (left) and Runyan, Dogpatch commanders.

supplied additional clothing and allowed the prisoners to build fires in their rooms to warm themselves and to heat water for coffee. The food was generally better than at Hoa Lo, although rice replaced bread as the main staple because of the lack of baking facilities. The superintendent, the well-traveled veteran "Fox," limited courtyard time but let the men outside their cramped cells to mix with other prisoners in the hallway for several hours a day.

Despite greater physical discomforts, in most respects life went on at Dogpatch much as it had at Unity. Majs. John Stavast and Al Runyan, first and second in command, presided over an organization that was transplanted to the new camp without missing a beat. For diversion the men played cards and checkers they had carried with them from Hoa Lo. Plumb and a partner took advantage of the light deprivation to work up a slide show using a homemade projector. The approximately 55 Vietnamese personnel present, all of them having made the trip with the prisoners, treated the PWs well for the most part, coexisting with their charges in a "live and let live" atmosphere. One critical deficiency, especially given the high incidence of illness in the dank conditions, was a lack of access to doctors or a hospital in a medical emergency. John Frederick, a prisoner since 1965 who had survived all manner of torture and suffering in the intervening years, became a victim of a typhoid epidemic that hit the camp during the summer. The brawny Marine, who had taught Jim Mulligan the tap code at the

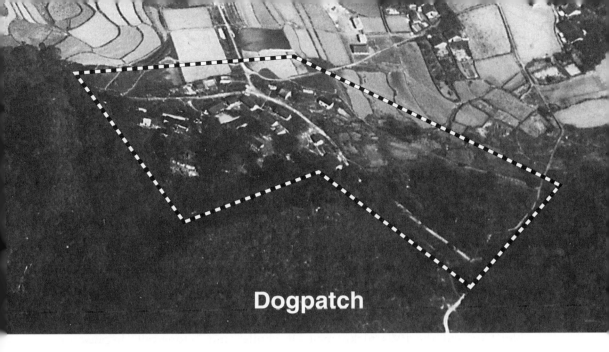

Dogpatch

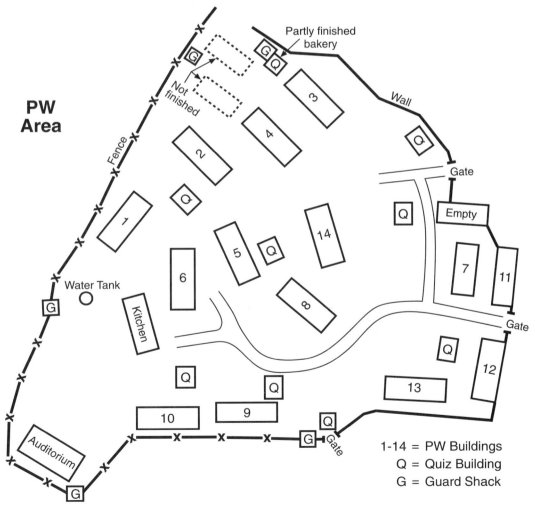

PW Area

Partly finished bakery

G Q

Not finished

Fence

3

Wall

4

Q

2

Gate

Q

Empty

1

Q

14

7   11

Water Tank

6

5   Q

Q

Kitchen

8

Q

Gate

Q

Q

Q

12

10

9

13

Auditorium

Q

G   Gate

G

1-14 = PW Buildings
Q = Quiz Building
G = Guard Shack

Zoo and impressed Stockdale with his courage at Vegas, was evacuated from Dogpatch in a delirious state with a high fever and, according to Vietnamese records, died days later, on 19 July, soon after reaching a hospital in Hanoi.[16]

As it turned out, the transfers from Unity were not the only Americans imprisoned a safe distance from the capital in 1972. In June and December 1971, the prison administration, possibly to create more berths for Unity's troublemakers at Skid Row, dispersed the two dozen Southern captures confined at the close-in facility since 1968 to two sites farther south and north of the city. The first group of 14, including Captain Thompson and most of the civilians who had been seized during the Tet offensive, were sent to a new camp 30 miles south of Hanoi that the Vietnamese called Noi Coc and the PWs nicknamed "Rockpile" and "Stonewall" because of the high masonry walls that surrounded it. Belying the grim name, the place was actually quite comfortable. Inside the heavy planked double doors that secured the entrance to the single cellblock building were two large sleeping quarters, a dining room, and a separate latrine and bathing area. Until Thompson and two of the civilians, Lewis Meyer and Cloden Adkins, attempted an escape in October 1971 (they managed to get over the wall but were captured within a couple of days), guards gave the prisoners considerable freedom to mingle and roam the compound. For a year after the incident the captives faced stricter supervision but no harsh reprisals.[17]

The remaining block of Southern captures at Skid Row, a group of nine led by Ben Purcell and including the two German civilians Diehl and Schwinn,* stayed until the end of 1971, when they were jeeped 50 miles north of Hanoi to a spot near Thai Nguyen. Their new camp, not as close to the Chinese border as Dogpatch but also in rugged mountainous country, they called "K-49," or simply "Mountain Camp." They spent all of 1972 at the tiny installation, isolated not only from the masses of other prisoners in the North but from each other, as they were kept in individual cells and took outside time in attached concrete "cages" topped with barbed wire. Purcell made covert contact with Gene Weaver in an adjacent cell, the pair able to communicate through a modified Morse code and swap notes through a drain hole that connected their outer compartments. They worried

---

* The others were Phil Manhard, Eugene Weaver, Charles Willis, Captain Gostas, Sergeant Rander, and another unidentified civilian (probably the Canadian Marc Cayer). Searching for a common link to explain why the Vietnamese separated them from the Rockpile group, Purcell concluded that the enemy believed the Americans in the bunch were all intelligence officers.

that K-49 seemed to be a state prison under civilian control rather than a military facility.

Despite the loneliness, Purcell considered the conditions "a spectacular improvement" over Skid Row. Each room had a table, stool, and water closet ("my own private bath," Purcell quipped) and a bed with a straw mattress. Tolerable as it was, Purcell immediately plotted another escape, this time intending to slip out through the barbed wire opening above his cage and, with an improvised compass, "head for the coast, borrow a fishing boat, and row out to sea." The tenacious colonel managed to break out on 18 March and elude his captors for 30 hours before being caught. The last months of his stay at K-49 were noteworthy for a running argument with Phil Manhard, the senior State Department official, over who was in charge of the Americans at the camp. They settled good-naturedly on a Communist-style arrangement that recognized the colonel as "unit commander" of the outfit and the civilian as "political commissar."[18]

The only Southern captures who spent 1972 in Hanoi were the Farnsworth group that had been at the Plantation since the close of 1970 and the dozen members of the Kushner entourage who had come to the Plantation directly from the Ho Chi Minh Trail in the spring of 1971.* When Brace's band of Lulus were brought back to Hanoi from Briarpatch in July 1971, they, too, were deposited in the Plantation,† bringing the former show camp's population to 72 by the summer of 1971. No camp had a more diverse makeup, with civilians Brace and Michael Benge, a preponderance of Army and Marine enlisted men, and more than a dozen officers from all four services—Kushner, Ted Guy, Marine Lieutenant DiBernardo and Captains Montague and Archer, Army Maj. Artice Elliott (captured at Pleiku in 1970) and Cambodian refugee Captain Leopold, and the shootdowns from Laos. The frictions at Farnsworth and within the Kushner group spilled over into the new community, the Vietnamese exploiting the situation to make Unity's divisions look mild by comparison.

Guy, who had been SRO at the Plantation during his previous residence there in 1968-69, was hampered in his efforts to organize the camp because of the same communications obstacles that the place presented earlier, the hodgepodge nature of the current aggregation, and his own isolation. Only when he got a roommate (Elliott, who became his deputy) and the Laos group (some of whom had experience at Unity) entered the camp did a "breakthrough" occur, although organization would continue

* See pp. 468, 517.
† See p. 535n. The Lulus acquired a sixth member at Plantation, Air Force Lt. Jack Butcher, who had been shot down over Laos in March. Counting Captain Leonard, who had been downed in Laos in 1968 but kept with the Tet captures at Portholes and Farnsworth, the fraternity numbered seven altogether.

Rockpile

Mountain
Camp

to suffer from what Guy perceived to be a lack of dedication and training on the part of the Army enlistees in particular. Guy's conversations with Elliott in their Gunshed cell convinced him "that the army did not put a great emphasis on training soldiers in resistance methods. A course in escape and evasion techniques was taught during infantry training but it was nothing like the survival school that air force personnel had to attend." Of course, the concentration of Air Force, Navy, and Marine aviators at Unity did not prevent disciplinary lapses there as well, but unquestionably the different training and preparation generally of the younger Army (and Marine) enlisted captives made them less disposed to follow a hardline officer of another service issuing orders on an intermittent basis in such unconventional circumstances.[19]

Although the show camp had become dusty and dirty during the several months it was vacant, it was a dramatic improvement over life at Farnsworth or, in the case of the Kushner group, in the jungle. In addition to a breakfast of bread and tea and other meals of canned meat, soup, and fresh vegetables, many of the prisoners received nuts, candy, and other sugar items for the first time. For those in worse shape, the Vietnamese supplemented the diet with milk, liver, and eggs, some individuals gaining 15 to 20 pounds in a matter of months. For PFC James Daly, after three years on the trail, the benefits of a roof over his head, a set of clean clothes, electricity, and a bath stall, not to mention "an honest-to-goodness basketball court," was "like going from hell to heaven." A medic visited each room of four to eight occupants daily and, beginning in September 1971, administered regular doses of medication, including cholera injections, to ward off disease.[20]

The generousness of the conditions, however, especially the amount of exercise and outdoor time, varied depending on a prisoner's behavior. Ironically, for those who assumed a resistance stance, treatment at what had been the "country club" of prisons in the difficult middle years became harsher as it was easing for headbutters everywhere else. The most striking example was the punishment of Guy in January 1972. Stripped of his clothes and flogged and beaten savagely over a period of five days to force information from him on organization and communication methods, he finally agreed to write an apology for his activities and an antiwar letter and to record a statement for the camp radio. (The enlistees whom Guy later accused of misconduct would cite the coerced confessions as evidence of the senior's own collaboration.) By contrast, those who appeared to be cooperating with the enemy by causing no trouble and freely producing propaganda material were given "rewards" of beer, ice cream, powdered milk, electric fans, and whole days outside.[21]

The main source of contention was a group of eight enlisted men the Vietnamese had tucked away in room 1 of the Warehouse, who were churning out a stream of pacifist cant. They either ignored or spurned the entreaties of Guy, Captain Leonard, and others who tried to reach them and get them to stop taping and reading on the radio. Some of their fellow prisoners believed they were also involved in actively subverting the organization by exposing members and communication techniques. Whether they were turncoats who willfully disobeyed orders, ratted on comrades, and bartered antiwar messages for special privileges, or were simply confused youngsters who sincerely opposed the war and saw no downside to expressing their feelings, depends on the perspective of the participants. Five of the men—Army Sgt. Robert Chenoweth and Specs. John Young and Michael Branch and Marine Sgt. Abel Kavanaugh and Cpl. Alfonso Riate—had raised eyebrows and provoked roommates with their antiwar declarations at Farnsworth, where they had been labeled the "Ducks" for seemingly following guards around the camp meekly in tow. With two more men from the Kushner group who came under their influence at Plantation—Daly and Marine Pvt. Fred Elbert—and a third man who joined them in the fall of 1971—Army Pvt. King Rayford—they became known as the "Peace Committee."[22]

Whether cowards, opportunists, or true believers, by 1972 the "PCs" had become totally controlled by the enemy, cultivated with Marxist literature and additional favors, including a separate study room and front-row seats at a city circus, and enlisted to make extreme statements condemning President Nixon and their own military leaders. Kushner and others who had reservations about the U.S. commitment and who were put off by Guy's gung-ho style nonetheless resisted overtures from the officer Cheese, who played the race card in an attempt to recruit Ike McMillan and Jose Anzaldua.* Four more enlistees—John Sparks, Dennis Tellier, Don MacPhail, and Jon Cavaiani,† the latter only recently captured—briefly consorted with the dissidents before having a falling-out. Toward the end of the captivity, increasingly segregated and estranged from the other Americans at Plantation, and fearing reprisals by their own officers on their return to the United States, the group requested asylum in Sweden or, if that was not feasible, possibly remaining in North Vietnam. Just before their release, Guy learned that several incensed comrades were plotting to execute them. According to one account, "It took the SRO two weeks to persuade them not to go through with their plan. A week later, he learned that the

---

* Among the eight belonging to the Peace Committee, Daly and Rayford were black and Riate and Kavanaugh were Hispanic. Daly remembered Cheese bringing to their room newspaper clippings on the Black Panthers and race riots.
† Cavaiani won the Medal of Honor for his heroics just prior to capture in June 1971.

plan had been changed to shaving their heads. The SRO talked them out of this plan by pointing out that he planned to court-martial the 'Ducks' after release and if their heads were shaved, the chances of a court-martial might be jeopardized." Guy did draft and file formal charges soon after homecoming, but the case was dismissed following the suicide of Sergeant Kavanaugh on 27 June 1973.* [23]

All the openings and closings, shuffles and splitups, during 1971 and 1972 left the PWs spread among a half dozen locations in the fall of 1972. The bulk of them were still distributed in and around Hanoi at Hoa Lo (Unity), Plantation, and the Zoo, with a large aggregate at Dogpatch by the Chinese border and a couple of smaller clusters at Rockpile and K-49 in the countryside south and north of the capital. The last punishment cases at Skid Row had returned to Hoa Lo earlier in the year, leaving the filthy penitentiary exclusively to its ARVN inhabitants. Except for the Schrump and Ramsey groups[†] and a handful of other, more recent captures being held deep in the South near the Cambodian border—they and Captain White in the Delta would not join the main body of PWs until release in 1973— all known surviving American prisoners seized in the South or Laos were now in North Vietnam.[‡]

And everywhere there were the surest signs yet that peace—and release —were at hand. At Unity Stockdale heard a broadcast reporting progress on a nine-point plan to end the war and knew that "something was in the wind." Through September and October workers took down the bamboo and tarpaper fences separating courtyards and the prisoners were allowed

---

* Defense attorneys were prepared to argue that Guy's claims were based largely on hearsay and circumstantial evidence and that Guy himself had been pressured into making concessions at Plantation. Even before the Kavanaugh tragedy, Pentagon officials were moving to drop the charges owing to the complex legal and policy issues that would have made conviction problematical and the damaging publicity that would have attended a long trial. Dismissal, the Army's Adjutant General advised the Chief of Staff in April, would "preserve the hero image of the returnees and diffuse the radicals and peace groups who are looking for a cause." See memo MajGen Verne L. Bowers for Chief of Staff, 9 Apr 73, sub: Whether Court-Martial Charges Should be Pressed Against Former PW for Alleged Misconduct, encl (6, quote); *NY Times*, 30, 31 May 73; *Washington Star & News*, 4 Jul 73; Solis, *Trial by Fire*, 218-19; Grant, *Survivors*, 334-43.

† See Chapter 21.

‡ Whether any Americans on the rolls of the missing were still alive and in custody in Laos, Cambodia, or South Vietnam remains the subject of speculation. Three late 1972 Laos captures would turn up among the releasees in 1973 (see Chapter 26), but the fate of numerous other servicemen and civilians (for example, four U.S. journalists missing in Cambodia) who were known or thought possibly to have been taken prisoner and whose bodies have never been recovered remains a mystery.

extra activity time outdoors, the result being that educational programs gradually gave way to basketball, volleyball, and ping-pong. Those preferring more sedentary pursuits now had access to American books and magazines, including baseball pitcher Jim Bouton's *Ball Four* and back issues of *Sports Illustrated* that had been confiscated from packages years earlier and were finally being dispensed; those wishing to continue their "studies" got pens and paper and language and mathematics textbooks. Also in October the prisoners received comprehensive medical examinations, including dental checks and chest X-rays on a portable East German machine. They even began preparing their own food, dicing meat and vegetables and developing their own kitchen schedules. Jack Fellowes recalled that as they also took to doing their own barbering, "we learned of the Mod look and started to taper our hair a bit."[24]

At Dogpatch a major reshuffling occurred during October that left the PWs there grouped according to shootdown date, triggering a surge of "release fever." The absence of radio at the remote camp denied them even filtered news, and without the telltale sound of airplanes and bombs going off so far from the war theater Nasmyth remarked that the stay there "was the most challenging we spent in terms of reading between the lines." By November Vietnamese officers were briefing them on "earnest" developments in Paris at the same time they were granting some extra privileges, convincing Plumb that "wheels were turning." Farther south at K-49, as Purcell remembered, "new indications that the war was winding down continued to appear on a regular basis." His guards were friendlier, the food got better, and "most significant" of all, on 1 November he met with the camp director, who informed him the six Americans at the facility would be able to spend time and eat together. In a crash effort to get Charles Willis back to health, a medic gave him 28 shots of vitamin B-1 within a period of about a week. The civilian recalled "they even sent a camp officer, by bicycle, into a village about five miles away to bring back limes and lemons to feed us." At Plantation, even the Lulus were being let out of the closet by fall, given more opportunity to mingle with one another and with non-Laos captives and to enjoy the same activities as the other prisoners, although at the screening of propaganda films they were still seated separately, said Brace, "in the back after everyone else had arrived." A bus that took a group of the PWs around town to survey bomb damage had a destination sign that read, with tongue-in-cheek optimism, HANOI, HUE, SAIGON.[25]

If the light at the end of the tunnel was now unmistakable, the tunnel still contained snags and pitfalls. A snapshot of prison life toward the end of 1972 would have shown daily routines and basic amenities much improved even over 1971, but, as Doremus had said about the caliber of the food on his entry into Unity, still "there was a great deal about which to complain." However much a luxury was their hole-in-cement toilet compared to the waste buckets of the earlier days, Rutledge "still dreamed of beautiful white toilet seats, white pillow cases, a soft bed with clean sheets, and chocolate-covered peanuts!"* The seniors in Rawhide and Blue remained physically removed from the other men in Unity and until just prior to release had to rely on covert communications for contact. Playing volleyball barefoot on a rough surface with blistered feet while propaganda photographers clicked pictures was not every PW's idea of fun. In what Day supposed was "the last roughing up of any of the old shootdowns," one Saturday afternoon in September, following a minor harassment incident, the aviator was screwed into manacles, banged around, and thrown into a solitary confinement cell fetid with rat droppings and mosquitos before guards returned him to his regular room the next day.[26]

The most regressive aspect of the last months of the captivity was an avalanche of propaganda that they were subjected to and coaxed to contribute to. As the peace talks gathered momentum, the American prisoners had once again been thrust to center stage, their status and condition having become a key topic on the agenda in Paris. Nixon's offer to withdraw U.S. troops from South Vietnam was contingent on the PWs being released. "Nixon's new proposal," Sam Johnson later observed, "made us the primary focus, the hinge on which the door to peace would swing open."[27] For the captives the psywar endgame meant two things: first, they were

---

* The receipt of one luxury item, a pair of turquoise paisley boxer shorts sent Sam Johnson by his wife Shirley, stirred a commotion. Wrote Johnson in his memoir:

> I couldn't believe my eyes when I saw them. Shirley knew I never wore anything but blah, basic white. This was so out of character that I shook my head and wondered if she had had some kind of breakdown. Or maybe she was trying to give me something to laugh about. Or maybe the shorts hid a message somewhere . . . .
>
> For weeks, we pored over those paisley turquoise boxers, looking for something—we had no idea what. We were convinced that military intelligence had sent them, not Shirley. And we were sure we would find something on them somewhere. The shorts passed from one pair of hands to another, each man convinced he would find the hidden message in a hem, under the elastic, in the paisley. We never found anything, and I never did put those boxer shorts on, even though they were a break from the non-colors of prison life. I just sat and stared at them from time to time, baffled (*Captive Warriors*, 262-63).

to be treated well, fattened up and left with as pleasant and grateful memories as possible—if not to become "Manchurian candidates," at least to be walking manifestations of the Communists' "humane and lenient" beneficence; second, they were wheedled, maneuvered, and in a few instances, as with Guy at the Plantation, threatened and coerced to supply the propaganda to fill the political warfare office's news releases and radio programming in a final flurry of image polishing. And so the playing out of their captivity, even as it brought them more recreation and better food, also witnessed a sharp increase in propaganda exposure and manipulation.

Through 1972 and into early 1973 the captor immersed prisoners at all the camps in a heavy schedule of propaganda movies, tours of Hanoi that spotlighted destruction inflicted by the recent bombing, and time in reading rooms that featured the latest leftist tracts and clipped newspaper articles of U.S. antiwar activities. The movies, some of them cultural films from China and Russia (including a Soviet production of *Othello*), reading materials, and music piped over camp speakers (ranging from Nancy Sinatra and Johnny Cash to Beethoven and Brahms) were the most eclectic the PWs had experienced and mixed genuine entertainment with both subtle and not so subtle indoctrination. "Pro-communist Americans began to rain on Hanoi," Day wrote, referring to the peace missions to Southeast Asia of Jane Fonda, Ramsey Clark, and other war critics during the summer and fall of 1972. The Vietnamese played tapes of Fonda's and Clark's interviews over PA systems again and again along with planks from the platform of Democratic presidential candidate George McGovern. Day recalled, "We were drowned with rhetoric, persuasion, and distortion . . . . Several POWs became quite emotional about the possibility of a Democratic victory, and threats of emigrating to Australia, England or Canada began to mount. The POW consensus was that we wanted to go home, but not at that price." Johnson was "amazed" that their handlers were still trying to brainwash them: "They continued to operate as though we were going to suddenly say, 'Okay, you're right. Democracy is bad, communism is good.'"[28]

As the "propaganda machinery went into perpetual motion early in the fall," captor and captives engaged in a familiar duel of wits. Those playing volleyball at Unity frustrated furtive cameramen by stopping the game upon spotting the interlopers, dispersing on the shout of the word "Kodak." Shortly before release, a Vietnamese advised the senior officers that as a demonstration of goodwill the camp authority had arranged to have a show performed by some of the country's top entertainers; the gala event played to an empty house ("hanging laundry," said Plumb) when the seniors, recognizing the potential for propaganda exploitation, instructed their men to stay in their rooms. As late as January 1973 the Vietnamese made propaganda movies of medical assistance being given to Air Force Sgt. Roy Madden, a B-52 gunner who suffered fractures and shrapnel wounds when shot down on 20 December. (By one account, doctors did little more than put a cosmetic cast on Madden's shattered leg, the lack of any further treatment costing the airman his limb after repatriation.)[29]

The closest the two sides came to a confrontation during this period occurred in late September when Colonels Flynn, Winn, and Gaddis and three of the other top seniors in Blue—Denton, Mulligan, and Rutledge—were rounded up for a visit to the War Museum. For weeks officials had been escorting small groups of the PWs, some of them in civilian dress, to the exhibition hall to view pictures of bomb damage and to be photographed taking the guided tour. To counter the propaganda stunt, the prisoners employed a tactic that peace demonstrators had used to advantage, a version of the sit-down strike whereby they forced their handlers to bodily drag them on and off buses and through the exhibits in full view of dignitaries and cameramen. When it came the seniors' turn, they resisted to the point that dozens of guards were needed to haul them onto the bus and drag them around the building. By the time they returned to Hoa Lo they had been kicked, pummeled, and put in handcuffs but had succeeded in causing the organizers such embarrassment that, Stockdale noted, "for all practical purposes that wiped out their museum trip program."[30]

The propaganda mill was busiest at the Zoo, where the new shootdowns were barely settled in before political officers exploited their lack of experience and organization (and, old-timers would argue, fuzzier convictions about the war and their resistance obligations) to extract statements and "show" the prisoners to visiting delegations. The Vietnamese may have wrung juicier material from the Peace Committee at Plantation but it was at the refurbished Zoo where they now concentrated the public relations campaign, staging big events such as celebrity interviews and touring outsiders in a program reminiscent of the old Plantation of the middle years. By fall 1972, a fresh coat of paint had given the camp's buildings an extra sheen, just in time to welcome Clark and a parade of international observers. In September an early release, the first in the North since 1969, sent Mark Gartley and two of the "new guys"—Air Force Maj. Edward Elias and Navy Lt. Norris Charles—home with peace activists Cora Weiss, David Dellinger, Richard Falk, and Rev. William Sloane Coffin.*[31]

---

* Why Gartley, Elias, and Charles were chosen from among many who by now were "going with the flow" is not clear. Charles was black; Gartley had been a member of the "Outer Seven" at Unity; all three were obviously hand-picked and cultivated prior to the release. Veterans like Day and Guarino fell on them with the same scorn they heaped on the Plantation early releases years before, taking special swipes at Gartley, whose mother accompanied the peace delegation (so did Charles's wife).

The Zoo in 1972 also had its own "Ducks," with Miller and Wilber ensconced there since the fall of 1971. The "Outer Seven" had been reduced to the "Outer Two," and the pair made no effort to repent or to renounce the cornucopia of privileges and favors that now included leather shoes, better quality beds, individual razors, exclusive use of a flush toilet facility, and virtually unlimited access and movement around the camp, the door of their cell kept unlocked all day. Through 1972, Ingvalson, Coffee, and the few older shootdowns still in touch with them tried to reason with them while at the same time attempting to contact the younger men and keep them from being influenced and corrupted by the bad example. By August Miller and Wilber were the only "old heads" left at the Zoo, the others having been returned to Unity (many gone on to Dogpatch in the spring).* Alvarez, one of the last to leave, remembered that the outcasts openly flaunted their independence and even enjoyed a kind of "trustee status" among the jailers; at least one of them met with representatives of a committee still pursuing evidence of U.S. war crimes. Although there was sentiment among some of their comrades that Wilber's behavior was less egregious than Miller's, both officers faced sweeping charges of mutiny and collaboration upon their return in 1973. Within weeks of repatriation Stockdale initiated legal proceedings against them, filing a formal indictment, but Navy and Marine Corps officials, for much the same reasons the services elected to drop charges against the Plantation eight, decided not to prosecute. The two retired with administrative letters of censure and in lasting disgrace. At a White House reception welcoming the PWs home, Chief of Naval Operations Admiral Elmo Zumwalt almost walked out when he realized he was seated next to Wilber.[32]

"POWs Caught in Swirl of U.S. Politics," the *Washington Post* headlined a lengthy article on 10 September 1972. "The American prisoners in North Vietnam are now political hostages to a greater degree than at any time in the Indochina war," wrote reporter George Wilson, " . . . caught in a swirl of politics that extends from the White House, to the McGovern camp, North Vietnam's politburo, to President Thieu's palace, to the Teamsters headquarters, to individual election campaigns all over the United States

---

* According to one post-homecoming report, 10 of the transfers who moved back into Hoa Lo volunteered to teach English to Vietnamese personnel: "Believing that the NVN knew the war was soon to end and would require trained linguists to assist in diplomatic contacts, the PWs volunteered on the condition that at no time would politics or views on the war be discussed. This condition was accepted by the NVN. The PWs also participated reasoning that the program would not harm other PWs, would afford a break in routine, and help pass the time." See Air Force Intelligence "Item of Interest" memo, 8 Mar 73.

and presumably to dark cells in North Vietnam."[33] Both the U.S. and North Vietnamese governments wielded the prisoner issue like a lightning rod through the fall to gain leverage in matters affecting other policy considerations, including the timetable for the American pullout from the South and the terms of the larger peace settlement. Nixon's reelection bought more time for hardliners convinced that intensified bombing was the way to force additional diplomatic concessions, but the sustained air attacks also brought weekly jumps in U.S. casualty statistics and left the prisoners in Hanoi nervously awaiting the outcome as a steady stream of new arrivals joined them. Even as the services announced plans at the end of October for the handling and processing of the prisoners upon their release, more hitches in the negotiations between presidential adviser Henry Kissinger and North Vietnamese representative Le Duc Tho again dampened expectations for an imminent settlement. To break the deadlock, the administration ordered a heavy bombardment of Hanoi and Haiphong in December.

The so-called Christmas bombing, the first involving the use of B-52s over the capital, lasted 11 days and caused extensive destruction and chaos despite efforts to target only military and industrial sites. The PWs reacted with mixed emotions, members of the Peace Committee horrified at the wreckage they spotted outside the Plantation's walls, the pilots at Unity gratified that their government had finally unleashed a display of "real air power." Most professed to be at least a little bit frightened by the day and night strikes that rattled their cells, shook buildings, and lit up the sky in what John McCain called "the most spectacular show I'll ever see." "Bombs began to fall in an awesome thundering pattern in every direction around the camp," Day recounted the onset of the raids on the evening of 18 December. As he and the others at Hoa Lo excitedly looked out their windows, the planes came "like locusts." To escape falling plaster the prisoners took cover in wooden bomb shelters that guards had them erect within their rooms. With a combination of luck and impressive execution, the attackers spared Hoa Lo significant damage.* [34]

The newly captured B-52 crews—15 of the planes went down, with 31 survivors entering captivity—updated the prisoners on the stalled peace talks, confirming that the end was in sight. By the end of December, with Hanoi out of SAMs to launch against the B-52s, the massive bombardment had accomplished its purpose. Both sides by now weary of the stalemate and the accumulating casualties, Kissinger and Le Duc Tho resumed

---

* To refute North Vietnamese claims that bombs hit the PW prison, inmates found a way to signal reconnaissance aircraft of their safety, transmitting the message in Morse code: V LIE WE OK.

negotiations in early January and quickly resolved the remaining sticking points. On 27 January a peace agreement was signed that stipulated prisoner exchange and repatriation procedures. Over the next couple of days, as provided for in the pact, the Vietnamese delivered personal copies of the document and a release schedule to each of the PWs—including Navy Lt. Cdr. Phillip Kientzler, shot down the same day the truce was initialed in Paris and the last prisoner seized before the cease-fire took effect.[35]

26

Homeward Unbound

The exact time and place varies considerably from recollection to recollection, even among those confined at the same camp, but within a matter of days after the conclusion of the peace accords, the American prisoners everywhere, whether by receipt of the mimeographed protocols or from bulletins on camp radios, learned the war was over and they were going home.

The signs that last week in January 1973 were all positive. The lights on weather and communication towers in Hanoi were being left on at night, signaling an end to any bombing worries. In an evident victory gesture, the North Vietnamese hoisted a huge flag to the top of the tower at Hoa Lo; it flew upside down for a half hour before a soldier reclimbed the tower to correct the mistake. And the 200-plus inmates at Dogpatch had been driven back to the city, most of them returned to Unity, the more recent shootdowns among them winding up at the Plantation. Nasmyth called the ride through the mountains, in a caravan of 18 trucks bouncing along roads with hairpin curves and deep potholes, "a breeze." Plumb, perhaps in a different truck, remembered a "terrible trip" at dangerous speed with reeking gasoline fumes and the men squeezed into the vehicles "like college kids in a phone booth . . . . Only the hope of repatriation made the situation bearable."[1]

When they were assembled for the official announcement—in the courtyards at Hoa Lo and Plantation and in the Zoo's Auditorium—the prisoners reacted in the subdued fashion of men who already suspected as much, yet were still leery from so often having "their chains jerked" with false promises. Only when they mustered in parade formation, seniors at the front, with no objection from the Vietnamese did the reality sink in. Even then there was no loud cheering or celebration. Some were simply too physically and emotionally drained to feel any elation. Others minded the leadership's instruction to maintain discipline and control emotions in order to negate the enemy's certain picture-taking.[2]

Jerry Coffee sketched the dramatic scene at Unity on 31 January as, "we stood quietly, hardly breathing, dressed against the chill air and formed in ranks according to our cell blocks." With Dog presiding,* an interpreter read from a prepared text that "their departure shall take place in increments of approximately one hundred and twenty men at two-week intervals. The sick and wounded shall depart in the first increment, followed by the others in the order in which they were captured." As Dog dismissed them with the admonition to continue to obey regulations and "show good attitudes" right up to release, they remained impassive while Colonel Risner† "did a smart about-face with all the dignity and military bearing within him." As Risner barked, "Fourth Allied POW Wing, atten-hut!" and almost 400 men snapped to attention, "the thud of eight hundred rubber-tire sandals coming together smartly was awesome. . . ." And when the squadron commanders returned Risner's salute and in unison dismissed their units with a "Squadron, dis...missed!," the open display at last of their military organization "sounded damned good."[3]

Once back in their cells the PWs let loose laughter and tears. As Coffee's group entered their room, "some men were exchanging a wink and a smile or a light punch on the shoulders, but most, with minds racing unto themselves, already projected themselves twelve thousand miles away and considered the joyful and spooky prospect of reunions with loved ones." Sam Johnson remembered that his group at Hoa Lo "ran to each other, hugging and crying and whooping with joy," but at Plantation Al Stafford felt only "a kind of emptiness which changed, slowly, to profound, bottomless fatigue. He had never felt so tired, and so vacant, in his life. He wanted, more than anything else, to go back to his cell, lie down, and sleep." From long experience some, even now, leavened their excitement with a pinch of skepticism. Coffee's squadron commander Ted Kopfman asked, "What do you think, guys? Is this it?" to which Jim Pirie replied, "Hell, man, my bags are packed. If this is some kind of ruse, they've got me sucked in." Old Man of the North Ev Alvarez, finishing out eight-and-a-half years in captivity, confided to Coffee: "You know, I've been up and down so many times over the years that I'm not sure what to think. It looks good, everything seems right, but I'll believe it when I see it. I'm not ready to party it up . . . yet."[4]

A rush of activity the first week in February removed any lingering doubts. At Unity, the Vietnamese finally opened up Rawhide and Blue,

---

* The accounts of Unity residents differ markedly in both minor and major details. Others have cited Spot and even Cat as the presiding North Vietnamese officer and the date anywhere from 28 January to 2 February.
† Flynn was still in semi-isolation in Blue with the other 06s and apparently did not participate in the event.

the top seniors integrated into a PW community that no longer had to engage in covert organization and communication. Acknowledging rank and finally adhering in general to the Geneva PW conventions, camp staff met with the senior American officers to discuss an orderly implementation of the departure schedule. Colonel Flynn submitted a list of 73 prisoners who were sick or injured and should be included in the first release increment. (The list contained the names of several of the "Lonely Hearts," such as Storz and Connell, who had not been seen for years.) Stockdale later said the Vietnamese tried to honor the requests in a few instances but, except for extreme cases as provided for in the peace protocols, stuck basically to the rule of release in order of capture date, the sequence having been already carefully planned and "it was too late to reshuffle the whole thing." When Flynn and Stockdale asked to be the last prisoners released from their respective services "as a matter of service custom and propriety," the Unity commander (identified by Stockdale as "Weasel"*) politely responded that "this was beyond his control" and the seniors dropped the issue.[5]

The prison authority reorganized Unity according to date of capture, the seniors from Rawhide and Blue dispersed to appropriate cells so as to be in the correct release order. Those with shootdown dates before August 1966 were placed in cells 4, 6, and 7, and those seized between August 1966 and June 1967 were put in 1, 2, and 3. (Cell 5 was used as a storeroom.) The graybeards in cell 7 included Alvarez, Shumaker, Stockdale, Risner, Guarino, Hayden Lockhart, Vohden, Scotty Morgan, Smitty Harris, and two dozen others who were checking out of the Hilton after seven- and eight-year stays. Joined by so many high-rankers, Alvarez joked, "This is the weirdest organization I've ever been in. The longer I stay here, the further down the ladder I go in the chain of command." Coffee was reunited with his first cellmate, Larry Spencer, whom he had not seen since early 1968, and his partner in the Hanoi March, Art Cormier. Denton joined "Bill Tschudy, a face out of the distant past, and Ed Davis, a voice out of the distant past." Discovering tapping buddies whom he knew only from their muffled messages, he now "attached pale faces to whispering voices: Ray Merritt, Ralph Gaither, Bob Purcell, Phil Butler . . . ." The shakeup moved Flynn out of Unity to Plantation—it and the Zoo were to be staging centers for the later release groups—and put Risner fully in charge at Hoa Lo.[6]

With complete freedom to communicate and roam the compound, the prisoners spent their last days in Hanoi mixing hellos with farewells, exercising in the chilly sunshine, and feasting on fresh supplies of bread and vegetables, canned meat and fish, and unlimited cigarettes. Amid all the

---

* Not the lower-level interrogator known by that name at the Zoo during 1967-69.

handshaking Guarino admitted to still being in shock and "if the others were like me, then we were often lost in our own private thoughts." His uncertainty lifted, Alvarez took to daydreaming about "returning to a normal life" in which "we would make our own decisions and set our own agendas." The prospect of doing the most routine of daily activities—getting in a car and cruising down the highway or rolling in a haystack—filled him with "tingling anticipation. I would get up whenever I pleased, make my own selection of clothing, eat whatever I wanted, and go wherever I fancied." Helping to ease the transition, the Vietnamese passed out remaining cartons of books, letters, and other materials from home, from *MAD* comics to a copy of *To Kill a Mockingbird*, that had been withheld over the years. Included in the personal possessions they returned were rings and wedding bands that had been taken from the prisoners at capture. Plumb complained that the leftover packages had been picked clean or had corroded and were "worthless, often containing nothing more than a half-cup of splintered hard candy or a glob of melted bouillon cubes."[7]

While the captors conducted "exit interviews" with the first group ticketed for departure, Risner and the other seniors stressed the importance of avoiding both fraternization and confrontation. The SRO held daily meetings with the squadron commanders to discuss potential problems and resolve policy questions. Before Flynn left for the Plantation, the leadership had already determined that the prisoners would not attend the much-ballyhooed farewell show* and had reached an agreement with officials that the release process "not be propagandized in any way." To prevent incidents, both Flynn and Risner warned the camp officers to keep correspondents and cameramen away. When a battery of French newsmen and photographers showed up, by prearranged signal the PWs returned to their cellblocks and closed the doors. When the journalists persisted, Risner and Stockdale granted one picture of themselves in the doorway of the cell and tersely answered one question. One of the last matters to be negotiated was what the prisoners would wear on their sendoff. The PWs wanted to come out in their confinement uniform; the Vietnamese refused but, rather than insist on their preferred choice of bright sweaters or civilian suits, settled for a drab compromise of black shoes, dark trousers, and a gray windbreaker.[8]

The first returnees were scheduled to leave from Unity on 12 February. While Alvarez and others in the initial group sifted their thoughts and belongings and counted down the final days and hours, prisoners elsewhere were

* See Chapter 25.

going through their own, similar logistical preparation and psychological coming to terms.

Beginning in late December and during January, approximately 100 military and civilians captured in the South and Laos were brought into Hoa Lo from Plantation, Rockpile, and K-49. The Vietnamese collected them next door to Unity in the old Vegas compound that had been vacant for two years. The first to arrive was Guy's group from the Plantation, which moved into the new quarters the evening of 27 December.* Most of Vegas's interior walls had been knocked out, reducing the complex of several small buildings to a few large cells. Frank Anton remembered they were called into the courtyard around noon on 29 January for the peace announcement, the first time many of them had actually seen Guy. As David Harker pondered the experience of the 12 men in the Kushner group who had managed to survive their ordeal in the jungle, Ike McMillan crept up behind him and whispered, "Harker, you can have my one twelfth of the sunshine now." Reflecting a sentiment that was probably universal among captives who had endured so much together, even in the not always harmonious Kushner camp, Harker averred that there was much to cherish and much to forget. As they awaited processing, the members of the Peace Committee struggled with the decision of whether to pursue expatriation or return to the United States; in the end, they all opted to return, though not before enthusiastically attending a version of the farewell show that the prisoners at Unity had boycotted and, according to James Daly, exchanging teary goodbyes with their captor friends.[9]

The tiny band of Laos survivors picked up three additional members at Vegas. Air Force pilot Charles Riess, downed over the Plain of Jars on Christmas Eve, was brought in on 17 January, and on 6 or 7 February there arrived two young missionaries—Sam Mattix and Canadian Lloyd Oppel —seized after a Communist attack on the small village in which they were living.† Even as their number grew to 10, Brace wondered whether any of them were destined to make it back. They were confined to a separate section within the compound and were advised by a Vietnamese officer that the Paris agreements did not apply to their group. Moreover, their names were not included on the original list issued with the protocols. It would

* The Vietnamese actually closed Plantation following the move, then reopened it on 20 January to receive those from Dogpatch and Hoa Lo who were slated to leave in the third release increment.

† The two civilians had been detained for about three weeks at a location just southeast of downtown Hanoi. Analysts could not identify any other PWs who were held at this facility, designated Xom De or "Countryside" in homecoming reports. See "Countryside Camp," nd, File 719. The source does not identify the pair by name but one was Canadian and judging from the time frame they almost certainly were Mattix and Oppel.

not be until March that the Lulus learned they were to be released, the last Americans to leave Vegas.[10]

The Rockpile and K-49 transfers did not enter Hoa Lo until late January and were initially placed in the New Guy section of the prison. For two weeks they received hefty rations of canned ham and mackerel, chowder, and loaves of bread along with physical examinations, the PWs later speculating that the Vietnamese intended to fatten them up before uniting them with their fitter colleagues who had come over from the Plantation. On 9 February, they joined the other "Southerners" in Vegas. Several in the Plantation group had not seen Old Man of the South Jim Thompson since their post-Tet incarceration together at the Portholes camp in the jungle; recalling his poor condition, they were astonished to find him not only alive but looking healthy. Monika Schwinn described an emotional reunion as she and her compatriot Bernhard Diehl, Ben Purcell, and the others among the two dozen who had come in from the outlying camps linked up with Kushner, Anton, and other comrades from whom they had long ago become separated on the trail north:

> The survivors shook hands and embraced one another warmly. Many had never met face to face and knew one another only through the cargoes that had passed from cell to cell. Now they walked over to greet one another, all moving rather unsteadily, looking gray-faced and emaciated. Some needed canes and crutches. I saw many of them cry when they embraced. They all seemed faintly bewildered, as if freedom were a dazzling light that had blinded them, so that for a moment they had to close their eyes.

The German nurse was allowed her own cell. When she visited Diehl at mealtime in a room nearby, Purcell recalled that all the men stood to welcome her "and of course she would be the first to take her meal from the table. It was good to have a refresher course in gentlemanly behavior."[11]

Those prisoners in custody in the Tay Ninh region of the South who had never been transported into the North, comprising mainly the Schrump and Ramsey groups, were processed locally in the same area where they had spent most of their confinement. Near the end of January, captors holding the 11 PWs under Major Schrump and 9 in the Ramsey band consolidated the two groups at a camp near Kratie, Cambodia. Here they outfitted them in clean clothes, dispensed medical treatment, and mixed parting apologies with a final indoctrination lecture. On 9 February the party broke camp and traveled most of the night by truck across the border into South Vietnam to Loc Ninh, where the Americans were returned to U.S. control in time to join the Alvarez group in the first release increment.

Another group of seven prisoners captured in the same general area in 1972* and held at a separate site near Snuol, Cambodia, also came out through the Loc Ninh repatriation point.[12]

As it turned out, each of the four principal release stagings between 12 February and 29 March 1973 ended up including two installments—a main group drawn from the bulk of the prisoners, mostly Navy and Air Force pilots, who had spent their entire captivity in the North; and a second, smaller group culled from the roster of PWs, mostly Army and civilians, who were originally in the custody of the Viet Cong.† The Loc Ninh group departed directly from South Vietnam, moved by helicopter to Saigon's Tan Son Nhut airport and then transferred to a C-9 medevac aircraft for the flight to the services' joint processing center at Clark Air Base in the Philippines. In all the other instances, the two groups departed from the same Hanoi airfield, Gia Lam, though usually a day apart after separate processing and on separate airplanes.

Alvarez's group spent their last evening at Hoa Lo getting haircuts and showers, receiving their going-home clothes and shoes, and dining on a banquet of turkey, salad, and wine. The clothing, issued roughly to size, was distributed out of the Heartbreak section, the men visiting a supply room there a half dozen at a time; personnel measured their shoe size by having them stand on pieces of toilet paper and penciling lines around their feet. Coffee recalled they eyed the wardrobe "like a bunch of little kids in a toy store," playfully trying out the zippers on their jackets and lacing and un-lacing the shoes. Except for those outfitted in civilian garb for the occasional city tour on trips outside the prison, "we hadn't seen a zipper, buttons, or shoelaces for years." Each prisoner was issued, too, a small black tote bag in which they were allowed to pack what few possessions they had—cigarettes, letters, toiletries and other items accumulated from parcels, and any souvenir they could sneak through, several opting for the tin drinking cup. Alvarez said the tin had been with him "for so long that it had taken on

---

* Maj. Albert Carlson, Capts. David Baker, Johnnie Ray, Mark Smith, George Wanat, and James Walsh, and Sgt. Kenneth Wallingford. An eighth man, Sgt. Howard Lull, was believed to have been captured in the same battle as Carlson, Ray, Smith, Wanat, and Wallingford, but disappeared. For four years the Army listed him as missing before making a presumptive finding of death in October 1976 absent any new information on his fate.
† Among this group the order of release bore little resemblance to sequence of capture. Captain Thompson, for example, a prisoner six months longer than Alvarez, was in the third installment of repatriated Southerners. To differentiate the two elements, some of the aviators referred to the Southerners as "WOPs" (POWs spelled backward). See memo AsstChStaff AF Intell MajGen George J. Keegan, Jr., for Generals Ryan, Wade, and Russell, 16 Feb 73.

American PWs from South Vietnam and Cambodia being released at Loc Ninh.

the sentimental value of a baby's cup." Chesley brought out a set of black pajamas and tire sandals that he later gave to the Air Force Museum at Wright-Patterson Air Force Base. With his SRO's permission, Davis stuffed in his handbag a small puppy liberated from the camp after a standoff with prison officials—a little victory that told the PWs they finally had some clout. Stratton's biographer noted that he was one returnee who "had no desire to come home with any keepsakes of his prison years. He had enough permanent mementos on his body, he would remark later on."[13]

During a sleepless night the departing prisoners partied, reminisced, and said goodbyes to comrades they hoped they were only temporarily leaving behind; some of the latter passed messages to be delivered to their families. Coffee reflected not only on his captivity but on the whole issue of war and peace and what their sacrifice had accomplished. In a pensive mood a few days earlier, he had brooded over "what the hell had I done the last seven [years]? During the prime years of my life, I'd sat on my ass in some medieval dungeons, broken my teeth, screwed up my arm, contracted worms and God knows what else, and had gotten *old*. Well, I was almost thirty-nine. We sure as hell better have something to show for it down South." Now, based on his understanding of the Paris agreement, he felt a sense of gratification that his sacrifice had somehow helped further the "democratic process" in the South, not realizing how short-lived that development would be.[14]

At dawn the next morning, 12 February, Lincoln's birthday (also Dramesi's), the PWs awoke to a breakfast of warm milk, bread, and coffee. By 7:30 or 8:00 a.m., dressed and shaved, they filed out of Unity into Hoa Lo's main courtyard, guards arranging them two abreast by shootdown date and dividing them into platoons of 20 (the number of seats on the buses used to transport the PWs to the airfield). Those sick and injured who were slated to accompany the early shootdowns home hobbled out of the New Guy area, some on crutches and three on stretchers.* To everyone's surprise—and dismay—two who emerged with the group were Colonel Miller and Commander Wilber. Although Miller told his debriefer he had specifically asked the Vietnamese not to move him ahead on the list, the captors may have felt they owed a last favor to the two renegades who in a final act of obeisance had attended the same performance of the prison farewell show as the Peace Committee. Commander Vohden, himself badly crippled, was the senior in charge of the 29 men in New Guy designated sick or wounded, the Vietnamese including Miller and Wilber in that category; 8 of the 29, including the 3 litter cases, were casualties from the December 1972 bombing raids.[15]

When foggy weather delayed their exit, Johnson was "taut with fear that this whole thing was going to fall apart." After an hour's wait, Alvarez had to go to the bathroom, finishing just in time to join Bob Shumaker at the front of the lead column as the formation marched out Hoa Lo's main gate and boarded the idling buses. As the convoy wove its way through the downtown traffic to the airport, Coffee "felt a little weird, like a tourist on a tour bus." Denton remembered their being "subdued in the solemnity of our thoughts, almost hypnotized . . . ." During a stop at an administration building on the outskirts of Gia Lam, the prisoners were offered beer and sandwiches before reboarding the buses and arriving at the terminal around noon just as the first of three U.S. Air Force C-141s was landing. The spectacle of the giant transport touching down was "electrifying," Alvarez recalled. "It was the first C141 I had ever seen and it was love at first sight." Guarino remembered being more detached until the cargo door opened and "people started jumping down from the airplane, people I had forgotten existed, who looked to me like they were from another world. Yes, they were from another world . . . *our* world!"[16]

As the reception team, headed by Air Force Col. James Dennett, made its way onto the tarmac, the first bus of prisoners was escorted to a table where Vietnamese officials checked off each man's name before formally

---

* Alvarez noticed only two but three men were carried aboard the evacuation aircraft in litters: Capt. Thomas Klomann and Sgts. Roy Madden and James Cook. See *Washington Post*, 13 Feb 73.

releasing him into the custody of an American serviceman. In the crowd of dignitaries were members of the International Commission of Control and Supervision and the Four-Party Joint Military Commission representing the United States, North Vietnam, South Vietnam, and the Viet Cong—along with what a French news dispatch described as "scores" of North Vietnamese who "had left their ministries to cross the Red River to the airport" to be present for the historic moment. Although Coffee saw no familiar faces, more than one of the departing prisoners identified Rabbit as the individual calling out the names and Mulligan cited a lineup of old foes who showed up to see them off: Frenchy, Slick, Mickey Mouse, Bug, Lump, Rat, Dum Dum, Spot, and Slopehead.[17]

The ceremony was repeated for each busload until by 1:45 p.m. all 116* men were airborne, 40 in each of the first two C-141s and 36 in the third. Hearts pounded and eyes glistened as the planes raised their ramps, taxied down the runway, and lifted into the sky to freedom. During the three-hour trip to Clark, the former prisoners joked, cried, hugged flight nurses, drank American coffee, and sat awestruck as the Defense Department's Roger Shields[†] and liaison officers briefed them on what to expect once on the ground in the Philippines. Told who had just won Super Bowl VII, one of the veteran PWs replied, "That's great, what's the Super Bowl?" Mulligan, the senior man on the last plane out, "cried like a baby" as he took his seat and the engines revved up for takeoff. Once in the air, seated next to the State Department's top official on POW/MIA matters, Frank Sieverts, Mulligan recited his memory bank of prisoner names into a tape recorder. Others agonized over the absence of Storz and other missing comrades, Shields and Sieverts confirming that Storz was among the 55 servicemen (a total of 70 counting civilians) whom the North Vietnamese listed as having died in captivity. In the meantime, Denton, the senior ranking officer on the first plane, borrowed a piece of paper from a flight attendant and quickly scribbled the simple eloquent words that he would deliver on the ramp at Clark.[18]

The first C-141 touched down at Clark at 4:20 p.m. (3:20 a.m. EST), the others trailing behind it at 30-minute intervals. The Loc Ninh group repatriated from the South, minus civilian Richard Waldhaus, who elected to stay in Saigon, arrived later that evening, the 26 Americans deplaning close to midnight after a day marked by several false starts. All the ex-PWs, in

* The list of releasees in this first group was supposed to be 115. At the last minute the North Vietnamese agreed to include Navy Cdr. Brian Woods, a 1968 capture, whose early return was sought by U.S. officials so that he could arrive home in time to see his gravely ill mother.
† Shields, in the Office of the Assistant Secretary of Defense for International Security Affairs, headed the DoD task force charged with planning and coordinating the repatriation operation, originally called Egress Recap and renamed Operation Homecoming early in 1973.

this and subsequent increments, received a red-carpet welcome, then spent three to five days at Clark in debriefings, medical evaluations, calls to family, and general decompression before being cleared for the journey home. Although Pentagon planners had meticulously coordinated the arrangements at the processing center, down to diet and measurement for uniforms (or, in the case of civilians, polyester suits), the returnees soon established their own priorities. "For our first meal in freedom," wrote Chesley, "we had steak or chicken, corn on the cob, strawberry shortcake and ice cream, all in huge quantities." Sleeping in a bed with a mattress and sheets and eating with a knife and fork would take some getting used to, as would being around females, handling money, and using a telephone. For many the first order of business was getting clean. Nasmyth remembered locating a bathtub in a staff room, locking the door, and "wallowing" in hot water until it ran over the side. His first bath lasted an hour, one of a half dozen he took that first night.[19]

Back in Hanoi the 400-plus prisoners remaining in captivity at Hoa Lo, Plantation, and the Zoo anxiously awaited their turn to leave. In a break with the protocols, the North Vietnamese announced on 14 February a special release of 20 men from the Hilton as a goodwill gesture coinciding with the visit to the capital of a U.S. delegation headed by Dr. Kissinger. Because the so-called "Kissinger 20" seemed to have been chosen at random—none were in particularly serious condition, nor were any next in line in order of shootdown—the senior in the group, Lieutenant Commander Pirie, backed by Colonel Gaddis, now camp SRO at Unity, instructed the men to stay put. Only when a representative of the U.S. repatriation team, permitted to enter the prison after he strenuously argued with Vietnamese authorities, assured the PW leadership that the release had been approved in Washington—and informed Pirie that their resistance, however principled, might jeopardize further departures—did the prisoners relent. Still with some hesitation and concern that they would be stigmatized by what appeared to be accepting preferential treatment, in the end they obeyed an order to dress, shave, and "get your asses outa here." The 16 Air Force and 4 Navy PWs* walked out of a holding area in New Guy the morning of 18 February and were transferred to U.S. control at Gia Lam that afternoon.[20]

---

* Joseph Abbott, James Berger, Joseph Crecca, John Clark, John Davies, Hubert Flesher, Henry Fowler, Donald Heiliger, Jay Jensen, Michael Lane, Kevin McManus, Edward Mechenbier, Joseph Milligan, John Nasmyth, James Pirie, Herbert Ringsdorf, James Shively, Charles Plumb, Frederick Purrington, and James Bailey. Lieutenant Bailey replaced Lt. Robert Wideman on the list when American officials asked that his name be added for humanitarian reasons owing to his father's recent heart attack; instead of adding the extra name, the Vietnamese dropped Wideman and the total remained 20, once again to match the number of seats on the bus.

Above: "Kissinger 20" lined up by airport bus. *Below:* PWs on Gia Lam tarmac for release ceremony.

Clockwise from top left: SRO Flynn on way home with junior lieutenant Tim Sullivan, who helped care for Flynn in prison; Ed Davis napping on plane with puppy he brought out; PWs arriving at Clark Air Base; Risner (with hand raised) and Stockdale disembarking at Clark.

The next regularly scheduled round of releases, set for 27 February, was held up by wrangling over alleged cease-fire violations and other procedural problems, Hanoi and Saigon exchanging charges and countercharges until the United States demanded an end to the delay. After several days of posturing, the North Vietnamese finally yielded, notifying the U.S. government that the release would take place in two installments on 4-5 March. The first group, including 106 American military personnel and 2 Thai sergeants, strode out of Unity shortly before noon on 4 March, emptying the compound and closing the door on one of the most celebrated camps of the captivity. By 1:00 p.m., Kasler, Coker, Tanner, Fuller, Swindle, Stratton, Larson, Gaddis, Stockman, Red McDaniel, and eight dozen other late 1966 and early 1967 shootdowns were on the tarmac at Gia Lam, running the same ceremonial gauntlet and emotional gamut as their predecessors.

As he rode out of Hanoi, McDaniel saw the past "dissolve" behind him, "but the smells and sights and sounds would remain a long time, I knew." At the airfield he looked at Spot and now "did not think of the many hours of interrogation under him, the torturing, the harassment. He was just another man in another part of the world who had done his job." (Few were as forgiving toward their oppressors, and McDaniel himself was more emotionally scarred than he let on; a decade later he would emerge as a zealous crusader for the MIA cause and opponent of normalizing relations with Vietnam.) Stratton was both euphoric and edgy, up and down "like a yo-yo," worried about how his family and the Navy would receive him after the 1967 bowing incident. As Fellowes approached the ladder of the C-141, he noticed a uniformed nurse, later remarking that "it was that fragrance of an American woman wearing perfume that made me acutely aware, for the first time in all those years, how really dirty our place of captivity had been." Minutes after Rabbit read their names, those in the first transport were over the Gulf of Tonkin en route to the Philippines.[21]

The second installment included 34 of the "Southern" prisoners—27 U.S. servicemen and 3 civilians, plus the 2 West Germans and 2 Filipinos. On 5 March they were released from Vegas. One of the last off the plane at Clark was Monika Schwinn, who had an orange handbag and a yellow rose given her by Phil Manhard before the two separated, but otherwise was dressed in the same departure outfit as the other returnees. Unbeknownst to the Vietnamese, hidden in the handbag was a message from Colonel Purcell advising U.S. authorities that Captain Gostas was in urgent need of medical attention. As a result Gostas, who had been scheduled to return with the last increment, went out with the next group from the South. In the meantime, after comparing capture dates, Purcell took over from Guy as commander of the PWs still left at the Hilton.[22]

The third general release followed on time 10 days later. Those aviators shot down between August 1967 and December 1968 had been gathered at the Plantation since 20 January. Led by Colonel Flynn, 107 servicemen, joined by one civilian (Bobby Keesee,* seized in 1970 and somehow winding up with this group), boarded five buses around noon on 14 March. Bud Day remembered that within hours of his arrival at Clark he had two badly infected teeth extracted, got all his shots, and was fitted for glasses. As with so many others, Day's joy at reentry was tempered by news of the deaths of family members and apprehension over the first contact with his wife. When an escort officer placed the call home and he heard his wife's voice, the ex-PW "felt as if I might melt into the phone." In his case, the words were reassuring: "She came through strong and clear. She was well. The children were well. They were as anxious to see me as I was to see them. All of the important things in my existence were in order."[23]

Among the Viet Cong prisoners released on 16 March were Captain Thompson (finally freed a week short of his ninth anniversary in captivity), Dr. Kushner, Gostas, Manhard, Guy, and the Peace Committee enlistees. The eight Peace Committee members stayed close together during their last hours at Hoa Lo, then sat together on the airport bus. Following Guy's instructions to salute and obey standard military procedure, they traversed the flight line without incident. Although Colonel Dennett and the reception team were aware of the PCs' past behavior and were prepared for either their refusal of repatriation or a propaganda stunt, it turned out that the North Vietnamese themselves (according to Daly) had advised the enlistees not to do anything foolish, or it "could be bad for you." Only when the complete contingent of 27 servicemen and 5 civilians arrived in the Philippines were the PCs singled out for special handling, quartered in a separate section of the hospital and assigned extra personnel to monitor them.[24]

The same week that the Day and Thompson groups were repatriated, U.S. officials managed to obtain the release of two PWs from Communist China. Air Force Capt. Philip Smith and Navy Lt. Cdr. Robert Flynn had gone down over China in 1965 and 1967 respectively when they strayed over the border while flying missions over North Vietnam. They were recovered on 15 March when an American Red Cross representative met them at a bridge connecting the mainland with Hong Kong. Three days earlier, on 12 March, the Chinese released another American, civilian John Downey, who had been imprisoned by the Communists for more than 20 years, since the Korean War, on charges that he was a CIA agent. Smith and Flynn joined their fellow fliers at Clark; Downey

---

* According to State's Sieverts, Keesee arranged his own capture, hijacking an aircraft to North Vietnam. In 1999, after trying to steal another aircraft, he was charged with murder (*Washington Post,* 15 Jan 99).

returned home immediately to be at the bedside of his ailing mother in New Britain, Connecticut.*[25]

By 16 March, then, excluding the three returnees from China, 445 PWs, including foreigners, had been released since the start of Operation Homecoming. According to the official list furnished by the North Vietnamese in Paris, there remained some 140 Americans still in custody, not counting the 10 captured in Laos. Regarding the latter, Hanoi had not even acknowledged their existence until February, and then it insisted it had no authority over the individuals and that the U.S. government would have to negotiate with the Pathet Lao for the men's release. While continuing to deny responsibility for the Laotian prisoners, on 24 and 25 March the Viet Cong and North Vietnamese submitted rosters for the final round of releases that were to take place beginning 27 March. By the evening of 26 March, an agreement was finally reached by U.S., North Vietnamese, and Laotian delegates clarifying the status of the 10 Lulus and permitting their departure with the final increment.[26]

In this last staging, the Southern PWs—27 U.S. military personnel and 5 civilians still housed in Hoa Lo—were the lead element. Headed by Colonel Purcell and including Lieutenant Commander Kientzler, who had been shot down just south of the Demilitarized Zone the last day of the war and hence was considered a prisoner of the Viet Cong, the 32 Americans left Gia Lam the afternoon of 27 March while the U.S. Command in Saigon simultaneously began troop withdrawals from the South. The next morning, 28 March, the 10 prisoners captured in Laos, including the one Canadian, were set free.† Brace recalled they had had a "sumptuous dinner"

---

* These were not the first Americans let go by the Chinese during the Vietnam War. In December 1971, seeking a thaw in relations with the United States, they freed civilians Richard Fecteau, who had been captured the same time as Downey and was also accused of espionage, and Mary Ann Harbert, a young woman jailed in 1968 when her sloop sank in Chinese waters during a storm. Harbert's companion Gerald McLaughlin died in captivity. One other civilian taken prisoner by the People's Republic, English engineer George Watt, was released in August 1970 after almost three years' detention on spying charges; for part of his sentence he was celled next to Smith. See *Time*, 27 Dec 71 and "China" folder in OSD Hist, which contains comments of Fecteau and Smith that point up similarities and differences between captivity in Vietnam and China. Harbert detailed her experience in a 1973 memoir, *How I Survived 44 Months as a Prisoner of the Red Chinese*. In 1975 the Chinese gave President Gerald Ford information on other American fliers missing and killed over China during the conflict in Southeast Asia, including two deceased Navy personnel, Jimmy Buckley and Kenneth Pugh, whose remains were returned in December. See memo Vice Premier Teng Hsiao-ping for President Ford, 4 Dec 75; ltr Frank Sieverts to Roger Shields, 24 Dec 75.

† Besides the 9 in this bunch, none of the more than 300 Americans listed as "missing" in Laos (the figure is over 500 if one counts killed in action/body not recovered casualties) were ever recovered alive, despite skepticism by U.S. authorities that the Pathet Lao had turned over all captives under their control at the end of the war and persistent investigation and speculation in the years since. (See Chapter 15.) One U.S. civilian captured after Operation Homecoming, in May 1973, Emmet Kay, was released by the Laotians in September 1974.

in the Vegas courtyard the night before, served turkey legs, fish, and peach wine, with guards eating at the same table and refilling the Lulus' cups when they were empty. In a poignant moment they bid farewell to Chi Charn Harnavee, their Thai ally who with Brace had been held captive since May 1965; Brace promised to get him and a Thai cellmate out as soon as he could contact the U.S. State Department (the pair were released in September 1974). Brace wrote that he and Steve Long could not remember crying through all the years of beatings and persecution until they were informed at the processing center that their wives had left them.[27]

Also on 28 March, in addition to the Lulus, North Vietnam released the first 40 of 107 prisoners at the Zoo, which was the staging compound for the last group of aviators to exit Hanoi. Arriving at Clark behind Brace's group, they were led off the plane by Colonel Kittinger. The 67 remaining, all late 1972 shootdowns, followed on 29 March in an action timed to coincide with the completion of the U.S. withdrawal from the South. The last prisoner to board the second of two C-141s was Navy Lt. Cdr. Alfred Agnew; the last pilot seized in the war except for Kientzler, he had been a PW for only three months. To the end, the Vietnamese tried to use the Zoo for propaganda purposes, with daily attempts to indoctrinate the younger shootdowns and an unprecedented invitation to repatriation officials and Western correspondents to visit the prison and observe the release preparations and departure for the airport.[28]

Even as the *New York Times* headlined the evacuation of the final installment of PWs ("Thousands See Release of Last P.O.W."), reports surfaced of yet another U.S. serviceman still being held in Southeast Asia and in the unlikeliest of places, the Mekong Delta. On 29 March the Viet Cong announced that Army Capt. Robert White, unaccounted for since his disappearance in an operation in the Delta in November 1969, was alive and would be repatriated within the next couple of days. Years later White would say "they just plain forgot about me" until his captors reminded their superiors of his detention and asked what to do with him. The PW had been weakened by malaria and vitamin deficiency but otherwise was in good shape. On 1 April, after a journey on foot and by sampan to a transfer point not far from his capture site, he was helicoptered to Tan Son Nhut and then flown to Clark Air Base that afternoon. White in fact turned out to be the last American released during Operation Homecoming and (unless one counts Robert Garwood) the last known surviving U.S. prisoner of war in the Indochina conflict.[29]

Altogether, 600 prisoners—591 Americans and 9 foreign nationals—were repatriated during Operation Homecoming. The Americans included 77

Jubilation as C-141 takes off from Hanoi on 28 March.

Left: Captain White, the last to be set free.
Below: Montage of homecoming headlines.

Army, 138 Navy, 325 Air Force, 26 Marines, and 25 civilians. When added to the more than 100 military and civilians eventually classified as having died in captivity and the nearly 100 who had returned previously via the escape or early release route, that made a total of almost 800 Americans who spent time as prisoners—ranging from a few days to just short of nine years—during the Vietnam War. There remained the wrenching question of the fate of some 1,300 U.S. personnel who were missing in action (the figure would be set at 2,500 when the Pentagon added to the list those killed in action whose bodies had not been recovered). By 1983 the services would issue presumptive findings of killed in action for all but a handful of the missing, but the final accounting to this day continues to occupy hundreds of analysts as well as a swarm of polemicists and opportunists.*

From Clark the returnees left for destinations throughout the United States—on geographical and career paths that in many cases would never converge again. Bob Craner spoke in a postwar interview about what it was like to separate from comrades who shared such an extraordinary experience:

> Of course, getting out was what we had all anticipated and dreamed of and desired desperately for so many years. But I and everyone did establish friendships and very intimate personal relationships up there, which I don't believe any other set of circumstances would have allowed. And it was with just a little bit of melancholia that I finally said good-bye to John McCain at Clark . . . . Even at Clark, we were still a group, and we were still talking to ourselves, and the outsiders were trying to butt in, but we weren't having too much of that. We were still a pretty tight-knit group. On the night before I was to get on an airplane at 8:00 o'clock the following morning, I could sense that here was the end. Now this group is going to be busted wide open and spread all over the United States. It may be a long time, years, before we rejoin, and when we do, it won't be the same.

The prisoners did reconvene at a White House dinner in May (by far the largest seated dinner there ever) and one or two other high-profile events,

---

* As of March 1997, based on the return of over 300 sets of identifiable remains, the "unaccounted for" number had dropped to 2,127. For an official statement on the MIA issue from an immediate post-homecoming perspective, see Frank Sieverts's testimony in *American Prisoners of War and Missing in Action in Southeast Asia, 1973*, Hearings before House Foreign Affairs Subcommittee on National Security Policy and Scientific Developments, 93 Cong, 1 sess (May 73), pt 4, 68-76. Sieverts insisted, and subsequent administrations would reiterate, that the government had no confirmable evidence of any individual left behind in captivity. The most recent and most comprehensive reviews of the issue are *POW/MIA'S*, Report of the Senate Select Committee on POW/MIA Affairs, 103 Cong, 1 sess (13 Jan 93); "A Zero-Based Comprehensive Review of Cases Involving Unaccounted for Americans in Southeast Asia," ODASD(POW/MIA Affairs), 13 Nov 95.

then dispersed again to their respective hometowns and bases to resume more mundane relationships and activities—getting reacquainted with family and friends, sorting financial and legal affairs, and attending to medical and dental follow-ups. Reams of reports and studies have been written on the physical and psychological health of the returning prisoners. Depending in part on whether they were held captive in the North or South, their residual problems ran from bailout fractures that never healed to intestinal ailments that never disappeared; getting fitted for eyeglasses and having chipped or rotted teeth removed were common priorities. Although there were two early suicides (besides Sergeant Kavanaugh, Lieutenant Brudno took his life on 3 June 1973), on the whole the men adjusted remarkably well given the severity and longevity of their confinement.[30]

Still, the stresses of reentry were enormous. Stratton recalled that the "first hours of reunion and emotion . . . blended into days of reality, and fatigue . . . . Hanoi was so far away now, yet always close." During a stay at a stateside hospital, "a jingle of keys on an orderly's belt, or soft footsteps by his door in the middle of the night, brought him bolt-upright in bed, terror-stricken and soaked instantly with sweat." The White House fete was followed by local ceremonies and celebrations, lifetime passes to ball games, offers of free automobiles and vacations, and what one writer termed "a Disney-like procession of parties, speeches, television appearances* and toasts," but the ex-PWs would have gladly traded the tributes and hoopla for a measure of normalcy and the restoration of "some semblance of a career." Aviators, even those whose vision still enabled them to fly, had to get caught up on the many technical and mechanical advances that had occurred during their absence. Many went to flight training again and requalified in various aircraft.† All the "old guys" had to deal with political and cultural shocks that they had heard about through letters or late shootdowns but now had to face—a world, Scott Blakey noted, in which "old enemies like China were new friends" and "Oakland baseball players wore

---

* His first night home Nasmyth asked if Sonny and Cher were still together. A week later he was on their show. Many others also turned up on TV or at state fairs, holiday parades, and promotional events.

† Capt. Peter Camerota, shot down as a B-52 crewmember in the December 1972 raids, who had not qualified as a pilot earlier, got the chance to try again and made it. That he was only briefly a prisoner did not spare him a surprise on his return. During processing at Travis Air Base, California, he was told by an official that he would be paid five dollars for each of the 88 days he was a PW. He protested that he had been 98 days in the Hanoi area—10 of them hiding in a tiny cave before being taken captive. The official explained that the money was expressly for "substandard quarters and subsistence" and that during his 10 days evading capture he had *no* quarters and subsistence and therefore did not have *substandard* quarters and subsistence. With that bureaucratic explanation, Camerota would later say, "I knew I was home." (Interv with Kiley.)

Strong rebounds: Boyd (left) would make four-star; Peterson (right) would return to Hanoi as U.S. Ambassador.

white shoes." And then, of course, there were the awkward adjustments to families, especially spouses, who had not only grown older but also more independent.[31]

As with coping in prison, some would make the transition more easily than others. Some picked up their lives as normally as if they had merely served overseas for the better part of a decade, and some never recovered from dissolved marriages, missed career opportunities, or the awful memories. Flynn, Winn, Gaddis, Chuck Boyd (the only four-star), Stockdale, Denton, Risner, Lawrence, Fuller, and Shumaker were among a score who would attain flag rank. Stockdale and Day (along with Sijan and Cook posthumously) were awarded the Medal of Honor for actions while in captivity. Old Man of the North Alvarez went on to law school and after his retirement from the Navy in 1980 held a string of important posts in the Reagan administration. Stockdale, who had fretted about his future as his homecoming flight descended into San Diego ("My hair is totally white now. I can't see to read . . . . I'm forty-nine years old and crippled and can't raise my left arm."), went on to head the Naval War College and then The Citadel before becoming a senior research fellow at Stanford. Lawrence became superintendent of the Naval Academy and Deputy Chief of Naval Operations.

Among a slew who enrolled in graduate and professional schools, the punster Ringsdorf received a degree in medicine and Joe Milligan obtained a Ph.D. and became the chief veterinarian of the Air Force. A dozen of the returnees entered politics; Denton, McCain, Sam Johnson, and Douglas "Pete" Peterson were elected to the U.S. Congress, and Orson Swindle became campaign director for 1992 presidential candidate Ross Perot (Stockdale was Perot's running mate). In the spring of 1997, 24 years after his release, Peterson became the first U.S. ambassador to Hanoi. Dozens who came home to divorces quickly remarried; Brace's best man was his fellow Lulu Jim Bedinger. A few who were adapting well were overtaken by further misfortune: in 1974 Bob Schweitzer died in an automobile accident and Darrel Pyle in a private plane crash; Dick Ratzlaff's melanoma was removed but the cancer recurred, spread, and killed him soon after a successful career reorientation and remarriage.[32]

For a year or two after homecoming, as part of the debriefing process, the former prisoners were asked to participate in surveys that sought to draw "lessons learned" from their captivity experience. Along with comments on the importance of leadership and organization, they recommended changes in survival training and equipment, clearer delineation of senior authority and the chain of command in prisoner of war situations, and, usually at the top of the list, clarification of the Code of Conduct so that each prisoner knew more specifically what was expected of him especially under extreme conditions.[33] Eventually the Code was modified slightly,[34] but ultimately, as the Indochina PWs themselves had come to accept reluctantly in the special circumstances of their confinement, the Code could never be more than a guide, a standard to hew to insofar as soldierly and humanly possible. Many of the returnees wrongly believed they had lowered that standard. Although there were those who did not measure up even by a flexible guideline—and their number was greater than postwar memoirists remember or care to admit—by and large, it is fair to say that as a group they raised the bar to another level.

The company of men who walked the Hanoi March, trekked the Ho Chi Minh Trail at the point of a bayonet, and battled the enemy behind the lines from Briarpatch to Dogpatch survived the jails and jungles of Southeast Asia against great odds. Blessed in many instances with advantages of skills and seasoning when compared with U.S. PWs of previous generations, they were also endowed with qualities of heart and soul, grace and courage, that in the end mattered more than their relatively high ranks. Those who made it back gave their countrymen an occasion to celebrate patriotism and heroism unencumbered by the vexing moral and political issues that beclouded so much of the war effort. In helping to achieve a healing, uplifting closure to the bitterly divisive conflict, the PWs, even when they were no longer incarcerated, continued to wield a symbolic power out of proportion to their small numbers. Their proud return to a grateful nation remains one of the few truly shining moments of that troubled era.

Afterword

I fought in the Vietnam War for nine years, starting as a 40-year-old fighter squadron commander on the *Ticonderoga,* leading the first retaliatory raids against North Vietnam in August 1964, and then as commander of the *Oriskany's* Air Wing for eight months until I was shot down in September 1965 and became a prisoner of the North Vietnamese for seven and a half years.

I was the only wing commander in that long war to lead prisoner resistance and therefore the natural target for Major Bui—The Cat—commissar of North Vietnamese prison camps. The business of the commissar was extortion. He had to continually intimidate—to break—a number of PWs so that he had Americans at the ready to parade before press conferences for foreign "dignitaries" (often Americans from the antiwar movement) and to exploit for propaganda statements favorable to the communist agenda. Our job was to hold out as long as we could, to make it difficult for the Cat to exploit us.

To do this, he hired experienced "torture guards," who in 40 minutes or so, with bars and ropes, could reduce a self-respecting American officer to a sobbing wreck. We had to figure on that, but not let it get us down. There were avenues to decrease vulnerability, most of them in the field of dramatic arts. The Vietnamese could not afford to expose an emotionally unstable person to a visiting "dignitary" because he might start blurting out the truth. So flying off the handle when initially pressured sometimes landed a prisoner on the "wacko" list and denied Cat a victim. Self-disfiguration was another option: because Hanoi's official line was "humane and lenient" treatment for prisoners, scars and wounds would defeat that lie. However, unless you come by these instincts naturally there was a grave danger of the North Vietnamese detecting your faking it. They killed people over that. Even so, several of my fellow prisoners avoided exploitation by damaging themselves.

In that grim, sustained, and bloody struggle, the Vietnamese held all the trumps, save one: our determination to resist, to hang together, to communicate with and support each other, to bounce back when they broke us, and to frustrate them in their sordid mission. We had a few failures, but I will carry with me to my final day the fierce pride and deep admiration that grew during those years for the grit, the stamina, the inventiveness, the resourcefulness, the bone-raw courage, and the unconquerable souls of those valiant men in the North Vietnamese prisons. The commissar and his barbaric lackeys should have shut us out 10–0, but I think the final score was (as someone put it) Lions 2, Christians 8.

Living in South Vietnam as a prisoner was another story. There, most prisoners were kept on the move out in the elements. It was a grim struggle for survival—rain, heat, cold, mudslides, lack of medicine, sometimes alone, sometimes with two or three others, being herded and confined like animals, including being kept in animal cages. But there, too, despite horrible conditions and much illness and lacking senior leadership, the prisoners carved out a record that Americans could be proud of. More than two dozen successfully escaped in the South. More than 50 were forced to journey all the way to Hanoi before release in 1973, or death. Of the approximately 100 PWs to die in captivity, many were in the South. Two PWs, Sgt. Jon Cavaiani and Pvt. William Port, were awarded the Medal of Honor for gallantry in the actions during which they were captured; another, Capt. Donald Cook, was awarded the Medal of Honor for heroism in captivity. Port's and Cook's awards were posthumous.

The Viet Cong executed several prisoners in the South—"bad attitude" cases who would have fit in very comfortably with the hardline resisters in the North. They also released a good number of PWs—hoping to gain propaganda advantages by, for example, persuading black or Latino PWs to speak out against the war to minority soldiers. They had small successes and some resounding defeats in this effort.

Laos was a terrible place to fly. The country is so desolate, the population so sparse, that a pilot was just as likely to die of ejection injuries swinging in his parachute harness, hooked high on a triple-canopy tree, as to meet any other fate. I did my flying in Laos over a six-week period early in the summer of 1964, escorting low-flying Crusader photo planes as they monitored the movement of Pathet Lao troops threatening to take over the Plaine de Jars. More than 300 American personnel were reported lost in Laos. Only nine showed up for Homecoming, returning with us from Hanoi in 1973.

The North Vietnamese were versatile—they had a fix for everything. When I was running the Hoa Lo prison resistance out of Vegas in April 1967, the skies cleared and we were privileged to see the first of two world-class, long-running air shows. Our Navy and Air Force started pouring it on. There would be tactical air strikes day and night forever, we hoped. The town was being beaten to death. Water mains were ruptured, and the Yen Phu thermal power station north of town was bombed time and again, with resultant power outages. Hanoi's fix? Camp Dirty Bird, a hostage residence for about 30 American prisoners adjacent to the Yen Phu plant—the Vietnamese making a big show of our hostages beside it, hoping American intelligence would pick it up and lay off the plant. Fifteen days after our hostages were on station, the Vietnamese got a signal that America knew what was going on. Did we stop bombing? No! That was the American spirit we wanted to see. Prisoner morale soared. The end of Dirty Bird came when two of our hostage stalwarts—George McKnight and George Coker—took advantage of the fragile lockup they were in and escaped at night to swim down the Red River. They were discovered, 15 miles down the river, buried in sand the next morning, and that was that. Dirty Bird's longevity was short. It was closed by 26 October.

Meanwhile, our Vegas resistance organization was booming. We were refusing to comply with most everything and we all took a hammering, but those bombs kept falling and our spirits remained jubilant. It looked as if we could end this war before Christmas. The thing that blew the Cat's stack was learning that we were forwarding all my orders to outlying camps by passing notes to the many new shootdowns of 1967 as they came out of initial shakedown at Heartbreak Hotel. The Vietnamese reaction? Another special camp: "Send Stockdale, his eight primary deputies, plus McKnight and Coker, into exile within the walls of the National Army Headquarters of North Vietnam." We called our new prison Alcatraz, and we went there to be "Brer Rabbits in the Briar Patch." We got there on October 25, 1967. The downer was that our bombing had almost stopped the previous week. No guts, no glory.

The White House had halted the bombing just as North Vietnam was on its knees. Instead of release and an end to the war by early 1968, we had to wait until the B-52s started hitting the rail yards of Hanoi on December 18, 1972. By December 29, the Vietnamese had nothing left to shoot at our bombers. They were on their knees again. We were eyeball-to-eyeball with prison officials frequently throughout December. They were petrified with fright. The commissar apologized to some of the senior officers for the previous bad treatment and even asked what kind of improved treatment we would accept. He and his superiors may have been worried about war crimes. My reaction to the whole thing was, "Why didn't we bring those B-52s in during 1965 and have this whole thing over, within the 11 days it took to completely demoralize the Vietnamese this time?"

The question is, of course, moot now. What remains 25 years after Operation Homecoming is a terrible sense of waste—not only the 59,000 Americans commemorated on the Vietnam Memorial, the many wounded in that decade-long war, and the MIAs but also the incredible number of Vietnamese dead and MIAs (more than 300,000) and the destruction of so much of the country, North and South.

The first four chapters of *Honor Bound* are very important to understanding the overall prisoner-of-war saga that followed. They show how the Hanoi ideologues were able to cast the United States in the role of just another colonial power trying to replace France, when in fact the United States did not support France's continuing colonial domination of Indochina and did not aid the French at Dien Bien Phu in 1954. Thus American prisoners became victims of a propaganda war—a psychological warfare campaign—which against great odds they by and large won. The war itself was another matter. Vietnam today is unified, calling itself the Socialist Republic of Vietnam, and struggling toward some kind of economic development. Our first ambassador to the SVR sits in Hanoi. Ironically, he has been there before, having been shot down in 1966 and spending more than six years in North Vietnamese jails. The population of the country since the war has doubled, so most Vietnamese, like most Americans, now know little of the war.

But through the melancholy memories of what needn't have been and what might have been shines a story of incredible perseverance and bravery in the darkest of hours. That story is the subject of this book. I salute it, and I salute those who lived it and those who died in those distant lands. And I thank them for giving this nation the shining example that was theirs.

VICE ADM. JAMES BOND STOCKDALE, USN (RET.)

Appendix 1

American Prisoners of War in Major
U.S. Interventions Since World War I

	WWI	WWII	Korea	**Vietnam**	Persian Gulf	Total
Captured and Interned	4,120	130,201	7,140	**771**	23	142,255
Died in Captivity	147	14,072	2,701	**113**	0	17,033
Returned to U.S. Military Control	3,973	116,129	4,418	**658**	23	125,201

Note: The table does not include civilian casualties. Also not included are 92,527 military personnel and civilians lost in either combat or MIA status whose remains were never recovered. The MIA breakdown by wartime period (as of January 1995) is as follows: World War I, 3,350; World War II, 78,773; Korea, 8,177; Vietnam, 2,214; Persian Gulf, 13.

Sources: U.S. Department of Defense, *POW-MIA Fact Book*, Oct 1992; "American Prisoners of War in WWI, WWII, Korea, Vietnam, Persian Gulf, and Somalia," 1995, Annual Report prepared by Charles A. Stenger for U.S. Department of Veterans' Affairs.

Appendix 2

Prisoner of War Camps in North Vietnam

Camp	Location	Dates of Operation[1]
Bao Cao (Portholes)	Near Vinh	Sep 67—28 Aug 68
Bang Liet (Skid Row, Hughey, K-77)	5 miles SW of Hanoi	7 Jul 68—1 Jan 72
Citadel (Plantation)	N Central Hanoi	6 Jun 67—16 Mar 73
Cu Loc (Zoo) Annex	SW suburb of Hanoi	20 Sep 65—29 Mar 73 19 Oct 67—24 Aug 70
Dan Hoi (Faith)	9 miles NW of Hanoi	14 Jul 70—24 Nov 70
Duong Ke (Farnsworth, D-1)	18 miles SW of Hanoi	29 Aug 68—25 Nov 70
Hoa Lo (Hanoi Hilton) Heartbreak New Guy Village Vegas Unity	Central Hanoi	11 Aug 64—28 Mar 73 (open throughout) (open throughout) 26 Jan 67—5 Mar 73 24 Nov 70—4 Mar 73
Loung Lang (Dogpatch)	105 miles NE of Hanoi	14 May 72—31 Jan 73
Ministry of National Defense (Alcatraz)	N Central Hanoi	25 Oct 67—17 Aug 70
Mountain Camp (K-49)	50 miles N of Hanoi	12 Dec 71—28 Jan 73
Noi Coc (Rockpile, Stonewall)	30 miles S of Hanoi	21 Jun 71—14 Feb 73
Power Plant (Dirty Bird)	Northern Hanoi	25 Jun 67—25 Oct 67
Son Tay (Hope)	22 miles NW of Hanoi	23 May 68—14 Jul 70
Xom Ap Lo (Briarpatch)	35 miles W of Hanoi	31 Aug 65—2 Feb 67 5 Feb 71—9 Jul 71
Xom De (Countryside)	1 mile SE of Hanoi	16 Jan 73—6 Feb 73

[1] These are inclusive dates. In some instances there were brief closings and then reopenings, or intervals of reduced operation (and PW population) short of complete shutdowns.

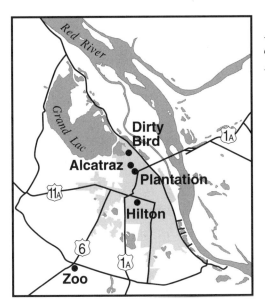

PW Prisons In and Around Hanoi

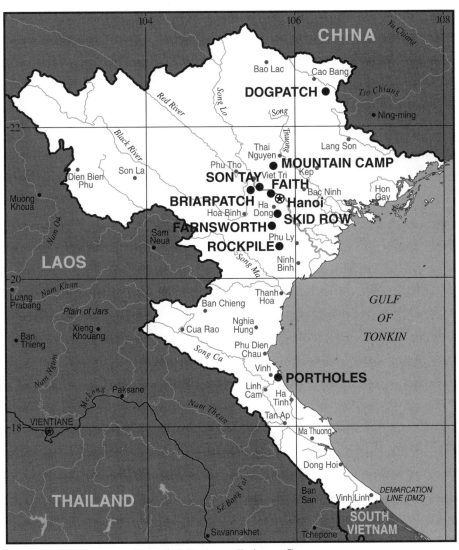

North Vietnam Prison Camps

Appendix 3

U.S. Personnel Captured in Southeast Asia, 1961-1973
(and Selected Foreign Nationals)

Name	Service	Capture Date	Release Date	Status
Abbott, John	N	660420		KR
Abbott, Joseph S Jr	F	670430	730218	RR
Abbott, Robert Archie	F	670430	730304	RR
Abbott, Wilfred Kesse	F	660905	730304	RR
Acosta, Hector Michael	F	721209	730329	RR
Adams, Samuel	F	651031		KK
Adkins, Cloden	V	680201	730305	RR
Agnew, Alfred Howard	N	721228	730329	RR
Agosto-Santos, Jose	M	670512	680123	RR
Aiken, Larry Delarnard	A	690513	690710	EE
Albert, Keith Alexander	A	700521	730212	RR
Alcorn, Wendell Reed	N	651222	730212	RR
Alexander, Fernando	F	721219	730329	RR
Allwine, David Franklin	A	710304	730327	RR
Alpers, John Hardesty Jr	F	721005	730329	RR
Alvarez, Everett Jr	N	640805	730212	RR

Service: A Army   F Air Force   M Marine Corps
       N Navy   V Civilian   W Foreign National

Status: KK Died in captivity   EE Escapee
       XX Presumptive finding   KR Died in captivity,
            of death   negotiated remains returned
       BR Body recovered   RR Returnee

Note: Information extracted from *DPMO Reference Document*, May 1997. Totals for military personnel captured and dying in captivity do not square exactly with the figures in Appendix 1 because of the inclusion of some and omission of other "discrepancy cases," where an individual was thought to be a prisoner for a day or two or even a few hours before dying, being killed, or disappearing. The treatment of such cases varies even among official sources and is constantly being updated based on new information, so that it is rare to find absolute consistency among PW lists produced at different times and by different agencies. Closure on the status of several civilians still awaits a final State Department determination; under the "status" column, these cases are indicated with a broken line.

Name	Service	Capture Date	Release Date	Status
Anderson, Gareth Laverne	N	670519	730304	RR
Anderson, John Thomas	A	680203	730305	RR
Anderson, John Wesley	F	721227	730212	RR
Anderson, Roger Dale	A	680103	680112	EE
Andrews, Anthony Charles	F	671017	730314	RR
Angus, William Kerr	M	720611	730328	RR
Anshus, Richard Cameron	A	710308	730327	RR
Anson, Robert	V	700803	700823	RR
Anton, Francis Gene	A	680105	730316	RR
Anzaldua, Jose Jesus Jr	M	700123	730327	RR
Archer, Bruce Raymond	M	680328	730316	RR
Arcuri, William Youl	F	721220	730212	RR
Arroyo-Baez, Gerasimo	A	690324		KR
Astorga, Jose Manuel	A	720402	730305	RR
Atterberry, Edwin Lee	F	670812		KR
Austin, William Renwick	F	671007	730314	RR
Ayres, Timothy Robert	F	720503	730328	RR
Badua, Candido Cardinez	W	680201	730305	RR
Bagley, Bobby Ray	F	670916	730314	RR
Bailey, James William	N	670628	730218	RR
Bailey, Lawrence Robert	A	610323	620815	RR
Baird, Bill Allen	A	680506	730305	RR
Baker, David Earle	F	720627	730212	RR
Baker, Elmo Clinnard	F	670823	730314	RR
Balagot, Arturo Mendoza	W	680201	730305	RR
Baldock, Frederick Charles	N	660317	730212	RR
Ballard, Arthur T Jr	F	660926	730304	RR
Ballenger, Orville Roger	A	610422	620815	RR
Barbay, Lawrence	F	660720	730304	RR
Barnett, Robert Warren	F	671003	730314	RR
Barrett, Thomas Joseph	F	651005	730212	RR
Barrows, Henry Charles	F	721219	730329	RR
Bartsch, Georg	W	690427		KK
Bates, Richard Lyman	F	721005	730329	RR
Baugh, William Joseph	F	670121	730304	RR
Bean, James Ellis	F	680103	730314	RR
Bean, William Raymond Jr	F	720523	730328	RR
Bedinger, Henry James	N	691122	730328	RR
Beekman, William David	F	720624	730328	RR
Beeler, Carroll Robert	N	720524	730328	RR
Beens, Lynn Richard	F	721221	730329	RR

Name	Service	Capture Date	Release Date	Status
Bell, James Franklin	N	651016	730212	RR
Benge, Michael	V	680128	730305	RR
Bennett, Harold George	A	641229		KK
Berg, Kile Dag	F	650727	730212	RR
Berger, James Robert	F	661202	730218	RR
Bernasconi, Louis Henry	F	721222	730329	RR
Biss, Robert Irving	F	661111	730304	RR
Black, Arthur Neil	F	650920	730212	RR
Black, Cole	N	660621	730212	RR
Black, Jon David	F	671027	680216	RR
Blevins, John Charles	F	660909	730304	RR
Bliss, Ronald Glenn	F	660904	730304	RR
Blood, Henry F	V	680201		KK
Bolstad, Richard Eugene	F	651106	730212	RR
Bomar, Jack Williamson	F	670204	730304	RR
Borling, John Lorin	F	660601	730212	RR
Boyd, Charles Graham	F	660422	730212	RR
Boyer, Terry Lee	F	671217	730314	RR
Brace, Ernest C	V	650521	730328	RR
Brady, Allen Colby	N	670119	730304	RR
Branch, Michael Patrick	A	680506	730316	RR
Brande, Harvey G	A	680207	730316	RR
Braswell, Donald Robert	A	670823	670824	EE
Brazelton, Michael Lee	F	660807	730304	RR
Breckner, William J Jr	F	720730	730329	RR
Brenneman, Richard Charles	F	671108	730314	RR
Brewer, Lee	A	680107	680108	EE
Bridger, Barry Burton	F	670123	730304	RR
Brigham, James W	A	680913	690101	RR
Brodak, John Warren	F	660814	730304	RR
Brookens, Norman J	V	680204	730212	RR
Brown, Charles A Jr	F	721219	730329	RR
Brown, Paul Gordon	M	680725	730314	RR
Browning, Ralph Thomas	F	660708	730212	RR
Brudno, Edward Alan	F	651018	730212	RR
Brunhaver, Richard Marvin	N	650824	730212	RR
Brunson, Cecil H	F	721012	730329	RR
Brunstrom, Alan Leslie	F	660422	730212	RR
Buchanan, Hubert Elliot	F	660916	730304	RR
Budd, Leonard R Jr	M	670821	730305	RR

Name	Service	Capture Date	Release Date	Status
Burdett, Edward Burke	F	671118		KR
Burer, Arthur William	F	660321	730212	RR
Burgess, Richard Gordon	M	660925	730305	RR
Burns, Donald Ray	F	661202	730304	RR
Burns, Frederick John	M	671225		KR
Burns, John Douglas	N	661004	730304	RR
Burns, Michael Thomas	F	680705	730314	RR
Burroughs, William David	F	660731	730304	RR
Butcher, Jack M	F	710324	730328	RR
Butler, Phillip Neal	N	650420	730212	RR
Butler, William Wallace	F	671120	730314	RR
Byrne, Ronald Edward Jr	F	650829	730212	RR
Byrns, William G	F	720523	730328	RR
Callaghan, Peter A	F	720621	730328	RR
Camacho, Issac	A	631124	650713	EE
Cameron, Kenneth Robbins	N	670518		KR
Camerota, Peter P	F	721222	730329	RR
Campbell, Burton Wayne	F	660701	730212	RR
Cannon, Francis Eugene	A	680108		KR
Carey, David Jay	N	670831	730314	RR
Carlson, Albert E	A	720407	730212	RR
Carpenter, Allen Russell	N	661101	730304	RR
Carpenter, Joe V	F	680215	680802	RR
Carrigan, Larry Edward	F	670823	730314	RR
Cassell, Harley M	A	680717	681219	RR
Cavaiani, Jon R	A	710605	730327	RR
Cayer, Marc Odilon	W	680201	730213	RR
Cerak, John P	F	720627	730328	RR
Certain, Robert G	F	721218	730329	RR
Chambers, Carl Dennis	F	670807	730314	RR
Chapman, Harlan Page	M	651105	730212	RR
Charles, Norris Alphonzo	N	711230	720925	RR
Chauncey, Arvin Ray	N	670531	730304	RR
Cheney, Kevin J	F	720701	730328	RR
Chenoweth, Robert Preston	A	680208	730316	RR
Cherry, Fred Vann	F	651022	730212	RR
Chesley, Larry James	F	660416	730212	RR
Chevalier, John R	A	680717	681219	RR
Chirichigno, Luis Genardo	A	691102	730327	RR
Christian, Michael Durham	N	670424	730304	RR

Name	Service	Capture Date	Release Date	Status
Cius, Frank E	M	670603	730305	RR
Clark, John Walter	F	670312	730218	RR
Clements, James Arlen	F	671009	730314	RR
Clower, Claude Douglas	N	671119	730314	RR
Cobeil, Earl Glenn	F	671105		KR
Coffee, Gerald Leonard	N	660203	730212	RR
Coker, George Thomas	N	660827	730304	RR
Collins, James Quincy	F	650902	730212	RR
Collins, Thomas Edward III	F	651018	730212	RR
Condon, James C	F	721228	730329	RR
Conlee, William W	F	721222	730329	RR
Connell, James Joseph	N	660715		KR
Cook, Donald Gilbert	M	641231		KK
Cook, James R	F	721226	730212	RR
Copeland, HC	F	670717	730314	RR
Cordier, Kenneth William	F	661202	730304	RR
Cormier, Arthur	F	651106	730212	RR
Cornthwaite, Thomas Guy	W	681105		KK
Coskey, Kenneth Leon	N	680906	730314	RR
Crafts, Charles	A	641229	670207	RR
Craner, Robert Roger	F	671220	730314	RR
Crayton, Render	N	660207	730212	RR
Crecca, Joseph	F	661122	730218	RR
Cronin, Michael Paul	N	670113	730304	RR
Crow, Frederick Austin	F	670326	730304	RR
Crowe, Winfred D	A	680717	681219	RR
Crowson, Frederick H	A	700502	730212	RR
Crumpler, Carl Boyette	F	680705	730314	RR
Curtis, Thomas Jerry	F	650920	730212	RR
Cusimano, Samuel B	F	721228	730329	RR
Cutter, James D	F	720217	730328	RR
Daigle, Glenn Henri	N	651222	730212	RR
Daly, James Alexander Jr	A	680109	730316	RR
Daniels, Verlyne Wayne	N	671026	730314	RR
Dat, Nguyen Quoc	W	660514	730319	RR
Daugherty, Lenard Edward	A	690511	730327	RR
Daughtrey, Robert Norlan	F	650802	730212	RR
Daves, Gary Lawrence	V	680201	730327	RR
Davies, John Owen	F	670204	730218	RR
Davis, Edward Anthony	N	650826	730212	RR

Name	Service	Capture Date	Release Date	Status
Davis, Thomas James	A	680311	730316	RR
Dawson, Donald	V	650401	650824	RR
Day, George Everette	F	670826	730314	RR
DeBruin, Eugene H	V	630905		– –
Deering, John Arthur	M	680203	730305	RR
DeLong, Joe Lynn	A	670518		KK
Deluca, Anthony J	N	700205	700228	RR
Dengler, Dieter	N	660201	660720	EE
Dennison, Terry Arden	N	660719		KR
Denton, Jeremiah Andrew	N	650718	730212	RR
Despiegler, Gale A	F	720415	730328	RR
Dexter, Bennie Lee	F	660509		KK
Dexter, Ronald James	A	670603		KK
DiBernardo, James Vincent	M	680203	730305	RR
Diehl, Bernhard	W	690427	730305	RR
Diehl, William C	F	671107		KR
Dierling, Edward A	A	680203	680223	EE
Dingee, David B	F	720627	730328	RR
Dodd, Joe Lee	V	651010	651025	EE
Dodge, Ward K	F	670705		KR
Dodson, James	M	660506	660618	EE
Donald, Myron Lee	F	680223	730314	RR
Doremus, Robert Bartsch	N	650824	730212	RR
Doss, Dale Walter	N	680317	730314	RR
Doughty, Daniel James	F	660402	730212	RR
Drabic, Peter E	A	680924	730316	RR
Dramesi, John Arthur	F	670402	730304	RR
Driscoll, Jerry Donald	F	660424	730212	RR
Drummond, David I	F	721222	730329	RR
Duart, David Henry	F	670218	730304	RR
Duffy, Charles J	V	610113		XX
Dunn, John Galbreath	A	680318	730212	RR
Dunn, John Howard	M	651207	730212	RR
Dusing, Charles Gale	F	651031		KK
Dutton, Richard Allen	F	671105	730314	RR
Eastman, Leonard Corbett	N	660621	730212	RR
Eckes, Walter W	M	660510	660618	EE
Eisenbraun, William F	A	650705		KK
Elander, William J Jr	F	720705	730329	RR
Elbert, Fred	M	680816	730316	RR

Name	Service	Capture Date	Release Date	Status
Elias, Edward K	F	720420	720925	RR
Elliott, Artice W	A	700426	730327	RR
Ellis, Jeffrey Thomas	F	671217	730314	RR
Ellis, Leon Francis	F	671107	730314	RR
Emberger, Collette	W	650401	650824	RR
Ensch, John C	N	720825	730329	RR
Estes, Edward Dale	N	680103	730314	RR
Ettmueller, Harry L	A	680203	730305	RR
Everett, David A	N	720827	730329	RR
Everson, David	F	670310	730304	RR
Fant, Robert St Clair	N	680725	730314	RR
Fellowes, John Heaphy	N	660827	730304	RR
Fer, John	F	670204	730304	RR
Ferguson, Walter Jr	A	680823		KK
Finlay, John Stewart	F	680428	730314	RR
Fisher, John B	A	690212	690311	RR
Fisher, Kenneth	F	671107	730314	RR
Fleenor, Kenneth Raymond	F	671217	730314	RR
Flesher, Hubert Kelly	F	661202	730218	RR
Flom, Fredric R	F	660808	730304	RR
Flora, Carroll E	A	670721	730305	RR
Flynn, John Peter	F	671027	730314	RR
Flynn, Robert J	N	670821	730315	RR
Forby, Willis Ellis	F	650920	730212	RR
Ford, David Edward	F	671119	730314	RR
Fowler, Henry Pope	F	670326	730218	RR
Francis, Richard L	F	720627	730328	RR
Frank, Martin S	A	670712	730305	RR
Franke, Fred Augustus	N	650824	730212	RR
Fraser, Kenneth J	F	720217	730328	RR
Frederick, John William	M	651207		KR
Friese, Lawrence Victor	M	680224	730314	RR
Frishman, Robert F	N	671024	690805	RR
Fritz, John J	V	690208	730212	RR
Fryett, George F	A	611226	620624	RR
Fuller, Robert Byron	N	670714	730304	RR
Fulton, Richard J	F	720613	730328	RR
Gabriel, James	A	620408		BR
Gaddis, Norman Carl	F	670512	730304	RR
Gaither, Ralph Ellis	N	651017	730212	RR

Name	Service	Capture Date	Release Date	Status
Galanti, Paul Edward	N	660617	730212	RR
Galati, Ralph W	F	720216	730328	RR
Gartley, Markham Ligon	N	680817	720925	RR
Garwood, Robert Russell	M	650928	790321	RR
Gauntt, William A	F	720813	730327	RR
Gaza, Ofelia	W	660624	670101	RR
Gaza, Vincente	W	660624		KK
Geloneck, Terry M	F	721220	730212	RR
George, James E Jr	A	680208		KK
Gerber, Daniel A	V	620530		– –
Gerndt, Gerald Lee	F	670823	730314	RR
Gideon, Willard Selleck	F	660807	730304	RR
Gillespie, Charles R	N	671024	730314	RR
Giroux, Peter J	F	721222	730212	RR
Glenn, Danny Elloy	N	661221	730304	RR
Glenn, Thomas Paul	N	700205	700228	RR
Godwin, Solomon Hughey	M	680205		KK
Goodermote, Wayne Keith	N	670813	730314	RR
Gostas, Theodore W	A	680201	730316	RR
Gotner, Norbert A	F	710203	730328	RR
Gough, James W	F	721228	730329	RR
Gouin, Donat Joseph	A	680203	730305	RR
Graening, Bruce A	A	670309	670318	EE
Grainger, Joseph W	V	640808		KR
Granger, Paul L	F	721220	730329	RR
Grant, David B	F	720624	730328	RR
Gray, David Fletcher	F	670123	730304	RR
Greene, Charles E	F	670311	730304	RR
Gregory, Kenneth R	A	680825	690526	RR
Griffin, James Lloyd	N	670519		KR
Grigsby, Donald E	A	680717	681219	RR
Grissett, Edwin R Jr	M	660122		KR
Groom, George Edward	A	620408	620501	RR
Grubb, Wilmer N	F	660126		KR
Gruters, Guy Dennis	F	671220	730314	RR
Grzyb, Robert H	V	671210		KK
Guarino, Lawrence Nicholas	F	650614	730212	RR
Guenther, Lynn	F	711226	730212	RR
Guffey, Jerry	A	690304	690304	EE
Guggenberger, Gary John	A	690114	730212	RR

Name	Service	Capture Date	Release Date	Status
Gurnsey, Earl F	A	681127	690106	RR
Guttersen, Laird	F	680223	730314	RR
Guy, Theodore Wilson	F	680322	730316	RR
Haines, Collins Henry	N	670605	730304	RR
Hall, George Robert	F	650927	730212	RR
Hall, Keith Norman	F	680110	730314	RR
Hall, Thomas Renwick	N	670610	730304	RR
Halyburton, Porter Alex	N	651017	730212	RR
Hamilton, Walter D	M	651018	651029	EE
Hammond, Dennis Wayne	M	680208		KK
Hanson, Gregg O	F	720613	730328	RR
Hanton, Thomas J	F	720627	730328	RR
Hardman, William Morgan	N	670821	730314	RR
Hardy, William H	A	670629	730212	RR
Harker, David Northrup	A	680108	730305	RR
Harnavee, Chi Charn	W	650521	740900	RR
Harris, Carlyle Smith	F	650404	730212	RR
Harris, Jessie B	A	690608	691020	RR
Hartman, Richard Danner	N	670718		KR
Hatch, Paul G	A	690824	690825	EE
Hatcher, David Burnett	F	660530	730212	RR
Hawley, Edwin A Jr	F	720217	730212	RR
Hayhurst, Robert A	A	680203	680223	EE
Heeren, Jerome D	F	720911	730329	RR
Hefel, Daniel	A	700205	730327	RR
Hegdahl, Douglas B	N	670406	690805	RR
Heggen, Keith R	F	721221		KR
Heilig, John	N	660505	730212	RR
Heiliger, Donald Lester	F	670515	730218	RR
Helle, Robert R	M	680424	730316	RR
Henderson, Alexander	V	680201	730316	RR
Henderson, William J	F	720403	730327	RR
Henry, Lee Edward	A	680717	681219	RR
Henry, Nathan Barney	A	670712	730305	RR
Herlik, Querin E	A	690212	690311	RR
Hertz, Gustav	V	650202		KK
Hess, Jay Criddle	F	670824	730314	RR
Hestand, James Hardy	A	710317	730212	RR
Hickerson, James Martin	N	671222	730314	RR
Higdon, Kenneth H	N	721221	730212	RR

Name	Service	Capture Date	Release Date	Status
Hildebrand, Leland	F	711218	730328	RR
Hill, Howard John	F	671216	730314	RR
Hinckley, Robert Bruce	F	680118	730314	RR
Hiteshew, James Edward	F	670311	730304	RR
Hivner, James Otis	F	651005	730212	RR
Hoffman, David Wesley	N	711230	730328	RR
Hoffson, Arthur Thomas	F	680817	730314	RR
Holt, Dewey Thomas	V	670823	670824	EE
Horinek, Ramon Anton	F	671025	730314	RR
Horio, Thomas Teruo	A	690511	730327	RR
Hrdlicka, David Louis	F	650518		XX
Hubbard, Edward Lee	F	660720	730304	RR
Hudson, Henry M	V	651220		EE
Hudson, Robert M	F	721226	730329	RR
Hughes, James Lindberg	F	670505	730304	RR
Hughey, Kenneth Raymond	F	670706	730304	RR
Hunsucker, James	N	700205	700228	RR
Hutton, James Leo	N	651016	730212	RR
Hyatt, Leo Gregory	N	670813	730314	RR
Hyland, Charles Keith	W	680206	681125	RR
Ingvalson, Roger Dean	F	680528	730314	RR
Intoratat, Phisit	W	630905	670107	EE
Iodice, Frank C	M	680530	680601	EE
Jackson, Charles A	F	720624	730212	RR
Jackson, James E	A	660705	671111	RR
Jacquez, Juan L	A	690511	730327	RR
James, Charlie Negus	N	680518	730314	RR
James, Gobel Dale	F	680715	730314	RR
Jayroe, Julius Skinner	F	670119	730304	RR
Jefcoat, Carl H	F	721227	730329	RR
Jeffrey, Robert Duncan	F	651220	730212	RR
Jenkins, Harry Tarleton	N	651113	730212	RR
Jensen, Jay Robert	F	670218	730218	RR
Johnson, Bobby Louis	A	680825	730212	RR
Johnson, Edward Robert	A	640721	671111	RR
Johnson, Harold E	F	670430	730304	RR
Johnson, Kenneth	F	711218	730314	RR
Johnson, Richard E	F	721218	730329	RR
Johnson, Samuel Robert	F	660416	730212	RR
Johnson, Sandra	V	680201	680331	RR

Name	Service	Capture Date	Release Date	Status
Jones, Edwin D	V	651220		EE
Jones, Murphy Neal	F	660629	730212	RR
Jones, Robert Campbell	F	680118	730314	RR
Jones, Thomas N	A	680825	690101	RR
Kalil, Tanos	V	690208		KK
Kari, Paul Anthony	F	650620	730212	RR
Kasler, James Helms	F	660808	730304	RR
Kavanaugh, Abel L	M	680424	730316	RR
Kay, Emmet James	V	730507	740918	RR
Keesee, Bobby Joe	V	700918	730314	RR
Keirn, Richard Paul	F	650724	730212	RR
Kerber, Marie Therese	W	690427		KK
Kernan, Joseph Eugene	N	720507	730328	RR
Kerns, Gail M	A	690327	730305	RR
Kerr, Michael Scott	F	670116	730304	RR
Key, Wilson Denver	N	671117	730314	RR
Kientzler, Phillip A	N	730127	730327	RR
Kirk, Thomas Henry	F	671028	730314	RR
Kittinger, Joseph W Jr	F	720511	730328	RR
Kjome, Michael H	V	680131	730212	RR
Klomann, Thomas J	F	721220	730212	RR
Klusmann, Charles F	N	640606	640831	EE
Knutson, Rodney Allen	N	651017	730212	RR
Kobashigawa, Tom Y	A	700205	730327	RR
Kopfman, Theodore Frank	N	660615	730212	RR
Kortmann, Hindrika	W	690427		KK
Kramer, Galand Dwight	F	670119	730212	RR
Kramer, Terry L	A	680717	681219	RR
Krause, Arthur E	V	630608	631118	RR
Kroboth, Alan J	M	720707	730327	RR
Kuhnen, Marie Renate	W	680304	690301	RR
Kula, James D	F	720729	730329	RR
Kushner, Floyd Harold	A	671130	730316	RR
Labeau, Michael H	F	721226	730329	RR
Lamar, James Lasley	F	660506	730212	RR
Lane, Michael Christopher	F	661202	730218	RR
Larson, Gordon Albert	F	670505	730304	RR
Lasiter, Carl William	F	680205	730314	RR
Latella, George F	F	721006	730329	RR
Latendresse, Thomas B	N	720527	730328	RR

Name	Service	Capture Date	Release Date	Status
Latham, James D	F	721005	730329	RR
Lawrence, William Porter	N	670628	730304	RR
Lebert, Ronald Merl	F	680114	730314	RR
LeBlanc, Louis E Jr	F	721222	730329	RR
Lehnrn, Gary Robert	N	700205	700228	RR
Lehrman, Ronald John	A	680520	680610	RR
Lengyel, Lauren Robert	F	670809	730314	RR
Lenker, Michael Robert	A	680208	730316	RR
Leonard, Edward W	F	680531	730328	RR
Leopold, Stephen Ryder	A	680509	730305	RR
Lerscth, Roger G	N	720906	730212	RR
Lesesne, Henry D	N	720711	730329	RR
Lewis, Earl Gardner	N	671024	730314	RR
Lewis, Frank D	F	721228	730329	RR
Lewis, Keith H	F	721005	730329	RR
Lewis, Robert	A	680105	730305	RR
Ligon, Vernon Peyton	F	671119	730314	RR
Lilly, Warren E	F	651106	730212	RR
Lockhart, Hayden James	F	650302	730212	RR
Logan, Donald K	F	720705	730329	RR
Lollar, James L	F	721221	730329	RR
Long, Julius Wollen Jr	A	680512	730316	RR
Long, Stephen G	F	690228	730328	RR
Low, James Frederick	F	671216	680802	RR
Luna, Jose David	F	670310	730304	RR
Lurie, Alan Pierce	F	660613	730212	RR
Lyon, James Michael	A	700205		KK
MacPhail, Don A	A	690208	730316	RR
Madden, Roy Jr	F	721220	730212	RR
Madison, Thomas Mark	F	670419	730304	RR
Makowski, Louis Frank	F	661006	730304	RR
Malo, Isaako F	A	710424	730327	RR
Manhard, Philip W	V	680201	730316	RR
Marchand, Wayne	A	620408		BR
Marshall, Marion A	F	720703	730329	RR
Martin, Donald Eugene	A	680302	680414	EE
Martin, Duane Whitney	F	650920		KK
Martin, Edward Holmes	N	670709	730304	RR
Martini, Michael R	F	721220	730329	RR
Marvel, Jerry Wendell	M	680224	730314	RR

Name	Service	Capture Date	Release Date	Status
Maslowski, Daniel F	A	700502	730212	RR
Masterson, Frederick J	N	720711	730329	RR
Mastin, Ronald Lambert	F	670116	730304	RR
Matagulay, Roque S	A	620723	621224	RR
Matheny, David P	N	671005	680216	RR
Matsui, Melvin K	F	720729	730329	RR
Mattix, Sam	V	721027	730328	RR
Mayall, William T	F	721222	730329	RR
Mayhew, William John	N	680817	730314	RR
McCain, John Sidney	N	671026	730314	RR
McClure, Claude D	A	631124	651128	RR
McCuistion, Michael K	F	670508	730304	RR
McCullough, Ralph W	A	680717	681219	RR
McDaniel, Eugene Baker	N	670519	730304	RR
McDaniel, Norman Alexander	F	660720	730212	RR
McDow, Richard H	F	720627	730328	RR
McGrath, John Michael	N	670630	730304	RR
McKamey, John Bryan	N	650602	730212	RR
McKnight, George Grigsby	F	651106	730212	RR
McManus, Kevin Joseph	F	670614	730218	RR
McMillan, Isiah	A	680311	730316	RR
McMorrow, John P	N	610515	620817	RR
McMurray, Cordine	A	670712	730305	RR
McMurray, Frederick C	F	720912	730329	RR
McMurry, William G	A	680207	730316	RR
McNish, Thomas Mitchell	F	660904	730304	RR
McSwain, George Palmer	N	660728	730304	RR
Means, William Harley	F	660720	730212	RR
Mechenbier, Edward John	F	670614	730218	RR
Mecleary, Read Blaine	N	670526	730304	RR
Mehl, James Patrick	N	670530	730304	RR
Mehrer, Gustav Alois	A	681225	730316	RR
Merritt, Raymond James	F	650916	730212	RR
Metzger, William John	N	670519	730304	RR
Meyer, Alton Benno	F	670426	730304	RR
Meyer, Lewis E	V	680201	730327	RR
Miller, Edison Wainright	M	671013	730212	RR
Miller, Edwin Frank	N	680522	730314	RR
Miller, Roger Alan	A	700415	730305	RR
Milligan, Joseph Edward	F	670520	730218	RR

Name	Service	Capture Date	Release Date	Status
Mitchell, Archie E	V	620530		– –
Mobley, Joseph Scott	N	680624	730314	RR
Moe, Thomas Nelson	F	680116	730314	RR
Molinare, Albert R	N	720427	730328	RR
Monahan, Robert W	V	660527	670101	RR
Monlux, Harold Deloss	F	661111	730304	RR
Montague, Paul Joseph	M	680328	730316	RR
Moon, Walter Hugh	A	610422		KK
Moore, Dennis Anthony	N	651027	730212	RR
Moore, Ernest Milvin	N	670311	730304	RR
Moore, Thomas	F	651031		KK
Morgan, Gary L	F	721222	730329	RR
Morgan, Herschel Scott	F	650403	730212	RR
Morrow, Michael	V	700507	700615	RR
Mott, David P	F	720519	730327	RR
Mullen, Richard Dean	N	670106	730304	RR
Mulligan, James Alfred	N	660320	730212	RR
Murphy, John S Jr	F	720608	730327	RR
Myers, Armand Jesse	F	660601	730212	RR
Myers, Glenn Leo	F	670809	730314	RR
Nagahiro, James Y	F	721221	730329	RR
Nakagawa, Gordon R	N	721221	730329	RR
Nasmyth, John Herbert	F	660904	730218	RR
Naughton, Robert John	N	670518	730304	RR
Neco-Quinones, Felix V	A	680716	730212	RR
Nelson, Marjorie	V	680201	680331	RR
Nelson, Steven N	M	680107	680121	EE
Neuens, Martin James	F	660812	730304	RR
Newcomb, Wallace Grant	F	670803	730314	RR
Newell, Stanley Arthur	A	670712	730305	RR
Newingham, James A	V	690208	730212	RR
Newsom, Benjamin B	F	660723		KR
Nichols, Aubrey Allen	N	720519	730328	RR
Niehouse, Daniel Lee	V	661125		KK
Nix, Cowan Glenn	F	661001	730304	RR
Norrington, Giles Roderick	N	680505	730314	RR
Norris, Thomas Elmer	F	670812	730314	RR
North, Joseph Jr	M	651018	651029	EE
North, Kenneth Walter	F	660801	730304	RR
Nowicki, James Ernest	A	691102	730327	RR

Name	Service	Capture Date	Release Date	Status
O'Connor, Michael Francis	A	680204	730305	RR
Odell, Donald Eugene	F	671017	730314	RR
Olsen, Betty Ann	V	680201		KK
Olsen, Robert F	V	680201	730327	RR
O'Neil, James W	F	720929	730329	RR
Oppel, Lloyd	W	721027	730328	RR
Ortiz-Rivera, Luis A	A	661227	680123	RR
Osborne, Dale Harrison	N	680923	730212	RR
Osburn, Laird P	A	690212	690311	RR
Overly, Norris M	F	670911	680216	RR
Padgett, James P	F	720511	730328	RR
Page, Jasper N	F	651030	651104	EE
Page, Russell J	V	680201	730316	RR
Paige, Gordon Curtis	N	720722	730329	RR
Parks, Joe	A	641222		KK
Parrott, Thomas Vance	F	670812	730314	RR
Parsels, John William	A	700205	730327	RR
Peel, Robert D	F	650531	730212	RR
Pemberton, Gene T	F	660723		KR
Penn, Michael Gene Jr	N	720806	730329	RR
Perkins, Glendon William	F	660720	730212	RR
Perricone, Richard Robert	A	670712	730305	RR
Peterson, Douglas Brian	F	660910	730304	RR
Peterson, Michael T	A	691102	691210	RR
Pfister, James F Jr	A	680105	730305	RR
Pirie, James Glenn	N	670622	730218	RR
Pitchford, John Joseph	F	651220	730212	RR
Pitzer, Daniel L	A	631029	671111	RR
Plumb, Joseph Charles	N	670519	730218	RR
Polfer, Clarence	N	720507	730328	RR
Pollack, Melvin	F	670706	730304	RR
Pollard, Ben M	F	670515	730304	RR
Pond, Elizabeth	V	700507	700615	RR
Port, William D	A	680112		KR
Potter, Albert J	M	680530	680601	EE
Prather, Phillip Dean	A	710308	730327	RR
Price, Donald E	A	680717	681219	RR
Price, Larry D	F	720730	730329	RR
Profilet, Leo Twyman	N	670821	730314	RR
Pryor, Robert J	A	690212	690311	RR

Name	Service	Capture Date	Release Date	Status
Purcell, Benjamin H	A	680208	730327	RR
Purcell, Robert Baldwin	F	650727	730212	RR
Purrington, Frederick R	N	661020	730218	RR
Pyle, Darrel Edwin	F	660613	730212	RR
Pyle, Thomas Shaw	F	660807	730304	RR
Quinn, Francis	A	620408	620501	RR
Raebel, Dale V	N	720817	730329	RR
Ragsdale, Thomas	V	680202		KK
Ramsey, Douglas	V	660117	730212	RR
Randall, Robert I	N	720711	730329	RR
Randcr, Donald J	A	680201	730327	RR
Ratzlaff, Brian M	F	720911	730329	RR
Ratzlaff, Richard Raymond	N	660320	730212	RR
Ray, James Edwin	F	660508	730212	RR
Ray, James Michael	A	680318		KK
Ray, Johnnie L	A	720408	730212	RR
Ray, Michele	W	670117	670206	RR
Rayford, King David Jr	A	670702	730316	RR
Reeder, William S	A	720509	730327	RR
Rehe, Richard Raymond	A	680109		KK
Rehmann, David George	N	661202	730212	RR
Reich, William J	F	720511	730328	RR
Reilly, Edward Daniel Jr	A	660426		KR
Reynolds, Jon Anzuena	F	651128	730212	RR
Riate, Alfonso Ray	M	670426	730316	RR
Rice, Charles Donald	N	671026	730314	RR
Ridgeway, Ronald Lewis	M	680225	730316	RR
Riess, Charles F	F	721224	730328	RR
Ringsdorf, Herbert Benjamin	F	661111	730218	RR
Risner, Richard F	M	680820	680822	EE
Risner, Robinson	F	650916	730212	RR
Rivers, Wendell Burke	N	650910	730212	RR
Robinson, Paul K	F	720701	730328	RR
Robinson, William Andrew	F	650920	730212	RR
Rodriquez, Ferdinand A	A	680414	730212	RR
Roha, Michael R	M	680107	680121	EE
Rollins, David John	N	670514	730304	RR
Rollins, James U	V	680205	730212	RR
Roraback, Kenneth M	A	631124		KK
Rose, George A	F	720621	730328	RR

Name	Service	Capture Date	Release Date	Status
Rose, Joseph	A	680208	730305	RR
Rottmers, Peter Schrader	W	690401	711108	RR
Rowe, James Nicholas	A	631029	681231	EE
Rudloff, Stephen A	N	720510	730328	RR
Ruhling, Mark John	F	681123	730314	RR
Rumble, Wesley L	F	680428	690805	RR
Runyan, Albert Edward	F	660429	730212	RR
Rushton, Thomas	V	680201	730327	RR
Russell, Kay	N	670519	730304	RR
Rutledge, Howard Elmer	N	651128	730212	RR
Salley, James Jr	A	710331		KK
Sandvick, Robert James	F	660807	730304	RR
Sawhill, Robert Ralston	F	670823	730314	RR
Scales, Thomas R	V	660527	670101	RR
Schierman, Wesley Duane	F	650828	730212	RR
Schmidt, Norman	F	660901		KR
Schoeffel, Peter vanRuyter	N	671004	730314	RR
Schrump, Raymond Cecil	A	680523	730212	RR
Schulz, Paul Henry	N	671116	730314	RR
Schumann, John Robert	A	650616		KK
Schweitzer, Robert James	N	680105	730314	RR
Schwertfeger, William R	F	720216	730328	RR
Schwinn, Monika	W	690427	730305	RR
Seeber, Bruce G	F	651005	730212	RR
Seek, Brian J	F	720705	730329	RR
Sehorn, James Eldon	F	671214	730314	RR
Sexton, John C	A	690812	711008	RR
Shanahan, Joseph Francis	F	680815	730314	RR
Shankel, William Leonard	N	651223	730212	RR
Shark, Earl E	A	680912		KK
Shattuck, Lewis Wiley	F	660711	730212	RR
Shelton, Charles Ervin	F	650429		XX
Shepard, Vernon C	A	691102	691210	RR
Sherman, Robert C	M	670624		KR
Shingaki, Tamotsu	F	720819	730329	RR
Shively, James Richard	F	670505	730218	RR
Shore, Edward R Jr	A	610515	620815	RR
Shumaker, Robert Harper	N	650211	730212	RR
Shuman, Edwin Arthur	N	680317	730314	RR
Sienicki, Theodore S	F	720503	730328	RR

Name	Service	Capture Date	Release Date	Status
Sigler, Gary Richard	F	670429	730304	RR
Sijan, Lance P	F	671109		KR
Sima, Thomas William	F	651015	730212	RR
Simms, Harold D	A	680717	681219	RR
Simonet, Kenneth Adrian	F	680118	730314	RR
Simpson, James Edward	V	681105		KK
Simpson, Richard T	F	721218	730329	RR
Singleton, Jerry Allen	F	651106	730212	RR
Sirion, Praphan X	W	660326	730304	RR
Smith, Bradley Edsel	N	660325	730212	RR
Smith, Dewey Lee	F	670602	730304	RR
Smith, Donald Glenn	A	680513	690101	RR
Smith, George Edward	A	631124	651128	RR
Smith, Homer Leroy	N	670520		KR
Smith, Mark A	A	720407	730212	RR
Smith, Philip E	F	650920	730315	RR
Smith, Richard Eugene	F	671025	730314	RR
Smith, Wayne Ogden	F	680118	730314	RR
Smith, William M	A	690303		KK
Sooter, David William	A	670217	730305	RR
Souder, James Burton	N	720427	730328	RR
Southwick, Charles Everett	N	670514	730304	RR
Sparks, John G	A	680424	730316	RR
Spaulding, Richard	V	680201	730316	RR
Spencer, Larry Howard	N	660218	730212	RR
Spencer, William A	F	720705	730329	RR
Sponeyberger, Robert D	F	721222	730329	RR
Spoon, Donald Ray	F	670121	730304	RR
Springman, Richard	A	700525	730212	RR
Stackhouse, Charles David	N	670425	730304	RR
Stafford, Hugh Allen	N	670831	730314	RR
Stamm, Ernest Albert	N	681125		KR
Stark, Lawrence J	V	680201	730305	RR
Stark, William Robert	N	670519	730304	RR
Stavast, John Edward	F	670917	730314	RR
Stephenson, Henry John	W	660913		KK
Sterling, Thomas James	F	670419	730304	RR
Stier, Theodore Gerhard	N	671119	730314	RR
Stirm, Robert Lewis	F	671027	730314	RR
Stischer, Walter Morris	F	680413	730328	RR

Name	Service	Capture Date	Release Date	Status
Stockdale, James Bond	N	650909	730212	RR
Stockman, Hervey Studdie	F	670611	730304	RR
Storey, Thomas Gordon	F	670116	730304	RR
Storz, Ronald Edward	F	650428		KR
Stratton, Richard Allen	N	670105	730304	RR
Strickland, James H	A	680108	691105	RR
Stutz, Leroy William	F	661202	730304	RR
Sullivan, Dwight Everett	F	671017	730314	RR
Sullivan, Timothy Bernard	N	671116	730314	RR
Sumpter, Thomas Wrenne	F	680114	730314	RR
Sweeney, Jon M	M	690219	700817	RR
Swindle, Orson George	M	661111	730304	RR
Sykes, Derri	A	680109		KK
Tabb, Robert Ernest	A	700412	730327	RR
Tadios, Leonard Masayon	A	641211		KK
Tallaferro, William P	M	680206	680213	EE
Talley, Bernard Leo	F	660910	730304	RR
Talley, William H	F	720511	730328	RR
Tangeman, Richard George	N	680505	730314	RR
Tanner, Charles Nels	N	661009	730304	RR
Taylor, William B	A	680320	680506	EE
Tellier, Dennis A	M	690619	730327	RR
Temperley, Russell Edward	F	671027	730314	RR
Terrell, Irby David	F	680114	730314	RR
Terrill, Philip B	A	710331		KK
Terry, Ross Randle	N	661009	730304	RR
Tester, Jerry Albert	A	680520	680610	RR
Thomas, William E	M	720519	730327	RR
Thompson, Dennis L	A	680207	730305	RR
Thompson, Floyd James	A	640326	730316	RR
Thompson, Fred N	F	680320	680802	RR
Thornton, Gary Lynn	N	670220	730304	RR
Thorsness, Leo Keith	F	670430	730304	RR
Tinsley, Coy R	A	690309	691105	RR
Tomes, Jack Harvey	F	660707	730212	RR
Torkelson, Loren H	F	670429	730304	RR
Towery, Herman	A	641022		BR
Trautman, Konrad Wigand	F	671005	730314	RR
Triebel, Theodore W	N	720827	730329	RR
Trimble, Jack R	F	721227	730329	RR

Name	Service	Capture Date	Release Date	Status
Tschudy, William Michael	N	650718	730212	RR
Tyler, Charles Robert	F	670823	730314	RR
Uom, Chem B	W	640818	730304	RR
Utecht, Richard W	V	680204	730212	RR
Uyeyama, Terry Jun	F	680518	730314	RR
Van Bendegom, James Lee	A	670712		KK
Van Loan, Jack Lee	F	670520	730304	RR
Vanputten, Thomas	A	680211	690417	EE
Varnado, Michael B	A	700502		KR
Vaughan, Samuel R	F	711218	730328	RR
Vavroch, Duane P	F	721226	730329	RR
Venanzi, Gerald Santo	F	670917	730314	RR
Versace, Humbert Roque	A	631029		KK
Vietti, Eleanor	V	620530		– –
Vissotzky, Raymond Walton	F	671119	730314	RR
Vogel, Richard Dale	F	670522	730304	RR
Vohden, Raymond Arthur	N	650403	730212	RR
Waddell, Dewey Wayne	F	670705	730304	RR
Waggoner, Robert Frost	F	660912	730304	RR
Waldhaus, Richard G	V	710804	730212	RR
Walker, Hubert C	F	680114	730314	RR
Walker, Michael James	N	700205	700228	RR
Walker, Orien J	A	650523		KK
Wallingford, Kenneth	A	720407	730212	RR
Walsh, James P	M	720926	730212	RR
Walters, Jack	N	670519		KR
Waltman, Donald G	F	660919	730304	RR
Wanat, George K Jr	A	720408	730212	RR
Ward, Brian H	F	721227	730329	RR
Warner, James Hoie	M	671013	730314	RR
Watkins, Willie A	A	680109	691105	RR
Watt, George	W	670901	700802	RR
Weatherman, Earl C	M	671108		KK
Weaver, Eugene	V	680201	730316	RR
Webb, Catherine M	W	710407	710430	RR
Webb, Ronald John	F	670611	730304	RR
Wells, Kenneth	F	711218	730328	RR
Wells, Norman Louross	F	660829	730304	RR
Wendell, John Henry	F	660807	730304	RR

Name	Service	Capture Date	Release Date	Status
Weskamp, Robert L	F	670425		KR
Wheat, David Robert	N	651017	730212	RR
White, Robert Thomas	A	691115	730401	RR
Wideman, Robert Earl	N	670506	730304	RR
Wieland, Carl T	N	721220	730329	RR
Wilber, Walter Eugene	N	680616	730212	RR
Williams, James W	F	720520	730328	RR
Williams, Lewis Irvng	N	670424	730304	RR
Williams, Richard F	A	680108		KR
Willis, Charles E	V	680201	730327	RR
Wilmoth, Floyd A	A	680717	681219	RR
Wilson, Glenn Hubert	F	670807	730314	RR
Wilson, Hal K	F	721219	730329	RR
Wilson, William W	F	721222	730329	RR
Winn, David William	F	680809	730314	RR
Wolfkill, Grant	V	610515	620815	RR
Womack, Sammie Norman	A	661008	670207	RR
Woods, Brian Dunstan	N	680918	730212	RR
Woods, Robert Deane	N	661012	730304	RR
Wright, Buddy	A	680922	681006	EE
Writer, Lawrence Daniel	F	680215	730314	RR
Young, James Faulds	F	660706	730212	RR
Young, John Arthur	A	680131	730316	RR
Young, Myron A	F	721012	730329	RR
Young, Robert M	A	700502		KK
Yuill, John H	F	721222	730329	RR
Zawtocki, Joseph S Jr	M	680208		KR
Ziegler, Roy Esper II	A	680208	730305	RR
Zuberbuhler, Rudolph U	F	720912	730329	RR
Zuhoski, Charles Peter	N	670731	730314	RR
Zupp, Klaus H	A	680717	681219	RR

Notes

Unless otherwise indicated, all documents and other unpublished materials, in original or copy form, are in the OSD Historical Office PW Collection (OSD Hist). Individual prisoner files are cited without reference to the particular source document where privacy restrictions apply. Full citations for published works appear in the bibliography.

1. THE HISTORICAL SETTING

1. *The Daily Worker* (London) of 11 August 1932 carried an obituary of Nguyen Ai Quoc, which became a cover for Ho Chi Minh's activities.

2. Two biographies of Ho Chi Minh written from disparate viewpoints are Nguyen Khac Huyen's *Vision Accomplished? The Enigma of Ho Chi Minh*, by a non-Communist Vietnamese expatriate to the United States, and Jean Lacouture's sympathetic *Ho Chi Minh: A Political Biography*. For a more balanced if somewhat simplistic estimate of Ho, see Jules Archer, *Ho Chi Minh: Legend of Hanoi*.

3. There are a number of excellent histories that examine both the political and military aspects of the Franco-Viet Minh War. On the background to the war, see P. J. Honey, *Genesis of a Tragedy*; Ellen J. Hammer, *The Struggle for Indochina*; John T. McAlister, Jr., *Vietnam: The Origins of Revolution*; Joseph Buttinger, *Vietnam: A Dragon Embattled*, vol 1, *From Colonialism to the Vietminh*. On the progress of the war itself, see Edgar O'Ballance, *The Indo-China War, 1945-1954: A Study in Guerilla Warfare*; Buttinger, vol 2, *Vietnam at War*; and the classic eyewitness account by Bernard B. Fall, *Street Without Joy: Indochina at War, 1946-54*. See also Ronald H. Spector, *Advice and Support: The Early Years, 1941-1960*, chs 3-10 passim, which provides a useful chronicle of the Franco-Viet Minh War in the context of early U.S. involvement in Vietnam.

4. The best accounts of Dien Bien Phu are Bernard B. Fall, *Hell in a Very Small Place: The Siege of Dien Bien Phu*; and Jules Roy, *The Battle of Dienbienphu*, translated by Robert Baldick.

5. For the roots of U.S. involvement in Vietnam in the postwar period, see *The U.S. Government and the Vietnam War, Executive and Legislative Roles and Relationships: Part I, 1945-1961*, Report of the Senate Foreign Relations Committee, 98 Cong, 2 sess (Apr 84), chs 2 and 3; Russell H. Fifield, *Americans in Southeast Asia: The Roots of Commitment*, 103-27, 173-204; Marvin Kalb and Elie Abel, *Roots of Involvement: The U.S. in Asia, 1784-1971*, ch 3; Steven L. Rearden, *History of the Office of the Secretary of Defense*, vol 1, *The Formative Years, 1947-1950*, 267-72; Archimedes L. A. Patti, *Why Viet Nam?*, ch 36. On the question of U.S. intervention at Dien Bien Phu, see Spector, *Advice and Support*, 182-214; *U.S. Government and the Vietnam War: Part I, 1945-1961*, ch 4; Fifield, *Americans in Southeast Asia*, 190-204; Dominique Moisi, "The Dienbienphu Crisis: American and French Behavior," Wilson Center International

621

Security Studies Program, Working Paper No 1 (1978?). *The Pentagon Papers: The Defense Department History of United States Decisionmaking in Vietnam*, Senator Gravel Edition, vol 1, chs 1, 2, and 4, cover these early years, including the debate over whether to intervene at Dien Bien Phu.

6. The most comprehensive treatment of the Geneva settlement is Robert F. Randle, *Geneva 1954: The Settlement of the Indochinese War*. See also Joseph Buttinger, *Vietnam: A Political History*, 369-83; Fifield, *Americans in Southeast Asia*, 207-26; Kalb and Abel, *Roots of Involvement*, 84-89; *Pentagon Papers* (Gravel ed), vol 1, ch 3; and, for a reappraisal, Richard H. Immerman, "The United States and the Geneva Conference of 1954: A New Look," *Diplomatic History* (Winter 90), 43-66.

7. The "falling domino" concept, in one metaphorical form or another, had for years been used by hardliners to rationalize containment; it quickly gained currency after the Eisenhower remark to a reporter on 7 April 1954, printed in *Public Papers of the Presidents of the United States: Dwight D. Eisenhower, 1954*, 383. Eisenhower later repeated the notion in *Mandate for Change: The White House Years, 1953-1956*, 333: ". . . If Indochina fell, not only Thailand but Burma and Malaya would be threatened, with added risks to East Pakistan and South Asia as well as to all Indonesia." The best treatment of the transition from French to American stewardship during these years is Spector, *Advice and Support*, chs 12-16. For a trenchant account of Diem's path to power, see Buttinger, *Vietnam: A Political History*, 384-415. See also *Pentagon Papers* (Gravel ed), vol 1, ch 4. Eisenhower's October 1954 message to Diem is in *Eisenhower Public Papers, 1954*, 948-49; for background, see "The United States Offer of Direct Military Assistance to South Vietnam: Background and Origins of the Eisenhower Letter to Diem of October 23, 1954," Research Project No 988, Sep 70, Hist Office, Dept of State.

8. Historians continue to argue over the extent of North Vietnamese complicity in the South Vietnam insurgency, some maintaining that Ho merely lent support to a spontaneous uprising in the South, others contending that Ho orchestrated events from the beginning. For a discerning assessment, see Guenter Lewy, *America in Vietnam*, 38-41. The U.S. State Department issued a report in February 1965 documenting the case for *Aggression From the North: The Record of North Viet-Nam's Campaign to Conquer South Viet-Nam.* An entire chapter is devoted to the origins of the insurgency in *Pentagon Papers* (Gravel ed), vol 1, ch 5.

9. David Halberstam in *The Best and the Brightest*, chs 9-15, discusses the debate within the Kennedy administration between a Ball-Harriman faction at State that was opposed to the use of U.S. troops in Vietnam (emphasizing the political nature of the conflict) and McNamara and the Joint Chiefs at Defense (who recommended in November 1961 that combat troops be introduced); the key role played by Walt W. Rostow and General Maxwell D. Taylor and their October 1961 fact-finding mission in persuading the president to expand the American commitment; and Kennedy's own self-doubts that yielded to a compromise whereby he decided to send additional U.S. support units and advisers but not combat troops. On Kennedy's soul-searching in the months prior to his assassination in November 1963, see also Kalb and Abel, *Roots of Involvement*, 142-51. William J. Rust, *Kennedy in Vietnam*, examines the administration's Vietnam policy and speculates on what course Kennedy might have pursued had his presidency not been foreshortened; for Clark Clifford's interesting conclusions in this regard, see his memoir *Counsel to the President*, 381-82. The *Pentagon Papers* (Gravel ed) reviews the background to the Kennedy buildup in vol 2, ch 1. See also *The U.S. Government and the Vietnam War, Executive and Legislative Roles and Relationships: Part II, 1961-1964*, Report of the Senate Foreign Relations Committee, 98 Cong, 2 sess (Dec 84), chs 1 and 2.

10. Southeast Asia Statistical Summary, Tables 3 and 50, OASD(Comp), Directorate for Information Operations, 5 Dec 73; Rochester memrcd, 1 Dec 81; DIA PW/MIA Automated File, 7 Sep 79.

11. Unless otherwise indicated, all figures on troop strength and casualties are from Southeast Asia Statistical Summary, OASD(Comp), Directorate for Information Operations, 5 Dec 73.

12. *American Prisoners of War in Southeast Asia, 1972*, Hearings before House Foreign Affairs Subcommittee on National Security Policy and Scientific Developments, 92 Cong, 2 sess (16 Mar 72), pt 3, 29.

13. See William Shawcross's scathingly critical *Sideshow: Kissinger, Nixon and the Destruction of Cambodia* and Kissinger's rebuttal in his *Years of Upheaval*, chs 2, 8, and app. Fifield, *Americans in Southeast Asia*, 303-07, offers a balanced summary of the circumstances surrounding the Cambodian and Laotian incursions.

14. Arthur M. Schlesinger, Jr., *A Thousand Days: John F. Kennedy in the White House*, 321.

15. *Prisoner of War Study: Step Two, The Functioning of the Law*, IV C. Mixed Civil and International Conflicts: Vietnam, prepared for Dept of Army by Harbridge House, May 69, 21.

16. Figures on civilian PWs are from information supplied OSD Hist by DIA, 3 Apr 85.

17. Japanese treatment of Marine PWs is discussed in Benis M. Frank and Henry I. Shaw, Jr., *History of U.S. Marine Corps Operations in World War II: Victory and Occupation*, app A; among more recent studies, see Gavan Daws, *Prisoners of the Japanese: POWs of World War II in the Pacific*. With regard to the Korean captivity, see *Communist Treatment of Prisoners of War: A Historical Survey*, Report of the Senate Judiciary Committee, 92 Cong, 2 sess (1972), 12-13; *Korean War Atrocities*, Report of the Senate Committee on Government Operations, 83 Cong, 2 sess (1954); *Communist Interrogation, Indoctrination, and Exploitation of Prisoners of War*, Dept of Army, May 56, 15-17; *Analysis of the Korean War Prisoner of War Experience*, USAF Program for Analysis of the Southeast Asia Prisoner of War Experience, Rpt A10-2, Mar 74; *Prisoner of War Study: Step Two, The Functioning of the Law*, IV B. Korea, 28-32, 37-60, 80-85, 116-30. For a comparison of captivity in Korea and Vietnam, see J. M. McGrath, "American POWs: North Korea and North Vietnam," Naval Postgraduate School paper, Monterey, Calif, nd. McGrath, a naval aviator, spent six years as a PW in Vietnam.

2. PWs OF THE VIET MINH, 1946-1954

1. As noted later in the chapter, estimates vary widely. See George J. Ho, "The Prisoner of War Issue in the First Indochina War, with Special Emphasis on the Release of Prisoners, 1954-1962," CRS Rpt 71-170F, 13 Jul 71, 6-7, 13-14. Bernard Fall's figure of 37,000 is the one most often cited. See, for example, *Communist Treatment of Prisoners of War*, 2, 15.

2. Claude Paillat, *Dossier Secret de L'Indochine*, 368-84; Jean Pouget, *Le Manifeste du Camp No. 1*, ch 13.

3. Claude Goeldhieux, *Quinze Mois Prisonier chez les Viets*, summary in OSD Hist, 1-2.

4. Ibid, 2-3.

5. Bernard B. Fall, "Communist POW Treatment in Indochina," *Military Review* (Dec 58), 4-7; Goeldhieux, *Quinze Mois Prisonier*, summary, 3.

6. Fall, "Communist POW Treatment in Indochina," 8, 10; Goeldhieux, *Quinze Mois Prisonier*, summary, 3; memo U/PW Frank A. Sieverts for AsstSecState David M. Abshire, 29 Nov 71, sub: French POWs and the Vietnam War. American intelligence agents would interview several of the Spanish ex-PWs after they had left Vietnam in 1967, learning from them the locations and architectural details of North Vietnamese prison camps.

7. *Communist Treatment of Prisoners of War*, 14; O'Ballance, *The Indo-China War*, 118.

8. Lucien Bodard, *The Quicksand War: Prelude to Vietnam*, 310.

9. Fall, *Street Without Joy*, 272-75; Pouget, *Le Manifeste*, ch 10; Paul Jeandel, "Deux Ans de Captivité chez les Viet-Minh," *Revue de l'Action Populaire* (Sep-Oct 55), 943-54; *Communist Treatment of Prisoners of War*, 15-16.

10. Bodard, *Quicksand War*, 311; Peter Scholl-Latour, *Death in the Ricefields: Thirty Years of War in Indochina*, 84.

11. Fall, *Street Without Joy* (1964 ed), 309-10. The material on the French PW training does not appear in the earlier edition.

12. Anita Lauve Nutt, *Prisoners of War in Indochina*, Rand study prepared for DoD (ARPA), Oct 68, vii; U.S. Military Assistance Command, Vietnam, *Command History, 1969*, vol 2, X-3.

13. *Communist Treatment of Prisoners of War*, 1-13; *Americans Missing in Southeast Asia*, Hearings before House Select Committee on Missing Persons in Southeast Asia, 94 Cong, 2 sess (7 Apr 76),

pt 4, 6-9. The final accounting for Korea showed that of 7,140 U.S. military personnel known to have been captured by the Communists, 2,701 (roughly 38 percent) died while in the hands of the enemy. See OASD(PA) News Release 150-83, 5 Apr 83.

14. Statement by Stephen S. Jackson, DASD(Manpower), in *Return of American Prisoners of War Who Have Not Been Accounted for by the Communists*, Hearing before House Foreign Affairs Subcommittee on the Far East and the Pacific, 85 Cong, 1 sess (27 May 57), 5; memo Harrison M. Holland for Paul Warnke, 22 Aug 67, sub: Korean POW Situation; "Facts Pertaining to American Servicemen Unaccounted for Since Cessation of Hostilities in Korea," DoD Fact Sheet, 9 Nov 70. Allegations that U.S. PWs were shipped to camps in China and the Soviet Union at the close of the war resurfaced in 1990. See *USA Today*, 25 Jun 90; *Washington Times*, 13 Jul 90; "An Examination of U.S. Policy Toward POW/MIAs," Senate Foreign Relations Committee Minority (Republican) Staff Report (23 May 91), ch 4.

15. Fall, *Street Without Joy*, 264, 268; Ho, "Prisoner of War Issue in the First Indochina War," 3-14; Randle, *Geneva 1954*, 458; *NY Times*, 24, 29 Aug, 19 Sep 54; "Release and Accounting of French PW/MIA—Indochina," DoD PW/MIA Task Force paper, 3 Jul 72, 1-2. There are those who view Fall's figures as suspect, noting his tendency to overdramatize, but he did have access to French government wartime files and is supported by Ely and others. On the French insistence in later years that nearly all native French PWs held by the North Vietnamese had been repatriated, see *Washington Post* and *NY Times*, 1 Jul 72; *Boston Globe*, 10 Sep 72; and Secretary of State William P. Rogers's testimony in *Foreign Assistance and Related Agencies Appropriations for 1972*, Hearings before House Appropriations Committee, 92 Cong, 1 sess (1 Jul 71), pt 2, 1165-66.

16. Edward G. Lansdale, *In the Midst of Wars: An American's Mission to Southeast Asia*, 151; Kiley conversation with Lansdale, Sep 75; Fall, *Street Without Joy*, 269; "Prisoner Release and Repatriation in Indochina," Interdepartmental Study Panel paper, Apr 72, 21-24; Nutt, *Prisoners of War in Indochina*, 7-10; *Americans Missing in Southeast Asia*, Final Report of the House Select Committee on Missing Persons in Southeast Asia, H Rpt 94-1764, 94 Cong, 2 sess (13 Dec 76), 78-79.

17. Ho, "Prisoner of War Issue in the First Indochina War," 4-5, 7-8; *Americans Missing in Southeast Asia* (7 Apr 76), pt 4, 13-14; Nutt, *Prisoners of War in Indochina*, 3, 32-33; Anita Lauve Nutt, *Troika on Trial*, 3 vols, Rand study of the International Control Commission, 1954-56, prepared for DoD(ISA), Sep 67, vol 1, 133-41. See, too, James L. Monroe, "The Communist Use of Prisoners and Hostages in the Truce Negotiations in Korea," unpub paper, Apr 56.

18. *Americans Missing in Southeast Asia* (7 Apr 76), pt 4, 1-8, 15-16.

19. Roy, *Battle of Dienbienphu*, 309.

20. Fall, "Communist POW Treatment in Indochina," 4.

21. *Washington Post and Times Herald*, 18 Jun 54; msg 2829 AmEmbSaigon for SecState, 18 Jun 54.

22. Msgs 2849 and 2893 AmEmbSaigon for SecState, 21, 24 Jun 54; msg 22 AmEmbSaigon for SecState, 2 Jul 54.

23. Msg 3166A Chief MAAG Saigon for Ridgway MG, 31 Aug 54; *Washington Post and Times Herald*, 1 Sep 54; Albert D. Biderman and Herbert Zimmer, "Treatment and Indoctrination of U.S. Prisoners Held by the Viet Minh," Air Force Personnel and Training Research Center paper, nd, 8-9.

24. Biderman and Zimmer, "Treatment and Indoctrination of U.S. Prisoners Held by the Viet Minh," 5-6, 24-26.

25. Ibid, i-iii, 12, 16-28; *Washington Post and Times Herald*, 1 Sep 54.

3. LAOS: PRISONERS OF THE SHADOW WAR

1. *Pentagon Papers* (Gravel ed), vol 2, 18; Kalb and Abel, *Roots of Involvement*, 106-07; Schlesinger, *A Thousand Days*, 320; W. W. Rostow, *The Diffusion of Power*, 265; *U.S. Government and the Vietnam War: Part II, 1961-1964*, 8-12. Eisenhower's comments on Laos are contained in a memorandum on the 19 January 1961 meeting prepared by Clark Clifford in 1967 for

President Lyndon B. Johnson, reprinted in *Pentagon Papers* (Gravel ed), vol 2, 635-37; see also Clifford, *Counsel to the President*, 342-43, and Dept of State, *Foreign Relations of the United States, 1961-1963*, vol 24, 19-25, which cites an earlier version of Clifford's memo and other participants' accounts of what transpired. On the controversy surrounding the meeting and what exactly was said, see Fred I. Greenstein and Richard H. Immerman, "What Did Eisenhower Tell Kennedy about Indochina? The Politics of Misperception," *Journal of American History* (Sep 92), 568-87.

2. *U.S. Government and the Vietnam War: Part II, 1961-1964*, 18-33; MajGen Oudone Sananikone, *The Royal Lao Army and U.S. Army Advice and Support*, 77-78; Earl H. Tilford, Jr., *Search and Rescue in Southeast Asia, 1961-1975*, 33-34.

3. Information on Duffy is limited to classified sources.

4. The following account of Bailey's captivity is based on his memoir, *Solitary Survivor*, and materials in File 719, OSD Hist.

5. The Pathet Lao photographed the ID card of one of the lost Air Force crew, Frederick Garside, and the passport of another, Ralph Magee. They later included this photo (which also shows part of a second ID card) in a propaganda film which the Defense Intelligence Agency obtained through a friendly foreign government in 1977. This and similar films, including one that shows Prince Souphanouvong viewing captured personal effects of Americans, refute Pathet Lao protestations of having no knowledge of Americans missing in Laos during the Indochina conflict. See DIA, U-48, 552/DB-4, apps H, Q.

6. Grant Wolfkill, *Reported To Be Alive*, 166. Wolfkill's memoir remains the best unclassified source on the details of his captivity as well as the experience of the others in his group (Shore, McMorrow, Moon, Ballenger, and Frigillano). Material for this section has also been drawn from File 719.

7. The Red Cross was continually hampered in its efforts in Indochina, in both Laos and Vietnam, because of the refusal of elements on both sides of the fight to accept the applicability of the Geneva Conventions or to recognize the organization as having any jurisdiction or authority in prisoner of war matters. However, as this episode illustrates, the Red Cross carried enough weight internationally so that the warring parties could not ignore it and occasionally conceded to it. For a summary of Red Cross activity on behalf of American PWs in Laos between February 1961 and August 1966, see ICRC memrcd, Oct 66, sub: ICRC intervention in favour of American nationals detained in Laos. See, too, msg U.S. Mission Geneva for State Dept, 11 Apr 65, sub: Summary of status of various U.S. prisoners of war in Far East; memcon DepDirISA(Far East Region) William C. Hamilton, 30 Jun 65; Alessandro Casella, "Prisoner Problems," *Far Eastern Economic Review* (14 Jul 66), 58.

8. Major Bailey, Captain Moon (posthumously), Sergeant Ballenger, and Wolfkill all received Army decorations after repatriation. Bailey and Ballenger received the first Bronze Stars awarded since the Korean War. As a result of testimony offered by Ballenger, Shore, and McMorrow, Wolfkill also was awarded the Medal of Freedom by President Kennedy.

9. Sources used for this section include Nutt, *Prisoners of War in Indochina*, 22-23; *Escape from Laos*, the memoir of Navy Lt. (j.g.) Dieter Dengler, who joined the group in 1966; the transcript of Dengler's press conference, San Diego, Calif, 13 Sep 66 (see also DoD news release re Dengler escape, 13 Sep 66); *Imprisonment and Escape of Lt. (jg.) Dieter Dengler, USNR*, Hearing before Senate Armed Services Committee, 89 Cong, 2 sess (16 Sep 66); the account of Pisidhi Indradat and a large file of reports and correspondence collected by DeBruin's brother Jerome, a professor at the University of Toledo who made a trip to Laos in 1971 to gather information about his missing relative and who interviewed Indradat in Laos and Thailand. All materials are in OSD Hist. There are considerable discrepancies between Dengler's and Indradat's accounts and even within Dengler's several versions.

10. The five prisoners were photographed together in July 1964. A letter to Souphanouvong, apparently in DeBruin's hand, dated 30 October 1964, appeared in the February 1965 edition of the Pathet Lao periodical *La Lutte du Peuple Lao, Contre L'Agression Des Imperialists Americans*. The accompanying story contained a statement attributed to DeBruin about his job as cargo kicker. That same month, Soth Pethrasi, Pathet Lao representative in Vientiane, relayed to the

U.S. Embassy a message from PL General Singkapo that "all prisoners are alive" and being held in the center of Savannakhet Province. The message, for the moment, was true.

11. Indradat, who was recaptured and later rescued, learned from guards that a villager had slain Martin, corroborating that aspect of Dengler's report. Official accounts later indicated that Martin had been beheaded. See, for instance, ltr SecDef Robert S. McNamara to House Armed Svcs Cte Chmn L. Mendel Rivers, 3 Sep 66. See, too, "Secrecy Cloaks Red Atrocities," *Northern Virginia Sun*, 4 Aug 66; Rod Colvin, *First Heroes: The POWs Left Behind in Vietnam*, 198.

12. *SERE Newsletter*, 5 Oct 66, 47. For the helicopter crew's account of the rescue, see *Washington Post*, 28 Jul 66.

13. In an interview with Kiley in February 1979, Dr. Jerome DeBruin cited a report placing his brother at a village named Muong Nong with other Americans from January 1967 to January 1968. See also ltr DASD(ISA) Roger E. Shields to J. Angus MacDonald, 25 Feb 76; memo J. V. Cricchi (DIA) for Kiley, 9 Nov 78; Colvin, *First Heroes*, 199-200.

14. See William M. Leary, "Mahaxay: Secret POW Rescue in Laos," *Vietnam* (Jun 95), 18-24.

15. Ltr Amb Unger to Prince Souphanouvong, 15 Jul 64; *NY Times*, 8 Jul 64. Actually, scattered reports of Klusmann's capture appeared in the American press almost immediately after his shootdown. See *Washington Post and Times Herald*, 8 Jun 64; *NY Times*, 8 Jun 64; *Time*, 19 Jun 64; *Newsweek*, 22 Jun 64.

16. The White House confirmed Klusmann's escape (see *Washington Post and Times Herald*, 2 Sep 64), but supplied no details, and no further information was forthcoming. The account here is drawn from materials in Klusmann file in OSD Hist, including interv with Kiley.

4. SOUTH VIETNAM: PRISONERS OF THE VIET CONG, 1961-1964

1. OASD(PA) News Release 204-62, 8 Feb 62; *NY Times*, 10 Feb 62.

2. Fryett account in South 1961-64 file; Bill Roberts, "Freedom Hard as Captivity for First POW," *Monterey Peninsula Herald*, 22 Oct 71, reprinted in *Washington Evening Star*, 26 Oct 71. Health and readjustment problems kept Fryett in the hospital for three months and plagued him after his discharge from the Army in October 1964, when he continued to have nightmares and suffer from anxiety related to his PW experience.

3. "Treatment of American Prisoners by the Vietnamese Communists (Viet Cong)," report to MajGen(USAF) Kuhfeld, 1963, 1-5; *NY Times*, 10 Apr 62; *Newsweek*, 23 Apr 62.

4. Fall ltr to *Washington Post and Times Herald*, 4 Sep 64; *NY Times*, 20 Oct 64; ltr DASD(ISA) Roger E. Shields to Rep Gillespie V. Montgomery, 19 Feb 76; Nigel Cawthorne, *The Bamboo Cage: The Full Story of the American Servicemen Still Held Hostage in South-East Asia*, 83. Mitchell's missionary wife Betty was herself captured near Ban Me Thuot in 1975, after the U.S. pullout, then marched north to Son Tay, where she was held for three months. Son Tay, site of the prison camp raid in 1970, was to have been a missionary post for both Mitchells until the war prevented that assignment. James and Marti Hefley, *Prisoners of Hope*, is an account of Mrs. Mitchell's experience.

5. Memo Col England for Chief, US Army Personnel Security Group, 4 Jan 66; memo TJAG for ACSI, 9 Mar 66, 3; Col McClanahan memrcd, 2 Jun 66; "Treatment of American Prisoners by Vietnamese Communists," 2-4.

6. Material on Krause and Grainger in South 1961-64 file; see especially Krause report dated 5 Mar 64. On Krause, see also *Newsweek*, 9 Dec 63, 58; on Grainger, *NY Times*, 10, 12 Aug 64, and *Washington Post and Times Herald*, 10 Aug 64.

7. "Prisoner Detention Sites in South Vietnam," encl DIA memo for JCS, NSA, and others, 18 May 67, sub: Prisoner Detention Sites in South Vietnam, 1; DIA Intelligence Appraisal, 8 May 73, fig 4.

8. Kushner did manage, by stealth and improvisation, to treat fellow PWs on occasion, using rusty razor blades for minor surgery and banana leaves and vines for bandages. See Floyd Kushner, "To Live or to Die," *SERE Newsletter*, Jun 76, 7 (the article appeared originally in

the medical periodical *Spectrum*, published by the Army Surgeon General's Office). For another view of Viet Cong medical practice, such as it was, see James N. Rowe interv with Air Training Command, Jul 69, printed in *Southeast Asia Survival Journal* (Apr 72), 51-54, 217-21.

9. Kushner, "To Live or to Die," 8.

10. The captivity experience in South Vietnam during the early years is described in "Treatment of American Prisoners by Vietnamese Communists," cited above; this report, prepared in 1963, is based largely on the accounts of Fryett, Mungada, Groom, Quinn, and Matagulay—all captured during late 1961 and 1962. For a more comprehensive analysis that includes later captures and that compares captivity in the South and the North, see S. William Berg and Milton Richlin, "Injuries and Illnesses of Vietnam War POWs. IV. Comparison of Captivity Effects in North and South Vietnam," *Military Medicine* (Oct 77), 757-60. Berg and Richlin observe that the captivity experiences in the North and the South differed not only because of separate geographical and logistical circumstances but also because of demographic contrasts between the captive groups themselves. Those captured in the North, mostly Navy and Air Force aviators, tended to be older, more mature, more homogeneous, and better trained in resistance techniques; those captured in the South were generally younger, had more diverse backgrounds (inhibiting solidarity), and included enlistees and civilians who, for reasons of lesser discipline and motivation, could be expected to have more trouble coping. Although North Vietnam PWs tended to enter captivity with more traumatic injuries (fractures and dislocations resulting from high-speed ejection from aircraft vs. bullet and shrapnel wounds acquired in firefights or in the crash of a helicopter), those in the South suffered more chronic illness, fungal infections, and malnutrition. See, too, Robert T. Browne, "Development of Prisoner of War Exploitation Techniques And Those Utilized by Guerrilla-Type Forces Against American Military Captives in the Republic of Vietnam," Naval War College thesis, Mar 69, ch 5; Claude Watkins and Charles Redman, "Captivity in Southeast Asia, 1964-1973," briefing paper for 7602 Air Intelligence Group, c. 1973, 3-4; Charles W. Hutchins, "The Captivity Experience of American Prisoners of War in Southeast Asia," Naval Health Research Center Publication 77-28, Aug 77, 11-12.

A sketchy but informative paper presented at a PW study conference at San Diego in January 1975 cautioned against overgeneralization and noted that prisoners encountered significant differences in their treatment and captivity conditions even within the South, the author (unidentified) dividing the list of PWs held by the Viet Cong into five separate groups based on the area of capture. See "An Overview of Free-World Personnel Captured in South Vietnam," paper delivered to SERE Conference, San Diego, Calif, Jan 75.

11. Material for this section is drawn from James N. Rowe, *Five Years to Freedom*; interv with Rowe by Air Training Command, Jul 69, in *Southeast Asia Survival Journal* (Apr 72); Pitzer testimony in *American Prisoners of War in Southeast Asia, 1971*, Hearings before House Foreign Affairs Subcommittee on National Security Policy and Scientific Developments, 92 Cong, 1 sess (3 Aug 71), pt 2, 51-83.

12. *American Prisoners of War in Southeast Asia, 1971*, 51.

13. Rowe, *Five Years to Freedom*, 120-21.

14. The story of this group is reconstructed largely from Smith's captivity account, *P.O.W.: Two Years With the Vietcong*. The book is essentially accurate in its details but must be used with caution because of Smith's bitterness toward the Army as a result of what he considered unfair court-martial charges (although they were later dropped) and his, and his publisher's, pronounced antiwar sentiments that intrude at points and color treatment of certain individuals and events. To balance the record, one must consult the case histories of the group developed by the Department of the Army; summaries of these are in attach to memo, DepUS/A (Manpower) Arthur W. Allen, Jr., for DASD(Military Personnel Policy) BrigGen William W. Berg, 21 Apr 67, sub: Prisoners of War in Southeast Asia.

See also Camacho testimony in *American Prisoners of War in Southeast Asia, 1971*, 50-78; Smith contribution to *The Winter Soldier Investigation: An Inquiry into American War Crimes*, 122-31; Craig Howes, *Voices of the Vietnam POWs: Witnesses to Their Fight*, 205-10. Other useful materials in OSD Hist PW Coll relate to the Smith (and McClure) court-martial charges.

Numerous discrepancies and contradictions in the testimony of the three surviving members of the group have never been fully explained, so that certain issues regarding their treatment and conduct while in captivity remain unresolved.

15. Smith, *P.O.W.*, 121.

16. Smith seems to have had something of a vendetta against Roraback, whom he savages in his book. See, for example, *P.O.W.*, 94-96, 116-17, 212-14. The hard feelings, again, may be traceable to bitterness over the court-martial charges.

17. Smith, *P.O.W.*, 131-32.

18. Burchett reported his visit in *Vietnam: Inside Story of the Guerilla War*, 101-06. See, too, his account in *NY Times*, 13 May 64. He quoted the Americans as astonished and grateful for the good treatment they received. Camacho, asked if he had any questions about life on the outside after being confined in the jungle for several months, only wanted to know the outcome of the heavyweight title fight between Cassius Clay and Sonny Liston. Burchett, with an obvious ax to grind (and perhaps missing what might well have been a sarcastic response from Camacho), contrasted the Americans' political indifference with the Viet Cong's keen interest in world affairs and in how other countries perceived their struggle.

    The journalist suggested that the VC intended the new camp as a permanent PW detention center so that prisoners could be held indefinitely rather than routinely released after a few weeks' indoctrination; intended or not, the permanent center never came about.

19. Smith, *P.O.W.*, 185.

20. Ibid, 197-98.

21. The *Washington Post and Times Herald* carried a report a year later of rescue efforts undertaken about this time (Christmas 1964) wherein U.S. helicopters spread a cloud of nonlethal but immobilizing gas over suspected Viet Cong camps in the Mekong Delta and Tay Ninh area; South Vietnamese ground troops pushed toward the targeted sites, but found no VC or prisoners. The report was based allegedly on U.S. intelligence sources. If it was accurate, the B-26 runs may have been designed to flush out the VC prior to the rescue attempt. See *Washington Post and Times Herald*, 4 Nov 65.

22. OSD Hist PW Coll contains an extensive file on Thompson; John G. Hubbell, *P.O.W.*, 383-93, 409-10, covers Thompson's captivity through the spring of 1968. Kiley interviewed Thompson in 1976.

5. FIRST ARRIVALS AT THE HANOI HILTON

1. Dept State *Bulletin*, 24 Aug 64, 268. The resolution was signed into law on 10 August.

2. OASD(PA) News Release 579-64, 6 Aug 64.

3. *Washington Post and Times Herald*, 12 Aug 64. Alvarez's story is reconstructed from interviews, survival training reports, and numerous articles that appeared in 1973 after his repatriation. Most of these materials may be found in OSD Hist. A narrative account of his first year's captivity is in Hubbell, *P.O.W.*, 3-33, 67-77. See, too, Alvarez's memoir, with Anthony S. Pitch, *Chained Eagle*; chs 2-7 recount his capture and first year in Hanoi.

4. Hubbell, *P.O.W.*, 10.

5. One of the best descriptions of Heartbreak, and of PW facilities in the North generally, is Armand J. Myers et al, *Vietnam POW Camp Histories and Studies*, vol 1, Air War College, Maxwell AFB, Ala, Apr 74. Heartbreak is described and diagrammed on 12, 14-15, 17-18.

6. Figures are from Carl Berger, ed, *The United States Air Force in Southeast Asia, 1961-1973*, 74. On the evolution of U.S. policy before and following Pleiku, and on the progress of the air war itself between February and June 1965, see *Pentagon Papers* (Gravel ed), vol 3, ch 3.

7. *Pentagon Papers* (Gravel ed), vol 3, 335 (Taylor quote); William C. Westmoreland, *A Soldier's Report*, 119 (Johnson quote); Berger, ed, *United States Air Force in Southeast Asia*, 69-70, 74-75; Lewy, *America in Vietnam*, 374-78; DIA PW/MIA Automated File, 7 Sep 79. On how bureaucratic politics and internal differences among competing organizations within the national

security apparatus hampered the air war, see James Clay Thompson, *Rolling Thunder: Understanding Policy and Program Failure*; 76-81 discuss the pernicious effects of interservice rivalry.

8. Material on Shumaker is drawn from File 719 and interviews; see also Hubbell, *P.O.W.*, 35-40.

9. Stephen A. Rowan, *They Wouldn't Let Us Die: The Prisoners of War Tell Their Story*, 22; Hubbell, *P.O.W.*, 44; DIA PW/MIA Automated File, 7 Sep 79. Butler's unpublished memoir devotes more than 50 pages to his evasion.

10. Myers, *Vietnam POW Camp Histories*, vol 1, 19, 21; Casella, "Prisoner Problems," 58.

11. Myers, *Vietnam POW Camp Histories*, vol 1, 18-21.

12. Shumaker file; *Vietnam Courier*, Feb, Apr 65.

13. Bill Surface, "Can We Free Our Vietnam War Prisoners?" *Parade*, 14 Nov 65, 4-5; "POWs in Vietnam: Forgotten Victims of a Nasty War," *National Observer*, 4 Oct 65; DoD Dir 7750.2, 3 Apr 53, sub: Battle Casualty Statistics; memo Dir for Statistical Services Foster Adams for Military Depts, 30 Sep 64, sub: Statistical Report of Casualties in Southeast Asia; memo Chief of Naval Personnel ViceAdm B. J. Semmes, Jr., for SecNav, 14 Jul 66, sub: Use of the Term "Prisoner of War"; memo ASD(Manpower) Thomas D. Morris for DepSecDef, 19 Jul 66, sub: Change in Reference to U.S. Personnel Captured in Vietnam; memo DepSecDef Cyrus Vance for ASD(Comp), 19 Jul 66, sub: Change in Reference to U.S. Personnel Captured in Vietnam.

6. ESTABLISHING COMMUNICATION: THE TAP CODE AND OTHER CHANNELS

1. Hubbell, *P.O.W.*, 40-41.

2. Hubbell, *P.O.W.*, 43-44; Myers, *Vietnam POW Camp Histories*, vol 1, 28-30.

3. Rowan, *They Wouldn't Let Us Die*, 84-85; Myers, *Vietnam POW Camp Histories*, vol 1, 30; Jim and Sybil Stockdale, *In Love and War: The Story of a Family's Ordeal and Sacrifice During the Vietnam Years*, 159-60; Hubbell, *P.O.W.*, 44-45; Everett Alvarez, Jr., "Sound: A POW's Weapon," U.S. Naval Institute *Proceedings* (Aug 76), 93.

4. James Bond Stockdale, "Communicating *Without* Technology," *Signal* (Oct 79), 30; Stockdale, *In Love and War*, 160, 186; Jeremiah A. Denton, Jr., *When Hell Was In Session*, 74.

5. Stockdale, "Communicating *Without* Technology," 29-30; Stockdale, *In Love and War*, 186. Gerald Coffee, *Beyond Survival: Building on the Hard Times—A POW's Inspiring Story*, 143, contains a humorous anecdote on one PW's botched first attempt to use the tap code.

6. James A. Mulligan, *Hanoi Commitment*, 64-65.

7. Stockdale, "Communicating *Without* Technology," 30; Stockdale, *In Love and War*, 186; Alvarez, "Sound: A POW's Weapon," 91-93.

8. Mulligan, *Hanoi Commitment*, 67-68, 85; Stockdale, "Communicating *Without* Technology," 32.

9. Denton, *When Hell Was In Session*, ix; Stockdale, "Communicating *Without* Technology," 32.

10. Robert B. Doremus, "Days to Remember," Industrial College of the Armed Forces paper, Mar 74, 50. Navy Lt. Cdr. Richard Stratton told interviewer Stephen Rowan how the prisoners frequently argued over nicknames for guards: "In fact we almost came to blows over whose name was going to reign for a new guard. For example, they got a new issue of Russian equipment including a fancy silver belt buckle, and, when we saw a new guard with this on, we called him Silver until about two days later, when every guard in the camp had the same belt buckle. My roommate was about to punch me in the nose. He said, 'You see, I told you it was a stupid name'" (*They Wouldn't Let Us Die*, 27).

11. Denton, *When Hell Was In Session*, 53.

12. Analysts would compile and correlate rosters of North Vietnamese prison camp personnel, with nicknames and characteristics, from PW debriefings. One of the most comprehensive lists is in Mulligan's homecoming account, app II; the most exhaustive is Kiley's in OSD Hist.

13. Stockdale file; Denton, *When Hell Was In Session*, 27, 82; Stockdale, *In Love and War*, 156-57.

14. Rivers file.

15. Hubbell, *P.O.W.*, 54. Hubbell discusses Guarino's experience at length; ch 3 covers the Air Force major's first month at Hoa Lo. Guarino's own account is in *A POW's Story: 2801 Days in Hanoi*, chs 3-4.

16. Hubbell, *P.O.W.*, 56, 58; Myers, *Vietnam POW Camp Histories*, vol 1, 28; Denton, *When Hell Was In Session*, 36-37 (Denton mistakenly identifies Vohden as one of the members of the Shumaker foursome and, on 27-28, possibly mistakes McKamey for Storz as the source of "Yankee Doodle").

17. Denton, *When Hell Was In Session*, ix-x, 1-10. Denton's memoir is brash, immodest, and in places downright conceited, as when the author describes his physical attributes and extols the expertise and intellectual qualities that made him "a good catch" for the North Vietnamese (17). There is no denying, however, his high standards of conduct as a PW and his outstanding leadership as a senior officer. Stockdale among others credited him with instituting the new tap code variation (see Chapter 17).

18. Denton, *When Hell Was In Session*, 15-19, 28-33 (16, quote). Tschudy's story is told in Rowan, *They Wouldn't Let Us Die*, ch 8.

19. Denton, *When Hell Was In Session*, 34-44 (44, quote); Hubbell, *P.O.W.*, 63-65.

20. Stockdale, "Communicating *Without* Technology," 29, 30; Myers, *Vietnam POW Camp Histories*, vol 1, 29; Denton, *When Hell Was In Session*, 37-38. One of the best sources of information on the range of PW communication options and tap code variations is Coffee, *Beyond Survival*, ch 9 (see esp 141-42).

21. File 719.

22. Keirn compares German and North Vietnamese treatment of PWs in "Treatment of World War II and Vietnam POWs," in Myers, *Vietnam POW Camp Histories*, vol 2, 311-27.

23. Berg file; a good description of Berg is in Alvarez and Pitch, *Chained Eagle*, 164.

24. Denton, *When Hell Was In Session*, 78; Hubbell, *P.O.W.*, 141-42, 159-61; Coffee, *Beyond Survival*, 149-50.

25. File 719; on Collins, see Norman A. McDaniel, *Yet Another Voice*, 33-34.

26. Kiley interv with Byrne; Aug 1965 Shootdowns file; Doremus, "Days to Remember," 6-14.

27. Davis file; Denton, *When Hell Was In Session*, 57.

28. Alvarez file; Hubbell, *P.O.W.*, 68-69; Alvarez and Pitch, *Chained Eagle*, 114-20. The details differ somewhat from source to source.

29. Doremus, "Days to Remember," 19.

30. Denton, *When Hell Was In Session*, 158; Alvarez, "Sound: A POW's Weapon," 91-93.

7. ADJUSTMENTS, RELOCATION, AND AN EMERGING LEADERSHIP

1. Karnow, *Vietnam*, 419-26; Herring, *America's Longest War*, 137-44.

2. Doremus, "Days to Remember," 6, 11-13; Mulligan, *Hanoi Commitment*, 66-67, 78; Jay R. Jensen, *Six Years in Hell: A Returned POW Views Captivity, Country, and the Nation's Future*, 52; Larry Chesley, *Seven Years in Hanoi*, 38-41. Schedules for shaving, baths, and haircuts varied considerably depending on the particular camp and time frame.

3. Jensen, *Six Years in Hell*, 51, 57; Doremus, "Days to Remember," 15-17, 24; Rowan, *They Wouldn't Let Us Die*, 25-26; Robinson Risner, *The Passing of the Night: My Seven Years As a Prisoner of the North Vietnamese*, 26.

4. Doremus, "Days to Remember," 25-26; Rowan, *They Wouldn't Let Us Die*, 26; Stockdale, *In Love and War*, 341; Ralph Gaither, *With God in a P.O.W. Camp*, 24. See also Charlie Plumb, *I'm No Hero*, 79, 203.

5. Stockdale, *In Love and War*, 193; Denton, *When Hell Was In Session*, 158, 160-62; Gaither, *With God in a P.O.W. Camp*, 44-45; Rowan, *They Wouldn't Let Us Die*, 110; Howard and Phyllis Rutledge, *In the Presence of Mine Enemies, 1965-1973: A Prisoner of War*, 32-33; Risner, *Passing of the Night*, 193-98; Coffee, *Beyond Survival*, ch 18.

6. Rowan, *They Wouldn't Let Us Die*, 110-11, 72-73; Rutledge, *In the Presence of Mine Enemies*, 33; Stockdale, *In Love and War*, 340-41; Mulligan, *Hanoi Commitment*, 100, 110; Denton, *When Hell Was In Session*, 159-60; Gaither, *With God in a P.O.W. Camp*, 20.

7. Mulligan, *Hanoi Commitment*, 66; Doremus, "Days to Remember," 21-24, 30-31; Rowan, *They Wouldn't Let Us Die*, 110, 113-14; Risner, *Passing of the Night*, 99-101, 197; Denton, *When Hell*

Was In Session, 159. There are some discrepancies in the prisoners' recollections of mealtimes; Risner, for example, places the morning meal at 9:30 and Stratton the afternoon meal at 2:30. Feeding times differed from camp to camp and sometimes seasonally within a camp, perhaps accounting for the varying reports.

8. Risner, *Passing of the Night*, ch 12; Jensen, *Six Years in Hell*, ch 8; Rowan, *They Wouldn't Let Us Die*, 20, 151; Doremus, "Days to Remember," 53-54. On the carrot-and-stick pattern of the Christmas meal, see, for example, Gaither, *With God in a P.O.W. Camp*, 32.

9. Myers, *Vietnam POW Camp Histories*, vol 1, 27; Mulligan, *Hanoi Commitment*, 110. Regarding the clumsy uniform, April 1966 shootdown Larry Chesley attributed its bagginess to the Vietnamese using hulking 260-pound Air Force Sgt. William Robinson as a model (*Seven Years in Hanoi*, 38).

10. On the trauma of "moving," see Doremus, "Days to Remember," 26-28; Coffee, *Beyond Survival*, 148-49; Mulligan, *Hanoi Commitment*, 147.

11. Myers, *Vietnam POW Camp Histories*, vol 1, 72-79; Hubbell, *P.O.W.*, 70-73, 75-77; Alvarez file.

12. Myers, *Vietnam POW Camp Histories*, vol 1, 31, 102-06, 121-22; Denton, *When Hell Was In Session*, 49-50; Risner, *Passing of the Night*, 63-64; Rutledge, *In the Presence of Mine Enemies*, 38; Hubbell, *P.O.W.*, 81; Alvarez and Pitch, *Chained Eagle*, 128-29. Alvarez cited Bob Purcell as the author of the "zoo" quote; Larry Guarino credited Scotty Morgan with the idea and the name (*A POW's Story*, 59).

13. James B. Stockdale, "Experiences as a POW in Vietnam," address to Executives' Club of Chicago, in *Naval War College Review* (Jan-Feb 74), 3.

14. Denton, *When Hell Was In Session*, 151; Risner, *Passing of the Night*, 100. The description of Stockdale's captivity that follows is drawn from File 719 and the Stockdales' memoir, *In Love and War*, previously cited.

15. *In Love and War*, 115.

16. Stockdale file.

17. Risner's captivity experience is recounted in his memoir, *The Passing of the Night*; ch 7 covers his earlier shootdown and rescue as well as his other activities in the intervening years between Korea and imprisonment in Vietnam. The *Time* piece, featuring him on the cover in flying gear, appeared in the 23 April 1965 issue. Hubbell's *P.O.W.* treats Risner's captivity extensively, and Denton's *When Hell Was In Session* makes frequent mention of Risner's resistance and leadership.

18. Risner, *Passing of the Night*, 20.

19. Ibid, 21.

20. Denton, *When Hell Was In Session*, 43-45; Mulligan, *Hanoi Commitment*, 107.

21. Hubbell, *P.O.W.*, 86-87; Risner, *Passing of the Night*, 72-74; Stockdale, *In Love and War*, 159; Denton, *When Hell Was In Session*, 53; Myers, *Vietnam POW Camp Histories*, vol 1, 112-13.

22. Risner, *Passing of the Night*, 74-75.

23. Hervey S. Stockman, "Authority, Leadership, Organization and Discipline Among U.S. POWs in the Hanoi Prison System," Air War College report, May 74, 7.

24. Risner, *Passing of the Night*, 203; Stockdale file; Westmoreland, *A Soldier's Report*, 416. Westmoreland's pecking order was off a bit. During the war a State Department FSO-3 was equivalent to a GS-14 in the civil service, and an Army lieutenant colonel equivalent to a GS-13. On the military/civilian PW relationship, see also "Lessons Learned Briefing to Chief of Staff, Army," 30 Aug 73; Ben and Anne Purcell, *Love and Duty*, 192.

25. Denton, *When Hell Was In Session*, 37; Risner, *Passing of the Night*, 206.

26. Denton, *When Hell Was In Session*, 37; Fourth Allied Prisoner of War Wing Debrief, 16 Apr 73, 5. On the "Room Responsible" program and a similar scheme known as the "Junior Liaison Officer" program, see Watkins and Redman, "Captivity in Southeast Asia," 28; John Fer, "Leadership and Followership in the Prisoner-of-War Environment," Air War College report, May 74, 22-28; Doremus, "Days to Remember," 32.

27. See, for example, Fer, "Leadership and Followership," 27-28, and Stockman, "Authority, Leadership, Organization," 29. See also Chapters 20 and 25.

8. TIGHTENING THE SCREWS: THE BEGINNINGS OF THE TORTURE ERA IN THE NORTH

1. Stockman, "Authority, Leadership, Organization," 7; Jon A. Reynolds, "Question of Honor," *Air University Review* (Mar-Apr 77), 107.

2. Denton, *When Hell Was In Session*, 50, 54, 55; Myers, *Vietnam POW Camp Histories*, vol 1, 121-22; Stockman, "Authority, Leadership, Organization," 8; Stockdale, *In Love and War*, 151-52. Several sets of regulations were issued, each successive one usually more stringent than the previous. The list cited by Stockdale as being posted on his door in October 1965 was actually distributed early in 1967. See Myers, app B.

3. Stockman, "Authority, Leadership, Organization," 8-9; Myers, *Vietnam POW Camp Histories*, vol 1, 123.

4. OSD Hist has extensive materials on the Code of Conduct relating to its roots in the Geneva PW Convention of 1949, promulgation following the Korean War, and effectiveness in Vietnam. An excellent analysis of its background and text and the problems it posed for American PWs in Vietnam is Howes, *Voices of the Vietnam POWs*, ch 1. See also Vernon E. Davis, *The U.S. Government and American PWs in Southeast Asia, 1961-1973* (forthcoming), ch 8 (ms).

5. Hubbell devotes an entire chapter to Knutson in *P.O.W.* See also Gaither, *With God in a P.O.W. Camp*, 8; Stockdale, *In Love and War*, 155-56.

6. Hubbell, *P.O.W.*, 98-105; "POW's Tell the Inside Story," *U.S. News & World Report*, 9 Apr 73; Stockdale, *In Love and War*, 156.

7. Hubbell, *P.O.W.*, 105-09; Knutson file.

8. "POW's Nightmarish Ordeal," *Washington Post*, 30 Mar 73; *American Prisoners of War and Missing in Action in Southeast Asia, 1973*, Hearings before House Foreign Affairs Subcommittee on National Security Policy and Scientific Developments, 93 Cong, 1 sess (23 May 73), pt 4, 3.

9. Wendy Rivers's homecoming report contains a torture summary and chronology that suggests the extent and variety of physical abuse to which they were subjected.

10. Risner in *Passing of the Night*, 26, comments on the size of the stocks: "built for Vietnamese ankles, and so were in many cases too small." On the wrist cuffs, see Plumb, *I'm No Hero*, 63.

11. Stockdale, *In Love and War*, 167, 181; Rowan, *They Wouldn't Let Us Die*, 232-33; Hubbell, *P.O.W.*, 323; Kiley interv with Shumaker.

12. Stockdale file; Stockdale, *In Love and War*, 156-57; Denton, *When Hell Was In Session*, 89.

13. Rowan, *They Wouldn't Let Us Die*, 44-46; Stockdale file; "POW's: The Price of Survival," *Newsweek*, 16 Apr 73; "POW's Nightmarish Ordeal," *Washington Post*, 30 Mar 73.

14. Hubbell, *P.O.W.*, 127-33; Stockdale, *In Love and War*, 235-36.

15. Rutledge's captivity chronicle, *In the Presence of Mine Enemies*, deals with his capture and initial torture experience in chs 1-3. See also Denton, *When Hell Was In Session*, 149; Hubbell, *P.O.W.*, 132-33. For another admiring profile of Rutledge, see Coffee, *Beyond Survival*, 186-87.

16. Hubbell, *P.O.W.*, 138; Alcorn and Shankel reports in OSD Hist.

17. Shumaker file; Hubbell, *P.O.W.*, 115-16.

18. Davis file; Denton, *When Hell Was In Session*, 57-58; Hubbell, *P.O.W.*, 114-15, 119-20, 140-41.

19. Gaither, *With God in a P.O.W. Camp*, 21-26, 32-34.

20. Denton, *When Hell Was In Session*, 56, 57-58; Hubbell, *P.O.W.*, 114, 120, 122-23, 141; Davis file; Risner, *Passing of the Night*, 100, 103.

21. Alvarez file; Hubbell, *P.O.W.*, 139, 143-44.

22. Denton, *When Hell Was In Session*, 58-59; Risner, *Passing of the Night*, 104-05; Stockdale, *In Love and War*, 161; Rivers file; Hubbell, *P.O.W.*, 144-45; Rutledge, *In the Presence of Mine Enemies*, 39-40, 43.

23. Risner, *Passing of the Night*, 105-06; Rivers file; Gaither, *With God in a P.O.W. Camp*, 32; Hubbell, *P.O.W.*, 143; Stockdale, *In Love and War*, 162-63; Doremus file; Denton, *When Hell Was In Session*, 53.

24. Rivers and Alvarez files; Hubbell, *P.O.W.*, 149; Myers, *Vietman POW Camp Histories*, vol 1, 127; Herring, *America's Longest War*, 164-66.
25. The statistical profile is drawn from DIA PW/MIA Automated File, 7 Sep 79, and Southeast Asia Statistical Summary, OASD (Comp), Directorate for Information Operations, 5 Dec 73. Abbott was seized on 20 April. The Vietnamese death certificate accompanying his remains to the United States in March 1974 listed 27 April as the date of his death and "Seriously injured on many parts of the body when parachuted" as the cause. Copies of enemy records in OSD Hist show that he was buried at Van Dien Cemetery, Hanoi, 28 April 1966 under a stone marked "Ta An Dong (J.A.)," then reburied in Ha Bac Province, 3 January 1973. On what is known of Schmidt's disappearance, see Hubbell, *P.O.W.*, 319, and Denton, *When Hell Was In Session*, 144; a North Vietnamese medical certificate dated 15 September 1967 listed the cause of his death as "contracted liver, acute yellowing of the skin with complications of cerebral swelling and collapse of cardial arteries," with no mention of contributing circumstances.
26. The North Vietnamese did not confirm Grubb's death until November 1970, but reports of his fate periodically filtered back to the United States through visitors to North Vietnam and other unofficial channels. Refusing to abandon hope and buoyed by a photograph showing her husband in apparent good health shortly after capture, Grubb's wife Evelyn became a leading spokeswoman for the families of PWs in the late 1960s. See her letter to United Nations Secretary General U Thant, 7 Jun 71, and an article on her efforts in Washington *Evening Star*, 31 Mar 72; these and other materials relating to Grubb's capture and death are in OSD Hist.
27. The informant showed Coffee Hanson's identification card. The Navy listed him as "missing in action" until July 1966, when his status was changed to "captured" because of the receipt of evidence that he had survived the shootdown. In January 1974, a year after Operation Homecoming, the Navy changed his status to "presumed killed in action." He may have died when U.S. aircraft unwittingly strafed the small boats that picked up him and Coffee, or he may have been shot by one of the captors.
28. Coffee discusses his capture and early captivity at length in *Beyond Survival*, chs 1-8 (133-38 introduce Risner). See, too, Hubbell, *P.O.W.*, 150; Mulligan, *Hanoi Commitment*, 109.
29. Mulligan, *Hanoi Commitment*, 9-60.
30. File 719.
31. Hubbell, *P.O.W.*, 159-61, 163-67; Denton, *When Hell Was In Session*, 78; Coffee, *Beyond Survival*, 150; Shankel file.
32. Myers, *Vietnam POW Camp Histories*, vol 1, 75, 79-89; Bell and Davis files; Hubbell, *P.O.W.*, 154-56; Gaither, *With God in a P.O.W. Camp*, 45-50; Kiley intervs with Bell and Ron Byrne. Alvarez's homecoming report has a good description of the camp.
33. Denton, *When Hell Was In Session*, 62-67, 81-88.
34. Stockdale, *In Love and War*, 163-85; Stockdale file.
35. Risner, *Passing of the Night*, 79-101; Stockdale, *In Love and War*, 158-60.
36. Risner, *Passing of the Night*, 110-21.
37. "POW's Nightmarish Ordeal," *Washington Post*, 30 Mar 73.
38. Stockdale, "Experiences as a POW in Vietnam," 5; ltr Denton to LtCol A. J. Myers, USAF, 5 Feb 74, cited in Stockman, "Authority, Leadership, Organization," 9; Denton, *When Hell Was In Session*, 105.
39. Denton, *When Hell Was In Session*, 106, 61-62.
40. Stockdale, "Experiences as a POW in Vietnam," 5.

9. INDOCTRINATION: TORTURING THE MIND

1. A. J. Barker, *Prisoners of War*, 164-65.
2. Edgar H. Schein, "Some Observations on Chinese Methods of Handling Prisoners of War," *Public Opinion Quarterly* (Spring 56), 321-27. See also Schein, "The Chinese Indoctrination

Program for Prisoners of War: A Study of Attempted Brainwashing," *Psychiatry* (May 56), 149-72; Albert D. Biderman, "Communist Attempts to Elicit False Confessions from Air Force Prisoners of War," *Bulletin of the New York Academy of Medicine* (Sep 57), 616-25; Col Walton K. Richardson, "Prisoners of War as Instruments of Foreign Policy," *Naval War College Review* (Sep 70), 53-54. OSD Hist files contain several folders of material on Chinese indoctrination practices and the "brainwashing" experiences of U.S. PWs in Korea. For a revealing look at the Chinese practices as they were applied to Indian Army personnel captured during border skirmishes between the two countries in the early 1960s, see "Chinese Brain-Washing Techniques and Their Effects on the Indian Prisoners of War," unpub paper, Aug 63.

Although an evaluation of Chinese "brainwashing" goes beyond the scope of this book, one should note that accounts by both journalists and historians in the years after the Korean War grossly exaggerated the nature and effect of the process. In fact, rare were instances where the Chinese employed drugs, hypnosis, or other extraordinary devices to alter mental states. Chinese indoctrination was protracted and intensive—in this sense a form of "brainwashing" indeed took place—but the notion of its subjects being reduced to robots mindlessly reciting party slogans was largely the creation of post-Korean War popularizers.

3. On North Vietnamese sensitivity to "brainwashing" charges, see File 719; Lewy, *America in Vietnam*, 339.

4. The 1969 capture and interrogation of Dr. Dang Tan, a North Vietnamese medical officer and party member, enabled U.S. intelligence agents to piece together a comprehensive picture of the DRV's political warfare organization and tactics. See memo ASD(ISA) G. Warren Nutter for SecDef, 28 May 70, sub: Rallier Report, with report; memo DirDIA ViceAdm V. P. de Poix for SecDef, 6 Apr 73, encl 4, 7-8; draft summary of Nov 69 debriefing of Dr. Tan.

5. Report attach to memo Nutter for SecDef, 28 May 70, sub: Procedures and Policies Relating to the Exploitation of American Prisoners of War, 4-6; draft summary of Nov 69 debriefing of Dr. Tan, 4-5; Gaither, *With God in a P.O.W. Camp*, 26. On the seeming inscrutability of Vietnamese actions, see, too, Doremus, "Days to Remember," 58-59; Coffee, *Beyond Survival*, 148, 169.

6. Report attach to memo Nutter for SecDef, 28 May 70, 13; draft summary of Nov 69 debriefing of Dr. Tan, 6; *USA Today*, 9 Apr 87.

7. Gaither, *With God in a P.O.W. Camp*, 74, 20; Rivers file; Guarino, *A POW's Story*, 171.

8. File 719; Myers, *Vietnam POW Camp Histories*, vol 2, 218.

9. "North Vietnamese (NVN) Exploitation of US Prisoners of War for Propaganda, 1964-1973," HQ USAF Analysis Program Rpt 700/JH/JK-1, Feb 76, 4, 102-05, 107 (quote); Byrne quotations from his chapter in Myers, *Vietnam POW Camp Histories*, vol 2, 226-27, 230.

10. Stockdale file. See also Watkins and Redman, "Captivity in Southeast Asia," 26.

11. Myers, *Vietnam POW Camp Histories*, vol 2, 217-19; Rivers file.

12. Myers, *Vietnam POW Camp Histories*, vol 2, 221; "North Vietnamese Exploitation of US Prisoners of War for Propaganda," 109; Doremus, Coffee, and Rivers files.

13. Alvarez and Pitch, *Chained Eagle*, 189; Michael Patrick Murray, "Historical Analysis and Critical Appraisal of the Code of Conduct," 190.

14. Byrne quote in Myers, *Vietnam POW Camp Histories*, vol 2, 225; Doremus, "Days to Remember," 29; Stockdale remarks at POW-SERE Study Conference, 15-16 Jan 75, 2.

15. See, for instance, Coffee and Shumaker observations in File 719; Doremus, "Days to Remember," 29; Myers, *Vietnam POW Camp Histories*, vol 2, 228-29.

16. See "Chinese Brain-Washing Techniques and Their Effects on Indian Prisoners of War," 2.

17. Mulligan, *Hanoi Commitment*, 111-13; File 719.

18. Rivers file; Byrne quotes in Myers, *Vietnam POW Camp Histories*, vol 2, 224.

19. "Chinese Brain-Washing Techniques and Their Effects on Indian Prisoners of War," 2-3; "North Vietnamese Exploitation of US Prisoners of War for Propaganda," 57, B-9-10; "Lessons Learned Briefing to Chief of Staff, Army," 30 Aug 73, 8-9; "Communist Propaganda Exploitation of U.S. Prisoners in Asia: A Handbook of Examples, 1967-1968," nd, tab E (quotes); Jackson testimony in *American Prisoners of War in Southeast Asia, 1971*, Hearings before House Foreign Affairs Subcommittee on National Security Policy and Scientific Developments, 92 Cong, 1 sess (3 Aug 71), pt 2, 58.

20. "POW's Hardest Task Was Forgetting He Was Black," *Jet*, 19 Apr 73; Denton, *When Hell Was In Session*, 104; *Washington Times*, 3 Apr 89; Margaret Eastman, "The Pain Lingers, Too," *Family*, 5 Sep 73, 12-13; "I Knew My Actions Would Affect 23 Million Blacks," *Pentagram*, 12 Apr 84. John Hubbell treats Cherry's post-capture ordeal and relationship with Halyburton in *P.O.W.*, 194-97; see, too, Guarino, *A POW's Story*, 124.

21. Denton, *When Hell Was In Session*, 104.

22. S/Sgt James E. Jackson, Jr., "18 Months As a Prisoner of the Viet Cong," *Ebony*, Aug 68; Rander quotes from *Pentagram* article, 31 Aug 89, 10. See also Howes, *Voices of the Vietnam POWs*, 131-32.

23. Myers, *Vietnam POW Camp Histories*, vol 2, 222-23; *Viet-Nam Documents and Research Notes*, Aug 69, app A, "Public Presentation of U.S. Prisoners of War," 58-65.

24. Myers, *Vietnam POW Camp Histories*, vol 1, 129, 280-81; File 719.

25. Myers, *Vietnam POW Camp Histories*, vol 2, 222; Watkins and Redman, "Captivity in Southeast Asia," 10; Coffee file; Myers, *Vietnam Camp Histories*, vol 1, 127, 140, 220, 278, 280. On the often fanciful nature of stories appearing in the *Vietnam Courier*, see Plumb, *I'm No Hero*, 134-36; Kiley interv with Hervey Stockman.

26. File 719; Plumb, *I'm No Hero*, 128.

27. Plumb, *I'm No Hero*, 129-32; Doremus, "Days to Remember," 34-35, 44-45; Myers, *Vietnam POW Camp Histories*, vol 1, 218-19; Murray, "Historical Analysis and Critical Appraisal of the Code of Conduct," 199; *Washington Times*, 3 Apr 89.

28. *USA Today*, 9 Apr 87; *Survival, Resistance, and Escape*, 23. For the manner in which the prisoners eventually learned of the moon shot, see Plumb, *I'm No Hero*, 109-10.

29. Doremus, "Days to Remember," 15; Plumb, *I'm No Hero*, 133; Chesley, *Seven Years in Hanoi*, 21; McDaniel, *Yet Another Voice*, 30; Rutledge, *In the Presence of Mine Enemies*, 39-40; Shumaker file.

30. McDaniel, *Yet Another Voice*, 29; Murray, "Historical Analysis and Critical Appraisal of the Code of Conduct," 237, n33; Hubbell, *P.O.W.*, 225-26; Plumb, *I'm No Hero*, 58; Doremus, "Days to Remember," 35.

31. File 719.

32. Ibid.

33. Denton, *When Hell Was In Session*, 89-94. Several American newspaper accounts of Denton's 2 May interview with the Japanese are cited in *Congressional Record*, 18 May 66, 10436-37.

34. Stockdale, *In Love and War*, 177-81.

35. "North Vietnam Exploitation of US Prisoners of War for Propaganda," 17-20; Risner, *Passing of the Night*, 175.

36. Staughton Lynd and Thomas Hayden, *The Other Side*, 106-07.

37. Gaither, *With God in a P.O.W. Camp*, 50-51; Stockdale file.

38. Myers, *Vietnam POW Camp Histories*, vol 2, 227-28; Watkins and Redman, "Captivity in Southeast Asia," 27; Coffee file.

39. Coffee file.

40. Butler file; Gaither, *With God in a P.O.W. Camp*, 51-52; Davis file.

41. Sam Johnson and Jan Winebrenner, *Captive Warriors*, 69-72, 79-85; Hubbell, *P.O.W.*, 180; Denton, *When Hell Was In Session*, 103-04; Gaither, *With God in a P.O.W. Camp*, 52.

42. Lewy, *America in Vietnam*, 339.

43. Myers, *Vietnam POW Camp Histories*, vol 2, 231.

10. THE HANOI MARCH AND THE ISSUE OF WAR CRIMES TRIALS

1. Msg U.S. Mission Geneva for State Dept, 11 Apr 65, sub: Summary of status of various U.S. prisoners of war in Far East, 4; Casella, "Prisoner Problems," 58; reply to ICRC appeal cited in *JAG Journal* (Spring 73), 253, n39; Foreign Broadcast Information Service (FBIS), Radio Hanoi in English, 1, 12 Nov 65; *Washington Post and Times Herald*, 30 Sep 65, 13 Feb 66.

2. Henry Kissinger, *White House Years*, 259.

3. Cited in *The Prisoner of War Problem*, American Enterprise Institute, Dec 70, 18-19. Published for use as a background report for congressional oversight committees, the AEI analysis provides an excellent summary not only of the Nuremberg application, but of other issues as well that had a bearing on the PWs' legal standing.

4. Ltr Rusk to Gonard, 10 Aug 65; memo AsstGenCoun Howard E. Hensleigh for DASD(ISA) Alvin Friedman, 11 Dec 65, sub: Trial as War Criminals of U.S. Pilots Shot Down in Vietnam; memo JCS for CSA and others, 9 Mar 66, sub: Code of Conduct and Related Matters; "The Legality of United States Participation in the Defense of VietNam," Dept State *Bulletin*, 28 Mar 66, 474-89; memo Dir(ISA)(Far East Region) RearAdm F. J. Blouin for DirJtStaff, 29 Jun 66, sub: Possible War Crimes Trials by the DRV: Scenario of USG Response, w/attach.

5. Barker, *Prisoners of War*, 18-19.

6. Democratic Republic of Vietnam, Ministry of Foreign Affairs, *US War Crimes in North VietNam*, Feb 66.

7. Herbert Aptheker, *Mission to Hanoi*; Lynd and Hayden, *The Other Side*. Lynd and Hayden contributed prefaces to Aptheker's work as well. The first excerpts of Aptheker's account appeared in the February issue of *Political Affairs*, about the same time Hanoi's *US War Crimes* was released.

8. Burchett, *Vietnam North*, ch 2; John Duffett, ed, *Against the Crime of Silence: Proceedings of the International War Crimes Tribunal*, 201-05 (Schoenman testimony); File 719. Schoenman's report of the meeting with Coffee, compared with Coffee's recollection, differs as day from night, Schoenman finding Coffee in good health, gently treated, regretting his participation in the war, and apprising his wife of his conversion in a lengthy mea culpa. In his memoir (*Beyond Survival*, 112-17), Coffee identifies his visitor as not Schoenman but Roger Schwinman, without explaining the discrepancy.

9. *U.S. MACV Command History, 1966*, 679; attach to memo Blouin for DirJtStaff, 29 Jun 66, 1.

10. *U.S. MACV Command History, 1966*, 679; memo Blouin for DirJtStaff, 29 Jun 66.

11. Alvarez and Pitch, *Chained Eagle*, 144; Gaither, *With God in a P.O.W. Camp*, 56; Risner, *Passing of the Night*, 125; Doremus, "Days to Remember," 37; Denton, *When Hell Was In Session*, 108; Mulligan, *Hanoi Commitment*, 79-80.

12. Typifying the discrepancies, Alvarez maintained as recently as 1990 that the Briarpatch group numbered 18, not 16. See *Chained Eagle*, 144-45. It should be noted that Alvarez's long-awaited memoir was something of a disappointment, its reliability diminished by careless errors. At least one other PW, however, has cited the 18 figure for Briarpatch.

13. Mulligan, *Hanoi Commitment*, 80; Sam Johnson and Jan Winebrenner, "Shot Down Over North Vietnam in 1966, Air Force Colonel Sam Johnson Survived Seven Years As a POW," *Vietnam* (Oct 90), 16; Chesley, *Seven Years in Hanoi*, 23.

14. This section is derived from reports and memoirs of those who participated in the march, with specific sources cited only as necessary or appropriate. Hubbell provides a lively account of the episode in *P.O.W.*, ch 11.

15. Risner, *Passing of the Night*, 126-27; Alvarez and Pitch, *Chained Eagle*, 145; Denton, *When Hell Was In Session*, 108-09; Coffee, *Beyond Survival*, 158. Risner reminded Alvarez of the movie actor Van Heflin: "Both had strong jaws, firm mouths and crew cuts with V-shaped hair lines."

16. Gaither, *With God in a P.O.W. Camp*, 61.

17. See Day, *Return With Honor*, 178. Alvarez's memoir credits Jerry Coffee with a similar remark, "Hey, does this happen every Saturday night?," suggesting he intended it as a wry comment to lighten the mood (*Chained Eagle*, 150).

18. See Risner, *Passing of the Night*, 130, and Denton's reference to the incident in *Baltimore News American* article, 4 Apr 73.

19. Gaither, *With God in a P.O.W. Camp*, 53; Denton, *When Hell Was In Session*, 112-13 (Kile Berg, in a cell adjacent to the room where Fox met with Denton, overheard much of the conversation and later corroborated Denton's report of the incident). Another lesson Denton drew from the session with Fox and Dum Dum was that the Vietnamese officers had to be careful not to give the enlisted men under them the impression that they were behaving sympathetically

toward fellow officers of the enemy, since the enlistees, who in many cases were more ideologically oriented, could and did lodge complaints against their superiors with the Party. Hence the more professional officers, although perhaps inclined to be lenient, were often hamstrung by political factors that ordained tougher treatment.

20. *Public Papers of the Presidents of the United States: Lyndon B. Johnson, 1966*, vol 2, 744; Rusk cables 10, 13 Jul 66, cited in *U.S. MACV Command History, 1966*, 679, 680.

21. *Congressional Record*, Sen, 15 Jul 66, 15123; *U.S. News & World Report*, 1 Aug 66, 20-21; *Newsweek*, 1 Aug 66, 35-36; *NY Times*, 13 Jul 66; *Philadelphia Inquirer*, 13 Jul 66. The Reston and *Inquirer* pieces appeared in the *Congressional Record*, Sen, 13 Jul 66, 14845, and app, 13 Jul 66, A3667, respectively.

22. See, for example, memo CJCS General Earle G. Wheeler for SecDef, 9 Oct 65, sub: Courses of Action with Respect to Executions of US Personnel; memo JCS ViceDir MajGen(USA) A. H. Manhart for ASD(ISA), 22 Oct 65, sub: Efforts on Behalf of US Prisoners in Vietnam; ltr Robert F. Kennedy to SecDef McNamara, 19 Oct 65.

23. *Americans Missing in Southeast Asia*, Final Report of the House Select Committee on Missing Persons in Southeast Asia, H Rpt 94-1764, 94 Cong, 2 sess (13 Dec 76), 134.

24. Memo DepUS/AF Philip F. Hilbert for AsstViceChStaff, 25 May 66.

25. *Washington Post and Times Herald*, 4 May 66; Statement by DepAsstSecState(PA) Robert J. McCloskey, 18 May 66, in Dept State *Bulletin*, 6 Jun 66, 888; Harriman memrcd 14 Mar 67, sub: USG Courses of Action Considered or Taken to Counter NVN Threats of Maltreatment of US PWs.

26. Memo ASD(ISA) John T. McNaughton for DirJtStaff, 19 Jul 66, sub: Defense Against Possible "War Crimes" Trial Charges; ltr Harriman to McNamara, 13 Jun 66. In the McNamara correspondence, Harriman referred specifically to the cases of Army Sergeants Smith and McClure, who following their release by the Viet Cong in December 1965 underwent a lengthy investigation, and Navy pilot Charles Klusmann, who after his escape from the Pathet Lao in 1964 also faced protracted legal proceedings.

27. The handling of enemy prisoners in the South, complicated by Washington-Saigon policy differences and jurisdictional disputes, would remain a troublesome issue for U.S. officials for the duration of the war, even as treatment improved significantly after the fall of 1966. OSD Hist files contain a large volume of materials on the subject. Two good summaries on the 1965-66 period are "The Historical Management of POWs: A Synopsis of the 1968 US Army Provost Marshal General's Study Entitled 'A Review of United States Policy on Treatment of Prisoners of War,'" ed Environmental Stress Branch, Center for Prisoner of War Studies, Naval Health Research Center, nd, 49-53; and Jeffrey J. Clarke, *Advice and Support: The Final Years, 1965-1973*, 118-20, 167-70. See, too, Casella, "Prisoner Problems," 58; *NY Times*, 25 Jan 67; *Prisoner of War Study: Step Two, The Functioning of the Law*, IV C, 17-18, 32-36.

28. The Nuremberg brief appeared as an article in the Communist newspaper *Nhan Dan* on 10 Jul 66. On the government's legal preparations, see memo McNaughton for DirJtStaff, 19 Jul 66, sub: Defense Against Possible "War Crimes" Trial Charges; *Prisoner of War Study: Step Two, The Functioning of the Law*, IV C, 59-60. Virginia W. Brewer wrote the Legislative Reference Service report, dated 27 Jul 66.

29. Memo Chief of Naval Personnel ViceAdm B. J. Semmes, Jr., for SecNav, 14 Jul 66, sub: Use of the Term "Prisoner of War"; memo Morris for Vance, 19 Jul 66, sub: Change in Reference to U.S. Personnel Captured in Vietnam; memo Vance for ASD(Comp), 19 Jul 66.

30. USAF homecoming briefing, nd, 1-3, summarizes PW intelligence activities through 1966. On the range of intelligence activities beyond 1966, see *Americans Missing in Southeast Asia*, 144-49. George J. Veith, *Code-Name Bright Light*, and Steve Edwards, "Operation Bright Light," *Vietnam* (Oct 91), 18 ff, discuss unsuccessful U.S. PW rescue efforts stemming from the intelligence operation.

31. Davis, *The U.S. Government and American PWs in Southeast Asia*, ch 7 (ms); USAF homecoming briefing, nd, 1-7; Bert H. Cooper, "Statistics on U.S. Participation in the Vietnam Conflict, With Addendum," CRS rpt, 15 Aug 72, 9-10; *Newsweek*, 1 Aug 66, 36. A French journalist back from a trip to Vietnam speculated in November 1966, accurately as it turned out, that there were "more than 150" PWs in the North. See msg 7761 AmEmbParis for

SecState, 22 Nov 66, sub: US Prisoners in North Vietnam. The final post-homecoming tally concluded that there were as many as 175 Americans in Northern prisons at year-end. Hervey Stockman, basing his figure on the 1972 CRS study, put the number at 174, but failed to distinguish between Northern and Southern captives and did not take into account those released, escaping, or dying while in captivity (Stockman, "Authority, Leadership, Organization," 12).

32. *Newsweek*, 1 Aug 66, 35-36; *U.S. News & World Report*, 1 Aug 66, 20; *Prisoner of War Study: Step Two, The Functioning of the Law*, IV C, 59; *U.S. MACV Command History, 1966*, 680; Davis, *The U.S. Government and American PWs in Southeast Asia*, ch 4 (ms).

33. *U.S. MACV Command History, 1966*, 680; DIA Weekly Summary for 29 Jul 66, 3; *NY Times*, 23-26 Jul 66; Davis, *The U.S. Government and American PWs in Southeast Asia*, ch 4 (ms).

34. *Newsweek*, 1 Aug 66, 35; Davis, *The U.S. Government and American PWs in Southeast Asia*, ch 4 (ms).

35. Salisbury's reports appeared in the *New York Times* between 26 December 1966 and 18 January 1967 and were published in *Behind the Lines—Hanoi*. For discussion of the controversy surrounding the account, see Karnow, *Vietnam*, 489-90; Lewy, *America in Vietnam*, 400-03.

36. Ashmore and William C. Baggs, editor of the Miami *News*, were recruited by the State Department to extend peace feelers to North Vietnam. See Blakey, *Prisoner at War*, 22.

37. The State Department was still pursuing this objective in December 1969. See memo Acting SecState for Henry A. Kissinger, 30 Dec 69, sub: Prisoners of War.

11. "MAKE YOUR CHOICE": ANOTHER ROUND OF TERROR

1. Mulligan, *Hanoi Commitment*, 80-81; memo DepAS/AF James P. Goode for ASD(ISA), 28 Nov 67, attach, 4-5, 8.

2. Foreign Broadcast Information Service (FBIS), Radio Hanoi in English, 7 Jul 66; *Nhan Dan* (Hanoi), 11 Jul 66. Errors in the newspaper article (Cole Black was identified incorrectly as a major) and stilted language plainly revealed to U.S. analysts that the statements were manufactured. A curiosity: Vietnamese political warfare experts latched onto "clique" as an insulting word, used it frequently in propaganda (four times in the cited article), and belabored the concept during PW indoctrination. One prisoner taught an interrogator to pronounce it "klee-Q," providing the men a chuckle when that pronunciation was used over the camp radio. When Frenchy pronounced it "klee-kway," referring to the "bad *assitude*" of the "John-SON klee-kway," a couple of the PWs admitted to being part of that "bad-ass LBJ klee-kway."

3. File 719.

4. Risner, *Passing of the Night*, 132-37.

5. Myers, *Vietnam POW Camp Histories*, vol 1, 88-90; Gaither, *With God in a P.O.W. Camp*, 66-67; Alvarez and Pitch, *Chained Eagle*, 158.

6. Myers, *Vietnam POW Camp Histories*, vol 1, 89-90; Doremus, "Days to Remember," 44-45; Gaither, *With God in a P.O.W. Camp*, 67.

7. Alvarez and Pitch, *Chained Eagle*, 158-62.

8. File 719.

9. Gaither, *With God in a P.O.W. Camp*, 69-73; Butler and Shumaker files; Butler oral history, USAF Academy. Hubbell, *P.O.W.*, 211-13, discusses the Shumaker and Knutson incidents; he places the Shumaker-Harris summons on the 16th rather than 15th, the discrepancy, here as elsewhere, possibly attributable to the author and the PWs using different time zones, Washington vs. Vietnam, as their frame of reference.

10. Doremus, "Days to Remember," 46; Gaither, *With God in a P.O.W. Camp*, 74; Alvarez and Pitch, *Chained Eagle*, 162-63; Myers, *Vietnam POW Camp Histories*, vol 1, 92-93, 97.

11. Myers, *Vietnam POW Camp Histories*, vol 1, 93-94; Alvarez and Pitch, *Chained Eagle*, 163, 164-65; Davis and Shankel files; Gaither, *With God in a P.O.W. Camp*, 75.

12. Shankel file; Myers, *Vietnam POW Camp Histories*, vol 1, 94-96, 97-98; Chesley, *Seven Years in Hanoi*, 26, 61; Hubbell, *P.O.W.*, 226-27.

13. Myers, *Vietnam POW Camp Histories*, vol 1, 98-99; Shankel file.
14. Gaither, *With God in a P.O.W. Camp*, 76; Alvarez and Pitch, *Chained Eagle*, 173-74; Myers, *Vietnam POW Camp Histories*, vol 1, 99-100; Hubbell, *P.O.W.*, 227-28; Chesley, *Seven Years in Hanoi*, 26.
15. Risner's "longest six weeks of my life" episode at Hoa Lo, involving more a mental than a physical test, is recounted in *Passing of the Night*, ch 16.
16. Mulligan, *Hanoi Commitment*, 80; Hubbell, *P.O.W.*, 201-03, 205-06; Rivers and Galanti files.
17. On "Lump," see Denton, *When Hell Was In Session*, 119; Mulligan, *Hanoi Commitment*, 111-12.
18. Most of the material used in this section is drawn from two published PW accounts, Denton's *When Hell Was In Session*, ch 13, and Mulligan's *Hanoi Commitment*, 80-132. Rutledge, *In the Presence of Mine Enemies*, 44-47, details one prisoner's experience at the Zoo in August 1966. Of course, the best sources on the Zoo captivity between July and December 1966 are the individual PW homecoming reports. See also Hubbell, *P.O.W.*, chs 12-13; Myers, *Vietnam POW Camp Histories*, vol 1, 133-39.
19. Rutledge, *In the Presence of Mine Enemies*, 45-46; Mulligan, *Hanoi Commitment*, 105-06; Hubbell, *P.O.W.*, 208.
20. Mulligan, *Hanoi Commitment*, 86-98, 104-06, 110; Denton, *When Hell Was In Session*, 120.
21. Denton, *When Hell Was In Session*, 117-23; Mulligan, *Hanoi Commitment*, 107-08.
22. Myers, *Vietnam POW Camp Histories*, vol 1, 134-35; Denton, *When Hell Was In Session*, 123-24; Hubbell, *P.O.W.*, 215-19; *NY Times*, 18 Sep 66; *Time*, 12 Aug 66, 9 Apr 73. French journalist Madeleine Riffaud visited Kasler and found him "arrogant and overbearing"; she reported to the U.S. Embassy in Paris that he was being given good care by the Vietnamese, with a fan in his room, a special diet, and vitamins to aid his recovery. See msg 7761 AmEmbParis for SecState, 22 Nov 66, sub: US Prisoners in North Vietnam.
23. Information on the Office PWs is from homecoming reports. Gregory arrived at Hoa Lo in an ambulance with Stutz and two other injured 2 December shootdowns, Maj. Hubert Flesher and Capt. James Berger. None ever saw Gregory again. Of the 13 aviators felled over North Vietnam that day, only 7 survived to homecoming.
24. Denton, *When Hell Was In Session*, 120-21; Mulligan, *Hanoi Commitment*, 108-09, 126; Hubbell, *P.O.W.*, 219-21; Rosario Rausa, "Home from Hanoi," *Naval Aviation News*, Dec 73 [Fellowes interv], 9-21.
25. Coffee, *Beyond Survival*, 151, 169-70; Mulligan, *Hanoi Commitment*, 108; Denton, *When Hell Was In Session*, 122-23; Rivers file; Hubbell, *P.O.W.*, 217; *Time*, 9 Apr 73.
26. Rausa, "Home from Hanoi," 13, 18; Denton, *When Hell Was In Session*, 118, 123; Mulligan, *Hanoi Commitment*, 100-02.
27. Coffee, *Beyond Survival*, 144; Mulligan, *Hanoi Commitment*, 82-85, 107, 109, 122-26; Johnson and Winebrenner, *Captive Warriors*, 105; Virginia and Spike Nasmyth, *Hanoi Release John Nasmyth*, 85-87.
28. Denton, *When Hell Was In Session*, 125-26; Mulligan, *Hanoi Commitment*, 126-32; Stockdale, *In Love and War*, 188; Rivers file; Myers, *Vietnam POW Camp Histories*, vol 1, 138-39.
29. Mulligan, *Hanoi Commitment*, 133 (quote), 148-49; McDaniel, *Yet Another Voice*, 30-31.
30. Rivers file; Alvarez and Pitch, *Chained Eagle*, 171, 174; Stockdale, *In Love and War*, 232-33.
31. Gaither, *With God in a P.O.W. Camp*, 79-82; Hubbell, *P.O.W.*, 230-32.
32. Mulligan, *Hanoi Commitment*, 135; Hubbell, *P.O.W.*, 235-36; Scott Blakey, *Prisoner at War: The Survival of Commander Richard A. Stratton*, chs 5, 10 (91, quote).
33. Risner, *Passing of the Night*, 150; Rivers file; Mulligan, *Hanoi Commitment*, 143-45; Denton, *When Hell Was In Session*, 129-30.
34. Mulligan, *Hanoi Commitment*, 144-47; Myers, *Vietnam POW Camp Histories*, vol 1, 101; "PW Camps in North Vietnam," encl 1, ltr DASD(ISA) Roger E. Shields to J. Angus MacDonald, 26 Apr 76.
35. Hubbell, *P.O.W.*, 224; Denton, *When Hell Was In Session*, 126.
36. Denton, *When Hell Was In Session*, 126; Gaither, *With God in a P.O.W. Camp*, 83.
37. Rowan, *They Wouldn't Let Us Die*, 86-87; Risner, *Passing of the Night*, 148-49.

12. THE MIDDLE YEARS IN THE SOUTH: NICK ROWE'S GROUP IN THE DELTA

1. On the 1965 buildup, see OASD(PA) News Release 10-66, 4 Jan 66. Figures on troop strength and casualties are from Southeast Asia Statistical Summary, OASD(Comp), Directorate for Information Operations, 5 Dec 73. Figures on civilian PWs are from information supplied OSD Hist Office by DIA, 3 Apr 85. See also Nutt, *Prisoners of War in Indochina* (Jan 69, rev ed), 57.

2. Neil Sheehan, *A Bright Shining Lie: John Paul Vann and America in Vietnam*, 565. Craig Howes observed that the Southern experience became subordinated or "marginalized" not only because there were fewer PWs in the South but because "the official story" was authored in the main by officer-memoirists confined in the North and then perpetuated by John Hubbell in *P.O.W.* See Howes, *Voices of the Vietnam POWs*, 77, 82, 98-102.

3. "Inside North Vietnam's Prisons—How Americans Coped" [with sidebar on "Life Under Viet Cong"], *U.S. News & World Report*, 26 Mar 73; Rowe interv in *Southeast Asia Survival Journal* (Apr 72), 73-74, 224-26; Browne, "Development of Prisoner of War Exploitation Techniques And Those Utilized by Guerrilla-Type Forces Against American Military Captives in Vietnam," ch 5. On the boredom factor, see, too, Rowe interv in *Southeast Asia Survival Journal*, 45-47. On VC interrogation and indoctrination from a later perspective than the 1963 report cited in Chapter 4, see Browne, 67-74; *U.S. MACV Command History, 1967*, vol 2, 973-75, 976-78; ibid, *1969*, vol 2, X-36-37; and *Survival, Resistance, and Escape*, Oct 69, chs 3 and 4 (see esp pp 30-31, where Rowe comments that "there's a great similarity between what they're trying to do up North and what they're trying to do down South").

4. On this point, see *U.S. MACV Command History, 1967*, vol 2, 973; ibid, *1969*, vol 2, X-34-35; CIA Rpt 314/03673-67, 14 Mar 67, sub: Viet Cong Policy Toward and Exploitation of U.S. Prisoners of War, 2; CIA Rpt 311/07262-68, 15 Aug 68, sub: Viet Cong Policy and Treatment of Prisoners of War, 1-2; encl 1, ltr McNamara to Rivers, 3 Sep 66, 3-4.

5. Rowe interv in *Southeast Asia Survival Journal*, 74, 98-99, 225-26; Murray, "Historical Analysis and Critical Appraisal of the Code of Conduct," 206-07.

6. Kushner, "To Live or to Die," 3; Stratton quote in *Washington Times*, 27 Jan 87. On the North-South comparison, see, too, "POW's: The Price of Survival," *Newsweek*, 16 Apr 73, which contains more Kushner impressions. Quotes from the voluble physician-prisoner were featured in a slew of postwar articles and provide some of the most graphic testimony of life on the run with the Viet Cong.

7. Browne, "Development of Prisoner of War Exploitation Techniques And Those Utilized by Guerrilla-Type Forces Against American Military Captives in Vietnam," 59-60, 75; *U.S. MACV Command History, 1967*, vol 2, 975-76; "Prisoner Retention Sites in South Vietnam," encl DIA memo for JCS, NSA, and others, 18 May 67, sub: Prisoner Detention Sites in South Vietnam, 1-2; Rowe interv in *Southeast Asia Survival Journal*, 7-10.

8. The Dodson-Eckes escape is discussed in Chapter 14; Vanputten's, Chapter 21; Camacho's, Chapter 13. On Graening, see Rochester note attached to msg 20774 AmEmbSaigon for SecState, 19 Mar 67, sub: Escape of U.S. PW. For a complete list of escapees (including civilians and the two servicemen who made it out of Laos, Charles Klusmann and Dieter Dengler) and the circumstances of their escapes, see attach ltr DASD(ISA) Roger E. Shields to J. Angus MacDonald, 22 Mar 76, "U.S. Escapees in Southeast Asia."

9. Official lists differ on the exact number, some including Klusmann and Dengler from the Laotian rolls in the VC count and others inexplicably omitting Army PFC Paul Hatch, who, records indicate, was captured by VC on 24 August 1969 and escaped the next day. Compare, for example, the Shields list cited in note 8 above and the data in DIA Intelligence Appraisal, 8 May 73, fig 8.

10. "An Overview of Free-World Personnel Captured in South Vietnam," 7-8; DIA Summary, "U.S. PW Movement to North Vietnam," nd, in *Americans Missing in Southeast Asia*, Hearings before House Select Committee on Missing Persons in Southeast Asia, 94 Cong, 1 sess (1976), pt 3, 307.

11. As in Chapter 4, we have relied principally on Rowe's published account *Five Years to Freedom* to treat this group's experience. The earliest of the Vietnam PW memoirs, it remains one of the best. See also the other sources cited in Chapter 4, note 11; Eric C. Ludvigsen, "Survival of an American Prisoner: An Extraordinary Exercise of Will," *Army*, Feb 70; memo James L. Monroe for LtCol Vince DiMauro, 10 Apr 69, sub: Special Report on Interview with Major James Nicholas Rowe USA; *Survival, Resistance, and Escape*, Oct 69; S/Sgt James E. Jackson, Jr., "18 Months As a Prisoner of the Viet Cong," *Ebony*, Aug 68.

12. *Survival, Resistance, and Escape*, 44-45; Rowe interv in *Southeast Asia Survival Journal*, 40-44.

13. *Five Years to Freedom*, 177.

14. Rowe discusses the broadcast and their reaction in *Five Years to Freedom*, 204-07. The three "patriots" were Communist sympathizers who had been convicted by a South Vietnamese Government tribunal of terrorist activities. News of the Americans' deaths spread abroad swiftly, reported in the *Washington Post and Times Herald* on 27 September and prompting a State Department press briefing the same day in which spokesman Robert J. McCloskey condemned the killings.

15. Rowe interv in *Southeast Asia Survival Journal*, 88-89. See, too, *Survival, Resistance, and Escape*, 14.

16. Rowe interv in *Southeast Asia Survival Journal*, 37.

17. *Five Years to Freedom*, 207.

18. Memo Monroe for DiMauro, 10 Apr 69, 1-2; *Five Years to Freedom*, 198; Rowe interv in *Southeast Asia Survival Journal*, 102-05 (on Code of Conduct), 148 (on physical conditioning), 151-87 passim (on diet).

19. Walker's death was confirmed by a VC defector, Phung Van Thuong. See *Washington Daily News*, 3 Jan 69. Quoted material is from *Five Years to Freedom*, 214, and Rowe interv in *Southeast Asia Survival Journal*, 220. In his memoir Rowe identifies Walker as Tim Barker, here as elsewhere in the book using pseudonyms to protect the identity of deceased comrades.

20. Rowe interv in *Southeast Asia Survival Journal*, 50. See, too, *Five Years to Freedom*, 221-25 (for Tadios, Rowe uses the name Dave Davila).

21. *Five Years to Freedom*, 257.

22. Rowe interv in *Southeast Asia Survival Journal*, 48. See, too, *Five Years to Freedom*, 258-59. For Jackson's version, see "18 Months As a Prisoner of the Viet Cong," *Ebony*, Aug 68.

23. *Five Years to Freedom*, 260-66. On Rowe's ability to obtain writing materials and maintain a diary of sorts, see *Survival, Resistance, and Escape*, 50-52. Parts of the notebook—which Rowe made available to the authors—are reproduced in *Five Years to Freedom*.

24. *Survival, Resistance, and Escape*, 54.

25. *Five Years to Freedom*, 271-74; Pitzer testimony in *American Prisoners of War in Southeast Asia, 1971*, 51-52; Browne, "Development of Prisoner of War Exploitation Techniques And Those Utilized by Guerrilla-Type Forces Against American Military Captives in Vietnam," 82-84.

26. U.S. Army troops did help to free dozens of South Vietnamese soldiers and civilians, but during the entire war only one American was recovered alive in such an operation—Army Spec. Larry Aiken, in July 1969—and he died two weeks later from a bludgeoning by a VC guard sustained shortly before or during the raid. Rescue and recovery efforts were coordinated at MACV Headquarters in Saigon by the Joint Personnel Recovery Center (JPRC). For a summary of these activities, see *Americans Missing in Southeast Asia*, Final Report (13 Dec 76), 149-56 (155-56 esp); Francis J. Kelly, *U.S. Army Special Forces, 1961-1971*, in Vietnam Studies Series, 148. See, too, Westmoreland, *A Soldier's Report*, 307; *Washington Post and Times Herald*, 4 Nov 65 (incident cited in Chapter 4, note 21). On the unfortunate Aiken episode, see materials in OSD Hist and *U.S. MACV Command History, 1969*, vol 2, X-50.

27. *Five Years to Freedom*, 290-94.

28. Ibid, 336. Rowe describes the mosquito assault vividly on 336-38.

29. Rowe's escape was reported in National Military Command Center memrcd, 31 Dec 68, sub: Liberation of a US Prisoner of War. For details, see *Five Years to Freedom*, 418-33; "Major Nick Rowe of Army," West Point *Assembly* (Spring 69), excerpted in *Survival, Resistance, and Escape*, 62-65.

30. *Five Years to Freedom*, 434-41 (435, 441, quotes); memo Monroe for DiMauro, 10 Apr 69, 3-4.
31. *Five Years to Freedom*, 457.
32. Caryle Murphy, "Manila Ambush Victim Had Foiled Viet Cong, Come Home a Hero," *Washington Post*, 23 Apr 89; "Targeting a U.S. Hero," *Newsweek*, 1 May 89, 42.

13. PWs IN SOUTH VIETNAM'S HEARTLAND, 1965-1967

1. "An Overview of Free-World Personnel Captured in South Vietnam," 5-7.
2. Crafts 6 Mar 67 interv; Maj Charles D. Melson and LtCol Curtis G. Arnold, *U.S. Marines in Vietnam: The War That Would Not End, 1971-1973*, 231.
3. Encl 1, ltr McNamara to Rivers, 3 Sep 66, 3; Crafts 4, 6 Mar 67 intervs; ibid, 2 Mar 67 interv, 20-21, 28, 89-90; Smith, *P.O.W.*, 228-29, 299; *NY Times*, 5 Sep 65.
4. Camacho file; Evasion and Escape Memo on Camacho experience, ACS/Intelligence, HQUSAF, 30 Dec 65, 15; Smith, *P.O.W.*, 225-27.
5. Smith, *P.O.W.*, 228, 231-32; Evasion and Escape Memo on Camacho experience, 16; *Winter Soldier Investigation*, 131. Smith and Crafts both indicated that the VC went to considerable trouble carrying the heavy packages on foot from Phnom Penh in Cambodia over 50 miles of jungle terrain to the Carefree location. Camacho was more skeptical of the Communists' motives (see E&E Memo, 23).
6. Crafts 10 Mar 67 interv; Smith, *P.O.W.*, 232-33; Evasion and Escape Memo on Camacho experience, 24.
7. Evasion and Escape Memo on Camacho experience, 17-18; Camacho file; Smith, *P.O.W.*, 233-37. Camacho's and Smith's accounts differ appreciably on details, but both suggest that Smith was instrumental in covering Camacho's getaway. See, too, *Winter Soldier Investigation*, 129; *Time*, 10 Dec 65, 39.
8. Smith, *P.O.W.*, 237-39.
9. Evasion and Escape Memo on Camacho experience, 19-21; Smith, *P.O.W.*, 300; *Washington Post and Times Herald*, 24 Aug 65; *NY Times*, 5 Sep 65.
10. Smith, *P.O.W.*, 239-42.
11. Ibid, 242-54; "Summary of Joint Experience of Personnel Captured at Hiep Hoa," attach memo Allen for Berg, 21 Apr 67, sub: Prisoners of War in Southeast Asia, 2; Crafts 9 Mar 67 interv and 2 Mar 67 interv, 46; *Washington Post and Times Herald*, 27 Sep 65. As with Bennett, there is no way of telling for certain—especially in the case of Versace, who had been in bad shape for some time—whether the Americans were in fact executed, or died from punishment or natural causes and were labeled reprisal victims for propaganda effect. Nick Rowe, whose group in the Delta learned about the "executions" from a radio furnished by guards, thought it "conceivable" that even Roraback "was sick or dead at the time . . . ." (see Rowe interv in *Southeast Asia Survival Journal*, 107-08), but Smith's firsthand account, which places Roraback at the scene and reasonably healthy the previous evening, makes that unlikely.
12. Smith, *P.O.W.*, 259-64. The two Cubans, Marta Rojas and Raul Valdes Viva, wrote a book about their visit to the guerrilla camp. Entitled *Vietnam del sur* and translated into English, it denigrated the American PWs and identified Oil Can Harry as Le Hoa, a hero of the Viet Minh war against the French.
13. Smith, *P.O.W.*, 264-85; *NY Times*, 1 Dec 65; *Time*, 10 Dec 65; *Newsweek*, 13 Dec 65. The *Time* piece covered the controversial press conference under the cynical title "Two for the Show."
14. A large file of material dealing with the Smith-McClure episode, much of it generated by Army Intelligence and still classified, is in OSD Hist. Smith's version of his stay on Okinawa and subsequent developments is recounted in *P.O.W.*, 285-92.
15. Ltr Harriman to McNamara, 13 Jun 66; ltr Vance to Harriman, 25 Jul 66.
16. The Dawson story is reconstructed here primarily from two *Life* articles that appeared 12 March and 8 October 1965 and Dawson's interview in August 1965 at Bien Hoa. The *NY Times* also reported on Dawson's activities; see articles 9, 12 May, 26 Aug 65.

17. The Hertz case is treated at length in Davis, *The U.S. Government and American PWs in Southeast Asia*, ch 5 (ms). For published reports of his changing status, see *Washington Post and Times Herald*, 28 Jun and 8 Nov 67, and *Life*, 21 Jul 67. Thirty years after his presumed death, Hertz's remains were still not recovered.

18. Scattered materials on the McLean case are in OSD Hist.

19. The principal source of the Wallis information is msg 252434 SecState Henry A. Kissinger for AmEmbSaigon, 5 Nov 74, sub: Reported Death of British National in SVN. Two Australian riflemen with a force supporting South Vietnamese troops—Richard Parker and Peter Gillson—and an Australian civilian—Peter Hunting—disappeared in the vicinity of the Wallis incident. They may have been captured, but intelligence reports are inconclusive. Hunting's body was later recovered.

20. Kiley interv with Page, Oct 79; *POW/MIA's*, Report of the Senate Select Committee on POW/MIA Affairs, 103 Cong, 1 sess (13 Jan 93), 584.

21. Materials on the civilian PWs, including accounts of Monahan and Scales, are in OSD Hist. See, too, *NY Times*, 6 Jan 67; *Washington Post and Times Herald*, 5 Jan 67.

22. Miscellaneous materials relating to these cases are in OSD Hist. Nolan is cited in the muckraking book by Mark Sauter and Jim Sanders, *The Men We Left Behind: Henry Kissinger, the Politics of Deceit and the Tragic Fate of POWs After the Vietnam War*, 227-30.

23. Ramsey's exceptional story is summarized here from various news reports and his own arresting post-homecoming commentaries. See, for example, "Inside North Vietnam's Prisons— How Americans Coped" [sidebar on "Life Under Viet Cong: Crude Bamboo Cages"], *U.S. News & World Report*, 26 Mar 73; "The Cruel Years—Two Exclusive Reports," *Nutrition Today*, May/Jun 73, printed in *American Prisoners of War and Missing in Action in Southeast Asia, 1973*, Hearings before House Foreign Affairs Subcommittee on National Security Policy and Scientific Developments, 93 Cong, 1 sess (May 73), pt 4, 223-33. Ramsey is treated admiringly in *A Bright Shining Lie*, Neil Sheehan's Pulitzer prize-winning account of U.S. adviser and Ramsey boss John Paul Vann. For another, less flattering view of both Ramsey and Vann that characterized the pair as sinister CIA operatives, see Ngo Vinh Long, "The American POWs: Their Glory Is All Moonshine," *Ramparts*, May 73.

24. Ramsey discusses the vicissitudes of food availability and distribution at length in the *Nutrition Today* article cited in the House hearing, 226-27 (226, quote).

25. Ramsey file; "The Cruel Years—Two Exclusive Reports," 224-25, 227, 230; Sheehan, *A Bright Shining Lie*, 661-64.

26. Ramsey file; Crafts 6 Mar 67 interv, 7.

27. Smith, *P.O.W.*, 232, 247; Crafts 9 Mar 67 interv; Ramsey file.

28. Ramsey file.

29. Ramsey graphically describes his near-fatal bout with malaria in the *Nutrition Today* article, 228.

30. Womack and Crafts case summaries attachs memo Allen for Berg, 21 Apr 67; Crafts 2 Mar 67 interv, 79. The most detailed description of VC personnel at this camp is in Crafts's interview of 10 Mar 67.

31. Womack and Crafts case summaries attachs memo Allen for Berg, 21 Apr 67.

32. Ibid; Crafts 6, 9 Mar 67 intervs; *Washington Post and Times Herald*, 24 Feb 67; OASD(PA) News Release 173-67, 27 Feb 67.

33. Crafts case summary attach memo Allen for Berg, 21 Apr 67; Crafts 6 Mar 67 interv; msg 18952 AmEmbSaigon for SecState, 25 Feb 67, sub: Letter from FSO Douglas K. Ramsey, Viet Cong PW, to His Parents.

34. Ramsey file; Crafts 6 Mar 67 interv, 8; "The Cruel Years—Two Exclusive Reports," 230-31.

35. Hardy file.

36. Ramsey file; "The Cruel Years—Two Exclusive Reports," 231.

37. Melson and Arnold, *The War That Would Not End*, 231.

38. *Washington Post and Times Herald*, 9 Nov 67.

14. PWs IN THE NORTHERN PROVINCES OF THE SOUTH, 1965-1967

1. "An Overview of Free-World Personnel Captured in South Vietnam," 1-4; DIA Summary, "U.S. PW Movement to North Vietnam," nd, in *Americans Missing in Southeast Asia*, Hearings before House Select Committee on Missing Persons in Southeast Asia, 94 Cong, 1 sess (1976), pt 3, 308-09.

2. Kushner, "To Live or to Die," 3-4.

3. This and other sections of the chapter draw heavily upon case summaries in the possession of the Marine Corps Historical Center, Washington, D.C.

4. OSD Hist has an extensive file on Garwood. Most of these materials are news clips and published articles relating to the PW's court-martial. The absence of witnesses makes it impossible to confirm Garwood's account of his capture and early mistreatment, but details of his behavior and activities after 1967 are known through the reports of surviving comrades and other hostages who lived with him. See, for example, Zalin Grant, *Survivors*, chs 7-8; James A. Daly and Lee Bergman, *A Hero's Welcome*, passim; Monika Schwinn and Bernhard Diehl, *We Came to Help*, 83-90; Hubbell, *P.O.W.*, 400-01. Gary D. Solis, *Marines and Military Law in Vietnam: Trial by Fire*, 223-30, supplies useful background on Garwood and his captivity experience in the context of examining the court-martial proceeding. Garwood elaborated on his version of events in *Playboy* interv, Jul 81, 69ff. See also Howes, *Voices of the Vietnam POWs*, 220-30.

    The definitive book about Garwood and his complicated story has yet to be written and perhaps never will be, owing to the subject's fuzzy memory and unreliable mental state and the difficulty in corroborating key aspects of his account. At his trial his lawyers took to distinguishing between "the historical truth" and "Bobby's truth." Even the authors of the most comprehensive Garwood biography to date, Winston Groom and Duncan Spencer, *Conversations With the Enemy: The Story of PFC Robert Garwood*, admit to the problem of separating fact from fiction: "Can anyone ever really know the whole of it? It is not likely. Probably even Garwood himself can't" (394).

5. Grant, *Survivors*, 87. Garwood remembered Grissett's capture circumstances differently (see *Conversations With the Enemy*, 100), suggesting that either Garwood manufactured parts of the story or Grissett himself had varying renditions he told different comrades.

6. *Conversations With the Enemy*, 158-59.

7. Schwinn and Diehl, *We Came to Help*, 86-87; Grant, *Survivors*, 111-16; Hubbell, *P.O.W.*, 401.

8. *Conversations With the Enemy*, 171-72; *Playboy*, Jul 81, 191.

9. *Washington Post and Times Herald*, 2 Aug 68; Zalin Grant, "American Defectors With the Viet Cong," *New Republic*, 7 Sep 68; Grant, *Survivors*, 145-49; Solis, *Trial by Fire*, 226; *Playboy*, Jul 81, 94f.

10. Garwood's court-martial was a drawn-out affair that is beyond the scope of this volume. Although the trial ended in a conviction, it left many questions unanswered regarding the extent of his transgressions and the issue of Code of Conduct standards generally. For a range of opinions on the controversial case, see, besides Solis's study, Smith Hempstone, "Court-Martial of a Traitor: Why Pvt. Garwood Deserves Mercy," *Washington Post*, 25 Jan 81; *Washington Post* news account of the verdict, 6 Feb 81, and editorial, 7 Feb 81; James Bond Stockdale, "What Not to Conclude From the Garwood Case," *Washington Post*, 9 Feb 81; *Conversations With the Enemy*, chs 24-27; Monika Jensen-Stevenson, *Spite House: The Last Secret of the War in Vietnam*.

11. The North Vietnamese released a letter to UPI on 29 May 1967 that had allegedly been written by Burgess and broadcast to American troops in the South, in which Burgess praised the treatment he received from his captors and condemned the U.S. involvement as "dirty, immoral, and illegal." See *NY Times*, 30 May 67.

12. We have only Budd's account to rely on as a gauge of how well he performed during this period, but there is no reason to doubt his story.

13. Garwood's impressions of the pair are in *Conversations With the Enemy*, 143-47.

14. Msg 60209 CINCPAC for JCS, 23 Jan 68, sub: Bright Light; *Washington Post and Times Herald*, 25 Jan 68.

15. Msg 5741 State for U.S. Mission Geneva, 12 Jul 67, sub: Mistreatment and Murder of PW's Grammar and Frits; *Washington Post and Times Herald*, 24 May 67.

16. Memo DepUS/N(Manpower) Richard A. Beaumont for DASD(Military Personnel Policy), 7 Apr 67, sub: Prisoners of War in Southeast Asia, with encl case summaries of North and Hamilton.

17. Ibid, with encl case summaries of Dodson and Eckes; *Newsweek*, 11 Jul 66, 36-37; news accounts cited in *Congressional Record*, 27 Jun 66, A3418-19; ltrs Eckes to NAMPOW, 15, 18, 24 Dec 98.

18. Sherman's story is pieced together from the accounts of Garwood and other fellow prisoners. See *Conversations With the Enemy*, 147-48, 213-14; Grant, *Survivors*, 81, 88-89, 123-28, 165; Daly and Bergman, *A Hero's Welcome*, ch 13. Because of considerable bickering and backbiting among this group, the sources must be used advisedly.

19. Solis, *Trial by Fire*, 223; Grant, *Survivors*, 91; *Conversations With the Enemy*, 163-66; Hubbell, *P.O.W.*, 418; Daly and Bergman, *A Hero's Welcome*, 110.

20. The escape episode is vividly related by Daly in *Survivors*, 123-27, and *A Hero's Welcome*, ch 13 (114-15, quote). See, too, Hubbell, *P.O.W.*, 419; PW Escape file. Again, there are discrepancies between accounts. Garwood later insisted the Vietnamese actually staged the Weatherman execution to intimidate the others and that Weatherman continued to serve the Communists after his faked death and even after the war when he remained in Vietnam. See Sauter and Sanders, *The Men We Left Behind*, 230-31.

21. *Conversations With the Enemy*, 167, 213; Grant, *Survivors*, 175-76.

22. Grant, *Survivors*, 81, 167-70 (170, quote); *Conversations With the Enemy*, 214-17, 377-78, 380. The cat story is recounted by Kushner in "POW's: The Price of Survival," *Newsweek*, 16 Apr 73.

23. *Conversations With the Enemy*, 393-94.

15. LAOS IN THE MIDDLE YEARS: LIVE AND VANISHED PWs

1. "The 'Twilight' War in Laos," *NY Times*, 24 Jan 65; "Reds Heat Up Laos—Real Key to Asia?" *U.S. News & World Report*, 17 Jun 68; Col Charles F. Brower IV, USA, "Strategic Reassessment in Vietnam: The Westmoreland 'Alternate Strategy' of 1967-1968," *Naval War College Review* (Spring 91), 24-26.

2. Arnold R. Isaacs, *Without Honor: Defeat in Vietnam and Cambodia*, ch 6; *The Vietnam Experience: War in the Shadows*, ch 5; "Air Attacks Secret for Two Years," Baltimore *Sun*, 4 May 66; "Reds Heat Up Laos," *U.S. News & World Report*, 17 Jun 68 (quote is from sidebar). A useful chronology of the "secret war" is in Robbins, *Ravens*, vii-xi. In a more investigative vein, though too polemical to be credible, is Monika Jensen-Stevenson and William Stevenson, *Kiss the Boys Goodbye: How the United States Betrayed Its Own PWs in Vietnam*; see ch 6 on Laos.

3. Coker's statement, 27 Oct 73, in *Americans Missing in Southeast Asia*, Hearings before House Select Committee on Missing Persons in Southeast Asia, 94 Cong, 1 sess (1975), pt 2, 117-18; Geoffrey Norman, *Bouncing Back*, 21.

4. Memo Sylvester for McNamara, 19 Jul 66, sub: Credibility and the Release of Casualty Statistics from Laos; memo Capt(USN) John W. Thornton for ASD(ISA) Paul Warnke, 22 Jan 68, sub: Greater Effort for Repatriation or Release of American PW's Held in Laos.

5. DoD *POW-MIA Fact Book*, Jul 89, 18, 19; msgs AmEmbVientiane for SecState, 21 Jun 65, 24 May 66; *Kiss the Boys Goodbye*, 106-07; Nigel Cawthorne, *The Bamboo Cage: The Full Story of the American Servicemen Still Held Hostage in South-East Asia*, 70-72; Marian Shelton ch in Sally Hayton-Keeva, ed, *Valiant Women in War and Exile*, 91-96; "Wife of only remaining POW in Southeast Asia dies in apparent suicide," *San Diego Union*, 6 Oct 90. Up until her death Marian Shelton had been a leading spokeswoman for the MIA cause and a prominent figure in the National League of Families of POW/MIA. Captain Shelton's status was finally changed in September 1994 to Killed in Action (see OASD(PA) News Release 533-94, 20 Sep 94).

6. *Americans Missing in Southeast Asia*, pt 2, 118; ltr SecDef McNamara to House Armed Svcs Cte Chmn Rivers, 3 Sep 66, encl 2.

7. *Americans Missing in Southeast Asia*, pt 2, 119; *Americans Missing in Southeast Asia*, Final Report (13 Dec 76), 36.

8. Laotian PW camps are described in *Americans Missing in Southeast Asia*, pt 3, 345. Civilian PW Ernest Brace took credit for devising the "Lulus" acronym as a code name for communications purposes. See his reference to the Lulus in Ernest C. Brace, *A Code to Keep: The True Story of America's Longest-Held Civilian Prisoner of War in Vietnam*, 201, 230; see also Hubbell, *P.O.W.*, 570.

9. Brace, *A Code to Keep*, 39.

10. A large folder of material on Brace is in OSD Hist Laos PW files. His in-depth main debrief remains classified but the relevant details appear in *A Code to Keep* and in his 1976 House testimony (see *Americans Missing in Southeast Asia*, pt 3, 163-83, 211-14). See also Rowan, *They Wouldn't Let Us Die*, ch 3. Kiley interviewed Brace on two occasions.

11. Brace file.

12. *A Code to Keep*, 85.

13. Quoted material from *A Code to Keep*, 138, 142, 143.

14. Brace file; Colvin, *First Heroes*, 196-97.

15. Case file on Cius in Marine Corps Historical Center, Washington, D.C.

16. See memo DirDIA ViceAdm V. P. de Poix for SecDef, 6 Apr 73, encl 4, 9-11 for Sijan case summary. A moving account of Sijan's experience is LtCol Fred A. Meurer, "Sijan! My Name Is Lance Peter Sijan!," which appeared originally in the June 1977 issue of *Airman* and has been reprinted many times since, most recently in *Retired Officer*, May 91, 38 ff. On Colonel Armstrong's fate, see *POW/MIA's*, Report of the Senate Select Committee on POW/MIA Affairs, 103 Cong, 1 sess (13 Jan 93), 702-03.

17. *A Code to Keep*, 162, 165 (quote), 168-69.

16. HIGHER STAKES: LITTLE VEGAS AT THE HILTON

1. Mulligan, *Hanoi Commitment*, 148; see also Brace, *A Code to Keep*, 189.

2. Stockdale, *In Love and War*, 238; Coffee file; Rutledge, *In the Presence of Mine Enemies*, 49; Mulligan, *Hanoi Commitment*, 147-48.

3. Stockdale file; Denton, *When Hell Was In Session*, 131; Myers, *Vietnam POW Camp Histories*, vol 1, 225-26; Gaither, *With God in a P.O.W. Camp*, 86-87; Johnson and Winebrenner, *Captive Warriors*, 121-22.

4. Mulligan, *Hanoi Commitment*, 148-49, 153; Denton, *When Hell Was In Session*, 131.

5. Denton, *When Hell Was In Session*, 134; Myers, *Vietnam POW Camp Histories*, vol 1, 215.

6. Rutledge, *In the Presence of Mine Enemies*, 48-49, 52 (quote); Gaither, *With God in a P.O.W. Camp*, 86-87; Stockdale, *In Love and War*, 237. On the Rutledge-McKnight pairing, see also Hubbell, *P.O.W.*, 272.

7. Myers, *Vietnam POW Camp Histories*, vol 1, 213, 217-18.

8. Chesley, *Seven Years in Hanoi*, 27-28; see, too, Shankel file.

9. Denton, *When Hell Was In Session*, 132-34; Stockdale, *In Love and War*, 245-46; Stockdale file.

10. Stockman, "Authority, Leadership, Organization," 13; Stockdale, *In Love and War*, 247.

11. Stockdale, *In Love and War*, 250-52. Stockdale credited his young roommate in Thunderbird, Navy Lt. (j.g.) Danny Glenn, with being "a sounding board and source of advice as I tried to build a foundation of fair and easily understood law." Glenn had been captured only two months earlier, in December 1966, and spent Christmas Day "suspended from the ceiling on a hook, upside down" when he refused to cooperate at his initial interrogation.

12. Mulligan, *Hanoi Commitment*, 155.

13. See Stockdale, *In Love and War*, 247-48 (247, quote); Rutledge, *In the Presence of Mine Enemies*, 51.

14. Myers, *Vietnam POW Camp Histories*, vol 1, 226; Rutledge, *In the Presence of Mine Enemies*, 51-52; Mulligan, *Hanoi Commitment*, 156-61; Gaither, *With God in a P.O.W. Camp*, 88; Stockman, "Authority, Leadership, Organization," 16.

15. Gaither, *With God in a P.O.W. Camp*, 88-94.

16. Butler file; Mulligan, *Hanoi Commitment*, 156-57; Coffee, *Beyond Survival*, 186-87, 189-90; Rutledge, *In the Presence of Mine Enemies*, 54-56. Coffee's memoir and debrief show two different dates for his move to the Mint, the memoir citing June and the debrief May; Rutledge was certain he entered the Mint on 21 May.

17. Denton, *When Hell Was In Session*, 150; Stockdale, *In Love and War*, 261-62 (Stockdale shared Denton's high regard for Tanner, calling him "the best, most stable landing-signal officer in the Pacific Fleet"); Coffee, *Beyond Survival*, 187-88; *Time*, 14 Apr 67, 34. The Ben Casey-Superman episode is recounted in detail in Hubbell, *P.O.W.*, 240-43, 265-69.

18. Stockdale, *In Love and War*, 255; Hubbell, *P.O.W.*, 276-77.

19. Murray, "Historical Analysis and Critical Appraisal of the Code of Conduct," 193. Murray is careful to state that even with the enhanced knowledge and expertise in interrogation matters, the Vietnamese still lacked sophistication and had only "varying success" at extracting substantive information. On the fate of new shootdowns during this period, see also Mulligan, *Hanoi Commitment*, 153; Denton, *When Hell Was In Session*, 134; Stockdale, *In Love and War*, 263; Hubbell, *P.O.W.*, 292-95. Mulligan's and Denton's time frames are somewhat off here.

20. McDaniel relates his story in *Before Honor*; chs 1-4 cover his capture and early captivity (23, quote). See also Rowan, *They Wouldn't Let Us Die*, ch 5. On the mystery surrounding Patterson's fate, see Cawthorne, *The Bamboo Cage*, 73-74.

21. Plumb recounts his initial torture episode in *I'm No Hero*, ch 4 (65, quotes). On Stark's ordeal, see Rowan, *They Wouldn't Let Us Die*, 234-40.

22. McDaniel, *Before Honor*, 41-42; see, too, Hubbell, *P.O.W.*, 278.

23. Once past the rough initiation, Milligan had one of the easier captivity experiences. Afflicted with toothache, diarrhea, and the usual ailments but spared further torture over the remaining six years, he attributed his good fortune to his junior officer status and a naturally quiet demeanor that may have caused the captor to overlook or ignore him. On Sterling, see McDaniel, *Before Honor*, 44-45.

24. Doremus file; Stockdale, *In Love and War*, 255; Rutledge, *In the Presence of Mine Enemies*, 48; Chesley, *Seven Years in Hanoi*, 41; Myers, *Vietnam POW Camp Histories*, vol 1, 214.

25. At Vegas as elsewhere, identification of Vietnamese prison personnel is made difficult by the several names the Americans used to refer to the same handler. For example, Myers, *Vietnam POW Camp Histories*, vol 1, 222, mentions the tubercular "Hack," while Red McDaniel alludes to a guard named "Ashley Asthmatic" (*Before Honor*, 51); almost certainly they were the same person. Likewise, Gaither and Stockdale call "Greasy" the officer whom Denton and Mulligan knew as "Flea." On "Abe," see Denton, *When Hell Was In Session*, 142-43.

26. Stockman, "Authority, Leadership, Organization," 16; Rowan, *They Wouldn't Let Us Die*, 95.

27. See Chapter 8, note 25. A year later at another camp, when Greasy tried to be friendly with some of the PWs he had tormented at Vegas, the prisoners judged that he had been held responsible and disciplined by superiors for Schmidt's death.

28. Denton, *When Hell Was In Session*, 139-42; Shumaker file; Rowan, *They Wouldn't Let Us Die*, 95. Shumaker eventually complied and did the movie but inserted obscene gestures throughout. "Ironically," his debriefer noted, "the movie roll [sic] called for a 'wounded American' and the Commander did their make-up work for them."

29. Stockdale, *In Love and War*, 265; Coffee, *Beyond Survival*, 192-94; Hubbell, *P.O.W.*, 297-300.

30. Hubbell describes this episode at graphic length in *P.O.W.*, 302-04; PW homecoming accounts, some based on hearsay, fill in other details.

31. Stockdale's summer 1967 ordeal is discussed in *In Love and War*, 256-76, app 4; see, too, File 719.

32. Stockdale, *In Love and War*, 258; Kiley interv with Fer, Aug 76; Mulligan, *Hanoi Commitment*, 158, 164. After the war Fer would follow Ray Vohden as principal adviser for PW-MIA matters in the Office of the Secretary of Defense.

33. File 719.

34. Myers, *Vietnam POW Camp Histories*, vol 1, 230-31; George E. Day, *Return With Honor*, 91; Plumb, *I'm No Hero*, 165.

35. Stockman, "Authority, Leadership, Organization," 22-23; Myers, *Vietnam POW Camp Histories*, vol 1, 227-28.

36. Gaither, *With God in a P.O.W. Camp*, 96-100; Chesley, *Seven Years in Hanoi*, 31-32; Coffee, *Beyond Survival*, 185, 224-25.

37. Hubbell, *P.O.W.*, 294-95, 369-70. By 1969 a healed Fuller would emerge as an effective senior in Stardust.

38. The reference to Day as "one of the toughest men alive" is especially noteworthy considering the source, Jack Fellowes, who himself had been called by Denton "one of the toughest men in prison." Fellowes's comment is in Rausa, "Home from Hanoi," 16. Day recounts his early escape and evasion and subsequent captivity through the move out of Vegas in late 1967 in *Return With Honor*, chs 1-8 (87, quote regarding Tanner's deception); on Overly, see 66, 68-69, 97-99.

39. Risner, *Passing of the Night*, 145-81 (quoted material is from 167, 168, 170, 180). See, too, memo DepAS/AF James P. Goode for ASD(ISA), 28 Nov 67, attach, 7.

40. Coffee, *Beyond Survival*, 136; Risner, *Passing of the Night*, ch 21; Stockman, "Authority, Leadership, Organization," 22; Larson statement in AF Special Report No 86, sub: NVN Fear of Col Risner, 15 Mar 73.

41. Stockman, "Authority, Leadership, Organization," 21-22; Reynolds, "Question of Honor," 108; John A. Dramesi, *Code of Honor*, 220; Johnson and Winebrenner, *Captive Warriors*, 217. Winn would reiterate Reynolds's point that the seniors learned the tap code belatedly and either missed or misconstrued earlier attempts to contact them; see Winn interv, nd, 6–7, and Winn, "The Angels Weep" (unpub ms), 161–66.

42. Stockdale, *In Love and War*, 343-48. Coffee gives his reaction to "The Bob and Ed Show" in *Beyond Survival*, 223-25; see also Hubbell, *P.O.W.*, 478-80.

43. Stockdale file; Stockman, "Authority, Leadership, Organization," 22; Stockdale, *In Love and War*, 240.

17. DIRTY BIRD AND ALCATRAZ: SPECIAL ARRANGEMENTS
FOR HOSTAGES AND HARDLINERS

1. Guarino, *A POW's Story*, 114.

2. A summary of intelligence reports about U.S. PWs at Yen Phu appears in a document titled "Thermal Power Plant (TPP) PW Camp Complex," DIA, DB-4.

3. Official sources and PW memoirs do little to clarify, and sometimes compound, the confusion. We have relied primarily on interviews to reconstruct the captivity experience at the power plant complex.

4. Coffee, *Beyond Survival*, ch 14 (201, quote); Myers, *Vietnam POW Camp Histories*, vol 1, 242, 245-46.

5. Gaither, *With God in a P.O.W. Camp*, 95-96; Myers, *Vietnam POW Camp Histories*, vol 1, 247-48, 258; Coffee, *Beyond Survival*, 201-02.

6. *U.S. MACV Command History, 1969*, vol 2, X-16; Coffee, *Beyond Survival*, 204; Myers, *Vietnam POW Camp Histories*, vol 1, 244-45, 254-55.

7. Kiley interv with LtCol Kevin McManus, 3 Feb 83. McManus was photographed by bystanders while on a street detail outside the power plant, but intelligence officers did not learn of his status until nearly two years later and from a different source.

8. Gaither, *With God in a P.O.W. Camp*, 95; Myers, *Vietnam POW Camp Histories*, vol 1, 257.

9. Kiley interv with Col Thomas Storey, Oct 82.

10. Coffee file; Myers, *Vietnam POW Camp Histories*, vol 1, 245.

11. Coffee file; Kiley interv with Storey.

12. Myers, *Vietnam POW Camp Histories*, vol 1, 252-54; Kiley interv with Storey.

13. Spike Nasmyth, *2355 Days: A POW's Story*, 121; Stockdale, *In Love and War*, 239; Dramesi, *Code of Honor*, 170.

14. See Denton, *When Hell Was In Session*, 126-27.

15. The Coker-McKnight escape incident was one of the more celebrated, and documented, PW episodes. It is treated at length in Hubbell, *P.O.W.*, 355-60, and elsewhere. Good summaries are in Stockdale, *In Love and War*, 460-61; and "U.S. Aircrew Members Escape from Permanent Detention Facilities in North Vietnam," USAF Series 700/KE, Nov 75, 5-10. The Hubbell quote cited here is from *P.O.W.*, 357.

16. "U.S. Aircrew Members Escape from Permanent Detention Facilities in North Vietnam," 9-10. The document makes a vague reference to "the functioning SRO" for Dirty Bird, but there is no evidence elsewhere that such an individual was present or privy to the escape.

17. Gaither, *With God in a P.O.W. Camp*, 96; Coffee file; Myers, *Vietnam POW Camp Histories*, vol 1, 255, 259.

18. Mulligan, *Hanoi Commitment*, 165-66; Denton, *When Hell Was In Session*, 144-47; Stockdale, *In Love and War*, 277.

19. Denton, *When Hell Was In Session*, 147; Rutledge, *In the Presence of Mine Enemies*, 58; Hubbell, *P.O.W.*, 361.

20. Stockdale, *In Love and War*, 277-78; Mulligan, *Hanoi Commitment*, 169; Denton, *When Hell Was In Session*, 148-52. Stockdale has a sketch of the compound and cell assignments in *In Love and War*, 280.

21. Mulligan, *Hanoi Commitment*, 169-70; Denton, *When Hell Was In Session*, 155-56.

22. Rutledge, *In the Presence of Mine Enemies*, 58; Mulligan, *Hanoi Commitment*, 167; Denton, *When Hell Was In Session*, 152-53.

23. Myers, *Vietnam POW Camp Histories*, vol 1, 301-02; Rutledge, *In the Presence of Mine Enemies*, 59-60; Denton, *When Hell Was In Session*, 154.

24. Johnson and Winebrenner, *Captive Warriors*, 164-65; Stockdale, *In Love and War*, 278-79. Stockdale took some pride in tying up such a large number of enemy personnel at Alcatraz (Kiley interv).

25. Johnson and Winebrenner, *Captive Warriors*, 164-65; Stockman, "Authority, Leadership, Organization," 17-18; Mulligan, *Hanoi Commitment*, 168; Denton, *When Hell Was In Session*, 155.

26. Hubbell, *P.O.W.*, 363; Johnson and Winebrenner, *Captive Warriors*, 196-97; Denton, *When Hell Was In Session*, 154; Stockdale, *In Love and War*, 291.

27. Stockdale ltr to Kiley, 24 Jul 85; Stockdale, *In Love and War*, 279, 281, 292; Myers, *Vietnam POW Camp Histories*, vol 1, 310-11; Denton, *When Hell Was In Session*, 156; Mulligan, *Hanoi Commitment*, 190-91.

28. Johnson and Winebrenner, *Captive Warriors*, 164, 166-67; Denton, *When Hell Was In Session*, 156-57; Mulligan, *Hanoi Commitment*, 173-78.

29. Denton, *When Hell Was In Session*, 158-59, 163-64; Stockdale, *In Love and War*, 281-85.

30. Myers, *Vietnam POW Camp Histories*, vol 1, 312-13; Stockdale file; Mulligan, *Hanoi Commitment*, 179, 181-82.

31. Stockdale file; Denton, *When Hell Was In Session*, 165-66; Myers, *Vietnam POW Camp Histories*, vol 1, 314-15; Stockman, "Authority, Leadership, Organization," 19; Hubbell, *P.O.W.*, 378-79.

32. Johnson and Winebrenner, *Captive Warriors*, 168, 172; Denton, *When Hell Was In Session*, 165, 166-67; Mulligan, *Hanoi Commitment*, 182-85; Myers, *Vietnam POW Camp Histories*, vol 1, 317.

33. Denton, *When Hell Was In Session*, 168; Johnson and Winebrenner, *Captive Warriors*, 172-73; Mulligan, *Hanoi Commitment*, 186-87; Stockdale, *In Love and War*, 285.

34. Denton, *When Hell Was In Session*, 168, 171-78; Myers, *Vietnam POW Camp Histories*, vol 1, 318-21; Johnson and Winebrenner, *Captive Warriors*, 173-76.

35. Stockdale file; Myers, *Vietnam POW Camp Histories*, vol 1, 321-22; Mulligan, *Hanoi Commitment*, 168, 195-96; Johnson and Winebrenner, *Captive Warriors*, 176; Denton, *When Hell Was In Session*, 178-81 (Denton places the Jenkins episode a day earlier, 23 January); Stockdale, *In Love and War*, 292-94.

36. Stockdale's riveting account of his 56 days in room 18 is in his homecoming report and, in shorter form, *In Love and War*, 326-39.

37. Stockman, "Authority, Leadership, Organization," 23; Shumaker file; Johnson and Winebrenner, *Captive Warriors*, 177-82.

38. Stockdale, *In Love and War*, 292; Rutledge, *In the Presence of Mine Enemies*, 63-64; File 719; Johnson and Winebrenner, *Captive Warriors*, 183-84, 199-200; Denton, *When Hell Was In Session*,

189-91, 195-96; Mulligan, *Hanoi Commitment*, 202-05, 208-09 (a slightly different version is in Mulligan's homecoming report). See also Risner's tribute to "A Hero Left Behind" in *Passing of the Night*, ch 9, and Guarino, *A POW's Story*, 274.

39. Johnson and Winebrenner, *Captive Warriors*, 183; Mulligan, *Hanoi Commitment*, 213; Denton, *When Hell Was In Session*, 192-97 (197, quote).

40. Rutledge, *In the Presence of Mine Enemies*, 65. See also Mulligan, *Hanoi Commitment*, 211; Johnson and Winebrenner, *Captive Warriors*, 212.

41. Johnson and Winebrenner, *Captive Warriors*, 211; Denton, *When Hell Was In Session*, 147.

18. PLANTATION: EXHIBITIONS AND EARLY RELEASES

1. Day, *Return With Honor*, 103 (diagram of the camp on 102); Blakey, *Prisoner at War*, 167-68; Myers, *Vietnam POW Camp Histories*, vol 1, 261, 264 (diagram on 262); Frishman summary report, 12-13; Project CHECO Southeast Asia Report: Enemy Capture/Release of USAF Personnel in SEA, 15 Mar 69, 13-16.

2. Myers, *Vietnam POW Camp Histories*, vol 1, 264-67, 271; Rumble summary report, 26-30.

3. Several returnees cited Slick as one of their more memorable antagonists. Hervey Stockman testified to his prowess in interv with Kiley, 4 Mar 76. Day paid him high respect in *Return With Honor*, 106-07. He had other nicknames besides "Soft Soap Fairy," including "Frenchy," but he was not the Frenchy of Briarpatch and the Zoo, who had a bad-guy reputation. The prisoners who called Slick Frenchy did not know the other interrogator and named him that because his good English nonetheless retained a French accent.

4. The celebrated bowing incident is recounted in Blakey, *Prisoner at War*, ch 12. See, too, Hubbell, *P.O.W.*, 245-47 (the date is miscited as 8 March), 263-64; Geoffrey Norman, *Bouncing Back*, 65-66; Blakey, "The Obsequious Bow," *American Heritage*, Aug/Sep 78 (excerpted from *Prisoner at War*). The famous still photograph first appeared in *Life* on 7 April, with an article by Lee Lockwood, the American freelance journalist who shot it; *Time* carried the photo and story a week later under the title "Hanoi's Pavlovians" (*Time*, 14 Apr 67, 33-34).

5. Hubbell, *P.O.W.*, 267-68; Larson, *Autobiography*, 13–20; "U.S. Fears Hanoi Is Brainwashing American P.O.W.'s," *NY Times*, 4 Apr 67; "Hanoi Displays 3 Downed Pilots," *NY Times*, 7 May 67; "Display of P.O.W.'s Protested by U.S.," *NY Times*, 9 May 67; Dept State Statement on Hanoi's Violation of Geneva POW Convention, 8 May 67, in Dept State *Bulletin*, 29 May 67, 825.

6. The best summary of the film's contents and impact is in "North Vietnamese Exploitation of US Prisoners of War for Propaganda," 76-91. The 1976 Air Force Intelligence report, citing its wide dissemination and translation, including its appearance, with Arab dubbing, in remote South Yemen, concluded that the film was "by any measure, the most sophisticated and potentially damaging propaganda piece produced by a Communist nation during the Vietnam conflict." See, too, Blakey, *Prisoner at War*, 176-78; Hubbell, *P.O.W.*, 283. Hubbell's derisive characterization of the shooting misses the point of the film's effectiveness. On the issue of U.S. television networks purchasing footage from the East Germans for commercial airing in the United States, see memo DepDirCIA ViceAdm Rufus Taylor for DirDIA LtGen Joseph F. Carroll, 6 Sep 67. The film was taped off the air by U.S. personnel in Germany and copies given to DIA and the services. A full-length copy exists in OSD Hist.

7. Hegdahl's post-release summary report, 1-3, deals with his capture and trip to Hanoi. Norman introduces him in *Bouncing Back*, 143-45 (143, quote); Hubbell, in *P.O.W.*, 252-60 (252, 253, quotes). See, too, Sam Johnson's description of Hegdahl in *Captive Warriors*, 188; and Scott Blakey's in *Prisoner at War*, 161-62 (the capture incident is discussed on 163-64).

8. Coffee, *Beyond Survival*, 228; Norman, *Bouncing Back*, 144-45; Blakey, *Prisoner at War*, 165-66.

9. Hubbell incorrectly places Stratton at the Zoo when he appeared in the movie. On the Dellinger interviews, see Blakey, *Prisoner at War*, 168-76; Hegdahl summary report, 7-8.

10. Blakey treats the relationship at length in *Prisoner at War*; see esp 182-85. Hubbell describes their unusual chemistry in *P.O.W.*, 286-87.

11. Blakey, *Prisoner at War*, 178; Hegdahl summary report, 9; Rowan, *They Wouldn't Let Us Die*, 24.

12. Hegdahl summary report, 9-10; Blakey, *Prisoner at War*, 170, 186-87; Norman, *Bouncing Back*, 146.

13. Hegdahl summary report, 10; Blakey, *Prisoner at War*, 186-89; Norman, *Bouncing Back*, 146-47.

14. Blakey, *Prisoner at War*, 189-92, 195, 198-99; Rowan, *They Wouldn't Let Us Die*, 66; Hubbell, *P.O.W.*, 315.

15. The Stratton controversy is treated most incisively in Blakey, *Prisoner at War*, ch 18 (ch 12, 119-22, recounts the circumstances surrounding the taping of the 6 March confession; the "confession" itself appears in app 1); and Dunn, "The POW Chronicles," 504-06. The "Captain Thaddeus B. Hoyt" referred to by Stratton in the Blakey volume was a pseudonym for Denton, who persisted to the end in his criticism of his Navy colleague, filing a negative report on Stratton at homecoming.

16. Hegdahl summary report, 10-11; Blakey, *Prisoner at War*, 195-97; Norman, *Bouncing Back*, 148; Hubbell, *P.O.W.*, 314-15, 317, 335-37, 354-55. There are unaccountable discrepancies between sources with respect to the dates and sequence of Hegdahl's activities here in the late summer and early fall of 1967. Blakey's chronology, for example, places Hegdahl with Crecca between 9 September and 30 November, whereas Hegdahl's debriefer cites the interval 9 September to 11 October.

17. Hubbell, *P.O.W.*, 337; Schoenbrun, *Vietnam: How We Got In, How to Get Out*, 209-11; memo DepAS/AF James P. Goode for ASD(ISA), 28 Nov 67, attach, 5; Risner, *Passing of the Night*, 174.

18. Risner, *Passing of the Night*, 161; Schoenbrun, *Vietnam: How We Got In, How to Get Out*, 211-12.

19. *Washington Post*, 24 Jan 91. The *Life* piece, a pictorial essay derived from the East German film and titled "U.S. Prisoners in North Vietnam," featured shots of the Plantation and, besides Galanti, PWs Stratton, Hegdahl, Kay Russell, Dave Hatcher, Art Cormier, Dave Rehmann, and Charles Boyd. All but Cormier and Boyd were Plantation residents. Boyd was shown in a capture sequence that U.S. analysts believed to be a reenactment. See *Life*, 20 Oct 67, 21-33; memo Goode for ASD(ISA), 28 Nov 67, attach, 1, 4.

20. File 719; Hubbell, *P.O.W.*, 337-39.

21. Blakey, *Prisoner at War*, 209; Rowan, *They Wouldn't Let Us Die*, 82.

22. See Stockman, "Authority, Leadership, Organization," 15.

23. Blakey, *Prisoner at War*, 208-09; Norman, *Bouncing Back*, 100.

24. Stockman, "Authority, Leadership, Organization," 15; Donald E. Welzenbach and Nancy Galyean, "Those Daring Young Men and Their Ultra-High-Flying Machines," in *Studies in Intelligence* (Fall 87), 106, 114-15.

25. Stockman's experience is reconstructed from PW accounts and Kiley interv, 4 Mar 76. Col. Norman Gaddis, in a nearby cell in Vegas, later testified to Stockman's extreme delirium, distinctly recalling the invalid speaking in French and ranting about traveling home to bury his father.

26. Stockman, "Authority, Leadership, Organization," 15; Plumb, *I'm No Hero*, 166.

27. Stockman, "Authority, Leadership, Organization," 15-16; Plumb, *I'm No Hero*, 166. Geoffrey Norman's Plantation narrative indicates that Stratton was a dominant influence even after Stockman officially took over as SRO and indeed all during his long stay at the Plantation, under Stockman's successors as well (see *Bouncing Back*, 83 and passim).

28. Norman, *Bouncing Back*, 155.

29. Rumble summary report, 20-21; Frishman summary report, 14. Physical security arrangements appeared to be lax in general at Plantation. See, for example, Hegdahl's observations in his summary report, I-1-2; Frishman report, III-4.

30. Norman, *Bouncing Back*, 69-71, 145-46; Day, *Return With Honor*, 112, 123.

31. Interv with Stockman, 4 Mar 76; Myers, *Vietnam POW Camp Histories*, vol 1, 272-73, 274-75.

32. Plumb, *I'm No Hero*, 8-11 (Van Loan foreword), 146-48; Stockdale file. On Plumb's inventiveness, see also Norman, *Bouncing Back*, 125-26.

33. Plumb, *I'm No Hero*, 149-51. On the variety of transmission methods employed at the Plantation, see, too, Rumble summary report, 35-36, 43-44.

34. Plumb, *I'm No Hero*, 9; Hegdahl summary report, II-1; Hubbell, *P.O.W.*, 372-73.

35. Norman, *Bouncing Back*, passim (21, 31, quotes); Hegdahl summary report, II-1. Norman discusses the Stafford-Hegdahl association in ch 10.

36. Norman, *Bouncing Back*, 82; Hubbell, *P.O.W.*, 368.

37. McCain recounts his dramatic story in "How the POW's Fought Back," *U.S. News & World Report*, 14 May 73, 46ff. (47, "football" quote). On his capture and early treatment, also see Hubbell, *P.O.W.*, 363-67 (363, quote). The Vietnamese enshrined the capture site with a statue of a kneeling pilot. Twenty years later it was still a major local attraction. "I've gotten letters from Vietnamese who claim to have pulled me from the lake," the ex-PW related after a visit to Vietnam as a U.S. senator in 1992. "I've been told . . . there are several thousand men who claim credit for it. It's like Roger Maris hitting his 61st home run. Everybody saw it" ("Pieces of the Puzzle," *People*, 9 Nov 92, 102).

38. Day, *Return With Honor*, 104-09; Kiley interv with Day, 27 May 78; Project CHECO Report, 15 Mar 69, 12.

39. McCain, "How the POW's Fought Back," 49-51; Grant, *Survivors*, 260.

40. *Time*, 9 Apr 73, 19; Norman, *Bouncing Back*, 167; Day, *Return With Honor*, 105-06.

41. Brace, *A Code to Keep*, ch 25 (175, quotes); McCain, "How the POW's Fought Back," 49-50, 52; Rowan, *They Wouldn't Let Us Die*, 52-53, 61; Frishman and Hegdahl news briefing, 2 Sep 69, 5; Rumble summary report, 11 Aug 69, 6. Brace demurred on the importance of the McCain contact in *They Wouldn't Let Us Die*, 84.

42. Rumble summary report, 33-34; Plumb, *I'm No Hero*, 154-55.

43. Day, *Return With Honor*, 123. Here again there are chronological discrepancies, Day dating the housecleaning to the springtime, Norman (*Bouncing Back*, 129-30) referring to "late in the summer." A likely explanation is that the transfers took place over a couple of months. See "Prisoner of War Camps in North Vietnam," DIA rpt, Nov 72, 12.

44. Myers, *Vietnam POW Camp Histories*, vol 1, 273, 275; Stockman, "Authority, Leadership, Organization," 23.

45. Grant, *Survivors*, 260-61, 269, 293. Guy later justified his "by-the-book" comportment. Discussing his interaction with Army Maj. Artice Elliott at the Plantation in 1971, he told interviewer Zalin Grant (*Survivors*, 270):

> I gave Major Elliott my policies, both official and private. When we were in the room, I told him, he could call me by my first name. Outside he would call me Colonel Guy and I would call him Major Elliott. He was to walk on my right and one step behind me in the proper military manner when we went to our baths and took exercise. I didn't particularly want to do this, but I thought it best so that if any POWs overheard or saw us they would know our ranks and who we were.
>
> I made it clear that I was the camp's senior ranking officer and, as such, in charge. I explained my policies concerning discipline. I was a very firm disciplinarian. I thought we had to have discipline in the camp in order to survive. The decisions I had to make, in my opinion, involved people's lives. This may be a hell of a thing to say, but I felt that in the military you had to act like a machine. You tell someone to do something and he has to react instantly . . . .

46. Norman, *Bouncing Back*, 94-99; Hegdahl summary report, 11.

47. Blakey, *Prisoner at War*, 197-98, 228, 229 ("Tom Smith" is used as a pseudonym for Black); Norman, *Bouncing Back*, 148; Hegdahl summary report, 12; Day, *Return with Honor*, 111-14; Myers, *Vietnam POW Camp Histories*, vol 1, 282-83; Project CHECO Report, 15 Mar 69, 35-37; Stockman, "Authority, Leadership, Organization," 18-19; *American Prisoners of War in Southeast Asia, 1971*, Hearings before House Foreign Affairs Subcommittee on National Security Policy and Scientific Developments, 92 Cong, 1 sess (23 Mar 71), 15-16.

48. Myers, *Vietnam POW Camp Histories*, vol 1, 283; Day, *Return With Honor*, 114; Project CHECO Report, 15 Mar 69, 37-38; memo DirDIA ViceAdm V. P. de Poix for SecDef, 6 Apr 73, encl 4, 8-9; Matheny summary report, 19-20; Blakey, *Prisoner at War*, 229.

49. Blakey, *Prisoner at War*, 229; Norman, *Bouncing Back*, 99; Stockdale file; Denton, *When Hell Was In Session*, 165; Coffee, *Beyond Survival*, 227-28.

50. The "early release" controversy consumed hours of discussion and rounds of memo exchanges at the Pentagon through 1969 and 1970, especially after the summer 1969 release of a third group of prisoners from Plantation, who informed debriefers that the PWs desired guidance on the U.S. government's position. Much of this material is in OSD Hist marked "Early Release." The Air Force view is stated in memo AS/AF(M&RA) Curtis W. Tarr for ASD(ISA), 16 Feb 70, sub: National Policy on Early Release of US Prisoners of War. See also Davis, *The U.S. Government and American PWs in Southeast Asia*, ch 12 (ms); Stockman, "Authority, Leadership, Organization," 19-20.

51. Stockman, "Authority, Leadership, Organization," 20.

52. Ibid, 19, 20; Blakey, *Prisoner at War*, 229-30; Norman, *Bouncing Back*, 100-05. Stockman may well have authorized the order in question, but with his removal to Hoa Lo in May it fell to Stratton, again assuming interim SRO responsibility, to follow it up. The real hero in this particular case appears to have been the "courier," Al Stafford, who volunteered to smuggle the order, carrying it on a string attached to his private parts, into the isolated cellblock where the men were being held.

53. Norman, *Bouncing Back*, 104; Stockman, "Authority, Leadership, Organization," 20; Myers, *Vietnam POW Camp Histories*, vol 1, 284; Blakey, *Prisoner at War*, 230. OSD Hist files contain the returnees' debriefings, official reports pertaining to the release, and copies of newspaper articles detailing the pacifists' involvement and chronicling the story up to and past the trio's homecoming; see esp Project CHECO Report, 15 Mar 69, chs 5-9.

54. Day, *Return With Honor*, 132-33; Grant, *Survivors*, 260-61; Brace, *A Code to Keep*, 179-83. Norman discusses the resourceful Hall in *Bouncing Back*, 109-12, and the amusing punster Ringsdorf on 137-40.

55. Brace, *A Code to Keep*, 180; Myers, *Vietnam POW Camp Histories*, vol 1, 279; Hegdahl summary report, 16-17; Hubbell, *P.O.W.*, 465-66; Norman, *Bouncing Back*, 141-42; Frishman summary report, 17. A copy of the Japanese film was obtained by the DIA in May 1969. The film showed Stratton and Stafford watering flowers and receiving mail in addition to decorating. In other clips, Abbott, Shively, Torkelson, and Crecca played games, peeled potatoes, and fixed dinner; Ringsdorf and Air Force Capt. James Berger planted a shrub; and others tended laundry or did other chores before participating in Christmas services.

56. Grant, *Survivors*, 262-63; Brace, *A Code to Keep*, 182-84; Myers, *Vietnam POW Camp Histories*, vol 1, 275-76; Blakey, *Prisoner at War*, 237-38; McCain, "How the POW's Fought Back," 110; Norman, *Bouncing Back*, 150, 155-59; Hegdahl summary report, 17-18.

57. Blakey, *Prisoner at War*, 231-38 (237, quote); Hegdahl summary report, 14-18; Hubbell, *P.O.W.*, 455-56 (Blakey also uses the MacArthur metaphor in *Prisoner at War*, 232); Norman, *Bouncing Back*, 153-54. Norman maintains that Hegdahl still resisted leaving, worrying that he was abandoning Stafford and needing assurances from the officer that he was okay before proceeding (see 161-63).

58. Hegdahl summary report, 18-20; Frishman summary report, 9-10, I-2; Rumble summary report, 45-49; Blakey, *Prisoner at War*, 238-41; McCain, "How the POW's Fought Back," 110-11; *U.S. MACV Command History, 1969*, vol 2, X-22-23; "The Plight of the Prisoners," with sidebar "How the Prisoners Were Released," *Time*, 15 Aug 69, 21-23.

59. Frishman and Hegdahl news briefing, 2 Sep 69; Lt Robert Frishman, "I Was a Prisoner in Hanoi," *Reader's Digest* (Dec 69), 111-15; Blakey, *Prisoner at War*, 240-41, 245-52 (241, 247, quotes).

60. Ltr Chief of Naval Personnel ViceAdm Charles K. Duncan to Navy Wives and Parents, 11 Sep 69; Blakey, *Prisoner at War*, 266-70; Norman, *Bouncing Back*, 163-66.

61. Many of the Plantation PWs clung to this conviction even after homecoming, when they had a better perspective on the other factors accounting for their improved situation. See, for example, Brace, *A Code to Keep*, 186; McCain, "How the POW's Fought Back," 111.

62. Brace file; see, too, Blakey, *Prisoner at War*, 257.

63. "Prisoner of War Camps in North Vietnam," Nov 72, 12; Brace, *A Code to Keep*, 187; McCain, "How the POW's Fought Back," 112; Grant, *Survivors*, 265; Myers, *Vietnam POW Camp Histories*, vol 1, 286.

64. Johnson, *Captive Warriors*, 8, 152-53.

65. Ibid, 170.

66. The release of the first group not only served as a humanitarian gesture to win approval. It was also meant to discourage retaliatory air strikes in the wake of Tet on the Hanoi-Haiphong area (under consideration at the time), the Vietnamese believing Washington would be less inclined to authorize such attacks once officials realized how many PWs were confined in or around Hanoi. They figured correctly. Assistant Secretary of Defense Paul Warnke, citing testimony from the released men on the location of prison camps around the capital, argued against expanded bombing raids on the grounds that such an action would jeopardize the prisoners' lives. For this and other reasons, the retaliation plan was dropped. See Berger, ed, *United States Air Force in Southeast Asia*, 327. The Vietnamese dangled the release prospect continually over the next two years as a tradeoff for the U.S. forgoing or ceasing bombing operations. On the public relations maneuvering over the second release, see Stanley Karnow, "Hanoi Hints at Deal For Release of Pilots," *Washington Post and Times Herald*, 22 May 68; Murrey Marder, "Hanoi Claims Pilots' Release Shows 'Humanitarian' Policy," ibid, 4 Jul 68.

67. Day, *Return With Honor*, 123; Blakey, *Prisoner at War*, 209; Norman, *Bouncing Back*, 188; Rowan, *They Wouldn't Let Us Die*, 82-83.

68. Norman, *Bouncing Back*, 78, 99; McCain, "How the POW's Fought Back," 50; Hubbell, *P.O.W.*, 284; "How One Man Survived a Special Kind of Hell," *National Observer*, 12 Oct 70.

69. Blakey, *Prisoner at War*, 209.

19. THE ZOO, 1967-1969: THE CUBAN PROGRAM AND OTHER ATROCITIES

1. The best camp history of Hope (Son Tay) is in Myers, *Vietnam POW Camp Histories*, vol 1, ch 10. See, too, "Summary of Son Tay Escape Plan and Operation Mole," DIA rpt, nd, 1; Gaither, *With God in a P.O.W. Camp*, 104-13 (quote, 104); Chesley, *Seven Years in Hanoi*, 33, 111; Warner and Doremus files. Chesley's ambivalence about the camp was typical, ranging from abhorrence of the poor conditions to pleasant surprise at the close contact with mates.

   Doremus suggested that the Son Tay assignees were "stashed" there because they weren't "famous or exceptional," as opposed to more publicized captives like Risner and Alvarez, who were more likely to be kept under a watchful eye in the capital. While there may be some truth to the observation, it is not particularly illuminating. Only a handful of the PWs had an exploitable celebrity stature, so by this explanation almost anyone could have wound up at Son Tay. More relevant is the fact that many of the assignees were previously together at other compounds and that the Vietnamese tended, probably for accounting or tracking purposes, to keep groups of prisoners intact throughout their stay in captivity, even when large-scale shuffles occurred.

2. Stockman, "Authority, Leadership, Organization," 14.

3. Day, *Return With Honor*, 125, 130; Guarino, *A POW's Story*, 138; Dramesi, *Code of Honor*, 74; Myers, *Vietnam POW Camp Histories*, vol 1, 107-08, 122. John Nasmyth offers salty profiles of the Zoo's staff in *2355 Days*, 84-86. See also Captor Personnel file.

4. Guarino, *A POW's Story*, 118-24 (119, 124, quotes); McKamey file; Alvarez and Pitch, *Chained Eagle*, 175-76.

5. Myers, *Vietnam POW Camp Histories*, vol 1, 142; Guarino, *A POW's Story*, 119; memo DepAS/AF James P. Goode for ASD(ISA), 28 Nov 67, attach, 5, 7; Rivers file. The "new twist" was actually not so new; see, for example, reference to Denton May 1966 interview rehearsal in Chapter 9.

6. Nasmyth, *2355 Days*, 63-68 (64, 68, quotes); Rivers file; Dramesi, *Code of Honor*, 76; Kiley interv with Jim Bell, 4 Sep 84.

7. Myers, *Vietnam POW Camp Histories*, vol 1, 139, 144; McKamey file; Kiley interv with Dewey Waddell, Feb 77. B. O. Plenty and Elf may have been one and the same.

8. Blakey, *Prisoner at War*, 111 (Mullen quote); Hubbell, *P.O.W.*, 308-09, 317-18; "Beyond the Worst Suspicions," *Time*, 9 Apr 73, 25; Guarino, *A POW's Story*, 155-56.

9. Blakey, *Prisoner at War*, 142-43, 147, 149; Myers, *Vietnam POW Camp Histories*, vol 1, 140-41; Nasmyth, *2355 Days*, 80; Brunhaver file.

10. Nasmyth, *2355 Days*, 80; Guarino, *A POW's Story*, 118, 170; Alvarez and Pitch, *Chained Eagle*, 178-79; Davis file; McDaniel, *Before Honor*, 80.

11. Material on the victimization of seniors during the summer 1967 communications purge at the Zoo is contained in a series of Air Force homecoming reports under the heading "Penalties incurred by individuals who attempted to exercise rank and leadership." See also Rivers file; Armand J. Myers, "POW Doctrine for Survival With Honor," Air War College report, Jun 75, 33; Myers, *Vietnam POW Camp Histories*, vol 1, 141; Dramesi, *Code of Honor*, 83-84.

12. Guarino, *A POW's Story*, 74, 119, 136; Plumb, *I'm No Hero*, 211; John L. Frisbee, "Surviving in Hanoi's Prisons," *Air Force Magazine* (Jun 73), 30; Day, *Return With Honor*, 176-77, 180.

13. Guarino graphically recounts his and Byrnes's 1967 ordeal in *A POW's Story*, 125-38. See also Hubbell, *P.O.W.*, 309-12.

14. Alvarez and Pitch, *Chained Eagle*, 177; McDaniel, *Yet Another Voice*, 32-33; and various other accounts. On Rollins, see Jensen, *Six Years in Hell*, 98-99; J. M. Heslop and Dell R. Van Orden, *From the Shadow of Death: Stories of POWs*, ch 12.

15. Myers, *Vietnam POW Camp Histories*, vol 1, 193-95 (a diagram of the Annex is shown on 104); ibid, vol 2, 103-04; McDaniel, *Before Honor*, 65-66.

16. Rivers and Shankel files; Myers, *Vietnam POW Camp Histories*, vol 1, 145.

17. Myers, *Vietnam POW Camp Histories*, vol 1, 195-96, 198; Butler and Brunhaver files; McDaniel, *Before Honor*, 66-69.

18. Guarino, *A POW's Story*, 148; McKamey, Davis, and Shankel files; Myers, *Vietnam POW Camp Histories*, vol 1, 147-48, 196-97.

19. Myers, *Vietnam POW Camp Histories*, vol 1, 197-99; McDaniel, *Before Honor*, 70-72; Shankel file.

20. Guarino, *A POW's Story*, 148-52, 162; Day, *Return With Honor*, 123, 127, 132; Stockman, "Authority, Leadership, Organization," 23; Rivers file.

21. Butler file; Alvarez and Pitch, *Chained Eagle*, 190; Day, *Return With Honor*, 125-27, 131, 140. On Stag, see Alvarez file; Kiley notes on conversation with Jim Lamar. In his case Lamar believed that Stag was attempting to produce an 05 for early release. Alvarez had a more generous view of Stag than most.

22. This section is based on interviews, Operation Homecoming transmissions (Air Force messages are identified with the code name "EGRESS RECAP"), after-action reports and analyses, and scattered secondary accounts as indicated. The most useful document, an analysis and evaluation prepared by Air Force Intelligence, is *The Special Exploitation Program for Selected United States Prisoners of War in Southeast Asia, 1967-1968*, Rpt A10-2, Series 700/JP-1, Jun 75. Waltman contributed an excellent chapter on Fidel and his associates in Myers, *Vietnam POW Camp Histories*, vol 2, under the title "Third Country Program," 287-310.

23. Guarino, *A POW's Story*, 149; Alvarez and Pitch, *Chained Eagle*, 181; Hubbell, *P.O.W.*, 319; J. David Truby, "Now It Can Be Told . . . Cubans Torture U.S. POW's in Vietnam," *Soldier of Fortune* (May 78), 39. Three photos in the Truby article show a Cuban man and woman posing with Vietnamese; the identity of the pair is unknown but the man is not Fidel.

24. Alvarez recounts the incident in *Chained Eagle*, ch 13. See, too, Hubbell, *P.O.W.*, 320-22, in which details differ slightly. For a good description of Fidel and Chico, see "Third Country Program," 289-90.

25. Alvarez and Pitch, *Chained Eagle*, 186; "Third Country Program," 291-92; McDaniel, *Yet Another Voice*, 15, 32; Hubbell, *P.O.W.*, 340-42; Glendon Perkins, "Hanoi Nightmare: American POW's Year of Terror," *Soldier of Fortune* (Aug 90), 25 ff.

26. "Third Country Program," 291-92, 296-99, 306-08; *Special Exploitation Program*, 7-9; memo DirDIA ViceAdm V. P. de Poix for SecDef, 6 Apr 73, encl 4, 3-4 ; Murray, "Historical Analysis and Critical Appraisal of the Code of Conduct," 203. Vohden stressed the cross-section aspect in an interview with Kiley.

27. Alvarez and Pitch, *Chained Eagle*, 186; Hubbell, *P.O.W.*, 342.

28. *Special Exploitation Program*, 11; Naval Center for Prisoner of War Studies, "The Cuban Program," nd (probably 1973), 2-3. The latter report is based upon the accounts of four Navy officers—Vohden, Spencer, and two officers added to the program later, Charles Rice and Earl Lewis—and one Marine Corps pilot, Harlan Chapman, who was not in the program.

29. *Special Exploitation Program*, 8-16; "Third Country Program," 292-97, 307; "Cuban Program," 3; Hubbell, *P.O.W.*, 345-48. Quote is from Truby, "Now It Can Be Told," 39. On Bomar's experience, see, too, "Vietnam P.O.W. Says Cuban Tortured Him," *NY Times*, 21 Aug 77, 17.

30. Truby, "Now It Can Be Told," 39; *Special Exploitation Program*, 17-18; "Third Country Program," 300; EGRESS RECAP Special Rpt 8, 22 Feb 73.

31. *Special Exploitation Program*, 18-19; "Third Country Program," 301, 310; "Cuban Program," 4-6; Hubbell, *P.O.W.*, 432-33. Details of the 21 May incident and other aspects of Cobeil's treatment vary from one account to another. Compare Hubbell's version, for instance, with Day, *Return With Honor*, 187-88; Guarino, *A POW's Story*, 152-53; "Cuban Program," 6; and Murray, "Historical Analysis and Critical Appraisal of the Code of Conduct," 204-05. Lt. Connell was the main source of information on Cobeil's 21 May bludgeoning, eyeing the activity in the torture shed from his location in the Gatehouse and relaying word to the other prisoners.

32. The "electric shock" reference is in Plumb, *I'm No Hero*, 208; Guarino, *A POW's Story*, 154; and EGRESS RECAP Special Rpt 131, 22 Mar 73. All three sources indicate that Cobeil (Guarino calls him "Corley") was extremely difficult to handle and that he soon became both a physical and psychological burden for his mates.

33. EGRESS RECAP Special Rpt 130, 22 Mar 73; EGRESS RECAP Special Rpt 8, 22 Feb 73; Hubbell, *P.O.W.*, 430-31; Truby, "Now It Can Be Told," 39. Hubbell has an amusing passage on how the oven and fish projects provided the prisoners some comic relief.

34. "Third Country Program," 305; EGRESS RECAP Special Rpt 8, 22 Feb 73.

35. EGRESS RECAP Special Rpt 130, 22 Mar 73; Hubbell, *P.O.W.*, 80, 191; Rivers file.

36. Hubbell, *P.O.W.*, 436-37; EGRESS RECAP Special Rpt 131, 22 Mar 73.

37. Nasmyth, *2355 Days*, 74; Guarino, *A POW's Story*, 160-61; Hubbell, *P.O.W.*, 435-37; EGRESS RECAP Special Rpt 8, 22 Feb 73.

38. Kasler's own account, beginning with the session with Spot on 25 June, is in "Beyond the Worst Suspicions," *Time*, 9 Apr 73; see also his statement in *Restraints on Travel to Hostile Areas*, Hearings before House Committee on Internal Security, 93 Cong, 1 sess (10 May 73), 32-33. Hubbell describes the confrontations with both Spot and Fidel in *P.O.W.*, 437-46. Guarino's "Gary Cooper" comparison is in *A POW's Story*, 155; 159 deals with the Fidel encounter. See, too, "Third Country Program," 303-04. In a 1976 interview with Kiley, Kasler elaborated on the information appearing in the published accounts; at that time he was still receiving medical treatment for injuries caused by Fidel.

39. Fidel made the comment to Perkins during Christmas 1967. See EGRESS RECAP Special Rpt 8, 22 Feb 73.

40. Hubbell, *P.O.W.*, 442.

41. Day, *Return With Honor*, 188. See also Hubbell, *P.O.W.*, 447-48; EGRESS RECAP Special Rpt 131, 22 Mar 73; Plumb, *I'm No Hero*, 206, 207 (drawing).

42. Guarino, *A POW's Story*, 161, 167-68; Stockman, "Authority, Leadership, Organization," 20.

43. Hubbell, *P.O.W.*, 449; Guarino, *A POW's Story*, 154, 161; EGRESS RECAP Special Rpt 131, 22 Mar 73; Plumb, *I'm No Hero*, 208-09.

44. Kiley and Rochester conversation with Robert J. Destatte, Washington, D.C., Mar 97; Alvarez and Pitch, *Chained Eagle*, 187, 189; "Third Country Program," 306-07, 309; memo DirDIA ViceAdm V. P. de Poix for SecDef, 6 Apr 73, encl 4, 3-4; "POWs Tortured by 'Fidel'," *Washington Star*, 3 Apr 73.

45. Kiley interv with Kasler, 25 Aug 76; Alvarez and Pitch, *Chained Eagle*, 189; "Third Country Program," 305.

46. Truby, "Now It Can Be Told," 39; Johnson, *Captive Warriors*, 124; *Special Exploitation Program*, 23-24.

47. Myers, *Vietnam POW Camp Histories*, vol 2, 100-01; Day, *Return With Honor*, 136-37; Johnson, *Captive Warriors*, 174.

48. Myers, *Vietnam POW Camp Histories*, vol 1, 149, 200-01; Day, *Return With Honor*, 139.

49. McDaniel, *Yet Another Voice*, 34; Hubbell, *P.O.W.*, 466-67; EGRESS RECAP Special Rpt 131, 22 Mar 73; Guarino, *A POW's Story*, 181, 183-84; Nasmyth, *2355 Days*, 89-90; Myers, *Vietnam*

POW Camp Histories, vol 1, 150. Alvarez wrote in *Chained Eagle*, 192-93, that the Vietnamese settled for the PWs' signing "a mimeographed, watered-down version of the statement."

50. Brunhaver and Rivers files; McDaniel, *Before Honor*, 105; Guarino, *A POW's Story*, 185-90; Myers, *Vietnam POW Camp Histories*, vol 2, 101-02 (Bolstad co-authored this section of the Myers study with Air Force Capt. William Baugh); Day, *Return With Honor*, 148-51; Johnson, *Captive Warriors*, 175.

51. Guarino, *A POW's Story*, 190-94; Myers, *Vietnam POW Camp Histories*, vol 1, 150, 201; Nasmyth, *2355 Days*, 75 (his time frame is off by several months).

52. Plumb, *I'm No Hero*, ch 19 (Plumb uses the pseudonym "Palmer" for McSwain; quoted material on 210-11); Nasmyth, *Hanoi Release John Nasmyth*, 166.

53. Nasmyth, *Hanoi Release John Nasmyth*, 166.

20. COPING: THE DAILY GRIND

1. Stockdale, "The Melting Experience," *National Review*, 25 Dec 81, 1534-37.

2. Mulligan, *Hanoi Commitment*, 141; Norman, *Bouncing Back*, 109; Stockdale, *In Love and War*, 276; Denton, *When Hell Was In Session*, 186.

3. Mulligan, *Hanoi Commitment*, 142, 181; Stockdale, *In Love and War*, 275; see also Denton, *When Hell Was In Session*, 160. On the possibility of drug-induced hallucinations, see memo DirDIA ViceAdm V. P. de Poix for SecDef, 6 Apr 73, encl 4, 6-7; Murray, "Historical Analysis and Critical Appraisal of the Code of Conduct," 236; Rowan, *They Wouldn't Let Us Die*, 196-97. In the Rowan account, Brady mentions Jim Hughes as another who maintained he had been drugged.

4. Rowan, *They Wouldn't Let Us Die*, 78; Mulligan, *Hanoi Commitment*, 141; Johnson and Winebrenner, *Captive Warriors*, 149 (see also 11-13).

5. Stockdale, *In Love and War*, 276. See, too, Day, *Return With Honor*, 131-32, 136-38.

6. Johnson and Winebrenner, *Captive Warriors*, 151, 170-73 (see also, for example, Coffee, *Beyond Survival*, 226); Day, *Return With Honor*, 116.

7. Blakey, *Prisoner at War*, 191; Stockdale, "The Melting Experience," 1534, 1536; Johnson and Winebrenner, *Captive Warriors*, 120, 138, 183; Stockdale, *In Love and War*, 286-91. On the special demands of solitary confinement, see John E. Deaton et al, "Coping Activities in Solitary Confinement of U.S. Navy POWs in Vietnam," *Journal of Applied Social Psychology* (1977), 239-57.

8. Denton, *When Hell Was In Session*, 187; Guarino, *A POW's Story*, 133; Plumb, *I'm No Hero*, 78, 226-29; Rutledge, *In the Presence of Mine Enemies*, 34-35; Rowan, *They Wouldn't Let Us Die*, 118, 149; Gaither, *With God in a P.O.W. Camp*, 42, 96; Chesley, *Seven Years in Hanoi*, 32; McDaniel, *Before Honor*, 42 (on McDaniel's own pivotal religious experience, see 118-24). On the importance of faith to a prisoner in the South, see James Rowe's account in *Army Digest* (May 69), excerpted in *Survival, Resistance, and Escape*, 66-67.

9. Rutledge, *In the Presence of Mine Enemies*, 52-53; Flynn remarks at POW seminar, National War College, Fort McNair, Washington, D.C., 6 Jan 88. Plumb knew of three professed atheists in his PW group (*I'm No Hero*, 230). On the Stockdale theme, see, for example, "The Melting Experience"; "The World of Epictetus: Reflections on Survival and Leadership," *Atlantic* (Apr 78); "Experiences as a POW in Vietnam," *Naval War College Review* (Jan-Feb 74). Stockdale "jobs" quote from "Experiences as a POW in Vietnam," 5. See, too, Frisbee, "Surviving in Hanoi's Prisons," 32-33.

10. Stockdale, "The World of Epictetus," 102; Johnson and Winebrenner, *Captive Warriors*, 164; Mulligan, *Hanoi Commitment*, 189; Doremus, "Days to Remember," 16; Louis H. Bernasconi et al, "Morale and Human Endurance," in Myers, *Vietnam POW Camp Histories*, vol 2, 157-58; Grant, *Survivors*, 256; Norman, *Bouncing Back*, 116.

11. Plumb, *I'm No Hero*, 174-76; Coffee, *Beyond Survival*, 98-99.

12. Norman, *Bouncing Back*, 114-16; Plumb, *I'm No Hero*, 85, 176-77; "P.O.W.'s Felt Their Mission Was to Resist," *NY Times*, 30 Apr 73; Nasmyth, *Hanoi Release John Nasmyth*, 168-69

(the same anecdote is in Nasmyth's *2355 Days*, 125-26). On Bridger's handwalking, see Nasmyth, *2355 Days*, 194.

13. McDaniel, *Yet Another Voice*, 47; Norman, *Bouncing Back*, 73; McCain interv in *USA Today*, 9 Apr 87; Coffee, *Beyond Survival*, 142. See also Gaither, *With God in a P.O.W. Camp*, 47-48; Doremus, "Days to Remember," 49-50; Frisbee, "Surviving in Hanoi's Prisons," 32; Heslop and Van Orden, *From the Shadow of Death*, ch 8.

14. Charles Redman report, 7602 AINTELG, 26 Mar 73; Bernasconi et al, "Morale and Human Endurance," 156-57; Joe V. Carpenter, "A Special Report on My Experiences as a POW in North Vietnam," Project Corona Harvest, Jan 70, 28.

15. Johnson and Winebrenner, *Captive Warriors*, 89; a typical prison schedule during the middle years is delineated by Norm McDaniel in *Yet Another Voice*, 26-27 (see also Bernasconi et al, "Living Conditions," in Myers, *Vietnam POW Camp Histories*, vol 2, 253-54); Kiley interv with Tom Collins; on the uniform change, see Chesley, *Seven Years in Hanoi*, 38, and Frishman debriefing, II-1.

16. Nasmyth, *Hanoi Release John Nasmyth*, 78; Gaither, *With God in a P.O.W. Camp*, 42; Blakey, *Prisoner at War*, 180; Hegdahl debriefing, II-2.

17. Frisbee, "Surviving in Hanoi's Prisons," 32; McDaniel, *Before Honor*, 98; Carpenter, "A Special Report on My Experiences as a POW in North Vietnam," 29; Rowan, *They Wouldn't Let Us Die*, 110; Coffee, *Beyond Survival*, ch 18. On the entertainment provided by their animal companions, see also other sources listed in Chapter 7, note 5; Bernasconi et al, "Morale and Human Endurance," 158.

18. Denton, *When Hell Was In Session*, 159-60; Mulligan, *Hanoi Commitment*, 181 (Denton's recollection of the cemetery story, presumably told to him by Mulligan, is somewhat different); Santoli, *Everything We Had*, 238; Grant, *Survivors*, 253-54.

19. Stockdale, *In Love and War*, 340; McCain, "How the POW's Fought Back," 49; Plumb, *I'm No Hero*, 179; Rausa, "Home from Hanoi," 16; McDaniel, *Before Honor*, 98 (Mike Goliat was the second baseman).

20. Plumb, *I'm No Hero*, 178; Rutledge, *In the Presence of Mine Enemies*, 60; Rowan, *They Wouldn't Let Us Die*, 72-73; Norman, *Bouncing Back*, 127-28. See also Jensen, *Six Years in Hell*, 58. "A nut on house plans," Jensen designed and remodeled several homes, "then . . . remodeled my parents' home, my brother's home, and my sister's home."

21. Norman, *Bouncing Back*, 121-25.

22. Stockdale, *In Love and War*, 340-41; Denton, *When Hell Was In Session*, 159; Risner, *Passing of the Night*, 154, 178-79.

23. Coffee, *Beyond Survival*, 190-91; Plumb, *I'm No Hero*, 179-80; Norman, *Bouncing Back*, 120-21; Kiley interv with Dave Burroughs, Jun 73; Howes, *Voices of the Vietnam POWs*, 122-23; "Inside North Vietnam's Prisons—How Americans Coped," *U.S. News & World Report*, 26 Mar 73; "P.O.W.'s Felt Their Mission Was to Resist," *NY Times*, 30 Apr 73; Bernasconi et al, "Morale and Human Endurance," 160-63; Guarino, *A POW's Story*, 291-92.

24. Nasmyth, *2355 Days*, 73-75; Guarino, *A POW's Story*, 289; Bernasconi et al, "Morale and Human Endurance," 159-61, 169.

25. McDaniel, *Before Honor*, 101, 98; Norman, *Bouncing Back*, 121, 137-40 (139, quote); "Inside North Vietnam's Prisons—How Americans Coped," *U.S. News & World Report*, 26 Mar 73; Howes, *Voices of the Vietnam POWs*, 123.

26. Coffee, *Beyond Survival*, 177; Norman, *Bouncing Back*, 180-83; Rowan, *They Wouldn't Let Us Die*, 90-93, 115-17, 146-47 (116, Doremus quote; 91, Brace quote). In the memoir literature, see Alvarez and Pitch, *Chained Eagle*, and Denton, *When Hell Was In Session*, both passim; Dramesi, *Code of Honor*, 141-43; Guarino, *A POW's Story*, 140-41; Coffee, *Beyond Survival*, ch 12. For a critique of PW memoirists' attitudes toward women in the context of cultural stereotyping, see Elliott Gruner, *Prisoners of Culture*, 100-08; Howes, *Voices of the Vietnam POWs*, 136-41, which also examines the issue of homosexuality.

27. Coffee, *Beyond Survival*, 181; "Field Survival Medicine Techniques Employed by American Prisoners-of-War in the Southeast Asia Prison Systems," report by Environmental Information Division, Maxwell AFB, Ala, Dec 75, 1; Grant, *Survivors*, 316; Rowan, *They Wouldn't Let Us Die*, 90-91, 115-16.

28. Plumb, *I'm No Hero*, 200; Bernasconi et al, "Morale and Human Endurance," 171; Nasmyth, *Hanoi Release John Nasmyth*, 262 (also in *2355 Days*, 192-93); Norman, *Bouncing Back*, 118-19; Denton, *When Hell Was In Session*, 158, 170. Jenkins and Stockdale returned Denton's money.

29. Coffee, *Beyond Survival*, 189; "P.O.W.'s Felt Their Mission Was to Resist," *NY Times*, 30 Apr 73; McDaniel, *Before Honor*, 97; Plumb, *I'm No Hero*, 199.

30. Heslop and Van Orden, *From the Shadow of Death*, 117-19 (Rollins quote on 118); Norman, *Bouncing Back*, 111-12; Nasmyth, *2355 Days*, 190-92. On the PWs' interest in needlemaking for "tailoring" and embroidery purposes, see, too, Plumb, *I'm No Hero*, 192.

31. Plumb, *I'm No Hero*, ch 17; Norman, *Bouncing Back*, 125-27.

32. Coffee file; Johnson and Winebrenner, *Captive Warriors*, 54; "Prisoner of War Detention Installations in the Hanoi Area," 45-47, DIA Rpt AP-365-6-1-68-INT, May 68, 45-47; Jensen, *Six Years in Hell*, 57; Guarino, *A POW's Story*, 42; Plumb, *I'm No Hero*, 189; Nasmyth, *Hanoi Release John Nasmyth*, 64.

33. McDaniel, *Yet Another Voice*, 30-31; Jensen, *Six Years in Hell*, 57; Nasmyth, *Hanoi Release John Nasmyth*, 62; Plumb, *I'm No Hero*, 189, 192, 204; Norman, *Bouncing Back*, 110.

34. Norman, *Bouncing Back*, 112; "Field Survival Medicine Techniques," 22-23; Bernasconi et al, "Living Conditions," 236-38, 240-42; McDaniel, *Before Honor*, 93; Denton, *When Hell Was In Session*, 44.

35. Bernasconi et al, "Living Conditions," 239; Chesley, *Seven Years in Hanoi*, 39-41; Alvarez and Pitch, *Chained Eagle*, 165; Plumb, *I'm No Hero*, 204, 186.

36. Plumb, *I'm No Hero*, 186; Norman, *Bouncing Back*, 111.

37. Plumb, *I'm No Hero*, 193; Bernasconi et al, "Living Conditions," 243; Heslop and Van Orden, *From the Shadow of Death*, 115; Chesley, *Seven Years in Hanoi*, 40.

38. Bernasconi et al, "Living Conditions," 238-39, 249-50; Chesley, *Seven Years in Hanoi*, 38-39; Jensen, *Six Years in Hell*, 51-52; Mulligan, *Hanoi Commitment*, 66-67, 78-79. An excellent study of PW "dental" characteristics and problems is James F. Kelly and Norman H. Tracy, "An Overview of Dental Findings and Experiences in Repatriated American Prisoners of War from Southeast Asia," Navy Center for Prisoner of War Studies, 1974, printed in *Military Medicine* (Oct 75), 699-704.

39. Kelly and Tracy, "An Overview of Dental Findings and Experiences," 699-704; McDaniel, *Before Honor*, 91-92; Nasmyth, *2355 Days*, 153.

40. Kelly and Tracy, "An Overview of Dental Findings and Experiences," 700; "Field Survival Medicine Techniques," passim; Rutledge, *In the Presence of Mine Enemies*, 59-60; Norman, *Bouncing Back*, 113; "POW's Tell the Inside Story," *U.S. News & World Report*, 9 Apr 73; Plumb, *I'm No Hero*, 188-89. Guarino called Doremus "a helluva guy, who took his job as medic very seriously" (*A POW's Story*, 301).

41. Stockdale, *In Love and War*, 267; McDaniel, *Before Honor*, 93-95; Gaither, *With God in a P.O.W. Camp*, 107-08; Plumb, *I'm No Hero*, 183; Bernasconi et al, "Living Conditions," 247; Chesley, *Seven Years in Hanoi*, 47-48. On the vision problem, see also "POW's: The Price of Survival" *Newsweek*, 16 Apr 73.

42. Blakey, *Prisoner at War*, 272-73; Frishman debriefing, II-3. The best survey of PW medical problems and the extent of enemy treatment in both the North and South is a series of articles by S. William Berg and Milton Richlin, under the heading "Injuries and Illnesses of Vietnam War POWs," that appeared in the July through October 1977 issues of *Military Medicine*. Other useful overviews on the Northern situation are Bernasconi et al, "Living Conditions," 243-50, and Coffee and Warner summaries in File 719.

43. In addition to Frishman's summary report, see his "Medical Journal of a Returned P.O.W.," *Medical World News*, 6 Nov 70, 44-47; Rumble summary report, 15, 30-32; Day, *Return With Honor*, 69; Bernasconi et al, "Living Conditions," 248-49; McDaniel, *Before Honor*, 91-92; Rivers file; transcript of Flynn press conference, 6 Apr 73, 19-20.

44. Coker testimony from his statement before the Board of Directors of the National League of Families, 27 Oct 73, excerpted in *Americans Missing in Southeast Asia*, Hearings before House Select Committee on Missing Persons in Southeast Asia, 94 Cong, 1 sess (1975), pt 2, 115; Mulligan, *Hanoi Commitment*, 170; on Osborne, besides Guarino's account, see Heslop and

Van Orden, *From the Shadow of Death*, chs 20-21, Jensen, *Six Years in Hell*, 141-42, and Hubbell, *P.O.W.*, 457-62. Guarino also credited Ralph Gaither with contributing to Osborne's rehabilitation.

45. H. Bruce Franklin, *M.I.A. or Mythmaking in America*, 105. Franklin discusses the "amputee" myth on 103-04.

46. Vohden, "Stress and the Viet Nam P.O.W.," 29-32; Chesley, *Seven Years in Hanoi*, 101.

47. Plumb, *I'm No Hero*, 181-82, 190; McDaniel, *Before Honor*, 85-86; Nasmyth, *2355 Days*, 118, 190-91; Hubbell, *P.O.W.*, 372; Robert J. Naughton, "Motivational Factors of American Prisoners of War Held by the Democratic Republic of Vietnam," *Naval War College Review* (Jan-Feb 75), 8; Dramesi, *Code of Honor*, 231; Fer, "Leadership and Followership," 85-86; Rowan, *They Wouldn't Let Us Die*, 48.

48. Fer, "Leadership and Followership," 86-87; Vohden, "Stress and the Viet Nam P.O.W.," 31-32; Chesley, *Seven Years in Hanoi*, 101; Guarino, *A POW's Story*, 174-75; Johnson and Winebrenner, *Captive Warriors*, 175; Denton, *When Hell Was In Session*, 170, 206; Grant, *Survivors*, 298.

49. Dramesi, *Code of Honor*, 76-78; Howard Dunn and W. Hays Parks, "If I Become a Prisoner of War . . .," U.S. Naval Institute *Proceedings* (Aug 76), 21.

50. Warner file; Hubbell, *P.O.W.*, 480-83, 524-27; Day, *Return With Honor*, 134; Alvarez and Pitch, *Chained Eagle*, 234-35; Coffee, *Beyond Survival*, 225. On Schweitzer's redemption, for two opposing viewpoints see Guarino, *A POW's Story*, 305-06 ("Forrester" is Schweitzer), and Dramesi, *Code of Honor*, 237-39 ("Brudino" is Guarino).

51. Rowan, *They Wouldn't Let Us Die*, 54-55; Nasmyth, *Hanoi Release John Nasmyth*, 244; Mulligan, *Hanoi Commitment*, 191; Coffee, *Beyond Survival*, 171-72; Bernasconi et al, "Morale and Human Endurance," 174-81; Plumb, *I'm No Hero*, 158. On the disappointment that letters sometimes brought, see *I'm No Hero*, 160; *Hanoi Release John Nasmyth*, 244; Alvarez and Pitch, *Chained Eagle*, 193.

52. Hubbell, *P.O.W.*, 379-80; Guarino, *A POW's Story*, 154 (Guarino reported on other feuding as well; see 242-43, 252); Mulligan, *Hanoi Commitment*, 259.

53. Guarino, *A POW's Story*, 253; Rowan, *They Wouldn't Let Us Die*, 153.

54. Dunn and Parks, "If I Become a Prisoner of War. . .," 20.

55. Coffee, *Beyond Survival*, 98; Chesley, *Seven Years in Hanoi*, 45-46; "Inside North Vietnam's Prisons—How Americans Coped," *U.S. News & World Report*, 26 Mar 73; Plumb, *I'm No Hero*, 188; Doremus, "Days to Remember," 15; McDaniel, *Before Honor*, 97.

56. Jensen, *Six Years in Hell*, 151; Naughton, "Motivational Factors," 4; Blakey, *Prisoner at War*, 181; Flynn remark at POW seminar at National War College, Fort McNair, Washington, D.C., 6 Jan 88; Alvarez and Pitch, *Chained Eagle*, 165; Nasmyth, *2355 Days*, 157-58; Plumb, *I'm No Hero*, 87-88.

57. Alvarez, "Sound: A POW's Weapon," 91-92 (in a similar vein, see Coffee's chapter in *Beyond Survival* entitled "Peepholes and Cracks," 219-20); *Time*, 3 Jul 78, 6; Plumb, *I'm No Hero*, 84-85; Rutledge, *In the Presence of Mine Enemies*, 32.

58. McDaniel, *Before Honor*, 84; Nasmyth, *Hanoi Release John Nasmyth*, 132; Guarino, *A POW's Story*, 294. On Venanzi, see Heslop and Van Orden, *From the Shadow of Death*, 56; Jensen, *Six Years in Hell*, 72; Nasmyth, *2355 Days*, 147.

59. Plumb, *I'm No Hero*, 180; Guarino, *A POW's Story*, 307.

21. PWs IN THE SOUTH, 1968-1971: BONDAGE AND VAGABONDAGE

1. Attach ltr DASD(ISA) Roger E. Shields to J. Angus McDonald, 22 Mar 76, "U.S. Escapees in Southeast Asia."

2. Grant, *Survivors*, 1-21, 53-58 (54, quote).

3. Grant, *Survivors*, 23-31; Daly and Bergman, *A Hero's Welcome*, 69-96.

4. Kushner's own capture is detailed in his homecoming account; see also Hubbell, *P.O.W.*, 393-94, and Grant, *Survivors*, 82. In his memoir Daly describes his and Watkins's arrival at the Kushner camp in March and their impressions of their new companions, including Garwood,

who, to Daly's surprise, was carrying a rifle; see *A Hero's Welcome*, ch 12. For other observations on Garwood during this period, see Grant, *Survivors*, ch 7; for Anton's and Harker's early impressions of the Kushner group, see *Survivors*, ch 5.

5. "Prisoner Release and Repatriation in Indochina," Interdepartmental Study Panel paper, Apr 72, 42; "American Civilians Missing or Captured in South Vietnam, Laos and Cambodia," composite list, undated but as of Aug 72. Both of these reports list 21, omitting the names of 2 women, Sandra Johnson and Marjorie Nelson, who were captured on 1 February and released two months later.

6. Benge was the only one of the trio to live to tell their story. See "The Cruel Years—Two Exclusive Reports," *Nutrition Today*, May/Jun 73, printed in *American Prisoners of War and Missing in Action in Southeast Asia, 1973*, Hearings before House Foreign Affairs Subcommittee on National Security Policy and Scientific Developments, 93 Cong, 1 sess (May 73), pt 4, 216-23. Hubbell treats their experience in *P.O.W.*, 397-99, 424-28.

7. "The Cruel Years—Two Exclusive Reports," 219-22 (221, quote).

8. Post-1968 Southern Captivity file. See also Winnie Wagaman and Norman J. Brookens, *Civilian POW: Terror and Torture in South Vietnam.*

9. Karnow, *Vietnam*, 531; Post-1968 Southern Captivity file. Besides his service in Korea, Manhard had spent time in Communist China helping to extradite U.S. citizens trapped there during the revolution. Both his diplomatic skills and experience dealing with Asian Communists would come in handy. See Schwinn and Diehl, *We Came to Help*, 239.

10. Post-1968 Southern Captivity file; Rander story in *Pentagram*, 31 Aug 89. There are gaps and inconsistencies in member accounts of this group's capture and captivity, indicative of the difficulty in reconstructing Southern captivity narratives with any exactitude.

11. See Willis's story in Heslop and Van Orden, *From the Shadow of Death*, ch 18; it is riveting, though marred by misspellings of names and other errors (he calls Dr. Nelson "Carlson"). The usually reliable comprehensive PW list compiled by DIA shows the DiBernardo five captured on 3 February, but their homecoming reports state 5 February.

12. According to Willis, Nelson and Johnson were nearly executed in reprisal for the Hayhurst-Dierling escape, saved when the French-speaking Cayer pleaded with an NVA officer to spare them. They were released on 31 March. Upon returning to U.S. control, they briefed officials on their confinement and, augmenting Hayhurst's and Dierling's input, helped identify other U.S. personnel captured at Hue, although this intelligence break failed to aid U.S. units in finding the various PW groups either in camps or on the move northward.

13. Participant accounts differ sharply. See Post-1968 Southern Captivity file; Heslop and Van Orden, *From the Shadow of Death*, 168-69.

14. Post-1968 Southern Captivity file.

15. The three captives' homecoming reports are in OSD Hist. Hubbell, calling Brande and Thompson "storybook soldiers who might have been invented by Rudyard Kipling," treats the pair's capture and subsequent experience in *P.O.W.*, ch 23.

16. Hubbell, *P.O.W.*, 407-08; Grant, *Survivors*, 210-11; McMurry file.

17. Purcell recounts their early experience through their arrival at Portholes in *Love and Duty*, chs 2-3, 5-6.

18. Purcell, *Love and Duty*, 44, 53-55.

19. Post-1968 Southern Captivity file.

20. Ibid.

21. The description of Bao Cao's physical layout and cellblock characteristics is drawn from PW recollections of the camp; see Bao Cao file. It is necessarily a composite sketch, as the accounts are fragmented and conflict in many details.

22. Hubbell, *P.O.W.*, 410. See also Thompson file; in Thompson's long alphabetized sequence of camps, Bao Cao is designated as "Camp India."

23. Bao Cao file; Purcell, *Love and Duty*, 59.

24. Bao Cao file; Manhard and Rander files. The subway anecdote is from Kiley interv with Rander. In *Pentagram* interv, Aug 89, Rander related: "When they asked me the names of commanders and stuff like that, I used names from the roster of the 1951 World Series Dodgers: All the infielders were officers . . . and all the outfielders were NCOs."

25. Brande and Thompson files; Hubbell, *P.O.W.*, 412-15.
26. Myers, *Vietnam POW Camp Histories*, vol 1, 451, 454, 475, 477; Hubbell, *P.O.W.*, 421.
27. An excellent summary that tracks the locations and movements of the major groupings of US PWs in the South, although it contains some minor errors, is memo DirDIA ViceAdm V. P. de Poix for SecDef, 6 Apr 73, encl 4, 1-3. See also "An Overview of Free-World Personnel Captured in South Vietnam," previously cited.
28. The experience at Bravo is best recapitulated by Kushner himself in his homecoming account and in a large folder of testimony and articles by and about him in OSD Hist. See also Daly and Bergman, *A Hero's Welcome*, chs 12-15; Grant, *Survivors*, chs 5-10; and Hubbell, *P.O.W.*, ch 24 (Hubbell uses pseudonyms for Sherman and Williams). There is some confusion on the exact number who died at Bravo because Kushner sometimes omits the escape casualty Weatherman and includes Hammond and Zawtocki, who died at a subsequent camp.
29. Grant, *Survivors*, 86 (Harker quotes), 92-95, 131-35; Groom and Spencer, *Conversations With the Enemy*, 376.
30. Groom and Spencer, *Conversations With the Enemy*, 377-78; "POW's: The Price of Survival," *Newsweek*, 16 Apr 73; "POW's Pleaded for Death," *Washington Post*, 4 Apr 73; Grant, *Survivors*, 155; Daly and Bergman, *A Hero's Welcome*, 107. On the skin problem see, too, Harker's account in *Survivors*, 159. On Williams's decline, see *Conversations With the Enemy*, 211-13; *Survivors*, 139-40, 164-65; Hubbell, *P.O.W.*, 400, 416-18, 419-20, 422-24.
31. Daly and Bergman, *A Hero's Welcome*, 107, 120-21, 133-37; Grant, *Survivors*, 134-36, ch 9. In *Survivors*, 183, there is even a hint of anti-Semitism directed toward Kushner, who was Jewish.
32. The deaths of Sherman, Grissett, and Burns are detailed in Chapter 14. On the others, see Groom and Spencer, *Conversations With the Enemy*, 211-15 (the sequence is incorrect); Daly and Bergman, *A Hero's Welcome*, 122-23, 131-32; Grant, *Survivors*, 164-65, 170-71 (171, McMillan quote). Kushner's comment on the manioc is from "To Live or to Die," 5; see, too, *Survivors*, 119-20, 185-86; one source (*Conversations With the Enemy*, 230-31) says that the brunt of the manioc "planting" was done by ARVN PWs and a sole American, Garwood.
33. Grant, *Survivors*, 187-97 (194-95, quote); Schwinn and Diehl, *We Came to Help*, 3-128; Groom and Spencer, *Conversations With the Enemy*, 224-32. On the extent of "sexist" conduct toward the female prisoners by the captors and male captives, see Gruner, *Prisoners of Culture*, 119-23.
34. Daly and Bergman, *A Hero's Welcome*, 152-56 (155, quote); Grant, *Survivors*, 198-99, 225-30; Kushner file.
35. Daly and Bergman, *A Hero's Welcome*, 157-74 (174, quote); Grant, *Survivors*, 231-49, 284-85.
36. The experience at Camps 101 and 102 is reconstructed from the Benge report in *Nutrition Today* (see note 6), 222, and the accounts of McMurray, Perricone, and Leopold in Post-1968 Southern Captivity file. On Grzyb, see *POW/MIA'S*, Report of the Senate Select Committee on POW/MIA Affairs, 103 Cong, 1 sess (13 Jan 93), 607-08. Hubbell introduces Leopold, a recent Stanford graduate seized only a month after his arrival in Vietnam, in *P.O.W.*, 427-28.
37. Leopold file; "The Cruel Years—Two Exclusive Reports," 223; memo DirDIA ViceAdm V. P. de Poix for SecDef, 6 Apr 73, encl 4, 2.
38. Vanputten and Dunn materials in Post-1968 Southern Captivity file.
39. Schrump file. Hereafter the section relies mainly on Schrump's homecoming account and Kiley intervs with Schrump, with other sources cited as pertinent.
40. On Vanputten's escape, see *Washington Post*, 20 Apr 69; msg 7364 AmEmbSaigon for SecState, 17 Apr 69, sub: Escape of US PW; msg 24242 MACV for JCS, 22 Apr 69, sub: Bright Light; "Lessons Learned Briefing to Chief of Staff, Army," 30 Aug 73, app H, 1-2. All, incidentally, misspell Vanputten's name. The quotes in the asterisk note are from the *Washington Post* article.
41. All of those mentioned here who returned home contributed accounts that help piece together the tangled history of this group's captivity. See Post-1968 Southern Captivity file.
42. Sexton's release coincided with the release of a North Vietnamese PW held in the South. Why he was selected, especially in light of his escape history, is not clear. A separate file on the

unusual case is in OSD Hist. See, too, the spate of newspaper stories on the subject in *Washington Post*, 9, 13 Oct 71; *NY Times*, 12 Oct 71; *Philadelphia Inquirer*, 25 Jan 72.

43. On Ramsey's and Hardy's pre-1968 captivity, see Chapter 13. The sources cited there are used here as well.

44. Ramsey and Hardy files; *Washington Post*, 30 Mar 73.

45. The quotes are from the Ramsey report in *Nutrition Today*, 226, 228.

46. See the relevant portions of the Hardy and Ramsey homecoming reports. The two differ on when Albert arrived, with Hardy's February date appearing to be the more accurate.

47. Ramsey file.

48. *U.S. MACV Command History, 1969*, vol 2, X-51-60. Whether out of genuine gratitude or concern for the welfare of colleagues left behind—perhaps both—the releasees generally praised their treatment by the Viet Cong. See, for instance, the comments by Peterson and Shepard in *Washington Post*, 12, 14 Dec 69.

49. Clips on both the Gregory and Sweeney cases are in Post-1968 Southern Captivity file. On Sweeney, a good summary, though written from a prosecution bias, is Solis, *Trial by Fire*, 221-23.

50. DoD *POW-MIA Fact Book*, Oct 92, 15; "A Sampling of 'Discrepancy Cases' Still on the Books," *Defense 92*, Jan/Feb, 9; Cawthorne, *The Bamboo Cage*, 76-77. For a comprehensive listing of such cases, see *POW/MIA'S*, Report of the Senate Select Committee on POW/MIA Affairs (13 Jan 93).

22. 1969: A WATERSHED YEAR IN THE NORTH

1. Norman, *Bouncing Back*, 149.

2. Dramesi recounts his formative years in *Code of Honor*, ch 5; his first escape attempt is discussed in ch 2 and the Meyer quote appears on 98. On the ambivalence with which comrades viewed his "iron man" conceit, see Dunn's excellent bibliographic essay, "The POW Chronicles," 503, and Jon Reynolds's incisive article "Question of Honor," esp 105, 109. Craig Howes takes a somewhat sympathetic if strained "diehard as scapegoat" look at Dramesi in *Voices of the Vietnam POWs*, 193-99. More critical of Dramesi's vainglory and his denigration of even decorated heroes like Risner and Coker is Maj. W. Hays Parks, USMC, "Code of Conduct vs. *Code of Honor*," *Armed Forces Journal International* (Nov 76), 27-28.

3. Howes, *Voices of the Vietnam POWs*, 194; Denton, *When Hell Was In Session*, 127; Guarino, *A POW's Story*, 195; *U.S. MACV Command History, 1969*, vol 2, X-28.

4. McDaniel, *Before Honor*, 103-05; Guarino, *A POW's Story*, 195-96 (Guarino uses the pseudonyms "Scorpio" and "Atherton" for Dramesi and Atterberry). For a fuller treatment of the "escape dilemma," both in historical context and as applied specifically to the situation in North Vietnam, see "U.S. Aircrew Members Escape from Permanent Detention Facilities in North Vietnam," Nov 75; a useful summary is on 50-53.

5. On the organization and preparation leading up to the escape, see Dramesi, *Code of Honor*, 88-113; Kiley interv with Bill Baugh; "U.S. Aircrew Members Escape from Permanent Detention Facilities," 37-43; Myers, *Vietnam POW Camp Histories*, vol 2, 104-09.

6. On Trautman's agonizing and the circumstances surrounding the final decision, Dramesi's version is in *Code of Honor*, 113-14; for Trautman's version and from the perspective of Dramesi's cellmates, see "U.S. Aircrew Members Escape from Permanent Detention Facilities," 43-44, and Kiley interv with Baugh. Guarino offers his thoughts on the decision and Trautman's handling of it in *A POW's Story*, 283-84.

7. Dramesi, *Code of Honor*, 120-35 (134, quote); Stockdale, *In Love and War*, 343, 460; Day, *Return With Honor*, 151-52; copy of Atterberry death certificate in OSD Hist.

8. Myers, *Vietnam POW Camp Histories*, vol 2, 116-18.

9. Myers, *Vietnam POW Camp Histories*, vol 2, 105-06; "U.S. Aircrew Members Escape from Permanent Detention Facilities," 45; Day, *Return With Honor*, 152; Plumb, *I'm No Hero*, 223.

10. The escape aftermath at the Zoo's main compound is portrayed in several lengthy postwar accounts that agree substantially on what occurred but differ somewhat on the chronological

sequence. See Myers, *Vietnam POW Camp Histories*, vol 1, 152-59; ibid, vol 2, 110-16; Guarino, *A POW's Story*, ch 13; Day, *Return With Honor*, 151-54.

11. Hubbell, *P.O.W.*, 495; Day, *Return With Honor*, 153, 157 (quote), 166; Guarino, *A POW's Story*, 217-18, 199 (quote), 212. Day refers to an interim commander named "Moses" who he says launched the purge before Buzzard's arrival, but this officer is mentioned nowhere else.

12. Guarino, *A POW's Story*, 200-14 (208-09, quote); Day, *Return With Honor*, ch 13 (159, 162, quotes).

13. McDaniel's experience is recounted in *Before Honor*, ch 7. See also Myers, *Vietnam POW Camp Histories*, vol 2, 111; Hubbell, *P.O.W.*, 499-501.

14. Guarino, *A POW's Story*, 274-75; Nasmyth, *Hanoi Release John Nasmyth*, 166; Plumb, *I'm No Hero*, 216-17. Day incorrectly assumed that Connell was never compromised (see *Return With Honor*, 152).

15. On "Bug," see Risner, *Passing of the Night*, 155; Day, *Return With Honor*, 81; Rowan, *They Wouldn't Let Us Die*, 27; McConnell, *Into the Mouth of the Cat*, 191. On Stockdale's return to torture, see *In Love and War*, 349-52 (352, quote).

16. Stockdale file; *In Love and War*, 352-58. The September 1969 incident is specifically mentioned in Stockdale's Medal of Honor citation.

17. Myers, *Vietnam POW Camp Histories*, vol 1, 346-47, 478-80; "Summary of Son Tay Escape Plan and Operation Mole," DIA rpt, nd, 1; Hubbell, *P.O.W.*, 502-06, 508-10.

18. Plumb, *I'm No Hero*, 225; "U.S. Aircrew Members Escape from Permanent Detention Facilities," vi, 46-48; Myers, *Vietnam POW Camp Histories*, vol 2, 123.

19. Chesley, *Seven Years in Hanoi*, 109; Murray, "Historical Analysis and Critical Appraisal of the Code of Conduct," 218-19; Hubbell, *P.O.W.*, 519; "USAF Intelligence Highlights of Operation Homecoming," Apr 74, 38.

20. Stockman, "Authority, Leadership, Organization," 24; Hubbell, *P.O.W.*, 520; Alvarez and Pitch, *Chained Eagle*, 200. See, too, Day's comments in *Return With Honor*, 171.

21. "USAF Intelligence Highlights of Operation Homecoming," Apr 74, 38-39; Bernasconi et al, "Living Conditions," in Myers, *Vietnam POW Camp Histories*, vol 2, 236; Stockman, "Authority, Leadership, Organization," 25; Rowan, *They Wouldn't Let Us Die*, 151.

22. Stockman, "Authority, Leadership, Organization," 25; Myers, *Vietnam POW Camp Histories*, vol 1, 235; Howes, *Voices of the Vietnam POWs*, 45; Risner, *Passing of the Night*, 191; Samuel R. Johnson, "Deficiencies in Treatment of U.S. POW's in North Vietnam Under the Standards of the Geneva Conventions of 1949," National War College research paper, Mar 74, 75-76.

23. Doremus, "Days to Remember," 64; Hubbell, *P.O.W.*, 512, 514; Myers, *Vietnam POW Camp Histories*, vol 1, 347-48; Grant, *Survivors*, 263-64; McCain, "How the POW's Fought Back," 112; Norman, *Bouncing Back*, 170-71; Dramesi, *Code of Honor*, 143-44, 163-64, 167-69 (168, quote).

24. Guarino, *A POW's Story*, 231; Nasmyth, *2355 Days*, 95-96; Hubbell, *P.O.W.*, 514; McDaniel, *Before Honor*, 133-37 (133, quote).

25. Day, *Return With Honor*, 171-72. On the intriguing "tea warmer," see also Jensen, *Six Years in Hell*, 102; Dramesi, *Code of Honor*, 154; Denton, *When Hell Was In Session*, 195.

26. Denton, *When Hell Was In Session*, 192-95; Johnson and Winebrenner, *Captive Warriors*, 189-200 (193, quote).

27. Stockdale, *In Love and War*, 359, 393, 397-98; Denton, *When Hell Was In Session*, 198-99; Mulligan, *Hanoi Commitment*, 211, 213; Johnson and Winebrenner, *Captive Warriors*, 213; Blakey, *Prisoner at War*, 254-55. Stockdale discusses "Cat's demise," including a touching final encounter with him, in his homecoming report.

28. Day, *Return With Honor*, 176-77; Guarino, *A POW's Story*, 243-44.

29. Bernasconi et al, "Living Conditions," 175-76; Nasmyth, *Hanoi Release John Nasmyth*, 243-44; Day, *Return With Honor*, 179; mail statistics in fact sheet, "American Prisoners of War and Missing in Action in Southeast Asia (as of February 28, 1971)"; Berger, ed, *United States Air Force in Southeast Asia*, 337.

30. Myers, *Vietnam POW Camp Histories*, vol 1, 349-52; Guarino, *A POW's Story*, 244; Rivers file. Ralph Gaither had a different opinion about the Son Tay service; see *With God in a P.O.W. Camp*, 111.

31. Johnson and Winebrenner, *Captive Warriors*, 200-02.

23. "THE GOOD GUY ERA": THE NORTHERN PRISONS, 1970

1. Alvarez and Pitch, *Chained Eagle*, 218.
2. Blakey, *Prisoner at War*, 255.
3. The "Good Guy Era" is identified in Northern captivity accounts as the period between October 1969 and the closing of the Las Vegas section of Hoa Lo in December 1970. See Myers, *Vietnam POW Camp Histories*, vol 1, 234; Stockman, "Authority, Leadership, Organization," 25-28.
4. Myers, *Vietnam POW Camp Histories*, vol 1, 164-68; McDaniel, *Before Honor*, 138; Guarino, *A POW's Story*, 250; Coffee file.
5. Shankel and McKamey files; Guarino, *A POW's Story*, 250, 253; Myers, *Vietnam POW Camp Histories*, vol 1, 171; Alvarez and Pitch, *Chained Eagle*, 219.
6. Myers, *Vietnam POW Camp Histories*, vol 1, 169-73, 208; McDaniel, *Before Honor*, 138-39; Alvarez and Pitch, *Chained Eagle*, 223-24; McDaniel, *Yet Another Voice*, 40-41; Coffee file; Nasmyth, *2355 Days*, 131-32.
7. McDaniel, *Yet Another Voice*, 41-42; Alvarez file; Myers, *Vietnam POW Camp Histories*, vol 1, 173-75; Alvarez and Pitch, *Chained Eagle*, 224.
8. Chesley, *Seven Years in Hanoi*, 109; Myers, *Vietnam POW Camp Histories*, vol 1, 352-55; Schemmer, *The Raid*, 22; Gaither, *With God in a P.O.W. Camp*, 110. With respect to the water facility, some sources refer to tanks, others to an in-ground well.
9. Chesley, *Seven Years in Hanoi*, 110-11; Schemmer, *The Raid*, 22-24; Myers, *Vietnam POW Camp Histories*, vol 1, 42-43.
10. Myers, *Vietnam POW Camp Histories*, vol 1, 356-57; "Summary of Son Tay Escape Plan and Operation Mole," DIA rpt, nd, 1-2; Melson and Arnold, *The War That Would Not End*, 222. Clower's code name was "Dixie." Some of the techniques used to transmit information are described in Schemmer, *The Raid*, 24-25.
11. Myers, *Vietnam POW Camp Histories*, vol 1, 357-62; "Summary of Son Tay Escape Plan and Operation Mole," 1; "USAF Intelligence Highlights of Operation Homecoming," Apr 74, 41.
12. Myers, *Vietnam POW Camp Histories*, vol 1, 360 (diagram), 362-64; Stockman, "Authority, Leadership, Organization," 28.
13. McDaniel, *Before Honor*, 139; Myers, *Vietnam POW Camp Histories*, vol 1, 362-65, 369-70; Chesley, *Seven Years in Hanoi*, 116.
14. Gaither, *With God in a P.O.W. Camp*, 113-14; Myers, *Vietnam POW Camp Histories*, vol 1, 367-71.
15. Myers, *Vietnam POW Camp Histories*, vol 1, 365-67, 371-72; Gaither, *With God in a P.O.W. Camp*, 113, 115-16; Shankel file; McDaniel, *Before Honor*, 140-41.
16. McDaniel, *Before Honor*, 139, 141, 146; Myers, *Vietnam POW Camp Histories*, vol 1, 373.
17. Norman, *Bouncing Back*, 175-79 (176, quote); McDaniel, *Before Honor*, 141-42; Bernasconi et al, "Morale and Human Endurance," 163-65; "Summary of Son Tay Escape Plan and Operation Mole," 2.
18. Alvarez and Pitch, *Chained Eagle*, 225; Myers, *Vietnam POW Camp Histories*, vol 1, 373-74; Gaither, *With God in a P.O.W. Camp*, 116.
19. Myers, *Vietnam POW Camp Histories*, vol 1, 359, 374; Norman, *Bouncing Back*, 186; McKamey file.
20. Rutledge, *In the Presence of Mine Enemies*, 65; Johnson and Winebrenner, *Captive Warriors*, 212; Rivers file; Doremus, "Days to Remember," 65-66.

21. Johnson and Winebrenner, *Captive Warriors*, 215, 219; Rutledge, *In the Presence of Mine Enemies*, 67; Doremus, "Days to Remember," 66-67; Denton, *When Hell Was In Session*, 202; Mulligan, *Hanoi Commitment*, 223-24.

22. Denton, *When Hell Was In Session*, 203-05; Mulligan, *Hanoi Commitment*, 219-20, 224; McCain, "How the POW's Fought Back," 112-13; Santoli, *Everything We Had*, 239; Dramesi, *Code of Honor*, 179-80; Rivers file.

23. Rutledge, *In the Presence of Mine Enemies*, 67; Denton, *When Hell Was In Session*, 207 (also see Mulligan, *Hanoi Commitment*, 227); Doremus, "Days to Remember," 70; Grant, *Survivors*, 265-66; Johnson and Winebrenner, *Captive Warriors*, 220-28.

24. On the organizational chaos at Vegas at the outset of 1970, see Denton, *When Hell Was In Session*, 200-01; Johnson and Winebrenner, *Captive Warriors*, 213-14; Stockman, "Authority, Leadership, Organization," 26.

25. Denton, *When Hell Was In Session*, 200; Johnson and Winebrenner, *Captive Warriors*, 215-19; Mulligan, *Hanoi Commitment*, 219-22; Myers, *Vietnam POW Camp Histories*, vol 1, 231; Brace, *A Code to Keep*, 189-96; Risner, *Passing of the Night*, 205 (Risner misspells Bedinger's name and has the year of his capture as 1968 instead of 1969). One of the best sources on Vegas's revived communications network in 1970 is Bedinger's own paper, "Prisoner-of-War Organization in Hanoi," ch 4.

26. Denton, *When Hell Was In Session*, 205-06; Mulligan, *Hanoi Commitment*, 220, 222-25; Stockdale file; Johnson and Winebrenner, *Captive Warriors*, 229.

27. Stockdale file; Dramesi, *Code of Honor*, 183, 187; Mulligan, *Hanoi Commitment*, 223.

28. Guarino, *A POW's Story*, 260; Stockdale file; Stockdale, *In Love and War*, 399; Johnson and Winebrenner, *Captive Warriors*, 233-36; Mulligan, *Hanoi Commitment*, 225; Stockman, "Authority, Leadership, Organization," 27.

29. Guarino, *A POW's Story*, 266; Doremus, "Days to Remember," 69; Mulligan, *Hanoi Commitment*, 229; Stockdale, *In Love and War*, 400-01; Denton, *When Hell Was In Session*, 201, 205-06; Johnson and Winebrenner, *Captive Warriors*, 231 (on Shumaker, although somewhat later, see also *A POW's Story*, 293). On the October visit of the 05s to Cu Loc, see Franke and Stockdale homecoming reports. Stockdale believed they were sent to the Zoo "as trial cases and came out as rejects."

30. Stockman, "Authority, Leadership, Organization," 26-28; Risner, *Passing of the Night*, 203-06; Denton, *When Hell Was In Session*, 207.

31. Quoted material is from Day, *Return With Honor*, ch 13, which is the fullest published account of life in the Heartbreak section of Hoa Lo during the second half of 1970. For a more revealing record of their experience, see Pollard's account in Myers, *Vietnam POW Camp Histories*, vol 1, 41-68. Guarino (*A POW's Story*, 272) cited Pollard, with Shumaker, as possessing "two of the best sets of brains" at Hoa Lo. From long sessions in irons, Pollard had developed noticeable blotches on his neck and back.

32. The plight of Connell, Cameron, and Cobeil is described at length in the Day and Pollard accounts cited in note 31 (Day quote is on 189, Pollard quotes on 52, 59). Pollard refers to them as "A," "B," and "C" respectively; Day labels them "Jig," "Kilo," and "Max." Risner discusses the three in *Passing of the Night*, ch 23. Guarino treats Cameron under the pseudonym "Burl Flagler" in *A POW's Story*, 273.

33. Myers, *Vietnam POW Camp Histories*, vol 1, 49 (quote), 56, 65; Day, *Return With Honor*, 190.

34. Leopold file; Hubbell, *P.O.W.*, 528-29; Grant, *Survivors*, 266-67; Myers, *Vietnam POW Camp Histories*, vol 1, ch 15. There are inconsistencies and some factual errors among the several accounts.

35. Hubbell, *P.O.W.*, 530-35; Grant, *Survivors*, 272-79. Archer is identified in *P.O.W.* and elsewhere as a lieutenant but DIA's official tabulation has him listed in captivity as a captain.

36. Fortunately, several prisoners from different periods have written accounts (in addition to furnishing debriefings) of their experience at Skid Row, so that one can reconstruct the camp's PW movements and physical characteristics with a fair degree of confidence. The key sources are Purcell, *Love and Duty*, chs 8-18; Day, *Return With Honor*, ch 15; Heslop and Van Orden, *From the Shadow of Death*, ch 19; Schwinn and Diehl, *We Came to Help*, 203-07; and Myers, *Vietnam POW Camp Histories*, vol 1, ch 14.

37. Purcell, *Love and Duty*, 75; Day, *Return With Honor*, 210; Heslop and Van Orden, *From the Shadow of Death*, 172.

38. Heslop and Van Orden, *From the Shadow of Death*, 172-73, 176-77; Schwinn and Diehl, *We Came to Help*, 204-06; Thompson file.

39. Myers, *Vietnam POW Camp Histories*, vol 1, 455-56; Purcell, *Love and Duty*, 75-80, 87-90, 141; Heslop and Van Orden, *From the Shadow of Death*, 178.

40. Purcell recounts this first escape attempt in *Love and Duty*, ch 12 (102, quote). See also Westmoreland, *A Soldier Reports*, 307-08; "USAF Intelligence Highlights of Operation Homecoming," Apr 74, 30.

24. UNITY, CHAOS, AND THE "FOURTH ALLIED POW WING"

1. A description of the new section is in Myers, *Vietnam POW Camp Histories*, vol 1, 376-77. The 800 figure for the number of indigenous Vietnamese celled there prior to the arrival of the Americans appears in Ben Pollard's account in the Myers volume, 66; the lower figure is cited in Stockman, "Authority, Leadership, Organization," 28.

2. Rutledge, *In the Presence of Mine Enemies*, 72; Day, *Return With Honor*, 192; Myers, *Vietnam POW Camp Histories*, vol 1, 65-67, 384-86. The exact count varies from source to source, ranging between 340 and 350, owing in part to the inclusion by some talliers of several Thai prisoners and a South Vietnamese in the total population.

3. Guarino, *A POW's Story*, 270; Risner, *Passing of the Night*, 208; Dramesi, *Code of Honor*, 191; Rutledge, *In the Presence of Mine Enemies*, 75.

4. On the Fellowes-Coker reunion, see Rausa, "Home from Hanoi," 14. On the move of the Lulus from Vegas to Unity, see Brace homecoming account and *A Code to Keep*, 203-05. On the Thais and "Max," see Brace references and Denton, *When Hell Was In Session*, 222-23; Stockdale praises Harnavee in *In Love and War*, 358-59; Risner lauds Max in *Passing of the Night*, 230-32. There is some confusion as to whether there were two or three Thais in building 0, but the 4th Allied POW Wing's own compilation shows three at Unity and the likelihood is they were kept together.

5. Nasmyth, *2355 Days*, 142-45; Alvarez and Pitch, *Chained Eagle*, 225; Johnson and Winebrenner, *Captive Warriors*, 244. Some sources cite 46 or 47 instead of 45 as the number of men in cell 7. The discrepancy is puzzling; one or two may have been briefly at another location before joining the others.

6. Myers, *Vietnam POW Camp Histories*, vol 1, 380-82.

7. Nasmyth, *2355 Days*, 145-46; Myers, *Vietnam POW Camp Histories*, vol 1, 386.

8. Brace, *A Code to Keep*, 205-09; Bedinger, "Prisoner-of-War Organization in Hanoi," 52-55; Stockdale file; Myers, *Vietnam POW Camp Histories*, vol 1, 387.

9. Stockman, "Authority, Leadership, Organization," 29; on the skepticism that greeted Ligon and Flynn, see Dramesi, *Code of Honor*, 192-93, 219-20; Stockdale's comment on Ligon is in File 719.

10. Brace, *A Code to Keep*, 211; Denton *When Hell Was In Session*, 217; Myers, *Vietnam POW Camp Histories*, vol 1, 387-88; Stockman, "Authority, Leadership, Organization," 29-30.

11. Stockdale file; Stockman, "Authority, Leadership, Organization," 31; Denton, *When Hell Was In Session*, 217. See also Risner, *Passing of the Night*, 210-11.

12. Myers, *Vietnam POW Camp Histories*, vol 1, 388; Stockdale file; Guarino, *A POW's Story*, 276; Brace, *A Code to Keep*, 210; Bedinger, "Prisoner-of-War," 56-58. Dramesi frames the debate in ch 16 of *Code of Honor*, entitled "The Will and the Purpose."

13. In a section entitled "The Gathering Storm," Myers, *Vietnam POW Camp Histories*, vol 1, 390-406, recapitulates a series of incidents that occurred over the first month or so in Unity, including the bathing and coal ball flaps. Dramesi discusses the bathing problem in *Code of Honor*, 193. See also Rivers file; Risner, *Passing of the Night*, 210-14.

14. Guarino, *A POW's Story*, 288; Franke file; Myers, *Vietnam POW Camp Histories*, vol 1, 391, 395-97; Risner, *Passing of the Night*, 214.

15. A defining moment of the captivity, the church service revolt is discussed in affectionate detail in the memoir literature. See, for example, Risner, *Passing of the Night*, ch 26; Stockdale, *In Love and War*, 429-30; Dramesi, *Code of Honor*, 203-04, 209-10; Day, *Return With Honor*, 195-96; Johnson and Winebrenner, *Captive Warriors*, 246-47; Mulligan, *Hanoi Commitment*, 237-38; Denton, *When Hell Was In Session*, 219-20; Guarino, *A POW's Story*, 284. The details, including how much was planned and how much was spontaneous, vary from source to source, with different individuals taking or receiving credit as initiators and with embellishments befitting what would become a legendary episode.

16. Risner, *Passing of the Night*, 220-22; Stockdale file (see also *In Love and War*, 430); Mulligan, *Hanoi Commitment*, 239-41; Dramesi, *Code of Honor*, 210-15; Myers, *Vietnam POW Camp Histories*, vol 1, 409-13.

17. Denton, *When Hell Was In Session*, 220.

18. Risner, *Passing of the Night*, 223; Stockman, "Authority, Leadership, Organization," 30; Stockdale file.

19. Mulligan, *Hanoi Commitment*, 246; Stockman, "Authority, Leadership, Organization," 31; Stockdale file. Jim Lamar's comment on the subject of "PW Organization" supports Stockman's version. Assessments of Flynn's role and contribution reflect to some extent rival service perspectives and a pride of authorship factor as well as the hardline vs. softline proclivities of the evaluators. Stockman and Lamar were fellow Air Force officers; Stockdale, of course, was Navy, and the principal author of the existing guidelines. In general, however, Flynn got high marks, as did Winn and Gaddis, whom Navy man Mulligan also extolls.

20. Stockman, "Authority, Leadership, Organization," 31-33; Plumb, *I'm No Hero*, 169-72; Myers, *Vietnam POW Camp Histories*, vol 1, 415, 488. For a comparison of Stockdale's BACK US and the new Plums, see Howes, *Voices of the Vietnam POWs*, 31.

21. Stockman, "Authority, Leadership, Organization," 31, 33; Stockdale file; Myers, *Vietnam POW Camp Histories*, vol 1, 414-16.

22. Franke file; Mulligan, *Hanoi Commitment*, 241-43; Denton, *When Hell Was In Session*, 222-24.

23. Denton, *When Hell Was In Session*, 225; Risner, *Passing of the Night*, 224; Myers, *Vietnam POW Camp Histories*, vol 1, 70, 417; Stockman, "Authority, Leadership, Organization," 33. The sources differ on exactly when and why the colonels were pulled from Rawhide, as well as where they were sent and when they returned. In interviews with Kiley, both Flynn and Winn said that, although the move closely followed Flynn's letter of protest, that may have been coincidental and the Vietnamese may have had other reasons for making the change.

24. Dramesi, *Code of Honor*, 208; McDaniel, *Before Honor*, 149-50; Nasmyth, *Hanoi Release John Nasmyth*, 239; Myers, *Vietnam POW Camp Histories*, vol 1, 411-13; Davis file (the year is mistakenly cited as 1972 instead of 1971).

25. For a range of views on the letter moratorium, both its character and outcome, see Myers, *Vietnam POW Camp Histories*, vol 1, 398-400; Stockdale and Doremus files; Guarino, *A POW's Story*, 287; Jensen, *Six Years in Hell*, 143-44; Dramesi, *Code of Honor*, 220-21, 240; McDaniel, *Before Honor*, 151-52; Nasmyth, *Hanoi Release John Nasmyth*, 237-38. In an interview with Kiley, Winn expressed the opinion that the effort resulted in "dubious gains" and that the senior officers "went along with it because it made the group of junior PWs feel like they were contributing something positive to the resistance."

26. See Chapter 7, note 26. On the application of the concept here in 1971 at Unity, see Myers, *Vietnam POW Camp Histories*, vol 1, 417; Plumb, *I'm No Hero*, 173; McDaniel, *Before Honor*, 151; memo AsstChStaff AF Intell, MajGen George J. Keegan, Jr., for Generals Ryan and Dixon, 21 Mar 73, sub: Item of Interest.

27. Day, *Return With Honor*, 209.

28. Ibid, ch 15; McDaniel, *Before Honor*, 150; Guarino, *A POW's Story*, 289-90, 294; Myers, *Vietnam POW Camp Histories*, vol 1, 458-71; McCain, "How the POW's Fought Back," 113.

29. On the December Skid Row transfer, see Rivers file; Guarino, *A POW's Story*, 309-12; Myers, *Vietnam POW Camp Histories*, vol 1, 471-73. Rivers's dates are off by a week; Guarino uses pseudonyms for several of the men. On the reopening of the Zoo, see Myers, *Vietnam POW Camp Histories*, vol 1, 176-81, 420.

30. Stockman, "Authority, Leadership, Organization," 34; Johnson and Winebrenner, *Captive Warriors*, 248-49; Franke, Winn, and Stockdale files; Denton, *When Hell Was In Session*, 226-27; Mulligan, *Hanoi Commitment*, 245-52 (250, quote). Here again, chronological and other details vary considerably from source to source.

31. File 719; Stockdale, *In Love and War*, 400, 430-31.

32. Myers, *Vietnam POW Camp Histories*, vol 1, 418-19; Guarino, *A POW's Story*, 275, 294; Heslop and Van Orden, *From the Shadow of Death*, 121-22; Mulligan, *Hanoi Commitment*, 237.

33. Mulligan, *Hanoi Commitment*, 245-49; Rutledge, *In the Presence of Mine Enemies*, 82-83; Doremus, "Days to Remember," 74.

34. McDaniel, *Before Honor*, 152-53; Guarino, *A POW's Story*, 294, 296; Mulligan, *Hanoi Commitment*, 242, 252-53; Plumb, *I'm No Hero*, 193-94; Blakey, *Prisoner at War*, 272. Alvarez first noticed Ratzlaff's "strange skin growth" at the Zoo (see *Chained Eagle*, 197); the cancer was diagnosed at homecoming. Regarding Crayton, see *A POW's Story*, 301-03, 319 (Guarino identifies him as "Ray Saxton"); Dramesi, *Code of Honor*, 218, 245-46; and *Before Honor*, 153, where McDaniel doesn't mention him by name but is almost certainly referring to him.

35. Doremus, "Days to Remember," 73-74; Guarino, *A POW's Story*, 293, 307-08, 312-13; Rowan, *They Wouldn't Let Us Die*, 112, Kiley interv with Hildebrand; Johnson and Winebrenner, *Captive Warriors*, 260-61.

36. Plumb, *I'm No Hero*, 160, 163; Alvarez and Pitch, *Chained Eagle*, 227-30, 238-44; Norman, *Bouncing Back*, 180-82; Rowan, *They Wouldn't Let Us Die*, 203-05; Guarino, *A POW's Story*, 265-66, 319; Coffee, *Beyond Survival*, 174.

37. Johnson and Winebrenner, *Captive Warriors*, 252-54; Guarino, *A POW's Story*, 277-79; Day, *Return With Honor*, 231-32; Blakey, *Prisoner at War*, 274.

38. Day, *Return With Honor*, 199-200, 206-07, 231; Johnson and Winebrenner, *Captive Warriors*, 249. The "den mother" reference is John McCain's in "How the POW's Fought Back," 113.

39. Day, *Return With Honor*, 205-06, 208, 229; Dramesi, *Code of Honor*, 213; *Time*, 9 Apr 73.

40. Dramesi, *Code of Honor*, 215-18; Day, *Return With Honor*, 202-03, 207; Jensen, *Six Years in Hell*, 122-23; Bernasconi et al, "Morale and Human Endurance," 173; Nasmyth, *Hanoi Release John Nasmyth*, 262-63; Johnson and Winebrenner, *Captive Warriors*, 255, 261.

41. Guarino, *A POW's Story*, 281; Jensen, *Six Years in Hell*, 122; Bernasconi et al, "Morale and Human Endurance," 173-74; Plumb, *I'm No Hero*, 89-90; Heslop and Van Orden, *From the Shadow of Death*, 58. Guarino and Dramesi have two quite different accounts of cell 7's toastmasters' program: see *A POW's Story*, 303, 315 ("Scorpio" is Dramesi) and *Code of Honor*, 243, 246-47, 253-54 ("Brudino" is Guarino).

42. Bernasconi et al, "Morale and Human Endurance," 165-66, 174; Norman, *Bouncing Back*, 196-200; Jensen, *Six Years in Hell*, 120-22; Dramesi, *Code of Honor*, 215; Santoli, *Everything We Had*, 243; Geoffrey Norman, "Wine Tasting at the Hanoi Hilton," *Forbes* (Suppl No 1, 90), 68-69.

43. Norman, *Bouncing Back*, 196-98; Bernasconi et al, "Morale and Human Endurance," 166-67; Myers, *Vietnam POW Camp Histories*, vol 1, 421-22; Jensen, *Six Years in Hell*, 120-21; Heslop and Van Orden, *From the Shadow of Death*, 52.

44. Norman, *Bouncing Back*, 200-02; Doremus, "Days to Remember," 74.

45. Day, *Return With Honor*, 229-30; Norman, *Bouncing Back*, 203; Mulligan, *Hanoi Commitment*, 254.

25. DETOURS: DISSENSION AND DISPERSION

1. Howes, *Voices of the Vietnam POWs*, 107.

2. Stockman, "Authority, Leadership, Organization," 32; Norman, *Bouncing Back*, 187-88.

3. Day, *Return With Honor*, 201; Norman, *Bouncing Back*, 189-95; Nasmyth, *Hanoi Release John Nasmyth*, 234-40; Risner, *Passing of the Night*, 214.

4. Rowan, *They Wouldn't Let Us Die*, 55-56; Gaither, *With God in a P.O.W. Camp*, 109; Dramesi, *Code of Honor*, 231.

5. Guarino, *A POW's Story*, 297-301; Dramesi, *Code of Honor*, ch 17. For a third-party view of Guarino's rigidity on the escape question, see Johnson and Winebrenner, *Captive Warriors*, 251.

6. For details of the Tiger and Mole plans and the controversy they stirred, see "Summary of Son Tay Escape Plan and Operation Mole," DIA rpt, nd, 2-5; "U.S. Aircrew Members Escape from Permanent Detention Facilities," 49; Stockman, "Authority, Leadership, Organization," 34-35; Dramesi, *Code of Honor*, 244, 250-52. The Guarino quote is from *A POW's Story*, 301.

7. "USAF Intelligence Highlights of Operation Homecoming," Apr 74, 16; Alvarez and Pitch, *Chained Eagle*, 247; Guarino, *A POW's Story*, 323-24; Howes, *Voices of the Vietnam POWs*, 37-38.

8. Melson and Arnold, *The War That Would Not End*, 222-23; Howes, *Voices of the Vietnam POWs*, 71; Steven V. Roberts, "The P.O.W.'s: Focus of Division," *NY Times*, 3 Mar 73; Roberts, "Unshakable Will to Survive Sustained P.O.W.'s Over the Years," *NY Times*, 4 Mar 73; Roberts, "P.O.W.'s Felt Their Mission Was to Resist," *NY Times*, 30 Apr 73; Seymour M. Hersh, "P.O.W.'s Maintained Discipline but Had Some Quarrels," *NY Times*, 23 Feb 73.

9. Norman, *Bouncing Back*, 195.

10. The "Outer Seven" and the Unity phase of the Miller-Wilber controversy are discussed in Hubbell, *P.O.W.*, ch 32 (562, quote); Mulligan, *Hanoi Commitment*, 243-45; Guarino, *A POW's Story*, 305 ("Forrester" is Schweitzer); Johnson and Winebrenner, *Captive Warriors*, 256; Howes, *Voices of the Vietnam POWs*, 110-11. The silence of building 8 during the church riot is mentioned by Bedinger, "Prisoner-of-War Organization in Hanoi," 59, and Brace, *A Code to Keep*, 213 (both refer to building 8 as "000"); see also Day, *Return With Honor*, 196. Wilber alluded to the Nuremberg analogy in an interview with Stephen Rowan (*They Wouldn't Let Us Die*, 163-65), and reiterated it before the Code of Conduct Review Committee in 1976. On Schweitzer's "redemption," see also Chapter 20, note 50.

11. Norman, *Bouncing Back*, 195.

12. Day, *Return With Honor*, 230, 232-33; Myers, *Vietnam POW Camp Histories*, vol 1, 422-23; Stockdale, *In Love and War*, 430-31; Alvarez and Pitch, *Chained Eagle*, 245-46; Nasmyth, *Hanoi Release John Nasmyth*, 285-86. On Christian's previous run-ins, see Richard C. Barnard, "Coming Home from Hanoi," *Family*, 5 Sep 73, 8 ff. Regarding the "disaster" planning, which Dramesi apparently tried to turn into yet another vehicle for escape, see McDaniel, *Before Honor*, 155-59 (in places the "Tiger" escape plan and the disaster plan appear to be one and the same); Dramesi, *Code of Honor*, 254.

13. Stockdale file; Stockman, "Authority, Leadership, Organization," 34-35. On Kittinger, who joined the top seniors in Blue late in 1972, see Day, *Return With Honor*, 235; Guarino, *A POW's Story*, 324; Mulligan, *Hanoi Commitment*, 265-66.

14. The most complete account of the Dogpatch confinement is Myers, *Vietnam POW Camp Histories*, vol 1, ch 13. Myers lists 210 prisoners making the trip; other sources list 209, the discrepancy attributable to some not counting John Frederick, who died after arriving at the camp. Counting Frederick, 210 made the trip and 209 came back. Adding to the confusion, some sources cite a figure of 220; see, for example, memo DirDIA ViceAdm V. P. de Poix for SecDef, 6 Apr 73, encl 3, 3, subsequently cited in 1976 hearings by the House Select Committee on Missing Persons in Southeast Asia.

15. Myers, *Vietnam POW Camp Histories*, vol 1, 440 (diagram), 441-42; Jensen, *Six Years in Hell*, 146-47; Chesley, *Seven Years in Hanoi*, 117; Plumb, *I'm No Hero*, 247; Nasmyth, *2355 Days*, 208-10.

16. Myers, *Vietnam POW Camp Histories*, vol 1, 442-46 (on Frederick's death, see also vol 2, 246-47); Nasmyth, *2355 Days*, 209, 214-15; Jensen, *Six Years in Hell*, 147-48; Plumb, *I'm No Hero*, 247. See Gaither's tribute to Frederick in *With God in a P.O.W. Camp*, 105-07.

17. Rockpile is described in Thompson's and other accounts in OSD Hist. It apparently was located alongside a larger complex used to house South Vietnamese prisoners. On the escape attempt, which involved elaborate planning but got the escapees barely into the thick jungle outside the prison, see Thompson and Rushton files; Hubbell, *P.O.W.*, 564-66.

18. Purcell, *Love and Duty*, chs 19-21, 190-92; Heslop and Van Orden, *From the Shadow of Death*, 178-79; Schwinn and Diehl, *We Came to Help*, 222-23. Purcell was so impressed by the German nurses, whom he did not meet face to face until the group was brought back to Hanoi for release in 1973, that he wrote the foreword to their book.

19. Grant, *Survivors*, 267-70, 285-87; Stockman, "Authority, Leadership, Organization," 36; Myers, *Vietnam POW Camp Histories*, vol 1, 287; Brace, *A Code to Keep*, 228-32; Bedinger, "Prisoner-of-War Organization in Hanoi," 60-63.

20. Myers, *Vietnam POW Camp Histories*, vol 1, 286, 288-89, 481; Brace and Leopold files; Daly and Bergman, *A Hero's Welcome*, 172, 174-75; Grant, *Survivors*, 284-85.

21. Grant, *Survivors*, 302-06; Brace, *A Code to Keep*, 233, 236 (Brace overstates the extent and severity of the "torture" administered at the Plantation in 1971-72, but there is corroborating testimony to the brutality of Guy's beating); Hubbell, *P.O.W.*, 574-75.

22. The best profile of the Peace Committee and account of their experience from the standpoint of one of the members is Daly and Bergman, *A Hero's Welcome*, chs 18-22. For other views from both within and outside the group, see Grant, *Survivors*, 279-83, chs 15-16. See, too, Myers, *Vietnam POW Camp Histories*, vol 1, 290-92; Hubbell, *P.O.W.*, 566-74; Howes, *Voices of the Vietnam POWs*, 217-20; Brace, *A Code to Keep*, 231-36; Bedinger, "Prisoner-of-War Organization in Hanoi," 60-62, 65; Steven V. Roberts, "Antiwar P.O.W.'s: A Different Mold Scarred by Their Combat Experiences," *NY Times*, 15 Jul 73.

23. Grant, *Survivors*, 288-93, 316-17; Daly and Bergman, *A Hero's Welcome*, 206, ch 22; Myers, *Vietnam POW Camp Histories*, vol 1, 292.

24. Stockdale and Coffee files; Myers, *Vietnam POW Camp Histories*, vol 1, 427-29; Bernasconi et al, "Morale and Human Endurance," 167, 174; Dramesi, *Code of Honor*, 267; Day, *Return With Honor*, 240; Rausa, "Home from Hanoi," 18.

25. Myers, *Vietnam POW Camp Histories*, vol 1, 448-49; Nasmyth, *2355 Days*, 216-17; Chesley, *Seven Years in Hanoi*, 117; Jensen, *Six Years in Hell*, 151-52; Plumb, *I'm No Hero*, 250; Purcell, *Love and Duty*, 189-90; Heslop and Van Orden, *From the Shadow of Death*, 179; Brace, *A Code to Keep*, 237-38.

26. Doremus, "Days to Remember," 74, 85; Rutledge, *In the Presence of Mine Enemies*, 83; Myers, *Vietnam POW Camp Histories*, vol 1, 427; Day, *Return With Honor*, 236-37.

27. Johnson and Winebrenner, *Captive Warriors*, 260, 265.

28. Brace, *A Code to Keep*, 237-38; Myers, *Vietnam POW Camp Histories*, vol 1, 425-27; Day, *Return With Honor*, 237-39; Johnson and Winebrenner, *Captive Warriors*, 263-64.

29. Day, *Return With Honor*, 237; Plumb, *I'm No Hero*, 137-38; Johnson, "Deficiencies in Treatment of U.S. POW's in North Vietnam Under the Standards of the Geneva Conventions of 1949," 82-83 (see, too, *Captive Warriors*, 271-72).

30. Air Force Intelligence "Item of Interest" memo, nd, referencing Operation Homecoming Summary, 28 Mar 73; Mulligan, *Hanoi Commitment*, 262-65; Stockdale file; Stockman, "Authority, Leadership, Organization," 34-35.

31. Myers, *Vietnam POW Camp Histories*, vol 1, 181-82, 186-87; *National Observer*, 16 Sep 72; *NY Times*, 17, 18, 29 Sep 72; "The Battle of the POW's," *Time*, 9 Oct 72; Day, *Return With Honor*, 238; Guarino, *A POW's Story*, 325-26. In an interview with Kiley, Elias insisted he did nothing to encourage his early release. For Pentagon logisticians, the receiving and processing of the Gartley group provided a dry run for 1973's Operation Homecoming; see Berger, ed, *United States Air Force in Southeast Asia*, 339.

32. Myers, *Vietnam POW Camp Histories*, vol 1, 178-80, 183-87, 424; Alvarez and Pitch, *Chained Eagle*, 236-38; Hubbell, *P.O.W.*, 575-81 (Howes rips Hubbell's "official" version of the prisoners' interaction with the apostates in *Voices of the Vietnam POWs*, 109-12). On the differentiation between Miller's and Wilber's conduct, see Kiley interv with Winn. On the lodging and outcome of the misconduct charges, see Solis, *Trial by Fire*, 219-21; Melson and Arnold, *The War That Would Not End*, 231-33; *Washington Post*, 27, 29 Jun, 27 Sep 73.

33. George C. Wilson, "POWs Caught in Swirl of U.S. Politics," *Washington Post*, 10 Sep 72.

34. Daly and Bergman, *A Hero's Welcome*, 222-25; Day, *Return With Honor*, 243-46; McCain, "How the POW's Fought Back," 114; Myers, *Vietnam POW Camp Histories*, vol 1, 429-30; Larson file. Nearly every PW memoir focuses on the Christmas 1972 bombing as a climactic event; besides Day above, see Guarino, *A POW's Story*, 328-33; Mulligan, *Hanoi Commitment*, 266-76; Johnson and Winebrenner, *Captive Warriors*, 266-71; Blakey, *Prisoner at War*, ch 24. For the operation's historic importance and context, see Karnow, *Vietnam*, 652-54.

35. Day, *Return With Honor*, 246-47; Stockdale, *In Love and War*, 432; Blakey, *Prisoner at War*, 302. Not so fortunate as Kientzler was his co-pilot Harley Hall, a Blue Angels commander who was declared missing (later killed) in action in the 27 January incident; see Cawthorne, *The Bamboo Cage*, 79-80 on the controversy that lingers over Hall's status. Kientzler himself had some tense moments. Because of his late shootdown he was not on the list turned over to the American authorities in Paris. See Purcell, *Love and Duty*, 215-16.

26. HOMEWARD UNBOUND

1. Plumb, *I'm No Hero*, 138-39, 252-53 (quote); McDaniel, *Before Honor*, 163; Alvarez and Pitch, *Chained Eagle*, 250-51; Nasmyth, *Hanoi Release John Nasmyth*, 317. Plumb's view was shared by two other memoirists, Chesley (*Seven Years in Hanoi*, 118) and Jensen (*Six Years in Hell*, 145, 152).

2. Blakey, *Prisoner at War*, 301-02; McDaniel, *Before Honor*, 163-64; Alvarez and Pitch, *Chained Eagle*, 251-52; Doremus, "Days to Remember," 86; Myers, *Vietnam POW Camp Histories*, vol 1, 432; Norman, *Bouncing Back*, 212.

3. Coffee, *Beyond Survival*, 252-54.

4. Ibid, 254; Johnson and Winebrenner, *Captive Warriors*, 273; Norman, *Bouncing Back*, 212.

5. Stockman, "Authority, Leadership, Organization," 36-37; Risner, *Passing of the Night*, 241; Stockdale file.

6. Myers, *Vietnam POW Camp Histories*, vol 1, 433; Alvarez and Pitch, *Chained Eagle*, 250; Guarino, *A POW's Story*, 334; Coffee, *Beyond Survival*, 255-56; Denton, *When Hell Was In Session*, 232.

7. Coffee, *Beyond Survival*, 256-58; Denton, *When Hell Was In Session*, 232; Johnson and Winebrenner, *Captive Warriors*, 275; Guarino, *A POW's Story*, 335; Alvarez and Pitch, *Chained Eagle*, 253; Blakey, *Prisoner at War*, 302; Myers, *Vietnam POW Camp Histories*, vol 1, 434; Chesley, *Seven Years in Hanoi*, 118-19; Plumb, *I'm No Hero*, 162.

8. Alvarez and Pitch, *Chained Eagle*, 252; Myers, *Vietnam POW Camp Histories*, vol 1, 433-35; Stockdale file; Risner, *Passing of the Night*, 242-43; Coffee, *Beyond Survival*, 264-65.

9. Myers, *Vietnam POW Camp Histories*, vol 1, 237-38; Grant, *Survivors*, 320-22, 325; Daly and Bergman, *A Hero's Welcome*, 228-38; Hubbell, *P.O.W.*, 595-97.

10. Brace, *A Code to Keep*, 241-46; Brace file.

11. Willis file; Purcell, *Love and Duty*, 195-96, 206-10 (210, quote); Hubbell, *P.O.W.*, 597-98; Schwinn and Diehl, *We Came to Help*, 248.

12. Schrump, Ramsey, and Hardy files. On the 1972 captures, see Captain Wanat's extensive homecoming report. On the logistics of the evacuation of all 27 prisoners from Loc Ninh, see Davis, *The U.S. Government and American PWs in Southeast Asia*, ch 22 (ms).

13. Myers, *Vietnam POW Camp Histories*, vol 1, 434-35; Rutledge, *In the Presence of Mine Enemies*, 89; Plumb, *I'm No Hero*, 255; Coffee, *Beyond Survival*, 264-65; Alvarez and Pitch, *Chained Eagle*, 253; Mulligan, *Hanoi Commitment*, 278; Johnson and Winebrenner, *Captive Warriors*, 275; Chesley, *Seven Years in Hanoi*, 120; Blakey, *Prisoner at War*, 305.

14. Blakey, *Prisoner at War*, 303; Coffee, *Beyond Survival*, 262, 265-67.

15. Doremus, "Days to Remember," 87; Alvarez and Pitch, *Chained Eagle*, 254; Coffee, *Beyond Survival*, 267; Day, *Return With Honor*, 247; Daly and Bergman, *A Hero's Welcome*, 236; Miller file. The day's events remain a blur to many of the PWs, their recollections on wakeup, breakfast, and departure times varying significantly. On the initial puzzlement over the division of the departing PWs into groups of 20, see Davis, *The U.S. Government and American PWs in Southeast Asia*, ch 22 (ms).

16. Johnson and Winebrenner, *Captive Warriors*, 276-77; Alvarez and Pitch, *Chained Eagle*, 254-56; Guarino, *A POW's Story*, 336-37; Coffee, *Beyond Survival*, 267-69; Denton, *When Hell Was In Session*, 234; Mulligan, *Hanoi Commitment*, 278-79.

17. Alvarez and Pitch, *Chained Eagle*, 256; Johnson and Weinbrenner, *Captive Warriors*, 279; Blakey, *Prisoner at War*, 299-300; Mulligan, *Hanoi Commitment*, 280-82; Denton, *When Hell Was In Session*, 234-35; Rutledge, *In the Presence of Mine Enemies*, 92.

18. Davis, *The U.S. Government and American PWs in Southeast Asia*, ch 22 (ms); Alvarez and Pitch, *Chained Eagle*, 257-59; Johnson and Winebrenner, *Captive Warriors*, 280; Doremus, "Days to Remember," 87-88; Mulligan, *Hanoi Commitment*, 282-83; Denton, *When Hell Was In Session*, 235 (on Denton's writing of his statement en route, see also Guarino, *A POW's Story*, 335).

19. *Washington Post*, 13 Feb 73; *Christian Science Monitor*, 13 Feb 73; *Newsweek*, 26 Feb 73; *U.S. News & World Report*, 26 Feb 73; Chesley, *Seven Years in Hanoi*, 124; Norman, *Bouncing Back*, 218-26; Nasmyth, *Hanoi Release John Nasmyth*, 330; Alvarez and Pitch, *Chained Eagle*, 260-62. On the eating binge, see, too, Risner, *Passing of the Night*, 249. The best summary of the arrangements at Clark and other aspects of Operation Homecoming is Davis, *The U.S. Government and American PWs in Southeast Asia*, ch 22 (ms). An interesting observation on their medical evaluation is Ramsey's account in "The Cruel Years—Two Exclusive Reports," 233-37.

20. *Washington Post*, 14, 19 Feb 73; Plumb, *I'm No Hero*, 256-60; Jensen, *Six Years in Hell*, 154-55; report on "VN Early Release of 20 PW's," 18 Mar 73; Blakey, *Prisoner at War*, 303; Nasmyth, *Hanoi Release John Nasmyth*, 323-24.

21. *NY Times*, 27 Feb, 5 Mar 73; *Washington Post*, 26 Feb, 2, 5 Mar 73; *Washington Star & News*, 28 Feb 73; McDaniel, *Before Honor*, 164-67; Blakey, *Prisoner at War*, 306-07, 311-16; Rausa, "Home from Hanoi," 20.

22. *Washington Post*, 6 Mar 73; Schwinn and Diehl, *We Came to Help*, 249-50; Purcell, *Love and Duty*, 210-12.

23. Myers, *Vietnam POW Camp Histories*, vol 1, 293-95 (the release figure is incorrect); Day, *Return With Honor*, 248-53 (253, quote); McCain, "How the POW's Fought Back," 115.

24. Daly and Bergman, *A Hero's Welcome*, 238-41; Grant, *Survivors*, 325-31; Davis, *The U.S. Government and American PWs in Southeast Asia*, ch 22 (ms); *NY Times*, 17 Mar 73.

25. *Washington Post*, 13, 16 Mar 73; Philip E. Smith, "Internment in China," in Myers, *Vietnam POW Camp Histories*, vol 2, 40-41.

26. Davis, *The U.S. Government and American PWs in Southeast Asia*, ch 22 (ms); *NY Times*, 22 Mar 73; *Washington Post*, 25, 27 Mar 73.

27. Purcell, *Love and Duty*, 214-18; *Washington Post*, 28 Mar 73; Brace, *A Code to Keep*, 246-52.

28. *NY Times*, 29, 30 Mar 73; Myers, *Vietnam POW Camp Histories*, vol 1, 191-92.

29. Davis, *The U.S. Government and American PWs in Southeast Asia*, ch 22 (ms); *NY Times*, 29, 30 Mar 73; *Washington Post*, 2 Apr 73; *Orlando Sentinel*, 2 May 93.

30. Rowan, *They Wouldn't Let Us Die*, 56; White House "Fact Sheet" pertaining to POW Dinner, 24 May 73 (press release); Howes, *Voices of the Vietnam POWs*, 11-12. On the North vs. South medical comparison, see the Berg and Richlin study cited in Chapter 4, note 10; "POW's: The Price of Survival," *Newsweek*, 16 Apr 73; "POWs More Ill Than Suspected," *Washington Post*, 2 Jun 73. On the Brudno suicide, see *Voices of the Vietnam POWs*, 145; Barnard, "Coming Home from Hanoi," 9. In "Unfinished Business," *Newsweek*, 1 Jun 98, Robert J. Brudno cites societal attitudes in 1973 as contributing to his brother's death. OSD Hist files contain several folders of studies and other materials on the prisoners' medical outcomes.

31. Blakey, *Prisoner at War*, 306, 332; Barnard, "Coming Home from Hanoi," 8, 14; "Returning P.O.W.'s Are Flooded with Offers of Gifts and Other Benefits," *NY Times*, 15 Feb 73; Howes, *Voices of the Vietnam POWs*, 159-61 (criticizes the excessive materialism and star treatment surrounding the honoring of the PWs); Norman, *Bouncing Back*, ch 17; Steven V. Roberts, "P.O.W.'s a Year Later: Most Adapt Well," *NY Times*, 10 Feb 74; "The POW's: What a Difference a Year Makes," *Newsweek*, 25 Feb 74.

32. Alvarez and Pitch, *Chained Eagle*, 305-08; Stockdale, *In Love and War*, 438, 447; Norman, *Bouncing Back*, 234; "Pieces of the Puzzle," *People*, 9 Nov 92, 101-03 (on McCain); on Swindle's involvement in the Perot campaign, see *NY Times*, 11 Oct 92, *Washington Post*, 30 Sep 92; Brace, *A Code to Keep*, 257. On the Peterson appointment, see "U.S. Envoy Was Hanoi's 'Guest'," Baltimore *Sun*, 4 Jun 96; Mary McGrory, "Our Man in Vietnam," *Washington Post*, 20 Apr 97; "U.S. Again Has Envoy in Vietnam," *Washington Post*, 10 May 97.

33. See, for example, "Fourth Allied Prisoner of War Wing Debrief," 16 Apr 73; "USAF PW Comments on Training and Equipment," Aug 73.

34. See Harold L. Hitchens, "Factors Involved in a Review of the Code of Conduct for the Armed Forces," *Naval War College Review* (Winter 78), 47-70.

Selected Bibliography

Prisoner of war records from the Vietnam era are scattered throughout the federal government, most remaining in the custody of the military services' personnel, medical, and casualty reporting offices or, where consolidated, the service historical offices. Through research associated with this project and including its own substantial Vietnam War and PW Code of Conduct files, the Historical Office in the Office of the Secretary of Defense has assembled probably the most extensive archive anywhere on the experience of American prisoners in Southeast Asia. The collection contains interview transcripts; newspaper and magazine clippings; photo, film, and map holdings; press releases; official and personal correspondence; Defense Department, State Department, and intelligence agency memoranda, cables, directives, and other documents; and a vast assortment of other print and pictorial materials. Some of the most useful items, including returnee debriefings and still classified reports and records, can be consulted with the proper clearances but cannot be cited for security and privacy reasons.

Too voluminous to list separately is the large repository of unclassified but unpublished internal DoD reports and studies from both the captivity period and the post-captivity evaluation. Several items, however, bear special mention. For statistical details the authors relied primarily on the Southeast Asia Statistical Summary, 5 December 1973, Office of the Assistant Secretary of Defense (Comptroller), Directorate for Information Operations. Two indispensable references for individual PW information—names, ranks, dates of capture, confinement locations and durations, etc.—are the Defense Intelligence Agency's 7 September 1979 master list of all Vietnam War PWs/MIAs (in both alphabetical and chronological sequence), and an Air Force report dated June 1975 and entitled "Places and Dates of Confinement of Air Force, Navy, and Marine Corps Prisoners of War Held in North Vietnam, 1964-1973," produced by the 7602nd Air Intelligence Group. The best overall survey of North Vietnamese prison camps is the Air War College's two-volume *Vietnam POW Camp Histories and Studies*, Maxwell AFB, Ala., 1974, 1975; compiled and written by a group of returnees headed by Col. Armand J. Myers, it is unmatched as a general guide to reconstructing the chronology and distinguishing the physical characteristics and functioning of the separate camps in the North. Unfortunately, no comparable work is available on camps in South Vietnam or Laos.

Listed below are the more prominent published works on the captivity experience and related subjects as well as key congressional hearings and other unpublished sources the authors found particularly valuable. Also listed are full citations for histories and other background works identified in shorter form in the Notes.

MEMOIRS AND OTHER PERSONAL ACCOUNTS

Alvarez, Everett, Jr., with Anthony S. Pitch. *Chained Eagle*. New York: Donald I. Fine, 1989.

Bailey, Lawrence R., Jr., with Ron Martz. *Solitary Survivor: The First American POW in Southeast Asia*. Washington: Brassey's, 1995.

Brace, Ernest C. *A Code to Keep: The True Story of America's Longest-Held Civilian Prisoner of War in Vietnam*. New York: St. Martin's Press, 1988.

Chesley, Larry. *Seven Years in Hanoi*. Salt Lake City: Bookcraft, Inc., 1973.

Coffee, Gerald. *Beyond Survival: Building on the Hard Times—A POW's Inspiring Story*. New York: Putnam, 1990.

Daly, James A. and Lee Bergman. *A Hero's Welcome*. Indianapolis: Bobbs-Merrill, 1975.

Day, George E. *Return With Honor*. Mesa, Ariz.: Champlin Museum Press, 1989.

Dengler, Dieter. *Escape from Laos*. San Rafael, Calif.: Presidio Press, 1979.

Denton, Jeremiah, Jr. *When Hell Was In Session*. New York: Reader's Digest Press, 1976.

Doremus, Robert B. "Days to Remember." Paper submitted to Industrial College of the Armed Forces, Washington, D.C., 1974.

Dramesi, John A. *Code of Honor*. New York: Norton, 1975.

Frishman, Robert F. "I Was a Prisoner in Hanoi." *Reader's Digest*, December 1969, 111-15.

Gaither, Ralph. *With God in a P.O.W. Camp*. Nashville: Broadman Press, 1973.

Guarino, Larry. *A POW's Story: 2801 Days in Hanoi*. New York: Ivy Books, 1990.

Jackson, S/Sgt. James E., Jr. "18 Months As a Prisoner of the Viet Cong." *Ebony*, August 1968, 114 ff.

Jensen, Jay R. *Six Years in Hell: A Returned POW Views Captivity, Country, and the Nation's Future*. Bountiful, Utah: Horizon, 1978.

Johnson, Sam and Jan Winebrenner. *Captive Warriors*. College Station, Tex.: Texas A & M University Press, 1992.

_____. "Shot Down Over North Vietnam in 1966, Air Force Colonel Sam Johnson Survived Seven Years As a POW." *Vietnam*, October 1990, 16.

Kushner, Floyd. "To Live or to Die." *SERE Newsletter*, June 1976, 3-11.

Larson, Gordon Albert. *Autobiography*. San Antonio, Tex.: privately printed, 1996.

McCain, John S. III. "How the POW's Fought Back." *U.S. News & World Report*, 14 May 1973, 46 ff.

McDaniel, Eugene B., with James L. Johnson. *Before Honor*. Philadelphia: A. J. Holman, 1975.

McDaniel, Norman A. *Yet Another Voice*. New York: Hawthorn Books, 1975.

McGrath, John M. *Prisoner of War: Six Years in Hanoi*. Annapolis, Md.: Naval Institute Press, 1975.

Mulligan, James A. *The Hanoi Commitment*. Virginia Beach, Va.: RIF Marketing, 1981.

Nasmyth, Spike. *2355 Days: A POW's Story*. New York: Orion Books, 1991.

Nasmyth, Virginia and Spike. *Hanoi Release John Nasmyth*. Santa Paula, Calif.: V. Parr, 1984.

Plumb, Charlie. *I'm No Hero*. Independence, Mo.: Independence Press, 1973.

Purcell, Ben and Anne. *Love and Duty*. New York: St. Martin's Press, 1992.

Risner, Robinson. *The Passing of the Night: My Seven Years As a Prisoner of the North Vietnamese*. New York: Random House, 1973.

Rowe, James N. *Five Years to Freedom*. Boston: Little, Brown, 1971.

_____. Interview with Air Training Command, July 1969, in *Southeast Asia Survival Journal*, April 1972.

Rutledge, Howard and Phyllis. *In the Presence of Mine Enemies, 1965-1973: A Prisoner of War*. Old Tappan, N. J.: Fleming H. Revell, 1973.

Schwinn, Monika and Bernhard Diehl. *We Came to Help*. New York: Harcourt Brace, 1973.

Smith, George. *P.O.W.: Two Years With the Vietcong*. Berkeley: Ramparts Press, 1971.

Stockdale, Jim and Sybil. *In Love and War: The Story of a Family's Ordeal and Sacrifice During the Vietnam Years*. New York: Harper & Row, 1984.

Wagaman, Winnie, and Norman J. Brookens. *Civilian POW: Terror and Torture in South Vietnam*. Hagerstown, Md.: Warm Welcomes Designs, 1990.

Wolfkill, Grant. *Reported To Be Alive*. New York: Simon and Schuster, 1965.

Wyatt, Frederic A. and Barbara P., eds. *We Came Home*. Toluca Lake, Calif.: P.O.W. Publications, 1977.

CONGRESSIONAL HEARINGS AND REPORTS

American Prisoners of War and Missing in Action in Southeast Asia, 1973. Hearings before House Foreign Affairs Subcommittee on National Security Policy and Scientific Developments. 92 Cong., 1 sess., 1973.

American Prisoners of War in Southeast Asia, 1971. Hearings before House Foreign Affairs Subcommittee on National Security Policy and Scientific Developments. 92 Cong., 1 sess., 1971.

American Prisoners of War in Southeast Asia, 1972. Hearings before House Foreign Affairs Subcommittee on National Security Policy and Scientific Developments. 92 Cong., 2 sess., 1972.

Americans Missing in Southeast Asia. Final Report of the House Select Committee on Missing Persons in Southeast Asia. 94 Cong., 2 sess., 13 December 1976.

Americans Missing in Southeast Asia. Hearings before House Select Committee on Missing Persons in Southeast Asia. 94 Cong., 1 sess., 1975.

Americans Missing in Southeast Asia. Hearings before House Select Committee on Missing Persons in Southeast Asia. 94 Cong., 2 sess., 1976.

Communist Treatment of Prisoners of War: A Historical Survey. 92 Cong., 2 sess., 1972.

"An Examination of U.S. Policy Toward POW/MIAs." Senate Foreign Relations Committee Minority (Republican) Staff Report, 23 May 1991.

The Gulf of Tonkin, The 1964 Incidents. Hearing before Senate Foreign Relations Committee. 90 Cong., 2 sess., 1968.

Imprisonment and Escape of Lt. (jg.) Dieter Dengler, USNR. Hearing before Senate Armed Services Committee. 89 Cong., 2 sess., 1966.

Korean War Atrocities. Report of the Senate Committee on Government Operations. 83 Cong., 2 sess., 1954.

POW/MIA'S. Report of the Senate Select Committee on POW/MIA Affairs. 103 Cong., 1 sess., 13 January 1993.

Restraints on Travel to Hostile Areas H.R. 1594 . . . . Hearings before House Committee on Internal Security. 93 Cong., 1 sess., 1973.

Return of American Prisoners of War Who Have Not Been Accounted for by the Communists. Hearing before House Foreign Affairs Subcommittee on the Far East and the Pacific. 85 Cong., 1 sess., 1957.

The U.S. Government and the Vietnam War, Executive and Legislative Roles and Relationships: Part I, 1945-1961. Report of the Senate Foreign Relations Committee. 98 Cong., 2 sess., April 1984.

The U.S. Government and the Vietnam War, Executive and Legislative Roles and Relationships: Part II, 1961-1964. Report of the Senate Foreign Relations Committee. 98 Cong., 2 sess., December 1984.

BOOKS

Aptheker, Herbert. *Mission to Hanoi*. New York: International Publishers, 1966.

Archer, Jules. *Ho Chi Minh: Legend of Hanoi*. New York: Macmillan, 1971.

Barker, A. J. *Prisoners of War*. New York: Universe Books, 1974.

Berger, Carl, ed. *The United States Air Force in Southeast Asia, 1961-1973*. Washington: Office of Air Force History, 1977.

Biderman, Albert D. *March to Calumny*. New York: Macmillan, 1963.

Blakey, Scott. *Prisoner at War: The Survival of Commander Richard A. Stratton*. Garden City, N. Y.: Doubleday, 1978.

Bodard, Lucien. *The Quicksand War: Prelude to Vietnam*. Boston: Little, Brown, 1967.

Burchett, Wilfred. *Vietnam: Inside Story of the Guerilla War*. New York: International Publishers, 1965.

_____. *Vietnam North*. New York: International Publishers, 1966.

Buttinger, Joseph. *Vietnam: A Dragon Embattled*. 2 vols. New York: Praeger, 1967.

_____. *Vietnam: A Political History*. New York: Praeger, 1968.

Cawthorne, Nigel. *The Bamboo Cage: The Full Story of the American Servicemen Still Held Hostage in South-East Asia*. London: Leo Cooper, 1991.

Clarke, Jeffrey J. *Advice and Support: The Final Years, 1965-1973*. The United States Army in Vietnam Series. Washington: U.S. Army Center of Military History, 1988.

Clifford, Clark, with Richard Holbrooke. *Counsel to the President*. New York: Random House, 1991.

Colvin, Rod. *First Heroes: The POWs Left Behind in Vietnam*. New York: Irvington, 1987.

Davis, Vernon E. *The U.S. Government and American Prisoners of War in Southeast Asia, 1961-1973* (forthcoming), manuscript in OSD Historical Office, Washington, D.C.

Daws, Gavan. *Prisoners of the Japanese: POWs of World War II in the Pacific*. New York: Morrow, 1994.

Doyle, Robert C. *Voices from Captivity: Interpreting the American POW Narrative*. Lawrence, Kans.: University Press of Kansas, 1994.

Duffett, John, ed. *Against the Crime of Silence: Proceedings of the International War Crimes Tribunal*. New York: Simon and Schuster, 1968.

Eisenhower, Dwight D. *Mandate for Change: The White House Years, 1953-1956*. Garden City, N.Y.: Doubleday, 1963.

Falk, Richard A., ed. *The Vietnam War and International Law*. 4 vols. Princeton: Princeton University Press, 1967-76.

Fall, Bernard B. *Hell in a Very Small Place: The Siege of Dien Bien Phu*. Philadelphia: Lippincott, 1967.

_____. *Street Without Joy: Indochina at War, 1946-54*. Harrisburg, Pa.: Stackpole, 1961.

Fifield, Russell H. *Americans in Southeast Asia: The Roots of Commitment*. New York: Crowell, 1973.

Frank, Benis M. and Henry I. Shaw, Jr. *History of U.S. Marine Corps Operations in World War II: Victory and Occupation*. Washington: Marine Corps Historical Branch, 1968.

Franklin, H. Bruce. *M.I.A. or Mythmaking in America*. New York: Lawrence Hill, 1992.

Goeldhieux, Claude. *Quinze Mois Prisonier chez les Viets*. Paris: Julliard, 1953.

Goulden, Joseph C. *Truth Is the First Casualty: The Gulf of Tonkin Affair—Illusion and Reality*. Chicago: Rand McNally, 1969.

Grant, Zalin. *Survivors*. New York: Norton, 1975.

Groom, Winston and Duncan Spencer. *Conversations With the Enemy: The Story of PFC Robert Garwood*. New York: Putnam, 1983.

Gruner, Elliott. *Prisoners of Culture*. New Brunswick, N. J.: Rutgers University Press, 1993.

Halberstam, David. *The Best and the Brightest*. New York: Random House, 1969.

Hammer, Ellen J. *The Struggle for Indochina*. Stanford: Stanford University Press, 1954.

Hayton-Keeva, Sally, ed. *Valiant Women in War and Exile*. San Francisco: City Lights Books, 1987.

Hefley, James and Marti. *Prisoners of Hope*. Harrisburg, Pa.: Christian Publications, 1976.

Herring, George C. *America's Longest War: The United States and Vietnam, 1950-1975*. New York: John Wiley & Sons, 1979.

Heslop, J. M. and Dell R. Van Orden. *From the Shadow of Death: Stories of POWs*. Salt Lake City: Deseret, 1973.

Honey, P. J. *Genesis of a Tragedy*. London: Benn, 1968.

Howes, Craig. *Voices of the Vietnam POWs: Witnesses to Their Fight*. New York: Oxford, 1993.

Hubbell, John G. *P.O.W.: A Definitive History of the American Prisoner-of-War Experience in Vietnam, 1964-1973*. New York: Reader's Digest Press, 1976.

Isaacs, Arnold R. *Without Honor: Defeat in Vietnam and Cambodia*. Baltimore: Johns Hopkins University Press, 1983.

Jensen-Stevenson, Monika. *Spite House: The Last Secret of the War in Vietnam*. New York: Norton, 1997.

_____ and William Stevenson. *Kiss the Boys Goodbye: How the United States Betrayed Its Own PWs in Vietnam*. New York: Dutton, 1990.

Kalb, Marvin and Elie Abel. *Roots of Involvement: The U. S. in Asia, 1784-1971*. New York: Norton, 1971.

Karnow, Stanley. *Vietnam: A History*. New York: Viking, 1983.

Kelly, Francis J. *U. S. Army Special Forces, 1961-1971*. Vietnam Study Series. Washington: U. S. Department of the Army, 1973.

Kinkead, Eugene. *In Every War But One*. New York: Norton, 1959.

Kissinger, Henry. *White House Years*. Boston: Little, Brown, 1979.

_____. *Years of Upheaval*. Boston: Little, Brown, 1982.

Lacouture, Jean. *Ho Chi Minh: A Political Biography*. New York: Random House, 1968.

Lansdale, Edward G. *In the Midst of Wars: An American's Mission to Southeast Asia*. New York: Harper & Row, 1972.

Lewy, Guenter. *America in Vietnam*. New York: Oxford, 1978.

Lynd, Staughton and Thomas Hayden. *The Other Side*. New York: New American Library, 1966.

McAlister, John T., Jr. *Vietnam: The Origins of Revolution*. New York: Knopf, 1969.

McConnell, Malcolm. *Into the Mouth of the Cat: The Story of Lance Sijan, Hero of Vietnam*. New York: Norton, 1985.

McCubbin, Hamilton I. et al, eds. *Family Separation and Reunion: Families of Prisoners of War and Servicemen Missing in Action*. Washington: GPO, 1974.

Melson, Maj. Charles D. and Lt. Col. Curtis G. Arnold. *U. S. Marines in Vietnam: The War That Would Not End, 1971-1973*. Washington: History and Museum Division, U. S. Marine Corps, 1991.

Nguyen Khac Huyen. *Vision Accomplished? The Enigma of Ho Chi Minh*. New York: Macmillan, 1971.

Norman, Geoffrey. *Bouncing Back*. Boston: Houghton Mifflin, 1990.

O'Ballance, Edgar. *The Indo-China War, 1945-1954: A Study in Guerilla Warfare*. London: Faber and Faber, 1964.

Paillat, Claude. *Dossier Secret de L'Indochine*. Paris: Presses de la Cité, 1964.

Patti, Archimedes L. A. *Why Viet Nam?* Berkeley: University of California Press, 1980.

The Pentagon Papers: The Defense Department History of United States Decision-making in Vietnam. Senator Gravel Edition. Boston: Beacon Press, 1971.

Pouget, Jean. *Le Manifeste du Camp No. 1*. Paris: Fayard, 1969.

POW-MIA Fact Book. Washington: U. S. Department of Defense, October 1992.

The Prisoner of War Problem. Washington: American Enterprise Institute, 1970.

Randle, Robert F. *Geneva 1954: The Settlement of the Indochinese War*. Princeton: Princeton University Press, 1969.

Rearden, Steven L. *The Formative Years, 1947-1950*. Vol. I in *History of the Office of the Secretary of Defense*. Washington: Historical Office, Office of the Secretary of Defense, 1984.

Robbins, Christopher. *The Ravens: The Men Who Flew in America's Secret War in Laos*. New York: Crown, 1987.

Rojas, Marta and Raul Valdes Viva. *Vietnam del sur*. Havana: Book Institute, 1967.

Rostow, W. W. *The Diffusion of Power*. New York: Macmillan, 1972.

Rowan, Stephen A. *They Wouldn't Let Us Die: The Prisoners of War Tell Their Story*. Middle Village, N. Y.: Jonathan David, 1973.

Roy, Jules. *The Battle of Dienbienphu*. Translated by Robert Baldick. New York: Harper & Row, 1965.

Rust, William J. *Kennedy in Vietnam*. New York: Scribner's, 1985.

Salisbury, Harrison. *Behind the Lines—Hanoi*. New York: Harper & Row, 1967.

Sananikone, Maj. Gen. Oudone. *The Royal Lao Army and U. S. Army Advice and Support*. Washington: U. S. Army Center of Military History, 1981.

Santoli, Al. *Everything We Had*. New York: Random House, 1981.

Sauter, Mark and Jim Sanders. *The Men We Left Behind: Henry Kissinger, the Politics of Deceit and the Tragic Fate of POWs After the Vietnam War*. Washington: National Press Books, 1993.

Schemmer, Benjamin F. *The Raid*. New York: Harper & Row, 1976.

Schlesinger, Arthur M., Jr. *A Thousand Days: John F. Kennedy in the White House*. Boston: Houghton Mifflin, 1965.

Schoenbrun, David. *Vietnam: How We Got In, How to Get Out*. New York: Atheneum, 1968.

Scholl-Latour, Peter. *Death in the Ricefields: Thirty Years of War in Indochina*. London: Orbis, 1981.

Shawcross, William. *Sideshow: Kissinger, Nixon and the Destruction of Cambodia*. New York: Simon and Schuster, 1979.

Sheehan, Neil. *A Bright Shining Lie: John Paul Vann and America in Vietnam*. New York: Random House, 1988.

Solis, Gary D. *Marines and Military Law in Vietnam: Trial by Fire*. Washington: History and Museum Division, U. S. Marine Corps, 1989.

Spector, Ronald H. *Advice and Support: The Early Years, 1941-1960*. The United States Army in Vietnam Series. Washington: U. S. Army Center of Military History, 1983.

Taylor, Telford. *Nuremberg and Vietnam: An American Tragedy*. New York: Random House, 1970.

Terry, Wallace. *Bloods: An Oral History of the Vietnam War by Black Veterans*. New York: Ballantine, 1984.

Thompson, James Clay. *Rolling Thunder: Understanding Policy and Program Failure*. Chapel Hill: University of North Carolina Press, 1980.

Tilford, Earl H., Jr. *Search and Rescue in Southeast Asia, 1961-1975*. Washington: Office of Air Force History, 1980.

Trooboff, Peter D., ed. *Law and Responsibility in Warfare: The Vietnam Experience*. Chapel Hill: University of North Carolina Press, 1975.

US War Crimes in North Viet Nam. Hanoi: Democratic Republic of Vietnam, Ministry of Foreign Affairs, 1966.

Veith, George J. *Code-Name Bright Light: The Untold Story of U.S. POW Rescue Efforts During the Vietnam War*. New York: Free Press, 1998.

The Vietnam Experience: War in the Shadows. Boston: Boston Publishing Company, 1988.

Westmoreland, William C. *A Soldier's Report*. Garden City, N. Y.: Doubleday, 1976.

Windchy, Eugene G. *Tonkin Gulf*. Garden City, N. Y.: Doubleday, 1971.

The Winter Soldier Investigation: An Inquiry into American War Crimes. Boston: Beacon Press, 1972.

ARTICLES

Alvarez, Everett, Jr. "Sound: A POW's Weapon." United States Naval Institute *Proceedings*, August 1976, 91-93.

Barnard, Richard C. "Coming Home from Hanoi." *Family*, 5 September 1973, 8 ff.

Berg, S. William and Milton Richlin. "Injuries and Illnesses of Vietnam War POWs. IV. Comparison of Captivity Effects in North and South Vietnam." *Military Medicine*, October 1977, 757-60.

"Beyond the Worst Suspicions." *Time*, 9 April 1973, 20 ff.

Biderman, Albert D. "Communist Attempts to Elicit False Confessions from Air Force Prisoners of War." *Bulletin of the New York Academy of Medicine*, September 1957, 616-25.

Brower, Col. Charles F., IV. "Strategic Reassessment in Vietnam: The Westmoreland 'Alternative Strategy' of 1967-1968." *Naval War College Review*, Spring 1991, 20-51.

Casella, Alessandro. "Prisoner Problems." *Far Eastern Economic Review*, 14 July 1966, 58.

Deaton, John E. et al. "Coping Activities in Solitary Confinement of U. S. Navy POWs in Vietnam." *Journal of Applied Social Psychology*, 1977, 239-57.

Dunn, Howard and W. Hays Parks. "If I Become a Prisoner of War . . ." U. S. Naval Institute *Proceedings*, August 1976, 18-27.

Dunn, Joe. "The POW Chronicles: A Bibliographic Review." *Armed Forces and Society*, Spring 1983, 495-514.

Eastman, Margaret. "The Pain Lingers, Too." *Family*, 5 September 1973, 12-13.

Edwards, Steve. "Operation Bright Light." *Vietnam*, October 1991, 18 ff.

Falk, Richard A. "The American POWs: Pawns in Power Politics." *The Progressive*, March 1971, 13-21.

Fall, Bernard B. "Communist POW Treatment in Indochina." *Military Review*, December 1958, 4-7.

Frisbee, John L. "Surviving in Hanoi's Prisons." *Air Force Magazine*, June 1973, 28-33.

Grant, Zalin. "American Defectors With the Viet Cong." *New Republic*, 7 September 1968, 15-16.

Greenstein, Fred I. and Richard H. Immerman. "What Did Eisenhower Tell Kennedy about Indochina? The Politics of Misperception." *Journal of American History*, September 1992, 568-87.

Grumbach, Doris. "Fine Print: The Art of Reviewing by Innuendo." *New Republic*, 16 March 1974, 32-33.

"Hanoi's Pavlovians." *Time*, 14 April 1967, 33-34.

Hempstone, Smith. "Court-Martial of a Traitor: Why Pvt. Garwood Deserves Mercy." *Washington Post*, 25 January 1981.

Hersh, Seymour M. "P.O.W.'s Maintained Discipline but Had Some Quarrels." *New York Times*, 23 February 1973.

Hitchens, Harold L. "Factors Involved in a Review of the Code of Conduct for the Armed Forces." *Naval War College Review*, Winter 1978, 47-70.

"'I Knew My Actions Would Affect 23 Million Blacks.'" *Pentagram*, 12 April 1984, 9.

Immerman, Richard H. "The United States and the Geneva Conference of 1954: A New Look." *Diplomatic History*, Winter 1990, 43-66.

"Inside North Vietnam's Prisons—How Americans Coped." *U. S. News & World Report*, 26 March 1973, 58-61.

Jeandel, Paul. "Deux Ans de Captivité chez les Viet-Minh." *Revue de l'Action Populaire*, September-October 1955, 943-54.

Jordan, Kenneth N., Sr. "William D. Port." In *Heroes of Our Time*. Atglen, Pa.: Schiffer Military/Aviation History, n.d.

Kelly, James F. and Norman H. Tracy. "An Overview of Dental Findings and Experiences in Repatriated American Prisoners of War from Southeast Asia." *Military Medicine*, October 1975, 699-704.

Leary, William M. "Mahaxay: Secret POW Rescue in Laos." *Vietnam*, June 1995, 18-24.

"Life Under Viet Cong: Crude Bamboo Cages." *U. S. News & World Report*, 26 March 1973, 61.

Ludvigsen, Eric C. "Missing, Dead or Captured?" *Army*, February 1970, 24-32.

_____. "Survival of an American Prisoner: An Extraordinary Exercise of Will." *Army*, February 1970, 32 ff.

"Major Nick Rowe of Army." West Point *Assembly*, Spring 1969, 16 ff.

Maze, Rick. "Revelations in POW's Book Concern Pentagon Officials." *Air Force Times*, 8 October 1984.

"Medical Journal of a Returned P.O.W." *Medical World News*, 6 November 1970, 44-47.

Meurer, Lt. Col. Fred A. "Sijan! My Name Is Lance Peter Sijan!" *Airman*, June 1977, 8-16.

Murphy, Caryle. "Manila Ambush Victim Had Foiled Viet Cong, Come Home a Hero." *Washington Post*, 23 April 1989.

Naughton, Robert J. "Motivational Factors of American Prisoners of War Held by the Democratic Republic of Vietnam." *Naval War College Review*, January-February 1975, 2-14.

Ngo Vinh Long. "The American POWs: Their Glory Is All Moonshine." *Ramparts*, May 1973.

Norman, Geoffrey. "Wine Tasting at the Hanoi Hilton." *Forbes*, Supplement No. 1, 1990, 66-69.

Parks, Maj. W. Hays. "Code of Conduct vs. *Code of Honor*." *Armed Forces Journal International*, November 1976, 27-28.

Perkins, Glendon. "Hanoi Nightmare: American POW's Year of Terror." *Soldier of Fortune*, August 1990, 25 ff.

"Pieces of the Puzzle." *People*, 9 November 1992, 101 ff.

"POW's Hardest Task Was Forgetting He Was Black." *Jet*, 19 April 1973.

"POW's Nightmarish Ordeal." *Washington Post*, 30 March 1973.

"POW's Tell the Inside Story." *U. S. News & World Report*, 9 April 1973, 33-34.

"POW's: The Price of Survival." *Newsweek*, 16 April 1973, 26 ff.

Rausa, Rosario. "Home from Hanoi." *Naval Aviation News*, December 1973, 9-21.

Reynolds, Jon A. "Question of Honor." *Air University Review*, March-April 1977, 104-10.

Richardson, Col. Walton K. "Prisoners of War as Instruments of Foreign Policy." *Naval War College Review*, September 1970, 47-64.

Roberts, Bill. "Freedom Hard as Captivity for First POW." *Monterey Peninsula Herald*, 22 October 1971.

Roberts, Steven V. "Antiwar P.O.W.'s: A Different Mold Scarred by Their Combat Experience." *New York Times*, 15 July 1973.

_____. "P.O.W.'s a Year Later: Most Adapt Well." *New York Times*, 10 February 1974.

_____. "P.O.W.'s Felt Their Mission Was to Resist." *New York Times*, 30 April 1973.

_____. "The P.O.W.'s: Focus of Division." *New York Times*, 3 March 1973.

_____. "Unshakable Will to Survive Sustained P.O.W.'s Over the Years." *New York Times*, 4 March 1973.

Rogers, Warren. "North Vietnam: Are U. S. Prisoners Mistreated?" *Look*, 25 July 1967, 53-55.

"A Sampling of 'Discrepancy Cases' Still on the Books." *Defense 92*, January/February 1992, 9.

Schein, Edgar H. "Some Observations on Chinese Methods of Handling Prisoners of War." *Public Opinion Quarterly*, Spring 1956, 321-27.

_____. "The Chinese Indoctrination Program for Prisoners of War: A Study of Attempted Brainwashing." *Psychiatry*, May 1956, 149-72.

"Soldier Survives Five Years in POW Camp." *Pentagram*, 31 August 1989, 10.

Stockdale, James Bond. "Communicating *Without* Technology." *Signal*, October 1979, 26 ff.

_____. "Experiences as a POW in Vietnam." *Naval War College Review*, January-February 1974, 2-6.

_____. "The Melting Experience." *National Review*, 25 December 1981, 1534-37.

_____. "The World of Epictetus: Reflections on Survival and Leadership." *Atlantic Monthly*, April 1978, 98-106.

_____. "What Not to Conclude From the Garwood Case." *Washington Post*, 9 February 1981.

Surface, Bill. "Can We Free Our Vietnam War Prisoners?" *Parade*, 14 November 1965, 4-5.

"Targeting a U. S. Hero." *Newsweek*, 1 May 1989, 42.

"The Battle of the POW's." *Time*, 9 October 1972.

"The Plight of the Prisoners." *Time*, 15 August 1969, 21-23.

"The POW's: What a Difference a Year Makes." *Newsweek*, 25 February 1974.

Truby, J. David. "Now It Can Be Told . . . Cubans Torture U. S. POW's in Vietnam." *Soldier of Fortune*, May 1978, 38 ff.

"U. S. Prisoners in North Vietnam." *Life*, 20 October 1967, 21-33.

Van Dyke, Jon M. "Were They Tortured?" *Nation*, 6 October 1969, 334-35.

"Wife of only remaining POW in Southeast Asia dies in apparent suicide." *San Diego Union*, 6 October 1990.

Wilson, George C. "POWs Caught in Swirl of U. S. Politics." *Washington Post*, 10 September 1972.

Wubben, H. H. "American Prisoners of War in Korea: A Second Look at the 'Something New in History' Theme." *American Quarterly*, Spring 1970, 3-19.

Zinn, Howard. "The Petty Route Home." *Nation*, 1 April 1968, 431-37.

INTERVIEWS

Everett Alvarez

Thomas Barrett

William Baugh

James Bedinger

James Bell

Charles Boyd

Ernest Brace

William Breckner

Norman Brookens

David Burroughs

Phillip Butler

Ronald Byrne

Peter Camerota

Fred Cherry

Lawrence Chesley

Gerald Coffee

Thomas Collins

Kenneth Coskey

Render Crayton

George Day

Jerome DeBruin

James DiBernardo

John Downey

Edward Elias

Richard Fecteau

John Fellowes

John Fer

Hubert Flesher

John Flynn

Robert Frishman

Norman Gaddis

Mark Gartley

Donat Gouin

Lawrence Guarino

Porter Halyburton

Douglas Hegdahl

Leland Hildebrand

John Hubbell

Kenneth Hughey

Samuel Johnson

Murphy Jones

James Kasler

Thomas Kirk

Charles Klusmann

Floyd Kushner

James Lamar

Edward Lansdale

William Lawrence

Gunther Lewy

Lee Lockwood

Jose Luna

Thomas Madison

Philip Manhard

William Mayall

John McCain

Eugene McDaniel

Norman McDaniel

Angus McDonald

Kevin McManus

Isiah McMillan

Edward Mechenbier

Joseph Milligan

James Monroe

James Mulligan

Armand Myers

Anita Nutt

Norris Overly

Jasper Page

John Parsels

Glendon Perkins

Ross Perot

Douglas Peterson

Charles Plumb

Benjamin Pollard

Benjamin Purcell

Douglas Ramsey

Donald Rander

Charles Redman

Jon Reynolds

Lawrence Robison

Nicholas Rowe

Robert Sawhill

Benjamin Schemmer

Wesley Schierman

Raymond Schrump	Lawrence Stark	Gerald Venanzi
Robert Schweitzer	John Stavast	Raymond Vohden
Joseph Shanahan	James Stockdale	Dewey Waddell
Roger Shields	Hervey Stockman	Claude Watkins
Robert Shumaker	Thomas Storey	Ronald Webb
Frank Sieverts	Richard Stratton	Robert White
Philip Smith	Timothy Sullivan	David Winn
Charles Southwick	Orson Swindle	Frederic Wolfer
Lawrence Spencer	James Thompson	

UNPUBLISHED PAPERS, STUDIES, AND DISSERTATIONS

Analysis of the Korean War Prisoner of War Experience. USAF Program for Analysis of the Southeast Asia Prisoner of War Experience, Report No. A10-2, March 1974.

Bedinger, Henry James. "Prisoner-of-War Organization in Hanoi." M.B.A. thesis, San Diego State University, 1976.

Biderman, Albert D. and Herbert Zimmer. "Treatment and Indoctrination of U. S. Prisoners Held by the Viet Minh." Air Force Personnel and Training Research Center, Project No. 7732, n.d.

Browne, Robert T. "Development of Prisoner of War Exploitation Techniques and Those Utilized by Guerrilla-Type Forces Against American Military Captives in the Republic of Vietnam." Naval War College, Newport, R. I., 1969.

Communist Interrogation, Indoctrination, and Exploitation of Prisoners of War. Washington: Department of the Army, May 1956.

Cooper, Bert H. "Statistics on U.S. Participation in the Vietnam Conflict, With Addendum." Congressional Research Service, 15 August 1972.

Every, Martin G. and James F. Parker, Jr. "A Review of Problems Encountered in the Recovery of Navy Aircrewmen Under Combat Conditions." Office of Naval Research, Washington, D. C., 1973.

Fer, John. "Leadership and Followership in the Prisoner-of-War Environment." Air War College, Maxwell AFB, Ala., 1974.

"Field Survival Medicine Techniques Employed by American Prisoners-of-War in the Southeast Asia Prison Systems." Environmental Information Division, Maxwell AFB, Ala., 1975.

Ho, George J. "The Prisoner of War Issue in the First Indochina War, with Special Emphasis on the Release of Prisoners, 1954-1962." Congressional Research Service, 13 July 1971.

Hutchins, Charles W. "The Captivity Experience of American Prisoners of War in Southeast Asia." Naval Health Research Center Publication No. 77-28, August 1977.

Johnson, Samuel R. "Deficiencies in Treatment of U.S. POW's in North Vietnam Under the Standards of the Geneva Conventions of 1949." National War College, Washington, D. C., 1974.

McGrath, J. M. "American POWs: North Korea and North Vietnam." Naval Postgraduate School, Monterey, Calif., n.d.

Moisi, Dominique. "The Dienbienphu Crisis: American and French Behavior." Wilson Center International Security Studies Program, Working Paper No. 1 (1978?).

Monroe, James L. "The Communist Use of Prisoners and Hostages in the Truce Negotiations in Korea." Paper in OSD Historical Office Files, April 1956.

Murray, Michael Patrick. "Historical Analysis and Critical Appraisal of the Code of Conduct for Members of the Armed Forces of the United States." Naval War College, Newport, R. I., 1973.

Myers, Armand J. "POW Doctrine for Survival With Honor." Air War College, Maxwell AFB, Ala., 1975.

_____, et al. *Vietnam POW Camp Histories and Studies*. 2 vols. Air War College, Maxwell AFB, Ala., 1974, 1975.

Nutt, Anita Lauve. *Prisoners of War in Indochina*. Rand study prepared for DoD (ARPA), October 1968.

_____. *Troika on Trial*. 3 vols. Rand study of the International Control Commission prepared for DoD (ISA), September 1967.

"An Overview of Free-World Personnel Captured in South Vietnam." Paper delivered to SERE Conference, San Diego, Calif., January 1975.

"POW: The Fight Continues After the Battle." Report of the Secretary of Defense's Advisory Committee on Prisoners of War, August 1955.

Prisoner of War Study: Step Two, The Functioning of the Law. Prepared for Department of the Army by Harbridge House, 1969.

Stockman, Hervey S. "Authority, Leadership, Organization and Discipline Among U.S. POWs in the Hanoi Prison System." Air War College, Maxwell AFB, Ala., 1974.

Vohden, Raymond A. "Stress and the Viet Nam P.O.W." Industrial College of the Armed Forces, Washington, D. C., c. 1974.

Wolfer, Frederic F., Jr. "The Origins of Affinity for the Armed Forces Code of Conduct Among Prisoners of War Returned from Southeast Asia." Ph.D. dissertation, George Washington University, 1979.

FILMS

A number of films have treated aspects of the PW story. Some are accounts of individual captivity experience, others are documentary or inspirational. At least one commercial movie has been made on the subject. Most of these are beyond the purview of this book, but two films are noteworthy for research purposes: *Pilots in Pajamas* and *Return with Honor*. The first is the lengthy propaganda film made at the Plantation by an East German camera crew, mentioned in Chapter 18. A copy is in the OSD Historical Office PW Collection. The second, directed by Freida Lee Mock and Terry Sanders (Santa Monica, Calif.: American Film Foundation, 1998), is an outstanding documentary account of captivity in North Vietnam that blends U.S. film footage and still photography, North Vietnamese archival footage and photography released to Mock and Sanders in 1997, and selected interviews with former PWs.

Index

Abbott, Cdr. John, 156, 388n
Abbott, Capt. Joseph, 388, 388n, 581n
Abbott, Lt. Robert, 348, 351, 353 (photo), 388
Abbott, Capt. Wilfred, 220, 388n, 435n
Abe, 304
Adams, Sgt. Samuel, 253-54
Adkins, Cloden, 451, 452, 517n, 558
aging, 225n, 410-11, 442, 497, 511n, 541-42, 578, 590-91
Agosto-Santos, Cpl. Jose, 266, 270-71, 273, 449, 476
Agnew, Lt. Cdr. Alfred, 587
Aiken, Sen. George, 200
Air Force, U.S., 26, 93, 94, 119, 139, 156, 170, 368, 376, 439, 554n, 561, 589
air strikes (U.S.) and impact on PWs:
    in Laos, 282; in North Vietnam, 12, 88, 93-94, 128, 141, 156, 191n, 193, 212, 214, 223, 298-99, 301, 304, 317, 320-21, 323, 330, 340, 354, 377, 383, 411-12, 539, 554, 569; in South Vietnam, 229, 240, 243, 248, 259, 262, 454, 468, 471, 474-75
Ajax, 343
Al Capone, 118
Albert, Spec. Keith, 476
Alcatraz, 105, 309n, 316, 326-39, 328 (photo), 340, 343, 367, 380, 381, 411, 412, 413, 415, 426, 439, 479, 494
Alcorn, Lt. (j.g.) Wendell, 151, 158, 160n, 216, 381
Alkies, 339, 426, 439, 509. See also Alcatraz
Alvarez, Lt. (j.g.) Everett, Jr., 85, 88, 89 (photo), 105, 120, 178 (photo), 286, 424, 491, 497, 551, 591; at Briarpatch, 126, 128, 160n, 212-13, 214, 216, 224,

443-44; and coping, 431, 441, 444, 542-43; and Hanoi March, 194-97; at Hoa Lo after capture, 90-92, 94-96, 98, 107, 111, 119, 123; at Unity, 524, 529, 572, 573, 574, 577, 579; at Zoo, 153, 382, 383, 386, 388, 394, 395-96, 397, 499, 500, 568
Alvarez, Tangee, 153, 542-43
Anderson, Lt. (j.g.) Gareth, 302, 303 (photo), 321, 346, 358, 509
Anderson, Sgt. John, 452, 453
Anderson, Pvt. Roger, 447
Andrews, Capt. Anthony, 373
Angus, Capt. William, 552
antiwar movement in U.S., 84, 100, 177, 193, 239, 375n, 377; and impact on U.S. PWs, 100, 180-81, 188, 192-93, 411, 412, 552
Anton, WO Francis, 447, 448, 464, 466 (photo), 468n, 575, 576
Anzaldua, Cpl. Jose, 468, 562
Appice, Airman Giacomo, 25-27
Aptheker, Herbert, 192
Archer, Capt. Bruce, 457, 458 (photo), 462, 517, 559
Armstrong, Lt. Col. John, 289
Army, U.S., 78n, 240, 250, 276, 477, 561, 563n, 589. See also Special Forces
Army Post, 319
Arroyo-Baez, Sgt. Gerasimo, 274n
Ashmore, Harry, 207
Atterberry, Capt. Edwin, 481-85, 483 (photo), 489, 490, 516
Auditorium, 151, 158, 159, 160, 176, 194, 211, 218, 219, 223, 395, 397, 403, 404, 408, 484, 485, 486, 496, 571
Austin, Capt. William, 423, 481, 482